# THE EUROPEAN HANDBOOK ON ADVERTISING LAW

Cavendish
Publishing
Limited

London • Sydney

# THE EUROPEAN HANDBOOK ON ADVERTISING LAW

Edited by

**Lord Campbell of Alloway, ERD, QC, MA (Cantab)**

and

**Zahd Yaqub, MA, LLM, Barrister, Inner Temple**

Cavendish
Publishing
Limited

London • Sydney

First published in Great Britain 1999 by Cavendish Publishing Limited,
The Glass House, Wharton Street, London WC1X 9PX, United Kingdom
Telephone: + 44 (0) 20 7278 8000     Facsimile: + 44 (0) 20 7278 8080
E-mail: info@cavendishpublishing.com
Visit our Home Page on http://www.cavendishpublishing.com

Campbell of Alloway, Lord
European Handbook on Advertising Law
1. Advertising laws
I. Title  II. Yaqub, Zahd
342.3'82

ISBN 1 85941 287 4

Printed and bound in Great Britain

# INTRODUCTION

This book is an invaluable work of reference for all those in any way concerned with advertising in Europe. The laws, basic principles and practices of 15 European states are included. Each chapter is written by an acknowledged expert in this specialist field in his own country, with a weather eye open to future developments.

The contents of each chapter are broken down for ease of reference in an excellent table prepared by the publishers, with relevant EC Council Directives, interpretative communications of the Commission, the Green Paper, the unofficial consolidated version on television without frontiers all included. The European Convention on transfrontier television, the ICC Code of Advertising Practice, the European Parliament Council Directive on Consumer Interest Protection are all provided amongst the appendices.

A new dimension of advertising law and practice has now been made available for those who work in Europe and those who have commercial relationships with Europe, including those whose work involves the media and the Internet. Matters such as teleshopping, sponsorship, misleading advertising and the misuse of intellectual property are all within the scope of this work. A reliable encyclopedia of essential intrinsic works now exists to fill a a gap in the bookshelves not only of the law libraries, but of the great national and international advertising houses, the Chambers of Commerce and many of their members.

The mammoth task of assemblage, the brainchild of Zahd Yaqub, was undertaking by him with the help of Cavendish Publishing. It has been a singular privilege to have been associated with them in this venture as co-editor.

*Lord Campbell of Alloway*
*2 King's Bench Walk*
*Temple*
*London*
*April 1999*

# FOREWORD:
# WORLD FEDERATION OF ADVERTISERS

That commercial communications play a vital economic role of in our societies is indisputable. Given the importance of commercial communications, it is not surprising to see that a great number of laws have been passed to regulate it.

The legislative world is filled with paradoxes. The first of these is the most obvious. Most people share a certain aversion to undue intrusion of laws and regulations into their lives. Indeed, most of us would prefer to live in as free a space as possible, enjoying freedom of action, of expression, of choice, of movement. Some, however, believe that it is necessary to limit these freedoms because, supposedly, people are unable to manage such a system of freedoms. Politicians have, to a certain extent, transformed these aspirations into reality and we find ourselves today living in an increasingly regulated world.

The second paradox is the result of this flood of legislation. The more laws and regulations there are, the harder it is not only to abide by them, but also to enforce them. Abundance in this case does not equate with efficacy.

The third paradox is that self-regulation is more efficient than legislation. Conscious of the natural limits of freedom, industry leaders decided to give themselves codes of ethics or of good practice. These codes have in common qualities that laws often do not. They are created by the very people who will be required to abide by them as well as enforce them, by the very people who know best the real constraints of their activities. These codes will be all the more respectable and respected as they are self-regulated and can be rapidly and continuously adapted to meet the changes of society and technological progress. These rules of self-regulation have become instruments to gain the loyalty of consumers. Indeed, conscious of the fact that each and every time a consumer buys a product, a service, or a brand, he is in effect exercising his freedom to choose, CEOs therefore know that they must win the client's vote of confidence every day. This can only be done if there is respect for the client.

The fourth paradox is that in the field of commercial communications, self-regulation actually predates legislation. The first self-regulation codes for advertising date back to the 1930s. At that time, there were few laws, if any, to regulate commercial communications.

Even though self-regulation can often replace laws and regulations to good effect, self-regulation still requires a legal framework if it is to be efficacious.

The wisdom of governments and legislators will be to find the right balance between legislation and self-regulation. Industry is prepared to do its part for the better good of citizens/consumers.

We can only applaud the initiative taken by the editors in making available to professionals such a useful and practical a book as this one. This book certainly constitutes a worthwhile contribution to our endeavour to promote respect for the consumer.

*Bernhard Adriaensens*
*Managing Director*
*World Federation of Advertisers*
*April 1999*

# FOREWORD: EUROPEAN ADVERTISING STANDARDS ALLIANCE

This book constitutes a major review of the regulation of advertising by law and by self-regulation across Europe. It describes in detail the EU and national legislative frameworks and give in depth consideration to the legislation in each Member State of the EU. Attention is drawn to the ICC codes of advertising practice whose principles – that advertising should be legal, decent, honest and truthful with a due sense of social responsibility and respect for the rules of fair competition – have served as the basis of all self-regulatory systems across Europe.

This book highlights well the complementary nature between regulation undertaken by law and that performed by the self-regulatory bodies acting on behalf of the advertising industry, via the application of codes/principles of advertising practice in the form of self-regulation. Neither can perform its task well without the other and, indeed, the challenge in the future will arise from the dynamics of this relationship in tackling, for example, the regulation of internet based communications.

The responsible advertising practitioner will need to take account of both law and self-regulation when preparing a commercial communication. This book will be a practical tool in understanding what rules exist to produce responsible commercial communication which will hopefully enjoy both the confidence of consumers and governments alike.

*Prisca Ancion-Kors*
*Chairman*
*European Advertising Standards Alliance*
*April 1999*

## What is the European Advertising Standards Alliance (EASA)?

The EASA is a non-profit making organisation based in Brussels, Belgium and is the co-ordination point for the views of national advertising self-regulatory bodies across Europe. The Alliance has 27 members, of which 24 are from 22 European countries, including: all Member States of the EU; the Czech Republic; Hungary; the Slovak Republic; Slovenia; Russia; Switzerland; and Turkey.

**Why was it created?** It was created, in 1992, in response to a direct challenge from the then EU Competition Commissioner, Sir Leon Brittan, to show how the issues affecting advertising in the Single Market could be successfully dealt with through co-operation, rather than detailed legislation. The national self-regulatory bodies and the European advertising industry have endeavoured to respond by demonstrating their strong commitment to effective self-regulation as a means of promoting high standards in advertising across Europe and, thus, for safeguarding the consumer's interests. The Alliance was established with a clear mission to achieve these aims.

**Who created the Alliance?** The national self-regulatory bodies, with the support of the respective parts of the European advertising industry, with which it liaises on policy issues.

**What are its aims?** To promote and support the development of effective self-regulation; to co-ordinate the handling of cross-border complaints; and to provide information and support on advertising self-regulation in Europe.

**Who are its members?** Its members are the national self-regulatory bodies responsible for administrating their respective national self-regulatory systems and applying national codes of International Chamber of Commerce (ICC) principles of advertising practice.

**What are its publications?** It publishes a quarterly newsletter, the *Alliance Update*, which contains both Alliance and national self-regulatory news, including a regular report on cross-border complaints. This is sent free to interested parties. Trilingual brochures exist on the Alliance and the cross-border complaints system. Surveys of Alliance members have been published on: *National Regulatory Systems for Television, Self-Regulation for Advertising and Children, Self-Regulation for Advertising and the Portrayal of Women and Men*. The Alliance has recently published a *Guide to Self-Regulation* and a comprehensive 124 page analysis of advertising self-regulatory systems and their codes of practice in 20 European countries: *Advertising Self-Regulation in Europe*.

**Is the Alliance a pan-European authority?** No. The alliance has no regulatory function; it does not enforce codes, nor does it have any decision making responsibility or give copy advice.

| Contact details for, and information about, EASA | |
|---|---|
| 10a rue de la Pépinière | Tel: (32 2) 513 78 06 |
| B–1000 Brussels | Fax: (32 2) 513 28 61 |
| Belgium | |
| E-mail: library@easa-alliance.org | Website: www.easa-alliance.org |
| Bank: GB 210-0450150-25 | VAT: BE 450 933 006 |

# ACKNOWLEDGMENTS

I would like to thank all those who have helped to make this book possible, particularly the contributors for their understanding and patience at some very difficult and testing times: José M Alarcão Júdice; Enrico J Batalla, Robert Beatty; Walter Beatty; Vassilis S Constandinides; Jacoline Harmeling-de Maa; Ralf Dresel; Vincenzo Guggino; Rainer Herzig; Deborah Jarmain-Barbizet; Takis G Kommatas; Karen Larsen; Francis Meyrier; Camila Pinto de Lima; Lennart Lindström; Jan Ravelingien; José Manuel Rey; Riccardo Rossotto; Ursula Schildt; Alex Schmidt; and Mårten Stenström. In this connection, I should also like to thank Pim de Vos of de Vos and Partners, Amsterdam.

I am grateful for the invaluable assistance of Dr Margot Frohlinger, Head of Unit E5, DGXV of the European Commission; Kenneth Collins, MEP, Chairman of the Committee on the Environment, Public Health and Consumer Protection; and Philip Whitehead, MEP.

Particular thanks go to Helene Bellofatto for providing logistical support and the vital communication with people far and near in a host of different roles, in my absence. Thanks also to Cara Annett at Cavendish Publishing for her assistance.

Those who have not contributed directly, but without whose sustaining encouragement I could not have completed this task, have my special thanks: Klare and Quinton Gerwat-Clark, my ever loyal and supportive family and Dr Dawn Miller. I wish to thank Farha, Sara Sommaya and Tahir for all their loving support.

I must also express my appreciation and thanks to Bernhard Adriansens of the World Federation of Advertisers and Dr Oliver Gray of the European Advertising Standards Alliancefor the forewords.

My gratitude extends to all others whom I have not been able to acknowledge here, but who assisted in bringing this project to a successful conclusion.

# LIST OF CONTRIBUTORS

**José Miguel Alarcão Júdice** is a partner of AM Pereira, Sáragga Leal Oliveira Martins, Júdice e Associados, in Lisbon. He has been a member of the Portuguese Bar Association since 1977. He is a graduate of the University of Coimbra, and an arbitrator at the Centre of Commercial Arbitration of Lisbon (Portuguese Chamber of Commerce) and the Commercial Association of Oporto (Chamber of Commerce and Industry of Oporto). He has held several posts as an Assistant Professor: from 1972–77 of political science and constitutional law (Law School of Coimbra), from 1978–80 of international law, and from 1980–81 of political science (Lisbon University Law School). He is also a member of the International Bar Association, the International Commission of Jurists (Director of the Portuguese section, 1976–79), Commercial Law Affiliates (General Council, since 1995) and the High Council of the Judiciary (since 1997).

**Enrique Jimenez Batalla** was born in Málaga, Spain, on 5 July 1944. He is a graduate of the University of Granada, and other education includes study in international juridical practices in Washington DC (1972). Since 1973, he has been a member of the Madrid Bar Association. He is also a member of various associations, such as the LES, IPBA, AIPPI, ECTA, IBA International Associations; Hispano-Chinese, Hispano-Japanese and Hispano-Taiwanese Bilateral Committees and the Spanish Chambers of Commerce High Council. His working languages include Spanish and English. He is a partner in the law firm of Batalla Larrauri and López Ante, in Madrid. His specialist areas of practice are information technology, mercantile and administrative law.

**Robert Beatty**, BL, obtained a BA (Hons) in politics and philosophy in 1990 from University College, Dublin, an MSSc in Irish political studies from the Queen's University, Belfast in 1991 and thereafter studied law. He was called to the Irish Bar in 1996 and is a practising barrister in Dublin.

**Walter Beatty**, BA, LLM, FCI, ARB is a partner of Vincent and Beatty Solicitors in Dublin. Vincent and Beatty act for several of Ireland's leading advertising agencies and international advertising agencies.

**Lord Campbell of Alloway,** ERD, QC, MA (Cantab), Life Baron, UK, Bencher of the Inner Temple 1972; Recorder of the Crown Court, 1976–89; Member, House of Lords Committee for Privileges since 1982; House of Lords Select Committee on Murder and Life Imprisonment, 1988–89; Chairman, Legal Research Committee of Society of Conservative Lawyers, 1968–80; Co Patron, Inns of Court Conservative Society, 1996; Member, Management Committee of UK Association for European Law, 1975–89; Vice-President, Association des Juristes Franco-Britanniques, 1989–91; Member, Law Advisory Panel of British Council, 1974–79. Special interests: industrial relations; EEC affairs; restrictive trade practices and monopolies. Sometime legal consultant for the Legal Affairs Committee of the Council of Europe on Industrial Espionage.

**Vassilis S Constandinides** graduated in law from Athens University in 1990, followed by postgraduate study in Greece in the areas of business, labour and intellectual property law. He entered practice in 1992, and is an associate in the firm of Takis G Kommatas and Associates Law Offices. He specialises in the fields of civil, business, labour and intellectual property law.

**Ralf Dresel** founded the Dresel Consulting Group, Nuremberg, in 1998. He is working in co-operation with the law firm Dr Kreuzer and Coll, Nuremberg, founded in 1976, and has been a freelance worker at the chair for economic and social science public law department at the Friedrich Alexander University of Erlangen-Nuremberg. He has published various articles concerning German general economic law, European and intellectual property law. His interests include European and international private law. At present he is working on publications concerned with the new European currency, the euro, and medical law.

**Vincenzo Guggino** is the Secretary General of the Instituto di Autodisciplina Pubblicitaria (Italian Institute of Advertising Self-regulation (IAP)). His educational background includes a Diploma in Advertising, from the International Advertising Association; a master's degree in management lecturing ('Ma Te R', Formez); a master's degree in business administration, ISIDA; and a degree in political science from the University of Florence. Regarding his professional career, since June 1992, he has been employed by the IAP, initially, as External Relations Manager, later, in 1997, as Manager of the General Secretariat and, since June 1998, as its Secretary General. His published work includes examinations of Thanatos and advertising; advertising self-regulation in Italy; the *Parodi* case; advertising self-regulation and its arbitration panel; and considerations on the legal nature of self-regulation in advertising.

**Jacoline Harmeling-de Maa** is a graduate in law of the University of Utrecht. From 1992 until 1997, she was in legal practice, specialising in intellectual property and advertising law. From 1995 to 1997, she worked for the law firm of De Vos and Partners Advocaten, Amsterdam. Her experience at De Vos and Partners was applied during the writing of the chapter on Dutch advertising law in this book. At present, she works as a trade mark lawyer with Shield Mark, in Amsterdam. She is also the author of a chapter on comparative advertising in the Consumer Handbook (1992).

**Rainer Herzig** earned his doctorate of law from Vienna University in 1982. Since 1990, he has been a partner of the law firm of Preslmayr and Partners, in Vienna. He is a member of the Association Internationale des Jeunes Avocats (AIJA) and the Rechtsanwaltskammer Wien (Lawyers' Association of Vienna). He is a specialist in advertising law, European law and commercial law. He has written numerous legal publications, particularly in the field of advertising law.

**Deborah Jarmain-Barbizet** was educated at the University of Leicester (LLB with French) and the University of Strasbourg. She is a solicitor of the Supreme Court of England and Wales, and has been a member of the Paris Bar since 1993. Of British nationality, Mme Jarmain-Barbizet practises in France, at Meyrier Fayout Lacoste, Paris. Her areas of specialisation are: commercial and company law, as well as banking, finance, leasing and aircraft law.

**Takis G Kommatas** graduated in law from Athens University in 1969, *magna cum laude*. He began practice in 1971 and has been a lawyer of the Supreme Court of Athens since 1978. He is the senior partner in the law firm of Takis G Kommatas and Associates, which represents a wide variety of clients, including major Greek and international corporations. He specialises in corporate, civil and business law, foreign investment and acquisitions. He is founding member and present chairman of the Board of LAWSPAN International, an international network of lawyers. He has published several papers on legal matters, and has contributed to *The Legal Professions in the New Europe* (2nd edn, 1996, London: Cavendish Publishing) and *European Travel Law* (1997).

**Karen Larsen** is Partner in Dania Law Firm. She graduated from Copenhagen University in 1977, and has an additional degree in French from the Copenhagen Business School of Administration. Her career has encompassed a four year period as in-house counsel for an engineering and construction company and a project development company, assisting in establishing projects abroad. Further, she has lectured at the Copenhagen University, and the Copenhagen Business School of Administration as well as for various institutions. She has lectured on topics such as project export, marketing law and related issues. She is the author of a handbook on marketing law, updated semi-annually, and the author of a basic introduction to business law. In addition to marketing law, her practice concentrates on company/commercial matters, international contracts, projects and project finance, and telecommunications.

**Lennart Lindström** graduated with a degree in law (*jur kand*) from the University of Lund, Sweden, in 1971. He then obtained a postgraduate degree (LLM) in EC law from the Europa Institut of the University of Amsterdam in 1973. From 1973–76, he worked as an assistant judge in district courts in Sweden. He has been a member of the Swedish Bar Association since 1979, and he is a partner in the law firm of Landahl in Stockholm. In addition, he is a member of the International Bar Association (area reporter in banking law), the Danish Association of European Law and the Swedish Association of European Law. His specialist areas of practice include all aspects of Swedish and international commercial law, EC competition law and intellectual property law. He has, on his own, as well as in collaboration with others, completed legal research projects in the fields of, for example, energy and food law for Swedish companies; employers' associations; and interest groups. He is the author of a chapter in *The Legal Professions in the New Europe* (2nd edn, 1996, London: Cavendish Publishing).

**Francis Meyrier** has been a member of the Paris Bar since 1969. He was an equity partner in the firm of Shearman and Sterling, in New York, from 1981 to 1988. He is the founder and senior partner of Meyrier, Rentmeesters Fayout Lacoste, a leading firm in the areas of business law, located in Paris. His areas of practice include international corporate and commercial transactions, mergers and acquisitions, commercial litigation and arbitration – both as counsel and as an arbitrator.

**Camila Pinto de Lima** practises law in Lisbon at AM Pereira, Sáragga Leal Oliveira Martins, Júdice e Associados. She graduated in 1991 from the Catholic University of Lisbon and has been a member of the Portuguese Bar Association since 1992.

**Jan Ravelingien** studied law and political science at the University of Leuven (1985) and later specialised in international development law and international commercial arbitration (The Hague). He was called to the Bar in 1986. From 1986–89, he was an assistant professor of comparative and international commercial law at the University of Leuven. He practised at the Brussels law firm of Lafili and van Crombrugghe from 1986–91 and, in 1995, was a founding partner of Claes and Partners, where he was in charge of the commercial law department. In 1995, he established Ravelingien Heitkamp, a small commercial law firm, located in Brussels. Mr Ravelingien is now senior partner at Marx, Van Ranst, Vermeersch and Partners. His current practice is in the area of Belgian/German commercial and trade practice law, focusing on competition and trade practices, intellectual property, marketing, advertising, sales promotion, passing off, counterfeit, transactional and regulatory work. He also acts in these fields for several marketing and advertising agencies, and for some smaller corporations in computer hardware and software, entertainment, media and audio-visual entertainment. He has published work on contracts, product liability, advertising and competition law, and is the Belgian representative in the European Advertising Lawyers Association.

**José Manuel Rey** obtained a degree from the University of Madridb and a master's in tax law (1992). He has published work on Community regulation on intellectual property rights (1993); intellectual property in audio-visual media (1995). Since 1992, he has been a member of the Madrid Bar Association and, since 1994, a member of the National Association of Security in Computing Environments. His working languages are Spanish and English, and his specialist areas of legal practice, at Batalla, Larrauri and López Ante in Madrid, are information technology, industrial and intellectual property, advertising, administrative and mercantile law.

**Riccardo Rossotto** has been a member of the Bar since 1986. He practices in the Turin, Milan and Rome offices of the law firm of 'Rossotto and Partners'. He is a specialist in communications law, and is a consultant to many Italian associations active in the field. Since 1990, he has been working with Professor Giancarlo Rivolta, resident professor in commercial law in the Faculty of Political Science at the Milan State University. He is member of the Debating Commission for Italian Self-regulatory Advertising, and of the Committee of Legal Experts of the EAAA in Brussels. He is founding member of Adlaw, an international network of lawyers specialised in industrial and copyright law. He writes for specialist journals in the industrial and copyright fields, and has published widely in these areas, on, for example, the code on advertising self-regulation (1990); authorisations and prohibitions in the EEC countries (1992); advertising contracts (1994); client/agency contracts (1996); advertising and copyright (1997); and comparative advertising (1998).

**Ursula Schildt**, LLM, Advocate (Finland), Solicitor (England and Wales), was educated at the University of Helsinki and admitted to the Finnish Bar in 1993. She is a member of the Finnish Association for Copyright Law, the Finnish

Association of Industrial Property Rights, the European Lawyer's Association and the Association Internationale des Jeunes Avocats. She has contributed to various publications in the fields of commercial, civil litigation and intellectual property law. She has a Diploma in English commercial law with merit from the College of Law, London, and in 1997 qualified as a solicitor (England and Wales), the first Finnish lawyer resident in Finland to do so. Between 1989 and 1996, she was employed by Bützow and Co Ltd, in Helsinki, a leading firm widely recognised for its expertise in commercial, corporate and intellectual property law. Since 1998, she has been working for the Office for the Harmonisation of the Internal Market, Alicante, Spain.

**Alex Schmitt** is a member of the Brussels and Luxembourg Bars. He holds a degree in law, a master's degree in European law from the Université Libre de Bruxelles and an LLM degree from Harvard University. He is the managing partner of Bonn & Schmitt – one of the largest law firms in Luxembourg. His major interests include international tax, finance and banking law, as well as European and general commercial law. His main writing interests are in the fields of commercial, financial and banking law, as well as international taxation. He is a regular correspondent for many legal journals, including the *International Financial Law Review* and the *Revue de la Banque*. He holds a lectureship at the Université Libre de Bruxelles, and is active in teaching in several other academic and professional organisations.

**Mårten Stenström** graduated with a Master of Laws (*jur kand*) from the University of Stockholm. He thereafter served in the District Court of Linköping, Sweden. In 1995, he was admitted to the Swedish Bar Association. He practises law at the Advokatfiman Nordia, in Stockholm. His specialist areas of practice are civil litigation and arbitration, marketing law and intellectual property law.

**Zahd Yaqub,** BA, MA, LLM, is a Barrister-at-Law (England and Wales, Republic of Ireland). He is a specialist in EC and commercial law, and a major writer in issues of EC law. He is the editor of the *EC Travel Law Handbook* (1997); co-editor of *The Legal Professions in the New Europe* (2nd edn, 1996, London: Cavendish Publishing). He is presently in the Chambers of Lord Campbell of Alloway QC, 2 King's Bench Walk, Temple, London EC4Y 7DE.

# CONTENTS

# Contents

# Contents

# Contents

# Contents

# Contents

# Contents

# Contents

# TABLE OF CASES

# TABLE OF STATUTES

**Republic of Ireland**

# Table of Statutes

# TABLE OF INTERNATIONAL INSTRUMENTS

# TABLE OF CONVENTIONS

# EUROPEAN COMMUNITY*

*Lord Campbell of Alloway and Zahd Yaqub*

## ADVERTISING: THE OVERALL PERSPECTIVE

Advertising involves the process of persuasion, using the paid media, in which purchasers of goods, services and ideas are sought. Its primary aim is to convince consumers to acquire products or services and/or the specific brands being offered by the advertisers.

It is impossible to restrict advertisers to include purely objective information in their advertisements, as that runs counter to the very essence of advertising. It is, moreover, very difficult to assess the effect any advertisement has on its target group, but market research has shown that consumer choice is not always based on rational considerations; emotional factors also play a part Nevertheless, it is important that consumers receive correct and objective information.

On this basis, an advertisement must satisfy a number of objective standards (laid down by Directive 84/450/EC on Misleading Advertising):

(a) the statements in the advertisement must be factually correct (honest and true);

(b) they must not be misleading;

(c) the product concerned must be legal.

Objective information will also reach the consumer via other channels. These include: correct and comprehensive information on labels and packaging, brochures, etc; information on products and services derived from comparative tests on products; and communications from governments and consumer organisations. Government information often provides more than basic product information, and sometimes indicates environmental and health hazards, the social position of the consumer and other concerns. In sum, individual producers, governments and consumers all have a hand in the tasks and responsibilities.

Advertising also plays a vital role in the operation of the internal market and the free movement of goods, services, capital and persons. Completion of the internal market means increased supply and choice in goods and services.

---

\*    **Readers should note that the Amsterdam Treaty came into force in May 1999.**

Advertising enables the public to be aware of the larger range of choice, and it enables producers to have access to consumers and to plan for tomorrow's market.

It is essential to have a clear European framework of legislation to prevent unfair competition. Cross-frontier advertising has increased sharply with the growth of cross-frontier communication, but it is also hampered by the differences in legislation between the various EC Member States. National autonomy in this area is influenced by the principle of the free flow of information, as laid down in the Treaty of Rome (EC Treaty), and by the way it has been interpreted in European legislation. The Television Directive constituted a breakthrough in this regard, and has led to major changes for the broadcasting systems of some Member States.

In the context of the internal market and the need to find the right balance between the market principle and protecting consumers, policy decisions to restrict or ban advertising, where the arguments are based on special cases, for whatever good reason, should be excluded. Bans or restrictions on advertising must be designed to halt proven abuse. Speculation and suspicion are not sufficient reasons to take action. Bans and restrictions should be based on the principle of fairness, and even where there is the useful aim of limiting consumption, they must be formulated so that basic freedoms are not harmed (freedom of expression, the market principle, freedom to exercise a profession, etc). An advertising ban for a certain product also hampers the consideration and development of products or substitutes which could be less environmentally damaging, healthier, cheaper or more practical.

## THE SECTOR OF COMMERCIAL COMMUNICATIONS

Commercial communications take in all forms of communication seeking to promote either products, services or the image of a company or organisation to final consumers and/or consumers. In addition to advertising, it includes all forms of direct marketing, sponsorship, sales promotions and public relations. Also covered within commercial communications is the use of commercial communication services by all goods and service industries, as well as public and semi-public bodies, charities and political organisations.[1] Packaging, however, is not included.

Within this service sector, there are two general types of service:

---

1    This definition covers all forms of remunerated commercial communication services, irrespective of the nature of the paying company or organisation. Thus, for example, a political advertising campaign would be included, whereas party television broadcasts imposed by law and for which political parties/organisations do not pay would be excluded.

(a) those services offered by the commercial communications industry – the 'suppliers'. Suppliers include advertising agencies, all forms of direct marketing companies, sales promotion designers, media buyers, sponsorship agents and public relations companies. Other services are supplied by 'specialised suppliers', such as market research companies, producers of advertising films and mailing list brokers. The services of both kinds of supplier are provided to clients ('users') interested in making such communications to the public or a part thereof;

(b) the delivery services offered by 'carriers' of commercial communications. The providers of these services cover a wide range of organisations, including the media (television, radio, the printed word), organisers of sporting and cultural events, postal and telecommunication service providers, billboard site operators, etc, and they may work both for suppliers and users.

It is impossible to give precise figures on the operations of the whole sector of commercial communication services. In 1993, advertising expenditure reached 45,557 m ECU in the EC; the market for direct marketing was worth 26,760 m ECU.[2]

In the modern industrial and service economies of the EC, commercial communications serve the role of promoting brand identities and informing potential users/clients, by strengthening the market presence and the desired positioning of the brand or company, and providing, in appropriate detail, information on the product or service offered.

## COMMERCIAL COMMUNICATIONS AND THE FREE MOVEMENT OF GOODS

In certain circumstances, the activities of commercial communications could benefit from the application of Art 28 of the EC Treaty relating to the free movement of goods. The recognition by the European Court of Justice (ECJ) of the indirect economic link between commercial communication services and the sale of goods is clearly explained in the judgment in *Re Oosthoek's Uitgeversmaatschappij* (C-286/81, [1982] (4) ECR 4575 of 15.12.82) concerning the restriction of a sales promotion by a Belgian company into the Dutch market. The ECJ stated that this measure amounted to a quantitative restriction:

Legislation which restricts or prohibits certain forms of advertising and certain means of sales promotion may, although it does not directly affect imports, be such as to restrict their volume because it affects marketing opportunities for the imported products. The possibility cannot be ruled out that to compel a

---

2   European Advertising Agencies' Association.

producer either to adopt advertising or sales promotion schemes which differ from one Member State to another or to discontinue a scheme which he considers to be particularly effective may constitute an obstacle to imports even if the legislation in question applies to domestic products and imported products without distinction.

Article 30 (Title I, Free Movement of Goods, Ch 2) of the EC Treaty deals with the elimination of quantitative restrictions between Member States:

Quantitative restrictions on imports and all measures having equivalent effect shall, without prejudice to the following provisions, be prohibited between Member States.

The Treaty of Amsterdam, not in force at the time of writing, seeks to go a step further by amending the EC Treaty to prohibit quantitative restrictions between Member States:

**Prohibition of quantitative restrictions between Member States**

Article 28 (ex Art 30)

Quantitative restrictions on imports and all measures having equivalent effect shall be prohibited between Member States.

Articles 31 to 33 shall be repealed.

Article 29 (ex Art 34)

Quantitative restrictions on exports, and all measures having equivalent effect, shall be prohibited between Member States (*formerly* para 1 of Art 34).

Paragraph 2 shall be repealed.

Article 35 shall be repealed.

Article 30 (ex Art 36)

The provisions of Art 28 and 29 shall not preclude prohibitions or restrictions on imports, exports or goods in transit justified on grounds of public morality, public policy or public security; the protection of health and life of human, animals and plants; the protection of national treasures possessing artistic, historic or archeological value; or the protection of industrial commercial property. Such prohibitions or restrictions shall not, however, constitute a means of arbitrary discrimination or a disguised restriction on trade between Member States.

Article 31 (ex Art 37)

Member States *shall adjust* any State monopolies of a commercial character so as to ensure *that no* discrimination regarding the conditions under which goods are procured and marketed exists between nationals of Member States.

The provisions of this article shall apply to any body through which a Member State, in law or in fact, either directly or indirectly supervises, determines or appreciably influences imports or exports between Member States. These provisions shall likewise apply to monopolies delegated by the State to others.

Member States shall refrain from introducing any new measure which is contrary to the principles laid down in para 1 or which restricts the scope of the articles dealing with the *prohibition* of customs duties and quantitative restrictions between Member States.

Paragraph 3 shall be repealed.

If a State monopoly of a commercial character has rules which are designed to make it easier to dispose of agricultural products or obtain for them the best return, steps should be taken in applying the rules contained in this article to ensure equivalent safeguards for the employment and standard of living of the producers concerned. Remainder of sentence shall be deleted.

Paragraphs 5 and 6 shall be repealed.

In the case of *GB-INNO-BM v Confédération du Commerce Luxembourgeois* (C-362/88, [1990[ (2) ECR I-667 of 7.3.90) where the restriction bore on the content of advertising leaflets distributed in Luxembourg by a Belgian retailer, the ECJ made the link to Art 30 by way of the reminder that the free movement of goods across frontiers also depended upon the free movement of people. Since the banning of advertising directed at individuals from a neighbouring State would deprive them of the incentive to cross the border, it would, therefore, limit the possibilities for the goods to cross the same border. This judgment shows that the informational role of commercial communications is recognised in law. It also shows that restrictions in advertising related to goods are to be assessed under Art 30 of the EC Treaty.

This informational benefit was stressed in the case of *Scutzverband gegen Unwesen in de Wirtschaft eV v Yves Rocher GmbH* (C-126/91, [1991] (3) ECR I-2361 of 18.5.93). In deciding that price comparisons were not misleading, the ECJ remarked that such advertising practices were considered as being 'extremely useful to enable the consumer to make his choice in the full knowledge of the facts'.

Restrictions on commercial communications may, therefore, be open to challenge under Art 30 of the EC Treaty. In *Re Keck and Mithouard* (C-267 and C-268/91, [1993] (7) ECR I-6097 of 24.11.93), the ECJ imposed certain limits on the application of Art 30, by holding that Art 30 would not apply to national measures prohibiting or restricting 'certain selling arrangements', provided that such measures applied to all relevant traders operating within the national area, and so long as they affect in the same manner, in law or fact, the marketing of domestic products and those from other Member States. This case has been followed by a number of others, in which the same line has been taken by the ECJ.[3] In order to decide whether Art 30 applies, an examination of restrictions on commercial communications should be taken on a case by case basis.

---

3  Eg, Case C-292/92, *Ruth Hünermunde eV v Landesapothekerkammer Baden-Würtemberg* [1993] (8) ECR I-6787 of 15.12.93; *Société d'Importation Edouard Leclerc-Siplec v TF1 Publicité SA and M6 Publicité* [1995] ECR I-179 of 9.2.95.

# COMMERCIAL COMMUNICATIONS AND THE FREE MOVEMENT OF SERVICES

## Treaty provisions

The dismantling of barriers between Member States in the provision of services is dealt with by Arts 59 and 60 (Title III, Free Movement of Persons, Services and Capital, Ch 3) of the EC Treaty:

Article 59

Within the framework of the provisions set out below, restrictions on freedom to provide services within the Community shall be progressively abolished during the transitional period in respect of nationals of Member States who are established in a State of the Community other than that of the person for whom the services are intended.

The Council may, acting by a qualified majority on a proposal from the Commission, extend the provisions of this chapter to nationals of a third country who provide services and who are established within the Community.

Article 60

Services shall be considered to be 'services' within the meaning of this Treaty where they are normally provided for remuneration, in so far as they are not governed by the provisions relating to freedom of movement for goods, capital and persons.

'Services' shall in particular include:

(a) activities of an industrial character;

(b) activities of a commercial character;

(c) activities of craftsmen;

(d) activities of the professions.

Without prejudice to the provisions of the chapter relating to the right of establishment, the person providing a service may, in order to do so, temporarily pursue his activity in the State where the service is provided, under the same conditions as are imposed by that State on its own nationals.

The provisions of Treaty of Amsterdam dealing with amendments on to Ch 3 of services are as follows:

Article 49 (ex Art 59)

Within the framework of the provisions set out below, restrictions on freedom to provide services within the Community shall be *prohibited* in respect of nationals of Member States who are established in a State of the Community other than that of the person for whom the services are intended.

The Council may, acting by a qualified majority on a proposal from the Commission, extend the provisions of the chapter to nationals of a third country who provide services and who are established within the Community.

Article 50 (ex Art 60)

Services shall be considered to be 'services' within the meaning of this Treaty where they are normally provided for remuneration, in so far as they are not governed by the provisions relating to freedom of movement for goods, capital and persons.

'Services' shall in particular include:

(a) activities of an industrial character;

(b) activities of a commercial character;

(c) activities of craftsmen;

(d) activities of the professions.

Without prejudice to the provisions of the chapter relating to the right of establishment, the person providing a service may, in order to do so, temporarily pursue his activity in the State where the service is provided, under the same conditions as are imposed by that State on its own nationals.

Article 51 (ex Art 61)

1  Freedom to provide services in the field of transport shall be governed by the provisions of the title relating to transport.

2  Liberalisation of banking and insurance services connected with movements of capital shall be effected in step with the liberalisation of movement of capital.

Article 62 shall be repealed.

Article 52 (ex Art 63)

Paragraph 1 shall be repealed.

1  In order to *achieve the* liberalisation of a specific service, the Council shall, on a proposal from the Commission and after consulting the Economic and Social Committee and the European Parliament, issue directives acting by *a qualified majority.*

2  As regards the *directives* referred to in *para 1*, priority shall as a general rule be given to those services which directly affect production costs or the liberalisation of which helps to promote trade in goods.

Article 53 (ex Art 64)

The Member States declare their readiness to undertake the liberalisation of services beyond the extent required by the directives issued pursuant to Art 52(1), if their general economic situation and the situation of the economic sector concerned so permit.

To this end, the Commission shall make recommendations to the Member States concerned.

Article 54 (ex Art 64)

As long as restrictions on freedom to provide services have not been abolished, each Member State shall apply such restrictions without distinction on grounds of nationality or residence to all persons providing services within the meaning of the first paragraph of Art 49.

Article 55 (ex Art 66)

The provisions of Arts 45–48 shall apply to the matters covered by this chapter.

## Bond van Adverteerders v The Netherlands

The freedom to provide services under Arts 59 and 60 of the EC Treaty depends on the meaning of these articles as interpreted by the ECJ. In this respect, the case of *Bond* (C-352/85, [1988] (2) ECR 2085 of 26.4.88) is worth consideration. In *Bond*, the ECJ explained that for the application of free movement of services, it is necessary: (a) to identify the services in question; (b) to consider whether the services are transfrontier in nature for the purposes of Art 59 of the Treaty; and (c) to establish whether the services in question are services that are normally provided for remuneration, within the meaning of Art 60 of the Treaty.

The relevant text of the *Bond* judgment ([1989] 3 CMLR 147, pp 147–52) is as follows:

(a) The existence of services within the meaning of Arts 59 and 60 of the EEC Treaty

12 In its first question the national court seeks essentially to ascertain whether the distribution, by operators of cable networks established in a Member State, of television programmes supplied by broadcasters established in other Member States and containing advertisements intended especially for the public in the Member State where the programmes are received, involve the provision of a service or services within the meaning of *Arts 59 and 60* of the Treaty.

...

17 The reply to the first question put by the national court must [...] be that the distribution, by operators of cable networks established in other Member States and containing advertisements intended especially for the public in the Member State where the programmes are received, comprises a number of services within the meaning of *Arts 59 and 60* of the Treaty.

(b) The existence of restrictions on freedom to supply services contrary to Art 59 of the Treaty

18 In its second, third, fourth and fifth questions, the national court essentially seeks to ascertain whether prohibitions of advertising and subtitling, such as those contained in the Kabelregeling (cable regulation), constitute restrictions on freedom to supply services contrary to *Art 59* of the Treaty, regard being had to the fact the Omroepwet (broadcasting law) prohibits national broadcasters from broadcasting advertisements and restricts the right to broadcast advertisements to a foundation which is bound by its statute to transfer its receipts to the State, which uses them to subsidise national broadcasters and the press.

19 It is appropriate to answer those questions together in the light, first, of the prohibition on advertising and, secondly, of the prohibition on subtitling.

20 It appears from the specific circumstances mentioned by the national court that the prohibitions of advertising and subtitling contained in the Kabelregeling must be considered in the context of the national legislation relating to the broadcasting system.

...

26 It must ... be held that there is discrimination owing to the fact that the prohibition of advertising laid down in the Kabelregeling deprives broadcasters established in other Member States of any possibility of broadcasting on their station advertisements intended especially for the public in The Netherlands, whereas the Omroepwet permits the broadcasting of advertisements on national television stations for the benefit of all the Omroeporganisaties.

27 Accordingly, a prohibition of advertising such as that contained in the Kabelregeling entails restrictions on the freedom to supply services contrary to *Art 59* of the Treaty.

...

29 ... the prohibition of subtitling to which broadcasters in other Member States are subject simply has the aim of complementing the prohibition of advertising, which, as appears from the considerations set out above, entails restrictions on the freedom to provide services contrary to *Art 59* of the Treaty.

(c) The possibility of justifying restrictions such as those at issue on the freedom of suppliers

31 On the assumption that national rules of the type at issue are not discriminatory, the national court asks in its sixth question whether they must be justified on grounds relating to the public interest and proportional to the objectives which they set out to achieve. In its seventh and eighth questions it further asks whether those grounds might relate to cultural policy or to policy designed to combat a form of unfair competition.

...

39 It must ... be held that prohibitions of advertising and subtitling such as those contained in the Kabelregeling cannot be justified on grounds of public policy under Art 56 of the Treaty.

(d) General principles of Community law and fundamental rights recognised by Community law

40 In its ninth question, the national court essentially asks whether the principle of proportionality and the right of freedom of expression guaranteed by Art 10 of the European Convention on Human Rights in themselves impose obligations on the Member States, independently of the applicability of provisions of Community law.

41  It is clear from the answers given to the preceding questions that prohibitions of advertising and subtitling such as those contained in the Kabelregeling are incompatible with the provisions of *Art 59 et seq* of the EEC Treaty. Since the national court can resolve the dispute before it in the light of those answers alone, the ninth question has no purpose.

Activities of commercial communication involve the provision of different 'services', which can be classified according to whether they are provided by the suppliers (for example, advertising agencies), the carriers (for example, media) or the specialist suppliers (for example, list brokers). All these services could be provided on a transborder basis and against remuneration.

## *Re Giuseppe Sacchi*

The ECJ has already held that advertising is a service.[4] Moreover, in the case of *Sacchi* (C-155/73, [1974] (1) ECR 409 of 30.4.74), the ECJ held that the transmission of television signals, including those in the nature of advertisements, comes within the rules on services of the EC Treaty:

> Advertising should be regarded as an intangible asset in its own right, or at least as having, to the products to which it relates, the relationship of accessory to principal, and on this double basis it is subject to the customs union and the principle of the free movement of goods. It appears from the case law of this Court that intangible assets – such as electricity – come under the application of these rules (Case 6/64, *Costa/Enel*, Rec 1964, p 1157) and all products on which a monetary value can be placed, and which are as such capable of being the object of commercial transactions, must be regarded as goods (Case 7/68, *Commission v Italie*, Rec 1968, p 625). This assimilation of the advertisement with the product is indispensable for progressive unification of the market, effective equality of opportunity for penetration and distribution which is not beyond the means of all save the large multinational undertakings.

> The fact that the national court, in its first question, has referred to the principle of the free movement of goods, rather than to the various articles in the Treaty which apply it in detail, is because the instances do not on their own reveal the whole scope of the principle. The principle of the free movement of goods must indeed be understood and applied as one of the fundamental freedoms guaranteeing the functioning of the market.

> It follows that it cannot be reduced to a simple guarantee of the sale of goods within the Common Market, but it must likewise ensure their sale with a view to consumption, so that any measure is prohibited which, outside the strict circumstances laid down in the Treaty, restricts the use of certain goods. The principle of free movement must therefore cover everything for which different arrangements are not expressly provided. There is no doubt as to the

---

4  Case C-52/79, *Procureur du Roi v Marc JVC Debauvèe and Others* [1980] ECR 833 of 10.5.95.

direct effect of the fundamental rule thus recognised, since the general principle is as precise, clear and free from ambiguity as the particular applications which the Treaty makes of it.

In the light of this, an affirmative reply should be given not only to the first question relating to the direct effects of the principle of free movement, but also the first two parts (a) and (b) of the second question. The advertisement enjoys as an intangible asset the guarantee of free movement. It enjoys it also in its capacity of a support and accessory for the movement of products. This free movement implies the free preparation of the latter for sale and the free exercise of activities on which the movement of goods depends, such as distribution and marketing.

In a judgment concerning 'cold calling', namely unsolicited telephone advertising, the case of *Alpine Investments BV v Minister van Financiën* (Case C-384/93, [1995] ECR 833 of 10.5.95), it was held that a prohibition of cold calling would deprive the operators concerned of a rapid and direct technique for marketing and contacting potential clients in other Member States. Such a prohibition could, therefore, constitute a restriction on the freedom to provide cross-border services.

The principle of freedom to provide services guarantees that a Member State will not be able to restrict services emanating from another Member State, except where such restrictions fulfil certain conditions. Where these conditions are not fulfiled, such services only fall under the legislation of the Member State in which the service provider is established (that is, the legislation of the country of origin).[5] However, such restrictions on the freedom to provide services can, subject to certain conditions, be justified. Here, the ECJ draws a clear distinction between discriminatory and non-discriminatory measures.

# DISCRIMINATORY AND NON-DISCRIMINATORY MEASURES

Discriminatory measures are compatible with Community law only if:

(a) they can be brought within the scope of the exemptions set out in Art 56 of the EC Treaty (that is, public policy, public security or public health); and

(b) they comply with the principle of proportionality.

The text of Art 56 (Title III, Free Movement of Persons, Services and Capital, Ch 2) reads as follows:

1    The provisions of this chapter and measures taken in pursuance thereof shall not prejudice the applicability of provisions laid down by law,

---

5    See 'Commission Interpretative Communication Concerning the Free Movement of Services across Frontiers', OJ C 334, 9.12.93.

regulation or administrative action providing for special treatment for foreign nationals on grounds of public policy, public security or public health.

2   Before the end of the transitional period the Council shall, acting unanimously on a proposal from the Commission and after consulting the European Parliament, issue directives for the co-ordination of the above-mentioned provisions laid down by law, regulation or administrative action. After the end of the second stage, however, the Council shall, acting in accordance with the provisions referred to in Art 189b, issue directives for the co-ordination of such provisions as, in each Member State, are a matter for regulation or administrative action.

Non-discriminatory measures may arise as a result of the additional application of national rules to persons providing services established in the territory of another Member State who already have to satisfy that State's legislation. Such restrictions could be justified under Art 59 only if they are supported by overriding reasons relating to the public interest, and if the requirements embodied in the restrictive measures are not already satisfied by the rules imposed on those persons in the Member State in which they are established (mutual recognition).

The Treaty of Amsterdam provisions for the amendment of Art 59 of the EC Treaty are as follows:

Article 46 (ex Art 56)

1   The provisions of this chapter and measures taken in pursuance thereof shall not prejudice the applicability of provisions laid down by law, regulation or administrative action providing for special treatment for foreign nationals on grounds of public policy, public security or public health.

2   The Council shall, acting in accordance with the procedure referred to in Art 251, issue directives for the co-ordination of the above-mentioned provisions.

See Art 49 of the Treaty of Amsterdam for guidance.


## Mediawet

The *Mediawet* case (Case C-288/89, *Stichting Collectieve Antennevoorziening Gouda and Others v Commissariat voor de Media* [1991] (1) ECR 4007) discusses the application of Art 59 of the EC Treaty. The questions posed by the national court were whether conditions, such as those imposed by the Mediawet (media law), on the transmission by operators of cable networks of radio or television programmes broadcast from the territory of other Member States, came within Art 59, and, if so, whether the imposition of such conditions was justified.

10 [...] the Court has consistently held (see, most recently, the judgments in Case C-154/89, *Commission v France* [1991] ECR I-659, para 12; Case C-180/89, *Commission v Italy* [1991] ECR I-709, para 15; and Case C-198/89, *Commission v Greece* [1991] ECR I-727, para 16) that Art 59 of the Treaty entails, in the first place, the abolition of any discrimination against a person providing services on account of his nationality or the fact that he is established in a Member State other than the one in which the service is provided.

11 As the Court held in its judgment in Case 352/85, *Bond van Adverteerders* [1988] ECR 2085, paras 32 and 333, national rules which are not applicable to services without discrimination as regards their origin are compatible with Community law only if they can be brought within the scope of an express exemption, such as that contained in Art 56 of the Treaty. It also appears from that judgment (para 34) that economic aims cannot constitute grounds of public policy within the meaning of Art 56 of the Treaty.

12 In the absence of harmonisation of the rules applicable to services, or even of a system of equivalence, restrictions on the freedom guaranteed by the Treaty in this field may arise in the second place as a result of the application of national rules which affect any person established in the national territory to persons providing services established in the territory of another Member State who already have to satisfy the requirements of that State's legislation.

13 As the Court has consistently held (see, most recently, the judgments in *Commission v France*, cited above, para 15; *Commission v Italy*, cited above, para 18; and *Commission v Greece*, cited above, para 18), such restrictions come within the scope of Art 59 if the application of the national legislation to foreign persons providing services is not justified by overriding reasons relating to the public interest or if the requirements embodied in that legislation are already satisfied by the rules imposed on those persons in the Member State in which they are established.

14 In this respect, the overriding reasons relating to the public interest which the Court has already recognised include professional rules intended to protect recipients of the service (Joined Cases 110/78 and 111/78, *Van Wesemael* [1979] ECR 35, para 28); protection of intellectual property (Case 62/79, *Coditel* [1980] ECR 881); the protection of workers (Case 279/80, *Webb* [1981] ECR 3305, para 19; Joined Cases 62/81 and 63/81, *Seco v EVI* [1982] ECR 223, para 14; Case C-113/89, *Rush Portuguesa* [1990] ECR I-1417, para 18); consumer protection (Case 220/83, *Commission v France* [1986] ECR 3663, para 20; Case 252/83, *Commission v Denmark* [1986] ECR 3713, para 20; Case 205/84, *Commission v Ireland* [1986] ECR 3817, para 20; *Commission v Italy*, cited above, para 20; and *Commission v Greece*, cited above, para 21); the conservation of the national historic and artistic heritage of a country and the widest possible dissemination of knowledge of the artistic and cultural heritage of a country (*Commission v France*, cited above, para 17; and *Commission v Greece*, cited above, para 21).

15 Lastly, as the Court has consistently held, the application of national provisions to providers of services established in other Member States

must be such as to guarantee the achievement of the intended aim and must go beyond that which is necessary in order to achieve that objective. In other words, it must not be possible to obtain the same result by less restrictive rules (see, most recently, Case C-154/89, *Commission v France*, cited above, paras 14 and 15; Case C-180/89, *Commission v Italy*, cited above, paras 17 and 18; Case C-198/89, *Commission v Greece*, cited above, paras 18 and 19).

16 In the light of those principles, it should be examined whether a provision such as Art 66(1)(b) of the *Mediawet*, which, according to the national court, is not discriminatory, contains restrictions on freedom to provide services, and, if so, whether those restrictions may be justified.

'Overriding reasons relating to the public interest' (public interest objectives) can be summarised as:

(a) the protection of workers;[6]

(b) the protection of consumers;[7]

(c) the protection of intellectual property;[8]

(d) the protection of fair trading;

(e) the conservation of the national and historic artistic heritage;

(f) the widest possible dissemination of knowledge of the artistic and cultural heritage of a country;[9]

(g) professional rules designed to protect recipients of services;[10] and

(h) the protection of pluralism[11] and linguistic policy.[12]

In addition, the restrictions on the free movement of services cannot be imposed merely because of the existence of such public interest objectives. To be justified under Community law, the restrictions must be proportionate to the public interest objectives pursued. The ECJ has specified the meaning of proportionality: 'It is settled case law that requirements imposed on the providers of services must be appropriate to ensure achievement of the

---

6  Case C-279/80, *Re Alfred John Webb* [1981] ECR 3305, para 19; Joined Cases 62/8, 63/81, *Seco SA and Desquenne and Giral SA v Etablissement d'Assurance contre la Vieillesse et l'Invalidité* [1982] (1) ECR 223, para 14; Case C-113/89, *Rush Portuguesa Lda v Office National d'Immigration* [1990] (2) ECR I-1417, para 18.

7  Case C-220/83, *Commission v France* [1986] (4) ECR 3663, para 20.

8  Case C-6/79, *SA Compagnie Gènèrale pour la Diffusion de la Tèlèvision Coditel and Others* [1980] ECR 881, para 15.

9  Case C-180/89, *Commission v Italy* [1991] (2) ECR I-709, para 20; Case C-154/89, *Commission v France* [1991] (2) ECR I-659; para 17; Case C-198/89, *Commission v Greece* [1991] (2) ECR I-727, para 21.

10 Joined Cases C-110 and C-111/78, *Ministère Public and Chambre Syndicalr des Agents Artistiques et Impresarii de Belgique, ASBL v Willy van Wesmael and Others* [1979] (1) ECR 35, para 28.

11 Case C-288/89, *Stichting Collectieve Antennevoorziening Gouda and Others v Commissariat voor de Media*, [1991] (1) ECR 4007, para 23.

12 Case C-379/87, *Anita Groener v Minister for Education and City of Dublin Vocational Committee* [1989] (4) ECR 3967.

intended aim and must not go beyond that which is necessary in order to achieve that objective.'[13] In other words, it must not be possible to obtain the same result by less restrictive rules.[14]

It cannot be excluded that the ECJ will extend its reasoning in *Keck* (Case C-267 and Case C-268/91, 1993 (7) ECR I-6097 of 24.11.93) to Art 59 of the EC Treaty. The impact of such an extension will very much depend on the type of service involved.

# COMMERCIAL COMMUNICATIONS AND THE FREEDOM OF EXPRESSION

Commercial communications could benefit from the principle of freedom of expression as provided in Art 10(1) of the European Convention on Human Rights (ECHR) and in Art 19 of the UN's International Covenant on Civil and Political Rights (UN Covenant). Indeed, commercial communication services include opinions, information or ideas and so could benefit from the freedom to hold opinions and to receive and impart information and ideas, without interference by public authorities and regardless of frontiers. Interference by public authorities can be justified if it complies with the conditions set out in para 2 of Art 10 of the ECHR or Art 19 of the UN Covenant. In this context, the specific nature of commercial communications is accounted for through the application of the principle of proportionality.

The European Commission, the Court of Human Rights and the UN Human Rights Committee[15] have recognised that commercial communications could benefit from freedom of expression as thus defined.[16]

Regarding links between Art 10 of the ECHR, Art 19 of the UN Covenant and the EC Treaty, restrictions on the free movement of services should be interpreted in the light of Art 10 of the ECHR[17] and Art 19 of the UN Covenant.[18]

---

13  Case C-384/93, *Alpine Investments BV v Minister van Financiën* [1995] ECR 833 of 10.5.95, para 45.

14  Case C-288/89, *Stichting Collectieve Antennevoorziening Gouda and Others v Commissariat voor de Media* (the *Mediawet* case), [1991] (1) ECR 4007, para 13.

15  Communications Nos 359/1989 and 385/1989 Ballantyne Davidson McIntyre, decision of 31.3.93 CCPR/C47/D/359/1989 and 385/1889/Rev 1.

16  See cases *Markt intern Verlag GmbH and Klaus Beerman*, Series A No 165 of 20.11.89; and *Groppera Radio AG and Others v Switzerland*, Series A No 173 of 28.3.90. In recent case law, it appears that the European Commission of Human Rights considers that there is no doubt that advertising is protected under Art 10. In two recent decisions on the admissibility of applications to the European Court of Human Rights, under the ECHR, the Commission took the view that a restriction on advertising would fall under Art 10 ECHR (decision of 5.9.91 *Re Application No 15450/89* (*Cosado Coca v Spain*)).

17  Case C-260/89, *Elleniki Radiophonia Tilèorassi AE v Dimotiki Etaireia Pliroforissis and Sotiros Kouvelas* [1991] ECR I-2925 of 18.6.91, paras 41-44.

18  Case C-4/73 J, *Nold, Kohlen v Baustoffgroßhandlung v Commission* [1974] (1) ECR 491, para 13.

# THE INTERNAL MARKET: SECONDARY LEGISLATION

Wherever the application of the principles of free movement enshrined in the EC Treaty is insufficient to remove restrictive barriers (for example, where national restrictive measures are justified under Community law), secondary legislation is necessary. The aim of the legislation is to establish an equivalent level of protection of the public interest objectives (for example, consumer protection, protection of minors, protection of public health) in order to remove the legal barriers which make for disparities between national regulations. Some existing directives are relevant to commercial communications. They concern, *inter alia*, misleading advertising,[19] foodstuffs,[20] financial services,[21] medicinal products,[22] data protection,[23] and television broadcasts.[24]

# OTHER COMMUNITY OBJECTIVES AND THEIR INFLUENCE ON COMMERCIAL COMMUNICATIONS

Other objectives established by the EC Treaty, such as consumer protection (Art 129a) and public health (Art 129) can have an influence on commercial communications.

---

19  Council Directive 84/450/EEC of 10.9.84, on the approximation of laws, regulations and administrative provisions of the Member States concerning misleading advertising.

20  Council Directive 79/112/EEC of 18.12.78 on the approximation of the laws of Member States relating to the labelling, presentation and advertising of foodstuffs for sale to the ultimate consumer, OJ L 33, 1979.

21  Council Directive 92/96/EEC of 10.11.92 on the co-ordination of laws, regulations and administrative provisions relating to direct life assurance, and amending Directives 79/267/EEC and 90/619/EEC (third life assurance Directive), OJ L 360, 1992. Council Directive 92/49/EEC of 18.6.92 on the co-ordination of laws, regulations and administrative provisions relating to direct insurance other than life assurance, and amending Directives 73/239/EEC and 88/357/EEC (third non-life assurance Directive), OJ L 228, 1992; Council Directive 85/611/EEC of 20.12.85 on the co-ordination of laws, regulations and administrative provisions relating to the undertakings for collective investment in transferable securities, OJ L 375, 1985; Second Council Directive 89/646/EEC of 15.12.89 on the co-ordination of laws, regulations and administrative provisions relating to the taking up and pursuit of the business of credit institutions, and amending Directive 77/780/EEC, OJ L 386, 1989.

22  Council Directive 92/28/EEC of 31.3.92 on the advertising of medicinal products for human use, OJ L 113, 1992.

23  Directive of the European Parliament and the Council 95/46/EEC of 24.10.95 on the protection of individuals with regard to the processing of personal data and the free movement of such data.

24  Council Directive 89/552 EEC of 31.10.89 on the co-ordination of certain provisions laid down by law, regulation or administrative action in Member States concerning the pursuit of broadcasting activities, OJ L 298, 1989.

# Consumer protection policy

Article 129a of the EC Treaty (Title XI, Consumer Protection) reads as follows:

Article 129a†

1   The Community shall contribute to the attainment of a high level of consumer protection through:

   (a) measures adopted pursuant to Art 100a in the context of the completion of the internal market;

   (b) specific action which supports and supplements the policy pursued by the Member States to protect the health, safety and economic interests of consumers and to provide adequate information to consumers.

2   The Council, acting in accordance with the procedure referred to in Art 189b and after consulting the Economic and Social Committee, shall adopt the specific action referred to in para 1(b).

3   Action adopted pursuant to para 2 shall not prevent any Member State from maintaining or introducing more stringent protective measures. Such measures must be compatible with this Treaty. The Commission shall be notified of them.

Article 129a of the Treaty requires the Community to deal with the whole range of consumer issues, not just those related to the internal market. Such an obligation implies careful consideration of subsidiarity at all stages, so that appropriate solutions are adopted. With the advent of the information society, it is possible that effective consumer protection may require increased transnational regulatory co-operation. For those regulatory areas that fall beyond the remit of the internal market, the globalisation of supply which the information society heralds calls for a comparable adjustment of the regulatory system. This adaptation will be of crucial importance to consumers' willingness to participate: the Commission and Member States must address these issues. In this context, attention should be drawn to the fact that all measures based on Art 129a can take a minimal nature, such that Member States may adopt stricter provisions to ensure a higher level of consumer protection.

The Treaty of Amsterdam (Title XIV) provides for amendment of Art 129a of the EC Treaty:

Article 153 (ex Art 129a)

1   In order to promote the interests of consumers and to ensure a high level of consumer protection, the Community shall contribute to protecting the health, safety and economic interests of consumers, as well as to promoting their right to information, education and to organise themselves in order to safeguard their interests.

2   Consumer protection requirements shall be taken into account in defining and implementing other Community policies and activities.

The Community shall contribute to the attainment of the objectives referred to in para 1 through:

(a) measures adopted pursuant to Art 95 in the context of the completion of the internal market;

(b) measures which support, supplement and monitor the policy pursued by Member States.

4   The Council, acting in accordance with the procedure referred to in Art 251 and after consulting the Economic and Social Committee, shall adopt the measures referred to in para 3(b).

5   Measures adopted pursuant to para 4 shall not prevent any Member State from maintaining or introducing more stringent protective measures. Such measures must be compatible with this Treaty. The Commission shall be notified of them.

## Industrial policy

Industrial policy is the subject of Art 130 (Title XIII, Industry) of the EC Treaty:

Article 130

The Community and the Member States shall ensure that the conditions necessary for the competitiveness of the Community's industry exist.

For that purpose, in accordance with a system of open and competitive markets, their action shall be aimed at:

- speeding up the adjustment of industry to structural changes;

- encouraging an environment favourable to initiative and to the development of undertakings throughout the Community, particularly small and medium sized undertakings;

- encouraging an environment favourable to co-operation between undertakings;

- fostering better exploitation of the industrial potential of policies of innovation, research and technological development.

2   The Member States shall consult each other in liaison with the Commission and, where necessary, shall co-ordinate their action. The Commission may take any useful initiative to promote such co-ordination.

3   The Community shall contribute to the achievement of the objectives set out in para 1 through the policies and activities it pursues under other provisions of this Treaty. The Council, acting unanimously on a proposal from the Commission, after consulting the European Parliament and the Economic and Social Committee, may decide on specific measures in support of action taken in the Member States to achieve the objectives set out in para 1.

This Title shall not provide a basis for the introduction by the Community of any measure which could lead to a distortion of competition.

The EC Treaty incorporates legal bases for implementing industrial policy to 'ensure that the conditions necessary for the competitiveness of the Community's industry' (Art 130(1)). Article 130(2) adds that in order to attain these objectives, Member States are required 'to consult each other in liaison with the Commission and, where necessary, shall co-ordinates their action'. The Commission is assigned the specific duty of taking 'any useful initiative to promote such co-ordination'.

To support national action, the Community will generally help to achieve this objective of improving competitiveness by taking horizontal measures under a series of common policies (on research, cohesion, vocational training, networks and foreign trade). The Council may also, ruling unanimously on a proposal from the Commission, 'decide specific measures destined to support actions taken by Member States in order to attain stated objectives' (Art 130, para 1, COM (94) 319 Final).

Since efficient commercial communication services would generally, by improving marketing efficiency, assist industry in meeting these competitive goals, they could be covered by initiatives in this field.

The Treaty of Amsterdam provides for amendment of Art 130 of the EC Treaty:

Title XVI (ex Title XIII), Industry

Article 157 (ex Art 130)

1  The Community and the Member States shall ensure that the conditions necessary for the competitiveness of the Community's industry exist.

For that purpose, in accordance with a system of open and competitive markets, their action shall be aimed at:

- speeding up the adjustment of industry to structural changes;
- encouraging an environment favourable to initiative and to the development of undertakings throughout the Community, particularly small and medium sized undertakings;
- fostering better exploitation of the industrial potential of policies of innovation, research and technological development.

2  The Member States shall consult each other in liaison with the Commission and, where necessary, shall co-ordinate their action. The Commission may take any useful initiative to promote such co-ordination.

3  The Community shall contribute to the achievement of the objectives set out in para 1 through the policies and activities it pursues under other provisions of this Treaty. The Council, acting unanimously on a proposal from the Commission, after consulting the European Parliament and the Economic and Social Committee, may decide on specific measures in support of action taken in the Member States to achieve the objectives set out in para 1.

This Title shall not provide a basis for the introduction by the Community of any measure which could lead to a distortion of competition.

## Competition policy

Article 85 (Title V, Ch 1) of the EC Treaty deals with rules applying to undertakings:

Article 85

1 The following shall be prohibited as incompatible with the common market: all agreements between undertakings, decisions by associations of undertakings and concerted practices which may affect trade between Member States and which have as their object or effect the prevention, restriction or distortion of competition within the common market, and in particular those which:

   (a) directly or indirectly fix purchase or selling prices or any other trading conditions;

   (b) limit or control production, markets, technical development, or investment;

   (c) share markets or sources of supply;

   (d) apply dissimilar conditions to equivalent transactions with other trading parties, thereby placing them at a competitive disadvantage;

   (e) make the conclusion of contracts subject to acceptance by the other parties of supplementary obligations which, by their nature or according to commercial usage, have no connection with the subject of such contracts.

2 Any agreements or decisions prohibited pursuant to this article shall be automatically void.

3 The provisions of para 1 may, however, be declared inapplicable in the case of:

   • any agreement or category of agreements between undertakings;

   • any decision or category of decisions by associations of undertakings;

   • any concerted practice or category of concerted practices;

   which contributes to improving the production or distribution of goods or to promoting technical or economic progress, while allowing consumers a fair share of the resulting benefit, and which does not:

   (a) impose on the undertakings concerned restrictions which are not indispensable to the attainment of these objectives;

   (b) afford such undertakings the possibility of eliminating competition in respect of a substantial part of the products in question.

In general commercial communication, the activities of 'supplier', 'users' and 'carriers' are all covered by the competition rules of the EC Treaty. Given the competitive role of commercial communication in the internal market, anti-competitive agreements in the meaning of Art 85(1), which restrict the freedom of the parties to supply, carry, use or buy such communications are prohibited.

Nevertheless, anti-competitive agreements on commercial communications can be granted an exemption if they satisfy the conditions set out in Art 85(3). An example, which also illustrates the direct relevance of commercial communications in the market relationship between manufacturers and distributors, is cl 8(b) of Art 3 of the Commission Regulation on the application of Art 85(3) of the EC Treaty to certain categories of motor distribution and servicing agreements. This clause allows manufacturers to prohibit dealers from soliciting customers for contract goods or corresponding goods, outside their territory, by personalised advertising.

## Protection of public health

Policy on public health is set out in Art 129 (Title X, Public Health) of the EC Treaty:

Article 129

1　The Community shall contribute towards ensuring a high level of human health protection by encouraging co-operation between the Member States and, if necessary, lending support to their action.

Community action shall be directed towards the prevention of diseases, in particular the major health scourges, including drug dependence, by promoting research into their causes and their transmission, as well as health information and education.

Health protection requirements shall form a constituent part of the Community's other policies.

2　Member States shall, in liaison with the Commission, co-ordinate among themselves their policies and programmes in the areas referred to in para 1. The Commission may, in close contact with the Member States, take any useful initiative to promote such co-ordination.

3　The Community and the Member States shall foster co-operation with third countries and the competent international organisations in the sphere of public health.

4　In order to contribute to the achievement of the objectives referred to in this article, the Council:

- acting in accordance with the procedure referred to in Art 189b, after consulting the Economic and Social Committee and the Committee of the Regions, shall adopt incentive measures, excluding any harmonisation of the laws and regulations of the Member States;

- acting by a qualified majority on a proposal from the Commission, shall adopt recommendations.

Central to the Commission's role in the implementation of Art 129 is the obligation to liaise with the Member States in the co-ordination of their policies and programmes concerning prevention, including drug prevention, investigation and analysis of causes and modes of transmission of health scourges, health information and health education.

In its framework of action in public health, the Commission has overseen eight programme proposals of which:

(a) Council decision establishing a communicable diseases surveillance network;

(b) Council decision adopting an action programme on the prevention of AIDS and certain other communicable diseases (1996 to 2000);

(c) Council decision adopting an action plan to combat cancer (1996 to 2000);

(d) Council decision adopting an action programme on health promotion (1996 to 2000);

(e) Council decision adopting an action programme on the prevention of drug dependence (1996 to 2000);

(f) Council decision adopting an action programme on health monitoring (1997 to 2001);

(f) Council regulation establishing a European monitoring centre for drugs and drug addiction;

(h) Directive on the legal protection of biotechnological inventions.

General public health policy, particularly concerning health information and promotion, generates a number of commercial communication-related measures, particularly in the various Member States. The Commission has adopted a directive to ban advertising of tobacco and tobacco products under certain circumstances. In the context of public health programmes, major EC-wide campaigns such as European Cancer Week are organised. At Member State level, there are numerous other public health campaigns. Although funded by the State, these are commissioned from providers of commercial communication services. Likewise, public health considerations have led Member States to require health warnings to be placed in commercial communications which promote certain products. The use of commercial communication measures in this area can be expected, given the key role of health information and education.

## Audio-visual policy

Audio-visual policy within the EC has two main goals: to put in place and ensure the working of a true 'European audio-visual area', in particular by ensuring the free movement of broadcast services; and to strengthen the competitiveness of the European film and television production. Both objectives are pursued taking into account the specific cultural aspects of the audio-visual sector.

Audio-visual policy is implemented through two types of Community instrument. These are legal measures, such as the Directive on 'Television without Frontiers', and financial support initiatives, such as the MEDIA II programme.

The Directive commonly referred to as Television without Frontiers (Council Directive 89/552/EEC, amended by Directive 97/36/EC, see Appendix 9) on the co-ordination of laws, regulations and administrative action in Member States regarding television broadcasting, is the cornerstone of the legal arrangements for the 'European visual area'. Its primary objectives are to create the legal framework needed to ensure the free movement of broadcast services and to encourage their development throughout the EC.

Free movement is ensured through the following:

(a) each broadcaster can only be subject to the law of the Member State under whose jurisdiction he comes (that is, the Member State where the broadcaster is established), and he must comply with a minimum set of common rules (the 'co-ordinated fields');

(b) Member States must ensure the freedom of reception, and may not hinder the retransmission of broadcasts from other Member States for reasons that fall within the co-ordinated fields.

One of the co-ordinated fields is television advertising and sponsorship, so this Directive is of especial relevance to the sector of commercial communications. Advertising and sponsorship are integral parts of, and constitute the main source of funding for, many television broadcasts, whether they emanate from public or private broadcasters. The full implementation of this Directive, based as it is on the principle of the 'country of origin' (the only workable way in which transnational broadcasting can be developed) is, therefore, of fundamental importance for the development of commercial communications. In turn, the maximisation of the resources broadcasters earn through advertising and sponsorship revenues will contribute significantly to the attainment of the audio-visual policy's main goal: the development of the film and television programme industries. The economic interlinking of these sectors – broadcasting, commercial communications and programme production – means that the development of effective instruments for audio-visual and communication policy is in the interest of all three of them.

In the sector of commercial communications services, one of the main objectives of the review is to liberalise the rules that apply to teleshopping. Otherwise, the 1989 rules on advertising and sponsorship have proved robust and have provided a suitable framework for the development of television advertising and sponsorship, while providing a satisfactory level of consumer protection. The Commission has, therefore, proposed to leave them largely unchanged. It has also proposed to strengthen the country of origin principle established by the Directive, by clarifying the rules on how jurisdiction is determined.

# THE EXISTING REGULATORY ENVIRONMENT

The existing regulatory environment is based on differing national legal traditions. National measures derive from three main families of law: unfair competition, consumer protection and specific legislation for the protection of the wider public interest. The disparity between aims pursued by Member States partly reflects their differing emphasis on these sources of national law.

## Laws on unfair competition

The objective of these laws is to prevent abuses of the commercial and industrial freedom to compete. Thus, for example, all Member States tend to control strictly, and often prohibit, commercial communications that cause confusion or disparagement (libel and slander), or that exploit or dilute the reputation of competitors (for example, the unauthorised use of trade marks). By contrast, the treatment of comparative advertising (the comparison of products or services with the same products/services offered by a competitor) differs between Member States. It tends to be most tightly controlled (often entailing bans) in those countries where the definition of 'truthful' or 'misleading' is most limited in scope.

National legislation on unfair competition across the EC has developed either into a broader law of market behaviour (Denmark, Finland, Sweden) or commercial practices (Belgium), or sections of the original competition law have been separated and developed independently (Portugal, Spain: advertising law; Greece: consumer protection law). Some Member States are tightening their laws, for example, Sweden is attempting to reinstate the concept of the protection of competitors.

## Laws on consumer protection

This branch of law dates back in most Member States to the 1960s or 1970s. It is becoming the source of new regulations on commercial communication in some Member States (Sweden, Greece). The link between these laws and those on unfair competition needs to be kept in mind since, in many instances, the laws seek to protect consumers by regulating competition between manufacturers and retailers.

Consumer protection law applies to: misleading advertising, improper influencing of the consumer, undercutting, discounts, 'free gifts' and promotional offers. Some of these areas are also covered by unfair competition law, which may lead to a conflict of interests between the two objectives. For example, comparative advertising may seen as providing useful information for consumers, but may also be seen as undesirable, from the point of view of those competitors who are shown to be promoting less advantageous products or services.

## Specific legislation for the protection of the wider public interest

Certain laws have come into being which seek to protect the interests of society, rather than those of the hypothetical final consumer. These laws have a wide scope, although they may also be product-specific. They include the protection of fundamental human rights as laid down in the European Convention on Human Rights (for example, freedom of thought, conscience and religion, respect for private life, etc) and extend into: protection of public health and safety; protection of minors; protection of pluralism in the media; protection from anti-social behaviour (this would cover taste and decency and those general laws which seek to safeguard human dignity and prohibit sexual, racial or national discrimination); protection of culture and of national spiritual heritage, notably in Greece, and in France and Belgium, where specific measures dealing with language exist. Specific product laws have been developed with these categories in mind. For example, the various restrictions on the advertising of food, dangerous products (for example, firearms) and those on commercial communications relating to pharmaceuticals and on medical and paramedical services fall under public health and safety, as would restrictions on tobacco and alcohol advertising.

The examination of current national measures (Green Paper COM (96) 192 Final), reveals that:

(a) Member States justify their legislative initiatives differently;

(b) the level of restriction tends to reflect the objective pursued;

(c) measures may have spill-over effects into other objectives.

## The level of restriction reflects the objective pursued

According to the objective pursued, the level of restriction can vary significantly between Member States. For example, sponsorship restrictions are justified under several different public interest objectives across Member States. Although many seek the protection of pluralism (all except Finland, Luxembourg, Belgium and Austria), others pursue consumer protection (Sweden, Finland, UK, Ireland, The Netherlands, Belgium, Austria), the protection of minors (Sweden, UK, Ireland, Italy, Spain), the protection of public health (Italy, UK, Sweden, Denmark, Germany, France, The

Netherlands), IPR protection (Austria, Belgium, Sweden) and the protection of public morality (UK). Restrictions themselves vary in scope, application and degree of restriction. For example, the protection of pluralism leads to a wide application (for example, all television/radio programmes), but a limited degree of restriction (that is, clear identification). By contrast, the protection of public health leads to narrowly defined ranges of application (for example, tobacco or alcohol sponsorship) and very high degrees of restriction (even total bans).

## Spill-over effects into other objectives

Account has to be taken of how a measure may affect other objectives. A measure directed at one objective may encroach or contradict measures pertaining to other objectives. Thus, at a general level, a Member State which feels strongly that commercial communications are unduly influencing consumers' behaviour may regulate the activity restrictively, even though it recognises that this might have adverse effects on competition. The reverse situation may also occur. National regulators are continually having to balance the achievement of one objective with the effects, direct and indirect, that the relevant measure may have on other policy areas.

In view of the variety of legal traditions, and the divergence in priorities and political choices, it is hardly surprising that, when commercial communications cross a border, they can be confronted with a regulatory framework utterly unlike that of the country from which they originate. This may hinder, or make less attractive, the exercise of fundamental internal market freedoms.

# A REVIEW OF MEMBER STATES'
# COMMERCIAL COMMUNICATIONS

The legal reviews indicate that a number of measures dealing with specific types of commercial communications vary considerably across Member States, particularly in respect of type and degree of restriction.

## Misleading advertising

The wide differences in national measures in this area are reflected in the Directive on Misleading Advertising (Council Directive 84/450/EC of 10.9.84, OJ L 250, 1984) on the approximation of laws, regulations and administrative provisions of the Member States. Furthermore, a lack of agreement on the term 'unfair' would prevent any useful horizontal action being accomplished in this domain. Certain differences remain between Member States, which to some extent may be explained by the Directive's minimal harmonisation or by its definition of 'misleading', which some survey respondents (Green Paper COM (96) 192 Final) claim is lacking in precision. The different degrees of restriction arise, too, from different national definitions of 'misleading'. In Member States where the definition is narrow, advertising may be banned which, in another Member State, would be seen as informative advertising. Survey results suggest that these differences in interpretation across a number of Member States are creating real barriers to the flow of advertising services.

Measures which regulate the advertising of the professions (such as lawyers and doctors) seek to protect the consumer from being misled. They vary from a total ban on advertising, often imposed by self-regulation, as, for example, in the UK in respect of barristers, to limited restrictions in other countries, such as France, where Bar associations forbid advertising by individuals, but not by the profession as a whole. Survey respondents claim that such differences prevent transborder commercial communications. This problem will become more widespread as the possibilities for offering such services at a distance increase with the growth of the information society.

Numerous users of commercial communications also complain that they cannot use comparative advertising in certain Member States, and so are forced to redesign entirely their commercial communication campaigns in those territories. The complaints focus on Germany, Belgium, France and The Netherlands. On this, the Commission has proposed that comparative advertising should be permitted as long as it is based on objective comparisons that are not used to denigrate the trade mark or reputation of a competitor. At the level of the Council, political agreement on this proposed Directive was reached in November 1995 and was accompanied by the formal adoption of a common position by the Council adopting Directive 97/55/EC, amending 84/450/EEC to include comparative advertising.

## Price advertising, discounts, undercutting, etc

A wide divergence in degrees of restriction characterises this area. For example, Germany, under its rebate law (*Gesetz über Preisnachlässe (RabattG)*), limits cash discounts for 'end' consumers to 3%, and the advertising of special offers is also restricted. Austria, Belgium and Italy also have relatively strict regimes (often limited bans), whilst France has limited restrictions. Other Member States generally permit price advertising, subject to restrictions linked to the general provisions on misleading advertising and those against anti-competitive practices, such as dumping. The Nordic countries, whose legal traditions are more closely linked to consumer protection than to legislation on unfair competition, tend to encourage such advertising. For example, Swedish law promotes comparative price advertising between traders.

A large proportion of respondents felt that the measures were so disparate that they effectively prevented any form of transborder campaign using this technique. A number of specific examples were given, such as the extremely detailed and different regulations on trading stamps and discounts in Greece, Portugal, Spain and Italy, and the effective ban on 'three for the price of two' campaigns in those countries with very low value thresholds, such as Germany and Denmark.

## Intrusive advertising: telephone/mail advertising

Measures in respect of 'cold calling' (unsolicited telephone advertising) vary in degree of restriction from no specific measures (Spain) to limited bans (for example, in Denmark, cold calling is only permitted for books, subscriptions to newspapers/periodicals and insurance contracts, but resulting orders are not legally binding), through to total bans (for example, in Germany, telephone solicitation is not allowed, even if individuals are first informed in writing). Regarding direct mail, The Netherlands (through a self-regulatory code) and Italy have the most restrictive measures (often bans). The Council has recently reached a common position (Directive 97/7/EC) on distance contracts, which harmonises consumer protection provisions, to allow for the development of transfrontier distance sales techniques. However, Member States may apply stricter provisions in the interest of consumer protection. Another relevant Directive (95/46/EEC, in force from 25 October 1998) has recently been adopted by the Council on data protection. Its aim is to allow the free circulation of personal data, essential for the efficient operation of the European direct marketing sector, on the basis of a common set of rules protecting individual privacy. In particular, individuals are guaranteed the right to 'opt out' of the use of their data for marketing purposes.

Respondents to the survey (Green Paper COM (96) 192 Final) specifically identified the problem of differing regulations, which they claim put obstacles in the way of effective transborder direct marketing. Consumer interests highlighted the problems arising from non-domestic direct mail offers.

## Intrusive advertising: promotional gifts/offers and prize competitions

The measures concerning promotional gifts and offers again differ greatly in form and restrictive effect. In Germany, the practice is heavily restricted. In France, free of charge gifts are banned; coupons (for example, 'money off next purchase' offers) are regulated in a less restrictive manner. Belgium bans all tie-in offers (for example, the possibility of buying a product/service at a reduced price after making a commitment to future purchases), whereas in The Netherlands (through self-regulatory codes) such offers are permitted, although subject to Art 86 restrictions of the EC Treaty. Denmark has similar provisions requiring that promotions be of low value, and that the gift be closely associated with the product purchased (as in the Dutch system), although coupons are permitted. Sweden and Finland have a less restrictive approach to this activity, although there are restrictions concerning alcohol.

The remaining Member States have more liberal approaches towards sales promotions, but even here certain peculiarities exist, such as the manner in which all such promotions in Italy have to be agreed by the finance ministry, and the specific regulation on trading stamps/coupons found in the UK.

As with promotional offers, there are significant differences in relation to prize competitions. These range from broad bans, for example, in Denmark, Belgium and Finland, where games of pure chance (lotteries) are generally prohibited, and bans on lotteries without State permits (for example, in The Netherlands or Italy, where the finance ministry must be notified before any lottery is launched), to restricted bans, such as those on games involving stakes or requiring purchase for participation (for example, France and Germany). Other detailed restrictions relate to the types and values of prizes.[25] The survey results (Green Paper COM (96) 192 Final) for both sets of activities made reference to the very marked differences in regulations across the EC, and the barriers created. The common complaint from the detailed commentaries was that it was impossible to run any form of transborder competition, because of the detailed and different nature of prize and lottery rules.

## General media and 'carrier' restrictions

The levels of restriction vary significantly in relation to television advertising, from no advertising (for example, the BBC in the UK) or an advertising monopoly (in Belgium-Flanders and Denmark) through to those Member States (such as Greece and Portugal) who have copied the provisions of the Television without Frontiers Directive (89/552/EEC, OJ L 298, 1989); that is, a maximum of 15% daily and 20% of advertising spots per hour. This Directive (TVWF) provides for a minimal harmonisation clause which allows Member States to apply stricter or more detailed rules to the broadcasters under their jurisdiction. For broadcasters, the Directive has the advantage of ensuring that they only have to comply with the advertising measures applicable in the Member State of their establishment.

---

25   The ECJ ruled in the case of *Schindler* (Case C-275/92 [1994] ECR I-1039) that bans on the cross-border promotion of 'major' (in this case, State or regional State) lotteries could be justified because of the need to protect social order and to prevent fraud.

In general, divergence of national practices was seen as problematic, and certain States were criticised for being over-restrictive. Supply restrictions, such as certain monopoly situations, were criticised (for example, Denmark and Belgium-Flanders). Extreme variations in the permitted advertising time were felt to lead to problems in planning and executing transborder media buying campaigns. Apparent restrictions on the sales of airtime into neighbouring 'overspill' markets (into which the signal either naturally falls or is retransmitted by cable) were felt to be a regulatory problem. Teleshopping operators criticised the classification of their programmes as advertisements. Likewise, the producers of 'infomercials' (short promotional product presentations) objected to the fact that broadcasters cannot sell them 'downtime' (programming periods which are either replaced by the test card or have very low audience ratings) because of their categorisation as advertisements. Specific points were made about restrictions, particularly in France, preventing certain sectors from using television advertising.

## General sponsorship restrictions

Such restrictions apply to both television and event sponsorship. Restrictions in this area are often detailed, and disparity between the Member States is large. Aspects of sponsorship tightly controlled (or indeed banned) in some countries are treated not as requiring regulation at all in others. The difference extends as far as the applicable tax regime. The TVWF Directive lays down certain conditions on sponsoring television programmes (Art 17), which have been supplemented in many cases by the Member States, either by legislation or through self regulatory codes. In events sponsorship, the Netherlands was singled out as having restrictive measures (often such activities were effectively banned), whilst for broadcasting the United Kingdom and Denmark were felt to be restrictive.

## Product restrictions: commercial communications for alcoholic beverages

Three groups of countries can be distinguished.

The first group consists of those countries with stringent rules. In Sweden and Finland, spirits and non-light beers cannot be advertised in periodicals or on radio television. Class II beer can be advertised in print but not on audio-visual media. Direct advertising and outdoor advertising are banned. Denmark allows such advertising only in the press. In addition, restrictive measures are found in France and Austria.

A second group of Member States (UK, The Netherlands, Spain and Portugal) places restrictions (often bans, imposed or voluntary) on the content and style of television advertising of spirits (in The Netherlands, this covers all alcoholic beverages). Such measures are, however, less restrictive than those in operation in the first group of Member States. (The UK has recently lifted its voluntary ban on advertising spirits on television.)

Finally, Member States of the third group generally permit the advertising of alcohol, subject to conditions (on content of such advertising or the audience for whom it is intended).

Article 15 of the TVWF Directive harmonised rules on television advertising for alcoholic beverages. A Council Resolution requested interested parties to submit views on how to limit and reduce disparities in the other media. The Amsterdam Group responded to this by calling for greater co-operation through self-regulation.

Many detailed responses to the survey (Green Paper COM (96) 192 Final) expressed concern at the extent to which these differences are creating new barriers. It was felt that transborder campaigns would be legally hazardous, under present conditions. Specific complaints were aimed at measures affecting the advertising of spirits in the audio-visual media, which were said to cause a shift on to price competition, which favoured cheaper 'own label' domestic brands. The spread of restrictive measures was also of concern; radio stations said that restrictions on beer advertising in Germany could reduce their total advertising revenue by 10%. The effect on sports sponsorship was also raised, in the context of bans in France and The Netherlands.

## Product restrictions: commercial communications to children

The strictest rules are found in Sweden (where advertising, and sponsorship of programmes aimed at children below the age of 12, is prohibited) and in Greece (where television advertising of toys to children is banned between 7.00 am and 10.00 pm). Generally there are specific (often differing) measures aimed at ensuring that children are not excessively influenced by advertising (mainly related to the content or standard of such advertising). Provisions also apply to sponsorship of sports events. At the community level, the rules on television advertising are co-ordinated to ensure the free circulation of television broadcasts, as required by Art 16 of the TVWF Directive.

Generally, the survey results (Green Paper COM (96) 192 Final) highlighted the variations between Member States, and the problems resulting from the method of applying local copy clearance to such advertising. Specific problems were raised in relation to bans on toy advertising in general, and for specific types of toys (in Germany and Denmark). Concerns were expressed about the manner in which such restrictions reduce sponsorship and advertising revenues for children's programmes, and also about the restrictions on the use of sales promotions (merchandising).

## Product restrictions: commercial communications for food products

None of the Member States prohibits such commercial communications, but there are wide differences in the complexity of codes or laws that regulate the contents of such advertising, particularly with respect to claims. Certain differences in approach are interesting, the first being Member States that extend labelling measures into advertising (notably Germany, Austria, the UK, Ireland and The Netherlands) and those that limit them to 'pack' display (that is, restrictions that relate only to the packaging of products). These countries sometimes have restrictive content provisions. For example, in Belgium, references to health or illness are banned in such advertising.

Community legislation in this area includes the Directive on the Labelling, Presentation and Advertising of Foodstuffs (Directive 79/112/EC, OJ L 33, 1979, amended by Directive 97/4/EC). However, the scope of the harmonisation is limited, given that Art 15 of this Directive makes it clear that the text applies only to national rules on labelling and presentation and, in spite of its title, not to provisions relating to commercial communications. The Council Directive on Infant Formulae (91/321/EEC, 14.5.91) contains a minimal clause in relation to provisions taken by the Member States in relation to advertising for such products. The survey results have highlighted the barriers resulting from diverse restrictions on baby foods in general.

Specific problems highlighted in the replies include: measures requiring the same information content that is imposed 'on pack' to be used for commercial communications (respondents suggest that this prevents the use of common visuals in cross-border campaigns); problems relating to very diverse self-regulatory codes and laws for baby foods; very significant differences that cause problems for advertising of confectionery products (for example, requiring additional images of toothbrushes, which means that a separate television advertisement needs to be produced in the relevant country).

## Product restrictions: commercial communications for pharmaceuticals

National restrictive measures in this area are complex, but certain general points arise: a group of Member States bans non-prescribed or 'over the counter' (OTC) pharmaceuticals advertising on audio-visual media (including Belgium and Denmark); another group requires pre-notification for OTC advertising (Sweden, Italy and France); and a third group prohibits sales promotions for these products (including Belgium and France). Respondents complained that, because the list of prescription drugs and those on the national insurance lists are not the same from one Member State to another, it was only possible to advertise those OTC drugs that were not on either list on a pan-European basis. In addition, specific problems related to information 'tag' messages (warning messages about the product) that varied across the Member States. Spain and Germany were stated to have strict requirements which extended the required length of television advertisements by up to 25%. Media respondents also stated that these restrictions dissuaded potential advertisers. The length of time required for copy clearance was also raised as a problem. The prohibition of the use of umbrella brands (these are corporate or product type brands which are applied to both non-prescribed and prescribed pharmaceuticals) by some Member States was criticised, as it results in the obligation to launch a completely new brand (involving considerable expense).

The Directive (92/28/EEC, OJ L 33, 1979) on the Advertising of Medicinal Products for Human Use harmonises this situation by banning the advertising of prescribed pharmaceuticals, and of those containing psychotropic or narcotic substances. Member States are permitted to ban the advertising of pharmaceuticals that could be reimbursed under State insurance schemes. Advertising for non-prescribed pharmaceuticals is subject to the need for market authorisation of the relevant product. Prescribed pharmaceuticals may only be advertised in media aimed at medical professionals, whereas OTC pharmaceuticals may be advertised, but are subject to stringent conditions. As regards the rules on television advertising, these are co-ordinated to the extent needed to ensure the free circulation of television broadcasts by Art 14 of the TVWF Directive.

## Product restrictions: commercial communications for financial services

Although measures in this sector are generally restrictive, there are significant differences between each of the Member States. For example, the details required in relation to financial service 'products' differ greatly. These provisions are extremely detailed, being contained both in laws and in self-regulation. Community legislation tends to concern the right to establish branches and offer services in the other Member States. However, the directives in this area allow Member States to impose their differing national rules justified by the 'general good' of the commercial communications of such companies (for example, Art 41 of both the third Life Insurance (92/96/EEC, OJ L 360, 1992) and third Non-life Insurance (92/49/EEC, OJ L 228, 1992) Directives; Art 44(2) of the Council Directive on the Co-ordination of Laws, Regulations and Administrative Provisions Relating to the Undertakings for Collective Investment in Transferable Securities (UCITS: 85/611/EEC, OJ L 375, 1985); Art 21(1) of the second Banking Directive (of 15.12.89, amending Directive 77/780/EEC, OJ L 386, 1989).

From the survey responses (Green Paper COM (96) 192 Final), it is clear that the disparity between the measures prevented the development of transborder commercial communication services. Copy clearance (pre-vetting of press and television advertisements) is required in some Member States (for example, in Italy, prior approval by the national supervisory commission for businesses and the stock exchange (CONSOB) is required for investment advertising, including advertising of financial products, and in the UK, it is an offence under the Financial Services Act 1986 to issue an investment advertisement which has not been approved by an authorised person) and not in others. It has been suggested that the intricacy of detail of the relevant laws and codes was making their interpretation difficult and thus resulting in inconsistencies between positions taken in specific cases. This was said to lead to significant legal uncertainty as to what could or could not be undertaken in this market.

## Restrictions on commercial communications for reasons of social values

This area covers such diverse subjects as political advertising and issues of 'taste and decency'. In relation to all these areas, both the levels of restriction and the measures themselves vary enormously across the Member States. For example, political advertising in the UK is banned for audiovisual media (this applies to both advertisers, and advertising content).This ban stems from a self regulatory code. However, it does not apply to the press or to outdoor advertising. In Finland, by contrast, political advertising is permitted on television. Article 12 of the Television Directive (89/552/EC) was considered to incorporate the essential features of the rules generally accepted in the Member States by the circles concerned.

With respect to *sex discrimination*, the use of the female body in advertising is strictly controlled in certain Member States (such as the UK, the Netherlands, Spain and Denmark). In respect of *sanitary products and contraceptives*, restrictions differ in relation to showing the product, and the timing of such advertising. *Political advertising* is strictly controlled on audiovisual media in relation to political parties. However, respondents raised the issue of wide interpretations of 'political' advertising in certain Member States which prevented charities and pressure groups from advertising (such as the UK and Germany). As for the *protection of the professional ethics of commercial communications,* respondents were concerned that certain regulations (notably self-regulatory codes) in the area of taste and decency were, in their application, seeking to achieve another objective, viz, the 'good repute' or 'professional image' of the commercial communications (notably advertising) industry. This was felt to make regulation diverge from country to country such that it became difficult to create trans-border campaigns. The difference in measures affecting public relations was highlighted, despite the existence of an agreement between national PR trade associations to a common international code. For reasons of *language/cultural protection* certain Member States were identified as imposing language restrictions that created internal market barriers (notably Belgium and France).

The key finding arising from this preliminary review is that *there is a growing divergence between Member States in the way in which they develop their national regulatory frameworks*. It has shown how Member States, when regulating commercial communications, pursue a wide range of policy objectives which, at times, rely on approaches that are not entirely coherent or indeed contradictory with those adopted by other countries. This leads to different types of regulatory measures as well as differing levels of restriction and the laws and codes may be applied in such a way as to impede the flow of cross border commercial communications.

The preliminary regulatory review indicates that potential internal market barriers arise from the existence of non-discriminatory rather than discriminatory measures based on nationality. To the extent that such measures give rise to impediments of free movement, their compatibility with internal market law depends principally on the nature of the objectives these pursue and on the proportionality of the presumed restrictions. Given that the safeguarding of general interest objectives is the key aim of these measures, any assessment of the need for Union action, therefore, will normally focus on the application of the principle of proportionality. However, the range of potential actions in this field is very wide: the assessment of proportionality therefore requires a case by case approach.

Two joint EC actions could nevertheless be required to assist this step by step approach. First, it would be useful to have a framework on which the assessment of the proportionality of measures in the field of commercial communications might be based. A proposal for such a framework is made in Part IV. Secondly, a more extensive review of the types of measures that could give rise to problems in terms of proportionality would be useful.

From the preliminary review, three types of national measures have been identified as needing to feature in this review.

## REGULATORY BANS

Certain Member States ban particular types or content of commercial communications which are permitted in others. Such measures could give rise to a problem of disproportionality, if applied to services originating in another Member State.

Regulatory bans might include the following:

(a) regulations banning the use of discounts, loyalty premia and other price discounting forms of commercial communications. These relate to introductory or other price promotional offers (for example, 10% off), package offers (for example, 'three for the price of two') or loyalty offers (repeat purchase confers a benefit on the consumer (for example, with coupons) for a price reduction on a subsequent purchase);

(b) regulations banning the use of concessionary gifts. These cover 'free gifts' which are given with the purchase of a product or independently;

(c) regulations banning broadcasters from selling 'overspill audiences' to media buyers and advertisers. This kind of ban is found within television and radio licensing procedures and is applied to audiences in neighbouring markets that fall within the footprint of a transmission or via retransmission over a cable network;

(d) regulations banning the use of certain media by specific categories of advertisers in order to preserve pluralism in other media. Such regulations typically seek to divert certain advertising revenues away from television to support other media such as the regional press;

(e) regulations leading to bans in the use of commercial communications for the professions;

(f) regulations banning advertising on teleshopping channels or on-line services for reasons of protection of pluralism. These typically seek to ensure that television advertising revenues are not adversely affected;

(g) measures banning the use of foreign languages in commercial communications.

## Horizontal regulatory limitations

Some Member States have chosen to apply strict limitations on general forms of commercial communications. These include:

(a) regulations limiting the use of discounts, loyalty premiums and other price discounting forms of commercial communications;

(b) regulations limiting the value and nature of concessionary gifts;

(c) regulations limiting advertising to children;

(d) regulations limiting the content of teleshopping or on-line services for reasons of protection of pluralism;

(e) regulations on media buying limiting the possibilities for cross-border media buying services;

(f) regulations on misleading advertising limiting competitive advertising;

(g) regulations limiting the use of brand diversification;

(h) regulations (other than fiscal) limiting the sponsorship of both events and audio-visual programmes.

## Specific regulatory limitations

Several Member States have applied strict limitations on specific sector or product/service-related forms of commercial communications. These include:

(a) regulations limiting advertising by professions which could severely hamper their provision, especially when using the new on-line techniques being developed in the information society;

(b) regulations limiting non-prescribed pharmaceutical advertising. These measures appear, in certain cases, to present the effective use of umbrella brands across borders;

(c) regulations limiting alcohol advertising;

(d) regulations limiting commercial communications related to baby foods other than infant formulae;

(e) regulations limiting commercial communications associated with television advertising of retailing;

(f) regulations limiting the use of commercial communications by the financial services sector.

## THE PROPORTIONALITY TEST

According to ECJ case law, the proportionality test requires: first, verification of the appropriateness of the national restrictive measure vis à vis the pursued objective, in other words, it must be such as to guarantee the achievement of the intended aim; secondly, testing the national restrictive measure must not go beyond that which is necessary in order to achieve that objective, in other words, the same result cannot be obtained by less restrictive rules. The jurisprudence of the Court has not, as yet, provided more precisely defined elements that would allow the assessment of the proportionality of national or EC-wide measures.

## CASE LAW INTERPRETATION OF THE TVWF DIRECTIVE (89/552/EEC)

Two joined cases are of special interest with regard to the TVWF Directive: *Konsumentombudsmannen v De Agostini (Svenska) Forlag AB* (Case C-34/95, 9.7.97) and *Konsumentombudsmannen v TV-Shop I Sverige AB* (Case C-35/95 and Case C-36/95, 9.7.97).

De Agostini (a Swedish associate company of an Italian group) advertised a children's magazine on TV3 and TV4. Each issue of the magazine, printed in Italy, contained a part of a model dinosaur which readers could collect. TV3 was a UK company, broadcasting television programmes from the UK to Sweden. TV4 was a television broadcaster operating in Sweden. The Swedish consumer ombudsman applied, under domestic consumer protection legislation, for an order prohibiting De Agostini from:

(a) marketing the magazine in a way which aimed at children under 12 years of age;

(b) from making certain statements in connection with the advertising; and

(c) for an order requiring that the advertisement should include a statement of the full cost of collecting all parts of the model dinosaur.

It presented products in television spots after which consumers could place orders by telephone, the products being delivered by post.

TV-Shop (a Swedish associate company of TV-Shop Europe) placed 'infomercials' on TV3 and on Homeshopping (another broadcaster operating in Sweden) about certain skin care and detergent products. Its business consists of presenting products, such as the above, in television spots, after which consumers can order products by telephone; the products are delivered by post. The consumer ombudsman applied for an order:

(a) restraining TV-Shop from making certain claims for, and statements in connection with, the products; and

(b) requiring it to include in the skin care product advertisements a statement of postage and other additional charges. A preliminary ruling was sought from the European Court as to whether Art 30 or 59 EC or the TVWF Directive (89/552/EEC) prevented a Member State from taking such action against television advertisements broadcast from another Member State; and/or precluded the application of the Swedish law prohibiting advertisements directed at children.

The ECJ had held, in the case of *Leclerc Siplec* (Case C-412/93, [1995] ECR I-179), that the main purpose of the Directive, which was adopted on the basis of Arts 57(2) and 66 of the EC Treaty, is to ensure the freedom to provide television broadcasting services.

Article 1 of the Directive defines 'television broadcasting' as the initial transmission by wire or over the air, including that by satellite in unencoded or encoded form, of television programmes intended for reception by the public. It also defines 'television advertising' as including any form of announcement broadcast in return for payment and for similar consideration by a public or private undertaking in connection with, *inter alia*, a trade in order to promote the supply of goods or services in return for payment.

Finally, the same provision provides that, except for the purposes of Art 18 of the Directive, television advertising does not include direct offers to the public for the sale, purchase or rental of products or for the provision of services in return for payment.

Article 2 of the TVWF Directive provides as follows:

1   Each Member State shall ensure that all television broadcasts transmitted ... by broadcasters under its jurisdiction ... comply with the law applicable to broadcasts intended for the public in that Member State.

2   Member States shall ensure freedom of reception and shall not restrict retransmission on their territory of television broadcasts from other Member States for reasons which fall within the fields co-ordinated by this Directive. Member States may provisionally suspend retransmissions of television broadcasts if the following conditions are fulfiled:

  (a) a television broadcast coming from another Member State manifestly, seriously and gravely infringes Art 22;

  (b) during the previous 12 months, the broadcaster has infringed the same provision on at least two prior occasions;

  (c) the Member State concerned has notified the broadcaster and the Commission in writing of the alleged infringements and of its intention to restrict retransmission should any such infringement occur again;

  (d) consultations with the transmitting State and the Commission have not produced an amicable settlement within 15 days of the notification period provided for in point (c), and the alleged infringement persists.

The Commission shall ensure that the suspension is compatible with Community law. It may ask the Member State concerned to put an end to a suspension which is contrary to Community law, as a matter of urgency. This provision is without prejudice to the application of any procedure, remedy or sanction to the infringements in question in the Member State which has jurisdiction over the broadcaster concerned.

Finally, under Art 3(1) of the Directive, Member States remain free to require television broadcasters under their jurisdiction to lay down more detailed or stricter rules in the areas covered by the Directive. Under Art 3(2), Member States must ensure that television broadcasters under their jurisdiction comply with the provisions of the Directive.

The Court considered whether Art 30 (prohibiting quantitative restrictions on imports) or Art 59 (providing for free movement of services) of the EC Treaty or the TVWF Directive (89/552/EEC) allows a Member State:

(a) to prohibit television advertising broadcast from another Member State; and/or

(b) to prohibit television advertising designed to attract the attention of children less than 12 years of age (in the specific instance of Case 34/95).

The Court ruled as follows:

1   Council Directive 89/552 on the co-ordination of certain provisions laid down by law, regulation or administrative action in Member States concerning the pursuit of television broadcasting activities does not preclude a Member State from taking, pursuant to general legislation on protection of consumers against misleading advertising, measures against an advertiser in relation to television advertising broadcast from another Member State, provided that those measures do not prevent the retransmission, as such, in its territory of television broadcasts coming from that other Member State (see C-222/94, *EC Commission v UK* [1996] ECR I-4025, para 42, also the judgment of the EFTA Court in Joined Cases E 8-9/94 *Forbrukerombudet v Mattel Scandinavia and Lego Norge*, 1994 EFTA Court Report 113, paras 54–56, 58).

2   On a proper construction of Art 30 EC, a Member State is not precluded from taking, on the basis of provisions of its domestic legislation, measures against an advertiser in relation to television advertising, provided that those provisions affect in the same way, in law and in fact, the marketing of domestic products and of those from other Member States, are necessary for meeting overriding requirements of general public importance or one of the aims laid down in Art 36 EC, are proportionate for that purpose, and those aims or overriding requirements could not be met by measures less restrictive of intra-Community trade (see *Leclerc-Siplec* [1995] ECR I-179, para 22; also Joined Cases C267-268/91, *Keck and Mithouard* [1993] ECR I-6097 [1995] 1 CMLR 101, para 16; Case 120/78, *Rewe v Bundesmonopolver-Waltung für Branntwein (Cassis de Dijon)* [1979] ECR 649; [1979] 3 CMLR 494, para 8).

3   On a proper construction of Art 59 EC, a Member State is not precluded from taking, on the basis of provisions of its domestic legislation, measures against an advertiser in relation to television advertising. However, it is for the national court to determine whether those provisions are necessary for meeting overriding requirements of general public importance or one of the aims stated in Art 56 EC, whether they are proportionate for that purpose and whether those aims or overriding requirements could be met by measures less restrictive of intra-Community trade (see *Bond van Adverteerders* [1988] ECR 2085; [1989] 3 CMLR 113; Case C-288/89, *Collectieve Antennevoorziening Gouda* [1991] ECR I-4007, para 12; Case C-384/93, *Alpine Investments* [1995] ECR I-1141).

4   Directive 89/552 is to be interpreted as precluding the application to television broadcasts from other Member States of a provision of a domestic broadcasting law which provides that advertisements broadcast in commercial breaks on television must not be designed to attract the attention of children under 12 years of age.

This ruling risks disappointing those who had hoped for a sharp change of direction concerning the scope of application of Art 30 in the area of advertising.

The judgment reconfirmed the rule established since the *Keck and Mithouard* ruling of 1993, whereby the ECJ, anxious to put a brake on the multiplicity of cases bringing into question national restrictions on advertising, limited the scope of the application of Art 30. The ECJ took care to note that a ban on television advertising by a Member State could have a greater impact on the marketing of products originating from another Member State. This was no doubt deliberate, and could allow new cases to be brought forward under the scope of Art 30.

It would appear that Art 59 does not prohibit a Member State from implementing measures, based on national legislation, against an advertiser because of a television advertisement. However, these measures must be justified by a public interest objective and they must respect the principle of proportionality as defined by the Court.

The fact that the ruling with respect to Art 59 did not see the necessity to prove the discriminatory nature of the national legislation, both in its scope as well as in its impact, shows that this criterion, seen as a precondition for the application of Art 30, is not relevant to Art 59.

The impact on the development of cross-border advertising, in allowing the possibility of the host State to intervene on the basis of its legislation against misleading advertising, is that the ruling forces advertisers to comply, in cases of cross-border advertising, with the legislation of the host country with the most restrictive rules.

This means that an advertiser wishing to disseminate the same advertisement across the 15 Member States of the Union will be obliged to research in advance the legislation in force in each of the countries before defining the content of his advertisement in terms of the most restrictive national legislation, which could mean his having to renounce promotional techniques or practices which would be allowed in the 14 other States.

The disparities in the regulations will not encourage cross-border advertising. This ruling has the merit of showing the limits of the TVWF Directive, as well as the shortcomings of the Directive on Misleading Advertising (84/450/EC) which, in its current form, by failing to apply the principle of mutual recognition, does not ensure freedom of movement for advertisements in the EC.

## CASE LAW INTERPRETATION OF THE FREE MOVEMENT OF SERVICES AND THE FREEDOM OF ESTABLISHMENT

There follows an overview of the case law of the ECJ concerning Arts 59 *et seq* of the EC Treaty on the free movement of services, and Arts 52 *et seq* on the freedom of establishment, and their applicability to different situations. This overview is based on the *Guide to the Case Law of the European Court of Justice on Arts 59* et seq *of the EC Treaty – Free Movement of Services*, and *Guide to the Case Law of the European Court of Justice on Arts 52* et seq *of the EC Treaty – Freedom of Establishment*, both by the European Commission (1998, Luxembourg: Office for Official Publications of the European Communities).

## Article 59 (Title III, Ch 3, Services)

As the Court has held [see Joined Cases C-60 and C-61/84, *Cinéthèque v Fédération Nationale des Cinémas Français* [1985] ECR 2605, para 25, and Case C-12/86, *Demirel v Stadt Schwäbisch Gmund* [1987] ECR 3719, para 28], it has no power to examine the compatibility with the European Convention on Human Rights of national rules which do not fall within the scope of Community law. On the other hand, where such rules do fall within the scope of Community law, and reference is made to the Court for a preliminary ruling, *it must provide all the criteria of interpretation needed by the national court to determine whether those rules are compatible with the fundamental rights* the observance of which the Court ensures and which derive in particular from the European Convention on Human Rights.

Case C-260/89, ERT [1991] ECR I-2925, para 42

*The provisions of the chapter on services are subordinate to those of the chapter on the right of establishment* in so far, first, as the wording of the first paragraph of Art 59 assumes that the provider and the recipient of the service concerned are 'established' in two different Member States and, second, as the first paragraph of Art 60 specifies that the provisions relating to services apply only if those relating to the right of establishment do not apply ...

Case C-55/94, *Gebhard* [1995] ECR I-4165, para 22

## Definition of services: remuneration

*According to the first paragraph of that provision, services are to be considered to be 'services' within the meaning of the Treaty where they are normally provided for remuneration, in so far as they are not governed by the provisions relating to freedom of movement of goods, capital or persons.* Indent (d) of the second paragraph of Art 60 expressly states that activities of the professions fall within the definition of services.

Case C-159/90, *Grogan* [1991] ECR I-4685, para 17

The two services in question are also *provided for remuneration* within the meaning of Art 60 of the Treaty. First, the cable network operators are paid, in the form of the fees which they can charge their subscribers, for the service which they provide for the broadcasters. It is irrelevant that the broadcasters generally do not themselves pay the cable network operators for relaying their programmes. *Article 60 does not require the service to be paid for by those for whom it is performed*. Secondly, the broadcasters are paid by the advertisers for the service which they perform for them in scheduling their advertisements.

Case C-352/85, *Bond van Adverteerders* [1988] ECR 2085, para 16

According to the first paragraph of Art 59 of the EEC Treaty, the abolition of restrictions on the freedom to provide services within the Community concerns all services provided by nationals of Member States who are established in a State of the Community other than that of the person for whom the services are intended. The first paragraph of Art 60 provides that services are to be considered to be 'services' within the meaning of the Treaty where *they are normally provided for remuneration, in so far as they are not governed by the provisions relating to freedom of movement of goods, capital and persons*.

Case C-205/84, *Commission v Germany* [1986] ECR 3755, para 18

According to Art 60 of the Treaty, services are deemed to be 'services' within the meaning of the Treaty where they are normally provided for remuneration, in so far as they are not governed by the provisions relating to freedom of movement of goods, capital and persons. Within the context of Title III of Part Two of the Treaty (Free Movement of Persons, Services and Capital), the free movement of persons included the movement of workers within the Community and freedom of establishment within the territory of the Member States.

Cases C-286/82 and 26/83, *Luisi* and *Carbone* [1984] ECR 377, para 9

Where an undertaking *hires out, for remuneration, staff* who remain in the employ of that undertaking, no contract of employment being entered into with the user, its activities constitute an occupation which satisfies the conditions laid down in the first paragraph of Art 60. Accordingly, they must be considered as a 'service' within the meaning of that provision.

Case C-279/80, *Webb* [1981] ECR 3305, para 9

In the absence of express provision to the contrary in the Treaty, a television signal must, by reason of its nature, be regarded as provision of services. Although it is not ruled out that *services normally provided for remuneration* may come under the provisions relating to free movement of goods, such is however the case, as appears from Art 60, only in so far as they are governed by such provisions. It follows that the transmission of television signals, including those in the nature of advertisements, comes, as such, within the rules of the Treaty relating to services.

Case C-155/73, *Sacchi* [1974] ECR 409, para 6

## Services of a cross-border character

It is settled case law that the provisions of the Treaty on freedom of establishment and freedom to provide services *do not apply to purely internal situations* in a Member State [see judgment of 16 November 1995 in Case C-152/94, *Openbaar Ministerie v van Buynder* [1995] ECR I-3981, para 10].

Case C-17/94, *Gervais* [1995] ECR I-4353, para 24

... the wording of the first paragraph of Art 59 assumes that the provider and the recipient of the service concerned are 'established' in two different Member States ...

Case C-55/94, *Gebhard* [1995] ECR I-4165, para 22

*The freedom to provide services would become illusory if national rules were at liberty to restrict offers of services. The prior existence of an identifiable recipient cannot therefore be a condition for application of the provisions on the freedom to provide services.*

Case C-384/93, *Alpine Investments BV* [1995] ECR I-1141, para 19

In this case, *the offers of services are made by a provider established in one Member State to a potential recipient established in another Member State.* It follows from the express terms of Art 59 *that there is therefore a provision of services within the meaning of that provision.*

Case C-384/93, *Alpine Investments BV* [1995] ECR I-1141, para 21

The answer to the first question is therefore that, on a proper construction, *Art 59 of the EEC Treaty covers services which the provider offers by telephone to potential recipients established in other Member States without moving* from the Member State in which he is established.

Case C-384/93, *Alpine Investments BV* [1995] ECR I-1141, para 22

A prohibition such as that at issue is imposed by the Member State in which the provider of services is established and affects not only offers made by him to addressees who are established in that State or move there in order to receive services but also offers made to potential recipients in another Member State. It therefore directly affects access to the market in services in the other Member States and is thus capable of hindering intra-Community trade in services.

Case C-384/93, *Alpine Investments BV* [1995] ECR I-1141, para 38

In pursuance of those rules *the freedom to provide services may be relied on not only by nationals of Member States established in a Member State other than that of the recipient of the services but also by an undertaking against the State in which it is established where the services are provided to recipients established in another Member State* [see Case C-18/93, *Corsica Ferries Italia* [1994] ECR I-1783, para 30], *and more generally whenever a provider of services offers services in a Member State other than the one in which he is established* [see Case C-154/89, *Commission v France* [1991] ECR I-659, paras 9 and 10].

Case C-381/93, *Commission v France* [1994] ECR I-5145, para 14

*The circumstance that,* according to the Raad van State, *TV10 established itself in the Grand Duchy of Luxembourg in order to escape The Netherlands legislation does not preclude its broadcasts being regarded as services within the meaning of the Treaty.* That is distinct from the question of what measures a Member State may take to prevent a provider of services established in another Member State from evading its domestic legislation. The latter point is the subject of the Raad van State's second question.

Case C-23/93, *TV10 SA* [1994] ECR I-4795, para 15

The answer to Question 2 must therefore be that the rules of the Treaty on the free movement of persons and services do not apply to barriers affecting nationals of a Member State in that State, *where there is no connecting factor* between the situation of those nationals and any of the situations envisaged by Community law.

Case C-60/91, *José Antónia Morais* [1992] ECR I-2085, paras 7 and 9

In this connection, the Court has consistently held that the *Treaty provisions on the freedom of movement for persons cannot be applied to activities which are confined in all respects within a single Member State* [see, for example, Case C-41/90, *Hötner and Elser v Macrotron* [1991] ECR I-1979].

There is thus *no connecting factor* between such situations and any of those contemplated by Community law, and accordingly the Treaty rules on freedom of establishment are inapplicable.

Cases C-330 and 331/90, *López Brea* [1992] ECR I-323, paras 7 and 9

It must then be pointed out that the Court has consistently held that *the provisions of the Treaty on freedom of movement cannot be applied to activities which are confined in all respects within a single Member State and that the question whether that is the case depends on findings of fact which are for the national court to make* [see, in particular, Case 52/79, *Debauve* [1980] ECR 833, para 9].

Case C-41/90, *Höfner v Macrotron* [1991] ECR I-1979, para 37

Consequently, *the provisions of Art 59 must apply in all cases where a person providing services offers those services in a Member State other than that in which he is established, wherever the recipients of those services may be established.*

Case C-180/89, *Tourist Guides Italy* [1991] ECR I-709, para 9

Case C-198/89, *Tourist Guides Greece* [1991] ECR I-727, para 10

Case C-154/89, *Tourist Guides France* [1991] ECR I-659, para 10

Since the present case and the two situations described in para 5 of this judgment concern the *provision of services in a Member State other than that in which the person providing them is established,* Art 59 of the Treaty must apply.

Case C-180/89, *Tourist Guides Italy* [1991] ECR I-709, para 10

Case C-198/89, *Tourist Guides Greece* [1991] ECR I-727, para 11

Case C-154/89, *Tourist Guides France* [1991] ECR I-659, para 11

Each of those services are transfrontier services for the purposes of Art 59 of the Treaty. In each case *the supplier of the service [is] established in a Member State other than that of certain of the persons for whom it is intended.*

Case C352/85, *Bond van Adverteerders* [1988] ECR 2085, para 15

By virtue of Art 59 of the Treaty, restrictions on freedom to provide such services are to be abolished in respect of nationals of Member States who are *established in a Member State other than that of the person for whom the service is intended. In order to enable services to be provided, the person providing the service may go to the Member State where the person for whom it is provided is established or else the latter may go to the State in which the person providing the service is established.* Whilst the former case is expressly mentioned in the third paragraph of Art 60, which permits the person providing the service to pursue his activity temporarily in the Member State where the service is provided, the latter case is the necessary corollary thereof, which fulfils the objective of liberalising all gainful activity not covered by the free movement of goods, persons and capital.

Cases C-286/82 and 26/83, *Luisi* and *Carbone* [1984] ECR 377, para 10

However, it should be observed that *the provisions of the Treaty on the freedom to provide services cannot apply to activities whose relevant elements are confined within a single Member State. Whether that is the case depends on findings of fact which are for the national court to establish.* Since the tribunal correctionnel has concluded that in the given circumstances of this case the services out of which the prosecutions brought before it arose are such as to come under provisions of the Treaty relating to services, the questions referred to the Court should be examined from the same point of view.

Case C-52/79, *Debauve* [1980] ECR 833, para 9

## Services of a temporary character

The aim of those provisions is primarily to enable the person providing the service to pursue his activities in the host Member State without suffering discrimination in favour of nationals of that State. As the Court pointed out in its judgment in Case 279/80, *Webb* [1981] ECR 3305, para 16, *those provisions do not mean that all national legislation applicable to nationals of that State and usually applied to the permanent activities of persons established therein may be similarly applied in their entirety to the temporary activities of persons who are established in other Member States.*

Case C-294/89, *Commission v France* [1991] ECR I-3591, para 26

Articles 59 and 60 of the Treaty require not only the abolition of any discrimination against a person providing services on account of his nationality but also the abolition of any restriction on the freedom to provide services imposed on the ground that the person providing a service is established in a Member State other than the one in which the service is provided. In particular, the Member State cannot make the performance of the services in its territory subject to observance of all the conditions required for establishment; were it to do so, the provisions securing freedom to provide services would be deprived of all practical effect.

Case C-180/89, *Tourist Guides Italy* [1991] ECR I-709, para 15

Under Art 59 and third paragraph of Art 60 of the EEC Treaty a person providing a service may, in order to do so, *temporarily* pursue his activity in the State where the service is provided, under the same conditions as are imposed by that State on its own nationals. As the Court has repeatedly emphasised, most recently in its judgment of 17 December 1981 in Case 279/80, *Webb* [1981] ECR 3305, those provisions entail the abolition of all discrimination against a person providing a service on the grounds of nationality or the fact that he is established in a Member State other than that in which the service must be provided. Thus they prohibit not only overt discrimination based on the nationality of the person providing a service but also all forms of covert discrimination which, although based on criteria which appear to be neutral, in practice lead to the same result.

Cases C-62 and 63/81, *Seco v Evi* [1982] ECR 223, para 8

# Services: residual application

*The provisions of the chapter on services are subordinate to those of the chapter on the right of establishment* in so far, first, as the wording of the first paragraph of Art 59 assumes that the provider and recipient of the service concerned are 'established' in two different Member States and, second, as the first paragraph of Art 60 specifies that *the provisions relating to services apply only if those relating to the right of establishment do not apply* ...

Case C-55/94, *Gebhard* [1995] ECR I-4165, para 22

According to the first paragraph of that provision, services are to be considered to be 'services' within the meaning of the Treaty where they are normally provided for remuneration, in so far as they are *not governed by the provisions relating to freedom of movement of goods, capital or persons.* Indent (d) of the second paragraph of Art 60 expressly states that activities of the professions fall within the definition of services.

Case C-159/90, *Grogan* [1991] ECR I-4685, para 17

The two cases described above thus relate to the provision of services by the tour company to tourists and by the self-employed tourist guide to the tour company respectively. Such services, which are of limited duration and *are not governed by the provisions on the free movement of goods, capital and persons,* constitute activities carried on for remuneration within the meaning of Art 60 of the Treaty.

Case C-180/89, *Tourist Guides Italy* [1991] ECR I-709, para 6

Case C-198/89, *Tourist Guides Greece* [1991] ECRI-727, para 7

Case C-154/89, *Tourist Guides France* [1991] ECR I-659, para 6

According to the first paragraph of Art 59 of the EEC Treaty, the abolition of restrictions on the freedom to provide services within the Community concerns all services provided by nationals of Member States who are established in a State of the Community other than that of the person for whom the services are intended. The *first paragraph of Art 60* provides that services are to be considered to be 'services' within the meaning of the Treaty where they are normally provided for remuneration, in so far as they are *not governed by the provisions relating to freedom of movement for goods, capital and persons*.

Case C-205/84, *Commission v Germany* [1986] ECR 3755, para 18

## Recipients of services

It should be borne in mind that *the nationals of Member States of the Community have the right to enter the territory of the other Member States in the exercise of the various freedoms recognised by the Treaty and in particular the freedom to provide services which*, according to settled case law, *is enjoyed both by providers and by recipients of services* [see Cases 186/87, *Cowan v Trésor Public* [1989] ECR 195 and C-68/89, *Commission v Netherlands* [1991] ECR I-2637, para 10].

Case C-43/93, *Vander Elst* [1994] ECR I-3803, para 13

## Definition of 'restrictions'

It is important to note that the legislation in question *constitutes a barrier to the freedom to provide services* in that it *prevents* broadcasting stations established in other Member States from having programmes that are transmitted in *a language other than that of the country in which they are established* relayed by cable networks of the Flemish community.

Case C-211/91, *Commission v Belgium* [1992] ECR I-6757, para 5

Whilst Art 59 of the Treaty prohibits restrictions upon freedom to provide services, it does not thereby encompass limits upon the exercise of certain economic activities which have their origin in the application of national legislation for the protection of intellectual property, *save where such application constitutes a means of arbitrary discrimination or a disguised restriction on trade between Member States*. Such would be the case if that application enabled parties to an assignment of copyright to create artificial barriers to trade between Member States.

Case C-62/79, *Coditel* [1980] ECR 881, para 15

From information given to the Court during these proceedings it appears that the television broadcasting of advertisements is subject to widely divergent systems of law in the various Member States, passing from almost total prohibition, as in Belgium, by way of rules comprising more or less strict restrictions, to systems affording broad commercial freedom. In the absence of any approximation of national laws and taking into account the considerations of great general interest underlying the restrictive rules [in] this area, the application of the laws in question *cannot be regarded as a restriction upon freedom to provide services so long as those laws treat all such services identically whatever their origin or the nationality or place of establishment of the persons providing them*.

Case C-52/79, *Debauve* [1980] ECR 833, para 13

The answer must therefore be that Arts 59 and 60 of the Treaty do not preclude national rules prohibiting the transmission of advertisements by cable television – as they prohibit the broadcasting of advertisements by television – *if those rules are applied without distinction as regards the origin, whether national or foreign, of those advertisements, the nationality of the person providing the service, or the place where he is established.*

Case C-52/79, *Debauve* [1980] ECR 833, para 16

The restrictions to be abolished pursuant to this provision *include all requirements imposed on the person providing the service by reason in particular of his nationality or of the fact that he does not habitually reside in the State where the service is provided, which do not apply to persons established within the national territory or which may prevent or otherwise obstruct the persons providing the service.*

Case C-39/75, *Coenen* [1975] ECR 1547, para 6

The restrictions to be abolished pursuant to Arts 59 and 60 include all requirements imposed on the person providing the service by reason in particular of his nationality or of the fact that he does not habitually reside in the State where the service is provided, which do not apply to persons established within the national territory or which may *prevent or otherwise obstruct* the activities of the person providing the service.

Case C-33/74, *van Binsbergen* [1974] ECR 1299, para 10

## Discrimination

An analysis of the above-mentioned General Programmes for the abolition of restrictions on freedom of establishment and freedom to provide services reveals that the restrictions envisaged by those provisions are essentially measures *discriminating, directly or indirectly,* between nationals of other Member States and nationals of the host country.

Cases C-330 and 331/90, *López Brea* [1992] ECR I-323, para 13

It should first be pointed out that Art 59 of the Treaty requires not only the *elimination of all discrimination against a person providing services on the ground of his nationality* but also the abolition of any restriction, even if it applies without distinction to national providers of services and to those of other Member States, when it is liable to prohibit or otherwise impede the activities of a provider of services established in another Member State where he lawfully provides similar services.

Case C-76/90, *Dennemeyer* [1991] ECR I-4221, para 12

In this respect, the Court has consistently held [see also Cases C-154/89, *Commission v France* [1991] ECR I-659, para 12, C-180/89; *Commission v Italy* [1991] ECR I-709, para 15; C-198/89, *Commission v Greece* [1991] ECR I-727, para 16] that Art 59 of the Treaty entails, in the first place, the abolition of any discrimination against a person providing services on account of his nationality or the fact that he is established in a Member State other than the one in which the service is provided.

Case C-288/89, *Mediawet* [1991] ECR I-4007, para 10

As the Court held in its judgment in Case 352/85, *Bond van Adverteerders* [1988] ECR 2085, paras 32 and 33, *national rules which are not applicable to services without discrimination as regards their origin are compatible with Community law only if they can be brought within the scope of an express exemption,* such as that contained in Art 56 of the Treaty. It also appears from that judgment (para 34) that economic aims cannot constitute grounds of public policy within the meaning of Art 56 of the Treaty.

Case C-288/89, *Mediawet* [1991] ECR I-4007, para 11

In any event, that fact is not such as to exclude the preferential system enjoyed by the NOPB from the field of application of Art 59 of the Treaty. Moreover, it is not necessary for all undertakings in a Member State to be advantaged in comparison with foreign undertakings. *It is sufficient that the preferential system set up should benefit a national provider of services.*

Case C-288/89, *Mediawet* [1991] ECR I-4007, para 25

*It should next be pointed out that the rules relating to the freedom to provide services preclude national rules which have such discriminatory effects unless those rules fall within the derogating provision contained in Art 56 of the Treaty to which Art 66 refers.* It follows from Art 56, which must be interpreted strictly, that discriminatory rules may be justified on grounds of public policy, public security or public health.

Case C-260/89, *ERT* [1991] ECR I-2925, para 24

Accordingly, the reply to the national court must be that Art 59 of the Treaty prohibits national rules which create a monopoly comprising exclusive rights to transmit the broadcasts of the holder of the monopoly and to retransmit broadcasts from other Member States, *where such a monopoly gives rise to discriminatory effects* to the detriment of broadcasts from other Member States, unless those rules are justified on the grounds indicated in Art 56 of the Treaty, to which Art 66 thereof refers.

Case C-260/89, *ERT* [1991] ECR I-2925, para 26

It must therefore be held that there is *discrimination owing to the fact* that the prohibition of advertising laid down in the Kabelregeling [cable regulation] deprives broadcasters established in other Member States of any possibility of broadcasting on their stations advertisements intended especially for the public in The Netherlands whereas the Omroepwet [broadcasting law] permits the broadcasting of advertising of advertisements on national television stations for the benefit of all the Omroeporganisaties [broadcasting organisations].

Case C-352/85, *Bond van Adverteerders* [1988] ECR 2085, para 26

Under Art 59 and the third paragraph of Art 60 of the EEC Treaty a person providing a service may, in order to do so, temporarily pursue his activity in the State where the service is provided, under the same conditions as are imposed by that State on its own nationals. As the Court has repeatedly emphasised, most recently in its judgment of 17 December 1981 in Case 279/80, *Webb* [1981] ECR 3305, those provisions entail the *abolition of all discrimination* against a person providing a service on the grounds of his *nationality or the fact that he is established in a Member State other than that in which the service must be provided.* Thus they prohibit not only overt discrimination based on the nationality of the person providing a service but also all forms of covert discrimination which, although based on criteria which appear to be neutral, in practice lead to the same result.

Cases C-62 and 63/81, *Seco v Evi* [1982] ECR 223, para 8

## Non-discriminatory measures

Article 59 of the Treaty requires not only the elimination of all discrimination on grounds of nationality against providers of services who are established in another Member State but also the abolition of *any restriction*, even if it applies without distinction to national providers of services and to those of other Member States, which is liable to *prohibit, impede or render less advantageous the activities of a provider of services* established in another Member State where he *lawfully* provides similar services [see also Cases C-76/90, *Saeger v Dennemeyer* [1991] ECR I-4221, para 12, and C-43/93, *Vander Elst v Office des Migrations Internationales* [1994] ECR I-3803, para 14].

Case C-272/94, *Guiot v Climatec* [1996] ECR I-1905, para 10

However, *such a prohibition deprives the operators concerned of a rapid and direct technique for marketing and for contacting potential clients in other Member States. It can therefore constitute a restriction on the freedom to provide cross-border services.*

Case C-384/93, *Alpine Investments BV* [1995] ECR I-1141, para 28

*Although a prohibition such as the one at issue in the main proceedings is general and non-discriminatory and neither its object nor its effect is to put the national market at an advantage over providers of services from other Member States, it can none the less,* as has been held above (see para 28), *constitute a restriction on the freedom to provide cross-border services.*

Case C-384/93, *Alpine Investments BV* [1995] ECR I-1141, para 35

The answer to the second question is therefore that *rules of a Member State which prohibit providers of services established in its territory from making unsolicited telephone calls to potential clients established in other Member States in order to offer their services constitute a restriction on freedom to provide services* within the meaning of Art 59 of the Treaty.

Case C-384/93, *Alpine Investments BV* [1995] ECR I-1141, para 39

*It should first be pointed out that Art 59 of the Treaty requires not only the elimination of all discrimination against a person providing services on the ground of his nationality but also the abolition of any restriction, even if it applies without distinction to national providers of services and to those of other Member States, when it is liable to prohibit or otherwise impede the activities of a provider of services established in another Member State where he lawfully provides similar services.*

Case C-76/90, *Dennemeyer* [1991] ECR I-4221, para 12

## Restrictions on exportation

The first paragraph of *Art 59 of the Treaty prohibits restrictions on freedom to provide services within the Community in general.* Consequently, *that provision covers not only restrictions laid down by the State of destination but also those laid down by the State of origin.* As the Court has frequently held, the right freely to provide services may be relied on by an undertaking as against the State in which it is established if the services are provided for persons established in another Member State [see Cases C-18/93, *Corsica Ferries Italia v Corpo dei Piloti del Porto di Genova* [1994] ECR I-1783, para 30, and C-381/93, *Commission v France* [1994] ECR I-5145, para 14].

It follows that the prohibition of cold calling does not fall outside the scope of Art 59 of the Treaty simply because it is imposed by the State in which the provider of services is established.

Case C-384/93, *Alpine Investments BV* [1995] ECR I-1141, paras 30 and 31

*A prohibition* such as that at issue is *imposed by the Member State in which the provider of services is established and affects not only offers made by him to addressees who are established in that State or move there* in order to receive services *but also offers made to potential recipients in another Member State.* It therefore directly affects access to the market in services in the other Member States and is thus *capable of hindering intra-Community trade in services.*

Case C-384/93, *Alpine Investments BV* [1995] ECR I-1141, para 38

The answer to the second question is therefore that *rules of a Member State which prohibit providers of services established in its territory from making unsolicited telephone calls to potential clients established in other Member States in order to offer their services* constitute a restriction on freedom to provide services within the meaning of Art 59 of the Treaty.

Case C-384/93, *Alpine Investments BV* [1995] ECR I-1141, para 39

## Nationality

It should first be pointed out that Art 59 of the Treaty requires not only the elimination of all discrimination against a person providing services on the ground of his *nationality* but also the abolition of any restriction, even if it applies without distinction to national providers of services and to those of other Member States, when it is liable to prohibit or otherwise impede the activities of a provider of services established in another Member State where he lawfully provides similar services.

Case C-76/90, *Dennemeyer* [1991] ECR I-4221, para 12

Under Art 59 and the third paragraph of Art 60 of the EEC Treaty a person providing a service may, in order to do so, temporarily pursue his activity in the State where the service is provided, under the same conditions as are imposed by that State on its own nationals. As the Court has repeatedly emphasised, most recently in its judgment of 17 December 1981 in Case 279/80, *Webb* [1981] ECR 3305, those provisions entail the abolition of all discrimination against a person providing a service on the grounds of his *nationality* or the fact that he is established in a Member State other than that in which the service must be provided. Thus they prohibit not only overt discrimination based on the nationality of the person providing a service but also all forms of covert discrimination which, although based on criteria which appear to be neutral, in practice lead to the same result.

Cases C-62 and 63/81, *Seco v Evi* [1982] ECR 223, para 8

## Residence, establishment

In particular, a Member State may not make the provision of services in its territory subject to compliance with all the conditions required for establishment *and thereby deprive of all practical effectiveness the provisions of the Treaty whose object is, precisely, to guarantee the freedom to provide services.* Such restriction is all the less permissible where, as in the main proceedings, and unlike the situation governed by the third paragraph of Art 60 of the Treaty, the service is supplied without its being necessary for the person providing it to visit the territory of the Member State where it is provided.

Case C-76/90, *Dennemeyer* [1991] ECR I-4221, para 13

Those essential requirements abolish all discrimination against the person providing the service by reason of his nationality or the fact that he is established in a Member State other than that in which the service is to be provided.

Case C-279/80, *Webb* [1981] ECR 3305, para 14

## Exclusive rights and monopolies

*The obligation imposed on all national broadcasting bodies established in a Member State to use exclusively or to some extent the technical resources provided by a national undertaking prevents those bodies from using the services of undertakings established in other Member States or, in any event, limits their opportunities of doing so.* It therefore has a *protective effect* for the benefit of a service undertaking established in the national territory and, to that extent, disadvantages undertakings of the same kind established in other Member States.

Case C-353/89, *Mediawet II* [1991] ECR I-4069, para 23

As has been indicated in para 12 of this judgment, although *the existence of a monopoly in the provision of services is not as such incompatible with Community law*, the possibility cannot be excluded that *the monopoly may be organised in such a way as to infringe the rules relating to the freedom to provide services*. Such a case arises, in particular, where the monopoly leads to *discrimination* between national television broadcasts and those originating in other Member States, to the detriment of the latter.

Case C-260/89, *ERT* [1991] ECR I-2925, para 20

## Restrictive interpretation of exceptions

Having regard to the particular characteristics of certain provisions of services, specific requirements imposed on the provider, which result from the application of rules governing those types of activities, cannot be regarded as incompatible with the Treaty. However, *as a fundamental principle of the Treaty, the freedom to provide services may be limited only* by rules which are justified by imperative reasons relating to the public interest and which apply to all persons or undertakings pursuing an activity in the State of destination, in so far as that interest is not protected by the rules to which the person providing the services is subject in the Member State in which he is established. *In particular, those requirements must be objectively necessary in order to ensure compliance with professional rules and to guarantee the protection of the recipient of services and they must not exceed what is necessary to attain those objectives* [see also Cases C-154/89, *Commission v France* [1991] ECR I-659, C-180/89, *Commission v Italy* [1991] ECR I-709, and C-198/89, *Commission v Greece* [1991] ECR I-727].

Case C-76/90 *Dennemeyer* [1991] ECR I-4221, para 15

[...] however, *national measures liable to hinder or make less attractive the exercise of fundamental freedoms guaranteed by the Treaty must fulfil four conditions: they must be applied in a non-discriminatory manner; they must be justified by imperative requirements in the general interest; they must be suitable for securing the attainment of the objective which they pursue; and they must not go beyond what is necessary to attain it.*

Case C-55/94, *Gebhard* [1995] ECR I-4165, para 39, see also paras 27, 28, 37, 38

## Restriction justified in the general interest

Having regard to the particular characteristics of certain provisions of services, *specific requirements* imposed on the provider, which result from the application of rules governing those types of activities, *cannot be regarded as incompatible with the Treaty*. However, as a fundamental *principle of the Treaty, the freedom to provide services may be limited only by rules which are justified by imperative reasons relating to the public interest and which apply to all persons or undertakings pursuing an activity in the State of destination, in so far as that interest is not protected by the rules to which the person providing the services is subject in the Member State in which he is established*. In particular, those requirements must be objectively necessary in order to ensure compliance with professional rules and to guarantee the protection of the recipient of services and they must not exceed what is necessary to attain those objectives [see also Cases C-154/89, *Commission v France* [1991] ECR I-659; C-180/89, *Commission v Italy* [1991] ECR I-709, and C-198/89, *Commission v Greece* [1991] ECR I-727].

Case C-76/90, *Dennemeyer* [1991] ECR I-4221, para 15

The only derogation which may be contemplated in a case such as this is that provided in *Art 56* of the Treaty, to which Art 66 refers, under which the national provisions providing for special treatment for foreign nationals escape the application of Art 59 of the Treaty if they are justified on grounds of public policy.

Case C-352/85, *Bond van Adverteerders* [1988] ECR 2085, para 33

The Court has nevertheless accepted, in particular in its judgments of 18 January 1979 (Joined Cases 110 and 111/78, *Ministère Public and Another v van Wesemael and Others* [1979] ECR 35) and 17 December 1981 (Case 279/80, *Webb*, cited above) that regard being had to the particular nature of certain services, specific requirements imposed on the provider of the services cannot be considered to be incompatible with the Treaty where they have as their purpose the application of rules governing such activities.

Case C-252/83, *Commission v Denmark* [1986] ECR 3713, para 17

Case C-205/84, *Commission v Germany* [1986] ECR 3755, para 27

# Circumvention of establishment

Moreover, the Court has already held in connection with Art 59 of the Treaty on the freedom to provide services *that a Member State cannot be denied the right to take measures to prevent the exercise by a person providing services whose activity is entirely or principally directed towards its territory of the freedoms guaranteed by the Treaty for the purpose of avoiding the rules which would be applicable to him if he were established within that State* [see Case C-33/74, van Binsbergen [1974] ECR 1299].

Case C-23/93, *TV10 SA* [1994] ECR I-4795, para 20; see also para 26

It follows that a *Member State may regard as a domestic broadcaster a radio and television organisation which establishes itself in another Member State in order to provide services there which are intended for the first State's territory, since the aim of that measure is to prevent organisations which establish themselves in another Member State from being able, by exercising the freedoms guaranteed by the Treaty, wrongfully to avoid obligations under national law*, in this case those designed to ensure the pluralist and non-commercial content of programmes.

Case C-23/93, *TV10 SA* [1994] ECR I-4795, para 21

By prohibiting national broadcasting organisations from helping to set up commercial radio and television companies abroad for the purpose of providing services there directed towards The Netherlands, The Netherlands

legislation at issue has the specific effect, *with a view to safeguarding the exercise of the freedoms guaranteed by the Treaty, of ensuring that those organisations cannot improperly evade the obligations deriving from the national legislation* concerning the pluralistic and non-commercial content of programmes.
Case C-148/91, *Veronica* [1993] ECR I-487, para 13

## Articles 56 and 66: public policy, public security and public health justifications

[...] the rule in question entails discrimination based on the place of establishment. *Such discrimination can only be justified on the general interest grounds referred to in Art 56(1) of the Treaty,* to which Art 66 refers, and which do not include economic aims [see in particular Case C-288/89, *Stichting Collectieve Antennevoorziening Gouda and Others v Commissariat voor de Media* [1991] ECR I-4007, para 11].
Case C-484/93, *Svensson, Gustavsson* [1995] ECR I-3955, para 15

As the Court held in its judgment in Case 352/85, *Bond van Adverteerders* [1988] ECR 2085, paras 32 and 33, *national rules which are not applicable to services without discrimination* as regards their origin *are compatible with Community law only if they can be brought within the scope of an express exemption, such as that contained in Art 56* of the Treaty. It also appears from that judgment (para 34) that economic aims cannot constitute grounds of public policy within the meaning of Art 56 of the Treaty.
Case C-288/89, *Mediawet* [1991] ECR I-4007, para 11

Moreover, the justifications put forward by the Belgian government do not come within any of the grounds for exemption from the freedom to provide services permitted by Art 56, *namely public policy, public security and public health.*
As the Court has consistently held [see, in particular, Case 288/89, *Collectieve Antennevoorziening Gouda and Others v Commissariat voor de Media* [1991] ECR I-4007, para 11] *those exemptions alone can effectively be relied upon to justify national rules which are not applicable to services without distinction as regards their origin.*
Case C-211/91, *Commission v Belgium* [1992] ECR I-6757, paras 10 and 11

[...] the rules relating to the freedom to provide services preclude national rules which have such discriminatory effects unless those rules fall within the derogating provision contained in Art 56 of the Treaty to which Art 66 refers. *It follows from Art 56, which must be interpreted strictly, that discriminatory rules may be justified on grounds of public policy, public security or public health.*
Case C-260/89, *ERT* [1991] ECR I-2925, para 24

In particular, *where a Member State relies on the combined provisions of Arts 56 and 66 in order to justify rules which are likely to obstruct the exercise of the freedom to provide services, such justification, provided for by Community law, must be interpreted in the light of the general principles of law and in particular of fundamental rights.* Thus the national rules in question can fall under the exceptions provided for by the combined provisions of Arts 56 and 66 only if they are compatible with the fundamental rights of observance of which is ensured by the Court.

Case C-260/89, *ERT* [1991] ECR I-2925, para 43

The reply to the national court must therefore be that the limitations imposed on the power of the Member States to apply the provisions referred to in Arts 66 and 56 of the Treaty on grounds of public policy, public security and public health must be appraised in the light of the general principle of freedom of expression embodied in Art 10 of the European Convention on Human Rights.

Case C-260/89, *ERT* [1991] ECR I-2925, para 45

It is appropriate to point out in the first place that national rules which are not applicable to services *without distinction* as regards their origin and which are therefore discriminatory are compatible with Community law only if they can be brought within the scope of an express derogation.

*The only derogation which may be contemplated in a case such as this is that provided in Art 56 of the Treaty, to which Art 66 refers,* under which the national provisions providing for special treatment for foreign nationals escape the application of Art 59 of the Treaty *if they are justified on grounds of public policy.*

Case C-352/85, *Bond van Adverteerders* [1988] ECR 2085, paras 32 and 33

## Consumer protection

In this respect, it must be observed in the first place that restrictions on the broadcasting of advertisements, such as a prohibition on advertising particular products or on certain days, a limitation of the duration or frequency of advertisements or restrictions designed to enable listeners or viewers not to confuse advertising with other parts of the programme, may be justified by overriding reasons relating to the general interest. Such restrictions may be imposed *in order to protect consumers* against excessive advertising or, as an objective of cultural policy, in order to maintain a certain level of programme quality.

Case C-288/89, *Mediawet* [1991] ECR I-4007, para 27

## Economic justifications

[...] the rule in question entails discrimination based on the place of establishment. Such discrimination can only be justified on the general interest grounds referred to in Art 56(1) of the Treaty, to which Art 66 refers, and which do not include economic aims (see in particular Case C-288/89, *Stichting Collectieve Antennevoorziening Gouda and Others v Commissariat voor de Media* [1991] ECR I-4007, para 11).

Case C-484/93, *Svensson, Gustavsson* [1995] ECR I-3955, para 15

The first and third cultural policy objectives adduced by the Belgian Government reveal that *in reality the purpose of the measure complained of is to restrict genuine competition* with the national broadcasting stations in order to maintain their advertising revenue. As regards the objective of preserving and developing the artistic heritage, suffice it to note, as does the Commission, that the measure complained of is *in reality likely to reduce demand* for television productions in Dutch.

Case C-211/91, *Commission v Belgium* [1992] ECR I-6757, para 9

As the Court held in its judgment in Case 352/85, *Bond van Adverteerders* [1988] ECR 2085, paras 32 and 33, national rules which are not applicable to services without discrimination as regards their origin are compatible with Community law only if they can be brought within the scope of an express exemption, such as that contained in Art 56 of the Treaty. *It also appears from that judgment (para 34) that economic aims cannot constitute grounds of public policy within the meaning of Art 56 of the Treaty.*

Case C-288/89, *Mediawet* [1991] ECR I-4007, para 11

Unlike the Kabelregeling [cable regulation], the provisions of the Mediawet [media law] at issue in this case no longer reserve to the STER all the revenue from advertising intended specifically for the Dutch public. However, by laying down rules on the broadcasting of such advertisements they *restrict the competition* to which the STER may be exposed in that market from foreign broadcasting bodies. Accordingly the result is that they protect the revenue of the STER – albeit to a lesser degree than the Kabelregeling – and therefore pursue the same objective as the previous legislation. As the Court held in Case C-352/85, *Bond van Adverteerders* [1988] ECR 2085, para 34, *that objective cannot justify restrictions on the freedom to provide services.*

Case C-288/89, *Mediawet* [1991] ECR I-4007, para 29

The reply to the national court must therefore be that *Community law does not prevent* the granting of a television monopoly *for considerations of a non-economic nature relating to the public interest.* However, the manner in which such a monopoly is organised and exercised must not infringe the provisions of the Treaty on the free movement of goods and services or the rules on competition.

Case C-260/89, *ERT* [1991] ECR I-2925, para 12

## The general interest protected in the country of origin

As the Court has consistently held [see, for example, Cases C-154/89, *Commission v France* [1991] ECR I-659, para 18, C-180/89, *Commission v Italy* [1991] ECR I-709, para 18, and C-198/89, *Commission v Greece* [1991] ECR I-727, para 18], such restrictions come within the scope of Art 59 if the application of the national legislation to foreign persons providing services is not justified by overriding reasons relating to the public interest or if the requirements embodied in that legislation are already satisfied by the rules imposed on those persons in the Member State in which they are established.

Case C-288/89, *Mediawet* [1991] ECR I-4007, para 13

# The principle of proportionality

It should next be stated that the public interest in the protection of the recipients of the services in question against such harm justifies a restriction of the freedom to provide services. However, such a provision goes beyond what is necessary to protect that interest if it makes the pursuit, by way of business, of an activity such as that at issue, subject to the possession by the persons providing the service of a professional qualification which is quite specific and *disproportionate* to the needs of the recipients.

Case C-76/90, *Dennemeyer* [1991] ECR I-4221, para 17

# Television, radio and film

*A cultural policy understood in that sense may indeed constitute an overriding requirement relating to the general interest* which justifies a restriction on the freedom to provide services. The maintenance of the pluralism which that Dutch policy seeks to safeguard is connected with freedom of expression, as protected by Art 10 of the European Convention on Human Rights and Fundamental Freedoms, which is one of the fundamental rights guaranteed by the Community legal order [Case 4/73, *Nold v Commission* [1974] ECR 491, para 13].

Case C-288/89, *Mediawet* [1991] ECR I-4007, paras 22 and 23

However, it should be observed that there is no necessary connection between such a *cultural policy* and the conditions relating to the structure of foreign broadcasting bodies. In order to *ensure pluralism in the audio-visual sector* it is not indispensable for the national legislation to require broadcasting bodies established in other Member States to align themselves on the Dutch model should they intend to broadcast programmes containing advertisements intended for the Dutch public. In order to secure the pluralism which it wishes to maintain The Netherlands Government may very well confine itself to formulating the statutes of its own bodies in an appropriate manner.

Case C-288/89, *Mediawet* [1991] ECR I-4007, para 24

Conditions affecting the structure of foreign broadcasting bodies cannot therefore be regarded as being objectively necessary in order to safeguard the general interest in maintaining a national radio and television system which secures pluralism.

Case C-288/89, *Mediawet* [1991] ECR I-4007, para 25

In this respect, it must be observed in the first place that restrictions on the broadcasting of advertisements, such as a prohibition on advertising particular products or on certain days, a limitation of the duration or frequency of advertisements or restrictions designed to enable listeners or viewers not to confuse advertising with other parts of the programme, may be justified by overriding reasons relating to the general interest. Such restrictions may be

imposed *in order to protect consumers against excessive advertising or, as an objective of cultural policy, in order to maintain a certain level of programme quality.*
Case C-288/89, *Mediawet* [1991] ECR I-4007, para 27

In the absence of express provision to the contrary in the Treaty, a television signal must, by reason of its nature, *be regarded as provision of services.*

Although it is not ruled out that services normally provided for remuneration may come under the provisions relating to free movement of goods, such is however the case, as appears from Art 60, only in so far as they are governed by such provisions.
Case C-155/73, *Sacchi* [1974] ECR 409, para 6

The answer must therefore be that national rules prohibiting the transmission by cable television of advertisements cannot be regarded as constituting either a disproportionate measure in relation to the objective to be achieved, in that the prohibition in question is relatively ineffective in view of the existence of natural reception zones, or discrimination which is prohibited by the Treaty in regard to foreign broadcasters, in that their geographical location allows them to broadcast their signals only in the natural reception zone.
Case C-52/79, *Debauve* [1980] ECR 833, para 22

Unlike the Kabelregeling [cable regulation], the provisions of the Mediawet [media law] at issue in this case no longer reserve to the STER all the revenue from advertising intended specifically for the Dutch public. However, by laying down rules on the broadcasting of such advertisements *they restrict competition* to which the STER may be exposed in the market from foreign broadcasting bodies. Accordingly the result is that *they protect the revenue* of the STER – albeit to a lesser degree than the Kabelregeling – and therefore pursue the same objective as the previous legislation. As the Court held in Case C-352/85, *Bond van Adverteerders* [1988] ECR 2085, para 34, *that objective cannot justify restrictions on the freedom to provide services.*
Case C-288/89, *Mediawet* [1991] ECR I-4007, para 29

The reply to the national court must therefore be that *Community law does not prevent* the granting of a television monopoly *for considerations of a non-economic nature relating to the public interest.* However, the manner in which such a monopoly is organised and exercised must not infringe the provisions of the Treaty on the free movement of goods and services or the rules on competition.
Case C-260/89, *ERT* [1991] ECR I-2925, para 12

It should be observed *in limine* that it follows from the *Sacchi* judgment that *television broadcasting falls within the rules of the Treaty relating to services and that since a television monopoly is a monopoly in the provision of services, it is not as such contrary to the principle of the free movement of goods.*
Case C-260/89, *ERT* [1991] ECR I-2925, para 13

As has been indicated in para 12 of this judgment, although the existence of a monopoly in the provision of services is not as such incompatible with

Community law, the possibility cannot be excluded that the monopoly may be organised in such a way as to infringe the rules relating to the freedom to provide services. Such a case arises, in particular, where the monopoly leads to discrimination between national television broadcasts and those originating in other Member States, to the detriment of the latter.

Case C-260/89, *ERT* [1991] ECR I-2925, para 20

It is apparent from the observations submitted to the Court that *the sole objective of the rules in question was to avoid disturbances due to the restricted number of channels available.* Such an objective cannot, however, constitute justification for those rules for the purposes of Art 56 of the Treaty, where the undertaking in question uses only a limited number of the available channels.

Case C-260/89, *ERT* [1991] ECR I-2925, para 25

The answer must therefore be that Arts 59 and 60 of the Treaty do not preclude national rules prohibiting the transmission of advertisements by cable television – as they prohibit the broadcasting of advertisements by television – *if those rules are applied without distinction* as regards the origin, whether national or foreign, of those advertisements, the nationality of the person providing the service, or the place where he is established.

Case C-52/79, *Debauve* [1980] ECR 833, para 16

Article 37 [of EC Treaty, Title I, Ch 2: Elimination of Quantitative Restrictions] concerns the adjustment of State monopolies of a commercial character.

It follows both from the place of this provision in the chapter on the elimination of quantitative restrictions and from the use of the words 'imports' and 'exports' in the second indent of Art 37(1) and of the word 'products' in Art 37(3) and (4) that it refers to trade in goods and cannot relate to a monopoly in the provision of services.

Thus *televised commercial advertising, by reasons of its character as a service, does not come under these provisions.*

Case C-155/73, *Sacchi* [1974] ECR 409, para 10

However, for the performance of their tasks, *these establishments remain subject to the prohibitions against discrimination* and, to the extent that this performance comprises activities of an economic nature, fall under the provisions referred to in Art 90 [EC Treaty, Title V, Ch 5: Rules on Competition] relating to public undertakings and undertakings to which Member States grant special or exclusive rights.

Case C-155/73, *Sacchi* [1974] ECR 409, para 14

Such would certainly be the case with an undertaking possessing a monopoly of television advertising, if it imposed unfair charges or conditions on users of its services or if it discriminated between commercial operators or national products on the one hand, and those of other Member States on the other, as regards access to television advertising.

Case C-155/73, *Sacchi* [1974] ECR 409, para 17

## Article 30 (Title I, Ch 2: Elimination of Quantitative Restrictions between Member States)

Such a prohibition *is not analogous to the legislation concerning selling arrangements held in* Keck and Mithouard *to fall outside the scope of Art 30 of the Treaty [...]. The reason is that the application of such provisions is not such to prevent access by the latter to the market of the Member State of importation or to impede such access more than it impedes access by domestic products [...]. A prohibition such as that at issue is imposed by the Member State in which the provider of services is established and affects not only offers made by him to addressees who are established in that State or move there in order to receive services, but also offers made to potential recipients in another Member State. It therefore directly affects access to the market in services in other Member States and is thus capable of hindering intra-Community trade in services.*

Case C-384/93, *Alpine Investments BV* [1995] ECR I-1141, paras 36, 37 and 38; see also Case C-415/93, *Bosman* [1995] ECR I-4921, para 103

The reply should accordingly be that, on a proper construction, Art 30 of the Treaty does not apply where a Member State, by statute or by regulation, prohibits the broadcasting of televised advertisements for the distribution sector.

Case C-412/93, *Edouard Leclerc-Siplec* [1995] ECR I-179, para 24

With regard to the fact that the servicing of a vehicle in another Member State may involve a supply of goods (spare parts, oil, etc), it should be noted that such a supply is not an end in itself, but is incidental to the provision of services. Consequently, it does not, as such, fall within the scope of Art 30 of the Treaty [see Case C-275/92, *Schindler* [1994] ECR I-1039].

Case C-55/93, *van Schaik* [1994] ECR I-2925, para 13

It should be observed *in limine* that it follows from the *Sacchi* judgment that television broadcasting falls within the rules of the Treaty relating to services and that since a television monopoly is *a monopoly in the provision of services, it is not as such contrary to the principle of the free movement of goods.*

Case C-260/89, *ERT* [1991] ECR I-2925, para 13

The situation in which student associations distributing the information at issue in the main proceedings are not in co-operation with the clinics whose addresses they publish can be distinguished from the situation which gave rise to the judgment in *GB-INNO-BM* [C-362/88, [1990] ECR I-667] in which the Court held that a prohibition on the distribution of advertising *was capable of constituting a barrier to the free movement of goods and therefore had to be examined in the light of Arts 30, 31 and 36 of the EEC Treaty.*

Case C-159/90, *Grogan* [1991] ECR I-4685, para 25

## Interpretation of Art 52: freedom of establishment

*The right of establishment*, provided for in Arts 52 to 58 of the Treaty, *is granted both to legal persons within the meaning of Art 58 and to natural persons who are nationals of a Member State of the Community.* Subject to the exceptions and conditions laid down, it allows *all types of self-employed activity to be taken up and pursued on the territory of any other Member State, undertakings to be formed and operated, and agencies, branches or subsidiaries to be set up.*

Case C-55/94, *Gebhard* [1995] ECR 4165, para 23

*The concept of establishment* within the meaning of the *Treaty is therefore a very broad one*, allowing a Community *national to participate, on a stable and continuous basis, in the economic life of a Member State other than his State of origin* and to profit therefrom, so contributing to economic and social interpenetration within the Community in the sphere of activities as self-employed persons [see also Case 2/74, *Reyners v Belgium* [1974] ECR 631, para 21].

Case C-55/94, *Gebhard* [1995] ECR 4165, para 25

## Fundamental rights

*It is settled law that fundamental rights,* including those guaranteed by the European Convention on Human Rights, *form an integral part of the general principles of law, the observance of which the Court ensures* [see, in particular, Cases C-260/89, *Elliniki Radiophonia Tilèorassi* [1991] ECR I-2925, para 41 and C-68/89, *Commission v Netherlands* [1991] ECR I-2637, para 10].

In *Commission v Netherlands* [[1991] ECR I-2637, para 30], the Court held that *the maintenance of the pluralism which The Netherlands broadcasting policy seeks to safeguard is intended to preserve the diversity of opinions, and hence freedom of expression, which is precisely what the European Convention on Human Rights is designed to protect.*

Case C-23/93, *TV10 SA* [1994] ECR I-4795, paras 24 and 25

The information to which the national court's questions refer is not distributed on behalf of an economic operator established in another Member State. On the contrary, the information constitutes a manifestation of freedom of expression and of the freedom to impart and receive information which is independent of the economic activity carried on by clinics established in another Member State.

Case C-159/90, *Grogan* [1991] ECR I-4685, para 26

According to, *inter alia*, the judgment of 18 June 1991 in *Elliniki Radiophonia Tilèorassi* [C-260/89 [1991] ECRI-2951, para 42], where national legislation falls within the field of application of Community law, the Court, when requested to give a preliminary ruling, must provide the national court with all the elements of interpretation which are necessary in order to enable it to assess the compatibility of that legislation with the fundamental rights – as laid down in particular in the European Convention on Human Rights – the observance of which the Court ensures. However, the Court has no such jurisdiction with regard to national legislation lying outside the scope of community law. In view of the facts of the case and of the conclusions which the Court has reached above with regards to the scope of Arts 59 and 62 of the Treaty, that would appear to be true of the prohibition at issue before the national court.

Case C-159/90, *Grogan* [1991] ECR I-4685, para 31

## The role and interpretation of directives

It follows from that provision that the implementation of a directive does not necessarily require legislative action in each Member State. In particular, the existence of general principles of constitutional or administrative law may render implementation by specific legislation superfluous, provided however that those principles guarantee that the national authorities will in fact apply the directive fully and that, where the directive is intended to create rights for individuals, the legal position arising from those principles is sufficiently precise and clear and the persons concerned are made fully aware of their rights and, where appropriate, afforded the possibility of relying on them before the national courts. That last condition is of particular importance where the directive in question is intended to accord rights to nationals of other Member States, because those nationals are not normally aware of such principles.

Case C-29/84, *Commission v Germany* [1985] ECR 1661, para 23

As the Court has held in its judgment of 13 December 1983 [Case 218/82, *Commission v Council* [1983] ECR 4063], when the wording of secondary Community law is open to more than one interpretation, preference should be given to the interpretation which renders the provision consistent with the Treaty rather than the interpretation which leads to its being incompatible with the Treaty. Consequently, the directive should not be construed in isolation and it is necessary to consider whether or not requirements in question are contrary to the above-mentioned provisions of the Treaty and to interpret the directive in the light of the conclusions reached in that respect.

Case C-252/83, *Commission v Denmark* [1986] ECR 3713, para 15

Case C-205/84, *Commission v Germany* [1986] ECR 3755, para 62

## External Community competence in the services sector

*Under Art I(2) of GATS, trade in services is defined, for the purposes of that agreement, as comprising four modes of supply of services:* (1) cross-frontier supplies not involving any movement of persons; (2) consumption abroad, which entails the movement of the consumer into the territory of the WTO member country in which the supplier is established; (3) commercial presence, that is, the presence of a subsidiary or branch in the territory of the WTO member country in which the service is to be rendered; (4) the presence of natural persons from a WTO member country, enabling a supplier from one member country to supply services within the territory of any other member country.

Opinion 1/94 [1994] ECR I-5267, para 43

*As regards cross-frontier supplies, the service is rendered by a supplier established in one country to a consumer residing in another. The supplier does not move to the consumer's country; nor, conversely, does the consumer move to the supplier's country. That situation is, therefore, not unlike trade in goods, which is unquestionably covered by the common commercial policy within the meaning of the Treaty. There is thus no particular reason why such a supply should not fall within the concept of the common commercial policy.*

Opinion 1/94 [1994] ECR I-5267, para 44

*The same cannot be said of the other three modes of supply of services covered by GATS,* namely, the consumption abroad, commercial presence and the presence of natural persons [...] the modes of supply of services referred to by GATS as 'consumption abroad', 'commercial presence' and the 'presence of natural persons' are not covered by the common commercial policy.

Opinion 1/94 [1994] ECR I-5267, paras 45 and 47

*Unlike the chapter on transport, the chapters on the right of establishment and on freedom to provide services do not contain any provision expressly extending the competence of the Community to 'relationships arising from international law'.* As has rightly been observed by the Council and most of the Member States which have submitted observations, *the sole objective of those chapters is to secure the right of establishment and freedom to provide services for nationals of Member States.* They contain no provisions on the problem of the first establishment of nationals of non-member countries and the rules governing their access to self-employed activities. *One cannot therefore infer from those chapters that the Community has exclusive competence to conclude an agreement with non-member countries to liberalise first establishment and access to services markets, other than those which are the subject of the cross-border supplies within the meaning of GATS, which are covered by Art 113.*

Opinion 1/94 [1994] ECR I-5267, para 81

*Whenever the Community has included in its internal legislative acts provisions relating to the treatment of nationals of non-member countries or expressly conferred on its institutions powers to negotiate with non-member countries, it acquires exclusive external competence in the spheres covered by those acts.*

Opinion 1/94 [1994] ECR I-5267, para 95

*The same applies in any event, even in the absence of any express provision authorising its institutions to negotiate with non-member countries, where the Community has achieved complete harmonisation of the rules governing access to a self-employed activity, because the common rules thus adopted could be affected within the meaning of the AETR judgment if the Member States retained freedom to negotiate with non-member countries.*

Opinion 1/94 [1994] ECR I-5267, para 96

*That is not the case in all service sectors, however, as the Commission has itself acknowledged.*
Opinion 1/94 [1994] ECR I-5267, para 97

*It follows that competence to conclude GATS is shared between the Community and the Member States.*
Opinion 1/94 [1994] ECR I-5267, para 98

# TOBACCO ADVERTISING DIRECTIVE (15/98/EC)

On 4 December 1992, the Council adopted its Common Position on a Commission proposal for a Directive on Tobacco Advertising, a proposal designed to harmonise internal market legislation under Art 100a of the Treaty.

Common Position 15/98/EC, adopted by the Council on 12 February 1998, sets out the following framework. In the Directive, Art 3 provides that, within three years, all tobacco advertising on boards and in cinemas and within four years, in newspapers and magazines, should be outlawed.

The Directive provides that Member States may continue to authorise the existing sponsorship of events or activities organised at world level, but this must end within five years – except for 'Formula One' motor racing, which has been given eight years. The sums devoted to such sponsorship decrease over the transitional period.

Measures of voluntary restraint are introduced, in order to reduce the visibility of advertising at the events or activities concerned.

The Directive aims to approximate the differing national provisions on advertising for tobacco products, taking as a basis a high level of health protection. The only exceptions to the ban are:

(a) those related to advertising within tobacco sales outlets having enclosed indoor premises for serving their customers;

(b) the presentation of tobacco products offered for sale and the indication of their prices at tobacco sales outlets;

(c) advertising aimed at purchasers in establishments specialising in the sale of tobacco products and on their shop fronts or, in the case of establishments selling a variety of articles or services, at locations reserved for the sale of tobacco products, and at sales outlets which, in Greece, are subject to a special system under which licences are granted for special reasons ('periptera');

(d) the sale of publications containing advertising for tobacco products which are published and printed in third countries, where those publications are not principally intended for the Community market.

The European Parliament approved the proposed Directive in a parliamentary vote on 22 April 1998. The ban was approved on 22 June 1998, with Germany and Austria voting against, and Spain and Denmark abstaining.

A parliamentary resolution calls for the introduction of an EC-wide age limit of 18 years for the purpose of tobacco products; a ban on tobacco vending machines and self-service displays; a ban on packaging that is particularly geared to attracting young people; and also increases in the price of tobacco in real terms. The Commission is also asked to propose the harmonisation of tobacco taxes upwards and to launch a co-ordinated campaign to force tobacco companies in the EC to pay American-style compensation for damage to smokers' health.

The resolution also calls for nicotine to be declared an 'addiction-inducing substance'; for more funding on anti-tobacco projects; and the establishment of a yearly European prize for the best tobacco-free project in the EC. The resolution also condemned the EC's export of poor quality tobacco to third countries. A call to halt subsidies to EC tobacco growers was rejected.

An amendment stating that there was no legal basis for a ban was rejected by 314 to 211 votes. A further impact of the ban will be that tobacco companies' logos on clothing must change too, to avoid direct linkage with cigarette packets' colours and designs. The directive has been challenged by Germany and the tobacco companies. We await a judgment from the court.

# COMPARATIVE ADVERTISING DIRECTIVE (97/55/EC)

The free movement of goods and services within the single market presupposes also a certain harmonisation of national rules concerning advertising. The Directive on Misleading Advertising dates from 1984 and, although it already sought to regulate all advertising that is unfair and misleading, specific provision was made (in Recital 6) for comparative advertising to be dealt with at a later stage.

The original proposal to amend the basic Directive to include comparative advertising dates from May 1991. After the Parliament's first reading in November 1992, it took the Commission until 1994 to amend its proposal, and the Council until March 1996 to adopt a Common Position. After the Common Position was transmitted to Parliament on 4 July 1996, 16 amendments were adopted at second reading on 23 October 1996. By a letter dated 29 January 1997, Council informed the Parliament that the conciliation committee would have to be convened, since it was not in a position to accept all the amendments.

A trialogue was held on 24 February 1997 to explore the Council's position on the amendments.

Finally, on 25 June 1997, the conciliation committee was able to meet to decide on amendments and changes to the proposed Directive.

On 6 October, the EU Council formally adopted a Comparative Advertising Directive. This will lead to pan-European comparative advertising campaigns.

The Directive introduces the concept of comparative advertising, which is defined as 'any advertising which explicitly or by implication identifies a competitor or goods or services offered by a competitor'. Comparative advertising is permitted if the following conditions are met:

(a) it is not misleading;

(b) it compares goods or services meeting the same needs or intended for the same purpose;

(c) it objectively compares one or more material, relevant, verifiable and representative features of those goods or services, which may include price;

(d) it does not create confusion in the market place between the advertiser and a competitor;

(e) it does not discredit or denigrate the trade marks, trade names or other distinguishing signs of a competitor;

(f) for products with designation of origin, it relates to products with the same designation;

(g) it does not take unfair advantage of the trade mark or other distinguishing sign of a competitor;

(h) it does not present goods or services as imitations or replicas of goods or services bearing a protected trade mark or trade name;

(i) the provisions for controlling misleading advertising apply also to prohibited comparative advertising;

(j) the Directive provides for the establishment of a system for dealing with cross-border complaints in respect of comparative advertising.

Member States must implement the Directive by 23 April 2000.


## DIRECTIVE ON ADVERTISING OF MEDICINAL PRODUCTS FOR HUMAN USE (92/28/EEC)

This Council Directive of 31 March 1992 provides that all advertising relating to a medicinal product:

(a) is forbidden if the medicinal product has not been granted a marketing authorisation;

(b) must be compatible with the information listed in the summary of the products' characteristics;

(c) must encourage the rational administration of the medicinal product;

(d) must not be misleading, within the meaning of Council Directive 84/450/EEC.

The following are prohibited:

(a) advertising to the general public of medicinal products which are only available on medical prescription;

(b) mentioning, when advertising to the general public, therapeutic indications where self-medication is not suitable;

(c) the distribution of free samples to the general public, as well as offers of gifts and bonuses.

Where authorised advertising is to the general public, it:

(a) must be set out in such a fashion that it is clear that the message is an advertisement, and that the product is clearly identified as a medicinal product;

(b) must include all the necessary information for correct administration of the medicinal product;

(c) must include an express invitation to read the instruction leaflet carefully;

(d) must not include elements incompatible with the rational administration of the medicinal product.

Any advertising to professionals and any documentation transmitted to them as part of the promotion of a medicinal product must include:

- essential information compatible with the summary of the product's characteristics;

- the classification of the medicinal product for supply purposes;

(e) during each visit, medical sales representatives must provide the persons visited with the summaries of product characteristics in respect of each medicinal product which they present;

(f) inducements to prescribe or supply medicinal products (such as gifts, pecuniary advantages or benefits in kind, including invitations to travel or to congresses, with the exception of objects of an insignificant intrinsic value) are prohibited;

(g) the supply of free samples to persons qualified to prescribe or supply medicinal products is subject to strict controls;

(h) pharmaceutical companies are required to establish within the company a scientific service in charge of information relating to medicinal products;

(i) provisions relating to the monitoring of pharmaceutical advertising are similar to those provided for in Directive 84/450/EEC on Misleading Advertising.

# DIRECTIVE ON DISTANCE CONTRACTS (97/7/EC)

Directive 97/7/EC (OJ L 44, 1997), in Art 10, para 1, merely prohibits unsolicited advertising by fax and voice mail, clearly leaving open the unsolicited dispatch of e-mails with a commercial content.

The Directive provides, in Art 14, that 'Member States may introduce or maintain, in the area covered by this Directive, more stringent provisions compatible with the Treaty to ensure a higher level of consumer protection. Such provisions shall, where appropriate, include a ban, in the general interest, on the marketing of certain goods or services, particularly medicinal products within their territory by means of distance contracts, with due regard for the Treaty.'

The State of Washington, in the US, has introduced one of the first laws to make it illegal to send false or misleading information by junk e-mail.

The law, which looks likely to be adopted by several other American States, covers any junk e-mail sent to or from an e-mail address in the State of Washington. It also lays down a fine of $1,500 for each violation – $500 to be paid by the sender and $1,000 by the internet service provider.

The law makes it illegal to use a false sender's address, to send e-mail with a misleading subject tag, or to make unauthorised use of a third party's e-mail address. How it will work in practice remains to be seen.

# THE INTERNATIONAL CHAMBER OF COMMERCE

The International Chamber of Commerce (ICC), founded in 1919, headquartered in Paris, is a non-governmental organisation which represents the interests of business enterprises of all sectors around the globe. Its purpose is to promote international trade, investment and the market economy system. It also provides essential services, such as the International Court of Arbitration (the world's leading body for the resolution of international commercial disputes), and has UN consultative status.

One of the ICC's main activities is the harmonisation of trade practices. The ICC promotes high standards in business self-regulation through its various codes of practice, the first code having been published as early as 1937. See Appendix 11, which contains the ICC codes dealing with advertising, sales promotion, sponsorship and marketing, as well as guidelines for advertising and marketing on the internet.

# A VIEW TO THE FUTURE

In March 1998, the European Commission adopted a Communication outlining a series of measures to facilitate the cross-border provision of commercial communications services while ensuring appropriate protection of public interest objectives such as health and protection of consumers and the environment. The measures include the application of a transparent method of assessing whether restrictions on cross-border commercial communications are proportional to the public interest objective and the creation of a group of Member States' experts which would, *inter alia*, seek solutions to restrictions. This is aimed at easing the cross-border restrictions in the different Member States and the opening up of their markets as part of the single market.

The commercial communications sector directly employs in excess of one million people, and it is growing rapidly thanks to the development of new communications technologies and buoyant demand. For example, in the specialised area of telemarketing, the current number of 193,500 employees in Europe is forecast to grow to 669,500 in the year 2001. Growth of internet-related commercial communications is similarly expected to increase. For France, Germany, The Netherlands and the UK alone, the value of these new commercial communications services is forecast to grow to 1.3 billion ECU in 2001.

## Proposed actions

The Commission saw that an internal market approach was required in this area, given that there existed no co-ordinated framework for the sector, even though it is regulated for a wide variety of public interest objectives and increasingly offering services across borders, thanks to the development of new communications channels.

Article 100a of the EC Treaty makes it clear that internal market measures which affect such public interest objectives must take as a base a high level of protection. The importance accorded to these public interest objectives by Community law is also reflected, as mentioned earlier, in Arts 129, 129a and 130r of the EC Treaty.

In accordance with the Single Market Action Plan endorsed by the European Council (see SMN 8), the Commission has agreed to implement the following actions.

### Applying a transparent assessment methodology

The Commission's services will, in future decisions taken in this field, apply, where appropriate, an assessment methodology which builds on that described in the Green Paper (COM (96) 192 Final), but it adds two further criteria, in recognition of cultural and social differences in the Member States and the need to ensure coherence across public interest objectives.

The methodology consists of two steps:

*Step 1: Analytical overview*

The objective of the first step is not to undertake the proportionality test as such, but to set out a complete 'picture' of the impacts of the measure. The aim is not to identify restrictions, but to provide a factual overview of all possible effects of a measure, in particular on activities that the measure is meant to regulate, and on the public interest objectives, such as consumer protection and public health. The first step characterises either (a) the relevant national measure restricting the free movement of commercial communication services, or (b) the harmonisation measure proposed by the Commission.

Seven criteria are proposed for this characterisation in step 1:

(a) What is the potential economic chain reaction and the resulting impact on consumers caused by the measure?

(b) What are the public interest objectives motivating the measure?

(c) Is the measure linked to the public interest objective invoked ?

(d) Does the measure affect other public interest objectives?

(e) How efficient is the measure in achieving the public interest objective invoked?

(f) Does the measure reflect cultural or social specificity?

(g) Is the measure coherent across all relevant public interest objectives, and notably those of consumer protection and public health?

*Step 2: Legal assessment*

On the basis of this overview and the factual information that it provides, the second step consists of an overall legal assessment of whether, for a national measure, it could be considered to be proportional or, in the case of a Community measure, it would be proportional and coherent with other Community measures. By knowing the key characteristics of the measure, the seven criteria above will help the relevant authority to be in a better position to assess its proportionality and coherence. The methodology will thus take particular account of the impact of commercial communications on the public interest objectives of the protection of consumers and public health.

This methodology is not an automatic test for assessing proportionality, which is left to the decision of the relevant authority. Nor is it a cost benefit or a mathematical analysis seeking to quantify the value of public interest objectives. It is only a means of ensuring that such evaluations are based on a complete overview of the effects of the measure concerned. In this respect, this methodology is not a substitute for the criteria developed by the ECJ, but rather assists in their application. Even if the application of this methodology is not rendered mandatory, as was explicitly requested by the European Parliament (EP), the Commission's services will, where appropriate, apply it when:

(a) considering infringement cases in the field of commercial communication services raising the issue of proportionality;

(b) providing analysis and discussing issues within the Commercial Communications Expert Group (see below).

The Commission plans that discussions on the regulatory problems for cross-border commercial communications brought to the attention of the Expert Group will be orientated on the basis of this methodology.

The Commission's services will, where appropriate, apply the assessment methodology when designing the Commission's own initiatives, which are directly linked to the provision of services in the area of commercial communications. It is hoped that the assessment methodology will facilitate the required application of the Treaty, achieve greater transparency and legal security and improve the protection of public interest objectives, thus increasing the speed and efficiency with which infringements are processed and improving the quality of any harmonisation initiatives proposed by the Commission in this field.

*Setting up a Commercial Communications Expert Group*

The Commission has recently established a Commercial Communications Expert Group with the aim of facilitating the exchange of views between the Commission and the Member States, and helping the Commission to identify solutions to problems in the field of cross-border commercial communication services. It will also provide data and facilitate information exchange on national measures in the field of cross-border commercial communication services in order to assist the Commission. It will provide information for the work of committees established by secondary Community law in the field of cross-border commercial communication services.

The Expert Group will be chaired by an official of the Commission. Its members will consist of two representatives appointed by each Member State. The Commission will invite groups, where they exist, made up of national representatives of interested parties (from all areas, including consumer associations) to present their positions on the issues being considered. The Expert Group will meet on a regular basis. The Commission will decide on its agenda, which will be made public via the information network where appropriate. The Expert Group should seek to reach an opinion on a specific point within six months. Its opinion, where appropriate, will be made public by the Commission's central contract point to interested parties, in particular, consumer associations, who will benefit from the Expert Group notably because they will have far easier access to information in this field and can submit written representations.

*Making available a contact point and information network*

The Commission will establish a central contact point in the Directorate General for the Internal Market and Financial Services, which will work closely with the other relevant Directorates General. Its role will be to respond to requests for information regarding the Commission's policy in this field. It will also collect information especially about problems regarding the efficient operation of the internal market in this domain. Formal complaints (Art 169 proceedings) will be sent to the Secretariat General of the Commission for registration. Complaints with respect to existing Directives will be passed to those services of the Commission responsible for their transposition and management.

The contact point will maintain communications between the Commission, the Parliament and the Member States. Other Commission services will be closely associated with, and be kept fully involved by, the central contact point, in order to ensure a better flow of information.

As a complement to the existing *Commercial Communications* newsletter, the Commission will establish a website. It will make available information on the Expert Group's work and give access to the database on European commercial communication regulations. The website will take a number of months to establish, so the Commission has already opened an e-mail address for queries or information from interested parties: comcom@dg15.cec.be.

The first meeting of the Expert Group took place on 27 May 1998 and at the second meeting, on 22 June 1998, considered regulations pertaining to discounts. Written submissions are invited to: The European Commission's Commercial Communications contact point, Directorate General XV C100 3/106, B-1049 Brussels, Belgium. Alternatively, responses can be faxed (+ 32 2 295 7712) or sent by e-mail to comcom@dg15.cec.be.

*Establishing a commercial communications database*

The Commission will establish a database on national and Community regulations and self-regulatory codes in this field. This initiative responds to the call for easier access to national and European regulations. The Commission believes that this database should de constructed on the basis of information exchanged between the Commission, national authorities and self-regulatory bodies. The database will be accessible via the commercial communications website. This would ensure that interested parties receive the most up to date regulatory information available from those competent for applying the relevant rules.

*Accelerating complaint resolution*

In line with its general policy, which seeks to improve its handling of infringements, the Commission will also seek to accelerate complaint resolution in this field. The Commission considers that the contact point, the information network and the proportionality assessment methodology should result in faster processing of complaints and thus greatly help the sector and its users, as well as the consumer, who are the receivers of such services.

## Setting up an expert network

The Commission will encourage the establishment of a network of independent experts interested in the various aspects of the commercial communications field in order to assist its work and that of the Expert Group. The network of academic experts will give views at the Commission's request. In order not to limit the number of experts, the Commission will use the new possibilities offered by the internet as a basis for organising the work and communication within this network.

## Clarifying issues of electronic commerce

The Commission is examining the specific legal issues relating to the use of cross-border commercial communication services in the information society and will propose possible clarification in the context of a proposal relating to electronic commerce and associated information society services.

Revenues generated from commercial communication services represent one of the major sources of funding for information society services. This form of funding needs to be promoted, in order to ensure that the distribution of high quality information will increase and remain accessible free of charge. There are already indications that cross-border commercial communication services on the internet are subject to legal insecurity and barriers. Other complex issues, such as those relating to intellectual property rights and branded domain names, also need to be addressed. Moreover, as regards new national proposals for regulations pertaining to on-line commercial communication services, the compatibility of these with the Treaty will be evaluated via the application of the currently proposed third amendment of Directive 83/189/EEC concerning regulatory transparency in the internal market for services in the information society. A Common Position was reached on this proposal in the Council on 26 January 1998:

> A proposal for a Directive to establish a coherent legal framework for the development of electronic commerce within the Single Market has been put forward by the European Commission. The proposed Directive would ensure that information security services benefit from the Single Market principles of free movement of services and freedom of establishment and could provide their services throughout the EU if they comply with the law in their country of origin. Such services are defined as those provided normally against remuneration, at a distance, by electronic means and in response to the individual request of a customer. The proposed Directive would establish specific harmonised rules only in those areas strictly necessary to ensure that businesses and citizens could supply and receive information society services

throughout the EU, irrespective of frontiers. These areas include definition of where operators are established, electronic contracts, commercial communications, liability of intermediaries, dispute settlement and role of national authorities. In other areas, the Directive would build on existing EU instruments which provide for harmonisation or on mutual recognition of national laws. The Directive would apply only to service providers established within the EU and not those established outside.

On 9 November 1998, the Internal Market Council adopted a European Parliament and Council Directive on the legal protection of services based on, or consisting of, conditional access (Directive 98/84 OJ L 320, 28.11.98, p 54). Adopted after just one year of negotiations, it will afford an equal level of protection to radio and television broadcasters and providers of information society services against piracy throughout the Union. The Directive will:

- require Member States to prohibit and provide appropriate sanctions against all commercial activities related to unauthorised access to a protected service, such as the sale of pirate decoders, smart cards or software;

- prohibit Member States from invoking 'anti-piracy' grounds to restrict the free movement of legitimate services and constitutional access devices originating in another Member State.

### Keeping the European Parliament informed

The Commission will inform the EP on the application of this approach, including an evaluation of the work carried out, and update the work programme. In its resolution, the EP explicitly asked to be kept informed by calling on the Commission to ensure that the Expert Group would work in a transparent manner and would have its results reported to the EP.

### Priority areas for the expert group's consideration

According to information and responses received during the consultation on the Green Paper (COM (96) 192 Final) (Commercial Communications in the Internal Market), and in order to ensure rapid and efficient results of its policy, the Commission will prioritise its work. During the two years following the adoption of this Communication, the Commission will call on the Expert Group to examine problems arising from cross-border commercial communications and the objectives, levels and means of protection of public interest objectives of differing national regulations pertaining to them in the following areas.

### (a) The protection of minors

In the field of television advertising, the Commission has already undertaken minimal harmonisation regarding advertising to minors (Directive 89/552 EEC, as amended by Directive 97/36/EC). However, further problems have been raised in the context of advertising regarding minors. The EP, in its resolution, has requested a more detailed assessment of the effects of commercial communications on children.

This issue has also been raised in a number of positions on the above-mentioned Green Paper. Consumer associations and public health bodies have called for harmonisation of regulations, and in some areas for strengthening of protection concerning commercial communications aimed at minors.

The key problem areas that will need to be addressed are:
- differing national regulations on sponsorship for educational programmes;
- differing national regulations on direct marketing targeted at minors;
- differing national regulations on television advertising aimed at minors (toys, snack foods, confectionery) in so far as these are not already covered by the TVWF Directive (89/552 EEC, as amended by Directive 97/36/EC) or by work of its contact committee;
- differing national regulations on the sponsorship of sports events by brands that are associated with products aimed at children, or that can have harmful effects on public health.

**(b) Laws of unfair competition and associated matters**

This issue was raised by the EP, which called for a framework of rules on dishonest marketing methods. Certain consumer associations also felt that harmonisation of laws preventing unfair marketing practices was necessary. This is a particularly important point, in view of the development of electronic commerce. Consumer associations also wished to ensure that fraudulent schemes and pyramid selling techniques are outlawed across the EC.

The following problem areas will be addressed:
- differing national regulations on discounts;
- differing national regulations on couponing;
- differing national regulations on free offers and gifts;
- differing national regulations on prize competitions, commercial lotteries and sweepstakes;
- differing national regulations on multilevel marketing and pyramid selling.

**(c) Sponsorship**

Whilst recognising that certain aspects of television sponsorship had already been subject to harmonisation by Directive 89/552 EEC, as amended by Directive 97/36/EC, the EP called for the different national regulations relating to sponsorship which are not harmonised by this Directive and patronage to be examined.

A number of interested parties noted the differences in definitions of sponsorship, or even their absence (whereby sponsorship is treated as identical to advertising), for regulatory purposes across the Member States. They complained of the legal uncertainty that arose as a consequence. Likewise, certain parties also noted that television sponsorship regulations vary significantly between countries.

The following problems will be addressed regarding differing national regulations:

- on sponsorship services related to particular products;
- on definition of sponsorship and patronage which restrict the development of cross-border services in this area;
- on television sponsorship in so far as they concern aspects which are not covered by Directive 89/552 EEC, as amended by Directive 97/36/EC or the work of its contact committee.

### (d) Claims and misleading advertising

The Green Paper (COM (96) 192 Final) noted that Directive 84/450 EEC has already harmonised misleading advertising and, more recently, comparative advertising. However, additional calls for action were made in this field as regards claims. Consumer associations and public health bodies wished to see stricter harmonised rules at the European level controlling the use of certain health and nutritional claims. Consumer organisations noted that differences remain in the interpretation of what is misleading advertising between the Member States. They pointed out that this leads to great difficulties in the processing of cross-border complaints.

Operators criticised differing national restrictions on requirements of packaging which went beyond the prescribed requirements of labelling legislation. These not only covered 'product information' (that is, claims) but also use of brand names (certain Member States have restrictions on brand diversification for brands associated with particular product categories), and the use of licensed graphics.

The following problems will be addressed:

- specific areas where differing national regulations are giving rise to divergent interpretations of 'misleading'. This is giving rise to evident legal uncertainty for cross-border commercial communication services and their recipients;
- differing national regulations on product or service 'claims' that have not been covered by legislation on labelling requirements;
- differing national regulations on brand diversification relating to particular products or services.

## (e) Systems of redress

The Commission has already proposed to improve access to justice with its Directive on injunctions for consumers' interests (Directive 98/26/EC). Whilst welcoming this action, consumer associations called for improvements in both judicial and extra-judicial cross-border redress systems against misleading and fraudulent commercial communication services. The purpose of this Directive is an infringement shall mean any act contrary to the Directives listed in the annex as transposed into the internal legal order of the EC Member States includes misleading advertising, television advertising of medicinal products.

The Expert Group will examine how existing redress and dispute settlement systems (including those operated by self-regulatory bodies) can be improved in a cross-border environment.

*Application of the proportionality assessment methodology at national level*

Some national authorities have indicated to the Commission their support for the application of the assessment methodology. The Commission would recommend its assessment methodology to be applied at national level by relevant national authorities. In this context, the members of the Expert Group will be invited to indicate how they apply the principle of proportionality, to what extent they are applying the Commission's methodology and, if not, whether they would be prepared to adopt this methodology.

# USEFUL ADDRESSES

Council of Europe
Point I F-67075
Strasbourg Cedex
France
Tel: + 33 388 41 2000
Website: http://www.coe.fr.index
E-mail: pointi@coe.fr

European Commission
Rue de la loi 200
B-1049 Brussels
Belgium
Tel: + 33 2299 11 11
E-mail: comcom@dg15.cec.be

*Advertisers*

IAA (International Advertising Association)
521 Fifth Avenue Suite 1807
New York NY 10175
Tel: + 1 212 557 lt 33
E-mail: isaglobal@worldnet.att.net
Website: www.iaaglobal.org

WFA (World Federation of Advertisers)
rue des Colonies 18-24 Bte 6
B-1000 Brussels
Tel: + 32 2 502 57 40
E-mail: info@wfa.be
Website: www.wfa.be

*Agencies*

EAAA (European Association of
Advertising Agencies)
rue Saint Quentin 3–5
B-1040 Brussels
Tel: + 32 2 280 16 03
E-mail: info@eaaa.be

*Media*

ACT (Association of Commercial
Television in Europe)
Square Ambiorix 7
B-1040 Brussels
Tel: + 32 2 736 00 52
E-mail: info@acto.be
Website: www.acto.be

EGTA (European Group of Television
Advertising)
rue Wiertz 30–50
B-1050 Brussels
Tel: + 32 2 286 9122
E-mail: michel.gregoire@skynet.be
Website: www.egta.com

ENPA (European Newspaper
Publishers' Association)
rue des Pierres 29 Bte 8
B-1000 Brussels
Tel: + 32 2 551 01 90
E-mail: michel.vanderstraeten@mail.
interpac.be
Website: www.enpa.com

EPC (European Publishers' Council)
49 Park Town
Oxford OX2 6SL
Tel: + 44 1865 310 732
Fax: + 44 1865 310 739
E-mail: angelamills.epc@btinternet.com
Website: www.epceurope.org

FAEP (Federation of Association of
Periodical Publishers in the EU)
Avenue de Tervuren 142–144
B-1150 Brussels
Tel: + 32 2 735 82 30
E-mail: julius.waller@eppa.com
Website: www.faep.org

*Direct marketing*

EMOTA (European Mail Order and
Distance Selling Trade Association)
Buro & Design Centre
Heizel Esplanade Bus 47
B-1020 Brussels
Tel: + 32 2 477 17 99
E-mail: adrian.weening@skynet.be

FEDMA (Federation of European
Direct Marketing)
Avenue de Tervaren 439
B-1150 Brussels
Tel: + 32 2 778 99 20
E-mail: info@fedma.org
Website: www.fedma.org

FEDSA (Federation of European
Direct Selling Association)
Avenue de Tervuren 14
B-1040 Brussels
Tel: + 32 20 736 10 14

*Sponsorship*

ESCA (European Sponsorship
Consultants Association)
Marash House
2–5 Brook Street
Tring
Herts HP23 5ED
Tel: + 44 1442 826 826
E-mail: eca@sponsorship.org

*Outdoor advertising*

FEPE (European Federation of
Outdoor Advertising)
c/o Gewista
Litfastrasse 6
A-61031 Vienna
Tel: + 43 1 795 97

*Self-regulation*

EASA (European Advertising
Standards Alliance)
10a Rue de la Pepiniere
B-1000 Brussels
Tel: + 32 2 513 78 06
E-mail: library@easa-alliance.org
Website: www.easa-alliance.org

ICC (International Chamber of
  Commerce)
38 Cours Albert 1er
F-75008 Paris
Tel: + 33 1 49 53 28 05
E-mail: viviane.schiavi@icewbo.org
Website: www.iccwbo.org

*Tripartites*

AA (Advertising Association )
Ablord House
15 Wilton Road
London SW1 1NJ
Tel: + 44 171 828 2771

AIG (Advertising Information
  Group)
c/o AA *see below*
E-mail: aig@adassoc.org.uk

Conseil de la Publicite
Rue des Colonies 18–24 bte 9
B-1000 Brussels
Tel: + 32 2 502 70 70

EAT (European Advertising
  Tripartite)
Avenue de Tervuren 267
B-1150 Brussels
Tel: + 32 2 779 21 30
E-mail: eat.sec.gen@infonie.be

Stichting Stuurgroep Reclame (NL)
Malietoren/Gebouw VNO-NCW
Beznidenhoutseweg 12
Den Haag
Post Bus 93002
2509 AA Den Haag
Tel: + 31 70 349 0145
E-mail: ssr@worldonline.nl

ZAW (Zentralverband des Deutschen
  Werbewirtschaft eV)
Vilichgasse 17
Postfach 201414
D-53177 Bonn
Tel: + 49 228 820 920
E-mail: zaw@zaw.de

*Others*

TAG (The Amsterdam Group)
The Hop Exchange
24 Southwark Street
London SE1 1TY
Tel: + 44 171 403 4225
E-mail : richard.owen@virgin.net

*Websites*

**General**

Access to Europe Direct: http://europa.eu.int/citizens. This site offers advice
  on individual rights in the internal market.

Agencies and other bodies: http://europa.eu.int/en/agencies.html

CELEX website: http://europa.eu.int/celex. This is a comprehensive site of
  information on EC law; present cost: 960 ECU per annum.

Committee of the Regions: http://www.cor.eu.int/

Court of Auditors: http://www.eca.eu.int/

Court of Justice: http://curia.eu.int/en/index.htm

Council of the EU: http://ue.eu.int/en/summ.htm

Economic and Social Committee: http://www.ces.eu.int/en/default.htm

Eur-Lex website: http://europa.eu.int/eur-lex. This website contains EC legislation in force. It will eventually provide complete contents of the Official Journal (C and L series).

European Commission: http://europa.eu.int/comm/index_en.htm

European Parliament: http://www.europarl.eu.int/sg/tree/en/default.htm

European Union website: http://www.europa.eu.int.index-en.htm. This site is that of the Europa server, which provides news, information on institutions, policies, etc, with many useful links to other sites.

Press releases: http://europa.eu.int/news-en.htm

What's new: http://europa.eu.int/geninfo/whatsnew.htm

**Directorate Generals of the Commission**

General address: http://europa.eu.int/comm/dgs–en.htm

DGX: Information, Communication, Culture, Audiovisual: http://europa.eu.int/en/comm/dg10/dg10.html

DGXV: information on the internal market and financial services: http://europa.eu.int/comm/ dg15/en/index.htm

DGXXIV: Consumer Policy and Consumer Health Protection: http://europa.eu.int/comm/dg24

European Parliament Legislative Observatory: http://www.europarl.eu.int/r/ors/oeil/en/default.htm

Inspectorate General: http://europa.eu.int/en/comm/igs

Legal Service: http://europa..eu.int/en/comm/sj/homesjen.htm

Office for Official Publications of the EC: http://eur-op.eu.int/

Secretariat General: http://europa.eu.int/comm/sg/index.htm

# EXTRACTS FROM THE TREATY OF AMSTERDAM (RIGHT OF ESTABLISHMENT, SERVICES)*

*OJ C 340, 10.11.97, p 195*

### Chapter 2 Right of establishment

Article 43 (ex Article 52)

Within the framework of the provisions set out below, restrictions on the freedom of establishment of nationals of a Member State in the territory of another Member State shall be prohibited. Such prohibition shall also apply to restrictions on the setting-up of agencies, branches or subsidiaries by nationals of any Member State established in the territory of any Member State.

Freedom of establishment shall include the right to take up and pursue activities as self-employed persons and to set op and manage undertakings, in particular companies or firms within the meaning of the second paragraph of Article 48, under the conditions laid down for its own nationals by the law of the country where such establishment is effected, subject to the provisions of the Chapter relating to capital.

Article 44 (ex Article 54)

1   In order to attain freedom of establishment as regards a particular activity, the Council, acting in accordance with the procedure referred to in Article 251 and after consulting the Economic and Social Committee, shall act by means of directives.

2   The Council and the Commission shall carry out the duties devolving upon them under the preceding provisions, in particular:

(a) by according, as a general rule, priority treatment to activities where freedom of establishment makes a particularly valuable contribution to the development of production and trade;

(b) by ensuring close co-operation between the competent authorities in the Member States in order to ascertain the particular situation within the Community of the various activities concerned;

(c) by abolishing those administrative procedures and practices, whether resulting from national legislation or from agreements previously concluded between Member States, the maintenance of which would form an obstacle to freedom of establishment;

(d) by ensuring that workers of one Member State employed in the territory of another Member State may remain in that territory for the purpose of taking up activities therein as self-employed persons, where they satisfy the conditions which they would be required to satisfy if they were entering that State at the time when they intended to take up such activities;

---

\*   **NOTE: came into effect May 1999.**

(e) by enabling a national of one Member State, insofar as this does not conflict with the principles laid down in Article 33(2);

(f) by effecting the progressive abolition of restrictions on freedom of establishment in every branch of activity under consideration, both as regards the conditions for setting up agencies, branches or subsidiaries in the territory of a Member State and as regards the subsidiaries in the territory of a Member State and as regards the conditions governing the entry of personnel belonging to the main establishment into managerial or supervisory posts in such agencies, branches or subsidiaries;

(g) by co-ordinating to the necessary extent the safeguards which, for the protection of the interests of members and other [sic], are required by Member States of companies or firms within the meaning of the second paragraph of Article 48 with a view to making such safeguards equivalent throughout the Community;

(h) by satisfying themselves that the conditions of establishment are not distorted by aids granted by Member States.

Article 45 (ex Article 55)

The provisions of this chapter shall not apply, so far as any given Member State is concerned, to activities which in that State are connected, even occasionally, with the exercise of official authority.

The Council may, acting by a qualified majority on a proposal from the Commission, rule that the provisions of this Chapter shall not apply to certain activities.

Article 46 (ex Article 56)

1  The provisions of this Chapter and measures taken in pursuance thereof shall not prejudice the applicability of provisions laid down by law, regulation or administrative action providing for special treatment for foreign nationals on grounds of public policy, public security or public health.

2  The Council shall, acting in accordance with the procedure referred to in Article 251, issue directives for the co-ordination of the above-mentioned provisions.

Article 47 (ex Article 57)

1  In order to make it easier for persons to take up and pursue activities as self-employed persons, the Council shall, acting in accordance with the procedure referred to in Article 251, issue directives for the mutual recognition of diplomas, certificates and other evidence of formal qualifications.

2  For the same purpose, the Council shall, acting in accordance with the procedure referred to in Article 251, issue directives for the co-ordination of the provisions laid down by law, regulation, or administrative action in Member States concerning the taking-up and pursuit of activities as self-

employed persons. The Council, acting unanimously throughout the procedure referred to in Article 251, shall decide on directives the implementation of which involves in at least one Member State amendment of the existing principles laid down by law governing the professions with respect to training and conditions of access for natural persons.

3   In the case of the medical and allied and pharmaceutical professions, the progressive abolition of restrictions shall be dependent upon the co-ordination of the conditions for their exercise in the various Member States.

Companies or firms formed in accordance with the law of a Member State and having their registered office, central administration or principal place of business within the Community shall, for the purposes of this Chapter, be treated in the same way as natural persons who are nationals of Member States.

'Companies or firms' means companies or firms constituted under civil or commercial law, including co-operative societies, and other legal persons governed by public or private law, save for those which are non-profit-making.

**Chapter 3 Services**

Article 49 (ex Article 59)

Within the framework of the provisions set out below, restrictions on freedom to provide services within the Community shall be prohibited in respect of nationals of Member States who are established in a State of the Community other than that of the person for whom the services are intended.

The Council may, acting by a qualified majority on a proposal from the Commission, extend the provisions of the Chapter to nationals of a third country who provide services and who are established within the Community.

Article 50 (ex Article 60)

Services shall be considered to be 'services' within the meaning of this Treaty where they are normally provided for remuneration, insofar as they are not governed by the provisions relating to freedom of movement for goods, capital and persons.

'Services' shall in particular include:

(a)  activities of an industrial character;

(b)  activities of a commercial character;

(c)  activities of craftsmen;

(d)  activities of the professions.

Without prejudice to the provisions of the Chapter relating to the right of establishment, the person providing a service may, in order to do so, temporarily pursue his activity in the State where the service is provided, under the same conditions as are imposed by that State on its own nationals.

### Article 51 (ex Article 61)

1   Freedom to provide services in the field of transport shall be governed by the provisions of the Title relating to transport.

2   The liberalisation of banking and insurance services connected with movements of capital shall be effected in step with the liberalisation of movement of capital.

### Article 52 (ex Article 63)

1   In order to achieve the liberalisation of a specific service, the Council shall, on a proposal from the Commission and after consulting the Economic and Social Committee and the European Parliament, issue directives acting by a qualified majority.

2   As regards the directives referred to in paragraph 1, priority shall as a general rule be given to those services which directly affect production costs or the liberalisation of which helps to promote trade in goods.

### Article 53 (ex Article 64)

The Member States declare their readiness to undertake the liberalisation of services beyond the extent required by the directives issued pursuant to Article 52(1), if their general economic situation and the situation of the economic sector concerned so permit.

To this end, the Commission shall make recommendations to the Member States concerned.

### Article 54 (ex Article 65)

As long as restrictions on freedom to provide services have not been abolished, each Member State shall apply such restrictions without distinction on grounds of nationality or residence to all persons providing services within the meaning of the first paragraph of Article 49.

### Article 55 (ex Article 66)

The provisions of Articles 45 to 48 shall apply to the matters covered by this Chapter.

# DIRECTIVE 79/112/EEC AND DIRECTIVE 97/4/EC (AMENDING 79/112/EEC) (LABELLING, PRESENTATION, ADVERTISING OF FOODSTUFFS)

*OJ L 33 of 8.2.79*

*Council Directive of 18 December 1978*

on the approximation of the laws of the Member States relating to the labelling, presentation and advertising of foodstuffs for sale to the ultimate consumer

(79/112/EEC)

The Council of the European Communities,

Having regard to the Treaty establishing the European Economic Community, and in particular Articles 100 and 237 thereof,

Having regard to the proposal from the Commission,

Having regard to the opinion of the European Parliament,

Having regard to the opinion of the Economic and Social Committee,

Whereas differences which exist at present between the laws, regulations and administrative provisions of Member States on the labelling of foodstuffs impede the free circulation of these products and can lead to unequal conditions of competition;

Whereas, therefore, approximation of these laws would contribute to the smooth functioning of the common market;

Whereas the purpose of this Directive should be to enact Community rules of a general nature applicable horizontally to all foodstuffs put on the market;

Whereas rules of a specific nature which apply vertically only to particular foodstuffs should be laid down in provisions dealing with those products;

Whereas, moreover, the field of applications of this Directive should be limited to foodstuffs intended for sale to the ultimate consumer, and the rules governing the labelling of products intended for subsequent processing or preparation should be fixed at a later stage;

Whereas the prime consideration for any rules on the labelling of foodstuffs should be the need to inform and protect the consumer;

Whereas, therefore, a list should be drawn up of all information which should be drawn up of all information which should in principle be included in the labelling of all foodstuffs;

Whereas, however, the horizontal nature of this Directive does not allow, at the initial stage, the inclusion in the compulsory indications of all the indications which must be added to the list applying in principle to the whole range of foodstuffs; whereas, during the second stage, Community provisions should be adopted, aimed at supplementing the existing rules, whereas it would accordingly seem necessary to adopt as a matter of priority. Community provisions regarding the indication of certain ingredients in the sales description or by indicating a quantity;

Whereas, furthermore, if in the absence of Community rules of a specific nature, Member States should retain the right to lay down certain national provisions which may be added to the general provisions of this Directive, nevertheless these provisions should be subject to a Community procedure;

Whereas the said Community procedure may consist simply in informing the Commission and the Member States when the matter concerns the maintenance of national provisions that precede this Directive, but must be that of a Community Decision when a Member State wishes to enact new legislation;

Whereas provisions should also be made for the Community legislator to derogate, in exceptional cases, from certain obligations that have been fixed generally;

Whereas the rules on labelling should also prohibit the use of information that would mislead the purchaser or attribute medicinal properties to foodstuffs; whereas, to be effective, the prohibition should also apply to the presentation and advertising of foodstuffs;

Whereas Member States should retain the right, depending on local conditions and circumstances, to lay down rules in respect of the labelling of foodstuffs sold in bulk; whereas, in such cases, information should nevertheless be provided for the consumer;

Whereas, with the aim of simplifying and accelerating the procedure, the Commission should be entrusted with the task of adopting implementing measures of a technical nature.

Whereas in all cases where the Council makes the Commission responsible for implementing rules laid down in respect of foodstuffs, provision should be made for a procedure instituting close cooperation between Member States and the Commission within the Standing Committee on Foodstuffs, set up by Decision 69/414/EEC;

Whereas foodstuffs in Greenland are manufactured and marketed under conditions fundamentally different from those prevailing in the other parts of the Community because of the island's general situation and, in particular, because of its commercial structures, low population, considerable area and special geographical situation,

HAS ADOPTED THIS DIRECTIVE:

*Article 1*

1  This Directive concerns the labelling of foodstuffs to be delivered as such to the ultimate consumer and certain aspects relating to the presentation and advertising thereof.

2  Without prejudice to the Community provisions to be adopted in this field, this Directive shall apply also to foodstuffs intended for supply to restaurants, hospitals, canteens and other similar mass caterers in so far as the Member States shall so decide.

3  For the purpose of this Directive:
   (a) 'labelling' shall mean any words, particulars, trade marks, brand name, pictorial matter or symbol relating to a foodstuff and placed on any packaging, document, notice, label, ring or collar accompanying or referring to such foodstuff;

(b) 'pre-packaged foodstuff' shall mean any single item for presentation as such to the ultimate consumer, consisting of a foodstuff and the packaging into which it was put before being offered for sale, whether such packaging encloses the foodstuff completely or only partially, but in any case in such a way that the contents cannot be altered without opening or changing the packaging.

### Article 2

1 The labelling and methods used must not:

(a) be such as could mislead the purchaser to a material degree, particularly:

(i) as to the characteristics of the foodstuff and, in particular, as to its nature, identity, properties, composition, quantity, durability, origin, or provenance, method of manufacture or production;

(ii) by attributing to the foodstuff effects or properties which it does not possess;

(iii) for suggesting that the foodstuff possesses special characteristics when in fact all similar foodstuffs possess such characteristics;

(b) subject to the provisions applicable to foodstuffs for particular nutritional uses, attribute to any foodstuff the property of preventing, treating or curing a human disease, or refer to such properties, Community provisions or, where there are none, national provisions may derogate from this rule in the case of natural mineral waters.

The procedure laid down in Article 16, shall apply to any such national provisions.

2 The Council, in accordance with the procedure laid down in Article 100 of the Treaty, shall draw up a non-exhaustive list of the claims within the meaning of paragraph 1, the use of which must at all events be prohibited or restricted.

3 The prohibitions or restrictions referred to in paragraphs 1 and 2 shall also apply to:

(a) the presentation of foodstuffs, in particular their shape, appearance or packaging, the packaging materials used, the way in which they are arranged and the setting in which they are displayed;

(b) advertising.

### Article 3

1 In accordance with Articles 4 to 14 and subject to the exceptions contained therein, indication of the following particulars alone shall be compulsory on the labelling of foodstuffs:

(1) the name under which the product is sold;

(2) the list of ingredients;

(3) in the case of prepackaged foodstuffs, the net quantity;

(4) the date of minimum durability;

(5) any special storage conditions or conditions of use;

    (6)  the name or business name and address of manufacturer or packager, or of a seller established within the Community.

        However, the Member States shall be authorised, in respect of butter produced in their territory, to require only an indication of the manufacturer, packager or seller.

        Without prejudice to the notification provided for in Article 22, Member States shall inform the Commission and the other Member States of any measure taken pursuant to this paragraph;

    (7)  particulars of the place of origin or provenance in the cases where failure to give such particulars might mislead the consumer to a material degree as to the true origin or provenance of the foodstuff;

    (8)  instructions for use when it would be impossible to make appropriate use of the foodstuff in the absence of such instructions.

2    Notwithstanding the previous paragraph, Member States may retain national provisions which require indication of the factory or packaging centre, in respect of home production.

3    The provisions of this Article shall be without prejudice to more precise or more extensive provisions regarding weights and measures.

## Article 4

1    Community provisions applicable to specified foodstuffs and not to foodstuffs in general may provide for derogations, in exceptional cases, from the requirements laid down in Article 3(1), points 2 and 4, provided that this does not result in the purchaser being inadequately informed.

2    Community provisions applicable to specified foodstuffs and not to foodstuffs in general may provide that other particulars in addition to those listed in Article 3 must appear on the labelling.

    Where there are no Community provisions, Member States may make provision for such particulars in accordance with the procedure laid down in Article 16.

## Article 5

1    The name under which a foodstuff is sold shall be the name laid down by whatever laws, regulations or administrative provisions apply to the foodstuff in question or, in the absence of any such name, the name customary in the Member State where the product is sold to the ultimate consumer, or a description of the foodstuff and, if necessary, of its use, that is sufficiently precise to inform the purchaser of its true nature and to enable it to be distinguished from products with which it could be confused.

2    No trade mark, brand name or fancy name may be substituted for the name under which the product is sold.

3    The name under which the product is sold shall include or be accompanied by particulars as to the physical condition of the foodstuff or the specific treatment which it has undergone (eg, powdered, freeze-dried, deep-frozen, concentrated, smoked) in all cases where omission of such information could create confusion in the mind of the purchaser.

*Article 6*

1  Ingredients shall be listed in accordance with this Article and the Annexes.

2  Ingredients need not be listed in the case of:
   (a) –  fresh fruit and vegetables, including potatoes, which have not been peeled, cut or similarly treated;
       –  carbonated water, the description of which indicates that it has been carbonated;
       –  fermentation vinegars derived exclusively from a single basic product, provided that no other ingredient has been added;
   (b) –  cheese;
       –  butter;
       –  fermented milk and cream,

   provided that no ingredient has been added other than lactic products, enzymes and micro-organism cultures essential to manufacture, or the salt needed for the manufacture of cheese other than fresh cheese and processed cheese.
   (c) products consisting of a single ingredient.

3  In the case of beverages containing more than 1.2% by volume of alcohol, the Council acting on a proposal from the Commission, shall, before the expiry of a period of four years following notification of this Directive, determine the rules for labelling ingredients and, possibly, indicating the alcoholic strength.

4  (a) 'Ingredient' shall mean any substance, including additives, used in the manufacture or preparation of a foodstuff and still present in the finished product, even if in altered form.
   (b) Where an ingredient of the foodstuff is itself the product of several ingredients, the latter shall be regarded as ingredients of the foodstuff in question.
   (c) The following shall not be regarded as ingredients:
       (i)  the constituents of an ingredient which have been temporarily separated during the manufacturing process and later re-introduced but not in excess of their original proportions;
       (ii) –  additives:
            –  whose presence in a given foodstuff is solely due to the fact that they were contained in one or more ingredients of that foodstuff, provided that they serve no technological function in the finished product,
            –  which are used as processing aids;
       –  substances used in the quantities strictly necessary as solvents or media for additives or flavouring.
   (d) In certain cases Decisions may be taken in accordance with the procedure laid down in Article 17 as to whether the conditions described in (c) (ii) are satisfied.

5  (a) The list of ingredients shall include all the ingredients of the foodstuff, in descending order of weight, as recorded at the time of their use in the

manufacture of the foodstuff. It shall appear preceded by a suitable heading which includes the word 'ingredients'.

However:

- added water and volatile products shall be listed in order of their weight in the finished product; the amount of water added as an ingredient in a foodstuff shall be calculated by deducting from the total amount of the other ingredients used. This amount need not be taken into consideration if it does not exceed 5% by weight of the finished product;

- ingredients used in concentrated or dehydrated form and reconstituted at the time of manufacture may be listed in order of weight as recorded before their concentration or dehydration;

- in the case of concentrated or dehydrated foods which are intended to be reconstituted by the addition of water, the ingredients may be listed in order of proportion in the reconstituted product provided that the list of ingredients is accompanied by an expression such as 'ingredients of the reconstituted product', or 'ingredients of the ready-to-use product';

- in the case of mixtures of fruit or vegetables where no particular fruit or vegetable significantly predominates in proportion by weight, those ingredients may be listed in another order provided that that list of ingredients is accompanied by an expression such as 'in variable proportion';

- in the case of mixtures of spices or herbs, where none significantly predominates in proportion by weight, those ingredients may be listed in another order provided that that list of ingredients is accompanied by an expression such as 'in variable proportion';

(b) ingredients shall be designated by their specific name, where applicable, in accordance with the rules laid down in Article 5.

However:

- ingredients which belong to one of the categories listed in Annex 1 and are constituents of another foodstuff need only be designated by the name of that category;

- ingredients belonging to one of the categories listed in Annex II must be designated by the name of that category, followed by their specific name or EEC number; if an ingredient belongs to more than one of the categories, the category appropriate to the principal function in the case of the foodstuff in question shall be indicated, amendments to this Annex based on advances in scientific and technical knowledge shall be adopted in accordance with the procedure laid down in Article 17;

- flavouring matter shall be described in accordance with the national provisions applicable thereto, until the entry into force of the Community provisions;

- the Community provisions or, where there are none, the national provisions applicable to certain specified foodstuffs, may also provide for categories additional to those specified in Annex 1. Without prejudice to the notification provided for in Article 22, Member States shall inform the

Commission and the other Member States of any measure taken pursuant to this indent.

6 Community provisions or, where there are none, national provisions may lay down that the name under which a specific foodstuff is sold is to be accompanied by mention of a particular ingredient or ingredients.

The procedure laid down in Article 16 shall apply to any such national provisions.

7 In the case referred to in paragraph 4(b), a compound ingredient may be included in the list of ingredients, under its own designation in so far as this is laid down by law or established by custom, in terms of its overall weight, provided that it is immediately followed by a list of its ingredients.

Such a list, however, shall not be compulsory:

- where the compound ingredient constitutes less than 25% of the finished product; however, this exemption shall not apply in the case of additives, subject to the provisions of paragraph 4(c);

- where the compound ingredient is a foodstuff for which a list of ingredients is not required under Community rules.

8 Notwithstanding paragraph 5(a), the water content need not be specified:

(a) where the water is used during the manufacturing process solely for the reconstitution of an ingredient used in concentrated or dehydrated form;

(b) in the case of a liquid medium which is not normally consumed.

*Article 7*

1 Where the labelling of a foodstuff places emphasis on the presence or low content of one or more ingredients which are essential to the specific properties of the foodstuff, or where the description of the foodstuff has the same effect, the minimum or maximum percentage, as the case may be, used in the manufacture thereof shall be stated.

This information shall appear either immediately next to the name under which the foodstuff is sold or in the list of ingredients in connection with the ingredient in question.

In accordance with the procedure laid down in Article 17, it may be decided that, in the case of certain ingredients, the percentage referred to in this paragraph shall be expressed in absolute terms.

2 Paragraph 1 shall not apply:

(a) in the case of labelling which is intended to categorise a foodstuff in accordance with Article 5(1) or which is required under Community provisions or, where there are none, under national provisions applicable to certain foodstuffs;

(b) in the case of ingredients used in small quantities only as flavourings.

3 Community provisions or, where there are none, national provisions may stipulate for certain foodstuffs, as well as in the case referred to in paragraph 2(a), that quantities of certain ingredients must be indicated either in absolute terms or as percentages and that, where appropriate, mention should be made of any alteration in the quantities of these ingredients.

The procedure laid down in Article 16 shall apply to any such national provisions.

*Article 8*

1    The net quantity of prepackaged foodstuffs shall be expressed:

–    in units of volume in the case of liquids;

–    in units of mass in the case of other products,

using the litre, centilitre, millilitre, kilogram or gram, as appropriate.

Community provisions as, where there are none, national provisions applicable to certain specified foodstuffs may derogate from this rule.

The procedure laid down in Article 16 shall apply to any such national provisions.

3    (a)  Where the indication of a certain type of quantity (eg, nominal quantity, minimum quantity, average quantity) is required by Community provisions or, where there are none, by national provisions, this quantity shall be regarded as the net quantity for the purposes of this Directive.

Without prejudice to the notification provided for in Article 22, Member States shall inform the Commission and the other Member States of any measure taken pursuant to this point.

(b)  Community provisions or, where there are none, national provisions may, for certain specified foodstuffs classified by quantity in categories, require other indications of quantity.

The procedure laid down in Article 16 shall apply to any such national provisions.

(c)  Where a prepackaged item consists of two or more individual prepackaged items containing the same quantity of the same product, the net quantity shall be indicated by mentioning the net quantity contained in each individual package and the total number of such packages. Indication of these particulars shall not, however, be compulsory where the total number of individual packages can be clearly seen and easily counted from the outside and where at least one indication of the net quantity contained in each individual package can be clearly seem from the outside.

(d)  Where a prepackaged item consists of two or more individual packages which are not regarded as units of sale,the net quantity shall be given by indicating the total net quantity shall be given by indicating the total net quantity and the total number of individual packages. Community provisions or, where there are none, national provisions need not, in the case of certain foodstuffs, require indication of the total number of individual packages.

Without prejudice to the notification provided for in Article 22, Member States shall inform the Commission, and the other Member States of any measure taken pursuant to this point.

3    In the case of foodstuffs normally sold by number, Member States need not require indication of the net quantity provided that the number of items can clearly be seen and easily counted from the outside or, if not, is indicated on the labelling.

Without prejudice to the notification provided for in Article 22, Member States shall inform the Commission and the other Member States of any measure taken pursuant to this paragraph.

4    Where a solid foodstuff is presented in a liquid medium, the drained net weight of the foodstuff shall also be indicated on the labelling.

For the purposes of this paragraph, 'liquid medium' shall mean the following products, possibly in mixtures, provided that the liquid is merely an adjunct to the essential elements of that preparation and is thus not a decisive factor for the purchase: water, salt water, brine, vinegar, aqueous solutions of sugars, and fruit or vegetable juices in the case of tinned fruit or vegetables.

Methods of checking the drained net weight shall be determined in accordance with the procedures laid down in Article 17.

5  It shall not be compulsory to indicate the net quantity in the case of foodstuffs:

    (a) which are subject to considerable losses in their volume or mass and which are sold by number or weighed in the presence of the purchaser;

    (b) the net quantity of which is less than 5g or 5ml; however,this provision shall not apply to spices and herbs.

Community provisions or, where there are none, national provisions applicable to specified foodstuffs may in exceptional cases lay down thresholds which are higher than 5g or 5ml provided that this does not result in the purchaser being inadequately informed.

Without prejudice to the notification provided for in Article 22, Member States shall inform the Commission and the other Member States of any measure taken pursuant to this paragraph.

6  Until the end of the transitional period during which the use of the imperial units of measurement contained in Chapter D of the Annex to Directive 71/354/EEC of 18 October 1971 on the approximation of the laws of the Member States relating to units of measurement, as last amended by Directive 76/770/EEC, is authorised in the Community, Ireland and the United Kingdom may permit the quantity to be expressed only in imperial units of measurement calculated on the basis of the following conversion rates:

    – 1ml = 0.0352 fluid ounces;

    – 1l = 1.760 pints or 0.220 gallons;

    – 1g = 0.0353 ounces (avoirdupois);

    – 1kg = 2.205 pounds.

## Article 9

1  The date of minimum durability of a foodstuff shall be the date until which the foodstuff retains its specific properties when properly stored.

It shall be indicated in accordance with the provisions of this Article.

2  The date shall be preceded by the words:

    – 'Best before ...' when the date includes an indication of the day;

    – 'Best before end ...' in other cases.

However, in the case of certain foodstuffs which, from the microbiological point of view, are highly perishable, Member States may require the words 'use before ...' to be indicated. Without prejudice to the notification provided for in Article 22, Member States shall inform the Commission and the other Member States any measure taken pursuant to this subparagraph.

Before the expiry of a period of six years from the date of notification of this Directive, the Council, acting on a proposal from the Commission, shall decide on the common date-indication arrangements for highly perishable foodstuffs of the sort referred to in the second subparagraph.

3   The words referred to in paragraph 2 shall be accompanied by:

- either the date itself, or
- a reference to where the date is given on the labelling.

If need be, these particulars shall be followed by a description of the storage conditions which must be observed if the product is to keep for the specified period.

4   The date shall consist of the day, month and year in uncoded chronological form.

However, in the case of foodstuffs:

- which will not keep for more than three months, an indication of the day and the month will suffice;
- which will keep for more than three months but not more than 18 months, an indication of the month and year will suffice;
- which will keep for more than 18 months, an indication of the year will suffice.

The manner of indicating the date may be specified according to the procedure laid down in Article 17.

5   In their own territories the Member States may permit the minimum durability period to be expressed otherwise than in terms of the date of minimum durability.

Without prejudice to the notification provided for in Article 22, Member States shall notify the Commission and the other Member States of any measure taken under this paragraph.

6   Subject to the Community provisions governing the products below, an indication of the date of minimum durability shall not be required for:

- fresh fruit and vegetables, including potatoes, which have not been peeled, cut or similarly treated;
- wines, liquor wines, sparkling wines, aromatised wines, fruit wines and sparkling fruit wines;
- beverages containing 10% or more by volume of alcohol;
- bakers' or pastry-cooks' wares which, given the nature of their content, are normally consumed within 24 hours of their manufacture;
- vinegar;
- cooking salt;
- solid sugar;
- confectionery products consisting of flavoured and/or coloured sugars.

*Article 10*

1   The instructions for use of a foodstuff shall be indicated in such a way as to enable appropriate use to be made thereof.

2 Community provisions or, where there are none, national provisions may, in the case of certain foodstuffs, specify the way in which the instructions for use should be indicated.

The procedure laid down in Article 16 shall apply to such national provisions.

*Article 11*

1 (a) When the foodstuffs are prepackaged, the particulars provided for in Article 3 and Article 4(2) shall appear on the prepackaging or on a label attached thereon.

(b) Notwithstanding point (a) and without prejudice to Community provisions on nominal amounts, Member States may authorise that all or some of the particulars provided for in Article 3 and Article 4(2) be given only on the relevant trade documents when the foodstuffs are prepackaged and marketed prior to their sale to the ultimate consumer.

Without prejudice to the notification provided for in Article 22, Member States shall inform the Commission and the other Member States of any measure taken pursuant to this point.

The Council, acting on a proposal from the Commission, shall lay down the provisions to apply subsequently in this connection not later than nine years after notification of this Directive.

2 These particulars shall be easy to understand and marked in a conspicuous place in such a way as to be easily visible, clearly legible and indelible.

They shall not in any way be hidden, obscured or interrupted by other written or pictorial matter.

3 (a) The particulars listed in Article 3(1), points 1, 3 and 4, shall appear in the same field of vision.

This requirement may be extended to the particulars provided for in Article 4(2).

(b) However, for glass bottles intended for re-use, upon which one of the particulars listed in point (a) is indelibly marked, this requirement shall not apply for a period of 10 years following notification of this Directive.

4 Member States may:

(a) permit that only the particulars listed in Article 3(1), points 1, 3 and 4, be indicated on packaging or containers, the largest surface of which has no area of less than $10cm^2$;

(b) require the indication of only some of the particulars listed in Article 3 in respect of milk or milk products in bottles intended for re-use; in this case they may also provide for derogations from paragraph 3(a).

Without ratification to the notification provided for in Article 22, Member States shall inform the Commission and the other Member States of any measure taken pursuant to this paragraph.

*Article 12*

Where foodstuffs are offered for sale to the ultimate consumer without prepackaging, or where foodstuffs are packaged on the sales premises at the consumer's request or prepackaged for direct sale, the Member States shall adopt detailed rules concerning the manner in which the particulars specified in Article 3 and Article 4(2) are to be shown.

They may decide not to require the provision of all or some of these particulars, provided that the consumer still receives sufficient information.

*Article 13*

This Directive shall not affect the provisions of national laws which, in the absence of Community provisions, impose less stringent requirements for the labelling of foodstuffs presented in fancy packaging such as figurines or souvenirs.

*Article 14*

Member States shall refrain from laying down requirements more detailed than those already contained in Articles 3 to 11 concerning the manner in which the particulars provided for in Article 3 and Article 4(2) are to be shown.

The Member States shall, however, ensure that the sale of foodstuffs within their own territories is prohibited if the particulars provided in Article 3 and Article 4(2) do not appear in a language easily understood by purchasers, unless other measures have been taken to ensure that the purchaser is informed. This provision shall not prevent such particulars from being indicated in various languages.

*Article 15*

1   Member States may not forbid trade in foodstuffs which comply with the rules laid down in this Directive by the application of non-harmonised national provisions governing the labelling and presentation of certain foodstuffs or of foodstuffs in general.

2   Paragraph 1 shall not apply to non-harmonised national provisions justified on grounds of:

   –   protection of public health;

   –   prevention of fraud, unless such provisions are liable to impede the application of the definitions and rules laid down by this Directive;

   –   protection of industrial and commercial property rights, indications of provenance, registered designations of origin and prevention of unfair competition.

### Article 16

Where reference is made to this Article, the following procedure shall apply:

(1) When a Member State maintains the provision of its national laws, it shall inform the Commission and the other Member States thereof within a period of two years after the notification of this Directive.

(2) Should a Member State deem it necessary to adopt new legislation, it shall notify the Commission and the other Member States of the measures envisaged and give the reasons justifying them. The Commission shall consult the Member States within the Standing Committee on Foodstuffs if it considers such consultation to be useful or if a Member State so requests.

Member States may take such envisaged measures only three months after such notification and provided that the Commission's opinion is not negative.

In the latter event, and before the expiry of the above-mentioned period, the Commission shall initiate the procedure provided for in Article 17 in order to determine whether the envisaged measures may be implemented subject, if necessary, to the appropriate modification.

### Article 17

1 Where the procedure laid down in this Article is invoked, the matter shall be referred to the Standing Committee on Foodstuffs (hereinafter called 'the Committee') by its chairman, either on his own initiative or at the request of a representative of a Member State.

2 The representative of the Commission shall submit to the Committee a draft of the measures to be taken. The Committee shall give its opinion on that draft within a time limit set by the chairman having regard to the urgency of the matter. Opinions shall be delivered by a majority of 41 votes,the votes of the Member States being weighted as provided for in Article 148(2) of the Treaty. The Chairman shall not vote.

3 (a) Where the measures envisaged are in accordance with the opinion of the Committee, the Commission shall adopt them;

(b) Where the measures envisaged are not in accordance with the opinion of the Committee, or if no opinion is delivered, the Commission shall without delay submit to the Council a proposal on the measures to be taken. The Council shall act by a qualified majority;

(c) If the Council has not acted within three months of the proposal being submitted to it, the proposed measures shall be adopted by the Commission.

### Article 18

Article 17 shall apply for 18 months from the date on which the matter was was first referred to the Committee pursuant to Article 17.

*Article 19*

If temporary measures prove necessary to facilitate the application of this Directive, they shall be adopted in accordance with the procedure provided for in Article 17.

*Article 20*

This Directive shall not affect Community provisions relating to the labelling and presentation of certain foodstuffs already adopted at the time of its notification.

Any amendments necessary to harmonise such provisions with the rules laid down in this Directive shall be decided in accordance with the procedure applicable to each of the provisions in question.

*Article 21*

The Directive shall not apply to products for export outside the Community.

*Article 22*

1   Member States shall make such amendments to their laws as may be necessary to comply with the provisions of this Directive and shall forthwith inform the Commission thereof; the laws thus amended shall be applied in such a way as to:

–   permit trade in those products which comply with the provisions of this Directive no later than two years after its notification;

–   prohibit trade in those products which do not comply with the provisions of this Directive four years after its notification.

2   However, Member States may:

(a)  in the case of certain foodstuffs, reduce the period specified in the second indent of paragraph 1;

(b)  in the case of certain foodstuffs which keep for a long time, extend the period specified in the second indent of paragraph 1;

(c)  without prejudice to the first indent of Article 23(1)(b), in the case of foodstuffs which will keep for more than 12 months, extend to six years the period laid down in the second indent of paragraph 1 above as regards the obligation to indicate the date of minimum durability;

3   In the case referred to:

(a)  in paragraph 2(a), the procedure laid down in Article 16(2) shall apply to any national provisions;

(b)  in paragraph 2(b) and (c), Member States shall inform the Commission and the other Member States of any measure taken pursuant to the said points.

4   Member States shall also ensure that the Commission receives the text of any essential provision of national law which they adopt in the field governed by this Directive.

*Article 23*

1   By way of derogation from the second indent of Article 22(1), Member States may make implementation of the provisions relating to the following matters option:

(a)  the designation, provided for in the second indent of Article 6(3)(b), of the specific name or EEC number of the ingredients belonging to one of the categories listed in Annex II;

(b)  the indication provided for in Article 9, of the date of minimum durability in the case of:

  –  foodstuffs whose minimum durability exceeds 18 months

  –  deep-frozen foodstuffs;

  –  ice-creams;

  –  chewing gums and similar chewing products;

  –  fermented cheese intended to ripen completely or partially in prepackaging;

(c)  the information provided for in Annex I to supplement the designation 'oil' or 'fat'.

2   Without prejudice to the information provided for in Article 22, Member States shall inform the Commission and the other Member States of any measure taken pursuant to paragraph 1.

3   After a period of five years following notification of this Directive, the Council shall, in accordance with the procedure laid down in Article 100 of the Treaty, decide upon the common rules to apply in the cases referred to in paragraph 1.

### Article 24

This Directive shall also apply to the French overseas departments.

### Article 25

This Directive shall not apply to foodstuffs marketed in Greenland, intended for local consumption.

### Article 26

This Directive is addressed to the Member States.

Done at Brussels, 18 December 1978.

*For the Council*
*The President*
*J ERTL*

*Annex I*

*Categories of ingredients which may be designated by the
name of the category rather than the specific name*

| Definition | Designation |
| --- | --- |
| Refined oils other than olive oil. | 'Oil', together with<br>– either the adjective 'vegetable' or 'animal', as appropriate, or<br>– an indication of their specific vegetable or animal origin.<br>The adjective 'hydrogenated' must accompany the indication of a hydrogenated oil where the vegetable origin or the specific vegetable or animal origin is mentioned.<br>However, in either case, Member States may lay down requirements which are more stringent in the case of foodstuffs consisting essentially of oils and fats, emulsified sauces or preparations where the oil serves as a liquid medium; in that case, the procedure laid down in Article 16 shall apply. |
| Refined fats. | 'Fat', together with<br>– either the adjective 'vegetable' or 'animal', as appropriate, or<br>– an indication of their specific vegetable or animal origin.<br>However, in either cases, Member States may lay down requirements which are more stringent in the case of foodstuffs consisting essentially of oils and fats or emulsified sauces; in that case, the procedure laid down in Article 16 shall apply. |
| Mixtures of flour obtained from two or more cereal species. | 'Flour', followed by a list of the cereals from which it has been obtained in descending order by weight. |
| Starches and starches modified by physical or enzymatic means. | Starch. |

| Definition | Designation |
|---|---|
| Fish. | All species of fish where the fish constitutes an ingredient of another foodstuff and provided that the name and presentation of such foodstuff does not refer to a specific species of fish. |
| Poultry meat. | All types of poultry meat where such meat constitutes an ingredient of another foodstuff and provided that the name and presentation of such a foodstuff does not refer to a specific type of poultry meat. |
| Cheese. | All types of cheese where the cheese or mixture of cheeses constitutes an ingredient of another foodstuff and provided that the name and presentation of such foodstuff does not refer to a specific type of cheese. |
| Spice(s) or mixed spices. | All spices and spice extracts not exceeding 2% by weight of the foodstuff. |
| Herb(s) or mixed herbs. | All herbs or parts of herbs not exceeding 2% by weight of the foodstuff. |
| Gum base. | All types of gum preparations used in the manufacture of gum base for chewing gum. |
| Crumbs or rusks as appropriate. | All types of crumbed baked cereal products. |
| Sugar. | All types of sucrose. |
| Dextrose. | Anhydrous dextrose and dextrose monohydrate. |
| Caseinates. | All types of caseinates. |
| Cocoa butter. | Press, expeller or refined cocoa butter. |
| Crystallised fruit. | All crystallised fruit not exceeding 10% of the weight of the foodstuff. |

*Annex II*

*Categories of ingredients which must be designated by the name of the category
to which they belong, followed by their specific name or EEC number*

Colour

Preservative

Antioxidant

Emulsifier

Thickener

Gelling agent

Stabiliser

Flavour enhancer

Acid

Acidity regulator

Anticaking agent

Modified starches

Artificial sweetener

Raising agent

Antifoaming agent

Glazing agent

Emulsifying sales

Flour improvers

*OJ L 43 of 14.2.97*

*Directive of the European Parliament and of the Council of 27 January 1997*

amending Directive 79/112/EEC on the approximation of the laws of the Member States relating to the labelling, presentation and advertising of foodstuffs

(97/4/EC)

THE EUROPEAN PARLIAMENT AND THE COUNCIL OF THE EUROPEAN UNION,

Having regard to the Treaty establishing the European Community, and in particular Article 100a thereof,

Having regard to Council Directive 79/112/EEC of 18 December 1978 on the approximation of the laws of the Member States relating to the labelling, presentation and advertising of foodstuffs, and in particular Article 6 (2)(c) and (3) and Article 7,

Having regard to the proposal from the Commission,

Having regard to the opinion of the Economic and Social Committee,

Acting in accordance with the procedure laid down in Article 189b of the Treaty in the light of the join text approved on 16 October 1996 by the Conciliation Committee,

Whereas, in the context of achieving the objectives of the internal market, the use of the name customary in the Member State in which a product is manufactured should also be allowed in the case of products to be sold in another Member State;

Whereas, with the twofold aim of providing the consumer with better information and ensuring fair trade, the labelling rules as regards the exact nature and characteristics of products need to be further improved;

Whereas, in accordance with the rules of the Treaty, the provisions applicable to sales names remain subject to the general rules on labelling in Article 2 and more particularly the principle that they must not be such as to mislead the consumer about the characteristics of the foodstuff;

Whereas the Court of Justice of the European Communities has delivered several judgments in which it recommends detailed labelling, in particular the compulsory affixing of suitable labels giving the nature of the product sold; whereas this course of action, which enables the consumer to make his choice in full knowledge of the facts, is the most appropriate since it creates fewest obstacles to free trade;

Whereas it is for the Community legislature to adopt measures deriving from that case law,

HAVE ADOPTED THIS DIRECTIVE:

*Article 1*

Directive 79/112/EEC is hereby amended as follows:

1    the following recital shall be inserted after the sixth recital:

'Whereas that need means that Member States may, in compliance with the rules of the Treaty, impose language requirements;';

2    the following shall be added to Article 3(1):

'2a the quantity of certain ingredients or categories of ingredients as provided for in Article 7;';

3    Article 5(1) shall be replaced by the following:

'1    The name under which a foodstuff is sold shall be the name provided for in the European Community provisions applicable to it.

(a)  In the absence of European Community provisions, the name under which a product is sold shall be the name provided for in the laws, regulations and administrative provisions applicable in the Member State in which the product is sold to the final consumer or to mass caterers.

Failing this, the name under which a product is sold shall be the name customary in the Member State in which it is sold to the final consumer or to mass caterers, or a description of the foodstuff, and if necessary of its use, which is clear enough to let the purchaser know its true nature and distinguish it from other products with which it might be confused.

(b)  The use in the Member State of marketing of the sales name under which the product is legally manufactured and marketed in the Member State of production shall also be allowed.

However, where the application of the other provisions of this Directive, in particular those set out in Article 3, would not enable consumers in the Member State of marketing to know the true nature of the foodstuff and to distinguish it from foodstuffs with which they could confuse it, the sales name shall be accompanied by other descriptive information which shall appear in proximity to the sales name.

(c)  In exceptional cases, the sales name of the Member State of production shall not be used in the Member State of marketing when the foodstuff which it designates is so different, as regards its composition or manufacture, from the foodstuff known under that name that the provisions of point (b) are not sufficient to ensure, in the Member State of marketing, correct information for consumers.';

4    Article 6(2)(c) shall be replaced by the following:

'(c) products comprising a single ingredient where:

–    the trade name is identical with the ingredient name, or

–    the trade name enables the nature of the ingredient to be clearly identified.';

5    the first indent of Article 6(5)(b) (Directive 79/112/EEC) shall be replaced by the following:

'–   ingredients which belong to one of the categories listed in Annex I and are constituents of another foodstuff need only be designated by the name of that category.

Alterations to the list of categories in Annex I may be effected in accordance with the procedure laid down in Article 17.

However, the designation "starch" listed in Annex I must always be complemented by the indication of its specific vegetable origin, when that ingredient may contain gluten,';

6 the second indent of Article 6(5)(b) (Directive 79/112/EEC) shall be replaced by the following:

'– ingredients belonging to one of the categories listed in Annex II must be designed by the name of that category, followed by their specific name or EEC number; if an ingredient belongs to more than one of the categories, the category appropriate to the principal function in the case of the foodstuff in question shall be indicated.

Amendments to this Annex based on advances in scientific and technical knowledge shall be adopted in accordance with the procedure laid down in Article 17.

However, the designation "modified starch" listed in Annex II must always be complemented by the indication of its specific vegetable origin, when that ingredient may contain gluten.';

7 Article 7 shall be replaced by the following:

'*Article 7*

1 The quantity of an ingredient or category of ingredients used in the manufacture or preparation of a foodstuff shall be stated in accordance with this Article.

2 The indication referred to in paragraph 1 shall be compulsory:

(a) where the ingredient or category of ingredients concerned appears in the name under which the foodstuff is sold or is usually associated with that name by the consumer; or

(b) where the ingredient or category of ingredients concerned is emphasised on the labelling in words, pictures or graphics; or

(c) where the ingredient or category of ingredients concerned is essential to characterise a foodstuff and to distinguish it from products with which it might be confused because of its name or appearance; or

(d) in the cases determined in accordance with the procedure laid down in Article 17.

3 Paragraph 2 shall not apply:

(a) to an ingredient or category of ingredients:

 – the drained net weight of which is indicated in accordance with Article 8(4), or

 – the quantities of which are already required to be given on the labelling under Community provisions,

 – which is used in small quantities for the purposes of flavouring,

 – which, while appearing in the name under which the food is sold, is not such as to govern the choice of the consumer in the country of marketing because the variation in quantity is not essential to characterise the foodstuff or does not distinguish it from similar foods. In cases of doubt it shall be decided by the procedure laid down in Article 17 whether the conditions laid down in this indent are fulfiled,

(b) where specific Community provisions stipulate precisely the quantity of an ingredient or of a category of ingredients without providing for the indication thereof on the labelling,

(c) in the cases referred to in the fourth and fifth indents of Article 6(5)(a),

(d) in the cases determined in accordance with the procedure laid down in Article 17.

4 The quantity indicated, expressed as a percentage, shall correspond to the quantity of the ingredient or ingredients at the time of its/their use. However, Community provisions may allow for derogations from this principle for certain foodstuffs. Such provisions shall be adopted in accordance with the procedure laid down in Article 17.

5 The indication referred to in paragraph 1 shall appear either in or immediately next to the name under which the foodstuff is sold or in the list of ingredients in connection with the ingredient or category of ingredients in question.

6 This Article shall apply without prejudice to Community rules on nutrition labelling for foodstuffs.';

8 The following Article shall be inserted:

'*Article 13a*

1 Member States shall ensure that the sale is prohibited within their own territories of foodstuffs for which the particulars provided for in Article 3 and Article 4(2) do not appear in a language easily understood by the consumer, unless the consumer is.in fact informed by means of other measures determined in accordance with the procedure laid down in Article 17 as regards one or more labelling particulars.

2 Within its own territory, the Member State in which the product is marketed may, in accordance with the rules of the Treaty, stipulate that those labelling particulars shall be given in one or more languages which it shall determine from among the official languages of the Community.

3 Paragraphs I and 2 shall not preclude the labelling particulars from being indicated in several languages.';

9 In Article 14, the second paragraph shall be deleted.

## *Article 2*

Member States shall, where appropriate, amend their laws, regulations and administrative provisions in order to:

- allow trade in products conforming to this Directive no later than 14 August 1998,

- prohibit trade in products not conforming to this Directive no later than 14 February 2000. However, trade in products not conforming to this Directive and labelled before that date shall be permitted until stocks are fully depleted.

The Member States shall forthwith inform the Commission of those provisions.

When Member States adopt these measures, they shall contain a reference to this Directive or shall be accompanied by such reference on the occasion of their official publication. The methods of making such reference shall be laid down by Member States.

### Article 3

This Directive shall apply as from the date of its publication in the Official Journal of the European Communities.

### Article 4

This Directive is addressed to the Member States.

Done at Brussels, 27 January 1997.

| | |
|---|---|
| *For the European Parliament* | *For the Council* |
| *The President* | *The President* |
| JM GIL-ROBLES | G ZALM |

# DIRECTIVE 92/28/EEC (ADVERTISING OF MEDICINAL PRODUCTS FOR HUMAN USE)

*OJ L 113, 30.4.92, p 13*

*Council Directive 92/28/EEC of 31 March 1992*

on the advertising of medicinal products for human use

THE COUNCIL OF THE EUROPEAN COMMUNITIES,

Having regard to the Treaty establishing the European Economic Community, and in particular Article 100a thereof,

Having regard to the proposal from the Commission,

In co-operation with the European Parliament,

Having regard to the opinion of the Economic and Social Committee,

Whereas Directive 84/450/EEC4 harmonised the laws, regulations and administrative provisions of the Member States concerning misleading advertising; whereas this Directive is without prejudice to the application of measures adopted pursuant to that Directive;

Whereas all Member States have adopted further specific measures concerning the advertising of medicinal products; whereas there are disparities between theses measures; whereas these disparities are likely to have an impact on the establishment and functioning of the internal market, since advertising disseminated in one Member State is likely to have effects in other Member States;

Whereas Council Directive 89/552/EEC of 3 October 1989 on the co-ordination of certain provisions laid down by law, regulation or administrative action in Member States concerning the pursuit of television broadcasting activities prohibits the television advertising of medicinal products which are available only on medical prescription the Member State within whose jurisdiction the television broadcaster is located; whereas this principle should be made of general application by extending it to other media;

Whereas advertising to the general public, even of non-prescription medicinal products, could affect public health, were it to be excessive and ill-considered; whereas advertising of medicinal products to the general public, where it is permitted, ought therefore to satisfy certain essential criteria which ought to be defined;

Whereas, furthermore, distribution of samples free of charge to the general public for promotional ends must be prohibited;

Whereas the advertising of medicinal products to persons qualified to prescribe or supply them contributes to the information available to such persons; whereas, nevertheless, this advertising should be subject to strict conditions and effective monitoring, referring in particular to the work carried out within the framework of the Council of Europe;

Whereas medical sales representatives have an important role in the promotion of medicinal products; whereas, therefore, certain obligations should be imposed upon them, in particular the obligation to supply the person visited with a summary of product characteristics;

Whereas persons qualified to prescribe medicinal products must be able to carry out these functions objectively without being influenced by direct or indirect financial inducements;

Whereas it should be possible within certain restrictive conditions to provide samples of medicinal products free of charge to persons qualified to prescribe or supply them so that they can familiarise themselves with new products and acquire experience in dealing with them;

Whereas persons qualified to prescribe or supply medicinal products must have access to a neutral, objective source of information about products available on the market; whereas it is nevertheless for the Member States to take all measures necessary to this end, in the light of their own particular situation;

Whereas advertising of medicinal products should be subject to effective, adequate monitoring; whereas reference in this regard should be made to the monitoring mechanisms set up by Directive 84/450/EEC;

Whereas each undertaking which manufactures or imports medicinal products should set up a mechanism to ensure that all information supplied about a medicinal product conforms with the approved conditions of use,

HAS ADOPTED THIS DIRECTIVE:

## Chapter I

### Scope, definitions and general principles

#### Article 1

1    This Directive concerns the advertising in the Community of medicinal products for human use covered by Chapters II to V of Council Directive 65/65/EEC of 26 January 1965 on the approximation of provisions laid down by law, regulation or administrative action relating to medicinal products.

2    For the purposes of this Directive:

- the definitions of the name of the medicinal product and of the common name shall be those laid down in Article 1 of Directive 92/27/EEC;

- the summary of product characteristics shall be the summary approved by the competent authority which granted the marketing authorisation in accordance with Article 4b of Directive 65/65/EEC.

3   For the purposes of this Directive, advertising of medicinal products shall include any form of door-to-door information, canvassing activity or inducement designed to promote the prescription, supply, sale or consumption of medicinal products; it shall include in particular:

–   the advertising of medicinal products to persons qualified to prescribe or supply them,

–   visits by medical sales representatives to persons qualified to prescribe medicinal products,

–   the supply of samples,

–   the provision of inducements to prescribe or supply medicinal products by the gift, offer or promise of any benefit or bonus, whether in money or in kind, except when their intrinsic value is minimal,

–   sponsorship of promotional meetings attended by persons qualified to prescribe or supply medicinal products,

–   sponsorship of scientific congresses attended by persons qualified to prescribe or supply medicinal products and in particular payment of their travelling and accommodation expenses in connection therewith.

4   The following are not covered by the Directive:

–   the labelling of medicinal products and the accompanying package leaflets, which are subject to the provisions of Directive 92/27/EEC;

–   correspondence, possibly accompanied by material of a non-promotional nature, needed to answer a specific question about a particular medicinal product;

–   factual, informative announcements and reference material relating, for example, to pack changes, adverse-reaction warnings as part of general drug precautions, trade catalogues and price lists, provided they include no product claims;

–   statements relating to human health or diseases, provided there is no reference, even direct, to medicinal products.

*Article 2*

1   Member States shall prohibit any advertising of a medicinal product in respect of which a marketing authorisation has not been granted in accordance with Community law.

2   All parts of the advertising of a medicinal product must comply with the particulars listed in the summary of product characteristics.

3   The advertising of a medicinal product:

–   shall encourage the rational use of the medicinal product, by presenting it objectively and without exaggerating its properties,

–   shall not be misleading.

*Chapter II*

Advertising to the general public

*Article 3*

1 Member States shall prohibit the advertising to the general public of medicinal products which:

   – are available on medical prescription only, in accordance with Directive 92/26/EEC,

   – contain psychotropic or narcotic substances, within the meaning of the international conventions,

   – may not be advertised to the general public in accordance with paragraph 2.

2 Medicinal products may be advertised to the general public which, by virtue of their composition and purpose, are intended and designed for use without the intervention of a medical practitioner for diagnostic purposes or for the prescription or monitoring of treatment, with the advice of the pharmacist, if necessary.

   Member States shall prohibit the mentioning in advertising to the general public of therapeutic indications such as:

   – tuberculosis,

   – sexually transmitted diseases,

   – other seriously infectious diseases,

   – cancer and other tumoral diseases,

   – chronic insomnia,

   – diabetes and other metabolic illnesses.

3 Member States shall also be able to ban on their territory advertising to the general public of medicinal products the cost of which may be reimbursed.

4 The prohibition referred to in paragraph 1 shall not apply to vaccination campaigns carried out by the industry and approved by the competent authorities of the Member States.

5 The prohibition referred to in paragraph 1 shall apply without prejudice to Articles 2, 3 and 14 of Directive 89/552/EEC.

6 Member States shall prohibit the direct distribution of medicinal products to the public by the industry for promotional purposes; they may however, authorise such distribution in special cases for other purposes.

*Article 4*

1 Without prejudice to Article 3, all advertising to the general public of a medicinal product shall:

   (a) be set out in such a way that it is clear that the message is an advertisement and that the product is clearly identified as a medicinal product;

   (b) include the following information:

- the name of the medicinal product, as well as the common name if the medicinal product contains only one active ingredient,
- the information necessary for correct use of the medicinal product,
- an express, legible invitation to read carefully the instructions on the package leaflet or on the outer packaging, according to the case.

2  Member States may decide that the advertising of a medicinal product to the general public may, notwithstanding paragraph 1, include only the name of the medicinal product if it is intended solely as a reminder.

*Article 5*

The advertising of a medicinal product to the general public shall not contain any material which:

(a) gives the impression that a medical consultation or surgical operation is unnecessary, in particular by offering a diagnosis or by suggesting treatment by mail;

(b) suggests that the effects of taking the medicine are guaranteed, are unaccompanied by side effects or are better than, or equivalent to, those of another treatment or medicinal product;

(c) suggests that the health of the subject can be enhanced by taking the medicine;

(d) suggests that the health of the subject could be affected by not taking medicine; this prohibition shall not apply to the vaccination campaigns referred to in Article 3(4);

(e) is directed exclusively or principally at children;

(f) refers to a recommendation by scientists, health professionals or persons who are neither of the foregoing but who, because of their celebrity, could encourage the consumption of medicinal products;

(g) suggests that the medicinal product is a foodstuff, cosmetic or other consumer product;

(h) suggests that the safety or efficacy of the medicinal product is due to the fact that it is natural;

(i) could, by a description or detailed representation of a case history, lead to erroneous self-diagnosis;

(j) refers, in improper, alarming or misleading terms, to claims of recovery;

(k) uses, in improper, alarming or misleading terms, pictorial representations of changes in the human body caused by disease or injury, or of the action of a medicinal product on the human body or parts thereof;

(l) mentions that the medicinal product has been granted a marketing authorisation.

*Chapter III*

Advertising to health professionals

*Article 6*

1   Any advertising of a medicinal product to persons qualified to prescribe or supply such products shall include:

–   essential information compatible with the he summary of product characteristics;

–   the supply classification of the medicinal product.

Member States may also require such advertising to include the selling price or indicative price of the various presentations and the conditions for reimbursement by social security bodies.

2   Member States may decide that the advertising of a medicinal product to persons qualified to prescribe or supply such products may, notwithstanding paragraph 1, include only the name of the medicinal product, if it is intended solely as a reminder.

*Article 7*

1   Any documentation relating to a medicinal product which is transmitted as part of the promotion of that product to persons qualified to prescribe or supply it shall include as a minimum the particulars listed in Article 6(1) and shall state the date on which it was drawn up or last revised.

2   All the information contained in the documentation referred to in paragraph 1 shall be accurate, up-to-date, verifiable and sufficiently complete to enable the recipient to form his or her own opinion of the therapeutic value of the medicinal product concerned.

3   Quotations as well as tables and other illustrative matter taken from medical journals or other scientific works for use in the documentation referred to in paragraph 1 shall be faithfully reproduced and the precise sources indicated.

*Article 8*

1   Medical sales representatives shall be given adequate training by the firm which employs them and shall have sufficient scientific knowledge to be able to provide information which is precise and as complete as possible about the medicinal products which they promote.

2   During each visit, medical sales representatives shall give the persons visited, or have available for them, summaries of the product characteristics of each medicinal product they present together, if the legislation of the Member State so permits, with details of the price and conditions for reimbursement referred to in Article 6(1).

3   Medical sales representatives shall transmit to the scientific service referred to in Article 13(1) any information about the use of the medicinal products they advertise, with particular reference to any adverse reactions reported to them by the persons they visit.

### Article 9

1   Where medicinal products are being promoted to persons qualified to prescribe or supply them, no gifts, pecuniary advantages or benefits in kind may be supplied, offered or promised to such persons unless they are inexpensive and relevant to the practice of medicine or pharmacy.

2   Hospitality at sales promotion must always be reasonable in level and secondary to the main purpose of the meeting and must not be extended to other than health professionals.

3   Persons qualified to prescribe or supply medicinal products shall not solicit or accept any inducement prohibited under paragraph 1 or contrary to paragraph 2.

4   Existing measures or trade practices in Member States relating to prices, margins and discounts shall not be affected by this Article.

### Article 10

The provisions of Article 9(1) shall not prevent hospitality being offered, directly or indirectly, at events for purely professional and scientific purposes; such hospitality must always be reasonable in level and remain subordinate to the main scientific objective of the meeting; it must not be extended to persons other than health professionals.

### Article 11

1   Free samples shall be provided on an exceptional basis only to persons qualified to prescribe them and on the following conditions:

(a)  a limited number of samples for each medicinal product each year on prescription;

(b)  any supply of samples must be in response to a written request, signed and dated, from the recipient;

(c)  those supplying samples must maintain an adequate system of control and accountability;

(d)  each sample shall be identical with the smallest presentation on the market;

(e)  each sample shall be marked 'free medical sample – not for resale' or bear another legend of analogous meaning;

(f)  each sample shall be accompanied by a copy of the summary of product characteristics;

(g)  no samples of medicinal products containing psychotropic or narcotic substances within the meaning of international conventions may be supplied.

2   Member States may also place further restrictions on the distribution of samples of certain medicinal products.

*Chapter IV*

*Monitoring of advertising*

*Article 12*

1  Member States shall ensure that there are adequate and effective methods to monitor the advertising of medicinal products. Such methods, which may be based on a system of prior vetting, shall in any event include legal provisions under which persons or organisations regarded under national law as having a legitimate interest in prohibiting any advertisement inconsistent with this Directive may take legal action against such advertisement, or bring such advertisement before an administrative authority competent either to decide on complaints or to initiate appropriate legal proceedings.

2  Under the legal provisions referred to in paragraph 1, Member States shall confer upon the courts or administrative authorities powers enabling them, in cases where they deem such measures to be necessary taking into account all the interests involved and in particular the public interest:

  –  to order the cessation of, or to institute appropriate legal proceedings for an order for the cessation of, misleading advertising, or

  –  if misleading advertising has not yet been published but publication is imminent, to order the prohibition of, or to institute appropriate legal proceedings for an order for the prohibition of, such publication, even without proof of actual loss or damage or of intention or negligence on the part of the advertiser.

  Member States shall also make provision for the measures referred to in the first subparagraph to be taken under an accelerated procedure:

  –  either with interim effect, or

  –  with definitive effect,

  on the understanding that it is for each Member State to decide which of the two options to select.

  Furthermore, Member States may confer upon the courts or administrative authorities powers enabling them, with a view to eliminating the continuing effects of misleading advertising the cessation of which has been ordered by a final decision:

  –  to require publication of that decision in full or in part and in such form as they deem adequate,

  –  to require in addition the publication of a corrective statement.

3  Under the legal provisions referred to in paragraph 1, Member States shall ensure that any decision taken in accordance with paragraph 2 shall state in detail the reasons on which it is based and shall be communicated in writing to the person concerned, mentioning the redress available at law and the time limit allowed for access to such redress.

4  This Article shall not exclude the voluntary control of advertising of medicinal products by self-regulatory bodies and recourse to such bodies, if proceedings before such bodies are possible in addition to the judicial or administrative proceedings referred to in paragraph 1.

*Article 13*

1   The marketing authorisation holder shall establish within his undertaking a scientific service in charge of information about the medicinal products which he places on the market.

2   The person responsible for placing the product on the market shall:

  –   keep available for, or communicate to, the authorities or bodies responsible for monitoring advertising of medicinal products a sample of all advertisements emanating from his undertaking together with a statement indicating the persons to whom it is addressed, the method of dissemination and the date of first dissemination,

  –   ensure that advertising of medicinal products by his undertaking conforms to the requirements of this Directive,

  –   verify that medical sales representatives employed by his undertaking have been adequately trained and fulfill [*sic*] the obligations imposed upon them by Article 8(2) and (3),

  –   supply the authorities or bodies responsible for monitoring medicinal products with the information and assistance they require to carry out their responsibilities,

  –   ensure that the decisions taken by the authorities or bodies responsible for monitoring advertising of medicinal products are immediately and fully complied with.

*Article 14*

Member States shall take the appropriate measures to ensure that all the provisions of this Directive are applied in full and shall determine in particular what penalties shall be imposed should the provisions adopted in the execution of this Directive be infringed.

*Article 15*

1   Member States shall take the measures necessary in order to comply with this Directive with effect from 1 January 1993. They shall forthwith inform the Commission thereof.

2   When Member States adopt the said measures, such measures shall contain a reference to this Directive or be accompanied by such reference on the occasion of their official publication. The methods of making such a reference shall be laid down by the Member States.

*Article 16*

This Directive is addressed to the Member States.

# DIRECTIVE 84/450/EEC AND DIRECTIVE 97/55/EC (AMENDING 84/450/EEC) (MISLEADING ADVERTISING)

Done at Brussels, 31 March 1992.

*For the Council*
*The President*
*Vitor MARTINS*

*OJ L 250 of 19.9.84, p 17*

*Council Directive of 10 September 1984*

relating to the approximation of the laws, regulations and administrative provisions of the Member States concerning misleading advertising

(84/450/EEC)

THE COUNCIL OF THE EUROPEAN COMMUNITIES,

Having regard to the Treaty establishing the European Economic Community, and in particular Article 100 thereof,

Having regard to the proposal from the Commission,

Having regard to the opinion of the European Parliament,

Having regard to the opinion of the Economic and Social Committee,

Whereas the laws against misleading advertising now in force in the Member States differ widely, whereas, since advertising reaches beyond the frontiers of individual Member States, it has a direct effect on the establishment and the functioning of the common market;

Whereas misleading advertising can lead to distortion of competition within the common market;

Whereas advertising, whether or nor it induces a contract, affects the economic welfare of consumers;

Whereas misleading advertising may cause a consumer to take decisions prejudicial to him when acquiring goods or other property, or using services, and the differences between the laws of the Member States not only lead, in many cases, to inadequate levels of consumer protection, but also hinder the execution of advertising campaigns beyond national boundaries and thus affect the free circulation of goods and provision of services;

Whereas the second programme of the European Economic Community for a consumer protection and information policy provides for appropriate action for the protection of consumers against misleading and unfair advertising;

Whereas it is in the interest of the public in general, as well as that of consumers and all those who, in competition with one another, carry on a trade, business, craft or profession, in the common market, to harmonise in the first instance national provisions against misleading advertising and that, at a second stage, unfair advertising and, as far as necessary, comparative advertising should be dealt with, on the basis of appropriate Commission proposals;

Whereas minimum and objective criteria for determining whether advertising is misleading should be established for this purpose;

Whereas the laws to be adopted by Member States against misleading advertising must be adequate and effective;

Whereas persons or organisations regarded under national law as having a legitimate interest in the matter must have facilities for initiating proceedings against misleading advertising, either before a court or before an administrative authority which is competent to decide upon complaints or to initiate appropriate legal proceedings;

Whereas it should be for each Member State to decide whether to enable the court or administrative authorities to require prior recourse to other established means of dealing with the complaint;

Whereas the courts or administrative authorities must have powers enabling them to order or obtain the cessation of misleading advertising;

Whereas in certain cases it may be desirable to prohibit misleading advertising even before it is published; whereas. however, this in no way implies that Member States are under an obligation to introduce rules requiring the systematic prior vetting of advertising;

Whereas provision should be made for accelerated procedures under which measures with interim or definitive effect can be taken;

Whereas it may be desirable to order the publication of decisions made by courts or administrative authorities or of corrective statements in order to eliminate any continuing effects of misleading advertising;

Whereas administrative authorities must be impartial and the exercise of their powers must be subject to judicial review;

Whereas the voluntary control exercised by self-regulatory bodies to eliminate misleading advertising may avoid recourse to administrative or judicial action and ought therefore to be encouraged;

Whereas the advertiser should be able to prove, by appropriate means, the material accuracy of the factual claims he makes in his advertising and may in appropriate cases be required to do so by the court or administrative authority;

Whereas this Directive must not preclude Member States from retaining or adopting provisions with a view to ensuring more extensive protection of consumers, persons carrying on a trade, business, craft or profession, and the general public,

HAS ADOPTED THIS DIRECTIVE:

*Article 1*

The purpose of this Directive is to protect consumers, persons carrying on a trade or business or practising a craft or profession and the interests of the public in general against misleading advertising and the unfair consequences thereof.

*Article 2*

For the purposes of this Directive:

1 'advertising' means the making of a representation in any form in connection with a trade, business, craft or profession in order to promote the supply of goods or services, including immovable property, rights and obligations;

2 'misleading advertising' means any advertising which in any way, including its presentation, deceives or is likely to deceive the persons to whom it is addressed or whom it reaches and which, by reason of its deceptive nature, is likely to affect their economic behaviour or which, for those reasons, injures or is likely to injure a competitor;

3 'person' means any natural or legal person.

*Article 3*

In determining whether advertising is misleading account shall be taken of all its features and, in particular, of any information it contains concerning:

(a) the characteristics of goods or services, such as their availability, nature, execution, composition, method and date of manufacture or provision,     fitness for purpose, uses, quantity. specification, geographical or commercial origin or the results to  be expected from their use, or the results and material features of tests or checks carried out on the goods or services;

(b) the price or the manner in which the price is calculated, and the conditions on which the goods are supplied or the services provided;

(c) the nature, attributes and rights of the advertiser, such as his identity and assets, his qualifications and ownership of industrial, commercial or intellectual property rights or his awards and distinctions.

*Article 4*

1 Member States shall ensure that adequate and effective means exist for the control of misleading advertising in the interests of consumers as well as competitors and the general public.

Such means shall include legal provisions under which persons or organisations regarded under national law as having a legitimate interest in prohibiting misleading advertising may:

(a) take legal action against such advertising; and/or

(b) bring such advertising before an administrative authority competent either to decide on complaints or to initiate appropriate legal proceedings.

It shall be for each Member State to decide which of these facilities shall be available and whether to enable the courts or administrative authorities to require prior recourse to other established means of dealing with complaints, including those referred to in Article 5.

2 Under the legal provisions referred to in paragraph 1, Member States shall confer upon the courts or administrative authorities powers enabling them, in cases where they deem such measures to be necessary, taking into account all the interests involved and in particular the public interest:

    – to order the cessation of, or to institute appropriate legal proceedings for an order for the cessation of, misleading advertising, or

- if misleading advertising has not yet been published but publication is imminent to order the prohibition of, or to institute appropriate legal proceedings for an order for the prohibition of, such publication,

even without proof of actual loss or damage or of intention or negligence on the part of the advertiser.

Member States shall also make provision for the measures referred to in the first subparagraph to be taken under an accelerated procedure:

- either with interim effect, or
- with definitive effect,

on the understanding that it is for each Member State to decide which of the two options to select.

Furthermore, Member States may confer upon the courts or administrative authorities powers enabling them, with a view to eliminating the continuing effects of misleading advertising the cessation of which has been ordered by a final decision:

- to require publication of that decision in full or in part and in such form as they deem adequate,
- to require in addition the publication of a corrective statement.

3 The administrative authorities referred to in paragraph 1 must:

(a) be composed so as not to cast doubt on their impartiality;

(b) have adequate powers, where they decide on complaints, to monitor and enforce the observance of their decisions effectively;

(c) normally give reasons for their decisions.

Where the powers referred to in paragraph 2 are exercised exclusively by an administrative authority, reasons for its decisions shall always be given. Furthermore in this case, provision must be made for procedures whereby improper or unreasonable exercise of its powers by the administrative authority or improper or unreasonable failure to exercise the said powers can be the subject of judicial review.

*Article 5*

This Directive does not exclude the voluntary control of misleading advertising by self-regulatory bodies and recourse to such bodies by the persons or organisations referred to in Article 4 if proceedings before such bodies are in addition to the court or administrative proceedings referred to in that Article.

*Article 6*

Member States shall confer upon the courts or administrative authorities powers enabling them in the civil or administrative proceedings provided for in Article 4:

(a) to require the advertiser to furnish evidence as to the accuracy of actual claims in advertising if taking into account the legitimate interests of the advertiser and any other party to the proceedings such a requirement appears appropriate on the basis of the circumstances of the particular case; and

(b) to consider factual claims as inaccurate if the evidence demanded in accordance with (a) is not furnished or is deemed insufficient by the court or administrative authority.

## *Article 7*

This Directive shall not preclude Member States from retaining or adopting provisions with a view to ensuring more extensive protection for consumers, persons carrying on a trade, business, craft or profession, and the general public.

## *Article 8*

Member States shall bring into force the measures necessary to comply with this Directive by 1 October 1986 at the latest. They shall forthwith inform the Commission thereof.

Member States shall communicate to the Commission the text of all provisions of national law which they adopt in the field covered by this Directive.

## *Article 9*

This Directive is addressed to the Member States.

Done at Brussels, 10 September 1984.

> *For the Council*
> *The President*
> P O'TOOLE

*OJ L 290 of 23.10.97, p 18*

*Directive 97/55/EC OF the European Parliament and of the Council
of 6 October 1997*

amending Directive 84/450/EEC concerning misleading
advertising so as to include comparative advertising

THE EUROPEAN PARLIAMENT AND THE COUNCIL OF THE EUROPEAN UNION,

Having regard to the Treaty establishing the European Community, and in particular Article 100a thereof,

Having regard to the proposal from the Commission,

Having regard to the opinion of the Economic and Social Committee,

Acting in accordance with the procedure laid down in Article 189b of the Treaty, in the light of the joint text approved by the Conciliation Committee on 25 June 1997,

(1) Whereas one of the Community's main aims is to complete the internal market; whereas measures must be adopted to ensure the smooth running of the said market; whereas the internal market comprises an area which has no internal frontiers and in which goods, persons, services and capital can move freely;

(2) Whereas the completion of the internal market will mean an ever wider range of choice; whereas, given that consumers can and must make the best possible use of the internal market, and that advertising is a very important means of creating genuine outlets for all goods and services throughout the Community, the basic provisions governing the form and content of comparative advertising should be uniform and the conditions of the use of comparative advertising in the Member States should be harmonised; whereas if these conditions are met, this will help demonstrate objectively the merits of the various comparable products; whereas comparative advertising can also stimulate competition between suppliers of goods and services to the consumer's advantage;

(3) Whereas the laws, regulations and administrative provisions of the individual Member States concerning comparative advertising differ widely, whereas advertising reaches beyond the frontiers and is received on the territory of other Member States; whereas the acceptance or non-acceptance of comparative advertising according to the various national laws may constitute an obstacle to the free movement of goods and services and create distortions of competition; whereas, in particular, firms may be exposed to forms of advertising developed by competitors to which they cannot reply in equal measure; whereas the freedom to provide services relating to comparative advertising should be assured; whereas the Community is called on to remedy the situation;

(4) Whereas the sixth recital of Council Directive 84/450/EEC of 10 September 1984 relating to the approximation of laws, regulations and administrative provisions of the Member States concerning misleading advertising states that, after the harmonisation of national provisions against misleading advertising, 'at a second stage ..., as far as necessary, comparative advertising should be dealt with, on the basis of appropriate Commission proposals';

(5) Whereas point 3(d) of the Annex to the Council Resolution of 14 April 1975 on a preliminary programme of the European Economic Community for a consumer protection and information policy includes the right to information among the basic rights of consumers; whereas this right is confirmed by the Council Resolution of 19 May 1981 on a second programme of the European Economic Community for a consumer protection and information policy, point 40 of the Annex, which deals specifically with consumer information; whereas comparative advertising, when it compares material, relevant, verifiable and representative features and is not misleading, may be a legitimate means of informing consumers of their advantage;

(6) Whereas it is desirable to provide a broad concept of comparative advertising to cover all modes of comparative advertising;

(7) Whereas conditions of permitted comparative advertising, as far as the comparison is concerned, should be established in order to determine which practices relating to comparative advertising may distort competition, be detrimental to competitors and have an adverse effect on consumer choice; whereas such conditions of permitted advertising should include criteria of objective comparison of the features of goods and services;

(8) Whereas the comparison of the price only of goods and services should be possible if this comparison respects certain conditions, in particular that it shall not be misleading;

(9) Whereas, in order to prevent comparative advertising being used in an anti-competitive and unfair manner, only comparisons between competing goods and services meeting the same needs or intended for the same purpose should be permitted;

(10) Whereas the international conventions on copyright as well as the national provisions on contractual and non- contractual liability shall apply when the results of comparative tests carried out by third parties are referred to or reproduced in comparative advertising;

(11) Whereas the conditions of comparative advertising should be cumulative and respected in their entirety, whereas, in accordance with the Treaty, the choice of forms and methods for the implementation of these conditions shall be left to the Member States, insofar as those forms and methods are not already determined by this Directive;

(12) Whereas these conditions should include, in particular, consideration of the provisions resulting from Council Regulation (EEC) No 2081/92 of 14 July 1992 on the protection of geographical indications and designations of origin for agricultural products and foodstuffs (1), and in particular Article 13 thereof, and of the other Community provisions adopted in the agricultural sphere;

(13) Whereas Article 5 of First Council Directive 89/104/EEC of 21 December 1988 to approximate the laws of the Member States relating to trade marks (2) confers exclusive rights on the proprietor of a registered trade mark, including the right to prevent all third parties from using, in the course of trade, any sign which is identical with, or similar to, the trade mark in relation to identical goods or services or even, where appropriate, other goods;

(14) Whereas it may, however, be indispensable, in order to make comparative advertising effective, to identify the goods or services of a competitor, making reference to a trade mark or trade name of which the latter is the proprietor;

(15) Whereas such use of another's trade mark, trade name or other distinguishing marks does not breach this exclusive right in cases where it complies with the conditions laid down by this Directive, the intended target being solely to distinguish between them and thus to highlight differences objectively;

(16) Whereas provisions should be made for the legal and/or administrative means of redress mentioned in Articles 4 and 5 of Directive 84/450/EEC to be available to control comparative advertising which fails to meet the conditions laid down by this Directive; whereas according to the 16th recital of the Directive, voluntary control by self-regulatory bodies to eliminate misleading advertising may avoid recourse to administrative or juridical action and ought therefore to be encouraged; whereas Article 6 applies to unpermitted comparative advertising in the same way;

(17) Whereas national self-regulatory bodies may coordinate their work through associations or organisations established at Community level and *inter alia* deal with cross-border complaints;

(18) Whereas Article 7 of Directive 84/450/EEC allowing Member States to retain or adopt provisions with a view to ensuring more extensive protection for consumers, persons carrying on a trade, business, craft or profession, and the general public, should not apply to comparative advertising, given that the objective of amending the said Directive is to establish conditions under which comparative advertising is permitted;

(19) Whereas a comparison which presents goods or services as an imitation or a replica of goods or services bearing a protected trade mark or trade name shall not be considered to fulfil the conditions to be met by permitted comparative advertising;

(20) Whereas this Directive in no way affects Community provisions on advertising for specific products and/or services or restrictions or prohibitions on advertising in particular media;

(21) Whereas, if a Member State, in compliance with the provisions of the Treaty, prohibits advertising regarding certain goods or services, this ban may, whether it is imposed directly or by a body or organisation responsible under the law of that Member State for regulating the exercise of a commercial, industrial, craft or professional activity, be extended to comparative advertising;

(22) Whereas Member States shall not be obliged to permit comparative advertising for goods or services on which they, in compliance with the provisions of the Treaty, maintain or introduce bans, including bans as regards marketing methods or advertising which targets vulnerable consumer groups; whereas Member States may, in compliance with the provisions of the Treaty, maintain or introduce bans or limitations on the use of comparisons in the advertising of professional services, whether imposed directly or by a body or organisation responsible under the law of the Member States for regulating the exercise of a professional activity;

(23) Whereas regulating comparative advertising is, under the conditions set out in this Directive, necessary for the smooth running of the internal market and whereas action at Community level is therefore required; whereas the adoption of a Directive is the appropriate instrument because it lays down uniform general principles while allowing the Member States to choose the form and appropriate method by which to attain these objectives; whereas it is in accordance with the principle of subsidiarity,

HAVE ADOPTED THIS DIRECTIVE:

*Article 1*

Directive 84/450/EEC is hereby amended as follows:

(1) The title shall be replaced by the following:

'Council Directive of 10 September 1984 concerning misleading and comparative advertising';

(2) Article 1 shall be replaced by the following:

'*Article 1*

The purpose of this Directive is to protect consumers, persons carrying on a trade or business or practising a craft or profession and the interests of the public in general against misleading advertising and the unfair consequences thereof and to lay down the conditions under which comparative advertising is permitted.';

(3) The following point shall be inserted in Article 2:

'2a "comparative advertising" means any advertising which explicitly or by implication identifies a competitor or goods or services offered by a competitor';

(4) The following Article shall be added:

'*Article 3a*

1  Comparative advertising shall, as far as the comparison is concerned, be permitted when the following conditions are met:

    (a) it is not misleading according to Articles 2(2), 3 and 7(1);

    (b) it compares goods or services meeting the same needs or intended for the same purpose;

    (c) it objectively compares one or more material, relevant, verifiable and representative features of those goods and services, which may include price;

    (d) it does not create confusion in the market place between the advertiser and a competitor or between the advertiser's trade marks, trade names, other distinguishing marks, goods or services and those of a competitor;

    (e) it does not discredit or denigrate the trade marks, trade names, other distinguishing marks, goods, services, activities, or circumstances of a competitor;

    (f) for products with designation of origin, it relates in each case to products with the same designation;

    (g) it does not take unfair advantage of the reputation of a trade mark, trade name or other distinguishing marks of a competitor or of the designation of origin of competing products;

    (h) it does not present goods or services as imitations or replicas of goods or services bearing a protected trade mark or trade name.

2  Any comparison referring to a special offer shall indicate in a clear and unequivocal way the date on which the offer ends or, where appropriate, that the special offer is subject to the availability of the goods and services, and, where the special offer has not yet begun, the date of the start of the period during which the special price or other specific conditions shall apply.';

(5) The first and second subparagraphs of Article 4(1) shall be replaced by the following:

'1  Member States shall ensure that adequate and effective means exist to combat misleading advertising and for the compliance with the provisions on comparative advertising in the interests of consumers as well as competitors and the general public.

Such means shall include legal provisions under which persons or organisations regarded under national law as having a legitimate interest in prohibiting misleading advertising or regulating comparative advertising may:

    (a) take legal action against such advertising, and/or

    (b) bring such advertising before an administrative authority competent either to decide on complaints or to initiate appropriate legal proceedings.';

(6) Article 4(2) is hereby amended as follows:

    (a) the indents in the first subparagraph shall be replaced by the following:

'– to order the cessation of, or to institute appropriate legal proceedings for an order for the cessation of, misleading advertising or unpermitted comparative advertising, or

– if the misleading advertising or unpermitted comparative advertising has not yet been published but publication is imminent, to order the prohibition of, or to institute appropriate legal proceedings for an order for the prohibition of, such publication,';

(b) the introductory wording to the third subparagraph shall be replaced by the following:

'Furthermore, Member States may confer upon the courts or administrative authorities powers enabling them, with a view to eliminating the continuing effects of misleading advertising or unpermitted comparative advertising, the cessation of which has been ordered by a final decision:';

(7) Article 5 shall be replaced by the following:

'*Article 5*

This Directive does not exclude the voluntary control, which Member States may encourage, of misleading or comparative advertising by self-regulatory bodies and recourse before such bodies are in addition to the court of administrative proceedings referred to in that Article.';

(8) Article 6 (a) shall be replaced by the following:

'(a) to require the advertiser to furnish evidence as to the accuracy of factual claims in advertising if, taking into account the legitimate interest of the advertiser and any other party to the proceedings, such a requirement appears appropriate on the basis of the circumstances of the particular case and in the case of comparative advertising to require the advertiser to furnish such evidence in a short period of time; and';

(9) Article 7 shall be replaced by the following:

'*Article 7*

1 This Directive shall not preclude Member States from retaining or adopting provisions with a view to ensuring more extensive protection, with regard to misleading advertising, for consumers, persons carrying on a trade, business, craft or profession, and the general public.

2 Paragraph 1 shall not apply to comparative advertising as far as the comparison is concerned.

3 The provisions of this Directive shall apply without prejudice to Community provisions on advertising for specific products and/or services or to restrictions or prohibitions on advertising in particular media.

4 The provisions of this Directive concerning comparative advertising shall not oblige Member States which, in compliance with the provisions of the Treaty, maintain or introduce advertising bans regarding certain goods or services, whether imposed directly or by a body or organisation responsible, under the law of the Member States, for regulating the exercise of a commercial, industrial, craft or professional activity, to permit comparative advertising regarding those goods or services. Where these bans are limited to particular media, the Directive shall apply to the media not covered by these bans.

5    Nothing in this Directive shall prevent Member States from, in compliance with the provisions of the Treaty, maintaining or introducing bans or limitations on the use of comparisons in the advertising of professional services, whether imposed directly or by a body or organisation responsible, under the law of the Member States, for regulating the exercise of a professional activity.'

*Article 2*

*Complaints systems*

The Commission shall study the feasibility of establishing effective means to deal with cross-border complaints in respect of comparative advertising. Within two years after the entry into force of this Directive the Commission shall submit a report to the European Parliament and the Council on the results of the studies, accompanied if appropriate by proposals.

*Article 3*

1    Member States shall bring into force the laws, regulations and administrative provisions necessary to comply with this Directive at the latest 30 months after its publication in the Official Journal of the European Communities. They shall forthwith inform the Commission thereof.

2    When Member States adopt these measures, they shall contain a reference to this Directive or shall be accompanied by such reference on the occasion of their official publication. The methods of making such reference shall be laid down by Member States.

3    Member States shall communicate to the Commission the text of the main provisions of domestic law which they adopt in the field governed by this Directive.

*Article 4*

This Directive is addressed to the Member States.

Done at Brussels, 6 October 1997.

*For the European Parliament*             *For the Council*

*The President*                          *The President*

JM GIL-ROBLES                           J POOS

# DIRECTIVE 97/7/EC (PROTECTION OF CONSUMERS RE DISTANCE CONTRACTS)

*OJ L 144 of 4.6.97, p 19*

*DIRECTIVE 97/7/EC OF THE EUROPEAN PARLIAMENT AND OF THE COUNCIL*
*of 20 May 1997*

on the protection of consumers in respect of distance contracts

THE EUROPEAN PARLIAMENT AND THE COUNCIL OF THE EUROPEAN UNION,

Having regard to the Treaty establishing the European Community, and in particular Article 100a thereof,

Having regard to the proposal from the Commission,

Having regard to the opinion of the Economic and Social Committee,

Acting in accordance with the procedure laid down in Article 189b of the Treaty, in the light of the joint text approved by the Conciliation Committee on 27 November 1996,

(1) Whereas, in connection with the attainment of the aims of the internal market, measures must be taken for the gradual consolidation of that market;

(2) Whereas the free movement of goods and services affects not only the business sector but also private individuals; whereas it means that consumers should be able to have access to the goods and services of another Member State on the same terms as the population of that State;

Whereas, for consumers, cross-border distance selling could be one of the main tangible results of the completion of the internal market, as noted, *inter alia*, in the communication from the Commission to the Council entitled 'Towards a single market in distribution'; whereas it is essential to the smooth operation of the internal market for consumers to be able to have dealings with a business outside their country, even if it has a subsidiary in the consumer's country of residence;

(4) Whereas the introduction of new technologies is increasing the number of ways for consumers to obtain information about offers anywhere in the Community and to place orders; whereas some Member States have already taken different or diverging measures to protect consumers in respect of distance selling, which has had a detrimental effect on competition between businesses in the internal market; whereas it is therefore necessary to introduce at Community level a minimum set of common rules in this area;

(5) Whereas paragraphs 18 and 19 of the Annex to the Council resolution of 14 April 1975 on a preliminary programme of the European Economic Community for a consumer protection and information policy point to the need to protect the purchasers of goods or services from demands for payment for unsolicited goods and from high-pressure selling methods;

(6) Whereas paragraph 33 of the communication from the Commission to the Council entitled 'A new impetus for consumer protection policy', which was approved by the Council resolution of 23 June 1986, states that the Commission will submit proposals regarding the use of new information technologies enabling consumers to place orders with suppliers from their homes;

(7) Whereas the Council resolution of 9 November 1989 on future priorities for relaunching consumer protection policy calls upon the Commission to give priority to the areas referred to in the Annex to that resolution; whereas that Annex refers to new technologies involving teleshopping; whereas the Commission has responded to that resolution by adopting a three-year action plan for consumer protection policy in the European Economic Community (1990–1992); whereas that plan provides for the adoption of a Directive;

(8) Whereas the languages used for distance contracts are a matter for the Member States;

(9) Whereas contracts negotiated at a distance involve the use of one or more means of distance communication; whereas the various means of communication are used as part of an organised distance sales or service- provision scheme not involving the simultaneous presence of the supplier and the consumer; whereas the constant development of those means of communication does not allow an exhaustive list to be compiled but does require principles to be defined which are valid even for those which are not as yet in widespread use;

(10) Whereas the same transaction comprising successive operations or a series of separate operations over a period of time may give rise to different legal descriptions depending on the law of the Member States; whereas the provisions of this Directive cannot be applied differently according to the law of the Member States, subject to their recourse to Article 14; whereas, to that end, there is therefore reason to consider that there must at least be compliance with the provisions of this Directive at the time of the first of a series of successive operations or the first of a series of separate operations over a period of time which may be considered as forming a whole, whether that operation or series of operations are the subject of a single contract or successive, separate contracts;

(11) Whereas the use of means of distance communication must not lead to a reduction in the information provided to the consumer, whereas the information that is required to be sent to the consumer should therefore be determined, whatever the means of communication used; whereas the information supplied must also comply with the other relevant Community rules, in particular those in Council Directive 84/450/EEC of 10 September 1984 relating to the approximation of the laws, regulations and administrative provisions of the Member States concerning misleading advertising; whereas, if exceptions are made to the obligation to provide information, it is up to the consumer, on a discretionary basis, to request certain basic information such as the identity of the supplier, the main characteristics of the goods or services and their price;

(12) Whereas in the case of communication by telephone it is appropriate that the consumer receive enough information at the beginning of the conversation to decide whether or not to continue;

(13) Whereas information disseminated by certain electronic technologies is often ephemeral in nature insofar as it is not received on a permanent medium; whereas the consumer must therefore receive written notice in good time of the information necessary for proper performance of the contract;

(14) Whereas the consumer is not able actually to see the product or ascertain the nature of the service provided before concluding the contract; whereas provision should be made, unless otherwise specified in this Directive, for a right of withdrawal from the contract; whereas, if this right is to be more than formal, the costs, if any, borne by the consumer when exercising the right of withdrawal must be limited to the direct costs for returning the goods; whereas this right of withdrawal shall be without prejudice to the consumer's rights under national laws, with particular regard to the receipt of damaged products and services or of products and services not corresponding to the description given in the offer of such products or services; whereas it is for the Member States to determine the other conditions and arrangements following exercise of the right of withdrawal;

(15) Whereas it is also necessary to prescribe a time limit for performance of the contract if this is not specified at the time of ordering,

(16) Whereas the promotional technique involving the dispatch of a product or the provision of a service to the consumer in return for payment without a prior request from, or the explicit agreement of, the consumer cannot be permitted, unless a substitute product or service is involved;

(17) Whereas the principles set out in Articles 8 and 10 of the European Convention for the Protection of Human Rights and Fundamental Freedoms of 4 November 1950 apply; whereas the consumer's right to privacy, particularly as regards freedom from certain particularly intrusive means of communication, should be recognised; whereas specific limits on the use of such means should therefore be stipulated; whereas Member States should take appropriate measures to protect effectively those consumers, who do not wish to be contacted through certain means of communication, against such contacts, without prejudice to the particular safeguards available to the consumer under Community legislation concerning the protection of personal data and privacy;

(18) Whereas it is important for the minimum binding rules contained in this Directive to be supplemented where appropriate by voluntary arrangements among the traders concerned, in line with Commission recommendation 92/295/EEC of 7 April 1992 on codes of practice for the protection of consumers in respect of contracts negotiated at a distance;

(19) Whereas in the interest of optimum consumer protection it is important for consumers to be satisfactorily informed of the provisions of this Directive and of codes of practice that may exist in this field;

(20) Whereas non-compliance with this Directive may harm not only consumers but also competitors; whereas provisions may therefore be laid down enabling public bodies or their representatives, or consumer organisations which, under national legislation, have a legitimate interest in consumer protection, or professional organisations which have a legitimate interest in taking action, to monitor the application thereof;

(21) Whereas it is important, with a view to consumer protection, to address the question of cross-border complaints as soon as this is feasible; whereas the Commission published on 14 February 1996 a plan of action on consumer access to justice and the settlement of consumer disputes in the internal market; whereas that plan of action includes specific initiatives to promote out-of-court procedures; whereas objective criteria (Annex II) are suggested to ensure the reliability of those procedures and provision is made for the use of standardised claims forms (Annex III);

(22) Whereas in the use of new technologies the consumer is not in control of the means of communication used; whereas it is therefore necessary to provide that the burden of proof may be on the supplier;

(23) Whereas there is a risk that, in certain cases, the consumer may be deprived of protection under this Directive through the designation of the law of a non-member country as the law applicable to the contract; whereas provisions should therefore be included in this Directive to avert that risk;

(24) Whereas a Member State may ban, in the general interest, the marketing on its territory of certain goods and services through distance contracts; whereas that ban must comply with Community rules; whereas there is already provision for such bans, notably with regard to medicinal products, under Council Directive 89/552/EEC of 3 October 1989 on the co-ordination of certain provisions laid down by law, regulation or administrative action in Member States concerning the pursuit of television broadcasting activities and Council Directive 92/28/EEC of 31 March 1992 on the advertising of medicinal products for human use,

HAVE ADOPTED THIS DIRECTIVE:

*Article 1*

*Object*

The object of this Directive is to approximate the laws, regulations and administrative provisions of the Member States concerning distance contracts between consumers and suppliers.

*Article 2*

*Definitions*

For the purposes of this Directive:

(1) 'distance contract' means any contract concerning goods or services concluded between a supplier and a consumer under an organised distance sales or service-provision scheme run by the supplier, who, for the purpose of the contract, makes exclusive use of one or more means of distance communication up to and including the moment at which the contract is concluded;

(2) 'consumer' means any natural person who, in contracts covered by this Directive, is acting for purposes which are outside his trade, business or profession;

(3) 'supplier' means any natural or legal person who, in contracts covered by this Directive, is acting in his commercial or professional capacity;

(4) 'means of distance communication' means any means which, without the simultaneous physical presence of the supplier and the consumer, may be used for the conclusion of a contract between those parties. An indicative list of the means covered by this Directive is contained in Annex I;

(5) 'operator of a means of communication' means any public or private natural or legal person whose trade, business or profession involves making one or more means of distance communication available to suppliers.

## Article 3

### Exemptions

1  This Directive shall not apply to contracts:
   - relating to financial services, a non-exhaustive list of which is given in Annex II,
   - concluded by means of automatic vending machines or automated commercial premises,
   - concluded with telecommunications operators through the use of public payphones,
   - concluded for the construction and sale of immovable property or relating to other immovable property rights, except for rental,
   - concluded at an auction.

2  Articles 4, 5, 6 and 7(1) shall not apply:
   - to contracts for the supply of foodstuffs, beverages or other goods intended for everyday consumption supplied to the home of the consumer, to his residence or to his workplace by regular roundsmen,
   - to contracts for the provision of accommodation, transport, catering or leisure services, where the supplier undertakes, when the contract is concluded, to provide these services on a specific date or within a specific period; exceptionally, in the case of outdoor leisure events, the supplier can reserve the right not to apply Article 7(2) in specific circumstances.

## Article 4

### Prior information

1  In good time prior to the conclusion of any distance contract, the consumer shall be provided with the following information:
   (a) the identity of the supplier and, in the case of contracts requiring payment in advance, his address;
   (b) the main characteristics of the goods or services;
   (c) the price of the goods or services including all taxes;
   (d) delivery costs, where appropriate;
   (e) the arrangements for payment, delivery or performance;
   (f) the existence of a right of withdrawal, except in the cases referred to in Article 6(3);

(g) the cost of using the means of distance communication, where it is calculated other than at the basic rate;

(h) the period for which the offer or the price remains valid;

(i) where appropriate, the minimum duration of the contract in the case of contracts for the supply of products or services to be performed permanently or recurrently.

2 The information referred to in paragraph 1, the commercial purpose of which must be made clear, shall be provided in a clear and comprehensible manner in any way appropriate to the means of distance communication used, with due regard, in particular, to the principles of good faith in commercial transactions, and the principles governing the protection of those who are unable, pursuant to the legislation of the Member States, to give their consent, such as minors.

3 Moreover, in the case of telephone communications, the identity of the supplier and the commercial purpose of the call shall be made explicitly clear at the beginning of any conversation with the consumer.

*Article 5*

*Written confirmation of information*

1 The consumer must receive written confirmation or confirmation in another durable medium available and accessible to him of the information referred to in Article 4(1)(a) to (f), in good time during the performance of the contract, and at the latest at the time of delivery where goods not for delivery to third parties are concerned, unless the information has already been given to the consumer prior to conclusion of the contract in writing or on another durable medium available and accessible to him.

In any event the following must be provided:

– written information on the conditions and procedures for exercising the right of withdrawal, within the meaning of Article 6, including the cases referred to in the first indent of Article 6(3),

– the geographical address of the place of business of the supplier to which the consumer may address any complaints,

– information on after-sales services and guarantees which exist,

– the conclusion for cancelling the contract, where it is of unspecified duration or a duration exceeding one year.

2 Paragraph 1 shall not apply to services which are performed through the use of a means of distance communication, where they are supplied on only one occasion and are invoiced by the operator of the means of distance communication. Nevertheless, the consumer must in all cases be able to obtain the geographical address of the place of business of the supplier to which he may address any complaints.

## Article 6

### Right of withdrawal

1    For any distance contract the consumer shall have a period of at least seven working days in which to withdraw from the contract without penalty and without giving any reason. The only charge that may be made to the consumer because of the exercise of his right of withdrawal is the direct cost of returning the goods.

The period for exercise of this right shall begin:

- in the case of goods, from the day of receipt by the consumer where the obligations laid down in Article 5 have been fulfiled,

- in the case of services, from the day of conclusion of the contract or from the day on which the obligations laid down in Article 5 were fulfiled if they are fulfiled after conclusion of the contract, provided that this period does not exceed the three-month period referred to in the following subparagraph.

If the supplier has failed to fulfil the obligations laid down in Article 5, the period shall be three months. The period shall begin:

- in the case of goods, from the day of receipt by the consumer,

- in the case of services, from the day of conclusion of the contract.

If the information referred to in Article 5 is supplied within this three-month period, the seven working day period referred to in the first subparagraph shall begin as from that moment.

2    Where the right of withdrawal has been exercised by the consumer pursuant to this Article, the supplier shall be obliged to reimburse the sums paid by the consumer free of charge. The only charge that may be made to the consumer because of the exercise of his right of withdrawal is the direct cost of returning the goods. Such reimbursement must be carried out as soon as possible and in any case within 30 days.

3    Unless the parties have agreed otherwise, the consumer may not exercise the right of withdrawal provided for in paragraph 1 in respect of contracts:

- for the provision of services if performance has begun, with the consumer's agreement, before the end of the seven working day period referred to in paragraph 1,

- for the supply of goods or services the price of which is dependent on fluctuations in the financial market which cannot be controlled by the supplier,

- for the supply of goods made to the consumer's specifications or clearly personalised or which, by reason of their nature, cannot be resumed or are liable to deteriorate or expire rapidly,

- for the supply of audio or video recordings or computer software which were unsealed by the consumer,

- for the supply of newspapers, periodicals and magazines,

- for gaming and lottery services.

4 The Member States shall make provision in their legislation to ensure that:
- – if the price of goods or services is fully or partly covered by credit granted by the supplier, or
- – if that price is fully or partly covered by credit granted to the consumer by a third party on the basis of an agreement between the third party and the supplier,

the credit agreement shall be cancelled, without any penalty, if the consumer exercises his right to withdraw from the contract in accordance with paragraph 1.

Member States shall determine the detailed rules for cancellation of the credit agreement.

## Article 7

### Performance

1 Unless the parties have agreed otherwise, the supplier must execute the order within a maximum of 30 days from the day following that on which the consumer forwarded his order to the supplier.

2 Where a supplier fails to perform his side of the contract on the grounds that the goods or services ordered are unavailable, the consumer must be informed of this situation and must be able to obtain a refund of any sums he has paid as soon as possible and in any case within 30 days.

3 Nevertheless, Member States may lay down that the supplier may provide the consumer with goods or services of equivalent quality and price provided that this possibility was provided for prior to the conclusion of the contract or in the contract. The consumer shall be informed of this possibility in a clear and comprehensible manner. The cost of returning the goods following exercise of the right of withdrawal shall, in this case, be borne by the supplier, and the consumer must be informed of this. In such cases the supply of goods or services may not be deemed to constitute inertia selling within the meaning of Article 9.

## Article 8

### Payment by card

Member States shall ensure that appropriate measures exist to allow a consumer:
- – to request cancellation of a payment where fraudulent use has been made of his payment card in connection with distance contracts covered by this Directive,
- – in the event of fraudulent use, to be recredited with the sums paid or have them returned.

## Article 9

### Inertia selling

Member States shall take the measures necessary to:

- prohibit the supply of goods or services to a consumer without their being ordered by the consumer beforehand, where such supply involves a demand for payment,
- exempt the consumer from the provision of any consideration in cases of unsolicited supply, the absence of a response not constituting consent.

### Article 10

#### Restrictions on the use of certain means of distance communication

1 Use by a supplier of the following means requires the prior consent of the consumer:
   - automated calling system without human intervention (automatic calling machine),
   - facsimile machine (fax).

2 Member States shall ensure that means of distance communication, other than those referred to in paragraph 1, which allow individual communications may be used only where there is no clear objection from the consumer.

### Article 11

#### Judicial or administrative redress

1 Member States shall ensure that adequate and effective means exist to ensure compliance with this Directive in the interests of consumers.

2 The means referred to in paragraph I shall include provisions whereby one or more of the following bodies, as determined by national law, may take action under national law before the courts or before the competent administrative bodies to ensure that the national provisions for the implementation of this Directive are applied:
   (a) public bodies or their representatives;
   (b) consumer organisations having a legitimate interest in protecting consumers;
   (c) professional organisations having a legitimate interest in acting.

3 (a) Member States may stipulate that the burden of proof concerning the existence of prior information, written confirmation, compliance with timelimits or consumer consent can be placed on the supplier.

   (b) Member States shall take the measures needed to ensure that suppliers and operators of means of communication, where they are able to do so, cease practices which do not comply with measures adopted pursuant to this Directive.

4 Member States may provide for voluntary supervision by self-regulatory bodies of compliance with the provisions of this Directive and recourse to such bodies for the settlement of disputes to be added to the means which Member States must provided to ensure compliance with the provisions of this Directive.

## Article 12

### Binding nature

1   The consumer may not waive the rights conferred on him by the transposition of this Directive into national law.

2   Member States shall take the measures needed to ensure that the consumer does not lose the protection granted by this Directive by virtue of the choice of the law of a non-member country as the law applicable to the contract if the latter has close connection with the territory of one or more Member States.

## Article 13

### Community rules

1   The provisions of this Directive shall apply insofar as there are no particular provisions in rules of Community law governing certain types of distance contracts in their entirety.

2   Where specific Community rules contain provisions governing only certain aspects of the supply of goods or provision of services, those provisions, rather than the provisions of this Directive, shall apply to these specific aspects of the distance contracts.

## Article 14

### Minimal clause

Member States may introduce or maintain, in the area covered by this Directive, more stringent provisions compatible with the Treaty, to ensure a higher level of consumer protection. Such provisions shall, where appropriate, include a ban, in the general interest, on the marketing of certain goods or services, particularly medicinal products, within their territory by means of distance contracts, with due regard for the Treaty.

## Article 15

### Implementation

1   Member States shall bring into force the laws, regulations and administrative provisions necessary to comply with this Directive no later than three years after it enters into force. They shall forthwith inform the Commission thereof.

2   When Member States adopt the measures referred to in paragraph 1, these shall contain a reference to this Directive or shall be accompanied by such reference on the occasion of their official publication. The procedure for such reference shall be laid down by Member States.

3   Member States shall communicate to the Commission the text of the provisions of national law which they adopt in the field governed by this Directive.

4   No later than four years after the entry into force of this Directive the Commission shall submit a report to the European Parliament and the Council on the implementation of this Directive, accompanied if appropriate by a proposal for the revision thereof.

*Article 16*

*Consumer information*

Member States shall take appropriate measures to inform the consumer of the national law transposing this Directive and shall encourage, where appropriate, professional organisations to inform consumers of their codes of practice.

*Article 17*

*Complaints systems*

The Commission shall study the feasibility of establishing effective means to deal with consumers' complaints in respect of distance selling. Within two years after the entry into force of this Directive the Commission shall submit a report to the European Parliament and the Council on the results of the studies, accompanied if appropriate by proposals.

*Article 18*

This Directive shall enter into force on the day of its publication in the Official Journal of the European Communities.

*Article 19*

This Directive is addressed to the Member States.

Done at Brussels, 20 May 1997.

| *For the European Parliament* | *For the Council* |
|:---:|:---:|
| *The President* | *The President* |
| JM GIL-ROBLES | J VAN AARTSEN |

## *ANNEX I*

### Means of communication covered by Article 2(4)

- Unaddressed printed matter
- Addressed printed matter
- Standard letter
- Press advertising with order form
- Catalogue
- Telephone with human intervention
- Telephone without human intervention (automatic calling machine, audiotext)
- Radio
- Videophone (telephone with screen)
- Videotext (microcomputer and television screen) with keyboard or touch screen
- Electronic mail
- Facsimile machine (fax)
- Television (teleshopping).

## *ANNEX II*

### Financial services within the meaning of Article 3(1)

- Investment services
- Insurance and reinsurance operations
- Banking services
- Operations relating to dealings in futures or options.

Such services include in particular:

- investment services referred to in the Annex to Directive 93/22/EEC(1); services of collective investment undertakings,
- services covered by the activities subject to mutual recognition referred to in the Annex to Directive 89/646/EEC(2);
- operations covered by the insurance and reinsurance activities referred to in:
  - Article I of Directive 73/239/EEC,
  - the Annex to Directive 79/267/EEC,
  - Directive 64/225/EEC,
  - Directives 92/49/EEC and 92/96/EEC.

*Statement by the Council and the Parliament re Article 6(1)*

The Council and the Parliament note that the Commission will examine the possibility and desirability of harmonising the method of calculating the cooling-off period under existing consumer-protection legislation, notably Directive 85/577/EEC of 20 December 1985 on the protection of consumers in respect of contracts negotiated away from commercial establishments ('door-to-door sales').

*Statement by the Commission re Article 3(1), first indent*

The Commission recognises the importance of protecting consumers in respect of distance contracts concerning financial services and has published a Green Paper entitled 'Financial services: meeting consumers' expectations'. In the light of reactions to the Green Paper the Commission will examine ways of incorporating consumer protection into the policy on financial services and the possible legislative implications and, if need be, will submit appropriate proposals.

# COMMON POSITION (EC) NO 15/98 (ADVERTISING AND SPONSORSHIP OF TOBACCO PRODUCTS)

*OJ C 91 of 26.3.98, p 34*

*COMMON POSITION (EC) No 15/98*

adopted by the Council on 12 February 1998

with a view to adopting Directive 98/15/EC of the European Parliament and of the Council on the approximation of the laws, regulations and administrative provisions of the Member States relating to the advertising and sponsorship of tobacco products

(98/C 91/03)

THE EUROPEAN PARLIAMENT AND THE COUNCIL OF THE EUROPEAN UNION,

Having regard to the Treaty establishing the European Community, and in particular Articles 57(2), 66 and 100a thereof,

Having regard to the proposal from the Commission,

Having regard to the opinion of the Economic and Social Committee,

Acting in accordance with the procedure laid down in Article 189b of the Treaty,

(1) Whereas there are differences between the Member States' laws, regulations and administrative provisions on the advertising and sponsorship of tobacco products; whereas such advertising and sponsorship transcend the borders of the Member States and the differences in question are likely to give rise to barriers to the movement between Member States of the products which serve as the media for such advertising and sponsorship and to freedom to provide services in this area, as well as distort competition, thereby impeding the functioning of the internal market;

(2) Whereas those barriers should be eliminated and, to this end, the rules relating to the advertising and sponsoring of tobacco products should be approximated, whilst leaving Member States the possibility of introducing, under certain conditions, such requirements as they consider necessary in order to guarantee the protection of the health of individuals;

(3) Whereas, in accordance with Article 100a of the Treaty, the Commission is obliged, in its proposals under paragraph 1 concerning health, safety, environmental protection and consumer protection, to take as a base a high level of protection;

(4) Whereas this Directive must therefore take due account of the health protection of individuals, in particular in relation to young people, for whom advertising plays an important role in tobacco promotion;

(5) Whereas in order to ensure the proper functioning of the internal market the Council adopted, on the basis of Article 100a, Directive 89/622/EEC (4) and

Directive 90/239/EEC concerning the labelling of tobacco products and the maximum tar yield of cigarettes, respectively;

(6) Whereas advertising relating to medicinal products for human use is covered by Directive 92/28/EEC (6); whereas advertising relating to products intended for use in overcoming addiction to tobacco does not fall within the scope of this Directive;

(7) Whereas this Directive will not apply to communications intended exclusively for professionals in the tobacco trade, the presentation of tobacco products offered for sale and the indication of their prices, and, depending on sales structures, advertising directed at purchasers at tobacco sales outlets and the sale of third-country publications which do not satisfy the conditions laid down in this Directive, provided, however, that they comply with Community law and the Community's obligations at international level; whereas it is for the Member States, where necessary, to take appropriate measures in these areas;

(8) Whereas, given the interdependence between the various forms of advertising – oral, written, printed, on radio or television or at the cinema – and in order to prevent any risk of distorting competition or circumventing rules and regulations, this Directive must cover all forms and means of advertising apart from television advertising already covered by Council Directive 89/552/EEC of 3 October 1989 on the co-ordination of certain provisions laid down by law, regulation or administrative action in Member States concerning the pursuit of television broadcasting activities;

(9) Whereas all forms of indirect advertising and sponsorship, and likewise free distribution, have the same effects as direct advertising, and whereas they should, without prejudice to the fundamental principle of freedom of expression, be regulated, including indirect forms of advertising which, while not mentioning the tobacco product directly, the brand names, trade marks, emblems or other distinctive features associated, with tobacco products; whereas, however, Member States may defer application of these provisions to allow time for commercial practices to be adjusted and sponsorship of tobacco products to be replaced by other suitable forms of support;

(10) Whereas, without prejudice to the regulation of the advertising of tobacco products, Member States remain free to allow the continued use, under certain conditions, for the advertising of products or services other than tobacco products, of a brand name which was already in use in good faith both for such products or services and for tobacco products before this Directive entered into force;

(11) Whereas existing sponsorship of events or activities which Member States may continue to authorise for a period of eight years after the entry into force of this Directive ending not later than 1 October 2006 and which will be subject to voluntary restraint measures and decrease of expenditure levels during the transitional period should include all means of achieving the aims of sponsorship as defined in this Directive;

(12) Whereas Member States must take adequate and effective steps to ensure control of the implementation of national measures adopted pursuant to this Directive in compliance with their national legislation,

HAVE ADOPTED THIS DIRECTIVE:

## Article 1

The objective of this Directive is to approximate the laws, regulations and administrative provisions of the Member States relating to the advertising and sponsorship of tobacco products.

## Article 2

For the purposes of this Directive, the following definitions shall apply:

1   'tobacco products': all products intended to be smoked, sniffed, sucked or chewed inasmuch as they are made, even partly, of tobacco;

2   'advertising': any form of commercial communication with the aim or the direct or indirect effect of promoting a tobacco product, including advertising which, while not specifically mentioning the tobacco product, tries to circumvent the advertising ban by using brand names, trademarks, emblems or other distinctive features of tobacco products;

3   'sponsorship': any public or private contribution to an event or activity with the aim or the direct or indirect effect of promoting a tobacco product;

4   'tobacco sales outlet': any place where tobacco products are offered for sale.

## Article 3

1   Without prejudice to Directive 89/552/EEC, all forms of advertising and sponsorship shall be banned in the Community.

2   Paragraph 1 shall not prevent the Member States from allowing a brand name already used in good faith both for tobacco products and for other goods or services traded or offered by a given undertaking or by different undertakings prior to ... to be used for the advertising to those other goods or services.

However, this brand name may not be used except in a manner clearly distinct from that used for the tobacco product, without any further distinguishing mark already used for a tobacco product.

3   (a) Member States shall ensure that no tobacco product bears the brand name, trademark, emblem or other distinctive feature of any other product or service, unless the tobacco product has already been traded under that brand name, trademark, emblem or other distinctive feature on the date referred to in Article 6(1).

(b) The ban provided for in paragraph 1 may not be circumvented, in respect of any product or service placed or offered on the market as from the date laid down in Article 6(1), by the use of brand names, trademarks, emblems and other distinguishing features already used for a tobacco product.

To this end, the brand name, trademark, emblem and any other distinguishing feature of the product or service must be presented in a manner clearly distinct from that used for the tobacco product.

4    Any free distribution having the purpose or the direct or indirect effect of promoting a tobacco product shall be banned.

5    This Directive shall not apply to:

  –   communications intended exclusively for professionals in the tobacco trade,

  –   the presentation of tobacco products offered for sale and the indication of their prices at tobacco sales outlets,

  –   advertising aimed at purchasers in establishments specialising in the sale of tobacco products and on their shop fronts or, in the case of establishments selling a variety of articles or services, at locations reserved for the sale of tobacco products, and at sales outlets which, in Greece, are subject to a special system under which licences are granted for social reasons ('periptera'),

  –   the sale of publications containing advertising for tobacco products which are published and printed in third countries, where those publications are not principally intended for the Community market.

*Article 4*

Member States shall ensure that adequate and effective means exist of ensuring and monitoring the implementation of national measures adopted pursuant to this Directive. These means may include provisions whereby persons or organisations with a legitimate interest under national law in the withdrawal of advertising which is incompatible with this Directive may take legal proceedings against such advertising or bring such advertising to the attention of an administrative body competent to give a ruling on complaints or to institute the appropriate legal proceedings.

*Article 5*

This Directive shall not preclude Member States from laying down, in accordance with the Treaty, such stricter requirements concerning the advertising or sponsorship of tobacco products as they deem necessary to guarantee the health protection of individuals.

*Article 6*

1    Member States shall bring into force the laws, regulations, and administrative provisions necessary to comply with this Directive not later than ... (1). They shall forthwith inform the Commission thereof.

     When Member States adopt these measures, they shall contain a reference to this Directive or shall be accompanied by such reference on the occasion of their official publication. The methods of making such reference shall be laid down by Member States.

2    Member States shall communicate to the Commission the text of the main provisions of domestic law which they adopt in the field covered by this Directive.

3    Member States may defer the implementation of Article 3(1) for:

  –   one year in respect of the press,

  –   two years in respect of sponsorship.

In exceptional cases and for duly justified reasons, Member States may continue to authorise the existing sponsorship of events or activities organised at world level for a further period of three years ending not later than 1 October 2006, provided that:

– the sums devoted to such sponsorship decrease over the transitional period,

– voluntary-restraint measures are introduced in order to reduce the visibility of advertising at the events or activities concerned.

*Article 7*

The Commission shall submit to the European Parliament, the Council and the Economic and Social Committee not later than ..., and subsequently every two years, a report on the implementation of this Directive, with particular reference to the implementation and effects of Article 3(2) and (3) and Article 6(3). Where appropriate, it shall submit proposals for the adaptation of this Directive to suit developments identified in the report. Such adaptation shall not affect the periods provided for in Article 6(3).

*Article 8*

This Directive shall enter into force on the day of its publication in the Official Journal of the European Communities.

*Article 9*

This Directive is addressed to the Member States.

Done at ...

| *For the European Parliament* | *For the Council* |
|:---:|:---:|
| *The President* | *The President* |

## STATEMENT OF THE COUNCIL'S REASONS

### I INTRODUCTION

1 Subsequent to and in place of an initial proposal presented in 1989 in this field, the Commission submitted on 15 May 1991 an amended proposal for a Council directive on the approximation of the laws, regulations and administrative provisions of the Member States relating to the advertising of tobacco products, based on Article 100a of the Treaty establishing the European Community.

2 The European Parliament delivered its opinion on 11 February 1992, and confirmed it on 3 December 1993 under the co-decision procedure provided for in Article 189b of the Treaty.

The Economic and Social Committee delivered its opinion on 23 September 1992.

In the light of the European Parliament's opinion, the Commission presented a new amended proposal on 30 April 1992.

3   On 12 February 1998, the Council adopted its common position in accordance with Article 189b of the Treaty.

## II   OBJECTIVE OF THE PROPOSAL

The proposal aims to approximate the differing national provisions on advertising for tobacco products, taking as a basis a high level of health protection.

The amended proposal submitted by the Commission, which takes into account the discussions held in the Council and the European Parliament on the initial proposal – which provided for limitations on advertising for tobacco products in the press and by means of bills and posters – and the situation regarding national laws in this field and their likely further development, aimed for full harmonisation, by banning such advertising, whatever the form or medium used.

The only exception (possibility of exemption) to this ban related to advertising within tobacco sales outlets having enclosed indoor premises for serving their customers.

The only limitation, introduced following the Parliament's opinion, related under certain conditions to the scope of the ban on indirect advertising in the case of non-tobacco products marketed under the same trademark as tobacco products.

## III   ANALYSIS OF THE COMMON POSITION

1   Overview

Within the framework of the proposed objective, the text adopted by the Council confines itself to amendments which are intended primarily to clarify and circumscribe the field of application and scope and/or which meet operational concerns.

These amendments relate primarily to:

(a)   sponsorship, which is explicitly covered;

(b)   specifications concerning the scope of the ban on indirect advertising by the use of trademarks (and other distinctive features);

(c)   the definition of certain fields or aspects – including the question of sales outlets – to which the Directive does not apply, which may be regulated at national level;

(d)   the special conditions governing the implementation and monitoring of certain provisions, particularly with regard to indirect advertising and sponsorship.

2   Content of the enacting terms

The enacting terms, the structure and components of which have not been substantially amended compared to the proposal, have been adjusted as follows, (Article 1 (new) is merely a formal addition):

(i)   Article 2 (former Article 1) – definitions:

–   the scope of the definition of advertising has not been amended. The more general wording adopted ('any form of communication') covers a broader field and the description 'commercial' is intended merely to specify that communications in the context of purely artistic or journalistic activities do not fall within the scope of advertising,

- a definition of sponsorship, formulated by analogy with that of advertising, is introduced for the purpose of the Directive and the rules relating thereto,
- the definition of tobacco sales outlets, for the purpose of the exceptions provided for in the second and third indents of Article 2(5), is expressed in more general and extensive terms than that proposed.

(ii) Article 3 (former Article 2) – substantive provisions:

(a) in paragraph 1, the general banning of all forms of advertising is extended to sponsorship;

(b) in paragraphs 2 and 3 (former paragraphs 2, 2a and 3), the specifications concerning the scope of the ban on indirect advertising through the use of trademarks (and other distinctive features) are reworded as follows:

- the possibility of limiting the scope of the ban – laid down in paragraph 2 – as regards the use under quite specific conditions of brand names in advertising for products (or services) other than tobacco products, is in line with the objective referred to in paragraph 2a of the proposal,
- paragraph 3(a) meets, in more specific and operational terms, the objective of the provision laid down in paragraph 3 of the proposal, as regards the use for tobacco products of brand names, trademarks (or other distinctive features) already used for other products (or services),
- paragraph 3(b), which refers to any use for any product (or service) of brand names, trademarks (or other distinctive features) associated with tobacco products under conditions likely to circumvent the ban on advertising, is intended to reinforce the scope of the objective of paragraph 2 of the proposal, which has not been incorporated as such as this provision in the given form is considered to be covered by the ban set out in paragraph 1 by reference to the definition of advertising given in Article 2;

(c) the wording of the ban on free distribution laid down in paragraph 4 has been adapted so as to target the objective more effectively by analogy with the definition of advertising;

(d) the fields not covered, which are for the Member States to regulate, if they so wish, are set out in paragraph 5 (new).

This paragraph, covering a broader field, replaces Article 3 of the proposal – which is deleted.

The scope of these exceptions is as follows:

- communications between professionals in the tobacco trade, addressed exclusively to them and not to the general public (first indent); such communications therefore do not fall within the scope of the definition of advertising for the purpose of the Directive,
- with regard to the provisions relating to sales outlets:

- in general, those relating to the presentation of products and to the indication of their price (second indent),
- more specifically, in accordance with the Commission proposal but making greater allowance for the different sales structures in the Member States, advertising aimed at purchasers (third indent),
- the sale of publications originating from third countries (fourth indent) – under conditions designed to prevent distortion; this exception is intended to ensure observance of the right to information which is part of freedom of expression.

(iii) The proposed provisions concerning the means of monitoring implementation (Article 4) and the possibility of laying down stricter requirements (Article 5) at national level were subject only to limited adjustments.

(iv) The provisions of Article 6 concerning the transposition and implementation of the provisions in the Member States have been reworded to allow for the necessary adjustments and adaptations of commercial practice and to take account of economic constraints.

The period specified for transposition is in general three years (paragraph 1), but paragraph 3 provides for the possibility of deferring implementation:

- in respect of the press, for one year,
- in respect of sponsorship in general, for two years, and, under certain conditions and within specific limits for existing sponsorship of events or activities organised at world level, for a further period of three years ending not later than 1 October 2006, the date on which all provisions of the Directive will be applicable.

(v) Provisions are introduced (new Article 7) with a view to appropriate monitoring (through reports and, where appropriate, proposals from the Commission for adaptation) of the implementation and effects of the Directive, particularly with regard to procedures concerning indirect advertising and conditions applicable to sponsorship.

## IV AMENDMENTS PROPOSED BY THE EUROPEAN PARLIAMENT

1    Amendment 10 accepted by the Commission

This amendment – one of the most substantial – which introduces under certain conditions a limitation on the ban referred to in Article 2(2) of the proposal, is the only one incorporated by the Commission in its proposal (Article 2(2a)).

The objective of this amendment is taken into account in the Council's text (Article 3(2)) in a different form and by different means (see point III(2)(ii)(b) above).

These means take particular account of the difficulties in implementing the conditions specified, linked in particular to the method of determining a company's annual turnover of tobacco products (following a full examination, these difficulties appeared to be insurmountable).

The provision adopted by the Council is not moreover a binding rule, but represents for Member States, which are free to impose stricter requirements.

2   Other amendments, not adopted by the Commission

(a) Amendments adopted, in full or in part, by the Council

- Amendment 4 (Article 1, first indent) concerning the mention of sponsorship, which is included under a specific definition, in Article 2(3),

- Amendment 8 (Article 5),

- Amendment 9 (Article 6(2a) (new)), in a more specific and detailed form, in Article 7 of the Council's text.

(b) Amendments not adopted as such by the Council

The Council, in general following the Commission and for the reasons given, has not adopted the other amendments.

## V CONCLUSION

The text of the common position, which is the outcome of full and difficult examination and discussions within the Council, largely meets the objective of the proposal, with adjustments primarily intended to clarify and specify its field of application and operational scope, taking into account the operating objectives of the internal market, the very specific characteristics of the sector and health requirements in a field in which health is an important factor.

# COMMISSION INTERPRETATIVE COMMUNICATION 93/C 334/03 (FREE MOVEMENT OF SERVICES ACROSS FRONTIERS)

*OJ C 334 of 9.12.93, p 3*

Commission interpretative communication concerning the
free movement of services across frontiers

93/C 334/03

## I  Introduction

The service sector is a cornerstone of the internal market. In an area without internal frontiers, not only must growth of the service sector be fostered in order to generate employment, but businesses and consumers must be afforded unhindered access to a broader range of services which are both cheaper, more efficient and more appropriate to their needs.

As the Commission stated in 1985, 'despite the provisions of Articles 59 and 62 of the Treaty, progress on the freedom to provide services across internal frontiers has been much slower than the progress achieved on free movement of goods' because 'firms and individuals have not yet succeeded in taking full advantage of this freedom'.

The Court of Justice recently handed down a series of important judgments concerning the interpretation of the provisions of the EEC Treaty on the free movement of services. This case-law, which the Court itself has felt ought to be summarised and consolidated, gives the Commission useful guidance on how the Treaty's rules should be applied with a view to ensuring the orderly functioning and development of the internal market.

The purpose of this communication is to inform the ordinary citizen about how Article 59 has been interpreted by the Court. It answers the need for transparency of Community rules as required by the Edinburgh European Council in that it facilitates a decentralised and correct application of the Treaty's rules in Member States with a minimum of intervention on the part of the Community authorities. As provided by the White Paper on completing the internal market, the communication will serve as a guide for public authorities as regards their obligations, and for Community citizens as regards the rights they enjoy.

## II  Field of application

Articles 59 and 60 of the Treaty establish the principle of free movement of services. This principle became directly applicable and unconditional on the expiry of the transitional period.

The Court has given a general definition of the obstacles to the free movement of services prohibited by Article 59 *et seq* of the EEC Treaty. These Articles cover cross-border trade in services of a temporary nature, as opposed to the right of establishment.

Where the service is of a 'permanent' nature, the rules on the right of establishment apply (Article 52). On the question of where to draw the dividing line between 'temporary' and 'permanent', the Court has held that the rules on the free movement of services may not be relied upon with a view to circumventing the rules which would be applicable were a person to establish himself in another Member State.

he Court has likewise held that a Member State may not make the provision of services in its territory subject to compliance with all the conditions required for establishment and thereby deprive of all practical effectiveness the provisions of the Treaty whose object is, precisely, to guarantee the freedom to provide services.

On this issue of the temporary nature of a service, the Court has ruled that Articles 59 and 60 of the Treaty cannot be interpreted as meaning that the domestic legislation applicable to nationals of a State which normally covers a 'permanent' activity pursued by persons established in that State may be applied in its entirety and in the same way to activities of a 'temporary' nature pursued by persons established in other Member States.

## III Principles of application

1   The prohibition of restrictions on the free movement of services

the Court's view, the concept of restriction on the free movement of services involves more than just discrimination. Unjustified or disproportionate restrictions are also prohibited even if they apply without distinction to services provided by nationals of the State in question and to those provided by non-nationals.

The Court has thus held that Article 59 requires 'not only the abolition of any discrimination against a person providing services on account of his nationality but also

- the abolition of any restriction on the freedom to provide services imposed on the ground that the person providing a service is established in a Member State other than the one in which the service is provided', and

- 'the abolition of any restriction, even if it applies without distinction to national providers of services and to those of other Member States, when it is liable to prohibit or otherwise impede the activities of a provider of services established in another Member State where he lawfully provides similar services'.

In principle, the expression 'liable to prohibit or otherwise impede' covers any measure which might hinder trade in services between Member States, eg, those which affect the ability of the service provider to provide a service, those which increase the cost of the service, or discourage its provision, and those which prevent potential customers from having recourse to the services of their choice. The freedom to provide services thus protects not only those who provide, but those who receive, services.

2   Exceptions, exemptions and derogations and the limits thereto: necessity and proportionality

That is not to say, however, that all such measures are prohibited outright by Article 59.

It is in the light of the principles of necessity and proportionality that it has to be examined whether a provision of domestic law contains restrictions on freedom to provide services and, if so, whether those restrictions are justified by overriding reasons relating to the public interest.

In its decisions, the Court thus introduces practical criteria for applying these principles, based, *inter alia*, on the specific situation of the service provider (who operates from the country in which he is established), the type of activity concerned (its simplicity) and protection of the recipient of the service (possibility of his suffering loss or damage in the event of non-compliance with the rules of the country in which the service is provided).

Restrictions are compatible with Article 59 only if it is established that:

(a) 'with regard to the activity in question, there are overriding reasons relating to the public interest which justify restrictions on the freedom to provide services'.

On the reasons that may be invoked, the Court draws a clear distinction between discriminatory and non-discriminatory measures.

'National rules which are not applicable to services without discrimination as regards their origin are compatible with Community law only if they can be brought within the scope of an express exemption, such as that contained in Article 56 of the Treaty'. These exemptions relate to public policy, public security or public health.

On the other hand, national rules which are applicable without discrimination may be justified, in the words used by the Court, by a number of other mandatory requirements or overriding reasons in the public interest. In view of the specific nature of certain professional activities, the imposition of specific requirements for the purpose of applying rules governing these types of activity is, therefore, not necessarily incompatible with the Treaty.

Such requirements are primarily those referred to in Article 56, but also those mentioned in other articles of the Treaty; they relate in particular to public morality, the protection of workers and consumers, industrial and commercial property and the protection of national treasures possessing artistic, historic or archeological value.

Other mandatory requirements and legitimate objectives worthy of protection may also qualify, such as professional rules designed to protect the recipients of services, the protection of intellectual property, the protection of workers, the protection of consumers, the taking into account of 'Coherence' in the tax system, 30 *bis* professional ethics, good standing and independence, the operation of the judicial system, the turning to account of the historical heritage and the widest possible dissemination of knowledge of a country's historical, artistic and cultural heritage.

On the other hand, 'economic aims cannot constitute grounds of public policy within the meaning of Article 56'. The same applies to considerations of an administrative nature aimed, for example, at making it easier for the authorities of the State in which the service is provided to perform their task. Such considerations 'cannot justify derogation by a Member State from the rules of Community law. That principle applies with even greater force where the derogation in question amounts to preventing the exercise of one of the fundamental freedoms guaranteed by the Treaty';

(b) 'the public interest is not already protected by the rules of the state of establishment'.

Admittedly, Member States have the right and indeed the duty to safeguard the public interest within their territory. This does not mean, however, that 'all national legislation applicable to nationals of the State and usually applied to the permanent activities of persons established therein may be similarly applied in their entirety to the temporary activities of persons who are established in other Member States'.

It should be emphasised that the conditions laid down by the Member State in which the service is provided 'may not duplicate equivalent statutory conditions which have already been satisfied in the State in which the undertaking is established' and that 'the supervisory authority of the State in which the service is provided must take into account supervision and verifications which have already been carried out in the Member State [sic] of establishment'.

Consequently, restriction on the freedom to provide services 'come within the scope of Article 59 if the application of the national legislation to foreign persons providing services is not justified by overriding reasons relating to the public interest or if the requirements embodied in that legislation are already satisfied by the rules imposed on those persons in the Member State in which they are established'; and

(c) 'the same result cannot be obtained by less restrictive rules'.

The very broad scope of the definitions of overriding reasons or mandatory requirements is counter-balanced by the fact that a national restriction on the free movement of services must not merely be imposed for such a reason: it must furthermore be 'proportionate' and 'justified', ie indispensable, objectively necessary, an appropriate means of attaining the objective and non-excessive.

The Court had held that a restriction is excessive where the requirements of the State in which the service is provided go beyond what is necessary for attaining the legitimate objectives. The restriction is excessive, for instance, if the same result can be obtained by less restrictive rules or rules that hinder trade less.

## IV Conclusions

Application of the principles established by the Court, which confirm the standpoints taken by the Commission, means that a Member State cannot normally prohibit the provision in its territory, of a service lawfully in another Member State, even if the conditions in which it is provided are different in the country where the service provider is established.

In so far as the service in question suitably and satisfactorily fulfils the legitimate objective pursued by its own rules (public safety, public policy, etc), a Member State 'cannot justify prohibiting the provision of a service in its territory by claiming that the way it fulfils the objective is different from that imposed on domestic service providers or service providers established in that Member State.

Any ban or restriction on the activities of a service provider established in another Member State must therefore be justified and not excessive.

# GREEN PAPER COM (96) 192 FINAL (COMMERCIAL COMMUNICATIONS IN THE INTERNAL MARKET)

Extracts from the Working Document (Part 1.E and Part 2)

Contents

*Part 1*

[...]

*A    Regulatory Reaction Tables: The Commercial Communications 'Chain Reaction'*

The following tables draw on the previous analysis to describe the potential reactions that could occur in the event of a regulatory restriction on commercial communications.

*TABLE 1*

Table 1 below demonstrates how users could react to a restriction, given their own strategies (drawn from Part A above) and those of suppliers (see Section B). The table considers the situation for the six types of branding sectors developed in Part A and considers, for each relevant type of commercial communications, the effect, in terms of users reactions to a restriction on its use. Note that, in the event that the restriction limits a particular type of user from using certain forms of commercial communications, the table can again be used to determine what he/she is most likely to respond with in terms of altering his/her commercial communications or marketing mix. Reactions are ranked in order of priority so the most likely reaction is listed first. Blank cells indicate that that particular type of commercial communications is unlikely to be relied upon to any significant degree by the relevant branding sector type. Finally, for potential restrictions on new on-line forms of commercial communications, given that these will resemble direct marketing and sales promotions, these two categories of commercial communications should be considered when examining the potential effect of the restriction.

TABLE 1
Potential reactions of users in the case of a regulatory restriction.

| Type of commercial communication affected by the restriction | BRANDING TYPE OF SECTOR (see Section A of text) | | | | | |
|---|---|---|---|---|---|---|
| | Type 1 | Type 2 | Type 3 | Type 4 | Type 5 | Type 6 |
| | Homogeneous product/service market where price competition is the norm | Homogeneous product/service market but with relatively little price competition | Heterogeneous consumer product/service markets with minor qualitative competition | Heterogeneous consumer product/service market with significant qualitative competition | Heterogeneous business product/service markets with minor qualitative competition | Heterogeneous business product/service markets with significant qualitative competition |
| Television advertising | | | Increase other types of advertising, increase TV sponsorship, increase other sponsorship, increase public relations, invest more in distribution contracts, invest less in qualitative improvements. Branded goods manufacturer could decide only to provide to own label retail sector. Increase price related sales promotions, decrease price | Increase other types of advertising notably magazine and weeklies, increase direct marketing, increase sponsorship (non-mass media related), increase public relations, increase non-price related sales promotions. Increase investment in distribution | Increase other types of advertising used by the sector, increase direct marketing, increase sponsorship (non-mass media related), increase public relations, increase non-price related sales promotions, invest more in distribution contracts. Invest less in qualitative improvements | |
| Radio advertising | | Increase price related sales promotions, decrease price. Invest more in distribution contracts, increase local press advertising, increase Press (dailies) advertising. Stop branding and move into supplying retailers own label | (Same as cell immediately above with advertising switch focused on local press advertising and increase in radio rather than TV sponsorship) | (Same as cell immediately above with advertising switch focused on local press advertising and increase in radio rather than TV sponsorship) | (Same as cell immediately above with advertising switch focused on local press advertising) | |

**TABLE 1 (continued)**

**Potential reactions of users in the case of a regulatory restriction.**

| Type of commercial communication affected by the restriction | TYPE OF USER | | | | | |
|---|---|---|---|---|---|---|
| | Type 1 | Type 2 | Type 3 | Type 4 | Type 5 | Type 6 |
| Press advertising | | Increase radio advertising, increase local press advertising, increase price related sales promotions, decrease price. Move into own label, invest more in distribution contracts | (Same as cell immediately above with advertising switch focused on radio advertising | (Same as cell immediately above with advertising witch focused on radio advertising | (Same as cell immediately above with advertising witch focused on radio advertising | |
| Magazine and weekly press advertising | (Specialised press) Decrease price, invest more in distribution contracts, increase direct marketing, increase local press advertising, increase PR | | (Same as cell immediately above with advertising switch focused on niche TV channel advertising | (Same as cell immediately above with advertising switch focused on niche TV channel advertising | (Same as cell immediately above with advertising switch focused on niche TV channel advertising). Increase investment in distribution | Increase direct marketing, increase public relations |
| Local press advertising | Increase price related sales promotions, decrease price. Invest more in distribution contracts, increase direct marketing, increase magazine (specialised press) advertising, increase PR | Increase radio advertising, increase Press (dailies) advertising, increase price related sales promotions, decrease price. Move into own label, invest more in distribution contracts | Invest more in distribution contracts, increase radio advertising, increase non-price related sales promotions, move into own label, increase price related sales promotions, decrease price | | | |
| Direct marketing (all forms) | Increase price related sales promotions, decrease price. Invest more in distribution contracts, increase magazine (specialised press) advertising, increase local press advertising, increase PR | | | | | |

TABLE 1 (continued)

Potential reactions of users in the case of a regulatory restriction.

| Type of commercial communication affected by the restriction | TYPE OF USER | | | | | |
|---|---|---|---|---|---|---|
| | Type 1 | Type 2 | Type 3 | Type 4 | Type 5 | Type 6 |
| Price related sales promotion | Decrease price, invest more in distribution contracts, increase magazine (specialised press) advertising, increase PR | Decrease price, increase radio, move into own label, invest more in distribution contracts decrease daily and local press advertising (because often associated with the price promotion) | Increase other types of advertising, increase non-price related sales promotions, invest more in distribution contracts. | | Increase other types of advertising, increase non-price related sales promotions, incest more in distribution contracts | |
| Other types of sales promotions | | | Increase other types of advertising, invest more in distribution contracts move into own label, increase price relate sales promotions, decrease price | Increase other types of advertising used by this sector, increase sponsorship (non-mass media related), increase public relations. Increase investment in distribution | Increase advertising, increase sponsorship (non-mass media related), increase public relations, invest more in distribution contracts | |
| Sponsorship (major cultural and sporting events covered by the mass media) | | | Increase non-price related sales promotions increase other types of advertising, try and increase non-sponsorship related public relations | | | |
| Sponsorship of other events | | | | Increase other types of advertising used by this sector, decrease public relations. Increase investment in distribution | Increase other types of advertising, decrease public relations | |
| Public relations | Increase price sales promotions, decrease price. increase advertising noted above invest more in distribution contracts | Increase price sales promotions, decrease price. increase local and daily press advertising, increase radio advertising, invest more in distribution contracts | Invest in forms of advertising remarked on above and non-price related promotions, invest more in distribution contracts, decrease sponsorship | Decrease sponsorship, increase other types of advertising used, increased non-price promotions. Increase investment in distribution | Decrease sponsorship, invest more in distribution contracts | Increase magazine (specialised press) advertising, increase direct marketing |

*TABLE 2*

Table 2 draws on part B and partially on part C above to summarise the links between different forms of commercial communication services that would have to be accounted for when evaluating potential impacts on suppliers of a regulatory initiative. These spill-over effects into other services should be accounted for in the reaction chain. Furthermore, if they are sufficiently large to affect the provision of the other forms of commercial communications then the consequences for carriers and users should also be followed through via Table 1 and Table 3.

For Internal Market measures, the third column in Table 2 summarises the key economies of scale and scope that could be restricted as a consequence of regulatory divergences across the Member States in the commercial communication services directly or indirectly (through the links identified in the second column) impacted upon by the relevant measure. Where these economies of scale and scope are affected, service provision will become relatively more expensive hence users may be forced to use less efficient marketing mixes. In the case of new fragmentation, the alterations in user strategies could then be checked for in Table 1 by checking for which substitutions they would make for the adversely effected type of commercial communications.

## TABLE 2

**Links between forms of Commercial Communications and potential scale economies in Commercial Communication services that could suffer from a fragmented Internal Market**

| Type of Commercial Communications services | | Link with other forms of Commercial Communication | Areas within the provision of the service where economies of scale and scope could exist and which could suffer (due to increases in average costs) due to fragmentation of the Internal Market |
|---|---|---|---|
| Advertising<br><br>Direct Marketing<br><br>Sponsorship<br><br>Public Relations | TV | Major sponsorship events/ Print advertising/Other advertising | Media Research and planning. Media buying. Scope economies in advertising agencies (same visuals, ie, creative ideas) used in more than one Member State |
| | Print/outdoor | TV advertising/DM | [As above] |
| | Radio | Print advertising/DM | Media Research and planning. Media buying |
| | Postal | Print and radio advertising. Sales promotions | List brokerage services (eg, pan-European profiled databases). Same visual design used across Member States. Same promotions and concessionary gifts used across Member States. Bulk packaging/postal rates, etc |
| | Mail Order | Sales promotions. Direct marketing | List brokerage services (eg, pan-European profiled databases). Same promotions and concessionary gifts used across Member States. Same visual design used across Member States. Bulk packaging/postal rates |
| | Telematic | Print and Radio advertising | List brokerage services (eg, pan-European profiled databases). Economies of scale in using the same approach across the Community |
| | Major (mass media coverage) events | TV, Press and Radio advertising PR and non-price sales promotions | Greater efficiency through pan-European media coverage of the event |
| | More targeted events | All the above except TV | |
| | TV/Radio | TV/Radio advertising/non-price related promotions | Same credits/promotions being used across all the Member States where programme sold/transmitted |
| All other Commercial Communications but notably sales promotions | Price promotions | Direct marketing, Press and Radio advertising | Common planning of a promotional campaign across various Member States. Same offer (discount) made over more than one market. Common trans-border communications campaign around the offer |
| | Other promotions | Direct marketing, Press advertising | Same as cell above but with same gift or competition being made available across all Member States |

*TABLE 3*

Table 3 summarises, on the basis of Sections B and C above, the potential reactions to a regulatory restriction by carriers of commercial communications. Both the reaction and the medium term effects of this reaction are listed in the Table. Again, in each case there could be spill-over effects into the service suppliers and the user strategies that should be checked for by using Tables 1 and 2.

As the text in Section C has demonstrated, the importance of commercial communication revenues for carriers cannot be underestimated. For this reason, this table should always be applied wherever the initial impact of the measure might be.

**TABLE 3**

**Potential reactions by carriers**

| Type of carrier | Type of restriction and direct effect | Potential short term reaction to restriction | Potential medium term effects |
|---|---|---|---|
| TV channel/ Radio channel | *Tightening of restrictions on advertising air-time.* TV/radio station loses air time and therefore revenue. | TV/radio station will seek to increase advertising rates, sponsorship possibilities (possibly both) and, where the restriction is very tight (for subscription TV channels) viewers subscriptions. | Likely to reduce potential market for commercial TV/radio as clients are dissuaded by higher rates from using the medium, high TV subscription fees (where applicable) restrict viewer demand and cost cutting in production due to lost revenues lead to lower level programme quality. These effects become far more amplified for a theme channel whose theme is attractive to the restricted advertiser category (may well resemble effect described immediately below). |
| | *Advertising content restriction.* TV/radio station suffers from diminished or lost revenues from the relevant advertiser type/category. | TV/radio station may regain some of revenue if the advertiser is allowed and wishes to use TV/radio sponsorship. If this is not possible, TV/radio station tries to substitute new accounts (users). | If TV/radio station cannot generate new business on existing schedule, it may change its schedule to make it more attractive to new users ( advertisers). Thus, programme sales/production of types that were attractive to the restricted advertisers might suffer. Finally, if all else fails, the TV/radio station may simply try to increase its advertising rate card to compensate for the lost revenue. This will clearly increase the commercial communication costs of all TV/radio advertisers or cause some to leave the media and thus incite second round effects. |

## TABLE 3 (continued)

### Potential reactions of carriers

| Type of carrier | Type of restriction and direct effect | Potential short term reaction to restriction | Potential medium term effects |
|---|---|---|---|
| | *Sponsorship by certain categories of advertisers limited.* Production arm of TV station or independent programme producers lose a source of finance. | If allowed, TV stations will try and get the sponsors to buy commercial airtime. | Lost source of programme finance may lead to reduction in such programming as other programmes that can be sponsored by other interests are substituted. |
| | *Sponsorship limited as a rule or indirectly because overtly strict rules on credits etc.* | TV stations lose a source of revenue aimed and at production and independent producers also suffer from reduced up front cash flow. | Lost potential revenue could be made up by increasing commercial airtime and/or rates or (where applicable) subscription levels. This obviously could dissuade certain smaller advertisers to use TV and might also reduce the reach of subscription channels. If this compensation cannot be achieved then the restriction on potential revenue implies that the TV market will be less developed than it otherwise would be. |
| Press | *Advertising content restrictions.* Same as for television. | Same as for television/radio but obviously without possibility of switching to sponsorship. | Possibility of changing newspapers content to attract new advertisers is very limited hence cover price may have to be increased to cover lost revenues but this obviously reduces circulation and can threaten the existence of the title. |
| Magazines | " | Same as for a newspaper but given that magazines already tend to be targeted at niches they have a far narrower range of advertisers than the Press to attract. It follows that the consequences are likely to be far worse for magazines than newspapers. | Due to restricted possibilities of substitution of new advertising, the need to increase cover prices may be far more likely in this case then the Press. Similarly the threat to the survival of the relevant title is proportionately greater. |
| Outdoor | Advertising content restrictions. Billboard operators lose revenue from restricted clients. | Similar to Press/Magazine situation. | Similar to Press/Magazine situation. |
| Post | Restrictions on direct marketing. Loss of bulk mailings to Postal services. | Postal service is a passive operator in this respect. Only a significant reduction in business through very strong restrictions are likely to force it to change its rate structure. | In so far as business to business mail cross-subsidises private mailing services, the reduction in the former may mean that the rates of the latter are kept higher than they would otherwise need to be. |

## TABLE 3 (continued)

### Potential reactions of carriers

| Type of carrier | Type of restriction and direct effect | Potential short term reaction to restriction | Potential medium term effects |
|---|---|---|---|
| Telemarketing (including fax marketing). | General restrictions on cold-calling etc. Loss of revenue to telephone operators although this is unlikely to represent much of their business. | Telephone companies unlikely to adjust rates as a consequence of reduction in marginal part of their total business. | No effect. |
| Video text, Teleshopping, Telemarketing and new on-line interactive services. | Content or horizontal restrictions. All the relevant service operators lose revenues from these sources. | Dedicated TV shopping channels or generalist channels carrying teleshopping programmes may try and substitute the teleshopping clients with airtime but this is unlikely to be successful given that teleshopping is currently scheduled during cheap low audience times. New on-line service providers loose business to traditional retail postal direct marketing and Press advertising. It should also be noted that these service combine commercial communications with distribution and therefore that overt restrictions on them will work in favour of the traditional retail sector. | Restrictions in these areas may threaten the development of existing services such as teleshopping. As for new services, if clients cannot 'test' their potential viability without having to be constrained by an overtly restrictive regulatory framework on such commercial communication channels then the establishment of such services might be threatened. |
| Major events | Restrictions on major events carrying certain forms of sponsorship or restrictions on the display of sponsorship credits at such events. Events organisers lose revenues from sponsors not only for display sites at the event but also because of lost coverage by mass media covering the event. | Events organisers may seek new sponsors interested in the same levels of high coverage offered by sponsorship of the event. If this is not possible, they may seek more money for broadcasting rights to compensate for the lost sponsorship revenues. | Particularly, in the area of sports where professional sports are becoming increasingly expensive, the potential loss of revenue from sponsorship may force the sports federations to increase broadcasting rights which are fast becoming the major source of their revenue. This may mean that the broadcasting of such events which would need to be maximised to maximise sponsorship revenues will be minimised to extract maximum amounts for exclusive TV rights. This may also go hand in hand with increased entrance charges at the events. |

## TABLE 3 (continued)

### Potential reactions of carriers

| Type of carrier | Type of restriction and direct effect | Potential short term reaction to restriction | Potential medium term effects |
|---|---|---|---|
| Specific events | As above. | Compensation for lost sponsorship revenues will again be sought by seeking new sponsors. However, where this is not possible, the only solution may be to increase entrance charges unless the event is sufficiently interesting to attract TV coverage in which case the increase of broadcasting rights may still remain a solution. For such events this possibility is rare and sponsorship revenues are far more important than in the previous category. | Small, non televised cultural and sporting events could be threatened by such limitations. In the sports field the grass-roots sports clubs may be subsidised by their more successful professional counterparts but if sponsorship restrictions are also affecting the latter then it may well mean that such associations will have to cease operating. |

*TABLE 4*

From the analysis above and Tables 1, 2 and 3, one can make a link between the potential reactions of each of the three types of operators in the commercial communications chain (suppliers, users and carriers) and public interest objectives that could be affected by these. In this manner, the spill-over effects of a measure into other public interest objectives as well as counterproductive effects can be accounted for in determining its proportionality and/or its coherence with other measures (see the assessment methodology explained in Part IV of the Green Paper).

Through using Tables 1, 2 and 3, effects of the measure in terms of strategic reactions or loss of economies of scale, etc, can be derived. Table 4 can then be used as a general guide to determine which general interest objectives will, in turn, be impacted upon by these alterations.

## TABLE 4

### Potential objective impact checklist

| Objective | Effects needing to be considered following strategic changes stimulated by a change to the European regulatory framework of commercial communications |
|---|---|
| Internal market (ensuring the principles of free movement) | Restriction on cross-border supply of commercial communication services. Restriction on cross-border supply of users products or services. Restriction on trans-border provision of carriers services. Effect on economies of scale/synergies within the commercial communications business resulting form the possibility to provide them on a trans-border basis. Effect on efficiency/economies of scale/synergies in users strategies. Effect on scale effects arising form the possibility of 'carriers' benefiting form cross-border commercial communications. |
| Consumer protection | Effect of changes of substituted forms of commercial communications on the consumer. Effect of changes in prices of promoted goods and services on the consumer. Effect of changes in the distribution of the promoted product or the service on the consumer. Effect of the changes in the price/availability to viewers or consumers of the carriers. |
| Safeguarding of competition | Effect on the balance of power between retailers and manufacturers using the commercial communications. Effect on the balance of power between traded branded goods and services and national unbranded products and services. |
| Protection of minors | Effect on minors of resulting changes in the commercial communications mix. Effect of minors of changes in prices of the users goods and services. Effect on minors of changes in the distribution of the products and services of the user. Effect on minors of the changes in programmes or events supported by the commercial communications. |
| Protection of public health | As for protection of minors. |
| Protection of pluralism | Effect on different media caused by losses of commercial communications revenues. Effect on radio and TV programme production caused by restrictions on advertising or sponsorship. |
| Protection of culture | Affect on cultural events funding caused by losses of sponsorship revenues. Note also that effects on major events may influence funding of non sponsored local grass roots activities. |
| Promotion of sports | Same as for cultural policy. |
| Protection of professional ethics | Effects on efficiency of provision and potential scale and competition effects. |
| Safeguarding of industrial competitiveness | Effects on costs and limitations in scale effects at the European level for both suppliers and users. |

*Part 2*

*National Regulatory Tables*

The tables below take each general category of national measure and assess under which public interest requirement of Community Law the national objective leading to the measure could be classified.

The measures taken by the Member States in this area follow a wide range of national policy objectives. This arises partly from the differing sources of national law, namely: unfair competition law, consumer protection law, and specific legislation for the protection of the wider public interest. The disparity of aims pursued by the Member States reflects, in part, their differing emphasis on these sources of national law but also reflects their differing political priorities.

The 'public interest objectives' used for these tables have been laid down by the EC Treaty or determined by the European Court of Justice in its case law. Restrictive measures may be justified by reference to one of these objectives (subject to proportionality).

The various national measures have been carefully examined to clearly identify the public interest objectives they could seek to protect. This scrutiny of the national measures demonstrates that most of these cross-reference to more than one public interest objective, and that measures relating to the same activity cross-reference to different public interest objectives from one Member State to another.

A '+' indicates that the national law specifically makes reference to the relevant public interest objective whereas a '?' indicates that this public interest objective is implied by the Member State's legislation.

I   Austria

| Categories of National Measures | General Interest Objections | | | | | | | | | | |
|---|---|---|---|---|---|---|---|---|---|---|---|
| | Privacy | Protection of minors | Public morality | Public health | Consumer protection | Protection of IPR | Professional ethics | Protection of national treasures | Dissemination of culture | Professional rules protecting recipients of services | Pluralism |
| Unauthorised use of trademarks and qualifiers | | | | | | + | | | | | |
| Misleading advertising | | | | | + | | | | | | |
| Misleading claims | | | | | + | | | | | | |
| Price advertising; discounts etc | | | | | + | | | | | | |
| Intrusive advertising coldcalling/telephone advertising | | | ? | | ? | | | | | | |
| Intrusive advertising: letterbox/mail marketing | | ? | | | + | | | | | | |
| Intrusive advertising: promotional gifts/concessionary offers | | | | | + | | | | | | |
| Intrusive advertising: prize competitions, draws and lotteries | | | | | ? | | | | | | |
| General media restrictions | | ? | ? | ? | ? | | | | | ? | |
| General sponsorship restrictions | | ? | ? | ? | ? | | | | | ? | |
| Product restrictions re commercial communications re tobacco | | ? | | ? | | | | | | | |
| Product restrictions re commercial communications for alcoholic beverages | | ? | | ? | + | | | | | | |
| Product restrictions re commercial communications to children | | | | | + | | | | | | |
| Product restrictions re commercial communications re food products | | | | ? | + | | | | | | |
| Product restrictions re commercial communications re pharmaceuticals | | | | ? | ? | | | | | | |
| Product restrictions re commercial communications re financial services | | | | | ? | | | | | | |
| Societal value | | | ? | ? | | ? | | | | | |

## II   Belgium

| Categories of National Measures | General Interest Objections | | | | | | | | | | |
|---|---|---|---|---|---|---|---|---|---|---|---|
| | Privacy | Protection of minors | Public morality | Public health | Consumer protection | Protection of IPR | Professional ethics | Protection of national treasures | Dissemination of culture | Professional rules protecting recipients of services | Pluralism |
| Unauthorised use of trademarks and qualifiers | | | | | ? | + | | | | | |
| Misleading advertising | | | | | + | + | | | | | |
| Misleading claims | | | | | + | + | | | | | |
| Price advertising: discounts etc | | | | | + | ? | | | | | |
| Intrusive advertising coldcalling/telephone advertising | | | | | + | ? | | | | | |
| Intrusive advertising: letterbox/mail marketing | | | | | + | ? | | | | | |
| Intrusive advertising: promotional gifts/concessionary offers | | | | | + | ? | | | | | |
| Intrusive advertising: prize competitions, draws and lotteries | | | | | + | ? | | | | | |
| General media restrictions | | | | | ? | | | | | | ? |
| General sponsorship restrictions | | | | | ? | ? | | | | | |
| Product restrictions re commercial communications re tobacco | | ? | | + | | | | | | | |
| Product restrictions re commercial communications for alcoholic beverages | | + | | + | | | | | | | |
| Product restrictions re commercial communications to children | | ? | | ? | | | | | | | |
| Product restrictions re commercial communications re food products | | | | + | + | + | | | | | |
| Product restrictions re commercial communications re pharmaceuticals | | + | | | + | ? | | | | | |
| Product restrictions re commercial communications re financial services | | | | | ? | | | | | | |
| Societal value | | | ? | | ? | | | | | | |

## III Denmark

| Categories of National Measures | General Interest Objections | | | | | | | | | | |
|---|---|---|---|---|---|---|---|---|---|---|---|
| | Privacy | Protection of minors | Public morality | Public health | Consumer protection | Protection of IPR | Professional ethics | Protection of national treasures | Dissemination of culture | Professional rules protecting recipients of services | Pluralism |
| Unauthorised use of trademarks and qualifiers | | | | | ? | + | | | | | |
| Misleading advertising | | | | | + | ? | | | | | |
| Misleading claims | | | | | + | ? | | | | | |
| Price advertising; discounts etc | | | | | + | ? | | | | | |
| Intrusive advertising coldcalling/telephone advertising | ? | | | | + | ? | | | | | |
| Intrusive advertising: letterbox/mail marketing | ? | | | | + | ? | | | | | |
| Intrusive advertising: promotional gifts/concessionary offers | | | | | + | ? | | | | | |
| Intrusive advertising: prize competitions, draws and lotteries | | | | | + | ? | | | | | |
| General media restrictions | | ? | | ? | ? | ? | | | | | ? |
| General sponsorship restrictions | | | | ? | | | | | | | ? |
| Product restrictions re commercial communications re tobacco | | ? | | ? | ? | | | | | | |
| Product restrictions re commercial communications for alcoholic beverages | | ? | | ? | ? | | | | | | |
| Product restrictions re commercial communications to children | | ? | | ? | | | | | | | |
| Product restrictions re commercial communications re food products | | | | + | + | | | | | | |
| Product restrictions re commercial communications re pharmaceuticals | | | | + | + | | | | | | |
| Product restrictions re commercial communications re financial services | | | | | | | | | | | |
| Societal value | | | | | ? | | | | | | |

**IV    Finland**

| Categories of National Measures | General Interest Objections | | | | | | | | | | |
|---|---|---|---|---|---|---|---|---|---|---|---|
| | Privacy | Protection of minors | Public morality | Public health | Consumer protection | Protection of IPR | Professional ethics | Protection of national treasures | Dissemination of culture | Professional rules protecting recipients of services | Pluralism |
| Unauthorised use of trademarks and qualifiers | | | | | | + | | | | | |
| Misleading advertising | | | | | + | ? | + | | | | |
| Misleading claims | | | | | + | ? | + | | | | |
| Price advertising: discounts etc | | | | | + | ? | + | | | | |
| Intrusive advertising: coldcalling/telephone advertising | | | | | | | | | | | |
| Intrusive advertising: letterbox/mail marketing | | | | | + | ? | ? | | | | |
| Intrusive advertising: promotional gifts/concessionary offers | | | | | + | ? | ? | | | | |
| Intrusive advertising: prize competitions, draws and lotteries | | | | | + | ? | + | | | | |
| General media restrictions | | ? | | ? | + | | + | | | | ? |
| General sponsorship restrictions | | | | | + | | | | | | |
| Product restrictions re commercial communications re tobacco | | ? | | + | | | | | | | |
| Product restrictions re commercial communications for alcoholic beverages | | ? | | + | | | | | | | |
| Product restrictions re commercial communications to children | | ? | | | | | | | | | |
| Product restrictions re commercial communications re food products | | | | ? | ? | | | | | | |
| Product restrictions re commercial communications re pharmaceuticals | | | | ? | + | | | | | | |
| Product restrictions re commercial communications re financial services | | | | | | | | | | | |
| Societal value | | | ? | | | | | | | | |

## V France

### Categories of National Measures

| Categories of National Measures | General Interest Objections | | | | | | | | | | |
|---|---|---|---|---|---|---|---|---|---|---|---|
| | Privacy | Protection of minors | Public morality | Public health | Consumer protection | Protection of IPR | Professional ethics | Protection of national treasures | Dissemination of culture | Professional rules protecting recipients of services | Pluralism |
| Unauthorised use of trademarks and qualifiers | | | | | ? | + | | | | | |
| Misleading advertising | | | | | + | ? | | | | | |
| Misleading claims | | | | | + | ? | | | | | |
| Price advertising; discounts etc | | | | | | | | | | | |
| Intrusive advertising coldcalling/telephone advertising | ? | ? | | | ? | | | | | | |
| Intrusive advertising; letterbox/mail marketing | ? | | | | ? | ? | | | | | |
| Intrusive advertising; promotional gifts/concessionary offers | | | | | | | | | | | |
| Intrusive advertising; prize competitions, draws and lotteries | | | | | + | | | | | | |
| General media restrictions | | | | ? | | | | | | ? | |
| General sponsorship restrictions | | | | + | | | | | | ? | |
| Product restrictions re commercial communications re tobacco | | ? | | + | | | | | | | |
| Product restrictions re commercial communications for alcoholic beverages | | ? | | + | | | | | | | |
| Product restrictions re commercial communications to children | | ? | | ? | | | | | | | |
| Product restrictions re commercial communications re food products | | | | ? | ? | ? | | | | | |
| Product restrictions re commercial communications re pharmaceuticals | | | | + | ? | | | | | | |
| Product restrictions re commercial communications re financial services | | | | | ? | | | | | | |
| Societal value | ? | | ? | | | | | | | | |

## VI    Germany

| Categories of National Measures | General Interest Objections | | | | | | | | | | |
|---|---|---|---|---|---|---|---|---|---|---|---|
| | Privacy | Protection of minors | Public morality | Public health | Consumer protection | Protection of IPR | Professional ethics | Protection of national treasures | Dissemination of culture | Professional rules protecting recipients of services | Pluralism |
| Unauthorised use of trademarks and qualifiers | | | | | ? | + | | | | | |
| Misleading advertising | | | | | ? | ? | | | | | |
| Misleading claims | | | | | ? | ? | | | | | |
| Price advertising; discounts etc | | | | | ? | ? | | | | | |
| Intrusive advertising coldcalling/telephone advertising | | | | | ? | ? | | | | | |
| Intrusive advertising: letterbox/mail marketing | | | | | ? | ? | | | | | |
| Intrusive advertising; promotional gifts/ concessionary offers | | | | | ? | ? | | | | | |
| Intrusive advertising; prize competitions, draws and lotteries | | | | | ? | ? | | | | | |
| General media restrictions | | ? | | | ? | ? | | | | | ? |
| General sponsorship restrictions | | ? | | ? | | | | | | | ? |
| Product restrictions re commercial communications re tobacco | | ? | | + | ? | ? | | | | | |
| Product restrictions re commercial communications for alcoholic beverages | | ? | | + | ? | ? | | | | | |
| Product restrictions re commercial communications to children | | ? | | ? | | | | | | | |
| Product restrictions re commercial communications re food products | | ? | | + | ? | ? | | | | | |
| Product restrictions re commercial communications re pharmaceuticals | | | | + | ? | | | | | | |
| Product restrictions re commercial communications re financial services | | | | | ? | | | | | | |
| Societal value | | | | | ? | | ? | | | | |

VII  Greece

| Categories of National Measures | General Interest Objections | | | | | | | | | | |
|---|---|---|---|---|---|---|---|---|---|---|---|
| | Privacy | Protection of minors | Public morality | Public health | Consumer protection | Protection of IPR | Professional ethics | Protection of national treasures | Dissemination of culture | Professional rules protecting recipients of services | Pluralism |
| Unauthorised use of trademarks and qualifiers | | | | | | + | | | | | |
| Misleading advertising | | | | | + | ? | | | | | |
| Misleading claims | | | | | + | ? | | | | | |
| Price advertising: discounts etc | | | | | ? | ? | | | | | |
| Intrusive advertising coldcalling/telephone advertising | | | | | ? | ? | | | | | |
| Intrusive advertising: letterbox/mail marketing | | | | | ? | ? | | | | | |
| Intrusive advertising; promotional gifts/concessionary offers | | | | | ? | ? | | | | | |
| Intrusive advertising; prize competitions, draws and lotteries | | | | | ? | ? | | | | | |
| General media restrictions | | ? | ? | ? | ? | | | | | | ? |
| General sponsorship restrictions | | ? | ? | ? | + | | ? | | | | ? |
| Product restrictions re commercial communications re tobacco | | | | | + | | | | | | |
| Product restrictions re commercial communications for alcoholic beverages | | | | ? | ? | ? | | | | | |
| Product restrictions re commercial communications to children | | | | | ? | ? | | | | | |
| Product restrictions re commercial communications re food products | | | | | + | ? | | | | | |
| Product restrictions re commercial communications re pharmaceuticals | | | | ? | ? | | | | | | |
| Product restrictions re commercial communications re financial services | | | | | | | | | | | |
| Societal value | | ? | | | ? | | | | | | |

**VIII Ireland**

| Categories of National Measures | General Interest Objections | | | | | | | | | | |
|---|---|---|---|---|---|---|---|---|---|---|---|
| | Privacy | Protection of minors | Public morality | Public health | Consumer protection | Protection of IPR | Professional ethics | Protection of national treasures | Dissemination of culture | Professional rules protecting recipients of services | Pluralism |
| Unauthorised use of trademarks and qualifiers | | | | | ? | + | | | | | |
| Misleading advertising | | | | | + | | | | | | |
| Misleading claims | | | | | + | | | | | | |
| Price advertising; discounts etc | | | | | + | ? | | | | | |
| Intrusive advertising coldcalling/telephone advertising | | | | | ? | | | | | | |
| Intrusive advertising; letterbox/mail marketing | | | | | ? | | | | | | |
| Intrusive advertising; promotional gifts/concessionary offers | | | | | + | ? | | | | | |
| Intrusive advertising; prize competitions, draws and lotteries | | | | | ? | | | | | | |
| General media restrictions | | ? | ? | ? | ? | | | | | | ? |
| General sponsorship restrictions | | | | | | | | | | | ? |
| Product restrictions re commercial communications re tobacco | | ? | | + | | | | | | | |
| Product restrictions re commercial communications for alcoholic beverages | | ? | | + | + | | | | | | |
| Product restrictions re commercial communications to children | | | | | | | | | | | |
| Product restrictions re commercial communications re food products | | | | + | + | | | | | | |
| Product restrictions re commercial communications re pharmaceuticals | | | | + | | | | | | | |
| Product restrictions re commercial communications re financial services | | | | | ? | | | | | | |
| Societal value | | | ? | | | | | | | | |

## IX  Italy

| Categories of National Measures | General Interest Objections | | | | | | | | | | |
|---|---|---|---|---|---|---|---|---|---|---|---|
| | Privacy | Protection of minors | Public morality | Public health | Consumer protection | Protection of IPR | Professional ethics | Protection of national treasures | Dissemination of culture | Professional rules protecting recipients of services | Pluralism |
| Unauthorised use of trademarks and qualifiers | | | | | | + | | | | | |
| Misleading advertising | | ? | | ? | + | ? | | | | | |
| Misleading claims | | | | | ? | ? | | | | | |
| Price advertising; discounts etc | | | | | | ? | | | | | |
| Intrusive advertising coldcalling/telephone advertising | ? | | | | | ? | | | | | |
| Intrusive advertising; letterbox/mail marketing | ? | | | | | ? | | | | | |
| Intrusive advertising; promotional gifts/concessionary offers | | | | | | ? | | | | | |
| Intrusive advertising; prize competitions, draws and lotteries | | | | | | ? | | | | | |
| General media restrictions | | ? | ? | ? | ? | | ? | | | | ? |
| General sponsorship restrictions | | + | ? | ? | ? | | | | | | ? |
| Product restrictions re commercial communications re tobacco | | ? | | ? | | | | | | | |
| Product restrictions re commercial communications for alcoholic beverages | | | ? | | + | | | | | | |
| Product restrictions re commercial communications to children | | | ? | | ? | | | | | | |
| Product restrictions re commercial communications re food products | | | ? | | + | + | | | | | |
| Product restrictions re commercial communications re pharmaceuticals | | | | | | | | | | | |
| Product restrictions re commercial communications re financial services | | | | | | ? | | | | | |
| Societal value | | | ? | ? | | | | | | | |

**X   Luxembourg**

| Categories of National Measures | General Interest Objections | | | | | | | | | | |
|---|---|---|---|---|---|---|---|---|---|---|---|
| | Privacy | Protection of minors | Public morality | Public health | Consumer protection | Protection of IPR | Professional ethics | Protection of national treasures | Dissemination of culture | Professional rules protecting recipients of services | Pluralism |
| Unauthorised use of trademarks and qualifiers | | | | | ? | + | | | | | |
| Misleading advertising | | | | | ? | ? | | | | | |
| Misleading claims | | | | | ? | ? | | | | | |
| Price advertising; discounts etc | | | | | ? | ? | | | | | |
| Intrusive advertising coldcalling/telephone advertising | | | | | ? | | | | | | |
| Intrusive advertising; letterbox/mail marketing | | | | | ? | | | | | | |
| Intrusive advertising; promotional gifts/concessionary offers | | | | | ? | ? | | | | | |
| Intrusive advertising; prize competitions, draws and lotteries | | | | | ? | ? | | | | | |
| General media restrictions | | ? | | ? | | | | | | | ? |
| General sponsorship restrictions | | | | | | | | | | | |
| Product restrictions re commercial communications re tobacco | | | | ? | | | | | | | |
| Product restrictions re commercial communications for alcoholic beverages | | | | + | | | | | | | |
| Product restrictions re commercial communications to children | | ? | | ? | | | | | | | |
| Product restrictions re commercial communications re food products | | | | + | ? | ? | | | | | |
| Product restrictions re commercial communications re pharmaceuticals | | ? | | + | ? | | | | | | |
| Product restrictions re commercial communications re financial services | | | | | ? | | | | | | |
| Societal value | | | | | ? | | | | | | |

## XI  The Netherlands

| Categories of National Measures | General Interest Objections | | | | | | | | | | |
|---|---|---|---|---|---|---|---|---|---|---|---|
| | Privacy | Protection of minors | Public morality | Public health | Consumer protection | Protection of IPR | Professional ethics | Protection of national treasures | Dissemination of culture | Professional rules protecting recipients of services | Pluralism |
| Unauthorised use of trademarks and qualifiers | | | | | ? | + | | | | | |
| Misleading advertising | | | | | + | ? | | | | | |
| Misleading claims | | | | | + | ? | | | | | |
| Price advertising: discounts etc | | | | | | ? | | | | | |
| Intrusive advertising coldcalling/telephone advertising | ? | | | | + | ? | | | | | |
| Intrusive advertising; letterbox/mail marketing | | | | | + | | | | | | |
| Intrusive advertising; promotional gifts/concessionary offers | | | | | + | ? | | | | | |
| Intrusive advertising; prize competitions, draws and lotteries | | | | | + | ? | | | | | |
| General media restrictions | | ? | | ? | + | | | | | | ? |
| General sponsorship restrictions | | | | ? | ? | | | | | | ? |
| Product restrictions re commercial communications re tobacco | | ? | | + | | | | | | | |
| Product restrictions re commercial communications for alcoholic beverages | | ? | | + | | | | | | | |
| Product restrictions re commercial communications to children | | ? | | ? | | | | | | | |
| Product restrictions re commercial communications re food products | | | | | + | ? | | | | | |
| Product restrictions re commercial communications re pharmaceuticals | | | | + | | | | | | | |
| Product restrictions re commercial communications re financial services | | | | | ? | | | | | | |
| Societal value | | | ? | | ? | | | | | | |

**XII Portugal**

| Categories of National Measures | General Interest Objections | | | | | | | | | | |
|---|---|---|---|---|---|---|---|---|---|---|---|
| | Privacy | Protection of minors | Public morality | Public health | Consumer protection | Protection of IPR | Professional ethics | Protection of national treasures | Dissemination of culture | Professional rules protecting recipients of services | Pluralism |
| Unauthorised use of trademarks and qualifiers | | | | | | + | | | | | |
| Misleading advertising | | | | ? | + | ? | ? | | | ? | |
| Misleading claims | | | | | + | + | | | | ? | |
| Price advertising: discounts etc | | | | | ? | + | | | | | |
| Intrusive advertising coldcalling/telephone advertising | | | | | ? | ? | | | | | |
| Intrusive advertising: letterbox/mail marketing | | | | | + | ? | | | | | |
| Intrusive advertising: promotional gifts/concessionary offers | | | | | | | | | | | |
| Intrusive advertising: prize competitions, draws and lotteries | | | | | ? | | | | | | |
| General media restrictions | | | | | ? | | | | | ? | |
| General sponsorship restrictions | | | | | | | | | | | |
| Product restrictions re commercial communications re tobacco | | | | ? | | | | | | | |
| Product restrictions re commercial communications for alcoholic beverages | | ? | | ? | | | | | | | |
| Product restrictions re commercial communications to children | | ? | | ? | | | | | | | |
| Product restrictions re commercial communications re food products | | | | | | | | | | | |
| Product restrictions re commercial communications re pharmaceuticals | | | | | | | | | | | |
| Product restrictions re commercial communications re financial services | | | | | | | | | | | |
| Societal values | | | | | | | | | | | |

## XIII Spain

| Categories of National Measures | General Interest Objections | | | | | | | | | | |
|---|---|---|---|---|---|---|---|---|---|---|---|
| | Privacy | Protection of minors | Public morality | Public health | Consumer protection | Protection of IPR | Professional ethics | Protection of national treasures | Dissemination of culture | Professional rules protecting recipients of services | Pluralism |
| Unauthorised use of trademarks and qualifiers | | | | | ? | + | | | | | |
| Misleading advertising | | ? | | | + | ? | | | | | |
| Misleading claims | | ? | | | + | ? | | | | | |
| Price advertising; discounts etc | | | | | + | ? | | | | | |
| Intrusive advertising coldcalling/telephone advertising | ? | | | | ? | | | | | | |
| Intrusive advertising; letterbox/mail marketing | ? | | | | ? | | | | | | |
| Intrusive advertising; promotional gifts/concessionary offers | | | | | + | ? | | | | | |
| Intrusive advertising; prize competitions, draws and lotteries | | | | | + | ? | | | | | |
| General media restrictions | | ? | ? | ? | ? | | | | | | ? |
| General sponsorship restrictions | | | | | | | | | | | ? |
| Product restrictions re commercial communications re tobacco | | | | + | ? | ? | | | | | |
| Product restrictions re commercial communications for alcoholic beverages | | | | + | ? | ? | | | | | |
| Product restrictions re commercial communications to children | | ? | | | ? | ? | | | | | |
| Product restrictions re commercial communications re food products | | | | ? | ? | | | | | | |
| Product restrictions re commercial communications re pharmaceuticals | | | | ? | ? | | | | | | |
| Product restrictions re commercial communications re financial services | | | | | ? | | | | | | |
| Societal value | | | ? | | ? | | | | | | |

## XIV Sweden

| Categories of National Measures | General Interest Objections | | | | | | | | | | |
|---|---|---|---|---|---|---|---|---|---|---|---|
| | Privacy | Protection of minors | Public morality | Public health | Consumer protection | Protection of IPR | Professional ethics | Protection of national treasures | Dissemination of culture | Professional rules protecting recipients of services | Pluralism |
| Unauthorised use of trademarks and qualifiers | | | | | ? | + | | | | | |
| Misleading advertising | | ? | | | + | ? | | | | | |
| Misleading claims | | ? | | | + | ? | | | | | |
| Price advertising; discounts etc | | | | | ? | | | | | | |
| Intrusive advertising coldcalling/telephone advertising | | | | | + | ? | | | | | |
| Intrusive advertising; letterbox/mail marketing | | | | | + | ? | | | | | |
| Intrusive advertising; promotional gifts/concessionary offers | | | | | + | ? | | | | | |
| Intrusive advertising; prize competitions, draws and lotteries | | | | | ? | | | | | | |
| General media restrictions | | ? | | ? | + | ? | | | | | ? |
| General sponsorship restrictions | | ? | | ? | + | ? | | | | | ? |
| Product restrictions re commercial communications re tobacco | | ? | | + | + | ? | | | | | |
| Product restrictions re commercial communications for alcoholic beverages | | ? | | ? | + | ? | | | | | |
| Product restrictions re commercial communications to children | | ? | | ? | ? | | | | | | |
| Product restrictions re commercial communications re food products | | | | ? | ? | | | | | | |
| Product restrictions re commercial communications re pharmaceuticals | | | ? | + | + | | | | | | |
| Product restrictions re commercial communications re financial services | | | | | ? | | | | | | |
| Societal value | | | ? | | | | | | | | |

## XV United Kingdom

| Categories of National Measures | General Interest Objections | | | | | | | | | | |
|---|---|---|---|---|---|---|---|---|---|---|---|
| | Privacy | Protection of minors | Public morality | Public health | Consumer protection | Protection of IPR | Professional ethics | Protection of national treasures | Dissemination of culture | Professional rules protecting recipients of services | Pluralism |
| Unauthorised use of trademarks and qualifiers | | | | | | + | | | | | |
| Misleading advertising | | | | | + | | | | | | |
| Misleading claims | | | | | + | | | | | | |
| Price advertising: discounts etc | | | | | + | | | | | | |
| Intrusive advertising coldcalling/telephone advertising | | | ? | | ? | | | | | | |
| Intrusive advertising: letterbox/mail marketing | | ? | | | + | | | | | | |
| Intrusive advertising: promotional gifts/concessionary offers | | | | | + | | | | | | |
| Intrusive advertising: prize competitions, draws and lotteries | | | | | ? | | | | | | |
| General media restrictions | | ? | ? | ? | ? | | | | | | ? |
| General sponsorship restrictions | | ? | ? | ? | ? | | | | | | ? |
| Product restrictions re commercial communications re tobacco | | ? | | ? | | | | | | | |
| Product restrictions re commercial communications for alcoholic beverages | | ? | | ? | + | | | | | | |
| Product restrictions re commercial communications to children | | | | | + | | | | | | |
| Product restrictions re commercial communications re food products | | | | ? | + | | | | | | |
| Product restrictions re commercial communications re pharmaceuticals | | | | ? | ? | | | | | | |
| Product restrictions re commercial communications re financial services | | | | | ? | | | | | | |
| Societal value | | | ? | | ? | | ? | | | | |

# CONSOLIDATED VERSION OF DIRECTIVES 89/552/82 AND 97/36/EC (TELEVISION WITHOUT FRONTIERS – UNOFFICIAL CONSOLIDATED VERSION)

*OJ L 298, 17.10.89, p 23; L 202, 30.7.97, p 60 (the authoritative texts)*

*EUROPEAN PARLIAMENT AND COUNCIL OF THE EUROPEAN UNION*

*COUNCIL DIRECTIVE (89/552/EEC) of 3 October 1989 on the co-ordination of certain provisions laid down by law, regulation or administrative action in Member States concerning the pursuit of television broadcasting activities*

*and*

*DIRECTIVE 97/36/EC OF THE EUROPEAN PARLIAMENT AND OF THE COUNCIL of 30 June 1997 amending Council Directive 89/552/EEC on the co-ordination of certain provisions laid down by law, regulation or administrative action in Member States concerning the pursuit of television broadcasting activities*

*Unofficial consolidated version prepared by the services of the Commission*

*RECITALS TO COUNCIL DIRECTIVE (89/552/EEC) of 3 October 1989 on the co-ordination of certain provisions laid down by law, regulation or administrative action in Member States concerning the pursuit of television broadcasting activities*

THE COUNCIL OF THE EUROPEAN COMMUNITIES,

Having regard to the Treaty establishing the European Economic Community, and in particular Articles 57(2) and 66 thereof,

Having regard to the proposal from the Commission,

In co-operation with the European Parliament,

Having regard to the opinion of the Economic and Social Committee,

1   Whereas the objectives of the Community as laid down in the Treaty include establishing an even closer union among the peoples of Europe, fostering closer relations between the States belonging to the Community, ensuring the economic and social progress of its countries by common action to eliminate the barriers which divide Europe, encouraging the constant improvement of the living conditions of its peoples as well as ensuring the preservation and strengthening of peace and liberty;

2  Whereas the Treaty provides for the establishment of a common market, including the abolition, as between Member States, of obstacles to freedom of movement for services and the institution of a system ensuring that competition in the common market is not distorted;

3  Whereas broadcasts transmitted across frontiers by means of various technologies are one of the ways of pursuing the objectives of the Community; whereas measures should be adopted to permit and ensure the transition from national markets to a common programme production and distribution market and to establish conditions of fair competition without prejudice to the public interest role to be discharged by the television broadcasting services;

4  Whereas the Council of Europe has adopted the European Convention on Transfrontier Television;

5  Whereas the Treaty provides for the issuing of Directives for the co-ordination of provisions to facilitate the taking up of activities as self-employed persons;

6  Whereas television broadcasting constitutes, in normal circumstances, a service within the meaning of the Treaty;

7  Whereas the Treaty provides for free movement of all services normally provided against payment, without exclusion on grounds of their cultural or other content and without restriction of nationals of Member States established in a Community country other than that of the person for whom the services are intended;

8  Whereas this right as applied to the broadcasting and distribution of television services is also a specific manifestation in Community law of a more general principle, namely the freedom of expression as enshrined in Article 10(1) of the Convention for the Protection of Human Rights and Fundamental Freedoms ratified by all Member States; whereas for this reason the issuing of Directives on the broadcasting and distribution of television programmes must ensure their free movement in the light of the said Article and subject only to the limits set by paragraph 2 of that Article and by Article 56(1) of the Treaty;

9  Whereas the laws, regulations and administrative measures in Member States concerning the pursuit of activities as television broadcasters and cable operators contain disparities, some of which may impede the free movements of broadcasts within the Community and may distort competition within the common market;

10  Whereas all such restrictions on freedom to provide broadcasting services within the Community must be abolished under the Treaty;

11  Whereas such abolition must go hand in hand with co-ordination of the applicable laws; whereas this co-ordination must be aimed at facilitating the pursuit of the professional activities concerned and, more generally, the free movement of information and ideas within the Community;

12  Whereas it is consequently necessary and sufficient that all broadcasts comply with the law of the Member State from which they emanate;

13  Whereas this Directive lays down the minimum rules needed to guarantee freedom of transmission in broadcasting; whereas, therefore, it does not affect the responsibility of the Member States and their authorities with regard to the organisation – including the systems of licensing, administrative authorisation or taxation – financing and the content of programmes; whereas the independence of

cultural developments in the Member States and the preservation of cultural diversity in the Community therefore remain unaffected;

14 Whereas it is necessary, in the common market, that all broadcasts emanating from and intended for reception within the Community and in particular those intended for reception in another Member State, should respect the law of the originating Member State applicable to broadcasts intended for reception by the public in that Member State and the provisions of this Directive;

15 Whereas the requirement that the originating Member State should verify that broadcasts comply with national law as co-ordinated by this Directive is sufficient under Community law to ensure free movement of broadcasts without secondary control on the same grounds in the receiving Member States; whereas, however, the receiving Member State may, exceptionally and under specific conditions provisionally suspend the retransmission of televised broadcasts;

16 Whereas it is essential for the Member States to ensure the prevention of any acts which may prove detrimental to freedom of movement and trade in television programmes or which may promote the creation of dominant positions which would lead to restrictions on pluralism and freedom of televised information and of the information sector as a whole;

17 Whereas this Directive, being confined specifically to television broadcasting rules, is without prejudice to existing or future Community acts of harmonisation, in particular to satisfy mandatory requirements concerning the protection of consumers and the fairness of commercial transactions and competition;

18 Whereas co-ordination is nevertheless needed to make it easier for persons and industries producing programmes having a cultural objective to take up and pursue their activities;

19 Whereas minimum requirements in respect of all public or private Community television programmes for European audio-visual productions have been a means of promoting production, independent production and distribution in the above mentioned industries and are complementary to other instruments which are already or will be proposed to favour the same objective;

20 Whereas it is therefore necessary to promote markets of sufficient size for television productions in the Member States to recover necessary investments not only by establishing common rules opening up national markets but also by envisaging for European productions where practicable and by appropriate means a majority proportion in television programmes of all Member States; whereas, in order to allow the monitoring of the application of these rules and the pursuit of the objectives, Member States will provide the Commission with a report on the application of the proportions reserved for European works and independent productions in this Directive; whereas for the calculation of such proportions account should be taken of the specific situation of the Hellenic Republic and the Portuguese Republic; whereas the Commission must inform the other Member States of these reports accompanied, where appropriate by an opinion taking account of, in particular, progress achieved in relation to previous years, the share of first broadcasts in the programming, the particular circumstances of new television broadcasters and the specific situation of countries with a low audio-visual production capacity or restricted language area;

21  Whereas for these purposes 'European works' should be defined without prejudice to the possibility of Member States laying down a more detailed definition as regards television broadcasters under their jurisdiction in accordance with Article 3(1) in compliance with Community law and account being taken of the objectives of this Directive;

22  Whereas it is important to seek appropriate instruments and procedures in accordance with Community law in order to promote the implementation of these objectives with a view to adopting suitable measures to encourage the activity and development of European audio-visual production and distribution, particularly in countries with a low production capacity or restricted language area; whereas national support schemes for the development of European production may be applied in so far as they comply with Community law;

23  Whereas a commitment, where practicable, to a certain proportion of broadcasts for independent productions, created by producers who are independent of broadcasters, will stimulate new sources of television production, especially the creation of small and medium-sized enterprises; whereas it will offer new opportunities and outlets to the marketing of creative talents of employment of cultural professions and employees in the cultural field; whereas the definition of the concept of independent producer by the Member States should take account of that objective by giving due consideration to small and medium-sized producers and making it possible to authorise financial participation by the co-production subsidiaries of television organisations;

24  Whereas measures are necessary for Member States to ensure that a certain period elapses between the first cinema showing of a work and the first television showing;

25  Whereas in order to allow for an active policy in favour of a specific language, Member States remain free to lay down more detailed or stricter rules in particular on the basis of language criteria, as long as these rules are in conformity with Community law, and in particular are not applicable to the retransmission of broadcasts originating in other Member States;

26  Whereas in order to ensure that the interests of consumers as television viewers are fully and properly protected, it is essential for television advertising to be subject to a certain number of minimum rules and standards and that the Member States must maintain the right to set more detailed or stricter rules and in certain circumstances to lay down different conditions for television broadcasters under their jurisdiction;

27  Whereas Member States, with due regard to Community law and in relation to broadcasts intended solely for the national territory which may not be received, directly or indirectly, in one or more Member States, must be able to lay down different conditions for the insertion of advertising and different limits for the volume of advertising in order to facilitate these particular broadcasts;

28  Whereas it is necessary to prohibit all television advertising promoting cigarettes and other tobacco products including indirect forms of advertising which, whilst not directly mentioning the tobacco product, seek to circumvent the ban on advertising by using brand names, symbols or other distinctive features of tobacco products or of undertakings whose known or main activities include the production or sale of such products;

29 Whereas it is equally necessary to prohibit all television advertising for medicinal products and medical treatment available only on prescription in the Member State within whose jurisdiction the broadcaster falls and to introduce strict criteria relating to the television advertising of alcoholic products;

30 Whereas in view of the growing importance of sponsorship in the financing of programmes, appropriate rules should be laid down;

31 Whereas it is, furthermore, necessary to introduce rules to protect the physical, mental and moral development of minors in programmes and in television advertising;

32 Whereas although television broadcasters are normally bound to ensure that programmes present facts and events fairly, it is nevertheless important that they should be subject to specific obligations with respect to the right of reply or equivalent remedies so that any person whose legitimate interests have been damaged by an assertion made in the course of a broadcast television programme may effectively exercise such right or remedy.

*RECITALS TO DIRECTIVE 97/36/EC of the European Parliament and of the Council amending Council Directive 89/552/EEC on the co-ordination of certain provisions laid down by law, regulation or administrative action in Member States concerning the pursuit of television broadcasting activities*

THE EUROPEAN PARLIAMENT AND THE COUNCIL OF THE EUROPEAN UNION,

Having regard to the Treaty establishing the European Community, and in particular Articles 57(2) and 66 thereof,

Having regard to the proposal from the Commission ,

Having regard to the opinion of the Economic and Social Committee,

Acting in accordance with the procedure laid down in Article 189b of the Treaty in the light of the joint text approved by the Conciliation Committee on 16 April 1997,

1 Whereas Council Directive 89/552/EEC constitutes the legal framework for television broadcasting in the internal market;

2 Whereas Article 26 of Directive 89/552/EEC states that the Commission shall, not later than the end of the fifth year after the date of adoption of the Directive, submit to the European Parliament, the Council and the Economic and Social Committee a report on the application of the Directive and, if necessary, make further proposals to adapt it to developments in the field of television broadcasting;

3 Whereas the application of Directive 89/552/EEC and the report on its application have revealed the need to clarify certain definitions or obligations on Member States under this Directive;

4 Whereas the Commission, in its communication of 19 July 1994 entitled 'Europe's way to the information society: an action plan', underlined the importance of a regulatory framework applying to the content of audio-visual services which would help to safeguard the free movement of such services in the Community and be responsive to the opportunities for growth in this sector opened up by new

technologies, while at the same time taking into account the specific nature, in particular the cultural and sociological impact, of audio-visual programmes, whatever their mode of transmission;

5   Whereas the Council welcomed this action plan at its meeting of 28 September 1994 and stressed the need to improve the competitiveness of the European audio-visual industry;

6   Whereas the Commission has submitted a Green Paper on the Protection of Minors and Human Dignity in audio-visual and information services and has undertaken to submit a Green Paper focusing on developing the cultural aspects of these new services;

7   Whereas any legislative framework concerning new audio-visual services must be compatible with the primary objective of this Directive which is to create the legal framework for the free movement of services;

8   Whereas it is essential that the Member States should take action with regard to services comparable to television broadcasting in order to prevent any breach of the fundamental principles which must govern information and the emergence of wide disparities as regards free movement and competition;

9   Whereas the Heads of State and Government meeting at the European Council in Essen on 9 and 10 December 1994 called on the Commission to present a proposal for a revision of Directive 89/552/EEC before their next meeting;

10  Whereas the application of Directive 89/552/EEC has revealed the need to clarify the concept of jurisdiction as applied specifically to the audio-visual sector; whereas, in view of the case law of the Court of Justice of the European Communities, the establishment criterion should be made the principal criterion determining the jurisdiction of a particular Member State;

11  Whereas the concept of establishment, according to the criteria laid down by the Court of Justice in its judgment of 25 July 1991 in the Factortame case, involves the actual pursuit of an economic activity through a fixed establishment for an indefinite period;

12  Whereas the establishment of a television broadcasting organisation may be determined by a series of practical criteria such as the location of the head office of the provider of services, the place where decisions on programming policy are usually taken, the place where the programme to be broadcast to the public is finally mixed and processed, and the place where a significant proportion of the workforce required for the pursuit of the television broadcasting activity is located;

13  Whereas the fixing of a series of practical criteria is designed to determine by an exhaustive procedure that one Member State and one only has jurisdiction over a broadcaster in connection with the provision of the services which this Directive addresses; nevertheless, taking into account the case law of the Court of Justice and so as to avoid cases where there is a vacuum of jurisdiction it is appropriate to refer to the criterion of establishment within the meaning of Articles 52 and following of the Treaty establishing the European Community as the final criterion determining the jurisdiction of a Member State;

14  Whereas the Court of Justice has constantly held that a Member State retains the right to take measures against a television broadcasting organisation that is established in another Member State but directs all or most of its activity to the

territory of the first Member State if the choice of establishment was made with a view to evading the legislation that would have applied to the organisation had it been established on the territory of the first Member State;

15 Whereas Article F(2) of the Treaty on European Union stipulates that the Union shall respect fundamental rights as guaranteed by the European Convention for the Protection of Human Rights and Fundamental Freedoms as general principles of Community law; whereas any measure aimed at restricting the reception and/or suspending the retransmission of television broadcasts taken under Article 2a of Directive 89/552/EEC as amended by this Directive must be compatible with such principles;

16 Whereas it is necessary to ensure the effective application of the provisions of Directive 89/552/EEC as amended by this Directive throughout the Community in order to preserve free and fair competition between firms in the same industry;

17 Whereas directly affected third parties, including nationals of other Member States, must be able to assert their rights, according to national law, before competent judicial or other authorities of the Member State with jurisdiction over the television broadcasting organisation that may be failing to comply with the national provisions arising out of the application of Directive 89/552/EEC as amended by this Directive;

18 Whereas it is essential that Member States should be able to take measures to protect the right to information and to ensure wide access by the public to television coverage of national or non-national events of major importance for society, such as the Olympic games, the football World Cup and European football championship; whereas to this end Member States retain the right to take measures compatible with Community law aimed at regulating the exercise by broadcasters under their jurisdiction of exclusive broadcasting rights to such events;

19 Whereas it is necessary to make arrangements within a Community framework, in order to avoid potential legal uncertainty and market distortions and to reconcile free circulation of television services with the need to prevent the possibility of circumvention of national measures protecting a legitimate general interest;

20 Whereas, in particular, it is appropriate to lay down in this Directive provisions concerning the exercise by broadcasters of exclusive broadcasting rights that they may have purchased to events considered to be of major importance for society in a Member State other than that having jurisdiction over the broadcasters, and whereas, in order to avoid speculative rights purchases with a view to circumvention of national measures, it is necessary to apply these provisions to contracts entered into after the publication of this Directive and concerning events which take place after the date of implementation, and whereas, when contracts that predate the publication of this Directive are renewed, they are considered to be new contracts;

21 Whereas events of major importance for society should, for the purposes of this Directive, meet certain criteria, that is to say be outstanding events which are of interest to the general public in the European Union or in a given Member State or in an important component part of a given Member State and are organised in advance by an event organiser who is legally entitled to sell the rights pertaining to that event;

22  Whereas, for the purposes of this Directive, 'free television' means broadcasting on a channel, either public or commercial, of programmes which are accessible to the public without payment in addition to the modes of funding of broadcasting that are widely prevailing in each Member State (such as licence fee and/or the basic tier subscription fee to a cable network);

23  Whereas Member States are free to take whatever measures they deem appropriate with regard to broadcasts which come from third countries and which do not satisfy the conditions laid down in Article 2 of Directive 89/552/EEC as amended by this Directive, provided they comply with Community law and the international obligations of the Community;

24  Whereas in order to eliminate the obstacles arising from differences in national legislation on the promotion of European works, Directive 89/552/EEC as amended by this Directive contains provisions aimed at harmonising such legislation; whereas those provisions which, in general, seek to liberalise trade must contain clauses harmonising the conditions of competition;

25  Whereas, moreover, Article 128(4) of the Treaty establishing the European Community requires the Community to take cultural aspects into account in its action under other provisions of the Treaty;

26  Whereas the Green Paper on 'Strategy options to strengthen the European programme industry in the context of the audio-visual policy of the European Union', adopted by the Commission on 7 April 1994, puts forward *inter alia* measures to promote European works in order to further the development of the sector; whereas the MEDIA II programme, which seeks to promote training, development and distribution in the audio-visual sector, is also designed to enable the production of European works to be developed; whereas the Commission has proposed that production of European works should also be promoted by a Community mechanism such as a Guarantee Fund;

27  Whereas broadcasting organisations, programme makers, producers, authors and other experts should be encouraged to develop more detailed concepts and strategies aimed at developing European audio-visual fiction films that are addressed to an international audience;

28  Whereas, in addition to the considerations cited above, it is necessary to create conditions for improving the competitiveness of the programme industry; whereas the communications on the application of Articles 4 and 5 of Directive 89/552/EEC, adopted by the Commission on 3 March 1994 and 15 July 1996 pursuant to Article 4(3) of that Directive, draw the conclusion that measures to promote European works can contribute to such an improvement but that they need to take account of developments in the field of television broadcasting;

29  Whereas channels broadcasting entirely in a language other than those of the Member States should not be covered by the provisions of Articles 4 and 5; whereas, nevertheless, where such a language or languages represent a substantial part but not all of the channel's transmission time, the provisions of Articles 4 and 5 should not apply to that part of transmission time;

30  Whereas the proportions of European works must be achieved taking economic realities into account; whereas, therefore, a progressive system for achieving this objective is required;

31 Whereas, with a view to promoting the production of European works, it is essential that the Community, taking into account the audio-visual capacity of each Member State and the need to protect lesser used languages of the European Union, should promote independent producers; whereas Member States, in defining the notion of 'independent producer', should take appropriate account of criteria such as the ownership of the production company, the amount of programmes supplied to the same broadcaster and the ownership of secondary rights;

32 Whereas the question of specific time scales for each type of television showing of cinematographic works is primarily a matter to be settled by means of agreements between the interested parties or professionals concerned;

33 Whereas advertising for medicinal products for human use is subject to the provisions of Directive 92/28/EEC;

34 Whereas daily transmission time allotted to announcements made by the broadcaster in connection with its own programmes and ancillary products directly derived from these, or to public service announcements and charity appeals broadcast free of charge, is not to be included in the maximum amounts of daily or hourly transmission time that may be allotted to advertising and teleshopping;

35 Whereas, in order to avoid distortions of competition, this derogation is limited to announcements concerning products that fulfil the dual condition of being both ancillary to and directly derived from the programmes concerned; whereas the term ancillary refers to products intended specifically to allow the viewing public to benefit fully from or to interact with these programmes;

36 Whereas in view of the development of teleshopping, an economically important activity for operators as a whole and a genuine outlet for goods and services within the Community, it is essential to modify the rules on transmission time and to ensure a high level of consumer protection by putting in place appropriate standards regulating the form and content of such broadcasts;

37 Whereas it is important for the competent national authorities, in monitoring the implementation of the relevant provisions, to be able to distinguish, as regards channels not exclusively devoted to teleshopping, between transmission time devoted to teleshopping spots, advertising spots and other forms of advertising on the one hand and, on the other, transmission time devoted to teleshopping windows; whereas it is therefore necessary and sufficient that each window be clearly identified by optical and acoustic means at least at the beginning and the end of the window;

38 Whereas Directive 89/552/EEC as amended by this Directive applies to channels exclusively devoted to teleshopping or self-promotion, without conventional programme elements such as news, sports, films, documentaries and drama, solely for the purposes of these Directives and without prejudice to the inclusion of such channels in the scope of other Community instruments;

39 Whereas it is necessary to make clear that self-promotional activities are a particular form of advertising in which the broadcaster promotes its own products, services, programmes or channels; whereas, in particular, trailers consisting of extracts from programmes should be treated as programmes; whereas self-

promotion is a new and relatively unknown phenomenon and provisions concerning it may therefore be particularly subject to review in future examinations of this Directive;

40 Whereas it is necessary to clarify the rules for the protection of the physical, mental and moral development of minors; whereas the establishment of a clear distinction between programmes that are subject to an absolute ban and those that may be authorised subject to the use of appropriate technical means should satisfy concern about the public interest expressed by Member States and the Community;

41 Whereas none of the provisions of this Directive that concern the protection of minors and public order requires that the measures in question must necessarily be implemented through the prior control of television broadcasts;

42 Whereas an investigation by the Commission, in liaison with the competent Member State authorities, of the possible advantages and drawbacks of further measures to facilitate the control exercised by parents or guardians over the programmes that minors may watch shall consider, *inter alia*, the desirability of:

- the requirement for new television sets to be equipped with a technical device enabling parents or guardians to filter out certain programmes,

- the setting up of appropriate rating systems,

- encouraging family viewing policies and other educational and awareness measures,

- taking into account experience gained in this field in Europe and elsewhere as well as the views of interested parties such as broadcasters, producers, educationalists, media specialists and relevant associations, with a view to presenting, if necessary before the deadline laid down in Article 26, appropriate proposals for legislative or other measures;

43 Whereas it is appropriate to amend Directive 89/552/EEC to allow natural or legal persons whose activities include the manufacture or the sale of medicinal products and medical treatment available only on prescription to sponsor television programmes, provided that such sponsorship does not circumvent the prohibition of television advertising for medicinal products and medical treatment available only on prescription;

44 Whereas the approach in Directive 89/552/EEC and this Directive has been adopted to achieve the essential harmonisation necessary and sufficient to ensure the free movement of television broadcasts in the Community; whereas Member States remain free to apply to broadcasters under their jurisdiction more detailed or stricter rules in the fields co-ordinated by this Directive, including, *inter alia*, rules concerning the achievement of language policy goals, protection of the public interest in terms of television's role as a provider of information, education, culture and entertainment, the need to safeguard pluralism in the information industry and the media, and the protection of competition with a view to avoiding the abuse of dominant positions and/or the establishment or strengthening of dominant positions by mergers, agreements, acquisitions or similar initiatives; whereas such rules must be compatible with Community law;

45 Whereas the objective of supporting audio-visual production in Europe can be pursued within the Member States in the framework of the organisation of their broadcasting services, *inter alia*, through the definition of a public interest mission

for certain broadcasting organisations, including the obligation to contribute substantially to investment in European production;

46 Whereas Article B of the Treaty on European Union states that one of the objectives the Union shall set itself is to maintain in full the 'acquis communautaire',

HAVE ADOPTED THIS DIRECTIVE:

**Chapter I Definitions**

Article 1

For the purpose of this Directive:

(a) 'television broadcasting' means the initial transmission by wire or over the air, including that by satellite, in unencoded or encoded form, of television programmes intended for reception by the public. It includes the communication of programmes between undertakings with a view to their being relayed to the public. It does not include communication services providing items of information or other messages on individual demand such as telecopying, electronic data banks and other similar services;

(b) 'broadcaster' means the natural or legal person who has editorial responsibility for the composition of schedules of television programmes within the meaning of (a) and who transmits them or has them transmitted by third parties;

(c) 'television advertising' means any form of announcement broadcast whether in return for payment or for similar consideration or broadcast for self-promotional purposes by a public or private undertaking in connection with a trade, business, craft or profession in order to promote the supply of goods or services, including immovable property, rights and obligations, in return for payment;

(d) 'surreptitious advertising' means the representation in words or pictures of goods, services, the name, the trade mark or the activities of a producer of goods or a provider of services in programmes when such representation is intended by the broadcaster to serve advertising and might mislead the public as to its nature. Such representation is considered to be intentional in particular if it is done in return for payment or for similar consideration;

(e) 'sponsorship' means any contribution made by a public or private undertaking not engaged in television broadcasting activities or in the production of audio-visual works, to the financing of television programmes with a view to promoting its name, its trade mark, its image, its activities or its products;

(f) 'teleshopping' means direct offers broadcast to the public with a view to the supply of goods or services, including immovable property, rights and obligations, in return for payment.

**Chapter II General provisions**

Article 2

1 Member State shall ensure that all television broadcasts transmitted by broadcasters under its jurisdiction comply with the rules of the system of law applicable to broadcasts intended for the public in that Member State.

2 For the purposes of this Directive the broadcasters under the jurisdiction of a Member State are:

- those established in that Member State in accordance with paragraph 3;

- those to whom paragraph 4 applies.

3 For the purposes of this Directive, a broadcaster shall be deemed to be established in a Member State in the following cases:

(a) the broadcaster has its head office in that Member State and the editorial decisions about programme schedules are taken in that Member State;

(b) if a broadcaster has its head office in one Member State but editorial decisions on programme schedules are taken in another Member State, it shall be deemed to be established in the Member State where a significant part of the workforce involved in the pursuit of the television broadcasting activity operates; if a significant part of the workforce involved in the pursuit of the television broadcasting activity operates in each of those Member States, the broadcaster shall be deemed to be established in the Member State where it has its head office; if a significant part of the workforce involved in the pursuit of the television broadcasting activity operates in neither of those Member States, the broadcaster shall be deemed to be established in the Member State where it first began broadcasting in accordance with the system of law of that Member State, provided that it maintains a stable and effective link with the economy of that Member State;

(c) if a broadcaster has its head office in a Member State but decisions on programme schedules are taken in a third country, or vice versa, it shall be deemed to be established in the Member State concerned, provided that a significant part of the workforce involved in the pursuit of the television broadcasting activity operates in that Member State.

4 Broadcasters to whom the provisions of paragraph 3 are not applicable shall be deemed to be under the jurisdiction of a Member State in the following cases:

(a) they use a frequency granted by that Member State;

(b) although they do not use a frequency granted by a Member State they do use a satellite capacity appertaining to that Member State;

(c) although they use neither a frequency granted by a Member State nor a satellite capacity appertaining to a Member State they do use a satellite up-link situated in that Member State.

5   If the question as to which Member State has jurisdiction cannot be determined in accordance with paragraphs 3 and 4, the competent Member State shall be that in which the broadcaster is established within the meaning of Articles 52 and following of the Treaty establishing the European Community.

6   This Directive shall not apply to broadcasts intended exclusively for reception in third countries, and which are not received directly or indirectly by the public in one or more Member States.

Article 2a

1   Member States shall ensure freedom of reception and shall not restrict retransmissions on their territory of television broadcasts from other Member States for reasons which fall within the fields co-ordinated by this Directive.

2   Member States may, provisionally, derogate from paragraph 1 if the following conditions are fulfiled:

(a)  a television broadcast coming from another Member State manifestly, seriously and gravely infringes Article 22(1) or (2) and/or Article 22a;

(b)  during the previous 12 months, the broadcaster has infringed the provision(s) referred to in (a)on at least two prior occasions;

(c)  the Member State concerned has notified the broadcaster and the Commission in writing of the alleged infringements and of the measures it intends to take should any such infringement occur again;

(d)  consultations with the transmitting Member State and the Commission have not produced an amicable settlement within 15 days of the notification provided for in (c), and the alleged infringements persists.

The Commission shall, within two months following notification of the measures taken by the Member State, take a decision on whether the measures are compatible with Community law. If it decides that they are not, the Member State will be required to put an end to the measures in question as a matter of urgency.

3   Paragraph 2 shall be without prejudice to the application of any procedure, remedy or sanction to the infringements in question in the Member State which has jurisdiction over the broadcaster concerned.

Article 3

1   Member States shall remain free to require television broadcasters under their jurisdiction to comply with more detailed or stricter rules in the areas covered by this Directive.

2   Member States shall, by appropriate means, ensure, within the framework of their legislation, that television broadcasters under their jurisdiction effectively comply with the provisions of this Directive.

3   The measures shall include the appropriate procedures for third parties directly affected, including nationals of other Member States, to apply to the competent judicial or other authorities to seek effective compliance according to national provisions.

Article 3a

1   Each Member State may take measures in accordance with Community law to ensure that broadcasters under its jurisdiction do not broadcast on an exclusive basis events which are regarded by that Member State as being of major importance for society in such a way as to deprive a substantial proportion of the public in that Member State of the possibility of following such events via live coverage or deferred coverage on free television. If it does so, the Member State concerned shall draw up a list of designated events, national or non-national, which it considers to be of major importance for society. It shall do so in a clear and transparent manner in due and effective time. In so doing the Member State concerned shall also determine whether these events should be available via whole or partial live coverage, or where necessary or appropriate for objective reasons in the public interest, whole or partial deferred coverage.

2   Member States shall immediately notify to the Commission any measures taken or to be taken pursuant to paragraph 1. Within a period of three months from the notification, the Commission shall verify that such measures are compatible with Community law and communicate them to the other Member States. It shall seek the opinion of the Committee established pursuant to Article 23a. It shall forthwith publish the measures taken in the Official Journal of the European Communities and at least once a year the consolidated list of the measures taken by Member States.

3   Member States shall ensure, by appropriate means, within the framework of their legislation that broadcasters under their jurisdiction do not exercise the exclusive rights purchased by those broadcasters following the date of publication of this Directive in such a way that a substantial proportion of the public in another Member State is deprived of the possibility of following events which are designated by that other Member State in accordance with the preceding paragraphs via whole or partial live coverage or, where necessary or appropriate for objective reasons in the public interest, whole or partial deferred coverage on free television as determined by that other Member State in accordance with paragraph 1.

### Chapter III Promotion of distribution and production of television programmes

Article 4

1   Member States shall ensure where practicable and by appropriate means, that broadcasters reserve for European works, within the meaning of Article 6, a majority proportion of their transmission time, excluding the time appointed to news, sports events, games, advertising, teletext services and teleshopping. This proportion, having regard to the broadcaster's informational, educational, cultural and entertainment responsibilities to its viewing public, should be achieved progressively, on the basis of suitable criteria.

2   Where the proportion laid down in paragraph 1 cannot be attained, it must not be lower than the average for 1988 in the Member State concerned.

However, in respect of the Hellenic Republic and the Portuguese Republic, the year 1988 shall be replaced by the year 1990.

3    From 3 October 1991, the Member States shall provide the Commission every two years with a report on the application of this Article and Article 5.

That report shall in particular include a statistical statement on the achievement of the proportion referred to in this Article and Article 5 for each of the television programmes falling within the jurisdiction of the Member State concerned, the reasons, in each case, for the failure to attain that proportion and the measures adopted or envisaged in order to achieve it.

The Commission shall inform the other Member States and the European Parliament of the reports, which shall be accompanied, where appropriate, by an opinion. The Commission shall ensure the application of this Article and Article 5 in accordance with the provisions of the Treaty. The Commission may take account in its opinion, in particular, of progress achieved in relation to previous years, the share of first broadcast works in the programming, the particular circumstances of new television broadcasters and the specific situation of countries with a low audio-visual production capacity or restricted language area.

4    The Council shall review the implementation of this Article on the basis of a report from the Commission accompanied by any proposals for revision that it may deem appropriate no later than the end of the fifth year from the adoption of the Directive.

To that end, the Commission report shall, on the basis of the information provided by Member States under paragraph 3, take account in particular of developments in the Community market and of the international context.

Article 5

Member States shall ensure, where practicable and by appropriate means, that broadcasters reserve at least 10% of their transmission time, excluding the time appointed to news, sports events, games, advertising, teletext services and teleshopping, or alternately, at the discretion of the Member State, at least 10% of their programming budget, for European works created by producers who are independent of broadcasters. This proportion, having regard to broadcasters' informational, educational, cultural and entertainment responsibilities to its viewing public, should be achieved progressively, on the basis of suitable criteria; it must be achieved by earmarking an adequate proportion for recent works, that is to say works transmitted within five years of their production.

Article 6

1    Within the meaning of this chapter, 'European works' means the following:

(a) works originating from Member States;

    (b)  works originating from European third States party to the European Convention on Transfrontier Television of the Council of Europe and fulfiling the conditions of paragraph 2;

    (c)  works originating from other European third countries and fulfiling the conditions of paragraph 3.

Application of the provisions of (b) and (c) shall be conditional on works originating from Member States not being the subject of discriminatory measures in the third countries concerned.

2    The works referred to in paragraph 1(a) and (b) are works mainly made with authors and workers residing in one or more States referred to in paragraph 1(a) and (b) provided that they comply with one of the following three conditions:

    (a)  they are made by one or more producers established in one or more of those States; or

    (b)  production of the works is supervised and actually controlled by one or more producers established in one or more of those States; or

    (c)  the contribution of co-producers of those States to the total co-production costs is preponderant and the co-production is not controlled by one or more producers established outside those States.

3    The works referred to in paragraph 1(c) are works made exclusively or in co-production with producers established in one or more Member States by producers established in one or more European third countries with which the Community has concluded agreements relating to the audio-visual sector, if those works are mainly made with authors and workers residing in one or more European States.

4    Works that are not European works within the meaning of paragraph 1 but that are produced within the framework of bilateral co-production treaties concluded between Member States and third countries shall be deemed to be European works provided that the Community co-producers supply a majority share of the total cost of the production and that the production is not controlled by one or more producers established outside the territory of the Member States.

5    Works which are not European works within the meaning of paragraphs 1 and 4, but made mainly with authors and workers residing in one or more Member States, shall be considered to be European works to an extent corresponding to the proportion of the contribution of Community co-producers to the total production costs.

Article 7

Member States shall ensure that broadcasters under their jurisdiction do not broadcast cinematographic works outside periods agreed with the rights holders.

Article 9

This Chapter shall not apply to television broadcasts that are intended for local audiences and do not form part of a national network.

## Chapter IV Television advertising, sponsorship and teleshopping

Article 10

1  Television advertising and teleshopping shall be readily available as such and kept quite separate from other parts of the programme service by optical and/or acoustic means.

2  Isolated advertising and teleshopping spots shall remain the exception.

3  Advertising and teleshopping shall not use subliminal techniques.

4  Surreptitious advertising and teleshopping shall be prohibited.

Article 11

1  Advertising and teleshopping spots shall be inserted between programmes. Provided the conditions set out in paragraphs 2 to 5 are fulfiled, advertising and teleshopping spots may also be inserted during programmes in such a way that the integrity and value of the programme, taking into account natural breaks in and the duration and nature of the programme, and rights of the rights holders are not prejudiced.

2  In programmes consisting of autonomous parts, or in sports programmes and similarly structured events and performances containing intervals, advertising and teleshopping spots shall only be inserted between the parts or in the intervals.

3  The transmission of audio-visual works such as feature films and films made for television (excluding series, serials, light entertainment programmes and documentaries), provided their scheduled duration is more than 45 minutes, may be interrupted once for each period of 45 minutes. A further interruption shall be allowed if their scheduled duration is at least 20 minutes longer than two or more complete periods of 45 minutes.

4  Where programmes, other than those covered by paragraph 2, are interrupted by advertising or teleshopping spots, a period of at least 20 minutes should elapse between each successive advertising break within the programme.

5  Advertising and teleshopping shall not be inserted in any broadcast of a religious service. News and current affairs programmes, documentaries, religious programmes and children's programmes, when their scheduled duration is less than 30 minutes, shall not be interrupted by advertising or by teleshopping. If their scheduled duration is 30 minutes or longer, the provisions of the previous paragraph shall apply.

Article 12

Television advertising and teleshopping shall not:

(a)  prejudice respect for human dignity;

(b) include any discrimination on grounds of race, sex or nationality;

(c) be offensive to religious or political beliefs;

(d) encourage behaviour prejudicial to health and safety;

(e) encourage behaviour prejudicial to the protection of the environment.

### Article 13

All forms of television advertising and teleshopping for cigarettes and other tobacco products shall be prohibited.

### Article 14

1   Television advertising for medicinal products and medical treatment available only on prescription in the Member State within whose jurisdiction the broadcaster falls shall be prohibited.

2   Teleshopping for medicinal products which are subject to a marketing authorisation within the meaning of Council Directive 65/65/EEC of 26 January 1965 on the approximation of provisions laid down by law, regulation or administrative action relating to medicinal products, as well as teleshopping for medical treatment, shall be prohibited.

### Article 15

Television advertising and teleshopping for alcoholic beverages shall comply with the following criteria:

(a) it may not be aimed specifically at minors or, in particular, depict minors consuming these beverages;

(b) it shall not link the consumption of alcohol to enhanced physical performance or to driving;

(c) it shall not create the impression that the consumption of alcohol contributes towards social or sexual success;

(d) it shall not claim that alcohol has therapeutic qualities or that it is a stimulant, a sedative or a means of resolving personal conflicts;

(e) it shall not encourage immoderate consumption of alcohol or present abstinence or moderation in a negative light;

(f) it shall not place emphasis on high alcoholic content as being a positive quality of the beverages.

### Article 16

1   Television advertising shall not cause moral or physical detriment to minors, and shall therefore comply with the following criteria for their protection:

(a) it shall not directly exhort minors to buy a product or a service by exploiting their inexperience or credulity;

(b) it shall not directly encourage minors to persuade their parents or others to purchase the goods or services being advertised;

(c) it shall not exploit the special trust minors place in parents, teachers or other persons;

(d) it shall not unreasonably show minors in dangerous situations.

2   Teleshopping shall comply with the requirements referred to in paragraph 1 and, in addition, shall not exhort minors to contract for the sale or rental of goods and services.

Article 17

1   Sponsored television programmes shall meet the following requirements:

(a) the content and scheduling of sponsored programmes may in no circumstances be influenced by the sponsor in such a way as to affect the responsibility and editorial independence of the broadcaster in respect of programmes;

(b) they must be clearly identified as such by the name and/or logo of the sponsor at the beginning and/or the end of the programmes;

(c) they must not encourage the purchase or rental of the products or services of the sponsor or a third party, in particular by making special promotional references to those products or services.

2   Television programmes may not be sponsored by undertakings whose principal activity is the manufacture or sale of cigarettes and other tobacco products.

3   Sponsorship of television programmes by undertakings whose activities include the manufacture or sale of medicinal products and medical treatment may promote the name or the image of the undertaking but may not promote specific medicinal products or medical treatments available only on prescription in the Member State within whose jurisdiction the broadcaster falls.

4   News and current affairs programmes may not be sponsored.

Article 18

1   The proportion of transmission time devoted to teleshopping spots, advertising spots and other forms of advertising, with the exception of teleshopping windows within the meaning of Article 18a, shall not exceed 20% of the daily transmission time. The transmission time for advertising spots shall not exceed 15% of the daily transmission time.

2   The proportion of advertising spots and teleshopping spots within a given clock hour shall not exceed 20%.

3   For the purposes of this Article, advertising does not include:

– announcements made by the broadcaster in connection with its own programmes and ancillary products directly derived from those programmes;

– public service announcements and charity appeals broadcast free of charge.

Article 18a

1   Windows devoted to teleshopping broadcast by a channel not exclusively devoted to teleshopping shall be of a minimum uninterrupted duration of 15 minutes.

2　The maximum number of windows per day shall be eight. Their overall duration shall not exceed three hours per day. They must be clearly identified as teleshopping windows by optical and acoustic means.

Article 19

Chapters I, II, IV, V, VI, VIa and VII shall apply mutatis mutandis to channels exclusively devoted to teleshopping. Advertising on such channels shall be allowed within the daily limits established by Article 18(1). Article 18(2) shall not apply.

Article 19a

Chapters I, II, IV, V, VI, VIa and VII shall apply mutatis mutandis to channels exclusively devoted to self-promotion. Other forms of advertising on such channels shall be allowed within the limits established by Article 18(1) and (2). This provision in particular shall be subject to review in accordance with Article 26.

Article 20

Without prejudice to Article 3, Member States may, with due regard for Community law, lay down conditions other than those laid down in Article 11(2) to (5) and Articles 18 and 18a in respect of broadcasts intended solely for the national territory which cannot be received, directly or indirectly by the public, in one or more Member States.

**Chapter V Protection of minors and public order**

Article 22

1　Member States shall take appropriate measures to ensure that television broadcasts by broadcasters under their jurisdiction do not include any programmes which might seriously impair the physical, mental or moral development of minors, in particular programmes that involve pornography or gratuitous violence.

2　The measures provided for in paragraph 1 shall also extend to other programmes which are likely to impair the physical, mental or moral development of minors, except where it is ensured, by selecting the time of the broadcast or by any technical measure, that minors in the area of transmission will not normally hear or see such broadcasts.

3　Furthermore, when such programmes are broadcast in unencoded form Member States shall ensure that they are preceded by an acoustic warning or are identified by the presence of a visual symbol throughout their duration.

Article 22a

Member States shall ensure that broadcasts do not contain any incitement to hatred on grounds of race, sex, religion or nationality.

Article 22b

1   The Commission shall attach particular importance to application of this Chapter in the report provided for in Article 26.

2   The Commission shall within one year from the date of publication of this Directive, in liaison with the competent Member State authorities, carry out an investigation of the possible advantages and drawbacks of further measures with a view to facilitating the control exercised by parents or guardians over the programmes that minors may watch. This study shall consider, *inter alia*, the desirability of:

   –   the requirement for new television sets to be equipped with a technical device enabling parents or guardians to filter out certain programmes;

   –   the setting up of appropriate rating systems,

   –   encouraging family viewing policies and other educational and awareness measures,

   –   taking into account experience gained in this field in Europe and elsewhere as well as the views of interested parties such as broadcasters, producers, educationalists, media specialists and relevant associations.

## Chapter VI Right of reply

Article 23

1   Without prejudice to other provisions adopted by the Member States under civil, administrative or criminal law, any natural or legal person, regardless of nationality, whose legitimate interests, in particular reputation and good name, have been damaged by an assertion of incorrect facts in a television programme must have a right of reply or equivalent remedies. Member States shall ensure that the actual exercise of the right of reply or equivalent remedies is not hindered by the imposition of unreasonable terms or conditions. The reply shall be transmitted within a reasonable time subsequent to the request being substantiated and at a time and in a manner appropriate to the broadcast to which the request refers.

2   A right of reply or equivalent remedies shall exist in relation to all broadcasters under the jurisdiction of a Member State.

3   Member States shall adopt the measures needed to establish the right of reply or the equivalent remedies and shall determine the procedure to be followed for the exercise thereof. In particular, they shall ensure that a sufficient time span is allowed and that the procedures are such that the right or equivalent remedies can be exercised appropriately by natural or legal persons resident or established in other Member States.

4   An application for exercise of the right of reply or the equivalent remedies may be rejected if such a reply is not justified according to the conditions laid down in paragraph 1, would involve a punishable act, would render the broadcaster liable to civil law proceedings or would transgress standards of public decency.

5   Provision shall be made for procedures whereby disputes as to the exercise of the right of reply or the equivalent remedies can be subject to judicial review.

## Chapter VIa Contact committee

Article 23a

1   A contact committee shall be set up under the aegis of the Commission. It shall be composed of representatives of the competent authorities of the Member States. It shall be chaired by a representative of the Commission and meet either on his initiative or at the request of the delegation of a Member State.

2   The tasks of this committee shall be:

(a) to facilitate effective implementation of this Directive through regular consultation on any practical problems arising from its application, and particularly from the application of Article 2, as well as on any other matters on which exchanges of views are deemed useful;

(b) to deliver own-initiative opinions or opinions requested by the Commission on the application by the Member States of the provisions of this Directive;

(c) to be the forum for an exchange of views on what matters should be dealt with in the reports which Member States must submit pursuant to Article 4(3), on the methodology of these, on the terms of reference for the independent study referred to in Article 25a, on the evaluation of tenders for this and on the study itself;

(d) to discuss the outcome of regular consultations which the Commission holds with representatives of broadcasting organisations, producers, consumers, manufacturers, service providers and trade unions and the creative community;

(e) to facilitate the exchange of information between the Member States and the Commission on the situation and the development of regulatory activities regarding television broadcasting services, taking account of the Community's audio-visual policy, as well as relevant developments in the technical field;

(f) to examine any development arising in the sector on which an exchange of views appears useful.

## Chapter VII Final provisions

Article 24

In fields which this Directive does not co-ordinate, it shall not affect the rights and obligations of Member States resulting from existing conventions dealing with telecommunications or broadcasting.

Article 25

1   Member States shall bring into force the laws, regulations and administrative provisions necessary to comply with this Directive not later than 3 October 1991. They shall forthwith inform the Commission thereof.

2    Member States shall communicate to the Commission the text of the main provisions of national law which they adopt in the fields governed by this Directive.

Article 25a

A further review as provided for in Article 4(4) shall take place before 30 June 2002. It shall take account of an independent study on the impact of the measures in question at both Community and national level.

Article 26

Not later than 31 December 2000, and every two years thereafter, the Commission shall submit to the European Parliament, the Council and the Economic and Social Committee a report on the application of this Directive as amended and, if necessary, make further proposals to adapt it to developments in the field of television broadcasting, in particular in the light of recent technological developments.

Article 27

1    Member States shall bring into force the laws, regulations and administrative provisions necessary to comply with this Directive not later than 30 December 1998. They shall immediately inform the Commission thereof.

When Member States adopt these measures, they shall contain a reference to this Directive or be accompanied by such reference on the occasion of their official publication. The methods of making such reference shall be laid down by Member States.

2    Member States shall communicate to the Commission the text of the main provisions of national law which they adopt in the field covered by this Directive.

Article 28

This Directive shall enter into force on the date of its publication in the Official Journal of the European Communities.

Article 29

This Directive is addressed to the Member States.

Done at Brussels.

*For the Parliament*          *For the Council*

*The President*          *The President*

# COUNCIL OF EUROPE: EUROPEAN CONVENTION ON TRANSFRONTIER TELEVISION

*No 132, Strasbourg, 5.5.1989*

PREAMBLE

The Member States of the Council of Europe and the other States party to the European Cultural Convention, signatory hereto,

Considering that the aim of the Council of Europe is to achieve a greater unity between its members, for the purpose of safeguarding and realising the ideals and principles which are their common heritage;

Considering that the dignity and equal worth of every human being constitute fundamental elements of those principles;

Considering that the freedom of expression and information, as embodied in Article 10 of the Convention for the Protection of Human Rights and Fundamental Freedoms, constitutes one of the essential principles of a democratic society and one of the basic conditions for its progress and for the development of every human being;

Reaffirming their commitment to the principles of the free flow of information and ideas and the independence of broadcasters, which constitute an indispensable basis for their broadcasting policy;

Affirming the importance of broadcasting for the development of culture and the free formation of opinions in conditions safeguarding pluralism and equality of opportunity among all democratic groups and political parties;

Convinced that the continued development of information and communication technology should serve to further the right, regardless of frontiers, to express, to seek, to receive and to impart information and ideas whatever their source;

Being desirous to present an increasing range of choice of programme services for the public, thereby enhancing Europe's heritage and developing its audio-visual creation, and being determined to achieve this cultural objective through efforts to increase the production and circulation of high-quality programmes, thereby responding to the public's expectations in the political, educational and cultural fields;

Recognising the need to consolidate the common broad framework of regulation;

Bearing in mind Resolution No 2 and the Declaration of the First European Ministerial Conference on Mass Media Policy;

Being desirous to develop the principles embodied in the existing Council of Europe recommendations on principles on television advertising, on equality between women and men in the media, on the use of satellite capacity for television and sound radio, and on the promotion of audio-visual production in Europe,

Have agreed as follows:

## CHAPTER I GENERAL PROVISIONS

Article 1

*Object and purpose*

This Convention is concerned with programme services embodied in transmissions. The purpose is to facilitate, among the Parties, the transfrontier transmission and the retransmission of television programme services.

Article 2

*Terms employed*

For the purposes of this Convention:

a    'Transmission' means the initial emission by terrestrial transmitter, by cable, or by satellite of whatever nature, in encoded or unencoded form, of television programme services for reception by the general public. It does not include communication services operating on individual demand;

b    'Retransmission' signifies the fact of receiving and simultaneously transmitting, irrespective of the technical means employed, complete and unchanged television programme services, or important parts of such services, transmitted by broadcasters for reception by the general public;

c    'Broadcaster' means the natural or legal person who composes television programme services for reception by the general public and transmits them or has them transmitted, complete and unchanged, by a third party;

d    'Programme service' means all the items within a single service provided by a given broadcaster within the meaning of the preceding paragraph;

e    'European audio-visual works' means creative works, the production or co-production of which is controlled by European natural or legal persons;

f    'Advertisement' means any public announcement intended to promote the sale, purchase or rental of a product or service, to advance a cause or idea or to bring about some other effect desired by the advertiser, for which transmission time has been given to the advertiser for remuneration or similar consideration;

g    'Sponsorship' means the participation of a natural or legal person, who is not engaged in broadcasting activities or in the production of audio-visual works, in the direct or indirect financing of a programme with a view to promoting the name, trademark or image of that person.

Article 3

*Field of application*

This Convention shall apply to any programme service transmitted or retransmitted by entities or by technical means within the jurisdiction of a Party, whether by cable, terrestrial transmitter or satellite, and which can be received, directly or indirectly, in one or more other Parties.

Article 4

*Freedom of reception and retransmission*

The Parties shall ensure freedom of expression and information in accordance with Article 10 of the Convention for the Protection of Human Rights and Fundamental Freedoms and they shall guarantee freedom of reception and shall not restrict the retransmission on their territories of programme services which comply with the terms of this Convention.

Article 5

*Duties of the transmitting Parties*

1   Each transmitting Party shall ensure, by appropriate means and through its competent organs, that all programme services transmitted by entities or by technical means within its jurisdiction, within the meaning of Article 3, comply with the terms of this Convention.

2   For the purposes of this Convention, the transmitting Party shall be:

a   in the case of terrestrial transmissions, the Party in which the initial emission is effected;

b   in the case of satellite transmissions:

i   the Party in which the satellite up-link is situated;

ii   the Party which grants the use of the frequency or a satellite capacity when the up-link is situated in a State which is not a Party to this Convention;

iii   the Party in which the broadcaster has its seat when responsibility under sub-paragraphs i and ii is not established.

3   When programme services transmitted from States which are not Parties to this Convention are retransmitted by entities or by technical means within the jurisdiction of a Party, within the meaning of Article 3, that Party, acting as transmitting Party, shall ensure, by appropriate means and through its competent organs, compliance with the terms of this Convention.

Article 6

*Provision of information*

1   The responsibilities of the broadcaster shall be clearly and adequately specified in the authorisation issued by, or contract concluded with, the competent authority of each Party, or by any other legal measure.

2.   Information about the broadcaster shall be made available, upon request, by the competent authority of the transmitting Party. Such information shall include, as a minimum, the name or denomination, seat and status of the broadcaster, the name of the legal representative, the composition of the capital, the nature, purpose and mode of financing of the programme service the broadcaster is providing or intends providing.

**CHAPTER II PROGRAMMING MATTERS**

Article 7

*Responsibilities of the broadcaster*

1   All items of programme services, as concerns their presentation and content, shall respect the dignity of the human being and the fundamental rights of others.

In particular, they shall not:

a   be indecent and in particular contain pornography;

b   give undue prominence to violence or be likely to incite to racial hatred.

2   All items of programme services which are likely to impair the physical, mental or moral development of children and adolescents shall not be scheduled when, because of the time of transmission and reception, they are likely to watch them.

3   The broadcaster shall ensure that news fairly present facts and events and encourage the free formation of opinions.

Article 8

*Right of reply*

1   Each transmitting Party shall ensure that every natural or legal person, regardless of nationality or place of residence, shall have the opportunity to exercise a right of reply or to seek other comparable legal or administrative remedies relating to programmes transmitted or retransmitted by entities or by technical means within its jurisdiction, within the meaning of Article 3. In particular, it shall ensure that timing and other arrangements for the exercise of the right of reply are such that this right can be effectively exercised. The effective exercise of this right or other comparable legal or administrative remedies shall be ensured both as regards the timing and the modalities.

2   For this purpose, the name of the broadcaster responsible for the programme service shall be identified therein at regular intervals by appropriate means.

Article 9

*Access of the public to major events*

Each Party shall examine the legal measures to avoid the right of the public to information being undermined due to the exercise by a broadcaster of exclusive rights for the transmission or retransmission, within the meaning of Article 3, of an event of high public interest and which has the effect of depriving a large part of the public in one or more other Parties of the opportunity to follow that event on television.

Article 10

*Cultural objectives*

1   Each transmitting Party shall ensure, where practicable and by appropriate means, that broadcasters reserve for European works a majority proportion of their transmission time, excluding the time appointed to news, sports events, games, advertising and teletext services. This proportion, having regard to the broadcaster's informational, educational, cultural and entertainment responsibilities to its viewing public, should be achieved progressively, on the basis of suitable criteria.

2   In case of disagreement between a receiving Party and a transmitting Party on the application of the preceding paragraph, recourse may be had, at the request of one of the Parties, to the Standing Committee with a view to its formulating an advisory opinion on the subject. Such a disagreement shall not be submitted to the arbitration procedure provided for in Article 26.

3   The Parties undertake to look together for the most appropriate instruments and procedures to support, without discrimination between broadcasters, the activity and development of European production, particularly in countries with a low audio-visual production capacity or restricted language area.

4   The Parties, in the spirit of co-operation and mutual assistance which underlies this Convention, shall endeavour to avoid that programme services transmitted or retransmitted by entities or by technical means within their jurisdiction, within the meaning of Article 3, endanger the pluralism of the press and the development of the cinema industries. No cinematographic work shall accordingly be transmitted in such services, unless otherwise agreed between its rights holders and the broadcaster, until two years have elapsed since the work was first shown in cinemas; in the case of cinematographic works co-produced by the broadcaster, this period shall be one year.

## CHAPTER III ADVERTISING

Article 11

*General standards*

1   All advertisements shall be fair and honest.

2   Advertisements shall not be misleading and shall not prejudice the interests of consumers.

3   Advertisements addressed to or using children shall avoid anything likely to harm their interests and shall have regard to their special susceptibilities.

4   The advertiser shall not exercise any editorial influence over the content of programmes.

Article 12

*Duration*

1 The amount of advertising shall not exceed 15% of the daily transmission time. However, this percentage may be increased to 20% to include forms of advertisements such as direct offers to the public for the sale, purchase or rental of products or for the provision of services, provided the amount of spot advertising does not exceed 15%.

2 The amount of spot advertising within a given one-hour period shall not exceed 20%.

3 Forms of advertisements such as direct offers to the public for the sale, purchase or rental of products or for the provision of services shall not exceed one hour per day.

Article 13

*Form and presentation*

1 Advertisements shall be clearly distinguishable as such and recognisably separate from the other items of the programme service by optical or acoustic means. In principle, they shall be transmitted in blocks.

2 Subliminal advertisements shall not be allowed.

3 Surreptitious advertisements shall not be allowed, in particular the presentation of products or services in programmes when it serves advertising purposes.

4 Advertisements shall not feature, visually or orally, persons regularly presenting news and current affairs programmes .

Article 14

*Insertion of advertisements*

1 Advertisements shall be inserted between programmes. Provided the conditions contained in paragraphs 2 to 5 of this article are fulfiled, advertisements may also be inserted during programmes in such a way that the integrity and value of the programme and the rights of the rights holders are not prejudiced.

2 In programmes consisting of autonomous parts, or in sports programmes and similarly structured events and performances comprising intervals, advertisements shall only be inserted between the parts or in the intervals.

3 The transmission of audio-visual works such as feature films and films made for television (excluding series, serials, light entertainment programmes and documentaries), provided their duration is more than forty-five minutes, may be interrupted once for each complete period of forty-five minutes. A further interruption is allowed if their duration is at least twenty minutes longer than two or more complete periods of forty-five minutes.

4 Where programmes, other than those covered by paragraph 2, are interrupted by advertisements, a period of at least twenty minutes should elapse between each successive advertising break within the programme.

5   Advertisements shall not be inserted in any broadcast of a religious service. News and current affairs programmes, documentaries, religious programmes, and children's programmes, when they are less than thirty minutes of duration, shall not be interrupted by advertisements. If they last for thirty minutes or longer, the provisions of the previous paragraphs shall apply.

Article 15

*Advertising of particular products*

1   Advertisements for tobacco products shall not be allowed.

2   Advertisements for alcoholic beverages of all varieties shall comply with the following rules:

   a   they shall not be addressed particularly to minors and no one associated with the consumption of alcoholic beverages in advertisements should seem to be a minor;

   b   they shall not link the consumption of alcohol to physical performance or driving;

   c   they shall not claim that alcohol has therapeutic qualities or that it is a stimulant, a sedative or a means of resolving personal problems;

   d   they shall not encourage immoderate consumption of alcohol or present abstinence or moderation in a negative light;

   e   they shall not place undue emphasis on the alcoholic content of beverages.

3   Advertisements for medicines and medical treatment which are only available on medical prescription in the transmitting Party shall not be allowed.

4   Advertisements for all other medicines and medical treatment shall be clearly distinguishable as such, honest, truthful and subject to verification and shall comply with the requirement of protection of the individual from harm.

Article 16

*Advertising directed specifically at a single Party*

1   In order to avoid distortions in competition and endangering the television system of a Party, advertisements which are specifically and with some frequency directed to audiences in a single Party other than the transmitting Party shall not circumvent the television advertising rules in that particular Party.

2   The provisions of the preceding paragraph shall not apply where:

   a   the rules concerned establish a discrimination between advertisements transmitted by entities or by technical means within the jurisdiction of that Party and advertisements transmitted by entities or by technical means within the jurisdiction of another Party; or

   b   the Parties concerned have concluded bilateral or multilateral agreements in this area.

## CHAPTER IV SPONSORSHIP

Article 17

*General standards*

1 When a programme or series of programmes is sponsored in whole or in part, it shall clearly be identified as such by appropriate credits at the beginning and/or end of the programme.

2 The content and scheduling of sponsored programmes may in no circumstances be influenced by the sponsor in such a way as to affect the responsibility and editorial independence of the broadcaster in respect of programmes.

3 Sponsored programmes shall not encourage the sale, purchase or rental of the products or services of the sponsor or a third party, in particular by making special promotional references to those products or services in such programmes.

Article 18

*Prohibited sponsorship*

1 Programmes may not be sponsored by natural or legal persons whose principal activity is the manufacture or sale of products, or the provision of services, the advertising of which is prohibited by virtue of Article 15.

2 Sponsorship of news and current affairs programmes shall not be allowed.

## CHAPTER V MUTUAL ASSISTANCE

Article 19

Co-operation between the Parties

1 The Parties undertake to render each other mutual assistance in order to implement this Convention.

2 For that purpose:

    a each Contracting State shall designate one or more authorities, the name and address of each of which it shall communicate to the Secretary General of the Council of Europe at the time of deposit of its instrument of ratification, acceptance, approval or accession;

    b each Contracting State which has designated more than one authority shall specify in its communication under sub-paragraph a the competence of each authority.

3 An authority designated by a Party shall:

    a furnish the information foreseen under Article 6, paragraph 2, of this Convention;

    b furnish information at the request of an authority designated by another Party on the domestic law and practices in the fields covered by this Convention;

    c co-operate with the authorities designated by the other Parties whenever useful, and notably where this would enhance the effectiveness of measures taken in implementation of this Convention;

d    consider any difficulty arising from the application of this Convention which is brought to its attention by an authority designated by another Party.

## CHAPTER VI STANDING COMMITTEE

Article 20

*Standing Committee*

1    For the purposes of this Convention, a Standing Committee shall be set up.

2    Each Party may be represented on the Standing Committee by one or more delegates. Each delegation shall have one vote. Within the areas of its competence, the European Economic Community shall exercise its right to vote with a number of votes equal to the number of its Member States which are Parties to this Convention; the European Economic Community shall not exercise its right to vote in cases where the Member States concerned exercise theirs, and conversely.

3    Any State referred to in Article 29, paragraph 1, which is not a Party to this Convention may be represented on the Standing Committee by an observer.

4    The Standing Committee may seek the advice of experts in order to discharge its functions. It may, on its own initiative or at the request of the body concerned, invite any international or national, governmental or non-governmental body technically qualified in the fields covered by this Convention to be represented by an observer at one or part of one of its meetings. The decision to invite such experts or bodies shall be taken by a majority of three-quarters of the members of the Standing Committee.

5    The Standing Committee shall be convened by the Secretary General of the Council of Europe. Its first meeting shall be held within six months of the date of entry into force of the Convention. It shall subsequently meet whenever one-third of the Parties or the Committee of Ministers of the Council of Europe so requests, or on the initiative of the Secretary General of the Council of Europe in accordance with the provisions of Article 23, paragraph 2, or at the request of one or more Parties in accordance with the provisions of Articles 21, sub-paragraph c, and 25, paragraph 2.

6    A majority of the Parties shall constitute a quorum for holding a meeting of the Standing Committee.

7    Subject to the provisions of paragraph 4 and Article 23, paragraph 3, the decisions of the Standing Committee shall be taken by a majority of three-quarters of the members present.

8    Subject to the provisions of this Convention, the Standing Committee shall draw up its own Rules of Procedure.

Article 21

*Functions of the Standing Committee*

The Standing Committee shall be responsible for following the application of this Convention. It may:

a    make recommendations to the Parties concerning the application of the Convention;

b    suggest any necessary modifications of the Convention and examine those proposed in accordance with the provisions of Article 23;

c    examine, at the request of one or more Parties, questions concerning the interpretation of the Convention;

d    use its best endeavours to secure a friendly settlement of any difficulty referred to it in accordance with the provisions of Article 25;

e    make recommendations to the Committee of Ministers concerning States other than those referred to in Article 29, paragraph 1, to be invited to accede to this Convention.

Article 22

*Reports of the Standing Committee*

After each meeting, the Standing Committee shall forward to the Parties and the Committee of Ministers of the Council of Europe a report on its discussions and any decisions taken.

## CHAPTER VII AMENDMENTS

Article 23

*Amendments*

1    Any Party may propose amendments to this Convention.

2    Any proposal for amendment shall be notified to the Secretary General of the Council of Europe who shall communicate it to the Member States of the Council of Europe, to the other States party to the European Cultural Convention, to the European Economic Community and to any non-Member State which has acceded to, or has been invited to accede to this Convention in accordance with the provisions of Article 30. The Secretary General of the Council of Europe shall convene a meeting of the Standing Committee at the earliest two months following the communication of the proposal.

3    The Standing Committee shall examine any amendment proposed and shall submit the text adopted by a majority of three-quarters of the members of the Standing Committee to the Committee of Ministers for approval. After its approval, the text shall be forwarded to the Parties for acceptance.

4    Any amendment shall enter into force on the thirtieth day after all the Parties have informed the Secretary General of their acceptance thereof.

## CHAPTER VIII ALLEGED VIOLATIONS OF THIS CONVENTION

Article 24

*Alleged violations of this Convention*

1    When a Party finds a violation of this Convention, it shall communicate to the transmitting Party the alleged violation and the two Parties shall

endeavour to overcome the difficulty on the basis of the provisions of Articles 19, 25 and 26.

2   If the alleged violation is of a manifest, serious and grave nature which raises important public issues and concerns Articles 7, paragraphs 1 or 2, 12, 13, paragraph 1, first sentence, 14 or 15, paragraphs 1 or 3, and if it persists within two weeks following the communication, the receiving Party may suspend provisionally the retransmission of the incriminated programme service.

3   In all other cases of alleged violation, with the exception of those provided for in paragraph 4, the receiving Party may suspend provisionally the retransmission of the incriminated programme service eight months following the communication, if the alleged violation persists.

4   The provisional suspension of retransmission shall not be allowed in the case of alleged violations of Articles 7, paragraph 3, 8, 9 or 10.

## CHAPTER IX SETTLEMENT OF DISPUTES

Article 25

*Conciliation*

1   In case of difficulty arising from the application of this Convention, the Parties concerned shall endeavour to achieve a friendly settlement.

2   Unless one of the Parties concerned objects, the Standing Committee may examine the question, by placing itself at the disposal of the Parties concerned in order to reach a satisfactory solution as rapidly as possible and, where appropriate, to formulate an advisory opinion on the subject.

3   Each Party concerned undertakes to accord the Standing Committee, without delay, all information and facilities necessary for the discharge of its functions under the preceding paragraph.

Article 26

*Arbitration*

1   If the Parties concerned cannot settle the dispute in accordance with the provisions of Article 5, they may, by common agreement, submit it to arbitration, the procedure of which is provided for in the appendix to this Convention. In the absence of such an agreement within six months following the first request to open the procedure of conciliation, the dispute may be submitted to arbitration at the request of one of the Parties.

2   Any Party may, at any time, declare that it recognises as compulsory ipso facto and without special agreement in respect of any other Party accepting the same obligation the application of the arbitration procedure provided for in the appendix to this Convention.

## CHAPTER X OTHER INTERNATIONAL AGREEMENTS AND THE INTERNAL LAW OF THE PARTIES

Article 27

*Other international agreements or arrangements*

1   In their mutual relations, Parties which are members of the European Economic Community shall apply Community rules and shall not therefore apply the rules arising from this Convention except insofar as there is no Community rule governing the particular subject concerned.

2   Nothing in this Convention shall prevent the Parties from concluding international agreements completing or developing its provisions or extending their field of application.

3   In the case of bilateral agreements, this Convention shall not alter the rights and obligations of Parties which arise from such agreements and which do not affect the enjoyment of other Parties of their rights or the performance of their obligations under this Convention.

Article 28

*Relations between the Convention and the internal law of the Parties*

Nothing in this Convention shall prevent the Parties from applying stricter or more detailed rules than those provided for in this Convention to programme services transmitted by entities or by technical means within their jurisdiction, within the meaning of Article 3.

## CHAPTER XI FINAL PROVISIONS

Article 29

*Signature and entry into force*

1   This Convention shall be open for signature by the Member States of the Council of Europe and the other States party to the European Cultural Convention, and by the European Economic Community. It is subject to ratification, acceptance or approval. Instruments of ratification, acceptance or approval shall be deposited with the Secretary General of the Council of Europe.

2   This Convention shall enter into force on the first day of the month following the expiration of a period of three months after the date on which seven States, of which at least five Member States of the Council of Europe, have expressed their consent to be bound by the Convention in accordance with the provisions of the preceding paragraph.

3   A State may, at the time of signature or at any later date prior to the entry into force of this Convention in respect of that State, declare that it shall apply the Convention provisionally.

4   In respect of any State referred to in paragraph 1, or the European Economic Community, which subsequently express their consent to be bound by it, this Convention shall enter into force on the first day of the month following the expiration of a period of three months after the date of deposit of the instrument of ratification, acceptance or approval.

Article 30

*Accession by non-Member States*

1  After the entry into force of this Convention, the Committee of Ministers of the Council of Europe, after consulting the Contracting States may invite any other State to accede to this Convention by a decision taken by the majority provided for in Article 20.d of the Statute of the Council of Europe and by the unanimous vote of the representatives of the Contracting States entitled to sit on the Committee.

2  In respect of any acceding State, this Convention shall enter into force on the first day of the month following the expiration of a period of three months after the date of deposit of the instrument of accession with the Secretary General of the Council of Europe.

Article 31

*Territorial application*

1  Any State may, at the time of signature or when depositing its instrument of ratification, acceptance, approval or accession, specify the territory or territories to which this Convention shall apply.

2  Any State may, at any later date, by a declaration addressed to the Secretary General of the Council of Europe, extend the application of this Convention to any other territory specified in the declaration. In respect of such territory, the Convention shall enter into force on the first day of the month following the expiration of a period of three months after the date of receipt of such declaration by the Secretary General.

3  Any declaration made under the two preceding paragraphs may, in respect of any territory specified in such declaration, be withdrawn by a notification addressed to the Secretary General. The withdrawal shall become effective on the first day of the month following the expiration of a period of six months after the date of receipt of such notification by the Secretary General.

Article 32

*Reservations*

1  At the time of signature or when depositing its instrument of ratification, acceptance, approval or accession:

a  any State may declare that it reserves the right to restrict the retransmission on its territory, solely to the extent that it does not comply with its domestic legislation, of programme services containing advertisements for alcoholic beverages according to the rules provided for in Article 15, paragraph 2, of this Convention;

b  the United Kingdom may declare that it reserves the right not to fulfil the obligation, set out in Article 15, paragraph 1, to prohibit advertisements for tobacco products, in respect of advertisements for cigars and pipe tobacco broadcast by the Independent Broadcasting Authority by terrestrial means on its territory.

No other reservation may be made.

3    A reservation made in accordance with the preceding paragraph may not be the subject of an objection.

4    Any Contracting State which has made a reservation under paragraph 1 may wholly or partly withdraw it by means of a notification addressed to the Secretary General of the Council of Europe. The withdrawal shall take effect on the date of receipt of such notification by the Secretary General.

5    A Party which has made a reservation in respect of a provision of this Convention may not claim the application of that provision by any other Party; it may, however, if its reservation is partial or conditional, claim the application of that provision in so far as it has itself accepted it.

Article 33

*Denunciation*

1    Any Party may, at any time, denounce this Convention by means of a notification addressed to the Secretary General of the Council of Europe.

2    Such denunciation shall become effective on the first day of the month following the expiration of a period of six months after the date of receipt of the notification by the Secretary General.

Article 34

*Notifications*

The Secretary General of the Council of Europe shall notify the Member States of the Council, the other States party to the European Cultural Convention, the European Economic Community and any State which has acceded to, or has been invited to accede to this Convention of:

a    any signature;

b    the deposit of any instrument of ratification, acceptance, approval or accession;

c    any date of entry into force of this Convention in accordance with the provisions of Articles 29, 30 and 31;

d    any report established in accordance with the provisions of Article 22;

e    any other act, declaration, notification or communication relating to this Convention.

In witness whereof the undersigned, being duly authorised thereto, have signed this Convention.

Done at Strasbourg, the 5th May 1989, in English and French, both texts being equally authentic, in a single copy which shall be deposited in the archives of the Council of Europe. The Secretary General of the Council of Europe shall transmit certified copies to each Member State of the Council of Europe, to the other States Party to the European Cultural Convention, to the European Economic Community and to any State invited to accede to this Convention.

## APPENDIX

*Arbitration*

1 A request for arbitration shall be notified to the Secretary General of the Council of Europe. It shall include the name of the other party to the dispute and the subject matter of the dispute. The Secretary General shall communicate the information so received to all the Parties to this Convention.

2 In the event of a dispute between two Parties one of which is a Member State of the European Economic Community, the latter itself being a Party, the request for arbitration shall be addressed both to the Member State and to the Community, which jointly shall notify the Secretary General, within one month of receipt of the request, whether the Member State or the Community, or the Member State and the Community jointly, shall be party to the dispute. In the absence of such notification within the said time-limit, the Member State and the Community shall be considered as being one and the same party to the dispute for the purposes of the application of the provisions governing the constitution and procedure of the arbitration tribunal. The same shall apply when the Member State and the Community jointly present themselves as party to the dispute. In cases envisaged by this paragraph, the time-limit of one month foreseen in the first sentence of paragraph 4 hereafter shall be extended to two months.

3 The arbitration tribunal shall consist of three members: each of the parties to the dispute shall appoint one arbitrator; the two arbitrators so appointed shall designate by common agreement the third arbitrator who shall be the chairman of the tribunal. The latter shall not be a national of either of the parties to the dispute, nor have his usual place of residence in the territory of either of those parties, nor be employed by either of them, nor have dealt with the case in another capacity.

4 If one of the parties has not appointed an arbitrator within one month following the communication of the request by the Secretary General of the Council of Europe, he shall be appointed at the request of the other party by the President of the European Court of Human Rights within a further one-month period. If the President of the Court is unable to act or is a national of one of the parties to the dispute, the appointment shall be made by the Vice-President of the Court or by the most senior judge to the Court who is available and is not a national of one of the parties to the dispute. The same procedure shall be observed if, within a period of one month following the appointment of the second arbitrator, the Chairman of the arbitration tribunal is not designated.

5 The provisions of paragraphs 3 and 4 shall apply, as the case may be, in order to fill any vacancy.

6 Two or more parties which determine by agreement that they are in the same interest shall appoint an arbitrator jointly.

7 The parties to the dispute and the Standing Committee shall provide the arbitration tribunal with all facilities necessary for the effective conduct of the proceedings.

8  The arbitration tribunal shall draw up its own Rules of Procedure. Its decisions shall be taken by majority vote of its members. Its award shall be final and binding.

9  The award of the arbitration tribunal shall be notified to the Secretary General of the Council of Europe who shall communicate it to all the Parties to this Convention.

10 Each party to the dispute shall bear the expenses of the arbitrator appointed by it; these parties shall share equally the expenses of the other arbitrator, as well as other costs entailed by the arbitration.

# CODES OF THE INTERNATIONAL CHAMBER OF COMMERCE (ICC)

ICC International Code of Advertising Practice

ICC International Code of Environmental Advertising

ICC Revised Guidelines on Advertising and Marketing on the Internet

ICC International Code of Sales Promotion

ICC International Code on Sponsorship

ICC International Code of Direct Marketing

ICC/ESOMAR International Code of Marketing and Social Research Practice

## ICC INTERNATIONAL CODE OF ADVERTISING PRACTICE

### Introduction

This edition of the ICC International Code of Advertising Practice follows the well-established policy of the ICC of promoting high standards of ethics in marketing via self-regulatory codes intended to complement the existing frameworks of national and international law.

The Code, which was first issued in 1937, and revised in 1949, 1955, 1966, 1973 and 1987, is an expression of the business community's recognition of its social responsibilities in respect of commercial communications. The globalisation of the world's economies, and the intense competition which ensues therefrom, require the international business community to adopt standard rules. The adoption of these self-disciplinary rules is the best way that business leaders have of demonstrating that they are motivated by a sense of social responsibility, particularly in light of the increased liberalisation of markets. A manifestation of this commitment to social responsibility is to be found in the ICC's decision to incorporate formally within this code the former ICC Guidelines for Advertising Addressed to Children.

This edition combines past experience with current thinking based on the concept of advertising as a means of communication between sellers and customers. In this respect the ICC considers freedom of communication (as embodied in article 19 of the United Nations International Covenant of Civil and Political Rights) as a fundamental principle.

The Code is designed primarily as an instrument for self-discipline but it is also intended for use by the Courts as a reference document within the framework of applicable laws.

The ICC believes that this new edition of the Code will promote adherence to high standards of commercial communications leading to efficient international markets and significant consumer benefits.

## Scope of the Code

The Code applies to all advertisements for the promotion of any form of goods and services. It should be read in conjunction with the other ICC Codes of Marketing Practice, namely:

ICC International Code of Sales Promotion

ICC International Code of Practice on Direct Marketing

ICC Code on Environmental Advertising

ICC Code on Sponsorship

ICC/ESOMAR International Code of Marketing and Social Research Practice

The Code sets standards of ethical conduct to be followed by all concerned with advertising, whether as marketers or advertisers, advertising practitioners or agencies, or media, and is to be applied against the background of the applicable law.

## Interpretation

The Code is to be applied in the spirit as well as in the letter.

Because of the different characteristics of the various media (press, television, radio and other broadcast media, outdoor advertising, films, direct mail, fax, e-mail, Internet and on-line services, etc) an advertisement which is acceptable for one medium may not necessarily be acceptable for another. Advertisements, therefore, should be judged by their likely impact on the consumer, bearing in mind the medium used.

The Code applies to the entire content of an advertisement, including all words and numbers (spoken and written), visual presentations, music and sound effects.

## Definitions

For the purpose of this code:

- the term 'advertisement' is taken in its broadest sense, and means any form of advertising for goods or services, regardless of the medium used;
- the term 'product' refers to any good or service;
- the term 'consumer' refers to any person to whom an advertisement is addressed or who can reasonably be expected to be reached by it whether as a final consumer or as a trade customer or user.

### Basic principles

Article 1

All advertising should be legal, decent, honest and truthful.

Every advertisement should be prepared with a due sense of social responsibility and should conform to the principles of fair competition, as generally accepted in business.

No advertisement should be such as to impair public confidence in advertising.

**Decency**

Article 2

Advertisements should not contain statements or visual presentations which offend prevailing standards of decency.

**Honesty**

Article 3

Advertisements should be so framed as not to abuse the trust of consumers or exploit their lack of experience or knowledge.

**Social responsibility**

Article 4

1   Advertisements should not condone any form of discrimination, including that based upon race, national origin, religion, sex or age, nor should they in any way undermine human dignity.

2   Advertisements should not without justifiable reason play on fear.

3   Advertisements should not appear to condone or incite violence, nor to encourage unlawful or reprehensible behaviour.

4   Advertisements should not play on superstition.

**Truthful presentation**

Article 5

1   Advertisements should not contain any statement or visual presentation which directly or by implication, omission, ambiguity or exaggerated claim is likely to mislead the consumer, in particular with regard to:

   (a)  characteristics such as: nature, composition, method and date of manufacture, range of use, efficiency and performance, quantity, commercial or geographical origin or environmental impact;

   (b)  the value of the product and the total price actually to be paid;

   (c)  delivery, exchange, return, repair and maintenance;

   (d)  terms of guarantee;

   (e)  copyright and industrial property rights such as patents, trade marks, designs and models and trade names;

   (f)  official recognition or approval, awards of medals, prizes and diplomas;

   (g)  the extent of benefits for charitable causes.

2   Advertisements should not misuse research results or quotations from technical and scientific publications. Statistics should not be so presented as to exaggerate the validity of advertising claims. Scientific terms should not be used to falsely ascribe scientific validity to advertising claims.

### Comparisons

Article 6

Advertisements containing comparisons should be so designed that the comparison is not likely to mislead, and should comply with the principles of fair competition. Points of comparison should be based on facts which can be substantiated and should not be unfairly selected.

### Denigration

Article 7

Advertisements should not denigrate any firm, organisation, industrial or commercial activity, profession or product by seeking to bring it or them into public contempt or ridicule, or in any similar way.

### Testimonials

Article 8

Advertisements should not contain or refer to any testimonial or endorsement unless it is genuine, verifiable, relevant and based on personal experience or knowledge. Testimonials or endorsements which have become obsolete or misleading through passage of time should not be used.

### Portrayal or imitation of personal property

Article 9

Advertisements should not portray or refer to any persons, whether in a private or a public capacity, unless prior permission has been obtained; nor should advertisements without prior permission depict or refer to any person's property in a way likely to convey the impression of a personal endorsement.

### Exploitation of goodwill

Article 10

Advertisements should not make unjustifiable use of the name, initials, logo and/or trademarks of another firm, company or institution nor should advertisements in any way take undue advantage of another firm, person or institution's goodwill in its name, trade name or other intellectual property, nor should advertisements take advantage of the goodwill earned by other advertising campaigns.

### Imitation

Article 11

1 Advertisements should not imitate the general layout, text, slogan, visual presentation, music and sound effects, etc, of any other advertisements in a way that is likely to mislead or confuse the consumer.

2 Where advertisers have established distinctive advertising campaigns in one or more countries, other advertisers should not unduly imitate these campaigns in the other countries where the former may operate, thus preventing them from extending their campaigns within a reasonable period of time to such countries.

**Identification of advertisements**

Article 12

Advertisements should be clearly distinguishable as such, whatever their form and whatever the medium used; when an advertisement appears in a medium which contains news or editorial matter, it should be so presented that it will be readily recognised as an advertisement.

**Safety and health**

Article 13

Advertisements should not without reason, justifiable on educational or social grounds, contain any visual presentation or any description of dangerous practices or of situations which show a disregard for safety or health.

**Children and young people**

Article 14

The following provisions apply to advertisements addressed to children and young people who are minors under the applicable national law.

*Inexperience and credulity*

(a) Advertisements should not exploit the inexperience or credulity of children and young people.

(b) Advertisements should not understate the degree of skill or age level generally required to use or enjoy the product.

(i) Special care should be taken to ensure that advertisements do not mislead children and young people as to the true size, value, nature, durability and performance of the advertised product.

(ii) If extra items are needed to use it (eg, batteries) or to produce the result shown or described (eg, paint) this should be made clear.

(iii) A product which is part of a series should be clearly indicated as should the method of acquiring the series.

(iv) Where results of product use are shown or described, the advertisement should represent what is reasonably attainable by the average child or young person in the age range for which the product is intended.

(c) Price indication should not be such as to lead children and young people to an unreal perception of the true value of the product, for instance by using the word 'only'. No advertisements should imply that the advertised product is immediately within reach of every family budget.

*Avoidance of harm*

Advertisements should not contain any statement or visual presentation that could have the effect of harming children and young people mentally, morally or physically or of bringing them into unsafe situations or activities seriously threatening their health or security, or of encouraging them to consort with strangers or to enter strange or hazardous places.

*Social value*

(a) Advertisements should not suggest that possession or use of a product alone will give the child or young person physical, social or psychological advantages over other children or young people of the same age, or that non-possession of the product would have the opposite effect.

(b) Advertisements should not undermine the authority, responsibility, judgment or tastes of parents, taking into account the current social values. Advertisements should not include any direct appeal to children and young people to persuade their parents or other adults to buy advertised products for them.

## Guarantees

Article 15

Advertisements should not contain any reference to a guarantee which does not provide the consumer with additional rights to those provided by law. Advertisements may contain the word 'guarantee', 'guaranteed', 'warranty' or 'warranted' or words having the same meaning only if the full terms of the guarantee as well as the remedial action open to the purchaser are clearly set out in the advertisements, or are available to the purchaser in writing at the point of sale, or come with the goods.

## Unsolicited products

Article 16

Advertisements should not be used to introduce or support the practice whereby unsolicited products are sent to persons who are required, or given the impression that they are obliged to accept and pay for these products (inertia selling).

## Environmental behaviour

Article 17

Advertisements should not appear to approve or encourage actions which contravene the law, self-regulating codes or generally accepted standards of environmentally responsible behaviour. Advertisers should respect the principles set forth in the ICC Code on Environmental Advertising.

## Responsibility

Article 18

1   Responsibility for the observance of the rules of conduct laid down in the Code rests with the advertiser, the advertising practitioner or agency, and the publisher, media owner or contractor.

 (a) Advertisers should take the overall responsibility for their advertising.

 (b) Advertising practitioners or agencies should exercise every care in the preparation of advertisements and should operate in such a way as to enable advertisers to fulfil their responsibilities.

(c) Publishers, medium-owners or contractors, who publish, transmit or distribute advertisements should exercise due care in the acceptance of advertisements and their presentation to the public.

2   Those employed within a firm, company or institution coming under the above three categories and who take part in the planning, creation, publishing or transmitting of an advertisement have a degree of responsibility commensurate with their positions for ensuring that the rules of the Code are observed and should act accordingly.

### Rules apply to entirety of advertisement

Article 19

The responsibility for observance of the rules of the Code embraces the advertisement in its entire content and form, including testimonials and statements or visual presentations originating from other sources. The fact that the content or form originates wholly or in part from other sources is not an excuse for non-observance of the rules.

### Effect of subsequent redress for contravention

Article 20

While an advertiser's subsequent correction and appropriate redress for a contravention of the Code are desirable, they cannot excuse the original contravention of the Code.

### Substantiation

Article 21

Descriptions, claims or illustrations relating to verifiable facts should be capable of substantiation. Advertisers should have such substantiation available so that they can produce evidence without delay to the self-regulatory bodies responsible for the operation of the Code.

### Respect of self-regulatory decisions

Article 22

No advertiser, advertising practitioner or agency, publisher, medium-owner or contractor should be party to the publication of any advertisement which has been found unacceptable by the appropriate self-regulatory body.

### Implementation

Article 23

This Code of self-discipline should be implemented nationally by bodies set up for the purpose and internationally by the ICC's International Council on Marketing Practice as and when the need arises.

Document no 240/381. Rev 21 April 1997.

# ICC INTERNATIONAL CODE OF ENVIRONMENTAL ADVERTISING

## Introduction

The ICC International Code of Advertising Practice is widely accepted as the basis for promoting high standards of ethics in advertising, by self-regulation against a background of national and international law. The Code recognises social responsibilities towards the consumer and the community, and is designed primarily as an instrument for self-discipline.

Because of the growing importance of environmental issues and the complexity of judging and verifying environmental claims, the ICC has decided to produce an Environmental Advertising Code, in order to extend the area of self-discipline and to help business to make responsible use of environmental advertising. National rules and guidelines, where applicable, have been taken into account, as well as the ICC's Business Charter for Sustainable Development, together with the ICC position paper on Environmental Labelling Schemes.

Definitions in environmental terminology have not crystallised yet and vary currently between countries, and between industrial sectors. Consequently, specific definitions are not included in the Code, but further work within the ICC may make it possible to recommend such definitions in a future edition which should then be incorporated into the International Code of Advertising Practice.

## Scope of the Code

This Code applies to all advertisements containing environmental claims, in all media. It thus covers any form of advertising in which explicit or implicit reference is made to environmental or ecological aspects relating to the production, packaging, distribution, use/consumption or disposal of goods, services or facilities (collectively termed products). All are covered by the Code.

This Code should be seen as an extension of the ICC Code of Advertising Practice which therefore remains applicable on any aspect not specifically dealt with in this Code. The Code on Environmental Advertising should also be read in conjunction with the other ICC Codes of Marketing Practice, namely:

Marketing Research Practice

Sales Promotion Practice

Direct Marketing Practice

Direct Sales Practice.

## Interpretation

The Code is to be applied in the spirit as well as in the letter.

## Basic principles

All environmental advertising should be legal, decent, honest and truthful. It should be consistent with environmental regulations and mandatory programmes and should conform to the principles of fair competition, as generally accepted in business.

No advertisements or claims should be such as to impair public confidence in the efforts made by the business community to improve its ecological performance.

## Rules

### Honesty

Article 1

Advertisements should be so framed as not to abuse consumers' concern for the environment, or exploit their possible lack of environmental knowledge.

### Environmental behaviour

Article 2

Advertisements should not appear to approve or encourage actions which contravene the law, self-regulating codes or generally accepted standards of environmentally responsible behaviour.

### Truthful presentation

Article 3

Advertisements should not contain any statement or presentation likely to mislead consumers in any way about the environmental aspects or advantages of products, or about the actions being taken by the advertiser in favour of the environment. Corporate advertisements can refer to specific products or actions, but not imply without justification that they extend to the whole performance of a company, group or industry.

Expressions such as 'environmentally friendly' or 'ecologically safe' implying that a product or activity has no impact – or only a positive impact – on the environment should not be used unless a very high standard of proof is available.

### Scientific research

Article 4

Advertisements should only use technical demonstrations or scientific findings about environmental impact, when backed by serious scientific work.

Environmental jargon or scientific terminology is acceptable provided it is relevant and used in a way that can be readily understood by consumers.

### Testimonials

Article 5

In view of the rapid developments in environmental science and technology, particular care should be taken to ensure that, when testimonials or endorsements are used to support an environmental claim in an advertisement, changes in product formulation or market circumstances have not made the testimonial out of date.

### Superiority

Article 6

Environmental superiority over competitors can only be claimed when a significant advantage can be demonstrated.

Claims in relation to competitive products, when based on the absence of a harmful ingredient or a damaging effect, are only acceptable when other products in the category do include the ingredient or cause the effect.

### Product ingredients and elements

Article 7

Environmental claims should not imply that they relate to more stages of a product-life cycle, or to more properties of a product, than justified and should where necessary clearly indicate to which stage or which property they refer.

When advertisements refer to the reduction of ingredients or elements having a negative environmental impact, it must be clear what has been reduced. Alternative elements, if any, must bring a significant ecological improvement.

### Signs and symbols

Article 8

Environmental signs or symbols should only be used in an advertisement when the source of these signs or symbols is clearly indicated, and there is no confusion over the meaning. Such signs and symbols should not falsely suggest official approval.

### Waste collection recycling and disposal

Article 9

Environmental claims referring to waste separation, collection, processing or disposal are acceptable provided that the recommended method of collection, processing or disposal is generally accepted or sufficiently available, or the extent of availability is accurately described.

### Substantiation

Article 10

Descriptions, claims or illustrations relating to verifiable facts should be capable of substantiation. Advertisers should have such substantiation available so that they can produce evidence without delay to the self-regulatory bodies responsible for the operation of the International Code of Advertising Practice.

International Chamber of Commerce

The World Business Organisation

# ICC REVISED GUIDELINES ON ADVERTISING AND MARKETING ON THE INTERNET

*Commission on Advertising, Marketing and Distribution*

Principles for responsible advertising and marketing over the Internet, World Wide Web, on-line services and electronic networks

## Introduction

The global promise of new communications technologies has become a subject of great public interest, as businesses and governments discuss the best ways of introducing these technologies and of sharing with consumers the benefits they offer. By marrying the user-friendliness of the computer/television screen to the instantaneous transmission of telecommunications, these technologies are providing a new means for the delivery of information, entertainment and business services, bringing consumers and business closer together. Consumers are being empowered, more than ever before, to dialogue with producers and to precisely express their particular needs and desires.

Advertisers and marketers are helping to develop the new media just as they helped to develop the traditional media of the past. Today, advertising represents the main source of revenue for traditional media. Similarly, advertising and marketing will make a vital contribution to the new interactive media by allowing it to offer more affordable goods and services to a wider, global audience.

The International Chamber of Commerce (ICC) is the world's foremost developer of self-regulatory codes of ethical conduct for advertising and marketing practices. The ICC believes that advertising and marketing on the Internet, World Wide Web, and on-line services should reflect the highest standards of ethical conduct as laid down in the ICC International Code of Advertising Practice and other relevant ICC self-regulatory Codes.

The global character and technological properties of the new media have created a unique business environment. Media owners, in the traditional sense, do not exist, which has led to the bypassing of traditional intermediaries such as publishers and broadcasters. Responsible advertisers and marketers (which, in this new context, will mean any person or company posting an electronic commercial message) should recognise that it is in their own interest to observe self-disciplinary guidelines specifically adapted for electronic or interactive advertising and marketing. Advertisers and marketers should strive to create an electronic environment which all the world's consumers can fully trust.

Consumers and marketers should seek to co-operate in order to minimise the potential cost and to enhance efficiency savings of electronic networks. By choosing to share pertinent data about themselves, consumers can be provided with relevant product information and efficient and economical services. This will enable consumers to choose goods and services better adapted to their needs and tastes.

The ICC recognises that advertising and marketing in the interactive media is at an early stage of development and acknowledges that the relevant principles and revised guidelines may have to change and evolve as we learn more about the new technologies and their specific uses. Thus, in light of experience acquired, the ICC presents hereafter an updated version of the 1996 Guidelines. The ICC commits itself to the regular review of these revised Guidelines to ensure their continued viability.

With the above in mind, the ICC recommends the worldwide promulgation of the revised Guidelines below, which intend to fulfil the following objectives:

- to enhance the confidence of the public at large in advertising and marketing provided over the new interactive systems;
- to safeguard an optimum of freedom of expression for advertisers and marketers;
- to minimise the need for governmental and/or inter-governmental legislation or regulations; and
- to meet reasonable consumer privacy expectations.

### Scope of the Guidelines

These Guidelines apply to all marketing and advertising activities on the Internet for the promotion of any form of goods or services. The Guidelines set standards of ethical conduct to be observed by all involved with advertising and marketing activities on the Internet.

### Definitions

For the purpose of these Guidelines:

- the term 'Internet' refers to the public network of computer networks which enables the transmission of information between users, or between users and a place on the network, as well as to all interactive media and electronic networks such as the World Wide Web and on-line services;
- the term 'content' means all forms of advertising and marketing information and covers text, pictures, animation, video and audio, and may also include software;
- the term 'World Wide Web' refers to the network of resources accessible on the Internet using the Hypertext Transfer Protocol ('http').

### Basic principles

Article 1

All advertising and marketing on the Internet should comply with the spirit as well as the letter of the principles set forth in the ICC's Codes on Advertising Practice, Sales Promotion, Direct Marketing, Environmental Advertising, and Sponsorship as well as the ICC-ESOMAR Code on Marketing and Social Research Practice.

All advertising and marketing should be legal, decent, honest and truthful. 'Legal', in the context of these Guidelines, is presumed to mean that advertising and marketing messages should be legal in their country of origin.

Advertising and marketing messages should be sensitive to issues of social responsibility and should in addition conform to generally accepted principles as regards ethical marketing.

Advertising and marketing messages should not be designed or transmitted in such a way as to impair overall public confidence in the Internet as a medium and marketplace.

## Rules

### Disclosure of identity

Article 2

Advertisers and marketers of goods and services who post commercial messages via the Internet should always disclose their own identity and that of the relevant subsidiary, if applicable, in such a way that the user can contact the advertiser or marketer without difficulty.

### Costs and responsibilities associated with electronic sales and marketing

Article 3

Advertisers and marketers should clearly inform users of the cost of accessing a message or a service where the cost is higher than the basic telecommunications rate. Users should be provided with such notice of cost at the time they are about to access the message or service. This notice mechanism should allow users a reasonable amount of time, as set by the marketer or mandated by applicable law, to disconnect from the service without incurring the charge.

### Respect for public groups

Article 4

Advertisers and marketers should respect the role of particular electronic news groups, forums or bulletin boards as public meeting places which may have rules and standards as to acceptable commercial behaviour. Advertising and marketing messages posted to public sites are appropriate:

- when the forum or site receiving the message has a fundamentally commercial nature or activity; or
- when the subject or theme of the bulletin board or news group is pertinent to the content of the advertising or marketing message; or
- when the forum or site has otherwise implicitly or explicitly indicated consent to the receipt of advertising and marketing messages.

### Users' rights

Article 5

1 Collection and use of data

   Advertisers and marketers should disclose the purpose(s) for collecting and using personal data to users and should not use the data in a way incompatible with those purposes. Data files should be accurate, complete and kept up to date.

2 Data privacy

   Advertisers and marketers should take reasonable precautions to safeguard the security of their data files.

3 Disclosure of data

   The user should be given the opportunity to refuse the transfer of data to another advertiser or marketer. Personal data should not be disclosed when the user has objected except by authority of law. On-line mechanisms should be put in place to allow users to exercise their right to opt-out by electronic means.

4    Correction and blocking of data

Advertisers and marketers should give the user the right to obtain data relating to him and, where appropriate, to have such data corrected, completed, or blocked.

5    Privacy policy statements

Advertisers and marketers are encouraged to post their privacy policy statement on their on-line site. When such privacy policy statements exist, they should be easy to find, easy to use and comprehensible.

6    Unsolicited commercial messages

Advertisers and marketers should not send unsolicited commercial messages on-line to users who have indicated that they do not wish to receive such messages. Advertisers and marketers should make an on-line mechanism available to users by which the users can make known to the advertisers and marketers that they do not wish to receive future on-line solicitations. Unsolicited on-line advertising or marketing commercial messages should be clearly identified as such and should identify the advertiser or marketer.

**Advertising to children**

Article 6

Advertisers and marketers offering goods or services to children on-line should:

*   not exploit the natural credulity of children or the lack of experience of young people and should not strain their sense of loyalty;

*   not contain any content which might result in harm to children;

*   identify material intended only for adults;

*   encourage parents and/or guardians to participate in and/or supervise their children's on-line activities;

*   encourage young children to obtain their parent's and/or guardian's permission before the children provide information on-line, and make reasonable efforts to ensure that parental consent is given;

*   provide information to parents and/or guardians about ways to protect their children's privacy on-line.

**Respect for the potential sensitivities of a global audience**

Article 7

Given the global reach of electronic networks, and the variety and diversity of possible recipients of electronic messages, advertisers and marketers should be especially sensitive regarding the possibility that a particular message might be perceived as pornographic, violent, racist or sexist.

**Note**

1 ICC Codes and Guidelines are always subordinate to existing national law. There is currently no international unanimity as to whether country of origin or country of destination applies to advertising and marketing on the Internet.

Document no 240/394 Rev 3

2 April 1998

ICC Commission on Advertising, Marketing and Distribution

# ICC INTERNATIONAL CODE OF SALES PROMOTION

## Introduction

This edition of the ICC International Code of Sales Promotion Practice continues the well-established policy of the ICC of promoting high standards of ethics in marketing by self-regulation against the background of national and international law. The Code, which was first issued in 1973, demonstrates that industry and commerce recognise their social responsibilities towards the consumer and the community.

The Code combines past experience with current thinking based on the concept of sales promotion as a useful means of competition, necessary in the market economy, and the need to establish a fair balance between the interests of all parties concerned – producers, distributors and consumers.

The ICC considers it to be fundamental and in the interest of society as a whole that business, while observing the principles of fair competition, be free to choose between different marketing methods. The Code is designed primarily as an instrument for self-regulation but is also intended for use by the Courts as a reference document within the framework of the appropriate laws.

The ICC believes that this new edition of the Code, like its predecessor, by promoting further harmonisation of standards of sales promotion practice, will facilitate the circulation of goods and services across frontiers to the benefit of consumers and the community throughout the world.

## Scope of the Code

This Code applies, irrespective of medium and form of distribution, to marketing devices and techniques which are used to make goods and services more attractive by providing some additional benefit whether in cash or in kind, or the expectation of such a benefit. The code also applies to sales and trade incentive promotions, to editorial promotional offers and to those made by audio-visual media.

Promotions are temporary activities, but the Code applies also to the long-term and permanent use of promotional techniques. Amongst others, the Code covers such forms of promotion as:

premium offers of all kinds

reduced price and free offers

the distribution of stamps, coupons, vouchers and samples

charity-linked promotions

and prize promotions of all types including incentive programmes

## Interpretation

The Code is to be applied in the spirit as well as in the letter, bearing in mind the varying degrees of knowledge, experience and discriminatory ability of those to whom promotions are directed.

## Definitions

Depending on the circumstances of the promotion, any producer, wholesaler, retailer or other person in the marketing process may be promoter, intermediary and/or beneficiary.

In this Code:

- the term 'promoter' refers to any person, company or organisation by whom or on whose behalf a promotion is initiated

- the term 'intermediary' refers to any person, company or organisation, other than the promoter, furthering the implementation of any form of sales promotion

- the term 'beneficiary' refers to any person, company or organisation to whom any sales promotion is directed, whether as an ultimate consumer or as a professional or trade customer

- the term 'main product' refers to the product, service, or facility (or combination thereof) which is being promoted

- the term 'additional benefit' refers to any product, service or facility (or combination thereof) which is offered for a promotional purpose.

## Basic principles

The Code sets standards of ethical conduct as part of the system of self-regulation in marketing and thereby complements existing legal regulations in the country or countries concerned.

All sales promotions should be legal, decent, honest, truthful and conform to the principle of fair competition as generally accepted in business:

(a) all sales promotions should deal fairly and honourably with consumers and other beneficiaries

(b) all sales promotions should be so designed and conducted as to avoid causing justifiable disappointment or giving any other grounds for reasonable complaint

(c) the administration of promotions and the fulfilment of any obligation arising therefrom should be prompt and efficient

(d) the terms and conduct of all promotions should be equitable to all participants

(e) neither the design nor the implementation of a promotion should be such as to provoke, or to appear to condone, violent or otherwise anti-social behaviour, or to encourage practices contrary to the public interest

(f) the presentation of a promotion should not be likely to mislead those to whom it is addressed

(g) any factor likely to affect the decision whether or not to participate in a promotion should be communicated in such a way that the beneficiary can take it into account before being committed to any purchase which may be necessary for participation.

## General rules

### Integrity

Article 1

Sales promotions should be so framed as not to abuse the trust of the beneficiaries or intermediaries or to exploit their possible lack of experience or knowledge.

### Terms of the offer

Article 2

Sales promotions should be so devised as to make it easy for the beneficiary to identify clearly the terms of the offer. Care should be taken not to exaggerate the value of the additional benefit and the price of the main product should not be concealed by the promotional activity.

### Presentation

Article 3

The presentation of sales promotions should not be misleading. Any advertisements, including any advertising devices used at the point of sale, should be framed in strict accordance with the ICC International Code of Advertising Practice.

### Servicing of promotions

Article 4

Sales promotions should be administered with adequate resources and supervision, including all possible precautions to ensure that beneficiaries have no valid grounds for complaint about the servicing of the offer.

In particular, the promoter should make sure:

(a) that the availability of the additional benefits is adequate to allow demand to be honoured within a reasonably short term. If delay is inevitable beneficiaries should be so advised and necessary steps be taken to adjust the advertising of the offer

(b) that faulty goods or inadequate services will be replaced or that appropriate financial compensation will be given. Costs incurred as a direct result of such inadequacy will be refunded immediately, on request

(c) that complaints are efficiently and properly handled.

### Protection of privacy

Article 5

Sales promotions should respect the right of privacy of any individual member of the public and any trader and should not impose on them any undue trouble or annoyance.

### Safety

Article 6

Sales promotions should be designed and conducted with proper regard to normal safety precautions, so that intermediaries, beneficiaries or any other persons are not exposed to any harm.

Instructions for use should, wherever appropriate, include safety warnings.

### Children and young people

Article 7

Sales promotions addressed to, or likely to influence, children and young people should be so framed as not to take advantage of their natural credulity or lack of experience. Furthermore such promotions should be so framed as not to harm children or young people mentally, morally or physically, nor to strain their sense of loyalty vis à vis their parents or guardians.

### Relations with employees of others

Article 8

The terms of sales promotions should be so designed as to respect the bond of loyalty between employees and their employers.

## Specific rules

### Presentation to beneficiaries

Article 9

The presentation of sales promotions should allow the beneficiary to take account of all relevant details of the promotions offer, before purchasing the main product.

In particular, the presentation should include, where applicable:

(a) the method of making use of, or obtaining, the promotional offer, eg, conditions for obtaining free gifts or premiums, or for taking part in competitions or lotteries

(b) any time-limit for taking advantage of the promotional offer, eg, closing date for competitions

(c) any limitation as to geographical area, quantity of promotional items or other additional benefits available, or any other limitations on quantity. In the case of a limitation on quantity any arrangements for substituting alternative items or refunding money should be stated

(d) the requirements for proof of purchase

(e) the value of any voucher or stamp offered where a monetary alternative is available

(f) expenditure involved, including costs of freight, delivery or postage and the terms of payment

(g) the full name and address of the promoter

(h) an address to which complaints can be directed (where different from (g) above).

## Presentation to intermediaries

Article 10

Sales promotions should be so presented to intermediaries that they are able to evaluate the services and commitments required of them. In particular, the promoter should give adequate details as to:

(a) the organisation and scope of the promotion including the timing and any time-limit

(b) the ways in which the promotion will be presented to the trade and to the public

(c) the conditions for participation

(d) the financial implications for intermediaries

(e) any special administrative task required of intermediaries.

Article 11

The outer packing of goods bearing promotional offers should be clearly identified and should state any closing date or time-limit so that the intermediary is able to effect the necessary stock control.

## Particular obligations of promoters

Article 12

Sales promotions should be devised and handled with due regard to the legitimate interests of intermediaries and should respect their freedom of decision.

Article 13

The promoter should always obtain the prior agreement of the intermediary or his responsible manager if he, *inter alia*, wishes to:

(a) invite the employees of the intermediary to assist in any sales promotion

(b) offer any inducement or any reward, financial or otherwise, to such employees for their assistance or for any sales achievements in connection with any sales promotion.

In the case of an offer addressed openly through public media, for which such prior permission cannot be obtained, it should be clear that employees must obtain their employer's permission before participating.

Article 14

All goods, including additional benefits and other relevant material, should be delivered to the intermediary within a period which is reasonable in terms of any time limitation on the promotional offer.

Article 15

Sales promotions involving active co-operation by intermediaries or their employees should be so devised as not to prejudice any contractual relationship which may exist between intermediaries and beneficiaries.

**Particular obligations of intermediaries**

Article 16

Sales promotions involving any specific responsibility on the part of intermediaries should be so handled by them that no misinterpretation is likely to arise as to the terms, value, limitations or availability of the offer.

Article 17

Sales promotions which have been accepted by the intermediary should be fairly and honestly handled, and properly administered by him and his employees.

In particular, the intermediary should adhere to the plan and conditions of the promotion as laid down by the promoter. No changes of the agreed arrangements, eg, alteration to the time-limit, should be made by the intermediary without the prior agreement of the promoter.

**Fair competition**

Article 18

Sales promotions should be framed in a way which is fair to competitors and other traders in the market.

Article 19

Sales promotions involving comparisons with any other product, where permitted, should not misrepresent, or denigrate, the qualities and value of either product.

**Responsibility**

Article 20

1. The prime responsibility for all aspects of sales promotions, whatever their kind or content, always rests with the promoter.

2. Anyone taking part in the planning, creation or execution of any sales promotion has a degree of responsibility commensurate with his position for ensuring the observance of the Code towards intermediaries, beneficiaries, and other parties affected or likely to be affected by the promotion.

3. Thus in addition to the promoter the Code should be duly observed by:

(a) any marketing practitioner, consultant, advertising or sales promotion agency, or their subcontractors, who contribute to the sales promotion

(b) any intermediary who takes part in the promotion

(c) any supplier of any additional benefit who is involved in the sales promotion.

### Article 21

Substantiation of verifiable facts needed to establish compliance of the sales promotion with the Code should be available and be produced when called for by the self-regulatory bodies responsible for administering the Code.

### Article 22

No promoter, intermediary, marketing practitioner, consultant or agency, publisher, medium owner or contractor should be party to the implementation of any sales promotion which has been found unacceptable by the appropriate self-regulatory organisation set up for the operation of the Code.

**Implementation**

### Article 23

This Code of self-discipline is to be applied nationally by bodies set up for the purpose and internationally by the ICC's International Council on Marketing Practice as and when the need arises.

International Chamber of Commerce

The World Business Organisation

# ICC INTERNATIONAL CODE ON SPONSORSHIP

**Introduction**

Sponsorship has become one of the major sources of funding for both local and international events involving sports, the arts, the environment, media, humanitarian and community projects, education and various other fields.

Sponsorship is also a useful way for companies and organisations to convey a broad message in association with the event, in a manner which is acceptable to their consumers.

Although sponsorship is an integral part of marketing strategy, it differs from advertising as well as from patronage with respect to objectives, message and control. Sponsorship benefits the general public by making possible events and activities which might not have been feasible otherwise. Successful sponsorship therefore benefits all the concerned parties, including sponsors, organisers, media and performers, and the general public.

The ICC Code on Sponsorship has the intention of setting down basic principles and guidelines for good practice and fairness in sponsorship so that sponsorship may play its proper role in the best interests of all concerned.

The Code is designed primarily as an instrument for self-discipline within the framework of national and international laws, and is also intended to complement existing self-regulation in the country or countries concerned. The Code, however, is also designed to serve as an interpretative aid for the parties in the clarification of uncertainties arising under the sponsorship, as well as a reference for courts or arbitrators in sponsorship disputes.

## Scope of the Code

The Code applies to all sponsorship related to corporate image, brands, products, services activities or events of any kind.

The Code does not apply to advertising, sales promotions, direct marketing or other areas which are already covered by other ICC Codes. This Code does not apply to any sort of funding which lacks a commercial or communication purpose, such as donations.

## Definitions

In the context of the ICC Code on Sponsorship certain key terms are defined as follows:

Sponsorship: any communication by which a sponsor, for the mutual benefit of sponsor and sponsored party, contractually provides financing or other support in order to establish a positive association between the sponsor's image, brands, products or services and a sponsored event, activity, organisation or individual.

Sponsor: any corporation or legal person providing financial or other sponsorship support.

Sponsored party: any individual or legal person receiving direct or indirect support from a sponsor in relation with an activity or event.

Audience: the public, individuals, or organisations to which a sponsorship is directed.

Other marketing terms used in the Code are defined as in the previously enacted ICC Codes.

## Basic principles

A   All sponsorship should be honest, truthful, legal and conform to the accepted principles of fair competition in business.

B   The terms and conduct of sponsorship should be based upon principles of fairness and good faith between all parties to the sponsorship.

C   The sponsorship should be based on contractual obligations between the parties. Sponsorship should be acknowledged and should not be misleading.

D   All categories of sponsors who are legally allowed to conduct business are free to sponsor any activity, event or programme of any kind and to define a set of sponsorship objectives, provided that such a sponsorship is consistent with the principles of fairness and good faith set out in this Code and other self-regulatory Codes.

# Rules

### Clarity and accuracy

Article 1

Sponsorship and all related communications should be subject to the principle of clarity and accuracy with respect to all persons and organisations taking part in the sponsorship and to any rights or other privileges granted to the sponsor.

### Autonomy and self-determination

Article 2

Sponsorship should respect the autonomy and self-determination of the sponsored party in the management of its own activities and properties, provided the sponsored party fulfils the objectives set out in the sponsorship agreement.

In particular, where the sponsored party's intellectual or creative properties are part of the sponsorship agreement, the sponsored party's creative freedom should be respected.

### Imitation and confusion

Article 3

Sponsors and sponsored parties, as well as other parties involved in a given sponsorship, should avoid imitation of the representation of other sponsorships where such imitation might mislead or generate confusion, even if applied to non-competitive products, companies or events.

### Parties to the sponsorship

Article 4

The sponsor should take particular care to safeguard the inherent artistic, cultural, sporting or other content of the sponsored activity or organisation and should avoid any abuse of its position which would damage the identity, dignity, or reputation of the sponsored party.

The sponsored party should never obscure, deform or impugn the image or trademarks of the sponsor nor should it jeopardise the goodwill or public appreciation these have already earned.

### The sponsorship audience

Article 5

The audience should be clearly informed of the existence of a sponsorship with respect to a particular event, activity, programme or person and the sponsor's own message should not deliberately offend the audience's religious, political or social convictions or professional ethics.

The foregoing does not imply any restriction on the sponsor to provide support for avant garde or potentially controversial artistic/cultural activities, nor is the sponsor thereby required or encouraged to exercise censorship over the sponsored party's message.

### Children and young people

Article 6

Sponsorship addressed to or likely to influence children and young people should not be framed so as to take advantage of their youth or lack of experience. Furthermore, such sponsorship should not be framed so as to harm children or young people mentally, morally or physically, nor to strain their sense of loyalty vis à vis their parents or guardians.

### Artistic and historical objects

Article 7

Sponsorship should never be operated in such a way as to endanger artistic or historical objects.

Sponsorship which aims to safeguard, restore, or maintain cultural, artistic or historical properties or their diffusion, should respect the public interest related thereto.

### Multiple sponsorship

Article 8

Where the activity or event requires or allows several sponsors, the individual contracts and agreements should clearly set out (and inform all sponsors of) the respective rights, limits and obligations of each sponsor. The sponsored party should be aware of the importance of keeping an appropriate balance between the sponsors.

In particular, each member of a pool or sponsors should scrupulously respect the defined sponsorship fields and the allotted communication tasks, abstaining from any interference that might unfairly alter the balance between the contribution of each sponsor.

The sponsored party should inform any possible future sponsors of any sponsors already a party to the sponsorship. The sponsored party shall not accept a new sponsor without the approval of sponsors who are already contractually parties to the sponsorship.

### Television, radio and cinema sponsorship

Article 9

The content and scheduling of sponsored programmes should not be influenced by the sponsor so as to abrogate the responsibility, autonomy or editorial independence of the broadcaster or programme producer.

Sponsored programmes should be identified as such by display of the sponsor's name and/or logo at the beginning and/or end of the programme.

Particular care should be taken to ensure that there is no confusion between sponsorship of an event or activity and the television, radio or cinema transmission of that event or activity.

### Environmental sponsorship

Article 10

Both sponsors and sponsored parties should take into consideration the potential environmental impact of the sponsorship when planning, organising and carrying out the sponsorship activities.

Any sponsorship message fully or partially based on a positive (or reduced negative) environmental impact should be substantiated in terms of actual benefits to be obtained. Parties to the sponsorship should respect the principles set out in the ICC Charter for Sustainable Development.

When advertising claims are made with respect to the sponsorship, the advertisements should conform to the principles set out in the ICC Code on Environmental Advertising.

**Implementation**

Article 11

This Code of self-discipline is to be applied nationally by bodies already in existence or set up for the purpose and internationally by the ICC International Council on Marketing Practice whenever:

A   A national body does not exist; or

B   The parties so agree; or

C   The parties belong to different countries.

International Chamber of Commerce

The World Business Organisation

# ICC INTERNATIONAL CODE OF DIRECT MARKETING

1998 Edition, updated by the Commission on Marketing, Advertising and Distribution.

**Introduction**

This edition of the ICC International Code of Direct Marketing Practice follows the well-established policy of the ICC of promoting high standards of ethics in marketing via self-regulatory codes intended to complement the existing frameworks of national and international law.

Like its predecessor, the 1978 Code of Direct Mail, this Code, which was first issued in 1992, is an expression of the business community's recognition of its social responsibilities in respect of commercial activities and communications. The globalisation of the world's economies, and the intense competition that ensues therefrom, require the international business community to adopt standard rules. The adoption of these self-disciplinary rules is the best way that business leaders have of demonstrating that they are motivated by a sense of social responsibility, particularly in light of the increased liberalisation of markets and the emergence of new media.

This edition combines past experience with current thinking based on the concept of direct marketing as a key factor in competition and communication, essential to the market economy. In the view of the ICC, the Code establishes a fair balance between the interests of all parties concerned – producers, distributors and consumers. The ICC considers it to be fundamental and in the interest of society as a whole that business, while observing the principles of fair competition, should be free to choose between different marketing methods.

The Code is designed primarily as an instrument for self-discipline, but it is also intended for use by legal or administrative bodies as a reference document within the framework of applicable laws.

The ICC believes that this new edition of the Code will promote adherence to high standards of direct marketing practice. Being a pointer to the direction of further international harmonisation, it will facilitate the free flow of products across frontiers, leading to efficient markets and significant consumer benefits.

**Scope of the code**

The Code applies to all direct marketing activities in their entirety, whatever their form, medium or content. It should be read in conjunction with the other ICC Codes of Marketing Practice, namely the:

ICC International Code of Advertising Practice

ICC International Code on Environmental Advertising

ICC International Code of Sales Promotion

ICC International Code on Sponsorship

ICC/ESOMAR International Code of Marketing and Social Research Practice

ICC Revised Guidelines on Advertising and Marketing on the Internet

ICC International Code of Direct Sales Practice

The Code sets standards of ethical conduct to be followed by all concerned with direct marketing, whether as marketers or sellers, distributors, practitioners or other contractors providing services for direct marketing purposes, or media, and is to be applied against the background of the applicable law.

**Interpretation**

The Code is to be applied in the spirit as well as in the letter, bearing in mind the different degrees of knowledge, experience and discriminatory ability of those to whom direct marketing activities are directed.

**Definitions**

For the purposes of this Code, direct marketing comprises all communication activities with the intention of offering goods or services or transmitting commercial messages presented in any medium aimed at informing and/or soliciting a response from the addressee, as well as any service directly related thereto.

- the term consumer refers to any person to whom direct marketing is addressed or who can reasonably be expected to be reached by it;
- the term data controller means the person or body responsible for the contents and/or use of the marketing file;
- the term data subject means any identified or identifiable natural person;
- the term Internet refers to the public network of computer networks which enables the transmission of information between users, or between users and a place on the network, as well as to all interactive media and electronic networks;
- the term marketing list means a data base created or used for direct marketing purposes;
- the term offer means any presentation or solicitation of goods or services;

- the term operator refers to any person, firm or company other than the seller that provides a direct marketing service for and on behalf of the seller;
- the term personal data means any information relating to an identified or identifiable individual;
- the term predictive dialler means an automated dialler which will adjust the rate at which it dials and deliver answered telephone calls immediately to match operator availability;
- the term preference service ['Robinson List'] means the administration and operation of a suppression file of consumers who have registered their wish not to receive unsolicited direct marketing approaches, against which marketing lists are matched;
- the term premium rate number means a telephone/fax number to which a call is charged at a higher rate than the standard telephone tariff;
- the term processing means any operation or set of operations which is applied to personal data;
- the term product refers to any goods or services;
- the term seller refers to any person, firm or company that offers and provides goods and/or services by direct marketing, either directly or through an operator;
- the term tele-operator means either a seller or an operator using the telephone for direct marketing purposes;
- the term third parties means any natural or legal person other than the data subject, the controller and any person authorised to process the data under the controller's authority or on his behalf.

## General Requirements

### Basic principles

Article 1

All direct marketing activities should be legal, decent, honest and truthful

Every direct marketing activity should be carried out with a due sense of social responsibility and should conform to principles of fair competition as generally accepted in business. Activities should not appear to condone or incite violence, nor to encourage unlawful or reprehensible behaviour.

No activity should be such as to impair public confidence in direct marketing.

### Honesty

Article 2

All direct marketing activities should deal fairly with consumers. Activities should be so designed and conducted to avoid giving ground for reasonable complaint.

Any factor likely to affect consumers' decisions should be communicated in such a way and at such a time that the consumers can take it into account before accepting an offer or making any other commitment.

The fulfilment of any obligation arising from a direct marketing activity should be equitable, prompt and efficient.

No direct marketing should be represented to the consumer as being a form of marketing research.

### Children and young people

Article 3

Direct marketing activities addressed to children and young people should not exploit their credulity or inexperience. No direct marketing activity should be undertaken which is likely to harm children mentally, morally or physically, or to strain their sense of loyalty vis-a-vis their parents or guardians.

Sellers and operators offering products to children should:

- identify material intended only for adults;

- encourage young children to obtain their parent's and/or guardian's permission before the children provide information, and make reasonable efforts to ensure that parental consent has been given; provide information to parents and/or guardians about ways to protect their children's privacy.

## Communication of the message

### Decency and Suitability

Article 4

Those using direct marketing techniques should take particular care, given the variety of audiences, to ensure that their messages will not be seen as indecent, offensive or inappropriate. Such messages should conform to prevailing standards of decency.

### Transparency

Article 5

Whenever information is gathered for direct marketing purposes, this should be made clear to the relevant consumers.

Whenever an offer is made, all the commitments undertaken by the seller, the operator and the consumer should be made clear to consumers, either directly or by reference to sales conditions available to them at the time of the offer.

Print which by its size or other visual characteristics is likely to affect substantially the legibility and clarity of the offer should be avoided

Wherever appropriate a simple statement of the essential points of the offer should be clearly displayed in the promotional material. The scattering of essential points of the offer throughout promotional material should be avoided.

### Presentation

Article 6

1   The presentation of the product should not contain any written, audio or visual element which directly or by implication is likely to mislead consumers, in particular with regard to such characteristics as nature, composition, method and date of manufacture, range of use, efficiency and performance, quantity, commercial or geographical origin and environmental impact.

When the presentation of an offer includes illustration of products not included in the offer, or where additional products need to be purchased for the consumer to be able to use the product on offer, this should be made clear in the offer.

2    The terms of any offer made should be clear, so that the consumer may know the exact nature of what is being offered.

3    High-pressure tactics which may be construed as harassment should not be used.

Any advertisements should be framed in strict accordance with the ICC International Code of Advertising Practice.

## Comparisons

Article 7

The presentation of an offer containing comparisons should be so designed that the comparison is not likely to mislead, and should comply with the principles of fair competition and with the protection of trade marks. Points of comparison should be based on facts which can be substantiated and should not be unfairly selected.

## Testimonials

Article 8

The presentation of the offer should not contain or refer to any testimonial or endorsement unless it is genuine, verifiable, relevant and based on personal experience or knowledge.

Testimonials or endorsements which have become obsolete or misleading through passage of time should not be used.

## Guarantees

Article 9

Offers may contain the word 'guarantee', 'guaranteed', 'warranty' or 'warranted' or words having the same meaning, only if the full terms of the guarantee as well as the remedial action open to the purchaser are clearly set out in the offer, or are available to the purchaser in writing.

The name and address of the guarantor and the duration of the guarantee should be clearly stated.

## After-sales service

Article 10

When after-sales service is offered, details of the service should be included in the guarantee or stated elsewhere in the offer. If the consumer accepts the offer, information should be given on how the consumer can activate the service and communicate with the service agent.

## Identity of the seller

Article 11

The identity and details of where the sellers and/or operators may be contacted should be given in the offer, so as to enable the consumer to communicate directly and effectively with them. At the time of delivery of the product, the seller's full name, address and telephone number should be made available to the consumer.

### Unsolicited products

Article 12

Neither the seller nor the operator should deliver products for which payment is requested without having first received an instruction for the supply of such products.

Offers that are likely to be mistaken for bills, invoices or similar documents relating to unordered products should not be made.

### Promotional incentives

Article 13

Direct marketing which utilises promotional incentives should conform with the relevant provisions of the ICC International Code of Sales Promotion.

### Safety and health

Article 14

Information provided with the product should include proper directions for use and full instructions covering health and safety warnings whenever necessary. The required health and safety warnings should be made readily understood by the use of pictures, text or a combination of both.

Goods and, where applicable, samples should be packaged in such a way as to be suitable for delivery to the customer – and possible return – in compliance with valid health and safety norms.

## Fulfilment

### Fulfilment of orders

Article 15

Orders should be fulfiled within 30 days from the date the order is received from the consumer, unless otherwise stipulated in the offer. Sellers or operators should inform the consumer of any undue delay as soon as it becomes known to them. In such cases, any request for cancellation of the order by the consumer should be granted, even when it is not possible to prevent delivery, and the deposit, if any, should be refunded immediately.

### Substitution of products

Article 16

If a product becomes unavailable for reasons beyond the control of the seller or the operator, another product may not be supplied in its place unless the consumer is informed that it is a substitution and unless such replacement product has materially the same or better characteristics and qualities, and is supplied at the same or a lower price. In such a case, an explanation of the substitution and of the right to return the substitute product at the seller's cost should be given to the consumer.

### Return of products

Article 17

1   The cost of return of faulty products damaged other than by the consumer is the responsibility of the seller, provided notice is given by the consumer within a reasonable period of time.

2   Sellers who undertake to supply products to the consumer on 'free examination', 'free trial', 'free approval' and the like should clarify in the offer who will bear the cost of returning such goods and should make the return as simple as possible. Any time restriction for the return should be clearly disclosed.

## Credit and debt collection

### Prices and credit terms

Article 18

Whether the offer is on a cash or installment basis, the price and terms of payment should be clearly stated in the offer together with the nature of any additional charges (such as postage, handling, taxes, etc) and, when possible, the amounts of such charges.

In the case of sales by installment, the credit terms, including the amount of any deposit or payment on account, the number, amount and periodicity of such installments and the total price compared with the cash price, if any, should be clearly shown in the offer.

Any information needed by the consumer to understand the cost, interest and terms of any other form of credit should be specified either in the offer or when the credit is offered.

Unless the duration of the offer and the price are clearly stated in the offer, prices should be maintained for a reasonable period of time.

### Payment and debt collection

Article 19

The procedure for payment and debt collection should be such as to avoid undue inconvenience to the consumer, making due allowance for delays outside the consumer's control.

Debtors should not be approached in an unreasonable manner and debt collection documents which might be confused with official documents should not be used.

## Costs of Communications

### Premium rates

Article 20

1   When promoting a premium rate number, such as an on-line message or telephone number, the seller or operator should state that the number is a premium rate and what the rate is, either as cost per minute or as cost per call. Sellers and operators should take particular care to ensure that the consumer not be kept waiting an unreasonable time in order to fulfil the purpose of the call.

2   When answering a call, a seller or operator should always begin by informing the consumer that it is a premium rate call. This should be done at the time the consumer is about to access the message or on-line service.

## Use of lists and databases

### Collection of data

Article 21

1   When collecting personal information from individuals, the seller and/or operator should ensure that the data subject is aware of the following:
  - the identity of the data controller;
  - the purposes of the collection;
  - any intention to transfer the data to third parties.

The data subject can be informed of this in the context of the collection, by a separate notice or message, contract, or by adequate collective notices.

2   When it is not possible to inform the data subject at the time of the collection, this should be done as soon as possible thereafter.

### Use of data

Article 22

Personal data collected in accordance with this Code shall be:

(a) collected for specified and legitimate purposes and not used in any manner incompatible with these purposes;

(b) adequate, relevant and not excessive in relation to the purpose for which they are collected and/or further processed;

(c) accurate and kept up to date;

(d) preserved no longer than is required for the purpose for which the data were collected or further processed.

The data controllers should take reasonable steps to ensure that their processors and third parties respect the data protection principles of this Code. Sales agents of the data controller are not considered third parties.

### Rights of the data subject

Article 23

Appropriate measures should be taken so as to enable consumers to exercise the following rights:
  - to opt out from marketing lists.
  - to require that their data are not made available to third parties.
  - to rectify incorrect data which are held on them.

### Preference services and suppression of data

Article 24

1   Sellers and/or operators should comply with the requests of data subjects that they not receive addressed mail, commercial telephone calls, faxes, e-mails or other addressed on-line communications by means of a preference service, in-house suppression file or by other means.

2   Names and other personal information contained in preference service suppression files should be used only to suppress matching information on promotional marketing lists which are to be used for making unsolicited marketing approaches. Names found in preference service lists should not be rented, sold or exchanged, except for suppression purposes.

3   When faxing or e-mailing or using any other form of on-line communication to consumers, particular care should be taken to reduce to the minimum any inconvenience likely to be caused by unwanted messages.

**Security of processing**

Article 25

Data controllers should ensure that they employ adequate security measures, having regard to the sensitivity of the information, to prevent unauthorised access or disclosure of the personal data.

Data controllers should satisfy themselves that any third party and/or processors they employ have adequate security measures.

**Transborder transactions**

Article 26

Particular care should be taken to maintain the data protection rights of the data subject when personal data is transferred from the country in which it is collected to another country.

When data controllers have processing conducted for them in another country, they should take all reasonable steps to ensure that adequate security measures are observed and that the data protection principles of this Code are respected. The use of the ICC model contract covering agreements between the originator of the marketing list and the processor or user in another country is recommended.

**Unaddressed direct mail**

**Respecting consumer wishes**

Article 27

Where a system has been established to enable consumers to indicate their wish not to receive unaddressed mail, this should be respected.

**The telephone in direct marketing**

**Content of the call**

Article 28

1   Outbound calls

When tele-operators call a consumer, they should promptly:

* state the name of the seller they represent;
* unambiguously state the purpose of the call;
* politely terminate the call when it is apparent that the receiver of the call is not competent, or does not wish to take the call or is a child (unless the tele-operator receives permission from an appropriate adult to continue).

2   Inbound calls

When tele-operators receive calls from consumers, tele-operators should state the name of the seller they represent.

**Reasonable hours**

Article 29

Outbound calls should, unless expressly otherwise requested, only be made during hours which are generally regarded as reasonable for the recipient.

**Monitoring of conversations**

Article 30

The monitoring, including taping, of telephone conversations made for telephone marketing purposes should be conducted only with appropriate safeguards, in order to verify the content of the call, to confirm a commercial transaction, for training purposes and for quality control. Marketers should ensure that the tele-operator is aware of monitoring; that, where practicable, the consumer is also aware of the possibility of monitoring; and that any taped recorded conversations are not played to a public audience without the knowledge of both parties.

**Unlisted numbers**

Article 31

Consumers with an unlisted number should not knowingly be contacted for marketing purposes, other than when the number is randomly picked for marketing research, and when the number was supplied by the consumer to the sellers or operators.

**Use of automatic dialling equipment**

Article 32

1    Where a predictive dialler is used, when a tele-operator is unavailable to take the call generated by the dialler, the equipment should abandon the call and release the line in not more than one second.

2    Where other automatic dialling equipment is used, it may be used to contact a consumer only where the call is initially introduced by a tele-operator or where the consumer has previously agreed to receive such calls without tele-operator intervention.

3    Neither predictive dialler nor any other automatic dialling equipment may be used unless the equipment immediately disconnects when the consumer hangs up. Dialling equipment should release each time before connecting to another number.

**On-line Communications**

Article 33

Sellers and/or operators should respect the role of particular news groups, forums or bulletin boards as public meeting places which may have rules and standards as to acceptable commercial behaviour.

Sellers and/or operators are encouraged to post their privacy policy statement on-line. Where such privacy policy statements exist, they should be easy to find easy to use and comprehensible.

Sellers and/or operators should make a suppression mechanism available to users who do not wish to receive future on-line commercial solicitations.

Unsolicited on-line addressed commercial messages should be clearly identified as such and should clearly identify the seller and or operator.

## Responsibility, substantiation and implementation

### Respecting consumer wishes

Article 34

1   The prime responsibility for all aspects of direct marketing activities, whatever their kind or content, always rests with the seller.

2   Those taking part in the planning, creation or execution of any direct marketing activity have a degree of responsibility commensurate with their position for ensuring the observance of the Code.

3   Thus in addition to the sellers the Code should be duly observed by:

  • operators or data controllers, or their subcontractors, who contribute to the activity or communication;

  • publishers, medium-owners or contractors who publish, transmit or distribute the offer or any other communication.

### Rules apply to entirety of direct marketing communication

Article 35

The rules of this Code embrace the direct marketing communication in its entire content and form, including testimonials, statements and visual presentations originating from other sources. The fact that the content or form of the direct marketing communication originates wholly or in part from other sources is not an excuse for non-observance of the rules.

### Respect of self regulatory decisions

Article 36

No seller, operator, publisher, medium-owner or contractor should be party to the implementation of any direct marketing activity or to the publication or distribution of any communication which they know to have been found unacceptable by the appropriate self-regulatory body or available dispute-resolution mechanisms.

### Effect of subsequent redress for contravention

Article 37

While subsequent correction and appropriate redress according to available dispute-resolution systems for a contravention of the Code are desirable, they cannot excuse the original contravention of the Code.

### Substantiation

Article 38

Substantiation of verifiable facts needed to establish compliance of the direct marketing activity with the Code should be available and be produced when called for by any appropriate self-regulatory body.

**Implementation**

Article 39

This Code of self-discipline should be applied and referred to nationally by bodies set up for that purpose, and internationally by the ICC's International Council on Marketing Practice as and when the need arises.

Document no 240/396 Rev 2

25 September 1998

Copyright 1998 ©. All rights reserved.

# ICC/ESOMAR INTERNATIONAL CODE OF MARKETING AND SOCIAL RESEARCH PRACTICE

## Introduction

Effective communication between the suppliers and the consumers of goods and services of all kinds is vital to any modern society. Growing international links make this even more essential. For a supplier to provide in the most efficient way what consumers require he must understand their differing needs; how best to meet these needs; and how he can most effectively communicate the nature of the goods or services he is offering.

This is the objective of marketing research. It applies in both private and public sectors of the economy. Similar approaches are also used in other fields of study: for example in measuring the public's behaviour and attitudes with respect to social, political and other issues by Government and public bodies, the media, academic institutions, etc. Marketing and social research have many interests, methods and problems in common although the subjects of study tend to be different.

Such research depends upon public confidence: confidence that it is carried out honestly, objectively, without unwelcome intrusion or disadvantage to respondents, and that it is based upon their willing co-operation. This confidence must be supported by an appropriate professional Code of Practice which governs the way in which marketing research projects are conducted.

The first such Code was published by the European Society for Opinion and Marketing Research (ESOMAR) in 1948. This was followed by a number of Codes prepared by national marketing research societies and by other bodies such as the International Chamber of Commerce (ICC), which represents the international marketing community. In 1976, ESOMAR and the ICC decided that it would be preferable to have a single International Code instead of two differing ones, and a joint ICC/ESOMAR Code was therefore published in the following year (with revisions in 1986).

Subsequent changes in the marketing and social environment, new developments in marketing research methods and a great increase in international activities of all kinds including legislation, led ESOMAR to prepare a new version of the International Code in 1994. This new version sets out as concisely as possible the basic ethical and business principles which govern the practice of marketing and social research. It specifies the rules which are to be followed in dealing with the general public and with the business community, including clients and other members of the profession.

ESOMAR will be glad to give advice on the implementation of this Code; and also offers an arbitration and expert assessment service to help resolve technical and other disputes relating to marketing research projects.

Other aspects of marketing – in particular Direct Marketing and Advertising – are covered by separate International Codes of Practice published by the ICC. Copies of these may be obtained from the ICC Secretariat in Paris.

**The International Code**

This Code sets out the basic principles which must guide the actions of those who carry out or use marketing research. Individuals and organisations who subscribe to it must follow not just the letter but also the spirit of these rules.

No Code can be expected to provide a completely comprehensive set of rules which are applicable to every situation which might arise. Where there is any element of doubt people should ask for advice and meanwhile follow the most conservative interpretation of these principles. No variation in the application of the rules is permissible without explicit authorisation by ESOMAR.

In certain countries there are additional national requirements laid down by legislation or by the local professional association which may affect the application of the International Code. Where they add to or differ from those set out in this Code such specific national requirements take precedence when carrying out research* in that country. This applies to all research in that country even when it is carried out by researchers or clients based elsewhere. National associations can provide information on any special requirements of these kinds which must be observed in their own country.

Individuals are always responsible for ensuring that the other people in their organisation who to their knowledge are concerned in any way with marketing research activities are aware of, and understand, the principles laid down in this Code. They must use their best endeavours to ensure that the organisation as a whole conforms to the Code.

Acceptance of this International Code is a condition of membership of ESOMAR and of all other national and international bodies which have officially adopted the Code. Members should also familiarise themselves with the Notes and Guidelines which ESOMAR produces to help in interpreting and applying the Rules of this Code.

* Throughout this Code the terms 'research' and 'researcher' are to be understood as relating to 'marketing research' and 'marketing researcher' (see 'Definitions')

**Definitions**

(a) Marketing research is a key element within the total field of marketing information. It links the consumer, customer and public to the marketer through information which is used to identify and define marketing opportunities and problems; generate, refine and evaluate marketing actions; improve understanding of marketing as a process and of the ways in which specific marketing activities can be made more effective.

Marketing research specifies the information required to address these issues; designs the method for collecting information; manages and implements the data collection process; analyses the results; and communicates the findings and their implications.

Marketing research includes such activities as quantitative surveys; qualitative research; media and advertising research; business-to-business and industrial research; research among minority and special groups; public opinion surveys; and desk research.

In the context of this Code the term marketing research also covers social research where this uses similar approaches and techniques to study issues not concerned with the marketing of goods and services. The applied social sciences equally depend upon such methods of empirical research to develop and test their underlying hypotheses; and to understand, predict and provide guidance on developments within society for governmental, academic and other purposes.

Marketing research differs from other forms of information gathering in that the identity of the provider of information is not disclosed. Database marketing and any other activity where the names and addresses of the people contacted are to be used for individual selling, promotional, fund-raising or other non-research purposes can under no circumstances be regarded as marketing research since the latter is based on preserving the complete anonymity of the respondent.

(b) Researcher is defined as any individual, research agency, organisation, department or division which carries out or acts as a consultant on a marketing research project or offers their services so to do.

The term includes any department, etc, which belongs to the same organisation as that of the client. A researcher linked to the client in this way has the same responsibilities under this Code vis à vis other sections of the client organisation as does one who is completely independent of the latter.

The term also covers responsibility for the procedures followed by any subcontractor from whom the researcher commissions any work (data collection or analysis, printing, professional consultancy, etc) which forms any part of the research project. In such cases the researcher must ensure that any such subcontractor fully conforms to the provisions of this Code.

(c) Client is defined as any individual, organisation, department or division (including one which belongs to the same organisation as the researcher) which requests, commissions or subscribes to all or any part of a marketing research project.

(d) Respondent is defined as any individual or organisation from whom any information is sought by the researcher for the purposes of a marketing research project. The term covers cases where information is to be obtained by verbal interviewing techniques, postal and other self-completion questionnaires, mechanical or electronic equipment, observation and any other method where the identity of the provider of the information may be recorded or otherwise traceable.

(e) Interview is defined as any form of direct or indirect contact, using any of the methods referred to above, with respondents where the objective is to acquire data or information which could be used in whole or in part for the purposes of a marketing research project.

(f) Record is defined as any brief, proposal, questionnaire, respondent identification, check list, record sheet, audio or audio-visual recording or film, tabulation or computer print-out, EDP disc or other storage medium, formula, diagram, report, etc,. in respect of any marketing research project, whether in whole or in part. It covers records produced by the client as well as by the researcher.

**Rules**

A   General

1   Marketing research must always be carried out objectively and in accordance with established scientific principles.

2   Marketing research must always conform to the national and international legislation which applies in those countries involved in a given research project.

B   The rights of respondents

3   Respondents' co-operation in a marketing research project is entirely voluntary at all stages. They must not be misled when being asked for their co-operation.

4   Respondents' anonymity must be strictly preserved. If the Respondent on request from the Researcher has given permission for data to be passed on in a form which allows that Respondent to be personally identified:

(a)   the Respondent must first have been told to whom the information would be supplied and the purposes for which it will be used, and also

(b)   the Researcher must ensure that the information will not be used for any non-research purpose and that the recipient of the information has agreed to conform to the requirements of this Code.

5   The Researcher must take all reasonable precautions to ensure that Respondents are in no way directly harmed or adversely affected as a result of their participation in a marketing research project.

6   The Researcher must take special care when interviewing children and young people. The informed consent of the parent or responsible adult must first be obtained for interviews with children.

7   Respondents must be told (normally at the beginning of the interview) if observation techniques or recording equipment are being used, except where these are used in a public place. If a Respondent so wishes, the record or relevant section of it must be destroyed or deleted. Respondents' anonymity must not be infringed by the use of such methods.

8   Respondents must be enabled to check without difficulty the identity and bona fides of the Researcher.

C   The professional responsibilities of researchers

9   Researchers must not, whether knowingly or negligently, act in any way which could bring discredit on the marketing research profession or lead to a loss of public confidence in it.

10   Researchers must not make false claims about their skills and experience or about those of their organisation.

11   Researchers must not unjustifiably criticise or disparage other Researchers.

12   Researchers must always strive to design research which is cost-efficient and of

adequate quality, and then to carry this out to the specifications agreed with the Client.

13 Researchers must ensure the security of all research records in their possession.

14 Researchers must not knowingly allow the dissemination of conclusions from a marketing research project which are not adequately supported by the data. They must always be prepared to make available the technical information necessary to assess the validity of any published findings.

15 When acting in their capacity as Researchers the latter must not undertake any non-research activities, for example database marketing involving data about individuals which will be used for direct marketing and promotional activities. Any such non-research activities must always, in the way they are organised and carried out, be clearly differentiated from marketing research activities.

D    The mutual rights and responsibilities of researchers and clients

16 These rights and responsibilities will normally be governed by a written Contract between the Researcher and the Client. The parties may amend the provisions of Rules 19–23 below if they have agreed to this in writing beforehand; but the other requirements of this Code may not be altered in this way. Marketing research must also always be conducted according to the principles of fair competition, as generally understood and accepted.

17 The Researcher must inform the Client if the work to be carried out for that Client is to be combined or syndicated in the same project with work for other Clients but must not disclose the identity of such Clients.

18 The Researcher must inform the Client as soon as possible in advance when any part of the work for that Client is to be subcontracted outside the Researcher's own organisation (including the use of any outside consultants). On request the Client must be told the identity of any such subcontractor.

19 The Client does not have the right, without prior agreement between the parties involved, to exclusive use of the Researcher's services or those of his organisation, whether in whole or in part. In carrying out work for different Clients, however, the Researcher must endeavour to avoid possible clashes of interest between the services provided to those Clients.

20 The following Records remain the property of the Client and must not be disclosed by the Researcher to any third party without the Client's permission:

(a) marketing research briefs, specifications and other information provided by the Client

(b) the research data and findings from a marketing research project (except in the case of syndicated or multi-client projects or services where the same data are available to more than one Client).

The Client has however no right to know the names or addresses of Respondents unless the latter's explicit permission for this has first been obtained by the Researcher (this particular requirement cannot be altered under Rule 16).

21 Unless it is specifically agreed to the contrary, the following Records remain the property of the Researcher:

(a) marketing research proposals and cost quotations (unless these have been paid for by the Client). They must not be disclosed by the Client to any third party, other than to a consultant working for the Client on that project (with the exception of any consultant working also for a competitor of the Researcher). In particular, they must not be used by the Client to influence research proposals or cost quotations from other Researchers.

(b) the contents of a report in the case of syndicated and/or multi-client projects or services where the same data are available to more than one Client and where it is clearly understood that the resulting reports are available for general purchase or subscription. The Client may not disclose the findings of such research to any third party (other than to his own consultants and advisors for use in connection with his business) without the permission of the Researcher.

(c) all other research Records prepared by the Researcher (with the exception in the case of non-syndicated projects of the report to the Client, and also the research design and questionnaire where the costs of developing these are covered by the charges paid by the Client).

22  The Researcher must conform to currently agreed professional practice relating to the keeping of such Records for an appropriate period of time after the end of the project. On request the Researcher must supply the Client with duplicate copies of such Records provided that such duplicates do not breach anonymity and confidentiality requirements (Rule 4); that the request is made within the agreed time limit for keeping the Records; and that the Client pays the reasonable costs of providing the duplicates.

23  The Researcher must not disclose the identity of the Client (provided there is no legal obligation to do so), or any confidential information about the latter's business, to any third party without the Client's permission.

24  The Researcher must on request allow the Client to arrange for checks on the quality of fieldwork and data preparation provided that the Client pays any additional costs involved in this. Any such checks must conform to the requirements of Rule 4.

25  The Researcher must provide the Client with all appropriate technical details of any research project carried out for that Client.

26  When reporting on the results of a marketing research project the Researcher must make a clear distinction between the findings as such, the Researcher's interpretation of these and any recommendations based on them.

27  Where any of the findings of a research project are published by the Client the latter has a responsibility to ensure that these are not misleading. The Researcher must be consulted and agree in advance the form and content of publication, and must take action to correct any misleading statements about the research and its findings.

28  Researchers must not allow their names to be used in connection with any research project as an assurance that the latter has been carried out in conformity with this Code unless they are confident that the project has in all respects met the Code's requirements.

29  Researchers must ensure that Clients are aware of the existence of this Code and of the need to comply with its requirements.

E  Implementation of the Code

Queries about the interpretation of this Code, and about its application to specific problems, should be addressed to the international Secretariats of the ICC or ESOMAR.

Any apparent infringement, if it applies solely to activities within a single country, should in the first place be reported immediately to the appropriate national body (or bodies) in that country. A list of such bodies which have adopted this Code will be found in the Appendix. That national body will then investigate and take any appropriate action, notifying the ICC/ESOMAR of the outcome in the case of proven infringement.

Apparent infringements should be reported directly to the Secretariats of the ICC or ESOMAR in cases where:

(a) there is no appropriate national body,

(b) the national body is unable to take action or prefers the issue to be dealt with by the international body,

(c) more than one country is involved, as with international projects.

One or both of these international bodies, as appropriate, will then investigate the complaint and take such further action as may be called for. This action can include suspension or withdrawal of membership of the relevant professional or trade associations, and in the case of an organisation its exclusion from the published Directory of such organisations.

## How the ICC/ESOMAR International Code should be applied

These Notes are intended to help users of the Code to interpret and apply it in practice. Any query or problem about how to apply the Code in a specific situation should be addressed to the Secretariats of ESOMAR or the ICC.

The German-language version of this Code is prefaced by a Declaration prepared by the ADM and BVM (the German national market research associations). This sets out certain additional requirements which must be followed in order to conform with German legislation when carrying out research in that country. Copies of this Declaration are available on request from the ESOMAR Secretariat, in the following languages: English, French, German and Spanish.

The ICC itself has published certain Codes of Practice which cover other aspects of marketing. In particular, the ICC's Code on Direct Marketing deals with the different rules which apply to that field of marketing activity.

The Notes, and the Guidelines referred to in them, will be reviewed and reissued from time to time. These revised versions will be circulated in draft to appropriate bodies for comment (and in the case of the ICC official approval, except in the case of purely technical papers before they are officially published as joint documents). The Notes and Guidelines will continue to be updated when it is necessary to take account of changing circumstances or important new issues.

## Section B

All Respondents are entitled to be sure that when they agree to co-operate in any marketing research project they are fully protected by the provisions of this Code and that the Researcher will conform to its requirements. This applies equally to

Respondents interviewed as private individuals and to those interviewed as representatives of organisations of different kinds.

### Rule 3

Researchers and those working on their behalf (eg, interviewers) must not, in order to secure Respondents' co-operation, make statements or promises which are knowingly misleading or incorrect – for example, about the likely length of the interview or about the possibilities of being re-interviewed on a later occasion. Any such statements and assurances given to Respondents must be fully honoured.

Respondents are entitled to withdraw from an interview at any stage and to refuse to co-operate further in the research project. Any or all of the information collected from or about them must be destroyed without delay if Respondents so request.

### Rule 4

All indications of the identity of Respondents should be physically separated from the records of the information they have provided as soon as possible after the completion of any necessary fieldwork quality checks. The Researcher must ensure that any information which might identify Respondents is stored securely, and separately from the other information they have provided; and that access to such material is restricted to authorised research personnel within the Researcher's own organisation for specific research purposes (eg, field administration, data processing, panel or 'longitudinal' studies or other forms of research involving recall interviews).

To preserve Respondents' anonymity not only their names and addresses but also any other information provided by or about them which could in practice identify them (eg, their Company and job title) must be safeguarded.

These anonymity requirements may be relaxed only under the following safeguards:

(a) where the Respondent has given explicit permission for this under the conditions of 'informed consent' summarised in Rule 4 (a) and (b).

(b) where disclosure of names to a third party (eg, a subcontractor) is essential for any research purpose such as data processing or further interview (eg, an independent fieldwork quality check) or for further follow-up research. The original Researcher is responsible for ensuring that any such third party agrees to observe the requirements of this Code – in writing, if the third party has not already formally subscribed to the Code.

It must be noted that even these limited relaxations may not be permissible in certain countries.

The definition of 'non-research activity', referred to in Rule 4(b), is dealt with in connection with Rule 15.

The particular issues which arise in the case of customer satisfaction surveys and 'Mystery Shopping' will be addressed in ESOMAR Guidelines on these subjects. These are currently under discussion.

## Rule 5

The Researcher must explicitly agree with the Client arrangements regarding the responsibilities for product safety and for dealing with any complaints or damage arising from faulty products or product misuse. Such responsibilities will normally rest with the Client, but the Researcher must ensure that products are correctly stored and handled while in the Researcher's charge and that Respondents are given appropriate instructions for their use.

More generally, Researchers should avoid interviewing at inappropriate or inconvenient times. They should also avoid the use of unnecessarily long interviews; and the asking of personal questions which may worry or annoy Respondents, unless the information is essential to the purposes of the study and the reasons for needing it are explained to the Respondent.

## Rule 6

This issue is addressed in detail in the ESOMAR Guideline on 'Interviewing Children'. The definitions of children' and 'young people' may vary by country but if not otherwise specified locally should be taken as 'under 14 years' and '14–17 years'.

## Rule 7

The Respondent should be told at the beginning of the interview that recording techniques are to be used unless this knowledge might bias the Respondent's subsequent behaviour: in such cases the Respondent must be told about the recording at the end of the interview and be given the opportunity to see or hear the relevant section of the record and, if they so wish, to have this destroyed.

A 'public place' is defined as one to which the public has free access and where an individual could reasonably expect to be observed and/or overheard by other people present, for example in a shop or in the street.

The more general issues which arise with the use of tape and video-recording of interviews are dealt with in the ESOMAR Guideline on this subject.

## Rule 8

The name and address/telephone number of the Researcher must normally be made available to the Respondent at the time of interview. In cases where an accommodation address or 'cover name' are used for data collection purposes arrangements must be made to enable Respondents subsequently to find without difficulty or avoidable expense the name and address of the Researcher. Wherever possible 'Freephone' or *similar facilities should be provided so that Respondents can check the Researcher's bona fides* without cost to themselves.

## Section C

This Code is not intended to restrict the rights of Researchers to undertake any legitimate marketing research activity and to operate competitively in so doing. However, it is essential that in pursuing these objectives the general public's confidence in the integrity of marketing research is not undermined in any way. This Section sets out the responsibilities which the Researcher has towards the public at large and towards the marketing research profession and other members of this.

**Rule 14**

The kinds of technical information which should on request be made available include those listed in the Notes to Rule 25. The Researcher must not however disclose information which is confidential to the Client's business, nor need he disclose information relating to parts of the survey which were not published.

**Rule 15**

The kinds of 'non-research activity' which must not be associated in any way with the carrying out of marketing research include:

- enquiries whose objectives are to obtain personal information about private individuals per se, whether for legal, political, supervisory (eg, job performance), private or other purposes
- the acquisition of information for use for credit-rating or similar purposes
- the compilation, updating or enhancement of lists, registers or databases which are not exclusively for research purposes (eg, which will be used for direct marketing)
- industrial, commercial or any other form of espionage
- sales or promotional approaches to individual Respondents
- the collection of debts
- fund-raising
- direct or indirect attempts, including by the design of the questionnaire, to influence a Respondent's opinions, attitudes or behaviour on any issue.

Certain of these activities – in particular the collection of information for databases for subsequent use in direct marketing and similar operations – are legitimate marketing activities in their own right. Researchers (especially those working within a client company) may often be involved with such activities, either directly or indirectly. In such cases it is essential that a clear distinction is made between these activities and marketing research since by definition marketing research anonymity rules cannot be applied to them.

Situations may arise where a Researcher wishes, quite legitimately, to become involved with marketing database work for direct marketing (as distinct from marketing research) purposes: such work must not be carried out under the name of marketing research or of a marketing research organisation as such. The ESOMAR Guideline on the subject of the differences between telephone research and telemarketing is being revised to deal with these issues.

**Section D**

This Code is not intended to regulate the details of business relationships between Researchers and Clients except insofar as these may involve principles of general interest and concern. Most such matters should be regulated by the individual business Contracts. It is clearly vital that such Contracts are based on an adequate understanding and consideration of the issues involved: the ESOMAR Guidelines on 'Selecting a Marketing Research Agency' and on 'Reaching Agreement on a Marketing Research Project' address these issues.

**Rule 18**

Although it is usually known in advance what subcontractors will be used, occasions do arise during the course of a project where subcontractors need to be brought in, or changed, at very short notice. In such cases, rather than cause delays to the project in order to inform the Client it will usually be sensible and acceptable to let the Client know as quickly as possible after the decision has been taken.

**Rule 22**

The period of time for which research Records should be kept by the Researcher will vary with the nature of the project (eg, ad hoc, panel, repetitive) and the possible requirements for follow-up research or further analysis. It will normally be longer for the stored research data resulting from a survey (tabulations, discs, tapes, etc) than for primary field records (the original completed questionnaires and similar basic records). The period must be disclosed to, and agreed by, the Client in advance.

In default of any agreement to the contrary, in the case of ad hoc surveys the normal period for which the primary field records should be retained is one year after completion of the fieldwork while the research data should be stored for possible further analysis for at least two years. The Researcher should take suitable precautions to guard against any accidental loss of the information, whether stored physically or electronically, during the agreed storage period.

**Rule 24**

On request the client, or his mutually acceptable representative, may observe a limited number of interviews for this purpose. In certain cases, such as panels or in situations where a Respondent might be known to (or be in subsequent contact with) the Client, this may require the previous agreement of the Respondent. Any such observer must agree to be bound by the provisions of this Code, especially Rule 4.

The Researcher is entitled to be recompensed for any delays and increased fieldwork costs which may result from such a request. The Client must be informed if the observation of interviews may mean that the results of such interviews will need to be excluded from the overall survey analysis because they are no longer methodologically comparable.

In the case of multiclient studies the Researcher may require that any such observer is independent of any of the Clients.

Where an independent check on the quality of fieldwork is to be carried out by a different research agency the latter must conform in all respects to the requirements of this Code. In particular, the anonymity of the original Respondents must be fully safeguarded and their names and addresses used exclusively for the purposes of backchecks, not being disclosed to the Client. Similar considerations apply where the Client wishes to carry out checks on the quality of data preparation work.

**Rule 25**

The Client is entitled to the following information about any marketing research project to which he has subscribed:

(1) Background
- for whom the study was conducted
- the purpose of the study
- names of subcontractors and consultants performing any substantial part of the work

(2) Sample
- a description of the intended and actual universe covered
- the size, nature and geographical distribution of the sample (both planned and achieved); and where relevant, the extent to which any of the data collected were obtained from only part of the sample
- details of the sampling method and any weighting methods used
- where technically relevant, a statement of response rates and a discussion of any possible bias due to non-response

(3) Data collection
- a description of the method by which the information was collected
- a description of the field staff, briefing and field quality control methods used
- the method of recruiting Respondents; and the general nature of any incentives offered to secure their co-operation
- when the fieldwork was carried out
- (in the case of 'desk research') a clear statement of the sources of the information and their likely reliability

(4) Presentation of results
- the relevant factual findings obtained
- bases of percentages (both weighted and unweighted)
- general indications of the probable statistical margins of error to be attached to the main findings, and of the levels of statistical significance of differences between key figures
- the questionnaire and other relevant documents and materials used (or, in the case of a shared project, that portion relating to the matter reported on).

The Report on a project should normally cover the above points or provide a reference to a readily available separate document which contains the information.

**Rule 27**

If the Client does not consult and agree in advance the form of publication with the Researcher the latter is entitled to:

(a) refuse permission for his name to be used in connection with the published findings and

(b) publish the appropriate technical details of the project (as listed in the Notes to Rule 25).

**Rule 29**

It is recommended that Researchers specify in their research proposals that they follow the requirements of this ICC/ESOMAR International Code and that they make a copy available to the Client if the latter does not already have one.

International Chamber of Commerce

The World Business Organisation

# DIRECTIVE 93/27/EC ON INJUNCTIONS FOR THE PROTECTION OF CONSUMERS' INTERESTS

*of 19 May 1998*

*on injunctions for the protection of consumers' interests*

THE EUROPEAN PARLIAMENT AND THE COUNCIL OF THE EUROPEAN UNION,

Having regard to the Treaty establishing the European Community, and in particular Article 100a thereof,

Having regard to the proposal from the Commission,

Having regard to the opinion of the Economic and Social Committee,

Acting in accordance with the procedure laid down in Article 189b of the Treaty,

(1) Whereas certain Directives, listed in the schedule annexed to this Directive, lay down rules with regard to the protection of consumers' interests;

(2) Whereas current mechanisms available both at national and at Community level for ensuring compliance with those Directives do not always allow infringements harmful to the collective interests of consumers to be terminated in good time; whereas collective interests mean interests which do not include the cumulation of interests of individuals who have been harmed by an infringement; whereas this is without prejudice to individual actions brought by individuals who have been harmed by an infringement;

(3) Whereas, as far as the purpose of bringing about the cessation of practices that are unlawful under the national provisions applicable is concerned, the effectiveness of national measures transposing the above Directives including protective measures that go beyond the level required by those Directives, provided they are compatible with the Treaty and allowed by those Directives, may be thwarted where those practices produce effects in a Member State other than that in which they originate;

(4) Whereas those difficulties can disrupt the smooth functioning of the internal market, their consequence being that it is sufficient to move the source of an unlawful practice to another country in order to place it out of reach of all forms of enforcement; whereas this constitutes a distortion of competition;

(5) Whereas those difficulties are likely to diminish consumer confidence in the internal market and may limit the scope for action by organisations representing the collective interests of consumers or independent public bodies responsible for protecting the collective interests of consumers, adversely affected by practices that infringe Community law;

(6) Whereas those practices often extend beyond the frontiers between the Member States; whereas there is an urgent need for some degree of approximation of national provisions designed to enjoin the cessation of the above-mentioned

unlawful practices irrespective of the country in which the unlawful practice has produced its effects; whereas, with regard to jurisdiction, this is without prejudice to the rules of private international law and the Conventions in force between Member States, while respecting the general obligations of the Member States deriving from the Treaty, in particular those related to the smooth functioning of the internal market;

(7) Whereas the objective of the action envisaged can only be attained by the Community; whereas it is therefore incumbent on the Community to act;

(8) Whereas the third paragraph of Article 3b of the Treaty makes it incumbent on the Community not to go beyond what is necessary to achieve the objectives of the Treaty, whereas, in accordance with that Article, the specific features of national legal systems must be taken into account to every extent possible by leaving Member States free to choose between different options having equivalent effect; whereas the courts or administrative authorities competent to rule on the proceedings referred to in Article 2 of this Directive should have the right to examine the effects of previous decisions;

(9) Whereas one option should consist in requiring one or more independent public bodies, specifically responsible for the protection of the collective interests of consumers, to exercise the rights of action set out in this Directive; whereas another option should provide for the exercise of those rights by organisations whose purpose is to protect the collective interests of consumers, in accordance with criteria laid down by national law,

(10)Whereas Member States should be able to choose between or combine these two options in designating at national level the bodies and/or organisations qualified for the purposes of this Directive;

(11)Whereas for the purposes of intra-Community infringements the principle of mutual recognition should apply to these bodies and/or organisations; whereas the Member States should, at the request of their national entities, communicate to the Commission the name and purpose of their national entities which are qualified to bring an action in their own country according to the provisions of this Directive;

(12)Whereas it is the business of the Commission to ensure the publication of a list of these qualified entities in the Official Journal of the European Communities; whereas, until a statement to the contrary is published, a qualified entity is assumed to have legal capacity if its name is included in that list;

(13)Whereas Member States should be able to require that a prior consultation be undertaken by the party that intends to bring an action for an injunction, in order to give the defendant an opportunity to bring the contested infringement to an end; whereas Member States should be able to require that this prior consultation take place jointly with an independent public body designated by those Member States;

(14)Whereas, where the Member States have established that there should be prior consultation, a deadline of two weeks after the request for consultation is received should be set after which, should the cessation of the infringement not be achieved, the applicant shall be entitled to bring an action before the competent court or administrative authority without any further delay;

(15) Whereas it is appropriate that the Commission report on the functioning of this Directive and in particular on its scope and the operation of prior consultation;

(16) Whereas the application of this Directive should not prejudice the application of Community competition rules,

HAVE ADOPTED THIS DIRECTIVE:

### Article 1 Scope

1    The purpose of this Directive is to approximate the laws, regulations and administrative provisions of the Member States relating to actions for an injunction referred to in Article 2 aimed at the protection of the collective interests of consumers included in the Directives listed in the Annex, with a view to ensuring the smooth functioning of the internal market.

2    For the purpose of this Directive, an infringement shall mean any act contrary to the Directives listed in the Annex as transposed into the internal legal order of the Member States which harms the collective interests referred to in paragraph 1.

### Article 2 Actions for an injunction

1    Member States shall designate the courts or administrative authorities competent to rule on proceedings commenced by qualified entities within the meaning of Article 3 seeking:

(a) an order with all due expediency, where appropriate by way of summary procedure, requiring the cessation or prohibition of any infringement;

(b) where appropriate, measures such as the publication of the decision, in full or in part, in such form as deemed adequate and/or the publication of a corrective statement with a view to eliminating the continuing effects of the infringement;

(c) insofar as the legal system of the Member State concerned so permits, an order against the losing defendant for payments into the public purse or to any beneficiary designated in or under national legislation, in the event of failure to comply with the decision within a time-limit specified by the courts or administrative authorities, of a fixed amount for each day's delay or any other amount provided for in national legislation, with a view to ensuring compliance with the decisions.

2    This Directive shall be without prejudice to the rules of private international law, with respect to the applicable law, thus leading nominally to the application of either the law of the Member State where the infringement originated or the law of the Member State where the infringement has its effects.

### Article 3 Entities qualified to bring an action

For the purposes of this Directive, a 'qualified entity' means any body or organisation which, being properly constituted according to the law of a Member State, has a legitimate interest in ensuring that the provisions referred to in Article I are complied with, in particular:

(a) one or more independent public bodies, specifically responsible for protecting the interests referred to in Article 1, in Member States in which such bodies exist and/or

(b) organisations whose purpose is to protect the interests referred to in Article 1, in accordance with the criteria laid down by their national law.

### Article 4 Intra-Community infringements

1 Each Member State shall take the measures necessary to ensure that, in the event of an infringement originating in that Member State, any qualified entity from another Member State where- the interests protected by that qualified entity are affected by the infringement, may seize the court or administrative authority referred to in Article 2, on presentation of the list provided for in paragraph 3. The courts or administrative authorities shall accept this list as proof of the legal capacity of the qualified entity without prejudice to their right to examine whether the purpose of the qualified entity justifies its taking action in a specific case.

2 For the purposes of intra-Community infringements, and without prejudice to the rights granted to other entities under national legislation, the Member States shall, at the request of their qualified entities, communicate to the. Commission that these entities are qualified to bring an action under Article 2. The Member States shall inform the Commission of the name and purpose of these qualified entities.

3 The Commission shall draw up a list of the qualified entities referred to in paragraph 2, with the specification of their purpose. This list shall be published in the Official Journal of the European Communities; changes to this list shall be published without delay, the updated list shall be published every six months.

### Article 5 Prior consultation

1 Member States may introduce or maintain in force provisions whereby the party that intends to seek an injunction can only start this procedure after it has tried to achieve the cessation of the infringement in consultation with either the defendant or with both the defendant and a qualified entity within the meaning of Article 3(a) of the Member State in which the injunction is sought. It shall be for the Member State to decide whether the party seeking the injunction must consult the qualified entity. If the cessation of the infringement is not achieved within two weeks after the request for consultation is received, the party concerned may bring an action for an injunction without any further delay.

2 The rules governing prior consultation adopted by Member States shall be notified to the Commission and shall be published in the Official Journal of the European Communities.

### Article 6 Reports

1 Every three years and for the first time no later than five years after the entry into force of this Directive the Commission shall submit to the European Parliament and the Council a report on the application of this Directive.

2 In its first report the Commission shall examine in particular:

- the scope of this Directive in relation to the protection of the collective interests of persons exercising a commercial, industrial, craft or professional activity,
- the scope of this Directive as determined by the Directives listed in the Annex,

- whether the prior consultation in Article 5 has contributed to the effective protection of consumers.

Where appropriate, this report shall be accompanied by proposals with a view to amending this Directive.

### Article 7 Provisions for wider action

This Directive shall not prevent Member States from adopting or maintaining in force provisions designed to grant qualified entities and any other person concerned more extensive rights to bring action at national level.

### Article 8 Implementation

1    Member States shall bring into force the laws, regulations and administrative provisions necessary to comply with this Directive no later than 30 months after its entry into force. They shall immediately inform the Commission thereof.

When Member States adopt these measures, they shall contain a reference to this Directive or shall be accompanied by such reference on the occasion of their official publication. The methods of making such reference shall be adopted by Member States.

2    Member States shall communicate to the Commission the provisions of national law which they adopt in the field covered by this Directive.

### Article 9 Entry into force

This Directive shall enter into force on the twentieth day following that of its publication in the Official Journal of the European Communities.

### Article 10 Addressees

This Directive is addressed to the Member States

Done at Brussels, 19 May 1998.

| For the European Parliament | For the Council |
|---|---|
| The President | The President |
| JM GIL-ROBLES | G BROWN |

### ANNEX

### LIST OF DIRECTIVES COVERED BY ARTICLE 1

1    Council Directive 84/450/EEC of 10 September 1984 relating to the approximation of the laws, regulations and administrative provisions of the Member States concerning misleading advertising (OJ L 250, 19.9.1984, p 17).

2   Council Directive 85/577/EEC of 20 December 1985 to protect the consumer in respect of contracts negotiated away from business premises (OJ L 372, 31.12.1985, p 31).

3   Council Directive 87/102/EEC of 22 December 1986 for the approximation of the laws, regulations and administrative provisions of the Member States concerning consumer credit (OJ L 42, 12.2.1987, p 48), as last amended by Directive 98/7/EC (OJ L 101, 1.4.1998, p 17).

4   Council Directive 89/552/EEC of 3 October 1989 on the coordination of certain provisions laid down by law, regulation or administrative action in Member States concerning the pursuit of television broadcasting activities: Article 10 to 21 (OJ L 298, 17.10.1989, p 23 as amended by Directive 97/36/EC (OJ L 202, 30.7.1997, p 60)).

5   Council Directive 90/314/EEC of 13 June 1990 on package travel, package holidays and package tours (OJ L 158, 23.6.1990, p 59).

6   Council Directive 92/28/EEC of 31 March 1992 on the advertising of medicinal products for human use (OJ L 113, 30.4.1992, p 13).

7   Council Directive 93/13/EEC of 5 April 1993 on unfair terms in consumer contracts (OJ L 95, 21.4.1993, p 29).

8   Directive 94/47/EC of the European Parliament and of the Council of 26 October 1994 on the protection of purchasers in respect of certain aspects of contracts relating to the purchase of the right to use immovable properties on a timeshare basis (OJ L 280, 29.10.1994, p 83).

9   Directive 97/7/EC of the European Parliament and of the Council of 20 May 1997 on the protection of consumers in respect of distance contracts (OJ L 144, 4.6.1997, p 19).

## CORRIGENDA

Corrigendum to Commission Regulation (EC) No 2571/97 of 15 December 1997 on the sale of butter at reduced prices and the granting of aid for cream, butter and concentrated butter for use in the manufacture of pastry products, ice-cream and other foodstuffs

*(Official Journal of the European Communities L 350 of 20 December 1997)*

On page 5 in Chapter II, Article 4(1)(b)(i), fifth line:

for:     ' ... eggs or egg yolk, ...',

read:    ' ... egg or egg yolk powder, ...'.

**Corrigendum to Decision No 1/98 of the EC-Turkey Association Council of 25 February 1998** *on the trade regime for agricultural products (98/223/EC)*

*(Official Journal of the European Communities L 86 of 20 March 1998)*

On page 4 in Annex 1:

for:

| 'ex 0701 90 | Potatoes, from 1 January to 31 March | 100 | – | |
|---|---|---|---|---|

read:

| 'ex 0701 90 51 | New potatoes, from I January to 31 March | 100 | – | |
|---|---|---|---|---|
| 0701 90 59 | New potatoes, from 16 May to 30 June | 0 | | |

On page 7 in Annex 1, column A, eighth and ninth entries:

for:      'ex 2007',

read:     'ex 2207',

and

for:      '2009 00',

read:     '2209 00'.

## CHAPTER 2

# AUSTRIA

*Rainer Herzig*

## INTRODUCTION

### Structure and organisation of media advertising

The Austrian advertising market increased from Sch 16.72 bn to Sch 18.32 bn in 1997. The increase has been not so significant as in 1996 (almost 25%), but was not far short of 10%.

The advertising market in Austrian media is shared between television (26%), radio (9.8%), magazines (24.4%), daily newspapers (32.7%) and billboard advertising (7.1%).

Austria's largest advertising agencies are as follows:

| Agency | Gross income 1997 (million Sch) |
|---|---|
| Lowe GGK Vienna/Salzburg | 196.0 (including Europe 312.0) |
| Demner, Merlicek and Bergmann | n/a (billing 1,701.4) |
| Wirz | 157.0 |
| Saatchi and Saatchi | 137.0 |
| Ammirati Puris Lintas | 127.6 |
| Euro RSCG Advertising Vienna | 122.0 |
| Young and Rubicam Vienna | 115.0 |
| Ogilvy and Mather Vienna | 114.0 (including Eastern Europe 353.0) |
| Publicis | n/a (billing 665.3) |
| Team/BBDO | 99.1 |

Austria's most advertised trade marks are as follows:

| Trade mark | Company/Type of business | Spend (million Sch) |
| --- | --- | --- |
| max.mobil | max.mobil Telecom/ telecommunications | 172.7 |
| Spar | Spar AG/retail | 171.4 |
| Media Markt | Media Markt Holding/retail | 170.3 |
| Bank Austria | Bank Austria/banking | 136.1 |
| Raiffeisen | RZB/banking | 132.5 |
| Renault | Renault/cars | 130.6 |
| Leiner | Leiner/furniture | 126.8 |
| Billa | Billa/retail | 125.8 |
| Kika | Kika/furniture | 125.0 |
| A1 GSM-network | Mobilkom Austria/ telecommunications | 124.8 |

## General information

Austrian competition law provides a set of provisions applicable to advertising media in general, such as the Act against Unfair Competition (*Gesetz gegen den unlauteren Wettbewerb* (UWG)) and the Media Act (*Mediengesetz*), as well as provisions applicable only to specific media, such as the Broadcasting Act (*Rundfunkgesetz* (RFG)) or only to specific products, such as the Tobacco Act (*Tabakgesetz*). The Austrian UWG corresponds closely to the German Act of the same name. Although there is a substantial similarity between these two laws, it does not necessarily mean that they are identical. There are differences in details (especially concerning the provisions on clearance sales, comparative advertising, premiums and discounts) and in court decisions. However, in cases when there are no reported Austrian decisions and there are no differences between the two laws, it may be assumed that Austrian courts would follow German decisions.

Austrian competition law regulates individual competitive breaches in a series of particular provisions. These particular provisions are found not only in the UWG, but also in other laws, including the Local Distribution Act (*Nahversorgungsgesetz*), the Cartel Act (*Kartellgesetz*) and the Prices Act (*Preisgesetz*).

In addition to these particular provisions, § 1 of the Austrian UWG (which is identical to § 1 of the German UWG) creates claims for cease and desist and for compensation against anyone who, 'in the course of business activity for purposes of competition, commits acts contrary to ethical practice'. Austrian courts subsume under this general clause deceptive practices, product placement, street canvassing, telephone advertising, delivery of unordered goods, certain kinds of door to door advertising and selling and lay advertising.

Based on § 32 of the UWG, a great number of merchandise labelling regulations have been implemented (for example, the Food Labelling Regulation (*Lebensmittelkennzeichnungsverordnung*)). These regulations also reflect the relevant directives of the EU. Violations of these regulations constitute violations of § 1 of the UWG, since it is contrary to ethical practice that someone should obtain a competitive advantage over law abiding competitors by not observing the law.

So called loss leader offers, where additional merchandise is offered at particularly favourable prices together with the main product, are treated as restrictive by Austrian courts under § 1 of the UWG.

The Austrian UWG, § 2(1), which is almost identical to § 3 of the German Act, prohibits deceptive practices. Austrian courts apply the law against deception fairly strictly, but perhaps not as strictly as the German courts. The criterion of deception is established by the understanding of the average casual observer and the burden of ambiguity is placed on the advertiser.

However, unlike in Germany, comparative advertising is permitted, and has been since the 1988 amendment to the UWG and a subsequent judgment of the Supreme Court (*Oberster Gerichtshof* (OGH)). Since this decision, the Supreme Court holds that comparative advertising which makes truthful claims of the superiority of one's own product, compared to the inferior performance of products of named competitors, is permissible when it is based on verifiable and objective data and is neither misleading, violating the requirement of objectivity, making disparaging remarks, nor unnecessarily disclosing competitors in some other manner. Comparative advertising which merely states that one's products are equal to the competitor's products may be regarded as unfair passing off. However, aside from price comparisons, comparative advertising is not very popular in Austria.

The Austrian UWG does not expressly restrict advertising price reductions. However, court decisions are strict, and when comparisons are made between one's own prices and list prices, the Act requires that it is clear with which prices the comparisons are being made, even for casual observers (§ 2(1) of the UWG). It is not permissible to use one's own (higher) prices that were valid only for short periods of time as a basis for price comparisons with one's own prices that have been subsequently reduced.

Because of the great promotional effectiveness of environmental claims, Austrian courts scrutinise such claims closely. Although they have not dealt with these claims to the same extent as their German counterparts, they have followed German decisions, and hold words such as 'environmentally aware' or environmental labels such as the 'blue angel' permissible only if the product is, in fact, compatible with the environment in all respects.

The UWG, § 9a allows certain kinds of promotional gifts and prize competitions. The following types of gifts or promotions are generally permitted: a fixed amount of money, which is not included with the goods or services; a fixed quantity of the same goods or services; information or advice; normal accessories for the goods and services; samples of merchandise; promotional products characterised as such by a visible and permanent designation of the advertising enterprise on them; miscellaneous items of low value; prize competitions where the total of the prizes does not exceed Sch 300,000 and the nominal value of a participation coupon, obtained by dividing the total prize value by the number of coupons, does not exceed Sch 5. Such prize competitions are not permitted in advertisements for newspapers and journals, but they are permitted for advertisements in newspapers and journals.

The Tobacco Act (Tabakgesetz), § 11 restricts advertising tobacco products to billboard, cinema and print media and excludes radio and TV advertising. Tobacco advertising has to include a legible warning of the dangers of smoking. The size of billboard advertising is limited, as well as the number of pages in print media. In addition, special restrictions apply as to the advertising of certain tobacco products and certain methods of direct advertising.

Advertising in mass media has to be identified as 'advertisement', 'paid for insertion' or 'advertising' unless the commercial nature is clear from the format or the arrangement (§ 26 of the Media Act (*Mediengesetz*)). Therefore, product placement is only permitted under certain conditions (see below, pp 291–93).

# ADVERTISING LAW

## Rules to be followed by advertising agencies/companies

As with most business activities in Austria, advertising agencies require a trade licence (*Gewerbeberechtigung*), which has to be applied for at the commencement of business. It requires a certificate of proficiency (*Befähigungsnachweis*), which may only be issued if certain educational criteria are met and previous practical experience has been gained. If the business is exercised by a corporation, it is necessary to name a person responsible for the correct conduct of the business, who fulfils these requirements. This person does not necessarily have to be a person authorised to represent the corporation, but can be an employee who works at least half time for the corporation. He is commonly referred to as *'gewerberechtlicher Geschäftsführer'*. The non-observance of the Trade Act (*Gewerbeordnung*) may constitute an infringement punishable by the administrative authorities with fines. Competitors may sue for cease and desist of the non-observance of the Trade Act under the UWG.

To obtain a certificate of proficiency, it is necessary to fulfil the requirements according to Ordinances 276 and 277/1978 in the current version (education, exam, practice time).

Citizens of EU Member States who do not fulfil these requirements may apply to the authority to hold that a proficiency certificate issued in their home country is equivalent to the Austrian requirements (§ 373d of the Trade Act (*Gewerbeordnung*)).

Advertising agencies entitled to do business in their home country may render services in Austria if ordered by Austrian clients (§ 373g of the Trade Act).

The Advertising Agencies Section of the Chamber of Commerce has created a kind of regulatory body named the *Österreichischer Werberat* (Austrian Advertising Council). This council may assess advertisements upon request. The council also may publish its decisions. The council applies the UWG, as well as some guidelines (women in advertising, children in advertising) which it has edited itself. However, the council does not have a substantial impact on the advertising industry and the public. Maybe this is due to the fact that Austrian jurisdiction applies the UWG very strictly and effectively and it is not possible for the council itself to enforce its recommendations.

## Television

Austria is one of the last countries in Europe to have only a public television network, the Austrian Broadcasting Corporation (*Österreichischer Rundfunk* (ORF)). The ORF provides two channels. There have been discussions about a proposed law on private television, as well as on the privatisation of one of the monopoly's channels, yet these have not led to legislation.

The Broadcasting Act (*Rundfunkgesetz* (RFG)), § 5(6) limits advertising time in a weekly average to a total of 20 minutes per day on each channel. Variations of up to 20% per day are permitted. Within a period of one hour, advertising time must not exceed 20%.

Commercials have to be placed together between programmes. Interruptions are allowed only under specific conditions (identification as advertising, no negative effect on the contents of the programme).

Commercials are prohibited on some holidays (Ash Wednesday, Maundy Thursday, Good Friday, 1 and 2 November and 24 December).

Commercials have to be separated from the programmes by a sign.

Sponsorship of programmes is permitted. Product placement and commercials for tobacco and spirits are prohibited.

The advertising guidelines of the ORF impose additional restrictions for (soft) alcoholic beverages, as they must not be aimed at young people or drivers and must not have sporting contents. The guidelines also restrict the use of children in advertisements.

## Radio

Under the Telecommunications Act (*Telekommunikationsgesetz*) broadcasting is subject to a licence. Such a licence is granted by law to the ORF.

Although a Private Broadcasting Act (*Regionalradiogesetz* (RRG)) was passed in 1993, the Act was partly overruled by the Constitutional Court (*Verfassungsgerichtshof*) in 1995, because the court did not find sufficient grounds for the apportionment of frequencies to regional broadcasters on the one hand and local broadcasters on the other hand, thus making the Act infringe the requirement of determination under the Austrian Constitution. In addition, the Act did not sufficiently determine the number of regional broadcasters per province. The overruled part of the RRG concerning the admission of private broadcasters and the apportionment of frequencies was amended in 1997, and as from 1 April 1998, private broadcasters started up in every federal province.

The public network, ORF, provides three radio channels. Advertising is limited to a maximum of 120 minutes per day in the weekly average. Variations of 20% per day are permitted. One of the channels has to be free of advertising.

Sponsorship and product placement, as well as the limitations, are the same as for television programmes (see above).

The RRG provides that advertising is limited to 15%, with a maximum of 90 minutes per day. Advertising is prohibited on Ash Wednesday, Maundy Thursday, Good Friday, 1 and 2 November and 24 December. Also prohibited are advertisements for tobacco products and hard liquor, as well as clandestine advertising. Advertising has to be identified by a sign. Product placement is prohibited.

## Satellite

There are no specific rules for satellite broadcasting into Austria (except the general rules of the Media Act, etc).

## Newspapers

As already mentioned (see above, p 290), § 26 of the Media Act (*Mediengesetz*) provides that advertisements in media have to be identified by the words 'advertisement', 'paid for insertion' or 'advertising', unless the commercial nature is clear from the format or the arrangement.

The UWG, § 9a(2), No 8, allowing certain prize competitions (the maximum value of the prizes must not exceed Sch 300,000, and the value of prizes divided by the number of participation coupons must not exceed Sch 5), is not applicable to advertisements for newspapers; however, it is allowed for advertisements for other products in newspapers.

## Video

There are no specific laws applicable to videos apart from the general rules as discussed above.

## International rules

### *European Convention on Human Rights*

Austria has adopted the European Convention on Human Rights by the Law of 5 August 1958.

### *Council of Europe's Trans-frontier Television Convention*

Although Austria has signed the Council of Europe's Convention on Trans-frontier Television, it has not ratified this Convention.

### *European Broadcasting Directive (89/552/EEC)*

To meet the provisions of the directive Austria has amended the Broadcasting Act and adopted the Private Radio Act (see above, pp 290–92).

## *Misleading Advertising Directive (84/450/EEC)*

Austria regards § 2 of the UWG and the court decisions based thereon as conforming to the EU Directive.

## *Directive on Comparative Advertising*

The criteria set up by Art 3a of the Directive do not correspond completely to the criteria set up by Austria's Supreme Court on comparative advertising. Therefore, § 2 of the UWG will need to be brought into line with the EU Directive (for example, currently it is permitted to compare sparkling wine and champagne, whereas this is not permissible under the Directive).

## *Directive on Advertising of Tobacco Products*

Although Austria (together with Germany) has opposed the advertising restrictions under the Directive, Austria will amend the Tobacco Act to transform the Directive when it comes into force.

# A STANDARD ADVERTISING CONTRACT

**Parties**

(1)    ('the Client').

(2)    ('the Agency').

**Definitions**

(1)  In this Agreement:

'The media' means television (including, but not limited to, satellite, cable and terrestrial), cinema, video, radio, internet, press, poster and outdoor advertising and any other recognised form of media as may from time to time exist;

'Media plan' means in relation to each campaign the media composition, timing and pre-agreed expenditure on the purchase of media space, together with an outline of the target audience profile and the timings for the campaign;

'Media space' means advertising space in the media.

## Introduction

(1) The Client hereby appoints the Agency and the Agency agrees to act as the Client's Advertising Agency in Austria upon the terms set out herein.

(2) The Agency shall act in all the contracts as a principal at law.

(3) The Agency shall not, without the Client's prior written consent, act for any other person or body in respect of any product or service, which is a similar product or service being a direct market competitor with any of the Client's products or services.

(4) The Agency shall co-operate fully with the Client and shall use the best efforts to make the Client's advertising successful. The Client shall make available to the Agency all relevant information and co-operate with them as necessary for the proper performance of their duties in accordance with this Agreement.

## Terms of appointment

(1) Subject to the provisions stipulated herein, this Agreement shall govern all work undertaken by the Agency from [date] and shall continue until [date]. It is understood that the assignments undertaken by the Agency relate to media plans as from [date].

(2) This Agreement shall be reviewed by both parties not later than [ weeks] prior to planning work on the [name of] campaign.

## Agency services

The Agency will perform the following services:

(a) evaluating advertising media; submitting media schedules; reserving and contracting for space in the Client's best interests, monitoring the placement of advertising and ensuring proper invoicing by media owners;

(b) advertising strategy;

(c) full preparation of all creative work from concept through to finished material for publication, radio and television stations;

(d) preparation of all creative and production estimates;

(e) control of budgets for each item in respect of paras (a), (c) and (d) above;

(f) checking and producing proper invoices and voucher copies;

(g) attending meetings with the Client relating to the preparation to the Client's advertising campaigns;

(h) maintaining guard books;

(i) the careful and continuous study of the Client's business and products, the analysis of the Client's present and potential markets and the identification of the Client's problems as they relate to advertising;

(j) all administrative work necessary to the provision of the aforementioned services.

### Duties of the parties

*Agency's duties*

(1) The Agency shall use its best endeavours to comply with the Client's instructions for the provision of the Agency services stated under clause 5 and shall include also:

 (a) discussing with the Client the recording and reviewing of media plans, provided the final responsibility for such media plans shall rest solely with the Client;

 (b) at the appropriate time, making all necessary bookings of media space, monitoring the proper invoicing by the media owners and giving full details thereof to the Client;

 (c) monitoring all media to ensure the correct placement of advertising in the media space purchased. In case of default, the Agency and the media owners will be liable for reimbursing the Client under the terms of standard agreements between the Agency and the media owners;

(2) the Agency will notify the Client of any changes in the rates or conditions of media or suppliers, of which the Agency is notified and which affect the Client's advertising. The Client's prior written approval for such changes is required;

(3) the Agency shall inform the Client should they have any reservations regarding the legality of any advertising or promotional material prepared by the Agency on behalf of the Client.

*Client's duties*

(1) The Client shall not itself nor shall it grant to any other person or company or undertaking the right to provide the Agency services or the right to purchase media space in Austria on behalf of itself or any of its associate companies.

(2) The Client shall supply the Agency with objective evidence in support of any product claim the Client wishes to make.

(3) The Client shall inform the Agency without delay, if the Client considers that any claim or trade description in any advertisement submitted to the Client by the Agency for approval is false or misleading in relation to the Client's product or service.

(4) The Client shall honour any contracts for the purchase of media space approved in writing in advance by the Client entered into by the Agency on behalf of the Client pursuant to the terms of this Agreement and in particular shall make all payments due thereunder in full and on time.

(5) The Client shall comply with all applicable laws and regulations relating to the advertising to be placed by the Agency.

## Client approval

### *Authority*

(1) The Client's prior written approval of copies, layouts and castings will be the Agency's authority to purchase production materials and to prepare proofs, and the Client's written approval of proofs, final media schedules and castings will be the Agency's authority to publish.

(2) The Client's prior written approval of television, cinema and radio scripts and/or storyboards, together with castings, will be the Agency's authority to make production materials and to prepare proofs and the Client's written approval of proofs, films, sound recordings and final media schedules will be the Agency's authority to publish.

(3) The Client's prior written approval of schedules and castings will be the Agency's authority to make reservations and contracts for space, time and other facilities under the terms and conditions required by media or suppliers.

### *Amendments and cancellations*

(1) The Client may request the Agency to change, reject, cancel or stop any and all plans, schedules or work in progress duly authorised by the Client and the Agency will take all possible steps to comply, provided that it can do so within its contractual obligations to media and suppliers.

(2) In the event of any cancellation or amendment effected with the Client's written approval giving rise to any costs, expenses, damages or losses, the Client shall reimburse the Agency for any and all such costs. In the case of force majeure under subclause 11.5, the Agency shall use its best endeavours to cancel or to postpone insertions so that the Client avoids incurring unnecessary financial losses.

**Agency remuneration**

### Media invoicing

(1) All rebates, discounts and commissions granted by the media owners are for the Client's account and benefit. The Agency shall bill to the Client this amount (net) as well as a 12% commission on net billings (that is, media invoices minus rebates and discounts) to the Client.

(2) The Agency undertakes to provide the Client with original invoices, together with third party invoices (copies or photocopies) showing the net amounts paid by the Agency.

### Production and artwork

(1) All photography, artwork, typesetting, block and plate making, press, radio, TV, video and cinema production costs and all other necessary costs incidental to such production work which are required for the performance of the services to be rendered to the Client according to clause 5 and which are within the agreed estimates, will be billed by the Agency to the Client at actual net cost exclusive of VAT and will be marked up by 12% (Agency's commission) if the work or time or item has been purchased outside the Agency. This will include items such as setting, finished drawings, prints, paste up, transparencies, blocks, photography, recording. All invoices will be supported by third party invoices (copies or photocopies). Invoices for production costs shall be issued separately for consumer, trade, conference, special reports, etc.

(2) For in-house production work (if any) the Agency will charge the Client at cost. Such production work, together with castings, will be submitted to the Client for prior written approval. In such cases the Agency will submit to the Client separate analytical invoices.

(3) Original invoices together with third party invoices (copies or photocopies), if any, showing the net amounts paid by the Agency shall be provided to the Client.

### Expenses for the preparation of proposals

Any expenses incurred by the Agency for the preparation of any proposals for the Client, which are not finally approved by the Client, will be borne by the Agency (for example, creative work, artwork, etc).

## *Travel and associated expenses*

Travel and associated expenses incurred by Agency's employees for meetings with the Client or other parties at the Client's office will be borne by the Agency.

## Other expenses

(1) Any trade, direct marketing, market research, consumer, quantitative or qualitative surveys including pre-testing or tracking studies, specifically designed for the Client, if undertaken by the Agency, will be at pre-agreed fees.

(2) Any other out-of-pocket expenses including delivery costs, incurred by the Agency at the Client's request, will be charged to the Client at cost, or at pre-agreed fees. These should be submitted to the Client in advance for written approval.

Terms of payment

## *Media (including TV)*

The Agency will submit to the Client invoices covering all charges. Payment will be made within 60 days of receipt of invoice.

## *Production*

Agency's production invoices together with third party invoices (copies or photocopies), if any, are due for payment within 60 days of receipt of invoice.

## *Stage payments*

The Client acknowledges that certain suppliers, particularly film production companies or market research organisations, require payment in advance or at various stages of production. The Client agrees to pay interim invoices in respect of such services on presentation of Agency's pro forma invoices (excluding Agency's commission) provided that Client's written approval for such services has been obtained in advance. A written acknowledgment of payment shall be provided by the Agency once payment has been made. Final payment of the balance (if any) will be made in the usual manner upon completion of the services rendered (including Agency's commission) and after the submission of the Agency's final invoices together with third party final invoices. Should the final costs be less than the money already paid by the Client, appropriate deduction will be made from subsequent payments to the Agency.

*Verifications*

The Agency undertakes to supply original invoices together with third party invoices (copies or photocopies) from the media as well as production invoices supported by third party invoices (copies or photocopies).

*Invoice queries*

(1) Any query on an invoice shall only be valid if notified to the Agency in writing within 21 days of receipt of invoice, and if so notified, only the payment of that portion of the invoice which is queried shall be deemed to be suspended until receipt of satisfactory clarifications by the Agency. Other items on an invoice which has in part been queried shall be paid in the normal manner. If payment has been made by the Client, such payment shall not preclude notification of a query if made within the said period, and if the query is proved justified, a refund of the payment, or the part queried, shall be made by the Agency. Otherwise, all invoices will be considered to be accepted by the Client and will be payable in the usual manner.

(2) Subject to the provisions of subclauses 9.5.1 and 9.6.1 the Agency reserves the right to charge interest on any sums payable by the Client and not paid by the due date at the rate of 12%.

**Terms of business with media owners**

Unless otherwise stated in this Agreement, the Agency's contracts with media owners and suppliers for the Client's advertising are made in accordance with pre-agreed rates or other standard or individual conditions and contracts. The Agency should act in the Client's best interests, negotiating the best possible discounts with media owners. The rights and liabilities between the Client and the Agency shall correspond to those between the Agency and the various media and suppliers under such conditions.

**Liability and indemnity**

(1) The Client hereby agrees to indemnify the Agency in respect of all costs, expenses, damages or other charges as a result of legal action brought against the Agency arising from the production, publication or transmission of any advertisement prepared for the Client and approved in writing by the Client before publication. It is hereby acknowledged that it is the Agency's duty to advise the Client in writing as to problems concerning the legality of specific advertising and promotional material that the Agency is involved in producing, publishing or transmitting.

(2) The Agency hereby agrees to indemnify the Client for any and all costs, expenses, damages and other charges brought against the Client and arising out of any breach or suspected breach of any third party's intellectual property rights, including, but not limited to, breach of such third party's copyright or trade marks.

(3) The Agency shall be liable to the Client for any delay in, or omission of, publication or transmission or any error in any advertisement, save where it can show that such delay or omission is not due to any default or neglect on its part.

(4) The Client shall not be liable for any expenses or additional expenses which were not included in the Agency's proposals, provided such omission was not caused by the Agency's default or neglect. The Client shall not be liable for any expenses or additional expenses incurred due to the Agency's negligence or omission.

(5) If, due to any act of force majeure, being war, strikes, lockouts, accidents, fire, blockage, import or export embargo, natural catastrophes or other obstacles over which the Agency has no control, the Agency fails to complete its assignments agreed with the Client in the manner and within the time required by the terms of this Agreement, the Agency shall not be held responsible for any loss or damage which may be incurred by the Client as a result of such failure.

**Ownership and custody of material**

(1) The Agency will keep in its care all advertising materials entrusted to it by the Client and shall be obliged to recover such property from media owners and other suppliers.

(2) Upon expiry of this Agreement, or at the request of the Client prior to the termination of this Agreement, the Agency undertakes to deliver to the Client's Vienna office all or part of advertising material commissioned by the Client.

**Copyright**

(1) The Agency shall negotiate for and shall seek to obtain the copyright in relation to such material comprised in work produced for the Client under this Agreement as is necessary for the purposes of the Client's advertising. In cases where the relevant copyright is owned by third party the Agency shall, wherever practicable, use all reasonable efforts to obtain an assignment of that copyright.

(2) The Client is to acquire the right of use for the planned use in Austria for all advertisements designed for the Client by the Agency, free of third party rights, in so far as the Agency holds the rights. This shall apply from the date of payment of all of the Agency's claims under this Agreement.

(3) For use of the advertisements designed by the Agency for the Client after the end of the Agreement, the Client has to pay 50% of the Agency fee which would have been payable had this Agreement continued. This shall also apply if the advertisement concerned enjoys no copyright protection or if the Client uses the advertisement in a modified or further developed state. The same shall apply accordingly for the use of advertising ideas which the Agency made known to the Client before the end of the Agreement.

The Client is required to pay the Agency the charge for the use of third party rights, and the Agency shall not be liable for any instances of infringement of third party rights.

### Advertising standards

The Agency hereby agrees to abide by the rulings of the radio authority code of advertising standards and practice of programme sponsorship (ORF-Geschäftsbedingungen) and other codes of advertising standards laid down voluntarily within the Austrian advertising industry to ensure that all advertising placed by the Agency is legal, decent, honest and truthful.

### Contractual obligations

The Agency acts in all its dealings with third parties as a principal at law. Unless otherwise stated, the Agency's contracts with media and suppliers for the Client's advertising are made in accordance with media rate card or other standard conditions. The rights and liabilities between the Client and the Agency shall correspond to those between the Agency and the various media and suppliers under such contracts.

### Confidential information

(1) The Agency acknowledges a duty not to disclose without the Client's written permission during or after the Agency's term of appointment any confidential information resulting from studies or surveys commissioned and paid for by the Client.

(2) During the continuance of this Agreement and after its termination the Agency acknowledges its responsibility to treat in complete confidence all the marketing and sales information and statistics with which the Client may supply the Agency in the course of any work for the Client.

**Termination provisions**

(1) Without prejudice to the rights of any party existing on termination, this Agreement may be terminated forthwith at any time by any party giving to the other party written notice in the event of:

(a) having gone into liquidation; or

(b) having suffered a receiver or administration order to be appointed over any of its assets; or

(c) having entered into a composition with its creditors; or

(d) having taken or suffered any step or event in a country in which it is incorporated or carries on business which is similar or analogous to any of the foregoing; or

(e) ceasing or threatening to cease to carry on its business; or

(f) being in breach of any substantial term condition or provision of this Agreement (relating to financial obligations and satisfactory completion of agreed work) and not having remedied the same within 14 days of being requested to do so in writing by the terminating party; or

(g) in the event of termination of this Agreement and unless the Agency is in breach under subclauses 17.1(a) and 17.1(e) above, the Client shall be liable for all work commissioned up to that date and all media space approved in writing by the Client and booked by the Agency which cannot be cancelled.

(2) Upon the termination of this Agreement and payment of all items properly chargeable to the Client hereunder, the Agency shall give all reasonable co-operation in transferring, with approval of third parties, all reservations, contracts and arrangements with media owners or others for space, time or materials yet to be used, and all rights and claims hereto, upon being duly released from the obligations thereunder.

(3) If, subsequent to the termination of this Agreement or its expiry and unless the Agency is in breach of this Agreement under subclauses 17.1(a) and 17.1(e) above, advertising or publicity material produced by the Agency is used in whole, or in substantial part, then the Client will pay the Agency according to clause 13 above.

(4) Termination of this Agreement under clause 17 shall be without prejudice to claims by either party.

(5) Waiver

The waiver by either party of any breach of any term of this Agreement shall not prevent the subsequent enforcement of that term and shall not be deemed a waiver of any subsequent breach.

(6) Notices

Any notice given under this Agreement shall be validly given in writing if sent or delivered personally to the addresses as appearing in clause 1 or by first class pre-paid post or by fax or by recorded delivery pre-paid post and such notice shall be deemed to have been served when received immediately where delivered personally or delivered by fax or two days later in all other cases.

(7) Complete Agreement

This document represents the entire Agreement between the two parties and no variation of any of its terms shall be valid unless made in writing and signed by both parties. The Agency shall in all cases act in the best interests of the Client in its dealing with production companies and media suppliers. Likewise, the Client will make every effort to meet its financial obligations promptly according to the terms of this Agreement.

(8) Clause headings

Clause headings are inserted for convenience only and shall not affect the interpretation of any clause.

(9) Governing law and jurisdiction

(a) This Agreement shall be governed by and construed in accordance with Austrian law.

(b) Any dispute arising out of or in connection with this Agreement or its termination shall be subject to the exclusive jurisdiction of the court competent for the first district of Vienna.

# FUTURE DEVELOPMENTS

The amendment to the Directive on Comparative Advertising will have to be implemented into the UWG. The amendment will reduce the possibilities of comparison in advertising. Also, the proposed Directive on Tobacco Advertising will need to be implemented into the Tobacco Act. Currently a substantial amendment to the Act on Trade Marks (*Markenschutzgesetz*) is in discussion, which implements the whole set of directives on trade marks, the most important change by this amendment is the introduction of the protection of highly renowned trade marks (*berühmte Marke*) into Austrian law.

# CODE OF CONDUCT

Austria's advertising industry has not published a code of conduct. However, the ORF has included provisions on advertising in its general terms and conditions and the Commission on Consumer Protection (*Konsumenten-politische Beirat*) has issued guidelines.

## ORF general terms and conditions (extract)

### Children in advertisements

Advertisements must not cause physical or moral harm to minors. Advertisements which cause minors to exercise a psychological obligation to buy products are prohibited. To protect minors, an advertisement must fulfil the following particular requirements:

(1) it must not make direct purchase appeals or appeals to consume to minors;

(2) it must not invite minors directly to induce their parents or third parties to buy the advertised product or service;

(3) it must not exploit the confidence minors have in their parents, teachers or other people;

(4) it must not show minors in dangerous situations without justified reason;

(5) it must not contain imitations of minors.

In addition, the international guidelines on advertising practice and the recommendations of the Commission on Consumer Protection are applicable.

## Recommendations of the Commission on Consumer Protection (extract)

These recommendations refer to the International Code of Conduct issued by the ICC as well as the international guidelines on advertising directed at children by the ICC and the OECD.

(a) Children and young people (Art 13 of the ICC Rules)

(1) Advertisements should not exploit the natural credulity of children or the lack of experience of young people and should not strain their sense of loyalty.

(2) Advertisements addressed to or likely to influence children or young people should not contain any statement or visual presentation which might result in harming them mentally, morally or physically.

(b) Truthful presentation (Art 4 of the ICC Rules)

(1) Advertisements should not contain any statement or visual presentation which, directly or by implication, omission, ambiguity or exaggerated claim, is likely to mislead the consumer, in particular with regard to:

(a) characteristics such as nature, composition, method and date of manufacture, fitness for purpose, range of use, quantity, commercial or geographical origin;

(b) the value of the product and the total price actually to be paid;

(c) other terms of payment, such as hire purchase, leasing, installment sales and credit sale ...;

(d) delivery, exchange, return, repair and maintenance;

(e) terms of guarantee ...;

(f) copyright and industrial property right such as patents, trade marks, designs and models and trade names;

(g) official recognition or approval; awards of medals, prizes and diplomas;

(h) the extent of benefits for charitable causes.

Advertisements should not misuse research results or quotations from technical and scientific publications. Statistics should not be presented so as to imply a greater validity than they really have. Scientific terms should not be misused; scientific jargon and irrelevancies should not be used to make claims appear to have a scientific basis which they do not possess.

# USEFUL ADDRESSES

Österreichischer Rundfunk (ORF)
ORF-Werbung
Würzburggasse 30
A-1136 Wien
Tel: + 4 31 87 87 8 4500

Fachverband Werbung Bundeswirtschaftskammer
Bauernmarkt 13
A-1011 Wien
Tel: + 4 31 63 57 63 260

Konsumentenpolitischer Beirat beim Bundesministerium für Gesundheit, Sport und Konsumentenschutz
Radetzkystraße 2
A-1030 Wien
Tel: + 4 31 711 72 0

## CHAPTER 3

# BELGIUM

*Jan Ravelingien*

## INTRODUCTION: THE LEGAL FRAMEWORK – THE TRADE PRACTICES ACT 1991

A comprehensive general regulatory framework for advertising has been in existence in Belgium since 1971 by way of the Act on Fair Trade Practices (TPA). That Act has been replaced by the Fair Trade Practices and Consumer Information and Protection Act of 14 July 1991. The TPA was published in the State Gazette on 29 August 1991 and contains 124 articles. Prior to the 1991 TPA, the 1971 TPA was the principal source of advertising law in Belgium.

The core rules are Arts 23, 93 and 94, which set out the limits of permitted advertising. Article 23 deals with the prohibition of particular forms of advertising, whilst Arts 93 and 94 are general catch-all formulations on fair trade practices and pertain to the protection of competitors and consumers.

In addition to Belgian national legislation, codes of conduct and self-regulation do play an important role in Belgium. In brief, the major legal difference between statutory instruments, which derive from economic and commercial laws, and self-discipline is that the former rules are judicially controlled, whilst the latter body of rules is an expression of the intention of the industry to impose usages and practices without the same coercive strength. The most important body of application of self-regulation is the *Jury Eerlijke Praktijken / Jury d'Ethique Publicitaire* (Jury of Advertising Ethics (JEP)).

The general purpose of this chapter is to provide an overview of the legal aspects of the most important modes of advertising, as well as of the instruments and forms of sanction prohibiting advertising conduct. What follows does not pretend to give an exhaustive overview of case law or doctrinal comments: it is merely a synthetic introduction to the advertising rules on a statutory and self-disciplinary level.

The word 'advertising' is construed in its broad meaning, since the borderline between advertising and other commercial communication practices through different media or sales promotion is not always clear-cut. Some sales promotions which relate to or closely accompany advertising are also included in this chapter. A detailed overview of labelling, trade marks, copyright and the regulation of the media is not covered in this chapter.

# PARTICULAR FORMS OF ADVERTISING AND ADVERTISING-RELATED SALES AND PRICE PROMOTION

## Product placement and sponsorship

The definition of advertising in Art 22 of the TPA includes the presentation of products in the form of product placement in radio and television advertising. Article 23.5 of the TPA prohibits any form of advertising which does not identify itself beyond doubt in a clear manner as being advertising. This general prohibition is amended through specific rules. For the Flemish community, a special regulation was put in place with the 'Maxi-Decree' of 12 June 1991, of which Art 8.1 allows unavoidable advertising in programmes, in other words, any form of presentation of products which are part of the normal living environment or of the normal street view, presented without emphasis or particular purpose. The image of such products should not be longer, more frequent or bigger than necessary and should not appear dominantly.

Product placement, whereby products are presented on television as available in competition prize shows, is allowed by Art 8.3 of the Maxi-Decree because the public should know what prizes can be won in the particular television programme. Special visual effects or moving emphasis are not allowed. Enlargement of trade marks or logos on the television screen or additional sound production is also prohibited. The prizes can only be shown twice. Price indication is prohibited.

### Sponsorship

On radio and television, only public institutions sponsor the public broadcaster and private companies sponsor private broadcasters. Any sponsorship needs to appear clearly at the beginning and the end of a programme and in the announcement spots (only the name and logo, without reference to a product or service). The maximum duration of animated images is five seconds per sponsor and 10 seconds in total. Sponsored programmes cannot be influenced by the sponsor to the extent that editorial independence is at stake and sponsored programmes cannot incite to buy or hire products or services of the sponsor or of third parties. News and political programmes may not be sponsored.

## Television and radio advertising

### Outline

Rules for television and radio advertising are not nationally uniform in Belgium, being set by the Flemish community and the French community, which are competent respectively as to Flemish broadcasters and broadcasters of the French community.

Generally, the rules are not spectacular and do not differ very much from the rules laid down in the EU 'Television Without Frontiers' Directive (in fact, they have been inspired by that Directive). However, some specific rules (as to Flemish broadcasters) must be mentioned:

(a) prohibition on mention of price;

(b) prohibition on mention of competitors' trade marks.

The Flemish decree also contains a prohibition on inserting advertisements *in* programmes for children or five minutes *before or after* programmes for children, which is unique in the EU.

A specific characteristic of rules for television and radio advertising is that these rules do not apply directly to the advertiser: it is the broadcasters who are obliged to follow the rules, and it is the broadcasters who can be sanctioned if they do not follow them. However, as an advertisement can be suspended, the advertiser has a vested interest in complying (apart from the fact that a broadcaster might not accept an advertisement contrary to the rules – though instances are known in which the broadcaster did not object to and did broadcast an advertisement manifestly contrary to the applicable rules).

What follows is an overview of the Flemish rules, the French rules, the rules as to the German-speaking community in Belgium, and some comments as to actual practice.

### Flemish advertising rules for radio and television

The Flemish Decree of 12 June 1991 on advertising and sponsorship on radio and television deals in Art 4 with the content of advertisements on radio and television. Article 4.8 of the Decree of 12 June 1991 also makes it obligatory to comply with the Advertising and Sponsorship Code. An Advertising Code for Radio and Television (the Code) had already been approved on 31 July 1990. The different Acts were co-ordinated through the Decree of 8 March 1995 (*State Gazette*, 31 May 1995, p 15346).

The following rules are worthy of mention:

(a) advertisements shall not incite behaviour which damages health, security, or the environment, or make improper use of arguments as to health, security, or the environment (Art 4.2 of the Decree);

(b) advertisements shall not mention price, unless these advertisements are made by companies not selling directly to the consumer (Art 4.3.d of the Decree);

(c) advertisements shall not damage minors (see also European Directive) (Art 4.5 of the Decree);

(d) advertisements shall not make use of persons who are known in the media through their participation in information programmes and, therefore, their appearance could mislead the audience (Art 4.7 of the Decree);

(e) advertisements shall not be misleading (Art 6 of the Code);

(f) advertisements shall not make a false or misleading use of results of scientific research or of quotes of scientific and technical publications; scientific and technical terms shall not be abused to provide certain claims with a pseudo-scientific basis (Art 7 of the Code);

(g) testimonies, certificates and recommendations used in an advertisement shall be genuine, shall not be placed out of context and shall not be outdated; using testimonies, certificates and recommendations is only possible if the author gives his permission (Art 10 of the Code);

(h) no use can be made in advertisements of the trade mark, name or initials of another company or organisation, without its permission (Art 12.1 of the Code) this prohibition is absolute.

An advertisement that does not use another company's trade mark is permissible under media law if it meets the criteria of points (a)–(g). However, the general tradition of prohibition of comparative advertising in Belgium might make a broadcaster hesitant to accept a comparative advertisement.

Article 15 of the Flemish Decree of 12 June 1991 established the Flemish Council for Advertising and Sponsorship on Radio and Television (the Flemish Council). The Flemish Council is competent as to safeguarding compliance with the rules on radio and television advertising, sponsorship and teleshopping. An Executive Decision of 31 July 1991 deals with the organisation of the Flemish Council. The chairperson, the vice chairperson and two members of the Council can decide to suspend the broadcasting of an advertisement until a final decision is taken. Parties must be heard. The Executive Decision of 31 July 1991 does not consider the advertiser as a party. The suspension decision must be confirmed by a two-thirds majority of the Flemish Council within seven days.

Article 17 of the Flemish Decree of 12 June 1991 stipulates that the broadcaster can be sanctioned with a fine of BFr 500 to BFr 100,000 if advertisements are broadcast contrary to the applicable rules.

Strictly speaking – but much attenuated in practice – an agreement whereby criminal liability is transferred from one person to another or by virtue of which the burden of criminal liability is transferred, infringes the Belgian public order and can be held null and void. The advertiser can hold the broadcaster free from the risk of civil damages (far more important than the risk of criminal damages). In a case where the broadcaster is confronted with a claim for damages (for example, tort), it must be expected that the broadcaster will turn to the advertiser.

## Time dedicated to adverts on radio and television in Flanders

(a) advertising has to be clearly recognisable as such and must be distinguished from the programmes. References to programmes in advertising is prohibited;

(b) advertising has to be grouped in non-consecutive time blocks of a limited duration. Every block is preceded and followed by an appropriate announcement that it is advertising;

(c) the broadcasting of audio-visual products such as cinema films and television films (excluded from this provision are series, serials, amusement programmes and documentaries) can be interrupted once per complete time span of 45 minutes, if the programmed duration is longer than 45 minutes;

(d) if such programmes are interrupted, there must be a time period of at least 20 minutes between any consecutive interruptions within the programmes;

(e) programmes of religious services, information programmes and parts of programmes for children cannot be interrupted for advertising. No advertising may be broadcast in the direct vicinity of children's programmes. 'Direct vicinity' means five minutes;

(f) the Flemish Executive decides the maximum duration of the advertising blocks and the maximum per hour and per day, within the limits of 15% per daily broadcasting and of 20% within one hour.

## French advertising rules as to radio and television

The French Decree of 17 July 1987 contains (in Arts 24 *quinquies* to 27 *decies*) stipulations as to advertising on radio and television in the French community in Belgium. These stipulations established an Ethical Advertising Commission (which can be compared to the Flemish Council). Advertising is dealt with for the broadcasters RTBF, RTL-TVi and CANAL PLUS TV.

The French Executive Decision of 21 November 1989 also deals with advertising in the French community, but only regarding public television (RTBF).

On 25 July 1996 (*Belgian Official Journal,* 16 October 1996, p 26627 *et seq*), an Act (*décret-programme*) was published on the taxation of television and radio advertising. The definition of advertising in Art 61.1 is very broadly construed.

The following rules of the French Executive Decision of 21 November 1989 are briefly summarised here:

(a) advertisements shall not refer to comparative tests which were performed by consumer organisations (Art 30);

(b) advertisements shall not be misleading (Art 31);

(c) technical or scientific terms shall not be used in an improper way or presented in a way which might provoke erroneous interpretation; recourse to results of research, to quotes of scientific works or to statistics can only be admitted if all risk of confusion, ambiguity or abusive generalisation is avoided (Art 32);

(d) the advertisers or their publicity agents shall, on demand, produce proof establishing that all the objective elements of the advertisements are well founded, as defined in Arts 31 and 32 of the Executive Decision (Art 33);

(e) recommendations, references, quotes and declarations can only be used with the agreement of the authors and must be genuine and truthful (Art 34);

(f) advertisements shall, in their visual or auditive aspect, not make use of persons employed on a regular basis by the RTBF (Art 19).

*Time dedicated to adverts on radio and television in the Walloon area*

According to the French Executive Decision of 21 November 1989:

(a) advertising may not interrupt programmes;

(b) the broadcasting time for advertising may not be longer than the average duration of eight minutes per hour of broadcasting;

(c) the broadcasting time for advertising within one hour cannot be longer than 12 minutes.

The 3 May 1991 Decree of the Executive on RTBF provides, in the relevant part:

(a) the time for advertising on radio is limited to 12 minutes per hour of broadcasting in 1993 and thereafter;

(b) advertising may not interrupt information programmes;

(c) advertising cannot interrupt dramatic productions or lyric art programmes, natural interruptions excepted;

(d) commercial advertising has to be national or regional and cannot be local.

Different rules exist for non-commercial advertising:

(a) the broadcasting of audio-visual products such as cinema and television films (except series, serials, amusement programmes and documentaries) can be interrupted once per complete time span of 45 minutes, if the programme's duration is longer than 45 minutes;

(b) if such programmes are interrupted, there must be a time period of at least 20 minutes between any consecutive interruptions within the programmes;

(c) programmes of religious services, information programmes and parts of programmes for children cannot be interrupted for advertising;

(d) the maximum per hour and per day for commercial and non-commercial advertising is to be decided by the Executive within certain limits, possibly 20% per day if teleshopping is included, on the condition that the time of advertising spots does not exceed 15%;

(e) teleshopping is possible, but limited to a maximum one hour per day. Radio advertisements are limited to maximum 12 minutes per hour.

## Advertising rules of the German-speaking community regarding radio and television

The Decree of 27 June 1986 of the German-speaking community deals with the Radio and Television Centre of the German-speaking Community, and contains in Art 3.2 some general advertising standards that only apply to 'non-commercial advertising' (for example, public institutions).

## Rules concerning radio and television advertising for the Region Brussels-Capital

The Act of 30 March 1995 does not explicitly define or regulate advertising. An application by analogy of the rules in the 'Television Without Frontiers' Directive and in the other Belgian statutory instruments can be made.

## Summary of practice

Far too many rules apply to Belgian audio-visual advertising. Generally speaking, the rules are not spectacular and do not differ very much from the EU Television Without Frontiers Directive. Very contentious, and subject to possible changes, is the prohibition in Flanders on the insertion of advertisements in programmes for children, or five minutes *before or after* programmes for children. The rules apply directly to the broadcasters, not to the advertiser.

As mentioned earlier, instances have occurred in which the broadcaster did not object to, and did broadcast, an advertisement manifestly contrary to the applicable rules. More specifically, the rule against the mention of price announcements has, in practice, not always been observed by VTM, a private television station in the Flemish community. Until now, the Flemish Council did not react – this is also a political issue: the regulations on television advertisements are not always strictly enforced. In certain instances, broadcasters also ask for prior clearance by the self-regulatory JEP. Broadcasters sometimes take a commercial point of view. Channels do, however, observe the time limits for advertising.

## Advertising through other audio-visual media

Cinema advertising is not the subject of particular Belgian statutory provisions. The same goes for advertising on video and other audio-visual media, such as CD-I, CD-ROM or the internet and other information highways. Television advertising regulation in Belgium remains rather unclear for new technologies in general, such as EPSIS systems and other technology and media for storage and treatment of synthetic image information, among others, in sports advertising.

## Journalistic advertising and market research

Advertising should be clearly presented in a manner distinct from journalistic information messages (Art 23.5 of the TPA).

Market research can be categorised as marketing/advertising for a service or product. Frequently, the last questions and, particularly, follow-up efforts during a subsequent telephone call, make clear that the direct and indirect purpose of the research/interview is the promotion of a product or service.

Article 22 of the TPA reads as follows:

> For purposes of the present law, advertising is any communication having as its direct or indirect purpose the promotion of the sale of products or services, including real estate, legal rights and legal obligations, irrespective of the place where disseminated or the means of communication used.

Serious argument exists as to whether concealed advertising, in the form of market research reports, or the research itself, falls under the prohibition of Article 23.5 of the TPA:

> Without limiting other provisions of the law or regulations, advertising is prohibited:
>
> ... which, by its overall effect, including its presentation, cannot be clearly discerned as such, and which does not mention 'advertising' in a legible, readily apparent and unequivocal manner.

Market research frequently contains elements of comparative advertising that unnecessarily identifies other merchants. If the market research is categorised as advertising, such identification is prohibited (Art 23.7 of the TPA).

The use in articles and reports, tests or interviews of parts of promotional material, without respecting the overall context of the original communication, tends to lead consumers to incorrect conclusions and can give the work a disparaging nature.

The unauthorised use of parts of marketing material can also infringe exclusivity (monopoly) rights, protected in Art 1 of the Act of 30 June 1994 on Copyright and Neighbouring Rights, and the commercial use of trade marks in pictures and texts without proper motive and in a manner which causes or can cause prejudice infringes the Benelux Trade Mark Act of 19 March 1962. Also, the use of a trade name in journalistic advertising and in particular methods of market research can be challenged.

## Advertising using test results of consumer organisations

The advertising of the results of tests, if truthful, is not prohibited by the TPA; no permissions are required. Article 23.12 of the TPA, however, clearly prohibits the use in advertising of the results of comparative testing carried out by consumers' organisations. Article 30 of the French Executive Decision of 21 November 1989 contains a comparable prohibition for television advertising on RTBF.

Pursuant to Art 24 of the TPA, the advertiser has the burden of proof that the claims in the advertising are true.

## Games and prize competitions

### *Principles*

Much like the distinctions made in the US, promotional games are classified into three categories in Belgium: lotteries, games of chance and contests.

*Lotteries*

A promotional game qualifies as a lottery (when the prize is money), or a raffle (when the prize is in kind), if the award of the prize entirely depends on chance (good luck) and does not require any effort on the part of the participant.

This kind of promotional game is, in principle, forbidden by the Criminal Act on Lotteries of 31 December 1851.

**Observations**

(a) Free method of entry (the 'no purchase necessary' option):

According to Belgian law and the case law of the Supreme Court, lotteries are prohibited in principle, regardless of whether or not the participation is free (contrary to recent French law, which legalised free lotteries, following the practice of case law over decades).

(b) Sweepstakes:

The Belgian term 'sweepstake' does not, necessarily, entirely correspond to the Anglo-American notion: in Belgium, 'sweepstake' indicates those lotteries where the random drawing is held before the lots are distributed.

This 'sweepstake' was allowed by Belgian case law until the Cour de Cassation (Supreme Court) judged in 1987 that this kind of promotional game is also to be considered as a lottery and so forbidden (landmark order of the Cour de Cassation of 24 September 1987, JT 1987, p 662).

(c) Not every random drawing for a prize is prohibited:

To be considered a lottery within the meaning of Belgian law, the game must be the result of an organised operation, have a public character and be destined to provide a profit to the participant (in money or in kind) by random drawing.

Failing one of these four constitutive elements, for example, the public character, no lottery exists. Traditional doctrine and case law hold the view that 'private circle' implies the circle of family members or friends, not a small circle of, for example, staff of a firm, members of a certain profession, or members of a club.

(d) Cost of participation:

It is not a prerequisite for qualification as a lottery that participation implies a cost in money for the participant.

(e) Some lotteries are permitted:

The only public lotteries which are legal are the lotteries of so called 'general interest' (Art 7 of the Criminal Act on Lotteries of 1851) and those organised by the National Lottery (Act of 6 July 1964, modified by Act of 12 July 1976).

Lists of organisations that received authorisation through Royal Decree to run lotteries – possibly jointly with commercial entities – are published in the Belgian Official Journal.

An option all too often overlooked is the lottery of general interest in terms of promoting a branch of industry.

(f) Lotteries and joint offers:

Article 56.7 of the TPA explicitly allows the combined offer (tied or joint offer) of a product or service with a title of participation to one of the above-mentioned legal lotteries.

### Games of chance

A promotional game qualifies as a game of chance when the luck factor is still dominant to win the prize, though some effort is required on the part of the participant.

This kind of promotional game is equally prohibited by another Act, the Criminal Act on Games of Chance of 24 October 1902.

## Observation

A game can be transformed into a lawful game of chance: Art 7 of the Criminal Act on Games of Chance of 1904 offers a very interesting exception to the principle of the prohibition of games of chance, as it allows the organisation of a game of forecasting the results of sporting competitions.

Article 1 of the Criminal Act of 26 June 1963 on the encouragement of physical education, sports, outdoor life and the supervision of organisers of bets on sports forecasts requires the free access of the participants, while the organisers must obtain a previous authorisation to organise the game from the Minister of Physical Education and Sports and give up to 20% of the profits to the National Sports Fund.

There can be no purchase obligation on the part of the participants, otherwise the game falls under the prohibition on combined offers, as laid out in the TPA.

### Contests

A promotional game qualifies as a contest when the award of the prize solely or mainly depends on the performance of the participants (put simply: the best/most intelligent/fastest wins; *bona fide* skill), and not, or only subsidiarily, on the chance factor.

This kind of promotional game is allowed on condition that:

(a) there is no (appearance of) purchase obligation of any product or service to participate. Courts not only examine whether or not a purchase obligation exists objectively, but also if there is a psychological purchase obligation or doubt in this respect. Otherwise, the contest falls under the general prohibition of combined offers (tied or joint offers; see Art 54 of the TPA 1991);

(b) if there are large numbers of participants, a serious (considerable) number of prizes are available. If the contrary applies, the award of the prizes would again mainly depend on the chance factor and, therefore, the game would qualify as a forbidden game of chance, and not as a real contest.

## Observation

A subsidiary question with an unpredictable answer could be added to select the winners. The disadvantage of this promotional game remains that it may not be linked with any purchase obligation on the part of the participants.

## Example

A promotion in the form of a free draw, whereby consumers apply for a premium product via the purchase of a promotional pack.

**Evaluation of the example**

The formula as such is to be considered a combined offer (a tying arrangement/joint offer) within the meaning of Art 54 of the TPA, as the benefits resulting from participation in the draw can only be obtained through purchase of the main product. Subject to exceptions, combined offers are generally prohibited. One exception is Art 56.6 of the TPA, which allows the offer, free, together with a main product, of a coupon which gives the right to participate in a lottery which is duly permitted by the Act on Lotteries of 31 December 1851 or in a lottery organised as part of the National Lottery.

A free draw is not a lottery within the meaning of Art 56.6 of the TPA. The only public lotteries which are legal are the lotteries of so called 'general interest' (Art 7 of the Criminal Act on Lotteries of 1851) and the ones organised by the National Lottery (Act of 6 July 1964, modified by Act of 12 July 1976). Article 56.7 of the TPA allows the combined offer of a product or service with a title of participation in one of these legal lotteries.

## Price indication and price advertising

### Price regulation

From a price regulation point of view, by virtue of a Ministerial Decree of 20 April 1993, the prices of all products, except the ones on a list of products, are free: producers can increase prices freely.

If the producer has a turnover in Belgium in excess of the BFr 300 m threshold, the producer is obliged to communicate the list of products and their new prices to the competent section of the Ministry of Economic Affairs no later than the date of entry into force of a new, increased price. This communication can be simply made by letter to the:

Ministère des Affaires Economiques
Administration de la Politique Commerciale
Division Prix et Concurrence
North Gate II
Bld E Jacqmain 154
1000 Bruxelles
Tel: + 32 2 206 41 11

### Price advertising

Price advertising is permitted. Article 25 of the TPA requires that any advertising for prepacked products which mentions the selling price must mention the price per unit or per number. The nominal content at the time of packaging should be fixed in a clear, legible and non-removable manner on each container or, alternatively, on the label or outside package. Exaggerated packaging in comparison to the content can be considered as a prohibited form of misleading advertising or misleading information to the consumer. The price must be indicated in a written, unambiguous and easily legible form in Belgian francs. The price must be the net price (including all taxes, such as VAT).

Additional mention of the price in a foreign currency is valid. A retailer is free to determine his price as long as he is not selling at a loss. It is not forbidden to suggest a particular price and to print the suggested price on the package. In the case of multiple prices being mentioned, the lowest price is the valid one and will be retained.

There are, in principle, no restrictions on making advertising claims on packaging. All rules applicable to advertising also apply to claims made on packaging: if the claims on the packaging would not be qualified as advertisements, the principles would be applied by analogy or on the basis of (generally) Art 93 of the TPA.

The *language(s)* to be used is, in principle, free, if the information is not mandatory. Article 13 of the TPA provides that labelling which is mandatory must, at least, be made in the language(s) of the region where the products are offered on the market. The mandatory labelling requirements must be easily legible and visible and clearly discerned from the advertising language.

This principle of use of the national language is superseded by virtue of the EU rules on the free movement of goods and precedents such as the *Piageme/Peeters* judgment of the ECJ (18 June 1991, Jur 1991, I-2971), and the *Piageme/Peeters* second judgment of the ECJ of 12 October 1995: the language requirement cannot be maintained if this requirement would lead to a substantial hindrance of free movement, and if the requirement reaches further than what is strictly necessary in the interest of the information of the consumer. At the least, the information which is directly addressed to the consumer should be in an *easily comprehensible language* for the latter, not necessarily in both Belgian national languages (Dutch and French). Other information, such as the detailed composition of the products, is aimed at professionals and for use of the controlling authorities, rather than for the consumer.

*Quantitative promotions and price reduction advertising*

*Principle 1*

A producer has the right to alter the quantity of prepacked products if the new quantity is mentioned and this in accordance with Art 8.1 of the TPA, which provides (free translation):

> Every pre-packed product, destined for sale, has to mention on the packaging ... the nominal quantity, expressed in a unit of measure, in a legible, easily visible and unequivocal manner.

*Principle 2*

Art 55.2 of the TPA provides that equal products can be offered jointly on condition that every product can be purchased separately in the same sales outlet at the regular price, that the consumer is informed about this possibility and that the price reduction does not exceed one-third of the combined price.

*Principle 3*

The rule of Art 5.2 of the TPA provides that:

> ... under no circumstances may the price reduction of a product or service be presented to the consumer as a free offer of a quantity of the product or of a part of the service.

*Principle 4*

The quantity referred to should in some way be recognisable to the consumer. The offer of a free quantity at the same price is possible, but – usually – the free quantity accompanies the 'regular' quantity. This follows also from the parliamentary preparations of the new TPA of 1991.

It follows that producers have the right to alter quantity of prepacked products if the new quantity is mentioned and this in accordance with Art 8.1 of the TPA.

*Principle 5*

Article 43 of the TPA contains the rule that the price reduction has to be real and requires that the announcement of a price reduction refers to the price used during a continuing period of one month immediately preceding the date of application of the reduced price for the *same* products.

*Principle 6*

It is permitted to affix a sticker with the price on the package in an extra large font if the package itself is not usually marked in this way.

*Principle 7*

The additional mention of words such as '*Offre d'essai/Proefaanbod*' (trial offer) is not problematic, since it is not prohibited to qualify a special offer as such, even if the product has been on the market for a while. The same applies to the expression '*offre de lancement/lanceeraanbod*' (launching offer).

*Principle 8*

It is prohibited to offer loss leaders (sales at a loss): a challenge for alleged sales at a loss (which includes sales at an extraordinarily low profit margin in comparison to what is normal for the market) is very difficult to substantiate against producers of the product. Producers do not have an own purchase price.

*Principle 9*

An *announcement* of the 'special' price (an implied price reduction in the perception of the average consumer) is held, by the majority of case law, by doctrine and in the opinion of the Ministry of Economic Affairs to be prohibited during the so called 'blocked period' preceding the end of season sales period.

*Principle 10*

In order to make controls on unlimited (in time) price reductions possible, the TPA requires that any explicit and implied *announcements* of price reductions mention *the date from which the special price starts*. In other words, any mention of the special price in advertising, on the *shelves* in shops, on *folders*, *leaflets* and other accompanying messages (supporting the mere mention on the packaging) will need to include this starting date (pursuant to Art 43.2 of the TPA). The maximum period of the price reduction is one month.

*Principle 11*

It follows from Art 45 of the TPA that producers and sellers can be obliged to compensate consumers who order products at the announced price (if the announcement was also made outside the normal sales outlets (shops)) for a reasonable time after the promotion, if the products are no longer available at this price.

## End-of-season sales

*Rules on the 'blocked period' preceding end-of-season sales*

Article 53 TPA provides that the blocked periods preceding end-of-season sales are from 15 November to 2 January and from 15 May to 30 June.

During this period, announcements of price reductions in any manner or form are prohibited. This article, as modified by the Act of 5 November 1993, advanced and prolonged the pre-sales period, but also extended the prohibition of price reductions and suggestions of price reductions during this period to all places and all means of communication of, in general terms, all non-food products.

With the exception of the Brussels Court of Appeal in its decision of 4 September 1996,[1] case law,[2] doctrine[3] and the administration of the Ministry of Economic Affairs[4] are all of the opinion that all products, regardless of their nature, apart from food products[5] fall within the ambit of the legal prohibition of Art 53 of the TPA. This position is based upon the parliamentary preparation works (Gedr St, Kamer, 1992–93, 1158/1, 2, 3 and 11583/3, 4).

The ambit of Art 53 of the TPA is even larger than that for the end-of-season sales period regulated by Art 52 of the TPA: while it is required for the 'soldes' (sales) that the seller previously had the product in his range at a regular price during the pre-sales period, the pre-sales regulation applies to all products, regardless of whether or not the seller offered them at a regular price prior to the pre-sales period.

*Announcement of price reduction during the blocked period*

In the new Art 53.1 of the TPA, the pre-sales period is characterised by a general prohibition, not only for announcements of price reductions, but also, through reference to Art 42 of the TPA, to all suggested price reductions. The new Art 53 of the TPA has also put an end to the practice of announcing, prior to the pre-sales period, price reductions having their effect during the pre-sales period.

It is permitted to launch a new product or a product with a new quality at a special 'launching price', even during the blocked period. In order to limit risks of recategorisation of the promotion into a (suggested) price reduction, the *packaging and advertising should highlight the product's newness*.

# Special offers or promotional offers through the use of titles, coupons and reduction cards

The use of titles, coupons and reduction cards in advertising and sales promotions is very important in the Belgian advertising world and a constant element of vetting and scrutiny by practitioners and courts, because Belgian

---

1 The Brussels Court of Appeal followed the opinion of the authors Dessard, D and Honhon, A-F, who had criticised the judgment at first instance, 'Annonces de réduction de prix et bons de valeur: même combat?', commentaire sur l'ordonnance du Prés Comm Bruxelles, 16 mai 1994, in *Pratiques du commerce et concurrence*, Annuaire 1994, p 238.

2 President of Commercial Court of Mons, *Pratiques du commerce et concurrence*, Annuaire 1994, p 174; President of Commercial Court of Mechelen, 17 February 1994, *Pratiques du commerce et concurrence*, Annuaire 1994, p 176).

3 De Bauw, H, *Nieuwsbrief handelspraktijken*, 25 December 1993, p 6, n 408; Ballon, E, 'Uitverkopen, opruimingen, openbare verkopen', *Handelspraktijken*, anno 1996, p 161.

4 *Circulaire*, 10 November 1994.

5 The exception for alimentary products is foreseen within the law itself (Art 53, para 2.4).

law is very severe in this respect. The most important forms are dealt with here.

Package offers or tie-ins (combined offers) to consumers are generally prohibited, but allowed in specific circumstances. In brief, goods or services can be offered as a package if they form one unit, if they are identical and available for sale separately and if the profit on the package does not exceed one-third.

Combined offers can either be simultaneous (for example, 'two chickens for the price of one') or postponed (for example, advertising with free air miles can be considered as a postponed combined offer). The TPA foresees four exceptions to the principle of prohibition of postponed combined offers:

(a) entitlement to an item or experience *identical* to the ones which were purchased, if the price reduction does not exceed one-third of the purchase price;

(b) entitlement to participate in legal lotteries and to items with very limited commercial value;

(c) entitlement to a price reduction in *money* only;

(d) entitlement to acquire free of charge, or at reduced price, a product or experience *similar* to the one which was purchased, on condition that at least two products or experiences were previously purchased at their normal price and that the benefit does not exceed one-third of the total amount of the purchases.

A licence or permit of the Ministry of Economic affairs must be obtained prior to distribution of entitlements (these are themselves subject to certain formalities).

**Example**

A joint promotion is run by a producer and a retailer, pursuant to which consumers can collect coupons for redemption at a later stage against a product of the consumer's choice (the premium product). The consumer can also post collected coupons for redemption of premium products free of charge or at reduced prices. Alternatively, each coupon has a value that would grant an immediate discount on the purchased (main) product.

The sales promotion of *cartes de fidélité* (conversion cards or fidelity cards) which can, under certain conditions, be transformed into price reduction coupons after the acquisition of a certain number of products, is regulated by Art 57.4 of the TPA:

> It is also permissible to offer, free of charge, together with a main product or service, titles in the form of documents that give the right, after acquisition of a certain number of products or services, to a free offer or to a reduction in price at the occasion of the acquisition of a similar product or service, on condition

that the advantage is granted by the same seller and does not exceed a third of the price of the products or services previously acquired [free translation].

The provision of similarity has been applied very broadly and the construction of the word 'similar' by courts – before and after the 1991 Act – is lenient. Products which are part of the regular range of the vendor can be included in loyalty promotions. In practice, comics are offered as premiums in loyalty promotions for nutritional products. An order of the President of the Court of Commerce of Brussels dated 30 March 1992 confirmed that the producer of fruit nectar can make a loyalty promotion for its fruit nectar, though distributed by wholesalers and not by the producer itself.

The promotion consisted of an offer whereby six collected coupons and a payment of the sum of BFr 247 gave the right to a watch. It should be added that the President ruled that the watch could be a non-similar product, compared to a fruit nectar, even if both products are part of the group of products regularly offered for sale by the distributor or producer.

One observes, in more recent case law, that products are compared as such in order to see similarities; the point of departure is no longer the regular product range of the company in question. This led to an overruling of the broad interpretation of the word similar and seems to require that the product belongs to the same industrial or commercial branch as the main product. The kind of gift that could be offered in such loyalty promotion without taking any risk would be a product from the regular product line of the organiser of the promotion, offered for sale in the same outlets as the main product of the combined offer. This was decided by the President of the Commercial Court of Brussels on 30 March 1992 in the *Punica* case involving Procter and Gamble. The President ruled that watches cannot be considered similar to a fruit nectar, regardless of the question of whether or not both products are part of the regular product line of Procter and Gamble. The President of the same court was invited a second time to rule on the similarity question on 13 October 1993, and decided that the petrol distributor SECA could not offer T-shirts together with coupons for petrol because both products are entirely different.

*Value coupons*

Under the TPA, distribution of reduction coupons is allowed:

(a) when the distribution of the coupons is done *without obligation to purchase*. These *bons de valeur* (value coupons) are submitted to the regulation of Art 63 *et seq* of the TPA (this is not a tied or joint offer);

(b) when the coupon concerns an identical product to the one to which it is linked (Art 57.1 of the TPA);

(c) when the coupon gives *exclusively* the right to an amount in money: value coupons. Pursuant to Art 57.3 of the TPA, it is permitted to combine the granting of entitlements which only give the right to receive an advantage in money with the purchase of a main product, if the following is clearly indicated:

- the value in money;
- the products involved and the details of the promotion in the sales outlet/shop;
- the period of validity;
- the identity of the author of/person issuing the coupons;
- the registration number, the name of the person holding the registration and his address.

Article 59 provides that, prior to implementing such a combined offer, a registration number should be applied for from the Ministry of Economic Affairs. The number, name of the person holding the registration and his address, as well as the conditions, should be clearly mentioned on the coupon, on the book containing the coupons and on any advertising for it.

*Alternative*

Under particular conditions, the premium product could be made into a special publicity object: Art 56.7 of the TPA provides that it is permissible to offer, free of charge, together with a main product or service, objects with non-erasable and clearly striking publicity inscriptions, that are not as such on the market, on condition that the offer does not exceed 5% of the sales price of the main product or services to which they are attributed.

According to case law, the purpose of the TPA is to remove all intrinsic sales value from the product; which is the case for a football with the name of a confectionery company. This would normally not be the case for a football with the name or the logo of a producer of sportswear or the producer of footballs. The courts have ruled that the inscription has to comply with the following conditions:

(a) the inscription may not be erasable and has to be of a permanent nature. A label which can be removed or an inscription on the packaging is not sufficient;

(b) the inscription should clearly be of a publicity nature. Courts will not accept the simple mention of the company name or logo, since the gift could then be taken for a normal commercial item bearing a brand name. The message can also be accompanied by a really striking and dominant advertising message (particularly for a useful object). Finally, logically following on from the above, the inscription should be clearly visible. The value of the promotional gift does not need to be mentioned.

## Advertising through direct marketing

Direct advertising as such is permitted. However, the Privacy Act of 8 December 1992 must be taken into account.

The Privacy Act is very general and stipulates that a person must be informed of the fact that personal data concerning him or her is stored in a database. The personal data can only be used for the purpose for which it was originally gathered.

## Advertising with free gifts

Handing out free promotional gifts is not restricted under the TPA when not tied to sales transactions.

## Sales at a distance

No later than at the time of delivery of the products, particular information must be given for the attention of the consumer. This is explained in more detail below.

### *Mandatory information*

The TPA first prescribes the information that has to be contained in a distance selling offer. The mandatory items are:

(a) the identity of the seller;

(b) the total price;

(c) the quantity;

(d) the identification of the product;

(e) the period of time during which the offer remains valid;

(f) the accepted methods of payment;

(g) the time for delivery. 'Time for delivery' means the time it takes for an order to be fulfiled. The object of this provision is to inform the customer of the normal time in which he can expect to receive his goods. One should always allow some extra margin when stating the delivery time, since the mention of a delivery time implies the obligation of delivering the goods within the said period;

(h) the seven day period to withdraw from the contract.

Since, in the case of a sale by mail order, a buyer cannot examine or see the product on offer, the TPA provides that the buyer has a seven day period to withdraw from the contract. It should be stressed that the seven day period starts to run, not from the day of the order, but from the day the customer has received the goods.

A statement about the seven day period to withdraw from the contract and the instructions to the customer on how to return the unwanted merchandise, and the costs relating thereto, should appear in the letter containing the offer (or the enclosed brochures).

No later than on delivery of the product, the seller should send a document, for example, an invoice or packaging slip, containing the following clause on the front, in large lettering, in a corner distinct from the remaining text and clearly surrounded by an outlined box:

> The consumer has the right during a seven day period starting the day after delivery to inform the seller that he withdraws from the purchase.

If such a document is not sent to the consumer, he has the right to keep the delivered products without having to pay the price.

It is permissible to charge the customer with the cost incurred in returning the unwanted merchandise, on condition that this is *explicitly mentioned in the offer and in the stipulations regarding the withdrawal from the purchase contract.*

It is prohibited to request an advance payment or payment from the consumer, prior to the expiry of the reflection period of seven working days from the day following the day of delivery.

According to some case law, it is sufficient to leave the consumer at least the option to pay after the seven working days' reflection period and withdrawal period, which starts running at the moment of delivery. This option for the consumer should be a real alternative to be able to make a free choice to pay later.

# ADVERTISING USING QUALITIES OF PRODUCTS OR SERVICES

Erroneous or misleading advertising can occur in relation to the identity, composition, geographic or commercial origin of a product or service. Advertising can also be misleading in relation to the qualities or characteristics of products.

Article 23.1 of the TPA prohibits advertising:

> ... that contains claims, data or representations that can mislead regarding the identity, type, composition, origin, quantity, availability, manner and date of producing, or the characteristics of a product ... it is to be understood under the word characteristics the advantages of a product, *inter alia,* from the perspective of its characteristics, its possibilities for use, the results that can be expected from its use, the conditions under which it can be purchased, such as the price ...

It suffices that there is a possibility (risk) of misleading the consumer: the relevant person is the normally attentive 'average' consumer (Memorandum of Explanation, Printed Doc, Senate, 947 (1984–85), No 1, p 16).

Article 23.4 of the TPA prohibits any advertising:

... whereby the seller deletes essential information with the purpose of misleading regarding the same data as those referred to under para 1 ...

For Art 23.4 of the TPA, it is not sufficient to demonstrate that a producer misleads the consumer by not mentioning certain characteristics of the (changed) product. It has further to be evidenced that the characteristics are essential and that the deletion occurred on purpose with the aim of misleading. The evidence of the knowing withholding of information (which is equal to bad faith) is not always easy to adduce. Essential information concerns elements that can influence the consumer in his/her decision to purchase or not.[6]

## Environmental type claims

Article 29.1 of the TPA explicitly prohibits advertising that misleads regarding the effects a product has on the environment. The article further provides for the constitution in the future of a Commission within the *Raad voor het Verbruik/Conseil de la Consommation* (Consumption Council) to draft an Environmental Advertising Code with which advertisers will have to comply. Also, in April 1992, a Code on Advertising with Reference to the Environment was drafted. This is not yet the Code in execution of Art 29. The relevant articles of the Code on Advertising with Reference to the Environment (which is in force) can be summarised as follows.

### Honesty

The advertiser shall not make abusive use of the preoccupation of the consumer for the environment; no abuse of a possible lack of environmental knowledge of the consumer shall be made.

### Correct presentation

No declaration or presentation shall be made which could mislead the consumer regarding the environmental aspects or advantages of products, or

---

6    Doc Parlem, Sénat (1986–87), p 68, n 464/2; De Gryse, L, 'De vernieuwingen inzake reklame', in *De nieuwe wet handelspraktijken*, 1992, Dordrecht: Kluwer, p 45). 'Not the intrinsic quality is important, but the authenticity of the information and the correctness of the presentation which is created through the communicated or suggested elements with the public' (Court of Appeal of Brussels, 8 December 1986, RW 1986–87, kol 2154).

regarding measures taken by the advertiser in favour of the environment. The advertiser shall not suggest without evidence that particular activities or products can count for the whole company or industry. Expressions such as 'environmentally friendly' or 'ecologically safe', which suggest that a product or activity has no influence or only a positive influence on the environment, shall not be used unless evidence of a high value is available.

## Scientific research

Advertisers shall only use technical developments or scientific results pertaining to environmental influence if these are substantiated by serious scientific work. The use of environmental technology or scientific terminology is allowed in so far as relevant, and if used in a manner easily understandable to the consumer.

## Certificates

In the light of the rapid development in the science of the environment and the technology involved, declarations or certificates in advertising for environmental claims shall be ascertained very carefully to establish whether changes in the composition of the product or in market circumstances have made the declarations outdated.

## Superiority

Superiority in environmental care vis à vis competitors shall only be claimed if substantial difference can be proved. Claims in comparison with competing products, based on the absence of a damaging part or a negative effect, shall only allowed if the other products of the same category indeed contain the parts described or cause the effect shown.

## Composition and elements of products

Environmental claims regarding the composition or elements of products shall be precise, clear and true. The information shall be given within a complete framework. Furthermore, the positive environmental influence of the elements in question shall be substantial.

## Signs and symbols

The meaning and origin of environmental signs and symbols in advertising shall be clear and not confusing. Those signs and symbols shall not suggest any official recognition.

*Waste collection – recycling and downcycling*

The environmental arguments in this respect shall be generally accepted and available or, if not, the availability shall be clearly indicated.

*Evidence*

Descriptions, claims or illustrations of ascertainable facts shall be proved by evidence. Advertisers shall have the evidence and shall be able to produce the evidence immediately to the self-regulatory institution, instructed with the execution of the International Code for Advertising.

# ADVERTISING RELATING TO OTHER COMPETITORS

## Statutory framework

Article 23.7 of the TPA contains the rule (actually, the prohibition) regarding comparative advertising. Articles 93 and 94 of the TPA more generally prohibit commercial activities that are contrary to 'honest trade practices'. Article 23.7 of the TPA is very concise in its wording as to the prohibition of comparative advertising. Advertising is prohibited if it contains comparisons which:

(a) are misleading (deceptive); or

(b) are disparaging (heavily critical); or

(c) permit identification of one or more 'vendors' where not necessary ('mere' comparative advertising).

Strictly speaking, a fourth form of (prohibited) advertising should be mentioned, namely confusing comparative advertising.

The rationale behind the tradition of prohibition in Belgium is the idea that every comparison is based on an affirmation of superiority, and thus implies a (more or less) heavily critical statement about a competitor.

In more recent years, another development has reinforced this tradition, namely, the prohibition of referring to another person (even for simply mentioning a truth) which can qualify as the parasitical use of the name of someone else (passing off).

The difference between (a) misleading; (b) heavily critical; and (c) comparative advertising is not always well made in case law. Courts, while prohibiting mere comparative advertising, tend to look for a heavily critical statement or a misleading element in the advertising, thus showing some reluctance to treat mere comparative advertising as a category of its own.

Advertising should not contain comparisons that permit identification of one or more 'vendors', if this not necessary. Two questions arise:

(a) when is a competitor identified? and

(b) when is such identification/comparison necessary?

It should be noted that the Belgian Government approved, on 24 July 1998, a draft for an Act which abolishes the prohibition of mere comparative advertising (see below, p 347).

## Identification

Case law rather easily concludes that identification is possible. Even collective references (such as 'the rails make the highway free' (challenged by the Federation of Road Transporters), or stressing the advantages of petrol over gas) have been condemned.

Doctrine has generally stated that neither the explicit terms of the TPA, nor the preparatory works, nor the historic rationale, make it possible to uphold this case law, which is unduly strict. In this respect, it should be mentioned that the court is often disturbed by a heavily or destructive critical element in advertising. For instance, the slogan 'the rails make the highway free' was accompanied by an image of a traffic jam on a motorway filled with lorries.

In the *Pepsi Cola* case (see below, p 332), the Court of Appeal considered that, if a company occupies 80% or more of the market share, any advertising for a competitor will entail an identification of the company holding a dominant position. The same is not necessarily true in the case of a company occupying 50–60% of the market. In the author's opinion, a market in which one company occupies 50% and five other companies occupy the rest of the market, identification is not automatic. However, identification can follow from the content of the advertisement.

Advertisements are evaluated based on the perception of the average, not the credulous, consumer. The fact that the particular market is dominated by only a few competitors and that the various brands will not all use the same promotion and advertising media is relevant. One precedent of the Antwerp Court of Appeal (October 1995) even states that if one cannot formally exclude identification in the mind of the consumer, the prohibition of Art 23.7 of the TPA applies.

## Necessity

Case law has been strict in interpreting the element of necessity.

The preparatory works to the TPA mention that an absolute necessity is required. In the following instances, necessity was recognised (and, therefore, the comparison was considered legitimate):

(a) the characteristics of a new product can only be properly discerned through comparison with an existing product (a comparison of margarine with butter was held legitimate in so far as the comparisons were true and indispensable for the definition of the new product);

(b) 'system comparison': the terminology is inspired by German case law and leads to confusion in Belgian legal doctrine – the examples that are sometimes quoted compare two methods for the opening and fixing of roof windows, or compare rail with road, or insurance without an intermediary with insurance through an intermediary agent.

(c) penetration in the market of a newcomer.

By far the most important and favourable precedent of comparative advertising during the last 10 years in Belgium is the *Coca Cola v Pepsi Cola* case, in which the Court of Appeal (decision of 7 June 1983) and the Belgian Cour de Cassation (Supreme Court) (decision of 21 March 1985) have ruled in favour of comparative advertising on the matter of a complaint by Coca Cola against a comparative advertisement by Pepsi Cola.

The challenged campaign concerned an important advertisement run in several media simultaneously (television, cinema, billboards, consumer tests in sales outlets), showing a comparative test of tastes of consumers for three similar drinks that were not quoted, nor explicitly identified. The commercial ended with the slogan: 'Take the Pepsi challenge, have your taste decide.'

At that time, Coca Cola enjoyed a market share of more than 80% and by virtue of such a dominant market position, any consumer could identify that one of the compared drinks was Coca Cola. The considerations of the Court of Appeal were:

(a) the unnecessary identification of a competitor can be an act of passing off, but the prohibition of comparing is not absolute, nor unconditioned;

(b) if a company occupies 80% or more of the market share, any advertising for a competitor will always entail an identification of the company holding a dominant position;

(c) an examination of the other possible ways of penetrating the market is relevant;

(d) the interest of the consumer in full and adequate information is relevant;

(e) whether the comparison has been largely tacit;

(f) whether the comparison was limited to only one subjective element (taste);

(g) Coca Cola apparently did not contest the existence of an adverse prejudice of the public towards Pepsi. The court ruled that the comparison was proportionate to the goal to be achieved, namely reversing a negative first opinion of consumers towards Pepsi Cola.

An objective product claim would entail greater risks.

The proportionality rule implies that the means have to be proportionate to the end one wants to reach, in other words, the means (the comparison) should not go further than necessary.

A second major recent precedent is the *Velux v Contichim* case (1990): this dismissed a challenge by Velux, a roof window producer, of an advertising campaign by Contichim. Velux, enjoying, in 1990, an 80% market share (dominant position), uses a method turning around one axis, whereas the competing company was offering a new technique. The court did not agree that the identification was necessarily present in the minds of the consumers, but continued that some degree of identification was clearly possible, even unavoidable, because of the dominant position of Velux, and ruled that it would be contrary to the *imperative rules on competition* to prohibit a small company from advertising in a manner allowing *a significant penetration* of a market dominated by a competitor. The court continued that Contichim could emphasise the advantages of the 'system' (easier to stick one's head out of the window) and could not demonstrate this advantage without contrasting its 'system' with the classic system existing in the market.

A third major dispute over the last 10 years shows that exceptions to the prohibition of comparative advertising are still relatively rare. The President of the Court of Commerce in Mons ruled, in a 1989 decision, in favour of the comparative advertising by CORA, giving as rationale that the standard of necessity has to be construed purely in the light of the consumers' interest to be fully informed (transparent market). CORA is a food retailer and conducted an advertising campaign in 1985, comparing the price for a number of its products with five different named competitors. Regarding the same campaign, however, the President of the Court of Commerce in Brussels ruled on 8 March 1985 that the comparison did not meet the necessity standard – and ordered the action to be dismissed.

It follows from the above analysis that there is a heavy burden to demonstrate the necessity to identify.

### Is the existing practice in the branch of activity relevant?

Reference to the existing advertising practice in the particular branch has also been held to be most relevant in the evaluation of challenging a comparative claim. In September 1994, the President of the Brussels Court of Commerce dismissed a Procter and Gamble claim against Henkel, *inter alia*, on the basis of references to former advertising claims in the market for household detergents. In the challenged advertisement, Henkel claimed that its product, Persil, was the most efficient detergent in comparison with all other existing products.

## The burden of proof

Important in the above-mentioned *Procter and Gamble v Henkel* case was the fact that the President evaluated the hyperbolic advertising for Persil upon scrutiny of tests of both products, Persil and Ariel.

It should be mentioned, however, that the difference is not to be proven in the absolute sense of the word, in view of advertising's customary exaggeration which consumers will approach with deserved scepticism. Belgian courts admit a certain degree of exaggeration, even on essential objective qualities, but using the words 'unique' and 'revolutionary' for products that are generally applied in all identical products is illegal.

## Disparagement

Heavily critical comparative advertising is illegal. For an advertisement to be denigrating, the casting of doubt on the value of competing products is required. If this is the case, it is not necessary to identify explicitly or impliedly one competitor.

In the case of a claim that margarine was healthier than butter, the court found that collective identification was given. A claim that the use of aluminium preserves the rain forest was held to identify and criticise the wood industry. An advertisement by a railway that 'the rails make the highways free' was found collectively to disparage the road transport industry. In this case, however, the image of a motorway full of stationary cars accompanied the phrase.

Courts stress the importance of the entire message: Procter and Gamble claimed that currently marketed lemonades were not thirst quenching or healthy. When evaluating the claim of a trade association of water and lemonade producers, the Court of Appeal of Brussels ruled on 13 October 1995 that the text as a whole counts.

## Deceptive advertising

Article 23.8 of the TPA prohibits any advertising containing elements which can create confusion with another seller, his products, his services or his activity. Case law and doctrine generally decide that advertising creates confusion or a real risk of confusion if the following three conditions are simultaneously and jointly met:

(a) the conflicting/confusing aspects of the advertising are distinctive and original. It is accepted that the distinctiveness can emerge from a long and notorious use of the creation, even if it is banal;

(b) the presentation of the concurring elements creates, or can create, in the mind of a consumer, a risk of substitution;

(c) there is a certain closeness in activities or place between the sellers, their products or the services.

It is the total impression of the normally cautious consumer that is taken into account. A synthetic evaluation of all elements together is made and it is sufficient that the similarities clearly dominate the differences to have a risk of confusion.

The intention of creating confusion and damage to competition are not required, the act being prohibited *in se*. This principle makes it more interesting to pursue action on the ground of Art 23.8 of the TPA (misleading advertising) than by virtue of the general Art 93 concerning unlawful trade practices, which requires damages.

## VOLUNTARY CODES OF PRACTICE OR STANDARDS: SELF-REGULATION

### The Jury of Advertising Ethics

The main voluntary self-regulatory authority of the advertising industry in Belgium is the JEP.

The JEP can be asked to intervene both before and after the advertising takes place. Pre-clearance by the JEP can be done free of charge on the initiative of the advertiser or the advertising agency on the one hand or of the advertising medium on the other hand. After implementation of the advertisement, an examination by the JEP occurs after a complaint filed by any interested person, the President, a member or the Secretary of the JEP.

Requests for advice or complaints should pertain to advertising which can damage the public. The JEP is not an arbitral jurisdiction to decide between particular private interests or competition disputes. The JEP is an advisory, self-disciplinary organ, whose decisions are formulated as advice and recommendations. It is not strictly required for the JEP to organise a hearing with the parties before taking a decision.

In the case of a preliminary request for advice on the initiative of the advertiser or the advertising agency, the dissemination of the advertisement under scrutiny needs to be suspended until the examination has been finished. The JEP can also ask the advertising medium to suspend the dissemination of the advertisement. Together with the communication of the advice, the Secretary will ask the advertiser or the advertising agency to communicate their intention to abide by the advice or to disregard it.

A refusal to abide by the advice could lead to a confidential disclosure of the decision by the Secretary of the JEP to the media concerned, inviting them to make use of their discretionary right to refuse the advertisement. The examination and deliberation of the JEP is confidential and secret.

The members of the JEP are appointed by the Board of Directors of the Council for Advertising from a list of persons proposed by the member associations of the Council for Advertising:

(a) the Union of Belgian Advertisers;

(b) the Association of Distance Sellers;

(c) the Belgian Association of Advertising Agencies;

(d) the Belgian Association of Newspaper Editors;

(e) the National Federation of Information Weekly Magazines;

(f) the Belgian Chamber of Audio-visual Advertising;

(g) the Association of Outdoor Billboards;

(h) the Belgian Association of Editors of Addresses and Yearbooks.

### Pre-clearance

Prior clearance of advertising is not required in Belgium, but is permitted, and it is possible to enter into discussion with the JEP by at least submitting several alternative and hypothetical questions for clearance (not necessarily showing the real intention of the advertiser). The evidentiary value of a pre-clearance in court is limited. In no way is the court bound by a JEP ruling. The number of requests for pre-publication advice and vetting has increased steadily over the past few years. In fact, the use of the JEP is increasingly becoming standard practice.

It is mentioned in the Rules of the JEP that the examination is always carried out as a matter of urgency. As a matter of principle, the JEP convenes every second week, but experience shows that an examination can last three weeks before the advertiser receives an answer, which can be a request for more ample information.

## CODES OF CONDUCT

The *Conseil de la Publicité* (Advertising Council) has adopted a self-regulatory code identical to that of the ICC Code.

Compliance with the product-specific codes is purely voluntary.

There are product-specific codes for given fields, such as:

(a) the AGIM/AVGI Code on medicinal products and medical treatments 1972, revised. Besides the provisions on medicinal products, the Code contains many rules concerning paramedical practices and on appliances presented as having preventive or curative properties;

(b) BELLUCO, the trade organisation of the Belgium and Luxembourg producers and distributors of soaps, detergents, maintenance products, hygienic and toilet articles, adhesives and similar products formulated an Advertising Code for Cosmetics and Hygienic Products in 1985, last renewed on 1 July 1994. Relevant in the BELLUCO Code are the provisions pertaining to arguments in advertising concerning the composition and production of the products, such as the requirements for using the words 'biological' or 'new';

(c) the JEP Rules on slimming products, appliances, treatments and methods 1987;

(d) the JEP Rules on the advertising in the press of loans and credit arrangements 1986;

(e) the JEP Recommendations on the advertising of insulation, fuel and heating products 1979;

(f) the JEP Rules on the advertising of charity appeals 1988;

(g) the FEBIAC Code on car advertising 1989;

(h) the JEP Rules on the advertising of talismans, amulets and similar products 1989;

(i) the JEP Rules on the use of health claims in the advertising of bedding 1989.

## RELIEF MEASURES – ENFORCEMENT

### Stop order: action to cease and desist

A cease and desist order can be issued by the President of the Commercial Court (Art 95 of the TPA). This fast track procedure is distinct from ordinary summary procedures because the action to cease and desist leads to a final judgment that is binding in subsequent proceedings. Also, there is no requirement of urgency. Appeal is possible.

Actions to cease and desist are a very widely practised remedy and found to be an efficient manner of sanctioning infringements. A stop order will generally be accompanied by a fine in the event of non-compliance.

These fines can be very high. A court could, for example, rule that BFr 5,000 must be paid for every magazine containing the illegal advertisements which is published after the court injunction. If it would appear that 1,000 copies of the magazine were nevertheless published, the advertiser would have to pay its competitor 1,000 x BFr 5,000, or a sum of BFr 5 m. The sole aim of such a lump sum is to prevent the advertiser from advertising in the illegal way in the future. The lump sum can, therefore, be substantially higher than the damage actually suffered by the competitors.

The President frequently orders the publication of the stop order or of an extract of the decision. This can be in any type of media, including audio-visual, which is rare, but not excluded (one of the first examples under the 1991 TPA was the *Punica* case, in which the President ordered the radio broadcasting of an excerpt of the order. The President took into consideration the scope of the advertising, more particularly its recurring character on radio and television). This is an additional cost for the infringer and can also form (good or bad) publicity.

A stop order can be obtained in a very short period of time. However, if the advertisement is published only once, a possible stop order will probably come too late (after the publication of the advertisement). Every infringement of the 1991 TPA can be sanctioned by this special stop order. However, when a party invokes his trade mark, the stop order cannot be issued (explicitly excluded by Art 96 of the TPA).

There is no requirement of urgency. Plaintiffs (every interested party, including competitors, consumers, consumer associations and the Minister for Economic Affairs) need only prove that injury or damage is possible. Article 100 of the TPA stipulates that the procedure is as in summary proceedings (which means that the delay of summons is two days, unless abbreviation is obtained) or by (almost always unilateral) *requête/verzoekschrift* (request) (in which case the adversary party has three days to be summoned). It is debatable whether a party can obtain an immediate *unilateral* stop order. Whereas, in fact, the preparatory works do mention this possibility, the text of Art 100 of the TPA does not mention the possibility of a unilateral procedure. Most case law excludes this possibility. Only in very exceptional circumstances can one imagine an *ex parte* stop order.

## Ordinary damages

Damages can be claimed in ordinary procedures in principal actions on the basis of the (general) Art 1382 of the Belgian Civil Code (torts).

Such an action for damages requires that the plaintiff prove fault, injury to the plaintiff and causation. In matters of infringements against the 1991 Act, every violation of the 1991 Act constitutes a fault. Competitors thus face the burden of proving they actually suffered harm because of the illegal advertising.

The court principally orders payment of money damages in order to put the plaintiff in the position that he would have been in had the illicit advertisement not occurred. The amount of the damages varies from case to case, but it has been commented that the courts sometimes condemn to a relatively limited amount. The court costs are relatively small and one party must never pay the other party's counsel's fee. An action to cease and desist usually precedes an action for damages.

## Criminal sanctions

Article 103 of the TPA penalises any infringement that is done 'with malicious intent'. This stipulation is very unclear and much criticised in legal doctrine.

## Warning

Article 101 of the TPA authorises particular civil servants of the Ministry of Economic Affairs to warn infringers of the TPA. The ministry acts on its own initiative, which can be triggered by (informal) private complaints; it remains in the discretion of the ministry whether a warning is issued. If the infringer of the TPA fails to follow the warning, the minister may commence expedited proceedings (an action to cease and desist), or may refer the matter to the Public Prosecutor. Royal Decree will also regulate the minister's power to propose a settlement with the infringer. In practice, this out of court mechanism will often lead to a spontaneous termination of the action or to a fine as a settlement.

## Seizure

Civil servants of the Ministry of Economic Affairs or the District Prosecutor's Office can order the seizure of the products that constitute a violation.

# ADVERTISING AND PROPERTY RIGHTS

## Copyright

*Copyright protection of an advertising theme*

*Principles*

Under the recently rewritten Belgian Copyright Act of 24 June 1994 (Moniteur Belge, 27 July 1994, in force since 1 August 1994 (the BCA)), a creation has to meet two general statutory requirements (one formal and one substantive) in order to be copyright protected:

(a) the work must be manifested in a *concrete form* (formal requirement); and

(b) the work must be *original* (substantive requirement). No definition of 'originality' is given in the BCA.

Hence, the protection of audio-visual works is explicitly dealt with in the BCA (Chapter 4). The copyright of advertising work can be assigned and the contract must not explicitly mention the different ways of exploitation, the remuneration, the extent nor the duration of the rights.

## Enforcement

The concept used in the BCA to encapsulate all forms of copyright infringement, whether civil or criminal, is *contre-façon* (counterfeit). If the infringement is fraudulent or malicious, it can be a misdemeanour, subject to a criminal sanction. Fraud is the intention to profit from the merits of the author; malice is the intention to damage the artistic reputation of the author.

The new BCA has introduced a cease and desist procedure to be heard before the President of the *Tribunal de première instance* (Civil Court of First Instance), who rules according to the referee procedure, but with the authority to rule on the merits (Art 87.1 of the BCA). The President cannot grant damages; these can be claimed before the civil court (not the commercial court, even when both parties are merchants – Art 569.7 of the Judicial Code). Damages are evaluated according to the generally applicable legal principles of foregone profits and losses caused.

Article 96 of the TPA explicitly precludes copyright infringements from the jurisdiction of the Commercial Court: the victim of a copyright infringement does not have the choice between a civil action and a cease and desist procedure under the TPA.

Articles 1481–88 of the Judicial Code provide for a special attachment (seizure) procedure in cases of infringement of intellectual property rights such as copyright. This special procedure has a twofold purpose:

(a) to allow the plaintiff to ascertain the extent of his damages (fact finding); and

(b) to avoid the disappearance of infringing/counterfeit objects.

## Concrete form

Case law and doctrine unanimously admit that ideas, principles, theories, systems and methods *are not copyrighted*. In order to be eligible for copyright protection, the idea/concept/theme needs to be communicated in a certain form. The work need not have received a fixed material and tangible form: any form of communication of the work will do.

## Originality

The notion of originality has been broadly construed by case law and doctrine. The Supreme Court has ruled that, in order to benefit from copyright protection, it is necessary but sufficient for the work to be the *expression of an intellectual effort* of its maker. The Supreme Court did not require that the work have any artistic merit.

In a second judgment of 1989, the Supreme Court ruled that, in order to warrant protection, the work must display *a personal mark*.

Case law and doctrine have also pointed out that the concept of originality is to be distinguished from the concept of novelty.

It is long since beyond dispute in case law and doctrine that creations in the field of *advertising* can be copyright protected if the two standards of materialisation and originality are fulfiled.

It has more particularly been recognised by case law that *the elaboration of a chosen theme* for an advertising campaign can be protected under the BCA if both the formal and substantial requirements are fulfiled.

Doctrine also underlines that the theme *in se* of an advertising campaign is not copyrighted, but only its expression. One author (Gotzen) gives the following example: Michelin would be able, by virtue of copyright law, to prohibit a competitor from using the 'Bibendum' character for publicity reasons, but could not prevent a competitor from using the idea and advertising with a different character.

## Use by a competitor of the same advertising theme through a different channel/medium

The courts of Brussels have ruled that copyright is violated when *even one of the elements* which makes the work original has been reproduced in a work of a *later date, even if there is no risk of confusion* between the two works. The civil Court of Charleroi ruled that there is counterfeit when the work has been conceived and elaborated in a way that creates, in the untrained mind and to the unfocused eye, an impression of a combination, similar to the one that was contained/present in a former/earlier work and attributes a *common origin* to the *originality* of the underlying work. Some authors are of the opinion – in this author's evaluation correctly – that the risk of confusion is not an appropriate standard for determining copyright infringement.

The concrete method used by case law in establishing copyright infringement is the analysis of the form of each work and, subsequently, the comparison of its concrete elements. In applying this method, courts and doctrine are not unanimous on whether only the similarities must be taken into account, or the similarities rather than the differences, or both in an equal way, but in general, the judge will examine the similarities between the two works. He will take the differences into account if these are significant and affect the protectable elements of the allegedly copied work, in order to decide if the structure and the characteristics of the work and the personality of the author or the protectable elements of the work are affected or imitated.

The change in medium is not relevant: in copyright law the medium is not the message and a change in medium does not preclude infringement. Since copyright laws are intended to protect the expression of the creator, it is immaterial what medium is used to convey the message.

Further, case law decides unanimously that no defence to a civil action is provided by the good faith of the defendant. Finally, even partial counterfeit remains a counterfeit.

## Copyright versus freedom to copy

In principle, all competitors have the freedom to copy: this is considered to be one of the cornerstones of genuine competition law. This freedom of imitation however, is not absolute: it is limited by legislation on intellectual property rights, such as copyright, and by the law on trade practices.

Traditional doctrine and case law hold that, if a product or creation is not directly protected/protectable by one of the particular laws on intellectual property rights, it cannot indirectly get equal protection through the common law. The imitation of a creation that is not protected/protectable by an intellectual property right, is thus *in se* not contrary to fair trade practices. The copying is only considered to be unlawful if:

(a) *it is accompanied by other, distinct prohibited acts,* such as misleading allegations, disparaging comparisons, the creation of (a risk of) confusion; or

(b) *it is accompanied by parasitic competition.*

## Parasitic competition

Article 93 of the TPA prohibits any act contrary to fair trade practices by which a seller damages or tries to damage the professional interest of one or several other sellers. It requires proof of damages, but not of intention: the notion covers acts exploiting the reputation of a seller (competitor or not) without creating any confusion and without disparagement to his merits. It is indeed felt to be an unfair trade practice when a seller procures himself a competitive advantage through an identical copy of the work of a competitor or other seller without making the least creative effort, enabling him to apply lower prices and make larger profits.

The derivation of profits from the investments or the success of another seller by the imitator, eventually his competitor, is what makes the parasitic competitor unlawful.

Sometimes, an act may both be parasitic and misleading advertising, but it is not necessary for the act to create confusion in order to be considered unlawful.

The theory of parasitic competition is based on the general principle of freedom to copy, which some authors and courts have perceived as a right to copy. In a ruling of 1982, the President of the Commercial Court of Brussels even proclaimed that imitation of a market leader may be a factor of progress, which is profitable to all consumers. Ten years later, his successor pertinently observed that this argument only counts when the copy allows a larger number of people to benefit from the advantages of certain achievements (products or services). This does not normally count in *the field of advertising*, where the copy can only benefit the imitator, whether or not he benefits from the position of market leader.

The theory of parasitic competition has been applied to all kinds of trade practices, and in the field of advertising, especially to slogans. In most cases where the copy of an advertisement was considered to be an unlawful parasitic practice, the accompanying factor of the *risk of confusion* was present. The Court of Appeal of Gent ruled that the imitation of the *ideas, conceptions and representations* of a seller's advertising is an unlawful trade practice, even if there is no risk of confusion. The facts of this case show, however, that it concerned *an identical copy*. In a case concerning specifically the copy of a *publicity theme*, it has been ruled that the prohibition of parasitic competition, being a limitation of the fundamental principle of free trade, asks for a reasonable application. Therefore, it was ruled that ideas cannot be protected under trade practice law, so that the imitation of a certain publicity method was not considered unlawful. In a matter involving a copy of a *publicity theme of a television advertisement*, brought before the Court of Brussels, the president ruled that the copy was indeed an unlawful practice, but it again was a servile copy, and furthermore, the behaviour was also considered a disparaging comparison and, thus, *in se* prohibited advertising. Finally, the President of the Brussels Court is quoted, in another case involving the copy of a publicity theme of a television advertisement, to conclude that in the particular case, the President had to decide that the act was not unlawful, because the underlying theme was not original and, therefore, not eligible for exclusive appropriation and because the difference in elaboration of the theme meant that there was no risk of confusion.

*Advertising agency vis à vis employees, creators of copyright protected work*

Only natural legal persons can have the quality of author of a copyrightable work. The employee as original owner of copyright can contractually assign his copyright. The agreement needs to be evidenced in writing, assignment is construed narrowly and the agreement must provide for a payment for each manner of commercialisation, with provisions on the scope and duration of the assignment. The assignment must be limited to known manners of commercialisation and the assignment must be limited in duration and to limited types of works if the assignment pertains to future works. If the creative work of the employee falls within the regular scope and purpose of the labour agreement, the above rules are attenuated: it is not necessary to make long, detailed enumerations of the assigned manners of commercialisation or use and the agreement does not have to provide for a payment for each manner of commercialisation, with provisions on the scope and duration of the assignment, and future forms of use and commercialisation can be included in the transfer. The assignment must provide for compensation of the employee, related to a percentage of the profits realised by the future manner of commercialisation. The amount of the percentage is free.

*Advertising agency vis à vis their employees as performing artists or who are at the origin of neighbouring rights*

The Copyright Act 1994 contains a distinct chapter on neighbouring rights and also provides a particular and extensive statutory regime regarding employees as performing artists or who are at the origin of neighbouring rights. Broadly speaking, the same reasoning as for copyright applies for the performing artists.

*Agencies/advertisers*

Article 3.3, ss 2 and 3 of the Copyright Act 1994 provides on copyright contracts between the independent author and the person, giving instructions and providing that in the non-cultural and advertising sector, assignment is possible if explicitly provided for and if the work will in fact be used for advertising. This article, however, is only valid if the advertising agency is simultaneously the creator and the original author of the copyright protected work. In practice, the advertising agency – virtually always being a company structure and not a natural legal person – can only be the assignee of copyright. Consequently, the assignment of copyright between agency and advertiser will not fall under the ambit of the Copyright Act 1994, thus, general principles of contract law and freedom of commerce govern the relationship.

*The rights of director/production company, for instance, in production of television commercials or other filmed commercials*

Under the Copyright Act 1994, all authors are presumed to have transferred the exclusive right of use to the producers, except for authors of music compositions and if otherwise explicitly provided for.

In the advertising world, it is not mandatory for the agency to give a distinct remuneration for every manner of use to the authors. In the cultural sector of audio-visual productions, remuneration is presumed to be a percentage of the gross turnover, the producer being obliged to give an overview per category of use at least once per year. This does not apply to advertising material. The following are presumed to be co-authors in audio-visual productions:

(a) the principal producer;

(b) the author of the scenario;

(c) the author of the adaptation;

(d) the author of the texts;

(e) the graphic author for the animation work;

(f) the author of the musical compositions specially realised for the work; and

(g) the authors of the original work if their work has been used in the new work.

*Model agreements*

The first UBA model agreement of 1983 (model of the Association of Belgian Advertisers) presumed that the copyright lay with the advertising agency. The 1991 model agreement, however, reverses the presumption into an automatic assignment of copyright in favour of advertiser. The UBA model agreement is not genuinely practised and there are other model agreements and guidelines. One of these guidelines emerges from the Association of Communication Professionals (ACP).

The ACP guidelines merely mention that the reproduction rights have to be clarified, namely, whether the they remain the agency's property or belong to the advertiser and, in that case, for which country, for which period and under which conditions. The ACP guidelines also mention the need to define whether it is up to the agency to negotiate production rights and in what kind of terms.

Furthermore, the profession does not stick to one generally accepted practice and, in view of this lack of unanimity, use and membership, the Court of Appeal of Brussels, in the case of *Côte d'Or v J Walter Thomson*, did not recognise the reference value of the model agreements.

## Patents and trade marks

Article 13.A.2 of the Benelux Trade Mark Law stipulates that the owner of a trade mark can object to every use *without any reason* of the trade mark in economic 'traffic' whenever damage is caused to the owner of the trade mark.

The condition of damage refers to the concept of possible damage; courts easily conclude that damage is possible. The discussion of whether the use of another's trade mark is legitimate is, therefore, mostly a discussion as to whether there is a *valid* reason for referring to the trade mark – in other words, if the reference (or comparison) is necessary. The concept of 'necessity' (see the discussion on comparative advertising below) is thereby revisited. No distinctions are made as to the verbal, written or visual representation of a trade mark. Case law has been very strict and practically does not permit the reference to another trade mark. Legal doctrine criticises this case law and supports the argument that the right of the public and the consumer to be informed can constitute a due reason.

A specific rule regarding radio and television advertising in the Flemish community should be kept in mind: no use can be made in advertisements of the trade mark, name or initials of an other company or organisation, without its permission (Art 12.1 of the Advertising Code for Radio and Television, approved on 31 July 1990 by the Flemish Government).

## Right of privacy

### Introduction

Following most other European countries, and under pressure of the Treaty of the Council of Europe of 28 January 1981 regarding the automated processing of private data and of the proposed directives of the Council of Ministers of the EU in this field, Belgium has had a Privacy Act since the end of 1992, the purpose of which is to protect natural legal persons from abuses in the processing of personal information.

### The general mechanism

The Act imposes, on the one hand, a number of obligations on everyone who deals with personal data and, on the other, grants a number of rights to the persons whose personal data is processed. The control and supervision of the Privacy Act is given to the Commission for the Protection of Personal Life (the 'Privacy Commission'), a Commission established within the Justice Ministry.

### Rule

The user/owner of a database is obliged to notify the Privacy Commission (Art 17 of the Privacy Act). At the moment of notification, the user/owner of the database has to mention the *principe de finalité* (particular purpose) of the database. Some particularly sensitive personal data cannot be used/stored, or is regulated very restrictively, such as that regarding race, ethnicity, sexual behaviour or conviction, political activity, religious or philosophical matters, membership of trade unions or social security membership (Art 6 of the Privacy Act).

*Prior notification to the persons whose data is processed*

Pursuant to Art 4 of the Privacy Act, a person whose personal data is collected, has to be notified/informed at the moment of the first collection/storage of his data. Important exceptions to the obligation of prior notification exist. No notification to the person whose data is stored is required in cases of a contractual relationship or in case of data which identifies persons with whom the user of the database intends to start and maintain *public relations*.

*Granting access to the database at the*
*request of a person whose data is included*

Article 10 of the Privacy Act grants a general right of access and correction to the person whose data is included in a database.

# ADVERTISING FOR PARTICULAR GROUPS OF PRODUCTS

## Pharmaceuticals

The Act of 25 March 1964 on Medicines and the Royal Decree of 9 July 1984 Concerning Information and Advertisements for Pharmaceuticals regulated advertising for both prescription and over-the-counter pharmaceuticals in a very restrictive manner. In line with the Council Directive on Advertising for Medicines (92/28/EEC, 31 March 1992), advertising of medicines is now regulated by the Royal Decree of 7 April 1995.

Advertising on radio/television, billboard advertising, advertising directed at children or advertising with contests is prohibited. The same prohibition applies to a large number of advertising claims, such as those promising positive results of treatment, pictures that have no direct connection to the product, etc. Advertising to consumers with certain diseases is completely prohibited.

## Tobacco

Radio and television advertising, advertising in films and distribution of free samples for tobacco products is totally forbidden. Magazine, newspaper and billboard advertising for tobacco is regulated. The pictures are regulated and particular information requirements, including a statement on the damage to health, are imposed. A mandatory system of pre-vetting by the Health Ministry is in place.

Most recent legislation prohibits virtually any form of advertising or promotion for tobacco products in Belgium. Also, the use of a logo for other products or services that present similarities with a tobacco brand are prohibited by the Act of 10 December 1997, Prohibition of Advertising for Tobacco Products, which came into force on 1 January 1999. Advertising of or sponsorship through tobacco, products having a tobacco basis or similar products is prohibited, except for foreign periodicals and newspapers, unless explicitly targeted at the Belgian market. Another exception is incidental advertising in the framework of communications of events abroad, and the display of brands inside and on the fascia of tobacco shops. The prohibition encompasses the use of tobacco brands for advertising in other fields, as long as the brand is still used for tobacco products. This prohibition does not apply if the tobacco turnover of the brand is less than half of the non-tobacco and if the brand was originally filed for products other than tobacco.

## Food products

Advertisements for products intended for human consumption may not include names of illnesses or any direct or indirect reference, even implied, to curative effects or to the medical world. The use of words such as 'biological' is subject to conditions. Detailed legislation exists for the commercialisation of nutriments and foodstuffs with nutritional additives, with lists of permitted oligo-elements and minerals.

Products with particular vitamins and minerals have to be notified prior to introduction into the Belgian market and detailed requirements for quantitative and qualitative lists of ingredients and other labelling provisions exist. Complete meal replacement products are regulated. There are detailed food labelling regulations (which implement the EU directives relating to labelling) on foodstuffs, prepacked foodstuffs, quick-frozen foodstuffs and nutriments.

# IMPLEMENTATION OF INTERNATIONAL ADVERTISING RULES

## Introduction

This section does not deal with the implementation of the numerous international (EU) special rules for particular goods and services, such as consumer credit, alcoholic beverages, food products and tobacco products. These rules have, in some form, found their implementation, partially or completely, in recent national laws and regulations which have been dealt with in the relevant sections above. The same goes for the international rules of self-regulation of the International Chamber of Commerce.

There are relatively few EU provisions that deal with advertising as such. There are, in the form of directives to Member States, three important directives which are considered here.

## Misleading Advertising, Council Directive of 10 September 1984 (84/450/EEC)

This has not been implemented in Belgian law. The European Commission instituted proceedings against Belgium for having failed to implement this Directive and the European Court of Justice held that this constituted a Treaty violation.

## Television Broadcasting, Council Directive of 3 October 1989 (89/552/EEC)

This has been pretty much implemented in Belgian regulations on television broadcasting activities, the main rules of which have been outlined above.

## Comparative Advertising, Directive of 6 October 1997 (97/55/EC)

This Directive provides that comparative advertising shall be permitted when the following conditions are met:

(a) it is not misleading;

(b) it compares goods or services meeting the same needs or intended for the same purpose;

(c) it objectively compares one or more material, relevant, verifiable and representative features of those goods and services, which may include price;

(d) it does not create confusion in the market place between the advertiser and a competitor or between the advertiser's trade marks, trade names, etc;

(e) it does not take unfair advantage of the reputation of a trade mark, trade name, etc.

The Belgian Government approved, on 24 July 1998, a draft Act which abolishes the prohibition of comparative advertising and which broadens the regulations on distance selling to include teleshopping and sales via the internet.

# USEFUL ADDRESSES

Conseil de la Publicité asbl
and
Jury d'Ethique Publicitaire
rue des Colonies 18–24, Box 9
1000 Bruxelles
Tel: + 32 2 502 42 20

Ministère des Affaires Economiques
Administration de la Politique Commerciale
Division Protection Consommateur et Réglementation du Commerce
North Gate III
Bld E Jacqmain 154
1000 Bruxelles
Tel: + 32 2 206 41 11

Ministerie van de Vlaamse Gemeenschap
Dept Welzign, Volksgezondheid en Cultuur
Adm Kunst, afd Media en Film
Koloniënstraat 31
1000 Bruxelles
Tel: + 32 2 510 35 61

Union Belge des Annonceurs (UBA)
rue des Colonies 18–24, Box 11
1000 Bruxelles
Tel: + 32 2 502 42 20

## CHAPTER 4

# DENMARK

*Karen Larsen*

## INTRODUCTION

For several years, the media and advertising business in Denmark has been expanding due to the growth in variety of media. Naturally, however, the growth of the business is subject to the state of the market in general, the overall growth depending on whether the market is in recession or growing. In 1988, a second public service television channel (TV2) was established, allowing television commercials, which had been prohibited until then. The television commercials are administered by a separate company, TV2 Reklame A/S. The possibility of showing commercials on Danish television has opened up a new market for film producers active in this field in addition to cinema commercials. After a very warm welcome by consumers, there is now a feeling that they are beginning to get irritated by commercials.

The accelerating development within information technology has also had an impact on the means of advertising and the market conditions. Teleshopping, teletext, etc, have been developing, and additional forms of advertising have been introduced accordingly. The internet represents enormous possibilities and the number of subscribers is increasing very rapidly in Denmark. A large number of companies are already represented on the internet and it is likely that it will be possible to buy and sell goods over the internet (once the security problems surrounding payment are solved). Advertising on CD-ROMs is expanding, and videos are still used in marketing campaigns.

Of course, all the traditional media – newspapers, magazines, leaflets and other printed matter, catalogues, direct mail, posters, outdoor advertising, exhibitions, company gifts, etc, are still used.

Sponsorship is growing in importance.

Almost all the international advertising firms are established one way or another in Denmark. In addition to the big agencies, a lot of smaller agencies exist. Establishment of an advertising agency requires no special licence but, naturally, general Danish legislation on the establishment and running of a business must be complied with.

The last decade has seen rather a lot of mergers and demergers, both nationally and internationally. It has been the trend in recent years for advertising agencies' clients to be less loyal than previously.

In addition to the advertising agencies, public relations consultants have emerged. The major task of a public relations consultant is to assist the business enterprise in developing its corporate image and strategy, including the advertising strategy. There is a lot of overlap between public relations agencies and advertising agencies, even though they belong to different associations.

Not all advertisers use the services of an advertising agency; in fact it is estimated that slightly less than 60% of all advertisers do so.

Besides the advertising agencies, media agencies are an important feature in the media advertising world. Their job is to buy space, thus, for instance, taking advantage of the rebates obtainable for large users. The advertising agencies pay a commission to the media agencies who procure the advertising space.

Publishers of Danish daily newspapers, publishers of Danish magazines, and publishers of Danish trade journals have each organised themselves into an association.

The objective of the Association of Danish Advertising Agencies (DRB) is to bring together Danish advertising agencies and safeguard their professional, organisational, and economical interests as well as to act as a service centre for the industry. DRB members do approximately 80% of all advertising work performed in Denmark. The Association has a seat on many related associations or boards, including Reklame Forum.

Reklame Forum is a co-operative association of the media, advertising agencies and advertisers to safeguard common interests, despite their differences. The Forum has no official status, but it issues statements which are often regarded as trade practice. All statements issued are unanimous.

# BASIC PRINCIPLES

## Contents and form

The basic principles applicable to advertising in Denmark, regardless of the media used or the product concerned, can be summarised as follows:

- advertising shall be conducted in accordance with generally accepted principles of fair marketing conduct, and advertising shall acknowledge its social responsibility towards the consumer and the society;
- advertising shall allow the consumer to form a correct first impression without close reading. Advertising shall be transparent, in order that the

consumer understands the complete offer and its contents, including price structure and the commitments involved if the offer is accepted;

- advertising must not be improper, untrue, misleading, deceptive, fraudulent, indecent or unjustly disparaging of competitors. Personal integrity shall be respected;

- advertising must not play on superstition, fear, credulity, discrimination (whether sex, race or others), and hate and violence must not be instigated; children must be protected, and lack of experience and knowledge of the consumer must not be exploited. Neither must his trust be abused;

- advertising shall be reasonably informative and provide the information necessary. Information given shall be true and verified upon request. Comparative advertising shall be relevant and verifiable;

- advertising must not sponge on business characteristics belonging to others or efforts invested by others;

- legislation applicable in any field shall be respected, including, but not limited to, special legislation related to the product or service advertised.

## Sanctions and other consequences

The sanctions applicable to an act (or omission) in contravention of Danish law within the advertising field vary, but – depending on the violation – the following can happen:

- the violation may be regarded as a criminal offence, typically subject to a fine. A specific provision to this effect must be contained in an Act or in administrative rules set out according to an Act allowing for the inclusion of stipulations making the offence criminal;

- the violation may incur payment of damages to the injured party;

- an injunction can be awarded against the offender;

- an order to redress, correct, or call back material distributed, destroy material, etc, can be issued;

- a contract entered into as a result of illegal or improper conduct may be invalid.

In addition, it must be taken into account that the contents of the advertising and promotional material may have an important impact on the advertiser's (seller's) liability with respect to the goods or services advertised and subsequently sold.

According to the Danish Sale of Goods Act, which incorporates the Convention on the International Sale of Goods, a buyer will be entitled to exercise certain remedial powers laid down in the Act if the goods are defective. A defect exists in the event that the goods are not as agreed, promised, requested, or justifiably expected. Accordingly, the contents of any promotional campaign and advertising material regarding the product may be of importance when judging whether a defect exists or not.

Regarding product liability, the evaluation of whether the product is dangerous or not will be based, *inter alia*, on how the product is marketed.[1]

There is currently a tendency in Denmark to increase the penalties where violation of the Marketing Practices Act has occurred.

# ADVERTISING LAW

The most important of the Danish laws and regulations dealing with marketing and advertising is the Marketing Practices Act. This Act was passed in 1974 and was amended in 1994, taking effect on 1 October of that year.[2]

It was expected that a proposal for a new Marketing Practices Act would be put forward in the autumn of 1998 but such proposal has been postponed. A major change is likely to be a tightening of the guarantee provisions, and the power of the ombudsman protecting consumers' rights of intervention.

Geographically, the Act extends to all actions having an impact on the Danish market. It covers almost all kinds of businesses, private or public, Danish or foreign. It covers any kind of promotional activity, although particular fields are covered by special legislation.

Special legislation applies to certain forms of products, for example, medicinal products, foodstuffs and toys, as well as to certain forms of advertising, for example, television and radio advertising, including sponsorship of a programme. The Act on certain Sales to Consumers regulates door to door sales and other unsolicited ways of approaching customers (including cold calling), agreements entered into outside the normal business location of the seller, postal sales (entered into on the basis of all readable media), and it contains certain specific rules on how to get out of a running contract. In addition, the Act on Price Marking is of general interest.

Data protection is of relevance, especially with regard to the direct marketing business and its use of databases. Denmark has rather strict legislation on data registers, see below, pp 374–75.The Danish Act on Contracts is of importance because it contains provisions on the validity of agreements. The way a product is advertised may influence the validity of the subsequent purchase contract. The Competition Act and the EC rules on

---

1    Denmark has implemented Directive 85/374/EC on Product Liability by Act No 371 on Product Liability issued on 7 June 1989.

2    Act No 428 issued on 1 June 1994.

competition may, of course, also have a certain impact on how to advertise, although rather limited.

Denmark is a member of the European Union. In the opinion of the Danish Government, all existing EC directives are implemented in the Danish legislation. This is also true for all directives related to advertising (including the Misleading Advertising Directive, the Comparative Advertising Directive and the Medicinal Products Directive).

Finally, it should be noted that the European Convention on Human Rights is implemented in Danish law directly by an Act incorporating the text of the Convention.

# THE MARKETING PRACTICES ACT

The main legislative instrument – the Marketing Practices Act – is fairly short. The main provision (Art 1) states, under the heading 'Fair Marketing Conduct':

> The Act is applicable to private business enterprises and public enterprises of equal nature. In such enterprises it is not allowed to act in contravention with fair marketing conduct.

This is the overall, general rule in Danish advertising law. The article should not just be regarded as an article to fall back on in case no other provision is applicable. It is considered to have its own life and its own meaning, see below, p 356.

Article 1 is a legal standard, changing when society changes, and shall be interpreted in accordance therewith. To assist in the interpretation of Art 1, all ICC Codes of Conduct are relevant, together with the many guidelines issued by the Danish authorities, see below. However, it should be noted that compliance with the ICC codes of conduct is not of itself sufficient to ensure compliance with Danish law.

Of almost equal importance is Art 2 of the Marketing Practices Act, which states that it is prohibited to use incorrect, misleading, or unreasonably inadequate statements.

Statements which, in isolation, are correct are prohibited if, due to their form or because of their lack of affinity to the subject matter, they are improper towards other business entities or towards customers.

Article 2 further contains a prohibition on the use of misleading procedures having an impact on supply or demand. Finally, it is stated that the advertiser must be able to document the correctness of any fact advertised.

Further prohibitions and guidelines are found in Art 3 *et seq* as follows:

*Article 3*

At the time of offering goods or services (or when entering into an agreement or – in certain circumstances – upon delivery) instructions of importance for the assessment of the character or quality of the goods or services, including their useful quality, durability, dangerousness, and maintenance possibilities, shall be provided.

*Article 4*

It is only allowed to mention 'warranty' and similar terms if the customer is put in an essentially better position than according to law.

*Article 5*

It is prohibited to make use of business characteristics belonging to others.

*Article 6*

It is prohibited to offer tokens (there is an exemption for 'frequent flyer' programmes).

*Article 7*

It is prohibited to limit the number of units for sale to one single buyer.

*Article 8*

It is prohibited, prior to a sale, to offer rebates or similar in the form of coupons or the like, unless they can be exchanged for cash.

*Article 9*

It is prohibited to arrange prize draws and/or competitions (the outcome of which is based on luck), if such prize draws and competitions put an obligation to purchase on the customer.

*Article 10*

It is prohibited to make use of trade secrets belonging to other business entities.

Articles 11 and 12 deal with certain aspects regarding marking and packaging, while Art 13 *et seq* deal with sanctions and control.

As it appears, the Marketing Practices Act concentrates on describing the prohibited acts. Accordingly, the Act would normally be interpreted such that, if an action is not prohibited, it is allowed. However, because many articles are very vague, and due to the fact that, in particular, Art 1 is a very general legal standard having its own legal life, it is sometimes extremely difficult to judge whether a particular activity is contrary to the law or allowed.

## THE OMBUDSMAN PROTECTING CONSUMERS

According to Art 15, the Marketing Practices Act is supervised by the Ombudsman Protecting Consumers (OPC). It is stated in the Act as a priority guideline that this supervision shall be conducted with particular regard to consumers. This supervision of the OPC comprises surveillance of the market, information, negotiation with industry, elaboration of guidelines, implementation of sanctions, issuing of injunctions, instituting law suits, and prosecuting violations. The OPC will himself decide which work to prioritise in compliance with the objects of the Act within the framework of the resources allocated. He can act on his own initiative, or upon receipt of a complaint. The OPC is the final administrative authority, whose decisions cannot be appealed to other administrative bodies. His decisions must be challenged by way of instituting a law suit.

The OPC can, of his own motion, intervene even in business-to-business marketing. However, his primary concern is to deal with consumers and, in practice, no resources are allocated to business to business marketing. Accordingly, and in reality, no specific administrative body is competent or supervisory with respect to business to business marketing matters, except when the Competition Act or the EC rules on competition are applicable.

If resources allow it, the OPC can, upon request, issue an 'advance ruling'. He is not obliged to do so and, in particular, not if the matter is extraordinary complicated and doubtful. In no circumstances is the advance ruling binding vis à vis the courts or others. If a marketing campaign has been launched, and a consumer files a complaint, it is not impossible for the campaign to be judged illegal after all. However, OPC can normally be relied upon not to change his mind.

An essential part of the activities exercised by the OPC is the issuance of guidelines within certain fields. Such guidelines have been issued, for instance, regarding environmental advertising, sex discrimination, rebates, prize draws, tokens and competitions, warranty declarations in adverts and as parts of agreements, use of portraits and other personal characteristics, and many others. All in all, more than 30 guidelines have been issued.

A special guideline has been issued, after negotiation with the industry, covering beer, wine, spirits and other drinks, imposing severe restrictions on advertising such products.

Further, the tobacco industry has entered into an agreement with the Ministry of Health regarding the advertising of tobacco products. This agreement is published as a guideline by the OPC. This agreement is not as strict as the proposed EC directive on tobacco advertising. For instance, it is permissible to distribute samples of pipe tobacco and cigars (although not cigarettes), and advertising generally is allowed under certain circumstances, provided always that a warning is placed very clearly.

The guidelines are not 'binding', in the sense that the courts cannot judge for themselves whether or not fair marketing conduct has been exercised.

However, they do normally provide very good guidance in conjunction with the ICC codes of conduct to help judge whether or not advertising as proposed will be legal. The OPC often refers to the ICC codes of conduct.

The OPC publishes a yearly report on his activities, including the decisions made in factual matters. Together with case law, these yearly reports are useful for interpreting and applying the Marketing Practices Act.

## Fair marketing conduct (Art 1)

The general prohibition against acting in contravention of fair marketing conduct is sanctioned with a liability to pay damages, and an injunction can be issued against continuing the conduct. No criminal sanctions are applicable.

Article 1 comprises a wide range of situations which can be deemed illegal as contravening this general rule. This article will, for instance, be used in unfair contract conditions, lack of respect for common security and lack of social responsibility. Marketing conduct which is of an obtrusive, aggressive, exploiting, bothersome, or discriminating nature, will equally be in contravention of Art 1. Protection of personal integrity and the sanctity of private life, the demand that the advertiser shall be identified and reachable, disloyal competition, use of customers as agents, pyramid sales, etc, are also matters encompassed by Art 1.

In order to protect consumers against dangerous products, only products which are safe may be marketed and sold (see the Act on Product Safety, which implements the corresponding EC directive and is supplemented by a guideline issued by the OPC). The Act contains, for instance, specific provisions on toys.

The provisions of this Act are complementary to other existing regulations on various special products, for instance, medicinal products, foodstuffs, traffic related equipment, chemical products, telecommunications apparatus, etc. Some of these additional acts contain special provisions regulating the advertising of the product in question. In the absence of special provisions, the marketing of products which, according to other legislation, cannot be legally sold or used, as well as the marketing of dangerous or substandard products, will constitute an act in contravention of fair marketing conduct under Art 1 of the Marketing Practices Act.

## Truthfulness (Art 2)

Article 2 states that the use of incorrect, misleading, or unreasonably inadequate statements is not permitted. Contrary to the wording of the ICC codes of conduct, the wording is thus negative. However, there is virtually no difference from the requirements of the ICC codes of conduct regarding truthfulness, etc, when it comes to the interpretation of how to apply Art 2. The overall requirement is, as stated by case law and the OPC in one of his yearly reports, that the correct understanding of the contents of an advert must be immediate and unambiguous to the consumer. All misleading information regarding prices, quality, and quantity is covered by Art 2. Regarding price, the provision is complementary to the Price Marking Act; see below, p 362. Information on 'price now/previous price', 'sale', or 'price reduction' shall be correct. Such indications must not be used in connection with goods not de facto offered at the higher price in the store. Goods acquired in order to be sold cheaper than the goods actually in stock, cannot be put in a 'sale', but they can be advertised, for instance, as a 'special offer'. The seller shall be able to verify upon request that the goods on sale have actually been offered at a higher price. First and second quality grades cannot be compared.

Any misleading statements regarding approvals, recommendations, testing, co-operation, copyright, etc, as well as misleading statements on terms of sale, the right to return goods, warranties, remedies, etc, will also be encompassed by Art 2.

The prohibition against inadequate statements has, for instance, been applied in a situation where a bank advertised a lowering of the interest rate without informing customers that, at the same time, the commission to be paid when establishing credit would be raised. A difference exists between information and 'praise'. Information covers the facts – it shall be true, correct, and not misleading. Upon request, the advertiser shall verify and document the correctness. Praise covers non-verifiable statements like 'excellent' or 'heavenly'. Such statements are legal, provided they are not negative, for instance, when used to compare other products: 'better than ...' Such comparisons must only be based on facts, the truth of which can be proved, and even then this form of comparative advertising is always in danger of being deemed contrary to the Marketing Practices Act.

## COMPARATIVE ADVERTISING

Disparagement of competitors and comparative advertising are also regulated by Art 2. Article 2 stipulates that it is not permissible to make use of statements which are improper towards other business entities or consumers due to their form or because of their lack of affinity to the subject matter. The guideline issued by the OPC on price information also covers, besides the general aspects on correct information on price, comparative advertising.

Article 2 is worded in general terms. Thus, the specific provisions contained in the EC Directive on Comparative Advertising are not found word for word in Danish legislation. However, all provisions laid down in the Directive may be considered covered by the wording of Art 2. The overall requirement of comparative advertising is that it must be based on essential factual information, the truth of which can be proven, and that the comparison is relevant and fair. The guideline issued deals, for instance, with the use of the phrase 'normal price'. This statement has as a prerequisite that the advertiser shall make clear whether he refers to his own price or the price of others. When comparing, the products compared with must be of exactly the same sort and quality. In addition, the compared products must be marketed in a way similar to the products of the advertiser, for instance, with respect to warranties and the like.

Implied comparisons which do not mention the competitor are considered unfair.Acts in contravention of Art 2 are subject to criminal sanctions.

When dealing with comparative advertising, Art 5 of the Marketing Practices Act (in addition to Arts 1 and 2) is also of relevance. Article 5 deals with abuse of business characteristics belonging to other businesses. As a general rule, it is not allowed to sponge on the merits of others, nor to use characteristics fit for creating confusion, see above, p 355.

# THE ACT ON CERTAIN SALES TO CONSUMERS

The Act on certain Sales to Consumers[3] regulates door-to-door sales, cold calling, etc. The Act only applies when business entities are selling to private persons and, accordingly, the Act is not applicable when the target is a business.

## Unsolicited personal approach

As a general rule, the Act forbids personal contact with a customer with a view to selling him goods or services (either now or later), unless the customer has specifically asked for the approach. It is not sufficient that the customer asks for additional information. This prohibition relates to personal contact or contact made by telephone, both in private homes and at work.

There are exceptions in respect of the sale of insurance, books, periodicals, life saving service, or ambulance transport.

It is a criminal offence to act in contravention of these provisions, sanctioned by way of fines.Further, in the event that an unsolicited approach results in a customer's agreement to buy the goods or services offered, the

---

3   Consolidated Act No 886 issued on 23 December 1987 (most recent amendment issued by Act No 1098 of 21 December 1994). The Act incorporates the provisions of Directive 85/577/EC on Consumer Protection.

customer is entitled to declare the agreement null and void. The seller, however, is bound by the 'agreement' and is not allowed to step back.

An agreement can be legally binding where the customer has asked for a visit, or under other applicable exceptions. For instance, it is legal to arrange promotional sales tours, provided the purpose is clearly stated. Purchases entered into on such occasions away from the seller's normal place of business are legal, but the customer is vested with the right to regret such a purchase and consequently, he is entitled to cancel the purchase within seven days from the day when the agreement was entered into.

This right to regret applies to all purchases made away from the seller's normal place of business.The Act obliges the seller to inform customers in a very precise way, in writing, of this right to cancel. In the absence of such information, the agreement entered into is not binding for the customer, who will be entitled to declare it null and void.

In public places, for instance in the street, a personal approach to a customer is not in contravention of the provisions of the Act on certain Sales to Consumers. However, such an approach may contravene other regulations, for instance, the police regulation in force in the local area (municipality). Also, for instance, the Act on the Danish Railroads contains a special provision stating that it is not allowed to be present in areas belonging to Danish Rail with the purpose of doing business.

## Postal sales

The right to regret is also vested in any customer buying goods by mail order on the basis of an offer from a seller by any readable medium, for instance, teledata, teletext, cable services, internet, etc. Catalogues or any other kind of promotional material or sales offers by mail or other readable media can legally be distributed, but precise information on the right to regret shall be given. The customer is entitled to cancel the purchase for seven days after receipt of the goods. If the agreement is null and void due to lack of information on the right to regret, the seller must pick up the goods at his own expense. If the right to regret is exercised, the purchaser shall return the goods at his expense.

## Unordered goods

The ICC code of conduct on direct marketing recommends that merchandise shall not be sent to a customer without the customer having requested it, except for samples, gifts, and the like. In this respect, it shall be noted, that a Danish customer, according to Art 4 of the Act on certain Sales to Consumers, is allowed to keep a product without paying for it if the product is forwarded unsolicited, except where it is obvious that he has received it by mistake.

## Supervisory body

With respect to agreements entered into relating to the Act on certain Sales to Consumers, complaints can be filed with the National Consumer Agency of Denmark, which is generally also the body which deals with disputes between buyers and sellers.

# PRICE MARKING

There is no specific provision obliging an advertiser to mention the price of the product or service in question. However, the Act on Price Marking[4] obliges a retail seller to display (in a conspicuous manner) the price of the merchandise or item offered. The price indicated shall include VAT and other taxes and dues (Art 1).

If price information is given in the course of advertising a product or service, the provisions of the Price Marking Act shall be complied with (Art 5). In addition, the OPC has issued guidelines to retailers on price information.

An example concerned a misleading advert for a printer. The price was stated in the advert, but the paperfeeder shown in the advert was not included in the price shown. Furthermore, the price excluded VAT, but the advert did not make this clear.

The advertiser was fined DKr 50,000 (in 1993) for contravention of Art 2 of the Marketing Practices Act (the advert was misleading).

The advertising agency responsible for the composition and insertion of the advert was acquitted. It was ruled that the agency did not have, and was not expected to have, such knowledge of the product that it should have realised that the picture of the printer was not in compliance with the other information contained in the advert. However, the agency was convicted for contravening the Price Marking Act, because the price advertised did not include the VAT. They were fined DKr 3,000.[5]

For certain products, the authorities can stipulate special rules requiring classification, measure and weight and units offered, quality grades, etc. Such special rules must, naturally, also be complied with.

Whether or not the advertiser will actually be obliged to sell the product at the advertised price will be judged neither in accordance with the Price Marking Act nor the Marketing Practices Act, but according to contract law.

---

4   Consolidated Act No 456 issued on 17 June 1991 (most recently amended by Act No 377 issued on 14 June 1995).

5   U 93.346 (*OPC v BFC Data A/S and Midt-Marketing Ikast A/S*).

# DANISH CONTRACT LAW

Entering into a contract is regulated by the Act on Contracts. An offer is made. This offer is binding for a certain period of time, starting from the time when the addressee becomes aware of the offer. Upon receipt by the offeror of an acceptance from a customer, an agreement is entered into. For common law readers it should be noted that Danish law does not apply the concept of consideration. As stated above, an offer is binding, and the binding effect is also attributed to a promise to donate a gift conveyed to the donee. Such a promise is binding, valid, and enforceable.It is legal to stipulate that an offer is not binding but can be withdrawn at any time, or that the offer is only valid for as long as the merchandise is in stock.

In addition, the Act on Contracts contains a special provision covering information which would normally be regarded as a binding offer, stipulating that such information can, under certain circumstances, be classified as an invitation to make an offer. If an offer is made as a result of a such an invitation, the receiver of this offer must refuse immediately (with or without cause) if he does not want to accept it. Under these specific circumstances, silence can be regarded as an acceptance.

It is not easy to judge whether advertising a product or a service shall be regarded as an invitation to make an offer or as an offer. Probably, ordinary catalogues, price lists, adverts, posters, etc, will be regarded as just invitations to make an offer. This has also applied to merchandise displayed in the window with a price mark. However, there is a tendency to regard such price labels as a binding offer. If the potential customer is informed immediately that it is a mistake, it is possible to avoid selling at the wrongly marked price. If the mistake is obvious, no agreement can be concluded on that basis.

Article 36 of the Act on Contracts stipulates that an agreement can be altered or disregarded (in part or totally) in the event that it will be unfair, or contrary to fair conduct, to enforce it. The decision shall also take into account the circumstances under which the agreement was entered into, the contents of the agreement, and subsequent events.

This clause was applied by the High Court in a ruling in June 1995.[6] The case concerned an agreement under which a married couple had bought a time share in a holiday apartment. The court made an overall assessment of the circumstances prevailing at the time the agreement was entered into, including the sales techniques used. These included an invitation to a promotional meeting, which they called an 'information evening' (at which meeting the sale was actually concluded). Further, tokens were offered in the form of flight tickets. The court ruled that such methods were not in

---

6    U 1995.799 Ø (*VBE Time-Share – Feriecentret Rågeleje Klit A/S v 'H and W'*).

compliance with the methods allowed under the Marketing Practices Act and the Act on certain Sales to Consumers. Thus, the court ruled that it was contrary to fair conduct to enforce the purchase agreement.

# TOKENS

Article 6 of the Marketing Practices Act states that a business is not allowed to offer tokens or free gifts or the like, unless the value of such tokens is almost nil. No exact figure on the permissible value of tokens is indicated in the Act. According to the guidelines issued by the OPC on tokens and free gifts, it is stated that the value shall be less than DKr 2. The value shall be considered in conjunction with the price which would have been payable by the customer, not the price paid by the advertiser.

Products or services identical to the main item are not considered to be tokens. The subject of tokens is normally considered a major obstacle in the promotion business, and the rules are often violated. Several decisions have been published in the yearly reports of the OPC. Recently, the OPC has been very keen on pursuing these violations. Naturally, advertising an illegal token is equally prohibited.

According to the wording of the Marketing Practices Act, a token is only prohibited in connection with a sale to consumers. However, even though Art 6 is not applicable in business to business matters, it should be noted that offering gifts to businesses in connection with purchases will probably be considered contrary to fair marketing conduct (Art 1), because such offers are considered to be hidden awards to distributors, making the price structure non-transparent.

A token can be offered if an alternative is presented in the form of an offer to reduce the price of the main item, thus allowing the buyer to choose between the additional item and the price reduction.

Offers whereby two or more products are combined are not contrary to the law, provided the products are interrelated (for example, toothbrush and toothpaste), or provided it is made clear that the products can be bought separately.

Furthermore, it is legal to offer services naturally connected to the product sold (for instance, installation of a washing machine, hanging of curtains, etc). However, it is not advisable to advertise that the service is free of charge. Such connected services shall be considered a combined sale.

Generally speaking, the words 'free of charge' or 'gratis' must be used with the utmost care, in order not to contravene Art 2 and in order not to suggest any affinity to illegal tokens, as prohibited by Art 6. If, for instance, the customer must pay the postage to receive a 'gift', the words 'free of charge' or similar may be regarded as misleading. It may be acceptable to ask the customer to pay the postage, but only provided that it is clearly and conspicuously stated close to the indication that the gift is free of charge.

Distribution of gifts is legal, provided it is made clear that the potential customers are not forced to buy the promoted main item as a condition of receiving the gift.

Tokens are legal in one context. It is expressly permitted to offer 'frequent flyer' programmes, provided they are offered internationally, and established in the course of the offeree's usual business. The main element in Denmark must be tokens offered in connection with air travel.

If the airline co-operates with other business entities, the programme may comprise tokens connected with hotel bookings and car rental. Thus, the legal tokens are confined to travel, hotels and car rental.

## REBATES

Quantity rebates are not considered tokens, and such forms of rebate are allowed. However, the Marketing Practices Act contains, in Art 8, specific prohibitions against offering rebates or similar benefits in the form of coupons and the like prior to a purchase, and the OPC has issued guidelines covering this provision. The ban makes it illegal to print coupons in, for instance, magazines and catalogues, which the customer can present in the store and by this means obtain a discount.

However, if a coupon of this kind is displayed in the store close to the goods to which such coupons relate, or close to the cash register, it is legal (but not if placed outside the store). Further, such coupons are legal if they can be exchanged for cash. It is also legal to stipulate a minimum. The permitted minimum is DKr 5.

## PRIZE DRAWS AND COMPETITIONS

The prohibition against prize draws and competitions was previously regarded as an obstacle when advertising and marketing products in Denmark. The 1994 amendment to the Marketing Practices Act liberalised the prohibition, making prize draws and competitions legal, provided always that no purchase obligation is attached to the event.

Competitions based on skill or, for instance, composition of a slogan, etc, in which the contributions are judged by an independent and qualified jury, and only a few winners are chosen, are legal under all circumstances, even if purchase is a prerequisite to enter the contest.

An exemption applies to periodical magazines. These are allowed to arrange prize draws in order to distribute awards in conjunction with competitions; they are typically used in connection with crosswords. It is not possible to bypass the ban by the periodical issue of an advertising paper. The periodical must contain editorial matter, and the prize draw must be arranged by the publisher (not the advertisers). The terms for entering the competition shall be stated correctly and in an informative way, including information on how the prizes are awarded or distributed as well as information on the chances of winning.

Even if a prize draw or competition is legal under the provisions of the Marketing Practices Act, regard must be had to other Danish legislation regulating lotteries. A lottery can be defined as a 'contract according to which an unconditional payment is made against the chance of winning'. Such lotteries cannot be conducted without special permission from the authorities. Accordingly, purchase requirements in order to participate in a prize draw, whether disguised as an extremely 'easy' competition or not, may be deemed contrary to the Lotteries Act.

Prizes and awards are subject to income tax (up to 62%). If the competition or the prize draw is open to the public, a special 15% tax applies instead, requiring the organiser to register, because he will be liable to the tax authorities that the tax is paid.

# BUSINESS CHARACTERISTICS

It is prohibited to use business characteristics or the like belonging to others, or to use one's own characteristics in a manner designed to create confusion.

Article 5 is complementary to the protection of intellectual property rights under other legislation, for instance, trade marks, and to the protection of your name (whether personal or a business name).

The protection covers anything which can reasonably be regarded as a business characteristic, including characteristics such as artistic presentations on a van, special colouring, ornamentation, and even sounds and smells.

In order to be classified as a business characteristic, distinction is required. The protection may be strengthened by use. If the use by a third party is unfair, the requirements of the level of distinction may equally be lowered.

A character developed by a Danish actor was more or less copied by a factory manufacturing cookies. The manufacturer used detachable stickers on the packing (60,000 copies were printed). The character's features were used on the stickers together with particular words used by the actor when in character. The case was judged according to Art 1 of the Marketing Practices Act, but Art 5 could have been applied as well. The court ruled that the character was not protected by the Copyright Act. However, the character had an economic value to the actor who was very selective about performing in marketing campaigns. It was ruled that his rights were infringed. Damages were awarded.[7]

# COPYRIGHT – PROTECTION OF PRIVACY, ETC

Under the Danish Copyright Act,[8] an author is vested with the copyright of his literary or artistic work ('author' includes writers of books, composers, actors, directors, photographers, and many others). In short, an author has the right to decide whether and how to make his work public.

An author is protected against his work being reproduced in an offensive way or in a context which can offend his literary or artistic reputation or distinction (see Art 3.2 of the Copyright Act). Use of the work in advertising will normally be in contravention of this provision, because the author will be in danger of being identified with the product advertised or a political view expressed.

Under the Copyright Act, a third party is entitled to quote without permission from a work already made public by the author, provided always that the use of the quote is considered in compliance with fair conduct and practice (Art 22). This restriction means, regarding the *droit moral*, that the right to quote normally cannot be exercised in connection with advertising (see above).

If, according to normal practice, appearance in the advert should have been paid for, the normal rule of thumb will be that use without prior consent from the author is deemed contrary to the Copyright Act or the Marketing Practices Act.

The OPC has issued guidelines on the use of portraits and other personal characteristics in advertising. It is specifically stated that in advertisements, including on packaging, gifts, or in relation to competitions, the use of portraits or persons, whether in private or public life, as well as the use of any other personal characteristics, will require consent. Further, references must not be made to a person in any way that suggests a personal recommendation.

However, if the use of a public person seems natural in the context, and provided the use is fair and not offensive, consent is not necessary.

Generally, privacy shall be respected. Invasion of privacy is penalised under the Penal Code, Art 264d, by means of a fine or imprisonment. For instance, it is not permitted to photograph a private person and publish the

---

7    U 76.282 SH (*Per Pallesen v Karen Volf A/S*).
8    Act No 194 issued on 11 March 1997.

picture. Accordingly, the copyright vested in the photographer according to the Copyright Act has as a prerequisite that the consent of the photographed person is obtained.

A model is, of course, performing as per consent. However, it should be noted that the use of the photograph, commercial, etc, can be restricted in certain ways, for instance, geographically, by type of media, etc.

Accordingly, the issue on rights is a very critical issue in advertising, because the advertiser has to be certain that all rights have been transferred to him in connection with the proposed use.

# LIABILITY

Advertising in contravention of Danish legislation is first and foremost the liability of the advertiser. Furthermore, the advertising agency is responsible that their work is in compliance with the legislation, and advisors, for instance, a lawyer, can also be held responsible.

The Media Responsibility Act[9] covers:

(a) national periodicals. In order to qualify as a 'periodical' in the sense of the Marketing Responsibility Act, the periodical must be issued at least twice a year, and it must contain editorial matter. Thus, for instance, booklets only containing adverts are not covered by the Media Responsibility Act, which also excludes books, posters, etc. Furthermore, the periodical must be printed, or mass produced in some other way; the technical method is not of essence;

(b) national broadcasts (Denmark Radio, TV2, regional television and enterprises holding a license to broadcast);

(c) text, picture or sound periodically distributed to the public if its character is that of news distribution similar to the periodicals and broadcast, provided the publisher has registered with the Press Council.

The Media Responsibility Act operates its own liability system. However, with respect to advertising (Art 27) it contains a reference to the system generally applicable, according to which the advertiser (and consultants) are liable to punishment according to other rules. The editor is co-responsible (but not on an objective basis, except that he will assume responsibility if he does not disclose the name of the advertiser upon request).

TV2 is not responsible for the activities of TV2 Reklame.

---

9    Act No 348 issued on 6 June 1991 (now consolidated Act No 85 issued on 9 February 1998).

If not covered by the Media Responsibility Act and the liability system laid down thereunder, the normal rules laid down in the Danish Penal Code will apply.

The Penal Code contains provisions which penalise assistance in the performance of a criminal act. Thus, the publisher/editor can be punished for printing an advert contrary to, for instance, the provisions of the Marketing Practices Act, provided these provisions involve criminal sanctions.

The Supreme Court has ruled in a case, the subject matter of which were adverts in a booklet containing only advertisements. The adverts inserted contained offers of illegal tokens, 'free' gifts which were not free, etc. The advertiser paid a considerable fine (DKr 100,000) and the court case concerned the responsibility of the publisher of the booklet. The publisher was convicted and fined (although acquitted on some counts).

It was ruled that the Media Responsibility Act was not applicable, because the booklet contained no editorial matter. However, the Penal Code provision regarding assistance in the performance of criminal acts was applied, because contravention of Art 2 by the advertiser is subject to criminal sanctions. Under this article of the Penal Code, the publisher was fined DKr 25,000.[10]

The counts on which the publisher was acquitted concerned mainly adverts where it was not obvious that the Marketing Practices Act had not been complied with.

It should be noted that the publisher argued that his production system did not allow him to check the contents of the adverts. It was ruled that the production system was the publisher's own risk.

# BROADCASTING (RADIO AND TELEVISION)

Broadcasting activities in Denmark are basically regulated by the Radio and Television Broadcasting Act.[11]

In addition to the two Danish public service channels – Denmark Radio and TV2 – many regional channels have been introduced. Today, about 50 local television stations and another 50 very small local television stations operate, as well as an increasing number of local radio stations. Satellite channels were introduced in 1985, and many households are able to receive such satellite programmes. At least 1.2 m households receive foreign programmes in addition to the Danish channels.

Broadcasting in Denmark requires a licence, for which anybody can apply. However, the licences are subject to certain conditions, and the licence holder

---

10   U 1996.209/2H.
11   Consolidated Act No 138 issued on 19 February 1998.

is obliged to ensure that the Radio and Television Broadcasting Act, and the conditions under which the licence is issued, including the regulations on Commercials and Sponsored Programmes, are not violated.

The Radio and Television Advertising Council is entrusted with the task of considering issues concerning the content of commercials. The Satellite and Cable Council is entrusted with the task of ensuring that the licensee abides by the provisions of the Radio and Television Broadcasting Act. This council can prosecute any violation of the Act. Furthermore, the Council can withdraw the licence to broadcast if the conditions are violated.

The Radio and Television Broadcasting Act regulates programming. More than 50% of the viewing hours, excluding news, sport, competitions, commercials and teletext, must be covered by European programmes. Further, the licensees must aim for 10% of the viewing hours, excluding news, sport, competitions, commercials and teletext, or 10% of the budget, being related to European programmes made by producers who are not broadcasting companies. This proportion of programmes must be of recent date.

Finally, the broadcasting company must ensure that programmes which may seriously harm the physical, mental and moral development of minors, are not broadcast. Programmes that in any way instigate hate, because of race, sex, religion or nationality are not allowed.

As mentioned above, it is the obligation of the licensee under the Radio and Television Broadcasting Act to ensure that the regulations on commercial and sponsored programmes are not violated. These regulations are quite strict, including, for instance, prohibitions against marketing alcohol and cigarettes.

Naturally, the broadcasting companies are responsible for observing any applicable Danish legislation, and any broadcasting company must have an editor responsible under the press laws. Of particular relevance is the Media Responsibility Act. The Press Council must be informed of the identity of the editor.

The author of text or a picture, the person who makes a statement, the responsible editor and/or the broadcasting company can all be held liable for the contents of a programme.

No commercials are broadcast on Denmark Radio or DR2. However, TV2 is partly financed by the income derived from selling commercial airtime.

## COMMERCIALS

Broadcast commercials are regulated by s 8 of the Radio and Television Broadcasting Act, as well as by other complementary and more detailed regulations.

With respect to all broadcasting, it is a basic rule that commercials must clearly be identified as such, and it must be clear who is the advertiser. In content and presentation, commercials must be distinguishable from non-commercial programmes.

As regards the content of commercials, the general rules applicable to all other forms of advertising apply. A commercial shall be legal, decent, honest and truthful, and show social responsibility. The Marketing Practices Act shall be obeyed, and advertising shall respect any generally accepted ethical codes applicable to advertising. Special regard shall be given to the effect that commercials presented on radio and television is expected to have on the consumer. The general prohibition against misleading advertising is particularly covered by the rules applicable to advertising on radio and television. For instance, it is particularly noted that any extra items (such as batteries) necessary for using the product advertised shall be highlighted.

Children under 14 years of age are only allowed to perform in television commercials if such performance is either a natural part of the environment shown or is necessary to explain or demonstrate how to use products relating to children. A television commercial promoting a shop, in which two children played shopkeeper and customer, was declared illegal, and the store had to re-take the commercial with adult performers.

Both broadcaster and advertiser are responsible for the legality of commercials. TV2 Reklame A/S offers an advance evaluation of commercials at a very early stage of the process, including foreign commercials not yet translated into Danish. Of course, such advance evaluation contains no guarantee of legality. Only the Radio and Television Advertising Council can rule, subject to the final decision of the ordinary courts.

In addition, very detailed rules are stipulated, for instance, regulating the protection of children and young people, and including references to rules generally applicable, such as those regarding the appearance of people without their prior consent.

The following specific rules apply regarding commercials broadcast by TV2, satellite television, and local television (not, however, applicable to teletext):

(a) advertising must only be broadcast in blocks placed between programmes;

(b) commercials must not account for more than 10% of the daily broadcasting time, to be understood as a restriction of a maximum of 12 minutes of commercials per hour;

(c) if the commercial is a direct offer to viewers with regard to the sale, purchase, or rental of products or services, such commercials must not exceed a total of one hour per day (this hour to be included in the 10% limit).

These restrictions are not applicable to radio broadcasting, whether satellite or local. Thus, radio programmes can be interrupted by commercials.

The advertising of beer, wine, spirits or tobacco is prohibited. This prohibition applies to all types of television and radio broadcasts.

Television commercials for medicinal products are prohibited.

With respect to radio broadcasts, commercials for medicinal products obeying the rules laid down in the Act on Medicinal Products are allowed.

Furthermore, it is not permitted to use television to advertise economic interest groups or to promote religious and political views. This prohibition does not apply to radio programmes, provided that the basic rules of fair marketing conduct are obeyed, despite the fact that the advertising is normally not conducted by a business entity.

Directive 89/552/EEC on the co-ordination of certain provisions laid down by law, regulation or administrative action in Member States concerning the pursuit of television broadcasting activities is implemented in Danish law.

According to the Council Directive, Member States are obliged to secure the freedom to receive broadcasts from other Member States, and re-transmission of such broadcasts must not be hindered for reasons stipulated in the Directive. The Directive lists basic requirements for the commercials. However, the Directive does not forbid Member States to impose stricter requirements on their national broadcasts, and Denmark has exercised this right.

However, according to the Directive, Denmark cannot hinder the reception and re-transmission of broadcasts from other EU Member States even if the programmes do not comply with the stricter Danish rules, provided that they comply with the rules applicable in the country of broadcast.

In a factual case, the EC Commission has confirmed that, for the purposes of Directive 89/552/EEC, it is a correct assumption that the broadcaster can only fall under the jurisdiction of one Member State. This clearly emerges from the system put in place by the Directive in general, and from Art 2, para 1 taken together with recitals 9–15 in particular. In this respect, recital 12 is particularly significant, 'whereas it is consequently necessary and sufficient that all broadcasters comply with the law of the Member State from which they emanate'. For this purpose, the Member State which has jurisdiction over any given broadcaster must be regarded as the Member State where the broadcaster is established.

This is the reason why TV3, broadcasting via the Astra satellite, primarily with a view to being received in Denmark, Sweden, and Norway, and having established subsidiaries in these three countries, is allowed to broadcast programmes interrupted by commercials and with a content not fulfiling the requirements of the Danish legislation. The decisive criterion is whether the broadcaster is established in Denmark or abroad, not the areas which receive the transmission. As regards TV3 Broadcasting Group Ltd, it was found that the company was actually managed in the UK.

# SPONSORSHIP

## Broadcasting

Sponsorship is specifically regulated in the executive order on advertising and sponsoring radio and television, 'Bekendtgørelse om reklame og sponsering i radio og fjernsyn', Executive Order No 489 amended on 11 June 1997.

Sponsorship is generally allowed, even for programmes broadcast by Denmark Radio. The provisions cover any contribution to the financing of radio and television broadcasts, direct or indirect, including contributions to text television pages from any physical or legal person who does not himself or itself do business as a broadcaster or producer of radio or television programmes, films, records, etc. The purpose of the sponsorship is to promote the name, logo, image, activities or products of the sponsor.

The programme shall be clearly identified as a sponsored programme by means of showing the name or logo of the sponsor at the beginning or end of the programme or both. It is not permitted to show the name or logo of the sponsor during the broadcast of the programme.With respect to text television, the name or logo of the sponsor will be marked on each single page sponsored.Physical or legal persons, whose main activity is to manufacture or sell alcohol (beer, wine, spirits or similar products), tobacco, or merchandise used primarily in connection with smoking, or medicinal products, are not allowed to act as sponsors.

Generally speaking, a sponsored programme must not be influenced by the sponsor in a way that has an impact on the responsibility of the radio and television broadcaster or its editorial independence regarding the programmes.

## In general

Sponsorship is, naturally, also used in other connections, for instance: sporting events; Copenhagen as the Culture City of Europe 1996; jazz festivals; concerts; foreign guest performances; development of technology; research, etc.

The ICC has issued a code of conduct regarding sponsorship which will be used in interpreting whether sponsorships have been agreed in accordance with the general rules laid down in the Marketing Practices Act.

# DATA PROTECTION

The Private Registers Act[12] is of great importance as far as direct marketing is concerned. The Act restricts the gathering, filing and use of data which could be useful in the process of selecting the targets of a marketing campaign. The areas covered by the Act are:

(a) registration of personal data by electronic means;

(b) systematic registration of data on private or financial matters concerning persons, institutions, associations/organisations or businesses, as well as matters which are generally expected to be kept from the public.

Computerised registration – even if any prerequisite laid down in the Act is fulfiled – cannot take place unless the business notifies the Data Surveillance Authority that such a register will be established.

Mailing houses are legal if registered in advance with the Data Surveillance Authority. However, such agencies are only allowed to register the name, address, title, profession and other data freely obtainable from a business register. Anyone registered by such an agency can demand to be deleted from the register.

Registration of data within a business is allowed, to the extent that such registration is considered a normal operation in the ordinary course of business. This means that files on customers, debtors, suppliers, employees, etc, are legal, even when registered electronically on computer, provided that the Data Surveillance Authority is notified of the establishment of the register. Information on purely private matters can only be legally registered if specific prerequisites are fulfiled. Race, skin colour, religion, political orientation, sexuality, crimes, health condition, essential social problems, abuse of drugs and the like are all considered private matters. Even information on sports and leisure activities will often be considered as private and thus protected. The prerequisites of legal registration of private matters are:

(a) that the information is obtained from the person in question or with his consent;

(b) that the person must have been made aware that the information will be registered;

(c) in addition, it must be of importance to the business to be in possession of this piece of information in order to permit justified safeguarding of the interests of both the business and others.

---

12 Consolidated Act No 622 issued on 2 October 1987 (most recently amended by Act No 389 of 14 June 1995).

Any person listed on a computerised register can demand to be informed about the data registered, and he can demand that wrong or obsolete data are deleted from the register.

Passing any registered data on customers to other businesses for marketing purposes is expressly prohibited. Such transmission requires the prior express consent from the customer in question who shall, at the same time, receive information on the business to which the data may be transmitted.

The ban on transmitting legally registered personal data to third parties, without the prior consent of the person registered, does not include a ban on transmitting such information to, for instance, the advertising agency working for the business, provided that the data is used by the agency exclusively when running campaigns for the business itself.

Matching of registers owned by different businesses or companies – including companies belonging to the same group – is prohibited.

Matching within a single business is allowed. Thus, a business may register its customers for its own use, in the course of ordinary business.

The Danish Act on private registers does not, of course, apply outside Denmark. However, it is not possible to bypass the rules by establishing a register abroad. Not only does the Act contain a ban on Danish businesses making use of such foreign registers, but it is also stipulated that such information cannot be legally gathered in Denmark with a view to registering data abroad (Art 21). This means, *inter alia*, that a Danish subsidiary cannot convey such data to its foreign parent company and cannot receive such data from other companies within the group. The corporate veil shall be respected.

On 30 April 1998, the Minister of Justice submitted a Bill proposing a new Act on the processing of private and personal data. The Bill was re-introduced with amendments in October 1998 when the Parliament reconvened, but it has not yet been passed. The Bill intends to incorporate EU Directive 95/46/EU dated 24 October 1995 on the protection of individuals with regard to the processing of personal data and on the free movement of such data and will replace both the Private Registers Act and the Public Registers Act. Member States must bring into force the laws, regulations and administrative provisions necessary to comply with the Directive by 24 October 1998 at the latest.

In addition to this, it is proposed that businesses selling mailing lists for marketing purposes are allowed to register personal data, provided an express consent from the customer in question is obtained. This does not include private data such as race, skin colour, drug abuse, etc. If adopted, this will – unlike today – enable direct marketing agencies in Denmark to gather and file data on the habits and interests of the customers in question.

# ADVERTISING CONTRACTS

The content of contracts varies according to the specific requirements of the parties and, naturally, the media and the purpose. Is it, for instance, a contract between an advertising agency and its customer, or is it a contract between the agency and the media or, for instance, a filmmaker?

Generally speaking, the following items should be addressed in a media advertising contract between a client and an advertising agency:

(a) scope and subject matter;

(b) exclusivity;

(c) performer;

(d) client's obligations;

(e) approvals;

(f) time limits;

(g) rights;

(h) liability, including liability for infringement;

(i) remuneration;

(j) expenses;

(k) confidentiality;

(l) assignment;

(m) breach and remedies;

(n) duration;

(o) disputes;

(p) law and jurisdiction.

## Scope and subject matter

The contract can relate to either a specific product, or constitute an ongoing co-operation. The contract must address whether the work relates to one or more specific product(s), corporate image, restricted to certain media, Denmark/abroad, etc. Does the work include campaigns, television commercials, newspaper advertisements, etc? With respect to an ongoing contract, the agency will normally assist the advertiser in creative and technical production, provide advice relating to advertising and handling of the media, as well as undertake all the relevant administrative functions.

# Exclusivity

The agency will often have to undertake an obligation not to work for other clients competing directly with this client during the contract period. Particularly in relation to an ongoing contract, the advertiser will normally be asked to undertake the same exclusivity obligation.

# Performance

Both parties will have to appoint a person responsible for the contract between them. In addition, sometimes the client may wish that named individuals within the agency work on his matters. In such cases, substitution rights must be dealt with.

The extent to which the agency can make use of freelancers and/or subcontractors must be covered. Normally the agency will wish to have the final choice regarding their partners and suppliers.

# Client's obligations

The client will often have to provide underlying material, allocate internal resources, approve drafts, etc. Milestones for approval ought to be stipulated, as well as the consequences of client approval.

Generally, it will be the responsibility of the client that special rules, regulations and customs within his trade are complied with.

In an ongoing contract, the initiating of a task will be subject to an order from the client, who will also be obliged to brief the agency.

# Time limits

Normally, milestones will be stipulated with respect to both parties. The time limits will be agreed when the work is ordered by the client. Consequences of non-observance of time limits should be stipulated.

# Rights

Rights are very important subject matter. The work done by the agency will sometimes reach the level necessary to be protected by the Copyright Act covering literary and artistic work, or sometimes, at least, it will be special enough to have some protection. By ordering the work, the client will assume that, against payment, he obtains the rights, but in the interest of both parties these matters should be regulated.

It is normally stipulated that, in consideration for the remuneration, the advertiser will be vested with the full and unrestricted right to use the work done within the activity area covered by the scope of the contract.

The right of use can be restricted, for instance, to apply to only certain geographical areas, by certain media, or in other ways.

Furthermore, the parties shall consider very carefully whether this right of use shall be a right of use during the period of co-operation, or whether the client shall be the owner with continued right of use afterwards. These considerations are to be made in conjunction with the provisions on remuneration.

Especially with respect to the advertising agency, it is of importance to remember to secure a transfer of ownership to all underlying rights when entering into contract with subcontractors and subsuppliers (filmmakers, model agencies, etc), including the necessary performers' rights, etc, and to secure that such assignment covers all media and geographic areas.

## Liability

Liability for infringement will normally be the responsibility of the advertising agency. Compliance with the rules laid down in the Marketing Practices Act will, to a certain extent, also be the liability of the agency, provided that the agency is, or ought to be, in possession of the information necessary to judge whether the regulations are being complied with. The agency undertakes responsibility for their advice.

With respect to material and information delivered by the advertiser, the correctness and completeness of such remain the responsibility of the advertiser.

## Remuneration, expenses, and budgets

Upon request, the agency shall draw up a budget related to every specific order placed by the advertiser, prior to initiating the work.

In addition, regarding ongoing contracts, a yearly budget will normally be agreed. The remuneration to the agency will often consist of four elements:

(a) work performed on an hourly basis, thus necessitating an appendix stipulating hourly rates. In this connection, it should be agreed how to treat, for instance, travelling time;

(b) the assignment of the rights to use the material will normally be remunerated as a percentage of the total media turnover (but, naturally, a lump sum can be agreed; or the assignment can be included in the rates). The percentage has to be agreed and will vary, for instance, according to the value of the creative performance and expected turnover. The royalty on the media turnover is a figure not connected to whether or not the agency takes care of the bookings. If not, the agency shall have access to the necessary documentation to be provided by the client, in order to check the accuracy of the calculation. If no media turnover is expected, the royalty can, alternatively, be calculated as a percentage in relation to the costs of production;

(c) handling of media booking will generally be remunerated by debiting a percentage of the cost to the client. (In addition thereto, the agency may receive a commission from the media. Such commission will normally be set off against payments due from the clients in order that this commission will be to the client's benefit.) Further, a fee per booking/change/ cancellation may be agreed. Such fees will often be calculated in absolute figures rather than percentages;

(d) the agency will handle external production. The remuneration is normally a percentage fee to be calculated on the basis of actual cost.

With respect to media booking and handling of external production, some clients will wish to take care of these matters themselves. In such situations, the agency will often demand to be credited with the commission which would have been payable from the media agency as well as demanding a special remuneration, at an agreed percentage, relating to the price obtained by the advertiser from the supplier chosen by him.

Finally, provisions shall be inserted on how to deal with expenses, and payment terms shall be stipulated.

## Assignment and duration

Advertising contracts will normally not be assignable. As regards ongoing contracts, termination notice periods shall be agreed.

# THE FUTURE

Development within advertising will be related to the development of new technologies, including internet structures, teleshopping, CD-ROMs and the like. 'Events' and sponsorships are growing as well, and generally, advertising is being used increasingly. Trades which were not previously allowed to market their services (such as lawyers) are now allowed to do so, due to the current abolition of restrictions pertaining hereto. Apart from the fact that additional legislation should be considered in relation to the use of the new information technology and apart from the increasing concern regarding ecology, environment, safety, etc, as well as the increasing efforts to protect consumers, no legislative changes of major importance relating to advertising can be expected in Denmark. As stated above, the main rule in Danish advertising law is an obligation to comply with fair marketing practices and conduct; this legal standard changes as society changes and will encompass the developments to be seen.

# USEFUL ADDRESSES

Dansk Markedsføringsforbund
(Danish Marketing Association)
St Strandstraede 21
1620 Copenhagen
Denmark
Tel: + 45 33 11 87 87

Danske Reklamebureauers Brancheforening
(Association of Danish Advertising Agencies)
Badstuestraede 20
1209 Copenhagen
Denmark
Tel: + 45 33 13 44 44

Dansk Annoncoerforening
(Association of Danish Advertisers)
Laederstraede 32–34
1201 Copenhagen
Denmark
Tel: + 45 33 14 43 46

Det Danske Handelskammer
(Danish International Chamber of Commerce)
Boersen
1217 Copenhagen
Denmark
Tel: + 45 33 95 05 00

Forbrugerstyrelsen
(National Consumer Agency of Denmark)
Amagerfaelledvej 56
2300 Copenhagen
Denmark
Tel: + 45 31 57 01 00

Forbrugerstyrelsens Rådgivning
(National Consumer Agency Consultancy)
Amagerfaelledvej 56
2300 Copenhagen
Denmark
Tel: + 45 32 96 07 00 (between 10.00 and 14.00)

Radio- og TV-Reklamenævnet
(Radio and Television Advertising Council)
Nybrogade 2
1203 Copenhagen
Denmark
Tel: + 45 33 92 33 70

Registertilsynet
(Data Surveillance Authority)
Christians Brygge 28, 4
1559 Copenhagen
Denmark
Tel: + 45 33 14 38 44

## CHAPTER 5

# FINLAND

*Ursula Schildt*

## INTRODUCTION

Finland is a civil law country. The substantive law regulating advertising can be divided into statutory and non-statutory regulation. The statutory regulation consists of Acts of Parliament and statutory instruments.

The courts, particularly a special tribunal called the Market Court,[1] interpret the statutes and the Market Court's decisions are important on determining the limits of fair and proper marketing.

The non-statutory regulation consists of a number of rules and guidelines of various national and international bodies. Instructions, guidelines and recommendations of the Consumer Ombudsman[2] are particularly important.

The decisions of the Chamber of Commerce Board on Business Practices[3] also play an important role in defining proper advertising practices. The Board is widely used by Finnish traders to resolve problems of unfair business practice. The Board's decisions are not binding but are generally accepted as expressing principles of fair competition and marketing.

In this chapter, the terms 'advertising' and 'marketing' are used interchangeably.

---

1 Finland is a bilingual country, the official languages being Finnish and Swedish. The Finnish statutes do not have official translations into English and all the translations used in this chapter are by the author. The original names of the statutes are indicated in the footnotes, carrying also the number of the Act (the number/year of publication of the Act). Many statutes have been amended since their enactment, but here, for the sake of simplicity, only the number of the original statute will be indicated.

The Finnish name for the Market Court is *Markkinatuomioistuin*, in Swedish, *Marknadsdomstolen*.

2 In Finnish, *Kuluttaja-asiamies*, in Swedish, *Konsumentombudsmannen*.

3 In Finnish, *Keskuskauppakamarin liiketapalautakunta*, in Swedish, *Centralhandelskammarens opinionsnämnd för affärssed*.

## National legislative supervision

Under this heading, the most important public organs supervising the legality of advertising are discussed first, then statutes on the field of consumer protection and unfair competition law.

## STATUTORY ORGANS SUPERVISING ADVERTISING

The most central public organs, basing their powers on statutes, are the Market Court and the Consumer Ombudsman.

### The Market Court

The powers of the Market Court are set out in the Market Court Act.[4] The Market Court can hear cases based on the Consumer Protection Act (CPA),[5] on the Unfair Business Practices Act (UBPA)[6] and some other special statutes.

The Market Court has powers to prohibit improper marketing and impose an order of fine. If the prohibition order is breached, the fine becomes enforceable. The Market Court does not have powers to order compensation of financial losses.

An ordinary court of first instance will normally have jurisdiction to grant damages in cases based on violation of the UBPA or the CPA.

There is no appeal from the decisions of the Market Court, save that an appeal to the Supreme Court on the amount of the fine imposed is allowed.

### The Consumer Ombudsman

The Consumer Ombudsman Act[7] provides the powers of the Consumer Ombudsman. His main duty is to supervise the legality of marketing and contract terms directed at consumers.

The Consumer Ombudsman is also entitled to assist a consumer in a prosecuting a particular case if he considers that it raises an important principle with regard to the application of laws or the public interest of consumers.

---

4   In Finnish, *Laki markkinatuomioistuimesta*, in Swedish, *Lagen om marknadsdomstol.*
5   In Finnish, *Kuluttajansuojalaki*, in Swedish, *Konsumentsskyddslagen.*
6   In Finnish, *Laki sopimattomasta menettelystä elinkeinotoiminnassa*, in Swedish, *Lagen om otillbörligt förfarande i näringverksamhet.*
7   In Finnish, *Laki kuluttaja-asiamiehestä*, in Swedish, *Lagen om konsumentombudsmannen.*

The Consumer Ombudsman also gives various guidelines on fair marketing.

The guidelines do not have the effect of a law as such, but are an important means of interpreting the vague wording of the CPA and the UBPA. These directions are discussed below.

The Consumer Ombudsman has wide powers to interfere with activity that is contrary to the CPA. If he notices that a trader is involved with activities in conflict with the law, the Consumer Ombudsman shall first seek to persuade the trader, by means of negotiations, to withdraw these activities voluntarily.

When necessary, the Consumer Ombudsman must take coercive measures or bring the matter to the Market Court.

When the matter is considered urgent, the Consumer Ombudsman is entitled to prohibit the use of any marketing measure or contract term. This is a temporary measure, and following his prohibition he is required to bring the matter before the Market Court within three days.

## Consumer Complaints Board

The Consumer Complaints Board[8] gives recommended decisions in disputes between traders and consumers concerning consumer products. The Board can also render statements to court dealing with these issues.

The Board decision's are recommendations. They are not enforceable and do not have the same legal effect as court decisions. The matter can be taken to court irrespective of proceedings in the Consumer Complaints Board. Courts, however, have a tendency to follow the opinion of the Board.

## Local consumer counselling

There are various public bodies dealing with the administration of consumer protection and controlling marketing and advertising at a local level.

The Act on Organising of Municipal Consumer Counselling[9] provides that local authorities are responsible for organising consumer counselling in the municipality, which includes control of advertising directed at consumers.

---

8   In Finnish, *Kuluttajavalituslautakunta*, in Swedish, *Konsumentklagonämnden*.
9   In Finnish, *Laki kuluttajaneuvonnan järjestämisestä kunnassa*, in Swedish, *Lagen om anordnande av konsumentrådgivning i kommunerna*, No 72/92.

# CONSUMER PROTECTION

## The Consumer Protection Act

Finnish law provides regulations on advertising relating to the marketing of consumer goods. The CPA has general provisions on what constitutes prohibited forms of advertising. As mentioned before, the Consumer Ombudsman provides guidance on the interpretation of the CPA.[10]

The provisions of the CPA concern cases where consumer goods are offered by a business to a consumer for private household use. The criteria for improper marketing and advertising will be different in the case of advertising directed by a business at other business consumers.

Criminal liability can be imposed for violation of the CPA. Criminal liability can be imposed only on natural persons and such cases are very rare.

According to s 2 of the CPA, advertising should not be improper from the consumer's point of view. The Market Court and the Consumer Ombudsman interpret this extremely wide rule in practice and their decisions and opinions form the body of advertising law. For example, the Market Court has held that advertising claiming that a magnetic bracelet would have healing powers is improper advertising.[11]

Another example of the very wide interpretation of prohibition against improper advertising is the Market Court's case 1984:7. A company manufacturing paints had a series of television commercials featuring a very curvaceous female character in various situations.

The court's reasoning was that advertising denigrating the female gender can be held improper from the consumer's point of view. Thus the court had jurisdiction, pursuant to s 2 of the Act, to prohibit the advertising. Further transmission of the advertisement was prohibited.

In the CPA, there is a general prohibition against advertising or promotions which contain a promise of a benefit or prize depending on luck, if the consumer would, in fact, have to make a purchase or a payment. An exemption is provided for puzzles and crosswords in newspapers and magazines.

The CPA prohibits the use of combined offers (that is, offering good X with good Y), if the goods do not have an obvious connection with each other. It also prohibits the offer of free gifts if the gift does not have an obvious connection with the main subject of the purchase.

---

10    In Finnish, Kuluttaja-asiamies, in Swedish, Konsumentombudsman.
11    The Market Court 1983:3.

There are plans to amend the Finnish CPA so that combined offers, perhaps in such a way that a certain maximum value of the 'free gift' is specified, will be introduced.

The Market Court has ruled that offers of free gifts are contrary to the CPA, even when the consumer is allowed to keep the free gift if he or she returns the product ordered.

According to the Consumer Ombudsman's practice, it should always be possible for the customer to participate in a competition without purchasing the goods or placing an order. Normal postage is not considered to be a purchase, but if participation in a competition is possible only by calling a toll telephone number, the competition is likely to violate the CPA.

Marketing may not go against good practice or be otherwise improper for consumers. Providing incorrect or misleading information is specifically prohibited.

No unreasonable contract term may be used and any court may vary such a term so that it accords with the principle of reasonableness under the CPA.

The CPA also provides rules pertaining to actual sales to consumers, the rights and obligations of the parties as well as consequences of a defect in the product sold. Furthermore, the CPA regulates mail order sales, as well as direct sales and the marketing of consumer credit.

The CPA also includes stipulations regarding certain consumer service agreements, building contracts and sale of building elements.

The Finnish CPA complies with the relevant EU directives, especially bearing in mind that the directives usually set forth the minimum level of protection required. In many respects, Finnish national law provides better protection for consumers than required by the directives.

## Product Liability Act

Consumer products or services which are manufactured, sold or imported by a trader are regulated by the Product Liability Act.[12]

A product or service is considered dangerous for health, for example, if it may cause injury, poisoning, illness or some other danger to health or damage to property due to untrue, misleading or insufficient information. The trader is responsible for taking care that no such danger is caused.

---

12  In Finnish, *Tuoteturvallisuuslaki*, in Swedish, *Produktsäkerhetslag*, No 914/86.

## Statutory Order on Information on Consumer Products

This statutory order[13] provides regulation on the information given on consumer goods in marketing. The order applies to second hand goods only to a certain extent.

## Statutory Order on Price Marking of Products

This statutory order[14] applies to all consumer products other than real estate. The marketing material for these products shall always contain the price. Prices shall be presented in a clear and unambiguous way, which can easily be understood and noticed by consumers.

When a retailer markets or advertises a product, he is obliged to indicate the price at the same time.

# UNFAIR COMPETITION LAW

## The Unfair Business Practices Act

Business activities in general are regulated by the UBPA. Acting against good business practice or otherwise in an improper manner with regard to other business is prohibited. Use of untrue or misleading expressions is also prohibited.

In the UBPA, there is a general prohibition against advertising or promotions which contain a promise of a benefit or prize depending on luck, if the purchaser would, in fact, have to make a purchase or a payment. An exemption is ordinary puzzles and crosswords in newspapers and magazines.

## The Competition Restrictions Act

The Competition Restrictions Act[15] may have some effect on advertising.

The Act prohibits such restrictions on business activities which would have harmful effects on healthy and effective economical competition. For example, abuse of a dominant position is prohibited, as well as arrangements

---

13  In Finnish, *Asetus kulutustavarasta annettavista tiedoista*, in Swedish, *Förordning om uppgifter om konsumtionsvaror*, No 97/87.

14  In Finnish, *Asetus kulutushyödykkeen hinnan ilmoittamisesta markkinoinnissa*, in Swedish, *Förordning om prisinformation vid marknadsföring av konsumtionsnyttigheter*, No 9/89.

15  In Finnish, *Laki kilpailunrajoituksista*, in Swedish, *Lagen om konkurrensbegränsningar*, No 480/92.

which affect pricing in an unfair way, reduce effectiveness, prevent trading or are in conflict with international treaties.

# LEGISLATION ON VARIOUS BUSINESSES AND PRODUCTS

There are various statutes on governing certain fields of business. Here, only the most central statutes are discussed.

## The Alcohol Act

There used to be a complete ban on advertising of alcohol products in Finland. This was related to the fact that previously, the import, wholesale and retail sale of alcohol products (everything stronger than 2.25%) was controlled by a State owned monopoly, Oy Alko Ab.

On 1 January 1995, it became possible for parties other than the State monopoly company to import alcoholic products and also to act as a wholesaler.[16] A certain relaxation in relation to advertising of alcohol products no stronger than 4.7% also took place.

For strong alcoholic products (more than 22%), advertising, indirect advertising and other promotions are totally prohibited. Advertising, indirect advertising and other promotions of weaker (less than 22%) alcoholic products are permitted, but subject to many restrictions.

Advertising of weaker alcoholic products is prohibited if it is directed to or depicts minors or people who are under age purchasing strong alcoholic drinks. Use of alcohol may not be combined with driving. The alcoholic content may not be described as a positive quality of an alcoholic drink.

Depicting extensive use of alcohol in a positive way, or temperance in a negative way, is also prohibited. Creating an image that the use of alcohol will increase the consumer's ability to perform or increase social success is not permitted.

Advertising for alcohol shall not create an image that alcohol has medicinal or therapeutic effect. Advertising of alcohol shall not give false or misleading information about alcohol.

The promotion of another product where an established sign of an alcoholic product, as such or identifiably modified, is used is considered an indirect advertisement of an alcoholic product.

---

16  The Alcohol Act No 1143/94 (in Finnish, *Alkoholilaki* and in Swedish, *Alkohollagen*) regulates sale and promotion of alcoholic products.

It is possible to obtain a special exemption granted by the National Product Control Agency for Welfare and Health[17] for advertising of alcoholic products in bars or in retail shops where alcoholic products are sold.

Foreign publications with alcohol advertising may be sold in Finland provided that the main objective of the publication is not promotion of alcoholic products.

## Credit institutions

The Act[18] regulates obligations for credit institutions when marketing services to their clients. In these marketing activities, all relevant information shall be forwarded to the client. The use of untrue or misleading information, or any otherwise improper manner of proceedings which goes against good practice, is prohibited.

## Medicine

The Medicine Act[19] sets out the general requirements for marketing of medicine. The CPA also applies to marketing of medicines to consumers.

The governmental National Agency of Medicine[20] controls the advertising of medicine. There is also extensive self-regulation applying to this kind of marketing (see below, p 397).

## Package tours

The Act on Package Tours[21] prescribes the information that must be contained in a package tour brochure. The brochure must contain information on general conditions and information particular to the tour in question. Before entering into a contract, the consumer must be given information on what the tour consists of, provided with certain documentation and be informed of regulations regarding medical matters relating to the tour and any foreign residence issues. The conditions must be given to the customer in writing if the conditions have not been published in the brochure.

---

17  In Finnish, *Sosiaali-ja Terveydenhuollon tuotevalvontakeskus*, in Swedish, *Social- och hälsovårdens produkttillsynscentral*. For this chapter, the author interviewed the representatives of the Agency on the telephone.

18  In Finnish, *Laki luottolaitostoiminnasta*, in Swedish, *Kreditinstitutslag*, No 1607/93.

19  In Finnish, *Lääkelaki*, in Swedish, *Läkemedelslagen*, No 395/87.

20  In Finnish, *Lääkelaitos*, in Swedish, *Läkemedelsverket*.

21  In Finnish, *Valmismatkalaki*, in Swedish, *Lagen om paketresor*, No 1079/94.

The brochure must give information on the period that the brochure is valid for, and the name, address and telephone number of the operator. The general conditions must be published in the brochure in easily legible print.

## Personal data

The Personal Data File Act[22] defines a personal data file as any set of data containing personal data, whether organised by means of automatic data processing or otherwise.

If the person's name and address are obtained from a personal data register and used in direct mailing or marketing (including marketing on the internet), the name and address of the person or company responsible for keeping the register shall be indicated.

A special public official, the Data Protection Ombudsman[23] controls use of data files in advertising, marketing and in other fields of life and the Data Protection Board may prohibit illegal use of personal data registers.[24]

## Estate agencies

The Act on Consumer Protection in the Business of Estate Agencies[25] applies to the relationship between estate agent and consumer when a consumer gives a sales or purchase assignment to the agent. The agent is obliged to furnish the sales advertisements with certain minimum information, for example, the requested price.

## Securities

The Act on Marketing of Securities and Bonds[26] prescribes that no false or misleading information shall be given in the marketing of bonds and securities. A special public organ, the Finance Inspection,[27] controls the marketing of bonds and securities and issues detailed directions on the marketing of securities.

---

22  In Finnish, *Henkilörekisterilaki*, in Swedish, *Personregisterlagen*, No 471/87.

23  In Finnish, *Tietosuojavaltuutettu*, in Swedish, *Dataskyddombudsmannen*.

24  The Board in Finnish is *tietosuojalautakunta*, in Swedish, *datasekretessnämnden*. The Personal Data File Act imposes restrictions on possibilities to collect and use personal data of internet users.

25  In Finnish, *Laki kuluttajansuojasta kiinteistönvälityksessä*, in Swedish, *Lagen om konsumentsskydd inom fastighetsförmedling*, No 686/88.

26  In Finnish, *Arvopaperimarkkinalaki*, in Swedish, *Värdepappersmarknadslagen*, No 495/89.

27  In Finnish, *Rahoitustarkastus*, in Swedish, *Finansinspektionen*.

When securities are marketed and offered to the public, a special brochure of the offer has to be prepared. This brochure provides interested parties with all the information that has an influence on the value of the securities. All information provided shall be truthful and not misleading. Marketing activities shall not go against good practice or be otherwise improper. The contents and minimum requirements of the brochure are subject to detailed regulation.

The Finance Inspection has wide powers to collect information from parties in order to evaluate the correctness of the brochure and other advertising. Breach of the liabilities imposed by the Act may lead to criminal liability.

The Market Court has competence to make orders of injunction and award fines against improper marketing of bonds and securities.

## The Tobacco Act

The manufacturer and/or importer of tobacco goods is obliged, before the sale, to mark the packages with warnings of the health risks caused by smoking as well as with test results on tar, nicotine and $CO_2$ levels.

Since 1977, there has been a total ban on direct tobacco advertising in Finland. All indirect tobacco advertising became prohibited when amendments to the Tobacco Act[28] became effective on 1 March 1995.

Indirect advertising, or other promotion, of a tobacco product is promotion of a product where an established sign of a tobacco product, as such or identifiably modified, is used. Advertising which would otherwise create the impression of advertising for a tobacco product is also considered to be indirect advertising.

The National Product Control Agency for Welfare and Health controls the marketing of tobacco products in Finland. The Agency has power to order the advertising to be removed, to grant injunctions and to award fines against advertising violating the Act.

The present view of the Finnish authorities is that an identical name to that of a tobacco product can be used for other products. However, a special figurative or typographical sign of the tobacco product may not be used for other products. This view is indicated in three very recent cases.

'CAMEL' is a well known trade mark for tobacco products as a figurative mark, particularly the word 'CAMEL' in a certain typographical form. The

---

28  The official name of the Tobacco Act is the Act on Measures Reducing Tobacco Smoking No 693/76 (in Finnish, *Laki toimenpiteistä tupakoinnin vähentämiseksi*, in Swedish, *Lagen om åtgärder för inskränkande av tobaksrökning*). Here the Act is simply called 'the Tobacco Act'.

National Product Control Agency for Welfare and Health prohibited a department store and two retailer shops from using the word 'camel' for advertising camel boots and bags when the word 'camel' was written in the identical typographical form as the well known trade mark 'CAMEL'. Use of a figurative 'CAMEL' mark (identical to that of the cigarette manufacturer) was also prohibited by the Agency.

The traders appealed to the Market Court. The court held that using the sign of a tobacco product for promotion of another product is contrary to the Tobacco Act.[29]

The court partially upheld the prohibition to use the word 'camel' in an identical typographical form and the figurative 'camel', identical to the signs for the cigarette brand 'CAMEL'. The traders were, however, not prohibited from using the word 'camel' as such in the advertising of camel bags and boots.

It is not prohibited to sell publications in Finland, which contain advertisements for tobacco products, provided that the main objective of the publication is not promotion of tobacco products.

## OTHER LEGISLATION INFLUENCING ADVERTISING

## Copyright

The author of a work has exclusive right to produce copies of the work or to decide on its public performance. The author of the work has the copyright even if an employee, within the course of the employment relationship, produces the work, unless otherwise agreed in the employment contract.

The only statutory exception to this in the Copyright Act[30] is a computer program created within the course of the employment relationship and for the purpose of fulfiling the obligations of the employment relationship. The copyright of this kind of work will be automatically transferred from the author to the employer.

### Use of pictures of banknotes in advertising

The Bank of Finland has copyright in Finnish banknotes. The colour and picture of the banknote in an advertisement should not be identical to a real banknote.

---

29  The Market Court 1998:1, 1998:2 and 1998:3.
30  In Finnish, *Tekijänoikeuslaki*, in Swedish, *Upphovsrättslagen*, No 404/61.

# LEGISLATION PERTAINING TO
# SPECIAL MEANS OF ADVERTISING

## Advertising on the internet

There is no explicit regulation on advertising on the internet in Finland. In the case of the sale of consumer goods to consumers, the CPA will apply to internet advertising.

It has been held that the CPA will even apply to an advertisement of a foreign company on the internet accessible in Finland. The applicability does not depend on the language of the advertisement. However, advertising in languages not widely understood in Finland may be regarded as advertising not directed at Finnish consumers.[31]

In addition to Finnish, Swedish, due to its position as the second official language of Finland, and English are so widely known in Finland that advertising in these languages may be regarded as directed at Finnish consumers.

Advertising on the internet has been considered as direct advertising. Furthermore, restrictions on the advertising of tobacco products and alcoholic products will also apply to advertising on the internet.

However, to date, there have not been any cases where a foreign company's internet advertisement has been subject to action by the Consumer Ombudsman based on a breach of the CPA.

Unsolicited e-mailing does not, as such, fall foul of the UBPA or the CPA, but it has not generally been seen as a desirable form of marketing. Should the e-mailing contain elements of unfair competition, such as unjustified comparative marketing, the normal rules shall apply.

## Cable broadcasting

The Cable Broadcasting Act[32] is applied to cable broadcasting activities in general, subject to certain exceptions. Advertising is allowed for each channel to the maximum level of 11% of the total broadcasting time, which is counted in six month periods.

Advertisements shall be presented clearly separated from actual programmes and in such a way that the integrity of programmes is not disturbed.

---

31 For this chapter, the author interviewed representatives of the Consumer Ombudsman's Office on the telephone.
32 In Finnish, *Kaapelilähetyslaki*, in Swedish, *Kabelsändningslag*, No 307/87.

All advertising in cable broadcasting shall be in line with good practice and truthful. No discrimination based on sex, race or nationality is allowed and no religious or political opinions may be criticised. Advertisements shall not encourage behaviour which is harmful to health, safety or environmental protection.

In advertising directed at children, no advantage may be taken of their immaturity or inexperience. Children may not be encouraged to buy the product or service nor encouraged to persuade their parents or other people to do so. The children's confidence in their parents and other people may not be shaken. Children may not appear in an advertisement in a dangerous situation without justified reason, and no violent behaviour may be presented as acceptable model behaviour.

The Consumer Ombudsman controls advertising in cable broadcasting.

Advertising is allowed without any restrictions in the case of a channel that is used only for advertising.

The Ministry of Transport and Communications controls cable broadcasting activities.

## Freedom of the press

According to the Freedom of the Press Act,[33] everyone has the right without any pre-restrictions to publish printed work in accordance with the stipulations of this Act. However, in each publication certain minimum information has to be provided. The editor-in-chief has responsibility for the editorial material only, not for advertisements published in the newspaper or magazine in question.

## Television and radio

There are four television channels in Finland. TV1 and TV2 are non-commercial nationwide State channels, and MTV3 is a commercial nationwide channel. Channel Four[34] is a commercial channel, but its coverage is not nationwide.

The first statutory regulation of television and radio advertising came into force on 1 January 1998. This regulation harmonises Finnish legislation with EU broadcasting television directives.

---

33  In Finnish, *Painovapauslaki*, in Swedish, *Tryckfrihetslagen*, No 1/19.

34  In Finnish the official name of the private limited company carrying commercial broadcasting activity is *Oy Ruutunelonen Ab*.

# SUPERVISION BASED ON INTERNATIONAL RULES

There are several Codes of Marketing Practice established by the International Chamber of Commerce, the stipulations of which are also applied to marketing in Finland.

## International Code of Advertising Practice

The Code is designed primarily as an instrument for self-discipline, but it is also intended for use by the courts as a reference document within the framework of the appropriate laws. The Code applies to all advertisements for any goods, services and facilities, including corporate advertising. Therefore the Code contains general and widely applicable guidelines. The Code sets standards of ethical conduct to be followed by all concerned with advertising, whether advertisers, advertising practitioners or agencies, or media.

The Board on Business Practice of the Finnish Central Chamber of Commerce applies this Code of self-discipline nationally in Finland.

There are separate *Guidelines for Advertising Addressed to Children*, which provide interpretation of relevant articles of the Code.

The *Code of Marketing Research and Social Research Practice* aims at ensuring that each market research is performed appropriately and that the principle of privacy is respected.

The International Chamber of Commerce *Code of Sales Promotion Practice* defines general ethical rules of sales promotion and complements the existing legislation.

The *Code of Sponsorship* of the International Chamber of Commerce applies to sponsorship as well as in disputes in arbitration or in court proceedings.

The Code is applied in practice nationally by the Board on Business Practice of the Finnish Central Chamber of Commerce and internationally by the International Marketing Council of the International Chamber of Commerce.

The *Code on Direct Marketing Practice* defines general ethical rules of direct marketing. The Board on Business Practices of the Finnish Central Chamber of Commerce also nationally interprets the Code on Environmental Advertising Practice.

# NATIONAL RULES PERTAINING TO SPECIFIC LINES OF BUSINESS

There are some national rules pertaining to specific lines of business. These rules do not, typically, have any statutory background but are drafted by the representatives of the specific line of business.

Sanctions for violations of these rules may not necessarily exist. These rules may serve as guidance for interpretation of best practice in the respective field in case of a dispute in court.

## Medicine

Special self-regulation exists for the advertising of medicine, namely the Code for the Marketing of Medicinal Products.[35] A self-regulatory body, the Supervisory Commission for the Marketing of Medicinal Products, applies the Code.[36]

The Commission has two Inspection Boards, one for the marketing of medicines to consumers. This Board pre-controls all radio and television advertisements of medicinal products.

The other Board is for the marketing of medicines to health care professionals. The Commission hears appeals from the decisions of the Inspection Boards.

The Commission consists of representatives of the Ministry of Trade and Industry, advertising agencies and health care professionals and manufacturers of pharmaceuticals. The Commission has competence to award fines if its rulings are not followed.

The rules define generally accepted marketing principles for pharmaceutical manufacturers. The purpose of these rules is to ensure that health care professionals and the general public will receive correct information about medicines and their use.

Slightly different criteria apply to the advertising of medicine to health care professionals and to the general public.

Only medicinal products that are available over the counter without prescription may be advertised to consumers. Advertising for a medicine aimed at the general public shall contain at least the name of the medicine and the name of the effective substance.

---

35 Author's translation of the Finnish name, which is *Lääkemarkkinoinnin ohjeet.*
36 In Finnish, *Lääkemarkkinoinnin valvontakunta.* According to the information received over the telephone, neither the Commission nor the Code has a Swedish name.

The necessary information for safe use of the medicine shall be indicated in the advertisement. An advertisement for a medicine shall also contain clear advice on reading the instructions for use as well as the name of the manufacturer, importer or the distributor of the medicine.

Advertising of medicines shall not be directed at children. Neither scientists' nor celebrities' recommendations, nor competitions with prizes or 'money back' offers may be used in the advertisement.

It is forbidden to give free samples of medicine to consumers. Comparisons between different medicines, agents, additives or other qualities shall be objective and trustworthy. Price comparisons are to be clearly justified.

Advertising to health care professionals is regulated slightly differently. The purpose of this kind of advertising is to maintain and develop expertise and to increase patient security.

No economic incentives or inducements may be directly or indirectly offered to practitioners or other personnel in public health service. The monetary value of prizes shall be reasonable. Distribution of free samples is restricted.

The Boards are entitled to reprimand parties acting against these rules as well as to request them to withdraw the activities in question. Furthermore, the Boards may refer the matter to the authorities and order fines.

## Natural products

The Rules on Advertising of Natural Products[37] define natural products as natural food products, natural cosmetics and other such products, goods or equipment, which are advertised to maintain health or prevent illnesses.

Application of the rules and objectivity of the advertising is supervised by the Natural Products Supervision Board.[38] The Board appoints a special Board to control and observe advertising. The Natural Products Supervision Board deals with appeals to the decisions of the Inspection Board and observes general developments in the field.

National laws and decisions of authorities as well as the International Code of Advertising Practice shall be applied to the advertising of natural products. The Board can give a notification in case it finds a violation of the Rules. The Board can also inform the appropriate national authorities on the improper marketing.

---

37  In Finnish, *Luontaistuotteiden markkinoinnin ohjeet*, in Swedish, *Regler för marknadsföring av naturprodukter*.

38  In Finnish, *Luontaistuotteiden markkinoinnin valvontakunta*, in Swedish, *Övervakningsnämnden för marknadsföring av naturprodukter*.

# Timeshares

The Consumer Ombudsman has negotiated instructions on the advertising and marketing of timeshares together with Finland's Timeshare Association.[39] The instructions apply to the advertising of timeshares in Finland.

1 Direct advertising of timeshares

1.1 In direct advertising of timeshares no marketing lotteries, gifts or other benefits shall be used as a main message of the advertising. The gifts are described according to their true value. The number of the most valuable lottery prizes must be stated.

1.2 Sufficient and clear information on the object of the offer shall be given. It must be clearly expressed that the addressee is offered timeshares. Relevant information on the holiday destination and shares are given. In advertising material, the name and address of the enterprise making the offer must be stated.

1.3 When gifts are promised in direct advertising, in presentations and sales exhibitions it shall be clearly stated that obtaining the gift does not require purchase of a timeshare or entry into an agreement.

1.4 Advertising material should not be sent to people who do not fulfil the requirements necessary to take advantage of the offer.

2 Brochures

2.1 Brochures will provide information according to certain statutory rules applicable to the marketing of housing.

2.2 When comparing the cost effectiveness of different ways of spending holidays, the marketing material must take into consideration the total costs.

2.3 In the context of the comparative calculation, the marketing material must clearly present the basis of calculations, such as level of interest rates, inflation and the expected rise in value.

2.4 When the advertising emphasises the future rise in value of the timeshares, the advertising material must also clearly present that timeshares are securities, the value of which is freely determined in the market according to supply and demand.

2.5 When the client is offered financing, the advertising must clearly point out all costs related to the credit, also the effective annual interest and the effective price of the timeshare.

The instructions also contain further provisions on sales exhibitions and conditions of sale of timeshares.

---

39 In Finnish, *Suomen Timeshare Yhdistys*, in Swedish, *Finlands Timeshare Förening*.

# NATIONAL RULES PERTAINING TO SPECIFIC MEANS OF ADVERTISING

As with the rules pertaining to specific lines of business, the national rules pertaining to specific means of advertising generally lack sanctions.

## Direct advertising

The Finnish Direct Marketing Association[40] has given rules on good conduct in direct mail advertising and use of mailing lists. The marketing material should clearly show the source for the address information of the addressee.

Finnish Direct Marketing Association has accepted the rules of fair play for advertising directed at consumers. The rules regard all forms of commercial communication, whether in writing, visual, electronic or oral. The fair play rules concern all direct advertising and marketing directed to consumers.

# THE CONSUMER OMBUDSMAN'S INSTRUCTIONS

The Consumer Ombudsman has given, often in co-operation with different organisations representing traders, several directions on acceptable marketing. The directions do have the effect of law, but they serve as guidelines. The courts tend, however, to consider the Consumer Ombudsman's directions as an important guideline for interpreting statutes.

Here, the Consumer Ombudsman's Directions and the relevant Market Court decisions are discussed together under the respective headings.

## Bargain sales and final clearance sales

The Consumer Ombudsman and Kaupan Keskusvaliokunta (the Central Board of Trade) have together drafted these directions.

The products on bargain sale must be clearly defined in any marketing material if the sale is only for a part of the selection of goods on offer.

Not only the original price and the discount percent must be stated, but also the new reduced price.

It is not allowed to use the word 'final clearance sale' when a trader has bought stock from a bankrupt's estate. The expression 'bankrupt clearance sale' is allowed only if the bankrupt's estate is selling the products.

---

40   In Finnish, *Suomen Suoramarkkinointiliitto.*

## Marketing lotteries and games

The CPA restricts use of benefits which depend on chance or games where participation is subject to the purchase of the product in advertising. From this it follows that it should be possible to participate in lotteries and games without the purchase of a product or even ordering a product.

For example, a travel agency's campaign, whereby free travel was to be disposed of by lottery among people who had made a reservation during a certain day, was against the law.

Organising a marketing lottery for public of a certain event, restaurant or sports game in such a way that the entrance ticket is the lottery ticket is prohibited because the participation is dependent on the purchase of a product.

A promise to refund the purchase price of a product or a part of it if a sportsman is successful in certain sports events is a benefit depending on chance and thus against the law, because the consumer cannot gain the benefit without first purchasing the product.

It is prohibited to use lotteries in the marketing of consumer credit.

The marketing material should state the organiser of the lottery or the game, the first and the final days of the lottery, how drawing the lots will take place and who will do it, when the lottery will take place and how the results of the lottery or the game are to be controlled.

The rules of the lottery are to be given prominence in the marketing material so that they will come to the attention of the consumer.

There are plans to restrict the possibility of arranging marketing lotteries but these plans have not yet come to the stage of a Government Bill.

## Marketing of special offers

The most common problems with special offer marketing are lack of information on the offer and misleading price comparisons.

The visual layout of an advertisement must not be misleading to a consumer.

Newspaper advertisements and advertisements outside a shop must be drafted in such a way that the consumer will not be misled to believe that products that are retailed at normal price are on special offer.

The campaign time must be announced clearly in advertising outside the shop and, if possible, also in the shop. Special offers may last for a maximum of one month.

## Expressions of price in advertising

According to the CPA, advertising is improper if it does not contain 'the necessary information for the financial safety of the consumers'. In other words, the price must be stated clearly.

In marketing and advertising of sales prices, a retail trade may use a 'suggested retail price' as a starting point for the reduction if it is the actual price used by that retail trade.

If a product or service is advertised with an expression 'from £X', the retail price of the individual product must always be given.

As regards 'from £X' prices at travel agencies, if the number of the trips available is less than 10 then the actual number must be given in the advertisement.

When marketing trips and cruises, the travel agency has to announce what departures and cabins the 'from £X' price concerns.

There are two prerequisites for using the concept of 'wholesale price' in marketing. The prices should in reality be more advantageous than the prices of the same products sold by other traders. Furthermore, the prices should be the same as the product is sold at by the wholesale traders to retail traders.

## Using the word 'free' in advertising

The word 'free' is often used when byproducts or giveaways are marketed.

Premiums and combined product offers are allowed only if the products are obviously connected with each other.

The Consumer Ombudsman recommends that, instead of using 'free gift', words such as 'at the same price', or 'without separate payment' are to be used.

## Premiums and combined product offers

Use of combined offers in Finnish marketing is limited and many forms of combined offers that are acceptable in other Member States of the EU are prohibited by the CPA.

When consumer goods are sold with another consumer product, it is required that the products in question are obviously connected with each other. In practice, only such offers where the simultaneous use of the products is either recommended or necessary are considered to be appropriate.

Bulk discounts or quantity discounts are generally accepted. Some discount arrangements between business traders may fall foul of the competition laws.

It is worth remembering that even offering a free gift may be prohibited if the gift does not have an obvious connection with the main subject of purchase.

For example, an offer by a furniture shop: 'Buy a sofa, get yourself a baked ham' was prohibited by the Consumer Ombudsman because there was not an obvious connection between the goods on sale (sofa) and the extra gift (a baked ham).

The fact that the products are used simultaneously or for the same purpose is not adequate proof of obvious connection. An obvious connection would occur if the simultaneous use of products were to be recommended for the financial security or health of the consumer.

Other prohibited combined offers have been:

- sports magazine with accident insurance, a nature guide and a sports drink;[41]
- women's magazine with tights and a toothbrush;[42]
- accident insurance with a waist bag;[43]
- a flat with a set of furniture;[44]
- a suit with a tie holder and a pair of diamond earrings;[45] and
- women's magazine with a T-shirt.[46]

An acceptable combined offer would be a free gift of a poster of a rock star with a magazine containing an article featuring the star. Another example of an acceptable free gift with an obvious connection would be a model of a gingerbread house with a magazine that contains a recipe for the gingerbread house.[47]

## Use of superlatives in advertising

Advertising should be truthful. Use of superlatives is justified if the suggested statement in advertising holds true.

When a superlative is used in advertising in such a way that a consumer may hold the superlative to be a statement of fact, the advertiser should be able to verify the truthfulness of the statement. Usually, the proof must be based on research that is impartial and scientifically conducted.

The Consumer Ombudsman has held that the use of the phrase 'the most popular' in advertising requires that the market share of the product or the

---

41   The Market Court 1981:14.
42   The Consumer Ombudsman 96/40/677.
43   The Consumer Ombudsman 96/41/573.
44   The Consumer Ombudsman 92/40/90.
45   The Market Court 1993:12.
46   The Market Court 1991:9.
47   The Consumer Ombudsman's guidelines for marketing of newspapers and magazines.

service in question is and has been consistently bigger than the market shares of other corresponding products. Temporary popularity due to an efficient sales campaign does not justify the use of this kind of expression in advertising.

As for the phrase 'the most advantageous', the Market Court has held that a generalising statement in 'X – the most advantageous in the market' cannot be used without research conducted by an impartial institute to support the statement.[48]

However, some appraisal of products is allowed without special proof. Thus, it is allowed to use expressions like 'the best product'. Other subjective superlatives allowed in advertising are 'the most beautiful', 'the most luxurious', 'the most delicious', etc.

## Use of tests in advertising

The Consumer Ombudsman has, in his guidelines, summed up the principles established in the decisions of the Market Court. The following principles can be held established:

- conclusions and expressions that the tester has not used cannot be presented in advertising;
- test results of a certain product model cannot be generalised with regard to other products;
- the test results must be easily available to customers;
- tests used in advertising must be current;
- if products of different classes are being compared in advertising, the difference must be announced clearly;
- a comparative test or research used in advertising must be representative of the products;
- one quality of a product cannot be presented to the neglect of other relevant qualities so that it gives a picture of general superiority of that product over other products;
- an outsider must conduct test or research that is referred to in advertising.

## Advertising of fuel consumption of cars

Since the fuel consumption affects consumers' decisions about the purchase of a product, the consumption must be announced as accurately as possible by using generally accepted measuring norms:

---

48   Eg, in cases 1987:10 and 1987:13 of the Market Court.

- if anything about fuel consumption of a car is claimed at all, nothing but the international EC norm consumption figures may be expressed. This includes television advertising;
- figures according to EC norms have to be used in all newspaper advertisements containing information about the capacity of the car. In car windows at exhibitions, and in direct mailing, brochures and manuals, these norms are to be used.

## Advertising of slimming preparations

The advertiser should always be able to prove reliably the claims used in advertising. Statements by private individuals, often used in the marketing of slimming preparations, are not considered to be proof of the healing effect of the preparation, but rather as statements of personal experience.

Before using the testimony of an individual as to the efficacy of a slimming preparation, the advertiser should be able, by impartial research results, to prove that the result reached by the individual in question is expressly due to using the advertised preparation.

The Consumer Ombudsman has not found animal tests conducted in Taiwan as sufficient proof of the slimming effect of a slimming tea. Nor has the Consumer Ombudsman held thank you letters from customers as sufficient proof of the slimming effect of the preparation.

## Mail order businesses

The Consumer Ombudsman has given instructions regarding several aspects of mail order businesses.

The advertising material must contain a full summary of all the conditions which must be clearly printed and easy to locate. The conditions must be printed on the part of the material that is not used for ordering.

On the order form, the most essential conditions of the order and also a reference to the complete conditions must appear. In a mail order catalogue, each two page spread must contain a reference to the full conditions.

The order forms for mail order business carry text which urges minors to obtain consent from the guardian for ordering the goods. If this is not done, the marketing may be held improper and unfair.

The full street address of the mail order business must be given in advertisements. The Market Court held that it is sufficient for the consumer to obtain the address of the mail order business at the latest on delivery of the goods.[49]

---

49   The Market Court 1981:3.

Prices must be presented clearly in advertisements and in mail order catalogues. The full price of the product must always be provided. All the costs must be also presented on the order form, such as handling costs, packaging costs and mail costs. It is not sufficient to express the additional costs only in the order form. If the product is delivered by post, the advertisement must contain information on the means of delivery and postage costs.

A mail order offer must be clear enough for the consumer easily to understand it to be an offer. It is unfair to characterise an offer as an 'experiment', 'marketing research' or 'poll' if the main purpose is sale of the products.

A mail order offer cannot be presented in a way that resembles an invoice or a completed order form. The consumer must easily be able to understand the mail order advertisement as an offer that need not to be replied to.

It is forbidden to state in the advertisement that the consumer is a part of a selected target group who is given 'a particularly profitable birthday offer' even though in reality anybody can purchase the same product with the same benefits.

It is also forbidden to call a mail order offer a 'game' or 'lottery' and charge the consumer for the delivery of the products advertised as prizes. Even though the payment is called 'postage costs', it is, in fact, a sale of a product, since lottery and game prices are usually delivered to winners without charge.

Furthermore, it is forbidden to call the cancellation time relating to mail order business as 'charge free probationary time'. This statement gives the impression that the consumer would be able to acquaint himself with the goods without paying anything.

However, if the consumer must pay the purchase price in advance to obtain the product, this expression is misleading. The misleading nature of this statement is not countered by the fact that the consumer is refunded the purchase price if he cancels the order.

## Advertising of newspapers and magazines

These Consumer Ombudsman's directions apply to all advertising media: newspapers, direct marketing, outdoor advertisements, television and radio, and also marketing and advertising of books.

In advertising material, it must be clearly shown that the consumer, when answering the offer, will be subscribing to a magazine. The conditions must be presented in advertising material clearly and visibly in one place.

Central conditions are, for example, the nature and length of subscription, the number of magazines belonging to the subscription, price, invoicing period and termination of subscription. A copy of the conditions must be left with the consumer. Such terms as a standing subscription or a fixed term subscription must be explained, as well as how the subscription can be terminated.

The contact information for customer service shall be clearly indicated to the customer.

Expressions such as 'for free', 'offer for free' or other expressions emphasising the gratuitous nature cannot be used when the order continues automatically after the first period of subscription.

The advertising must give information on the continuous nature of the subscription clearly and visibly.

If price comparison is used in an advertisement, the comparison must be clear and the comparative prices true. Comparative price can be only the normal price of the equivalent subscription. The subscription price cannot be compared with the price of an individual edition or the price of a standing subscription.

Marketing material sent to adults which is attractive to children is regarded as advertising to children. Lotteries directed at children are not allowed.

When advertising a magazine subscription, lotteries and games should not be the dominating part of the material.

The material should clearly present the possibility of participating in the game or lottery without purchasing the product.

Benefits depending on chance, or combined products that do not have an obvious connection with each other, are forbidden. A make-up box for the subscriber of a beauty magazine or a thermometer for the subscriber of a technical magazine are prohibited premiums, as are a book for the subscriber of a newspaper, an atlas for the subscriber of a dictionary or an encyclopedia for the purchaser of a book.

Posters of a rock star or a book of recipes published in the newspaper in question have been regarded as acceptable combined offers in conjunction with the subscription of a magazine.

## Teleshopping

A teleshopping broadcast must be clearly distinguished from ordinary broadcasts. Transmission times and the advertising nature of teleshopping broadcasts must also be seen in information on television programmes in newspapers, etc.

The following minimum information must be given in each teleshopping broadcast:

• the name and contact information of the seller;

- information of price and payment conditions of the product on sale;
- delivery time and conditions.

Ordinary rules on marketing, lotteries and premiums are applicable to teleshopping. Benefits which depend on chance or require purchase of a product are forbidden. Premiums and combined product offers are allowed only if the products in question are obviously connected with each other.

## Environmental advertising

Advertising must be based on facts. The advertiser must prove all environmental statements to be true. Expressions such as 'pro-environmental' or 'ecologically beneficial' require thorough investigation on the product.

Use of such arguments must be based on the results of research.

## Other directions

The Consumer Ombudsman has given directions on even very particular issues such as the advertising of mobile sales exhibitions, price advertising of second hand cars, marketing of gravestones, advertising of gold and jewellery and slimming products.

# OTHER RULES, INSTRUCTIONS AND RECOMMENDATIONS

Several organisations have given various rules of conduct and recommendations relating to advertising. Here, some of the most important of these rules of conduct are discussed.

## Principles for the Advertising Council for Equality

This Council[50] follows the international rules for marketing approved by the International Chamber of Commerce.

It is forbidden to discriminate against people because of their sex, religion or other such grounds in advertising.

Advertisements go against good conduct in advertising if a man or woman is used as a sex object in a discriminating way or any sexual promises are given that do not have anything to do with the advertised product.

---

50  In Finnish, *Tasa-arvoa markkinoinnissa valvova neuvosto.*

Advertisements stating or clearly suggesting that the role of one sex be socially, economically or culturally inferior to the other sex go against good advertising conduct.

Advertisements do not go against good advertising conduct only because there are naked people in an advertisement if the people have not been described in a discriminating way.

## Use of certain professional titles in advertising

Under the ethical rules of the Finnish Association of Architects, architects can use matter of fact advertising only.

Attorneys-at-law may, in their advertisements, only state their main field of activity and references under the ethical rules of the Finnish Bar Association.

If a non-Bar member is practising law, there are no restrictions to his/her advertising other than those set forth by the CPA and the UBPA.

The Association of Finnish Patent Attorneys follows the rules of the International Federation of Industrial Property Attorneys. Patent attorneys advertise in the reference publications under the Association's heading.

## INTERNATIONAL RULES

Finland's position vis à vis the International Chamber of Commerce Code of Advertising Practice is discussed above.

## Joint Nordic Regulation of Television Advertising

Legislation in all Nordic countries, as well as the practice based thereon, has set similar kinds of requirements to television advertising and other marketing directed at consumers.

It has been deemed necessary to protect conformity in all Nordic countries in this field, since commercial television programmes cross the borders between the Nordic countries.

The Joint Nordic Regulations of Television[51] include opinions of the Consumer Ombudsmen from Denmark, Finland, Norway and Sweden as well as the opinion of the Price and Competition Board of Iceland.

---

51 In Finnish, *Televisiomainonnan yhteispohjoismaalaiset säännöt*, in Swedish, *Gemensamma nordiska regler beträffande televisionreklam.*

Advertisements shall be clearly separate from the actual programmes. No action which could be understood as an incitement to act against the law is allowed.

The advertisement should neither encourage people to endanger health or safety at home, at work or in traffic, or generally to encourage them to some irresponsible activities or activities which could be in conflict with environmental protection.

Advertisements shall not go against good practice, insult human dignity, denigrate anyone on the basis of their sex, race, religion or nationality or offend people's religious or political opinions. Advertisements should not cause fear or show violent or aggressive behaviour, nor encourage such behaviour.

It should specifically be taken into consideration that children and young people are inexperienced and inclined to be influenced. Children may not be misled or encouraged to persuade anyone to buy the product or service.

Children may appear in advertisements only if they are a natural part of the environment shown, or if they are necessary in order to illustrate the product or service. Children shall not recommend any product or service.

# ADVERTISING CONTRACTS

Advertising in Finland is regulated by a number of national laws and rules as well as international codes. The appropriate contract depends largely on the media in which the advertising is to take place and the product in question. Therefore no standard contract can be presented, but the terms and provisions of an advertising contract should, in each case, be individually examined.

Some organisations in this field have models for advertising contracts. These contracts should not be copied, but be used only as a guideline and should always adapted to the relevant case.

In advertising, there is a strong trend towards the situation where the advertiser shall gain all copyright in advertisements, whether electronic, graphic or other forms of advertising are used.

## Future developments

Advertising experts presume that in the future, advertising and marketing via electronic media will become more and more important. Also, direct mail advertising through mailing lists will play an increasing role.

Advertising on the internet has raised new questions relating to the applicability of national laws to marketing emanating from abroad, but accessible in various jurisdictions.

The traditional view of certain public organs controlling advertising may became blurred in the future because of questions of jurisdiction. For the EU Member States, the Brussels Convention will offer possibilities to have judgments enforceable in other Member States.

For companies planning advertising in new media, the need to seek advice in advance will become paramount. It may be necessary for advertisers to restrict access to their home pages by registration means. Another option may be to limit the geographical application of lotteries, competitions and other marketing efforts to 'safe' jurisdictions.

## Code of conduct

In Finland there is no national code of advertising conduct, but advertising is regulated by separate laws and rules mainly applicable only to certain areas of advertising. The International Chamber of Commerce Code of Advertising Practice is widely recognised in Finland, together with other International Chamber of Commerce advertising codes.

## USEFUL ADDRESSES

*Radio*
Association of Finnish Radio Broadcasters
Lönnrotinkatu 11 A
FIN-00120 Helsinki
Tel: + 358 9 228 773 40

*Cinema*
State Office of Film Censorship
Jaakonkatu 5 B
FIN-00100 Helsinki
Tel: + 358 9 173 41

*Press*
Finnish Newspaper Publishers Association
Lönnrotinkatu 11
FIN-00120 Helsinki
Tel: + 358 9 228 77 300

Finnish Periodical Publishers Association
Lönnrotinkatu 11 A
FIN-00120 Helsinki
Mailing address:
PL 267
FIN-00121 Helsinki
Tel: +358-9-228 77 280

Finnish Urban Press Association
Kauppakartanonkatu 7A
FIN-00930 Helsinki
Tel: + 358 9 334 876

Regional Press Association
Vuorikatu 3 A 30
FIN-00100 Helsinki
Tel: + 358 9 179 064

*Outdoor*
Outdoor Advertising Association of Finland
Talttakuja 1
FIN-01650 Vantaa
Tel: +358 9 840 103

*Direct mail*
Finnish Direct Marketing Association
Vuorikatu 4A 6
FIN-00100 Helsinki
Tel: + 358 9 663 744

International Chamber of Commerce
Finnish Section
Fabianinkatu 14 A
FIN-00100 Helsinki
Tel: + 358 9 650 133

Suoramainosliitto ry
c/o Startual Oy
Mr Pertti Huhtala
Box 104
FIN-00381 Helsinki
Tel: + 358 9 122 33 11

*Consumer associations*
Elintarvikevirasto
(Foodstuffs Board)
PL 3
FIN-00531 Helsinki
Tel: + 358 9 77261

Keskuskauppakamarin Liiketapalautakunta
(Council on Business Practice/Central Chamber of Commerce)
PL 1000
FIN-00101 Helsinki
Tel: + 358 9 650 133

Kilpailuvirasto
(Competition Council)
Haapaniemenkatu 5
PL 332
FIN-00531 Helsinki
Tel: + 358 9 73 141

Kuluttaja-asiamiehen toimisto
(Consumer Ombudsman's Office)
PL 306
FIN-00531 Helsinki
Tel: + 358 9 77 261

Kuluttajavalituslautakunta
(Consumer Complaint Board)
PL 306
FIN-00531 Helsinki
Tel: + 358 9 7726 7977

Kuluttajat-Konsumenterna
(Consumer Association)
Vilhonkatu 6F
FIN-00100 Helsinki
Tel: + 358 9 626 206

Kuluttajatutkimuskeskus
(Centre of Consumer Research)
PL 5
FIN-00531 Helsinki
Tel: + 358 9 77 261

Markkinatuomioistuin
(Market Court)
Unioninkatu 16
FIN-00130 Helsinki
Tel: + 358 9 65 3079

Suomen Kuluttajaliitto ry
(Finnish Consumers' Association)
Mannerheimintie 15A
FIN-00260 Helsinki
Tel: + 358 9 448 288

Tasa-arvovaltuutetun toimisto
(Council for Equality)
Käenkuja 3-5 M
FIN-00500 Helsinki
Tel: + 358 9 1601

Tietosuojavaltuutettu
(Councillor of Privacy Protection)
Kauppakartan k 7 A
FIN-00930 Helsinki
Tel: + 358 9 343 2455

*Other specialist organisations*
Grafia ry
Uudenmaankatu 11 B
FIN-00120 Helsinki
Tel: + 358 9 601 941

Mainostajien Liitto ry
(Advertisers' Union)
Meritullinkatu 3 D
FIN-00170 Helsinki
Tel: + 358 9 662 622

Mainostoimistojen liitto (MTL) ry
(Union of Advertising Offices)
Vuorikatu 22 A 3
FIN-00100 Helsinki
Tel: + 358 9 625 300

Suomen audovisuaalisen alan tuottajat (SATU) ry
(Finnish Producers of the Audio-visual Branch)
Kanavaranta 3 D
FIN-00160 Helsinki
Tel: + 358 9 622 1690

Suomen Markkinointiliitto (SML) ry
(Finnish Marketing Union)
Fabianinkatu 4 B
FIN-00130 Helsinki
Tel: + 358 9 651 500

Suomen Suoramarkkinointiliitto (SSML) ry
(Finnish Direct Marketing Union)
Vuorikatu 46 A
FIN-00100 Helsinki
Tel: + 358 9 663 744

Suomen Tiedottajien Liitto (STL) ry
(Finnish Communicators' Union)
Meritullinkatu 13 C 64
FIN-00170 Helsinki
Tel: + 358 9 135 7775

## CHAPTER 6

# FRANCE

*Francis Meyrier and Deborah Jarmain-Barbizet*

## INTRODUCTION

As will be shown by those subjects covered in this chapter, advertising in France is a highly regulated activity. An advertising campaign requires careful consideration by each of the players in their various roles of the legal environment surrounding advertising and the implication of such laws and regulations on the manner in which they choose to advertise a particular product or service. French legislation has, over the last decade, become more strict in the manner in which it permits advertising, most particularly in protecting the targeted consumer.

Moreover, in parallel with the reinforcement of this protectionist environment, the multiplication of the types of media is progressively modifying the manner in which businesses are able to communicate on an international scale.

Such technological evolution will undoubtedly result in legislative change on both a national and European level.

## THE PROFESSIONALS: THE INSTITUTIONS

### Access to the profession

Access to the role of an advertising agency is legally unrestricted and no particular conditions are imposed under French law for the exercise of the profession.

The profession operates according to well entrenched principles of self-regulation within a framework of professional organisations and/or unions belonging to each of the advertising players.

### Professional organisations

Advertising players can be divided into four general categories:

(a) the advertiser;

(b) the advertising agency;

(c) the *régie publicitaire* (the advertising space sales intermediary) with the various media;

(d) the media.

Various professional unions or organisations group together the different types of advertising players depending on their particular role.

## Union des Annonceurs

The *Union des Annonceurs* is an organisation which represents advertisers, and seeks to protect their common interests with public authorities, supervisory bodies and consumers. In addition, it provides information and assistance facilities to its members.

## L'Association des Agences Conseils en Communication

The *Association des Agences Conseils en Communication* (AACC) is a professional organisation, the members of which are principally advertising and marketing agencies which have satisfied the relevant selection criteria. Although membership of the AACC is not a legal obligation, it is generally accepted as representing a professional benchmark, as each member agrees to respect the professional rules set out in the charter of the AACC and the practice of self-regulation common to the French advertising industry in general.

The AACC represents the interests of its members with the media, clients and public authorities, both in France and abroad, and generally promotes the profession. It comprises specialist committees to provide such representation and to promote current media topics.

It also provides a data and research service which regularly publishes advertising market studies and professional reference guides. It also has established its own training centre.

There are several categories of activity within the AACC, which each have their own set of professional rules and guidelines:

- *agence conseil en publicité* (advertising agency);
- *agence conseil en marketing direct* (direct marketing agency);
- *agence conseil en promotion des ventes* (sales promotion agency);
- *agence conseil en communication santé* (health communication agency)
- *agence conseil en partenariat* (partnerships/sponsorships agency).

A translation of the full text of the professional rules of the advertising agency is reproduced at the end of this chapter. Such rules define the qualifications necessary for membership and the role to be played by the agency. The professional rules of each type of agency described above are published and available from the AACC.

The AACC has produced a standard form contract, to be entered into between the advertising agency and the advertiser, which is available to its members. The form provides commentary on the law applicable to such contracts and examples of standard clauses. This type of contract is discussed below, p 440.

## The supervisory bodies

### Bureau de verification de la publicite (BVP)

The *Bureau de Vérification de la Publicité* (commonly known as the BVP) is an independent, self-regulatory, inter-professional body which controls advertising standards in France. Members of the BVP are advertisers, agencies and the media, and professional associations and unions.

It has several roles, covering principally advice on and control, a priori or a posteriori, of advertising in the context of the French legal environment (including the International Advertising Practices Code drawn up by the International Chamber of Commerce), the treatment of complaints and the drafting of professional codes.

Its goal is to promote loyal, honest and truthful advertising in the interest and respect of the public (BVP Bylaws, Art 1), through such advisory and supervisory role.

Members of the BVP may submit all types of advertising proposals to it prior to broadcast, in order to seek its confirmation that the proposal is in line with current French laws and regulations. Indeed, television advertisements are submitted to the BVP for approval in draft form prior to broadcast.

Following broadcast or publication, an advertisement may be subject to the control of the BVP. In the case of breach of French law or regulations, the BVP may request the advertiser to make the appropriate modifications to the advertisement in order to ensure proper compliance. The BVP will request the media support to cease its broadcast should the advertiser not adhere to the proposal of the BVP. The membership of a member who breaches the rules of the BVP may be cancelled.

In its advisory role, the BVP publishes recommendations to the industry. These constitute guidelines on proper practice with respect to a wide range of advertising subject matters such as, for example, advertising language, children, race, religion etc. They bind members of the BVP, but also act as a reference for non-members in the advertising industry and the judicial system, even though they do not have the force of law. Communiqués are also published, should case law or regulations change which have immediate effect on the advertising industry.

## *The conseil superieur de l'audiovisuel (CSA)*

The role of the CSA is to 'exercise control by all appropriate means over the object, the content and the methods of programming of advertisements' (Law No 86-1067 of 30 September 1986) in both the public and private audio-visual sector. Its control extends to both radio and television advertising.

The CSA publishes an annual report comprising commented case law. It also publishes technical notes relating to the laws and regulations for audio-visual advertising.

Advertisements are subject to post-broadcast control of the CSA. In the event that a broadcast advertisement breaches French rules, the CSA may prohibit further broadcasts and apply sanctions. The CSA is also responsible for policing the compliance with European legislation of retransmissions from other European Member States.

State owned radio and television broadcasting companies are also obliged to abide by their internal regulations with respect to advertising broadcasting rules and policies. Independent radio and television services are obliged to abide by the terms of their broadcasting authorisation agreement with the CSA which sets out, *inter alia*, the advertising rules applicable to and policy of the service in question. In respect of advertising, such rules and policies will generally include provisions relating to programming, advertising interruptions, sponsorship policies, etc. The CSA will supervise compliance with such internal regulations and broadcast authorisation agreements by the services in question.

It is to be noted that France is a member country of the European Advertising Standards Alliance and its practice of self-regulation is also based upon its adherence to the International Code of Advertising Practice of the International Chamber of Commerce.

# ADVERTISING MEDIA

This section deals with the rules relating to the types of media used in advertising and, particularly, the rules relating to radio and television advertising. Advertising in the written press and on hoardings have not been dealt with. In summary, precautions should be taken in the written press to distinguish press articles from advertising. The French legal regulations which apply to poster and hoarding advertising are essentially of an urban, ecological and highway security nature.

It should be noted that advertising in cinemas must have been granted a certificate from the Ministry of Cultural Affairs once reviewed by the commission for the control of cinema films (*'Commission de contrôle des films cinématographiques'*) prior to broadcast.

# Radio and television advertising

Advertising on such media support is essentially governed by Law No 86-1067 of 30 September 1986 as modified, and by the decrees passed under French law for its implementation. French law is in harmony with the provisions of the EEC Directive of 1989 concerning television which allows Member States to impose stricter rules in their national legislation. Moreover, those internal rules, and those of the broadcasting authorisation agreement of the radio and television service in question, must be taken into consideration.

## *Television advertising*

In respect of television advertising, the rules relating to content that are set out in Decree No 92-280 of 27 March 1992 generally apply to State owned and independent stations alike, in all their various forms of broadcast (terrestrial, satellite, cable, toll paying services, etc) with limited exceptions.

Television advertising is described by the Decree as:

... any form of television message broadcast for remuneration or other consideration with a view either to the promotion of the supply of products or services including those presented under their generic name in the context of a commercial, industrial, artisan activity or a profession, or to ensure the commercial promotion of a public or private business. This definition does not include direct offers to the public with a view to the sale, purchase or rental of products or with a view to the supply of services in exchange for remuneration.

Such advertising must comply with the rules set out in the Decree as follows:

Article 3

Advertising must conform to the requirements of truth, decency and respect of human dignity.

It must not prejudice the reputation or authority of the State.

Article 4

Advertising must be free from any discrimination by reason of race, sex or nationality, from any scenes of violence and from any incitement to behaviour prejudicial to health, to the security of persons and assets or to the protection of the environment.

Article 5

Advertising must not contain any element of a nature to shock the religious, philosophical or political convictions of television viewers.

Article 6

Advertising must be expressed in a manner which respects the interests of consumers. Any advertising containing, in any form whatsoever, allegations, indications or presentations which are false or of a nature to mislead consumers, is forbidden.

Article 7

Advertising must not prejudice minors.

To this end, it must not:

1 Directly incite minors to purchase a product or service by exploiting their inexperience or credulity.

2 Directly incite minors to persuade their parents or third parties to purchase the products or services in question.

3 Exploit or alter the special trust that minors have in their parents, teachers or other persons.

4 Present, without legitimate reason, minors in a dangerous situation.

Article 8

Advertising in respect of those products prohibited for television advertising by law and in respect of the following products and economic sectors is forbidden:

- drinks containing more than 1.2 degrees of alcohol;
- literary publishing;
- cinema (ie, films currently showing, or to be shown, and their derivative products);
- press;
- distribution (retail/wholesale).

Article 9

Clandestine (underhand) advertising is prohibited.

For the purposes hereof, clandestine (underhand) advertising is the verbal or visual presentation of merchandise, services, names, trade marks or activities of a producer of merchandise or provider of services during television programmes, when such presentation is made with the aim of advertising.

Article 10

Advertising must not use subliminal techniques.

Article 11

Advertising must not use, either visually or orally, those persons who regularly present television news related programmes.

Advertising on television must be clearly identifiable as such. Advertising slots must be clearly separated from the television programme before and after the broadcasting thereof by the use of screens which are recognisable by their image and sound. The sound volume of the advertising slot and the presentation screens must not exceed the average volume of the rest of the programme, during which the advertisement is screened.

# Radio advertising

The content of independent radio advertising is governed by the rules set out in Decree No 87-239 of 6 April 1987, which provide that:

Article 2

The content of advertising messages must conform with the requirements of truth, decency and respect for the person. It must not prejudice the credit of the State.

Article 3

Advertising messages must be free from any racial or sexual discrimination, scenes of violence or elements provoking fear or encouraging abuse, imprudence or negligence.

Article 4

Advertising messages must not contain any element of a nature to shock religious, philosophical or political convictions of listeners.

Article 5

Advertising must be expressed in a manner which respects the interests of consumers. Advertising messages must not, directly or indirectly, by exaggeration or omission, or by reason of their ambiguous nature, mislead a consumer.

Article 6

Advertising must not in any way exploit the inexperience or credulity of children and adolescents.

Children and adolescents may not recommend the product or service advertised. They may only be the principal actors if there is a direct relationship between them and the product or service in question.

Article 7

Advertising messages are broadcast in French.

Article 8

Advertising messages must be clearly announced and identified as such.

State owned radio generally obeys similar rules on the content of advertising as those described above, although it is important to note that French state owned radio is prohibited from broadcasting trade mark advertising and is restricted to public interest and public service type advertising. Local advertising is also subject to specific regulation.

## Frequency of advertising – interruptions

Special rules apply to the frequency of advertising and the interruptions of certain programme types on radio and television. These rules vary from service to service (depending on whether the service is State owned or independent, depending on the manner of broadcast, or its particular categorisation, or the method of access, for example, toll paying) and reference should therefore be made to the internal regulations or the broadcasting authorisation agreement of the service in question and any legislation specific to it.

With regard to television services, Arts 15 and 16 of Decree No 92-280 provide, with respect to interruptions, that:

Article 15

... without prejudice to the provisions specifically applicable to each organisation or service, advertising is broadcast on the following conditions:

I    Advertisements are inserted between programmes. However, they may be inserted within programmes, provided that this does not prejudice the integrity and the value of these programmes, that they take into account natural breaks in the programme as well its duration and its nature and that they do not prejudice the rights of interested third parties.

A period of at least 20 minutes must elapse between two successive interruptions within a programme.

II   In the programmes comprised of independent parts, or in sporting programmes, and in recorded events and shows comprising intervals, the advertisements are inserted between these independent parts or during these intervals.

III  The broadcasting of news programmes, religious programmes and children's programmes which have a duration of less than 30 minutes, may not be interrupted by advertising. When they have a duration longer than 30 minutes, the rules in paras I and II apply.

IV   When the broadcast of a film is interrupted by advertising, the interruption may not comprise advertisements exceeding a total duration of six minutes.

Article 16

No publicity may be inserted in religious service broadcasts.

In addition to the rules relating to the frequency of advertising (generally identifying the amount of advertising permitted on an average hourly basis) as set out in the internal rules and broadcasting authorisation agreements, such rules and agreements may also identify the maximum advertising airtime available to any one advertiser.

Particular rules apply to the interruption of cinema or television films on television which may not be subject to more than one advertising interruption without authorisation of the *Conseil Supérieur de l'Audiovisuel*. The advertising interruption may only contain advertisements to the exclusion of any other information or message of any nature, and in particular, previews of forthcoming programmes. Moreover, the broadcasting of a cinema film by certain State owned broadcasting companies and by toll paying television services may not be subject to any advertising interruption.

## CONTENT AND PRODUCT BASED RESTRICTIONS/PROHIBITIONS

We will deal in this section with:

(a) the use of the French language in advertising;

(b) the notions under French law of publicité trompeuse (false or misleading advertising);

(c) the content based restrictions on the advertising of: alcohol, tobacco and pharmaceutical products.

### Use of the French language

It is particularly important to note the restrictions on advertisers in France resulting from the French rules relating to the use of the French language. The provisions are applicable to the marketing in France of goods or services, whatever their origin.

The Law No 94-665 of 4 August 1994 (known as the *Loi Toubon*) sets out the rules relating to the use of the French language. A published ministerial circular of 19 March 1996 provides valuable insight into the interpretation to be made of this text of law.

The law provides for the compulsory use of the French language in all written, spoken and audio-visual advertising. This obligation covers all radio or television advertising, whatever the method of broadcasting used.

The 'naming, offer, presentation, the method of use, the description of and warranty conditions of goods, products or services, invoices and receipts' (Art 2.1) also fall within this requirement and the circular in fact lists in detail those documents and supports which are intended to be covered by the *Loi Toubon* in this respect.

Moreover, 'any inscription or announcement posted or made on the public highway, in a place open to the public or in public transport and intended to inform the public' falls within the requirement to use the French language (Art 3.1).

A corporate name or trade mark registered in a foreign language may be used in advertising. However, references and messages using the said trade mark are to be in the French language, even if such references or messages have been incorporated into and registered within the trade mark.

For the purposes of the application of the *Loi Toubon*, the circular describes 'reference' as the description used to describe the characteristics of a product or service or the generic commonly used to describe such product or service. 'Message' is described as meaning any message to inform the public or to draw to its attention the characteristics of a product or service.

In advertising, the law does, however, allow the use of a foreign language to the extent that the advertisement also contains the text in French in a form which is as readable, audible or intelligible as the foreign language presentation. In connection with this option for advertisers to translate the foreign language, the supervisory authorities will take into account colour, volume, graphics etc, to ensure that the foreign language version is no better understood than the French language version. The translation does not need to be literal, but should reflect the spirit of the original text; nor does it have to be presented in exactly the same way.

Other exceptions to the requirement to use the French language relate to advertising included in programmes for the learning of a foreign language or in those programmes designed for broadcast completely in a foreign language, for example, in foreign television broadcasts received in France. The law does not prevent the use of original film extracts or music in a foreign language in advertising.

Certain exceptions may also apply in the case of expressions which are in common international usage or which result from the application of international treaties. Article 2 is not considered as applying to typical products and specialities with a foreign name, for example, jeans or pizza, or to foreign product names protected by international treaties, for example, Scotch whisky.

Advertising in the written press, which is fully printed in a foreign language, is not covered by the *Loi Toubon*.

Breach of the rules relating to the use of the French language will result in criminal sanctions in the form of fines.

## False and misleading advertising

In addition to the obligation on advertisers and agencies alike to comply with the obligation under French law to respect the principle of decency in advertising, advertising which is false or misleading is prohibited.

The legal definition of *'publicité trompeuse'* (false or misleading advertising) and the rules relating thereto are clearly set out under French law in Arts 121-1 to 121-7 of the French Consumer Code.

The rules relating to *'publicité trompeuse'* are applicable to all forms of advertising media and the notion of advertising is widely interpreted by the courts for this purpose. The provisions of the Consumer Code cover all types of both goods and services and are destined to protect not only consumers, but users and competitors alike.

The Consumer Code describes as prohibited

... any advertising for goods or services comprising, in any form whatsoever, allegations, indications or presentations which are false or of a misleading nature, and which relate to one or several of the following elements: existence, nature, composition, substantial qualities, content of useful substances; type, origin, quantity, method and date of manufacture; properties, price and conditions of sale of the goods and/or services advertised; conditions of use; results that may be expected from their use; motives for or procedures of sale or service; extent of undertakings made by the advertiser; identity, qualifications, or aptitudes of the manufacturer; sellers, promoters or service providers [Art 121-1].

In considering whether the advertisement is false or misleading, the courts will not limit their assessment to the use of the written or spoken word but will include the use by the advertiser of image, graphics, music and colour. Also, the use of asterisks indicating offer restrictions and the form of presentation (size, print type, etc) will be analysed. The use of asterisks has been the subject of recommendations by the BVP. In addition to the comprehensive list of elements on the basis of which an advertisement may be challenged, omissions may also result in an advertisement being held as misleading and hence sanctionable. It is also to be noted that certain words describing products or services are regulated under French law and the use thereof restricted to the meeting of particular criteria by the product or service (for example, 'new', 'light', 'medicine', 'home made'). In general, the use of certain commonplace adjectives is therefore always to be considered in the light of existing French legislation.

French courts will apply the test of the average consumer in considering whether an advertisement is misleading unless the advertisement in question is directly targeted at a particular group of persons or professionals in the same field as the advertiser, in which case the particular vulnerability of the target may be taken into account. Regard will also be had to the humourous or exaggerated nature of the advertisement. Such humour or exaggeration is not liable to sanction if it can be easily identified as such.

An advertisement which is false or of a misleading nature exposes the advertiser to criminal sanctions and possible civil actions for damages. It is only necessary that the advertisement be of a misleading nature, not that it has actually misled. Breach of the Code is instantaneous and is deemed constituted irrespective of attempts to re-establish reality or provide consumers with additional information.

The Code provides that the advertiser on behalf of whom the advertising is made is principally liable for the offence committed. If the advertiser is a legal entity, liability falls upon its management (Art 121-5). The notion of advertiser may also extend to those persons who participated in the advertisement production and within companies, not only the directors, but also employees may be qualified as co-authors of the offence.

Third parties, such as advertising agencies, may be held liable as accomplices in the case of *'publicité trompeuse'*.

For the sanctions to apply, French law does not require that the advertiser have acted in bad faith and to have intentionally misled the public. Advertisers have been held liable by reason of their mere imprudence or negligence, and an advertiser and, indeed, its advertising agency, is required to be particularly vigilant in its advertising strategy.

The sanctions for *'publicité trompeuse'* consist of fines of up to FFr 250,000 and/or a maximum imprisonment of two years. The Code, in Art 121-6, also provides that the maximum amount of the fine may be increased to 50% of the expenses incurred in respect of the advertising campaign in question.

The court may also, prior to giving judgment, deliver an injunction for the ceasing of the advertisement in question until judgment is rendered.

An additional sanction constitutes the obligation to publish the judgment, in the case of conviction, at the expense of the convicted party. Moreover, the court may order the broadcasting of an announcement to rectify the position.

Finally, Art 121-5 of the Code provides that the offence is committed when the advertisement is 'made, received or perceived in France'. Advertisements broadcast or distributed in France from abroad and advertisements made in France and broadcast or distributed abroad may therefore be sanctionable, provided that, on a European level, and in connection with television advertising, the provisions of the *Télévision sans Frontières* Directive are respected.

## Product based restrictions

In addition to those restrictions under French law which result from the media to be used by the advertiser or the message to be conveyed to the public, there are also restrictions with respect to advertising which are dictated by the nature of the product or service in question. This section examines those relating to alcohol, pharmaceutical and tobacco products. It should be noted that restrictions and, in certain cases, prohibitions apply under French law in respect of a variety of products or services, for example with respect to the advertising of lotteries, firearms, baby food products, the provision of legal and financial services and offers of credit and employment. Advertising by the mechanism of price reduction and sale promotions is also regulated.

## *Alcohol*

Advertising of alcohol and related products has undergone extensive change over the last 10 years. Law No 87-588 of 30 July 1987, Law No 91-32 of 10 January 1991, known as the *Loi Evin*, and most recently Law No 94-679 of 8 August 1994 constitute the main framework within which such change has taken place. Today the provisions relating to the advertising of alcohol are codified in the Code des débits de boissons in Arts L 17 and L 18.

Article L 17 of the Code provides that:

Direct or indirect propaganda or advertising of alcoholic beverages, the manufacture and sale of which are not prohibited, is authorised exclusively:

1 In the written press, with the exception of children's publications (as defined in the first paragraph of Art 1 of Law No 49-956 of 16 July 1949).

2 By radio broadcast within specific time slots fixed by decree of the Conseil d'Etat (namely, midnight to 5 pm, with the exception of Wednesdays, when the approved time slots fall between midnight and 7 am).

3 In the form of posters and hoardings; in the form of displays and objects available inside places of specialised sales outlets (for example, licensed sellers of alcoholic beverages, fairs and hotels) upon the conditions set out by decree.

4 By producers, manufacturers, importers, wholesalers, dealers, warehouse merchants, by the sending of messages, marketing circulars, catalogues, brochures, to the extent that these contain only those references set out in Art 18 of the Code and the conditions of sale of the products proposed.

5 By notices on vehicles used for normal beverage deliveries, if the notice carries only the name of the product and the name and address of the manufacturer, agent or warehouse, to the exclusion of all other references.

6 By advertising of traditional fairs dedicated to local alcoholic beverages, under the conditions set out by decree.

7 Of museums, universities, fraternities or wine tasting courses of a traditional nature and of presentations and tastings under the conditions set out by decree.

8 In the form of an offer, whether free of charge or against payment, of objects strictly reserved for the consumption of drinks containing alcohol marked with their name, by producers and manufacturers of such drinks at the time of direct sales of their product to consumers and distributors or during a tourist visit at the place of manufacture.

It should be noted that the restrictions apply to both direct and indirect advertising; indirect advertising is defined by the same Code as including:

... any propaganda or advertising of an organisation, service, activity, product or article other than an alcoholic beverage which by its design, presentation, use of name, trade mark, advertising emblem or other distinctive feature, calls to mind an alcoholic beverage.

In addition, sponsorship of alcoholic beverages is prohibited.

The form and message content of permitted alcoholic beverage advertising is also regulated and the rules relating thereto are set out in Art 18 of the same Code. Such advertising messages are limited to the indication of the degree of alcohol by volume in the beverage, its origin, name and ingredients, the name and address of the manufacturer and agent together with the means of production and sale and mode of consumption. They may also make reference to the production area and any awards received for the product in question.

Packaging of the product may only be reproduced if such reproduction does not infringe the restrictions set out above.

The application by the French courts of the restrictions set out in Art 18 is strict and advertising which uses image or text which exceeds the boundaries of the specific information identified as admissible in the article is generally sanctioned.

In addition, any advertisement, with the exception of commercial circulars to professionals or personalised letters, small posters, tariffs, menus or objects inside specialised sales outlets, must be accompanied by a health warning that alcohol abuse is dangerous to health.

The penalties for breach of the provisions of the Code described above are pecuniary (fines of up to FFr 500,000) and the possible withdrawal, at the court's discretion, of the advertisement in question. The maximum amount of the fine may be increased to 50% of the amount spent on the advertising campaign. Moreover, in the case of repeated breach, the sale of the alcoholic product in question may be banned for one to five years.

There are limited exceptions to the restrictions set out above; the restrictions set out in Arts L 17 and L 18 of the Code:

(a) only apply to alcoholic products containing more than 1.2° of alcohol;

(b) do not apply to the advertisement of a trade mark identical or similar to that of an alcoholic beverage if the product advertised is not an alcoholic beverage and was put onto the market before 1 January 1990 by a business which is legally and financially distinct from any business which manufactures, imports or commercialises an alcoholic beverage. This exception is only tolerated if it does not constitute indirect advertising of an alcoholic beverage;

(c) do not prevent a producer, manufacturer or distributor of alcoholic beverages from carrying out certain types of charitable operations which fall within the definition of 'mécénat' under French law (humanitarian actions, natural and cultural heritage projects). Such entities may make known their participation therein in documentation distributed during the event or on commemorative products, relating to or which are the object of the mécénat. The manner in which such participation may be made known is, however, restricted;

(d) do not generally apply to the retransmissions on French television of foreign sports programmes containing alcohol advertising messages if the foreign State legislation is respected. The CSA has also drawn up guidelines for French television channels with respect to the procedure to be followed concerning retransmissions of sporting events which contain alcohol advertising.

## Pharmaceutical products

EEC Directive 92/28 of 31 March 1992 was adopted into French law by Law No 94-43 of 18 January 1994. The rules relating to the advertising of pharmaceutical products for human consumption are codified in Arts 551 to 556 of the *Code de la Santé Publique* (French Public Health Code) which cover advertising to the public and to professionals.

Advertising of medicines for human consumption to the public is restricted to those medicines which have been approved for market use and have obtained an advertising certificate issued by the appropriate French health authorities (*Agence du médicament*).

Advertising of a medicine to the public is only permitted if the medicine does not require a medical prescription and is not refundable by the health insurance organisations, and if its marketing licence does not impose restrictions on such advertising for public health reasons.

'Advertising' is described by the Code as:

> ... any form of information, including soliciting, prospecting or incitement which refers to the prescription, delivery, sale or consumption of such medicines, with the exception of information dispensed in the context of their profession by pharmacists managing a pharmacy and for use inside such pharmacy.

It must neither be misleading nor prejudice public health. Advertising must be presented objectively, encourage the proper use of the medicines in question and must carry a health message to seek medical advice should symptoms persist.

Advertising of products other than medicines, which are presented as assisting the diagnosis, prevention or treatment of illnesses or complaints relating to health also require an advertising certificate from the health authorities.

Failure to comply with the Code results in pecuniary and injunctive sanctions.

## Tobacco

Direct or indirect propaganda or advertising of tobacco and tobacco products in France is subject to a general prohibition. The legal provisions relating to this prohibition are set out in the French Public Health Code in Art L 355-24 *et seq*.

Tobacco products include those products designed to be smoked, taken, chewed or sucked when they are, even partially, constituted of tobacco and certain products designed to be smoked even if they do not contain tobacco.

The concept of indirect advertising is essentially the same as that described in connection with the restrictions on alcohol advertising, and covers all forms of tobacco related accessories, or indeed organisations which use a tobacco trade mark, even when the organisation in question provides a service or has an activity which is unrelated to the tobacco industry.

All sponsorship operations which have as their object or effect the direct or indirect propaganda or advertising of tobacco or tobacco products are prohibited.

There are limited exceptions to the general prohibition; such prohibition:

(a) does not apply to exterior signs at tobacco sales outlets (known as *carottes*) or to small posters inside such outlets which are not visible from the outside, as long as such signs or posters obey certain rules relating to their form and availability to the public;

(b) is limited with respect to the tobacco trade and professional journals;

(c) does not apply to advertising of products bearing trade marks which are identical or similar to those of tobacco or tobacco products, provided the product represented by the trade mark was put onto the market before 1 January 1990 by a business legally and financially distinct from any business which manufactures, imports or commercialises tobacco or tobacco products. The creation of any legal or financial link (an interpretation which is strict, and recently was held to include the existence of a trade mark licence) between these businesses renders the said exception null and void. Moreover, the exception is only tolerated if it does not constitute indirect advertising for tobacco products;

(d) pursuant to Law No 93-121 of 27 January 1993, does not apply to the televised retransmission of *mechanical* sporting competitions (motorcar and bike racing) which take place in countries where the advertising of tobacco is authorised, until such time as European regulations are passed in respect thereof. Until the passing of such regulations, no action may brought or sanction imposed with respect to such advertising.

The sanctions for breach of the provisions described above take the form of fines and injunctions on the same terms as those with respect to breaches of the legislation relating to alcohol advertising. They may be brought against any person who has participated in the production of the prohibited advertising, including persons who were acting in good faith.

# SPONSORSHIP

In France, a distinction is made, in particular from a tax treatment point of view, between sponsorship activities carried out by a business in the direct interest of its business activity (known as 'parrainage') and those made by a business through, in particular, donations, in the general public interest (known as 'mécénat').

In this summary of French rules relating to advertising, it is intended to deal only with parrainage, and the impact of French regulations on such sponsorship activities. Sponsors and the sponsored alike should consider carefully the nature of their contractual relationship in the context of such sponsorship and the French law implications resulting therefrom. In particular, sponsorship contracts should identify the respective obligations of the parties and the treatment and use of the intellectual and personal property rights which result from the sponsored event or the participation of sponsored individuals. In addition, any specific rules relating to the type of event sponsored should be analysed and any necessary authorisations obtained from trade unions or federations or pursuant to professional codes of practice relating to a sponsored event or personality; this is particularly true with respect to sporting events. It is also imperative that the restrictions relating to media advertising and advertising content should be respected when contemplating any sponsorship activity, for example, alcohol or tobacco.

French law sets out specific rules with respect to radio and television sponsorship. On State owned radio and television, only sponsorship which has an educational, cultural and social character is permitted. It should be noted that the conditions under which such sponsorship may be made will also be dictated by their internal regulations.

## Radio sponsorship

Article 9 of Decree No 87-239 of 6 April 1987 relating to advertising and sponsorship on independent radio stations (terrestrial or satellite) provides that public or private businesses are authorised to finance broadcasts with a view to improving their image and their activities as long as the radio station retains complete control over the programme planning of the broadcast.

The use of the corporate name of the business and reference to distinctive logos usually associated with the business may appear on an ad hoc basis during a sponsored programme.

## Television sponsorship

The rules and restrictions relating to State owned and independent television sponsorship are also set out by Decree No 92-280, which should be read in conjunction with the internal regulations and the broadcast authorisation agreements of the service in question.

The Decree defines sponsorship as 'any contribution by a business or a public or private legal entity, not exercising television broadcasting or audio-visual production activities, to the financing of television programmes in order to promote its name, trade mark, image, activities or productions' (Art 17).

Article 18 of Decree No 92-280 sets out clearly the rules to be respected in the sponsorship of television broadcasts:

I    Their content and programme planning may not be influenced by the sponsor upon conditions capable of causing prejudice to the liability and undermining the editorial independence of the television broadcasting company.

II   They must not incite the purchase or rental of the products or services of the sponsor or a third party and may not include references of a promotional nature specific to such products and services.

III  They must be clearly identified as such at the beginning or the end of the sponsored programme.

     Such identification may be made by making reference to the name of the sponsor, its corporate object, its sector of activity, its trade marks or its image or distinctive marks which are habitually associated with it, such as logo or jingle or signature tune, to the exclusion of any advertising slogan and the presentation of the product itself or its packaging.

     When the sponsorship is designed to finance a game show or competition, the products or services of the sponsor may, provided they are not the subject of an advertising pitch, be delivered free of charge to the participants.

IV  During the sponsored programme and in the trailers, the reference to the sponsor is only possible if such reference is on an ad hoc basis and discrete and is limited to recalling the contribution made by the latter and does not have recourse to other methods of identification than those mentioned in III above.

French television programmes may not be sponsored by businesses whose principal activity is the manufacture or the sale of alcoholic drinks, tobacco products, medicines available on prescription only or the supply of medical treatments available on prescription only. Moreover, news programmes and political information programmes may not be sponsored.

In France, it is increasingly commonplace that companies sponsor televised game shows and competitions or, indeed, co-produce television programmes,such as, for example, the presentation of weather forecasts, or popular television series followed by a competition linked to the episode in question. The CSA has given an indication of its interpretation of the conditions in which such types of sponsorship or co-production may take place, and general guidance as to the level of tolerance acceptable to the CSA with respect to sponsorship can be sought from existing jurisprudence and its published annual reports and circulars.

It is interesting to note that the restrictions preventing certain sectors of activity from advertising on television, as described above, do not apply to sponsorship; hence, television programmes are often sponsored in France by publishing houses and retail chains.

## COMPARATIVE ADVERTISING

French law authorises comparative advertising on the basis of the rules set out in Law No 92-60 of 18 January 1992, the terms of which have been codified in Arts 121-8 to 121-14 of the French Consumer Code.

Comparative advertising is described by the French Consumer Code as 'advertising which compares goods or services by either quoting or using the representation of the trade mark of another, or by quoting or using the representation of the corporate or business name or logo of another' and is only authorised if it is loyal, truthful and is not of a nature to mislead the consumer.

Comparative advertising must be limited to an objective comparison which may only concern essential, significant, pertinent and verifiable (that is, generally quantifiable) characteristics of goods or services of the same nature, available on the market. Whether the characteristics are essential, significant and pertinent will depend on whether it may be considered that they were a sufficiently determining factor in the mind of the consumer. Comparisons which are not objective and, for example, relate to smell or taste, etc, are considered as prohibited.

When the comparison relates to price, it must concern identical products, sold upon the same conditions, and indicate the period during which the prices put forward by the advertiser are in force. Comparative advertising may not use individual or collective opinions or appreciations as an advertising pitch.

Comparative advertising may not, as its principal objective, take advantage of the renown attached to the trade mark of the competitor in question. The comparison may not present products or services as the imitation or replica of products or services carrying a trade mark benefiting from a prior registration.

With respect to those products which benefit from a controlled certificate of origin, comparison is only authorised with products which also benefit from the same certificate.

It is forbidden, under French law, to print comparative statements on packaging, invoices, transport tickets, means of payment, or entry tickets to shows or places open to the public.

An advertiser on behalf of whom the advertisement is broadcast must be in a position to prove the exactness of its allegations, indications and representations. The advertiser is obliged to communicate the comparative advertisement to the competitor with whom the comparison is made. He must do this before broadcast or distribution, leaving enough time to allow cancellation of the advertisement booking, the exact time depending on the advertising media used.

To the extent that the advertisement does not satisfy or comply with the rules set out above, its author will be open to potential actions for unauthorised use of a trade mark and/or unfair competition or, indeed, misleading advertising.

Unfair competition constitutes a method by which, *inter alia*, an advertiser makes denigrating or unfair statements concerning its named competitor or, if unnamed, advertises in such a manner that it leaves no doubt in the consumers' mind that the statement is directed at a particular product or person. Methods designed to create confusion in the mind of the consumer with a view to attracting them away from a competitor, such as imitation, may also result in actions for unfair competition.

The sanctions for illegal comparative advertising are potentially:

(a) damages pursuant to the provisions of the French Civil Code, for prejudice incurred, in particular where the advertising is qualified as an act of unfair competition;

(b) the same criminal sanctions as those set out in the Consumer Code for *publicité trompeuse;*

(c) criminal sanctions for infringement of a third party's trade mark.

The use of advertising in which neither competitor nor the product or service compared is identified does not, in principle, fall within the definition of comparative advertising set out above. In general, such forms of advertising have not been held to constitute unfair competition, unless the competitor or the products can in fact implicitly be identified by reference to slogans or to other recognisable factors or, indeed, by way of elimination given the particular market within which the advertiser and its competitor or competitors operate.

On 6 October 1997, the European Directive 97/55 relating to comparative advertising was adopted and Member States have until April 2000 to harmonise their national legislation.

Although largely similar in concept to the European provisions, French legislation is currently more restrictive and, should total harmonisation be required, will necessitate change.

The main differences between current French legal provisions and the Directive concern the types of goods and services which may be compared, the advertising media available for comparative advertising, comparison based on price and the requirement to notify the competitor before broadcasting the advertisement.

## ADOPTION BY FRANCE OF EUROPEAN DIRECTIVES IN ADVERTISING

France has adopted into its legislation European directives which deal with the subjects discussed above, in the context of advertising.

With respect to misleading advertising, the provisions of the French Consumer Code comply with the minimum provisions set out in Directive 84/450 of 10 September 1984 on this subject. This Directive has been recently amended to include provisions relating to comparative advertising, as discussed above.

Directive 89/552 *'Télévision sans Frontières'* was incorporated into French law by Law No 92-61 of 18 January 1992 and various Decrees in March of the same year concerning television advertising and sponsorship. France adopted rules that are stricter than those provided for by the Directive. Recent European decisions and the adoption of the new version of the Directive in June 1997 confirm that the content of television advertising broadcast in France by a service governed by another European Member State will depend on the rules existing in the said Member State. Consequently, the restrictions on television advertising provided under French law which go beyond the terms of the Directive may not be enforceable by France against such a foreign service unless their application can be justified by the permitted public order exceptions.

In addition, the European Treaty on cross-border television signed in Strasbourg on 5 May 1989 was signed by France on 12 February 1991 and was the subject of Decree No 95-438 of 14 April 1995.

Given the strict terms of French law as far as tobacco advertising is concerned, France is also in line with the *Télévision sans Frontières* Directive with respect to the prohibition of tobacco advertising. However, until European legislation is passed to prohibit such practices, France does permit the retransmission of *mechanical* sporting competitions which take place in countries where tobacco advertising is authorised and which result in the retransmission of such tobacco advertising on French soil (Law No 93-121 of 27 January 1993).

With the passing of European Directive No 98/43 of 6 July 1998, for the harmonisation of tobacco product advertising, French legislation will undergo change.

With respect to those regulations applicable to products and services, France incorporated Directive 92/28 of 31 March 1992 into French law by Decree No 94-19 of 5 January 1994, thus modifying the French Public Health Code.

# CONTRACTUAL RELATIONSHIPS BETWEEN THE ADVERTISER AND THE ADVERTISING AGENCY

## The *Loi Sapin*

In 1993, Law No 93-122 of 29 January 1993, known as the *Loi Sapin*, modified the relationship between advertising agencies, client advertisers and the media, with respect to the purchasing of advertising space in all forms of media, in the quest for improved transparency in the relationship between such parties.

The rules resulting from the *Loi Sapin* are applicable whatever the place of business of the advertising agency if the advertisement is made on behalf of a French business and is principally received on French territory.

The *Loi Sapin* came into force on 31 March 1993 and applies to existing contracts. The law has led to certain difficulties of interpretation and, indeed, explanatory circulars have been drawn up which should be consulted in any reading of the *Loi Sapin*.

First, the *Loi Sapin* provides that 'any purchase of advertising space or of a service having as its object the publication or distribution of printed advertising material, by an intermediary may only be made on behalf of an advertiser and in the context of a *written* agency agreement' (Art 20).

The relationship must therefore take the form of a written contract.

The relationship between the advertising agency and its client was requalified, the agency being considered as the agent of the client when it carries out the purchase of advertising space on its behalf. The obligations of an agent are governed by Arts 1984 *et seq* of the French Civil Code. These rules also apply to contracts for the purchase by the agency on behalf of the advertiser of services comprising the publication or distribution of printed advertising material.

Secondly, the *Loi Sapin* imposes obligations on both the advertising agency and the media to provide information concerning the remuneration for their services.

In addition to the obligation on the agency and media to supply details of their tariffs, the contract for the purchase of advertising space by an advertising agency must set out the conditions of the remuneration of the agent, including the detail of the various services which will be carried out in the context of the contract and identifying the remuneration for each of the said services. The contract must also set out the other services to be provided by the agency independently of the purchase of advertising space, and identify the global remuneration in respect thereof. Moreover, any discount or tariff advantages granted by the media must be set out on the invoice delivered to the advertiser client, and may only be retained by the agency with the written agreement of the client advertiser, in the contract.

In all circumstances, invoices for the purchase of the media space must be delivered by the media directly to the client advertiser, even if the payment thereof is made through the agency as intermediary.

With respect to the remuneration of the agent for the provision of such advertising space purchasing services, the *Loi Sapin* provides that it may not 'receive any payment other than that paid to it by its principal for the remuneration of the exercise of its mandate, nor any remuneration or advantage whatsoever from the seller of the [advertising] space'. Moreover, the provider of media planning services or services for the recommendation of advertising media may not receive any remuneration or advantage whatsoever from the seller of such media space.

In addition, and in the interests of transparency, the law provides that:

Any person who provides advisory services on media planning or services for the recommendation of the advertising media must indicate in its general conditions of sale, the financial links that it holds or that its group holds with the sellers [of advertising space], stating the extent of such shareholdings [Art 24].

Within one month of the broadcast of the advertisement in question, the seller of the advertising space and the agency have an obligation to inform the client advertiser of the conditions under which the services have been rendered. Any modification in the broadcasting conditions gives rise to an obligation on the seller of the space and the agent to warn the client advertiser thereof and obtain his agreement on the said changes.

Breach of the provisions relating to remuneration by the seller of media space or the agent or media planner is sanctioned by fines of FFr 2 m, or FFr 10 m for legal entities. In general, other breaches of the provisions of the *Loi Sapin* result in fines of FFr 200,000, or FFr 1 m for legal entities.

## The contract for creation and advice relating to an advertising campaign

It is common for an agency to combine the role of intermediary for the purchase of advertising space for its client with the services of creation and execution of an advertising campaign.

The terms of such services are not regulated by the *Loi Sapin*. Contractual provisions relating thereto are subject to French common law principles and to industry practice.

In 1961, a standard contract was drawn up for use by the industry, which is still of limited guidance today in drafting and interpreting the contractual relationship between client advertisers and their advertising agency.

It should be noted that the UDA and the AACC have each drawn up forms of advertising contracts for their members, which provide useful commentary and alternative drafting formulae.

In general, the advertising contract will treat the following subjects:

(a) undertakings of the agency towards the advertiser, setting out how the campaign will be prepared, performed and followed through;

(b) undertakings of the advertiser;

(c) invoicing, remuneration and payment;

(d) intellectual property rights;

(e) duration of the relationship and its termination;

(f) applicable law and settlement of disputes.

(a) French case law has shown itself to be increasingly severe in its appreciation of the obligations of the agency towards its client. In particular, it is generally accepted that the agency is bound by an obligation towards its client to ensure compliance of the publicity campaign with the regulations in force, though the commercial success of the campaign in itself is not deemed to be guaranteed by the agency.

The agency must therefore take all precautions to verify that the proposed slogan, image, etc, do not contravene third party intellectual property rights or protected personal rights under French law.

(b) The strict legal framework of advertising, and particularly the rules on misleading advertising and comparative advertising, make an obligation on the client advertiser to provide the agency with all pertinent information relating to its product or service and details of any restrictions resulting from its own professional rules or otherwise, imperative in a contract of this nature.

(c) The method of remuneration should strictly comply with the provisions of the *Loi Sapin* as described above.

(d) With respect to intellectual property rights in the creation of an advertisement, the rules relating to ownership thereof are set out in the French Intellectual Property Code. Article 132-31 provides that 'in the case of an commissioned work used for advertising, the contract between the producer (that is, the advertiser) and the author results, except if provided to the contrary, in the transfer to the producer of the exploitation rights over the work. This is only the case if the contract states the distinct remuneration due for each method of exploitation of the work by reason in particular of the geographical zone, the duration of the exploitation, the importance of the circulation and the nature of the media'.

Generally, contracts provide for this transfer of rights to the advertiser for the purposes of the campaign.

The agency has an obligation to inform the advertiser if any intellectual property rights used, or to be used, for the campaign do not belong to it.

The agency should on behalf of and with the agreement of its client obtain appropriate third party rights, be it copyright or rights relating to the use of image, voice, sound, locations, works of art, etc, of participants, for the reproduction and adaptation of such works for such periods and locations as necessary for the campaign.

The contract should specify how the negotiation in order to obtain such rights will be remunerated and identify the responsibilities of the agency in respect of the obtaining of such rights on behalf of its client.

(e) The contract may take the form of a fixed or non-fixed term contract.

The non-fixed term contract may only be terminated on expiry of a fixed notice period negotiated by the parties. The period accepted by the profession is six months, except in the case of legitimate, serious reasons for termination.

The execution of the notice period does not generally prevent the agency from seeking new clients in spite of any non-competition clause, or the client from instructing a new agency to work on projects upon expiry of the said notice period.

Indemnities may be payable to the agency should the notice period not be respected.

With respect to fixed term contracts, their termination takes place on the date of expiry.

(f) The parties are free to choose the method of resolving disputes. Arbitration proceedings may be chosen in this respect.

Aside from the principal clauses referred to above, common contractual clauses which should also be considered by the parties are those relating to the exclusive nature of the relationship, to non-competition, confidentiality and the respective liabilities of the parties and any permitted limitations thereon.

# PROFESSIONAL RULES OF ADVERTISING AGENCIES

As explained above, the notion of *'Agences conseils en communication'* comprises various types of agency and the rules relating thereto are specific to the type of media advice given thereby.

A translation of those professional rules relating to *'Agences conseils en publicité'* (advertising agencies) is set out below:

**Professional rules: January 1993**

**DEFINITION OF ADVERTISING AGENCY AND THE MISSION OF *'AGENCE CONSEIL'*.**

*Role of advertising agencies*

The essential functions that an advertising agency must fulfil are four in number. They are distinct, indispensable and constitute the qualification as an 'advertising agency'. The capacity to assume them is closely linked to the professional skills of the individuals who run the agency and to the organisation thereof.

(a) *Research and programmes*

This function implies an in-depth knowledge and constant practice of the methods of marketing which are necessary for designing an advertising campaign. It guarantees to the advertiser the aptitude of the agency to analyse its commercial policy, to translate it in terms of advertising strategy and, where possible, to control the efficiency thereof.

(b) *Conception and creation*

This function includes:

- the general conception of the campaign and themes;
- the search for an advertising pitch and its expression by all graphic, script, sound and audio-visual means, etc;
- the production of basic material communication tools: documents for the preparation of blocks, films, on-air production, etc.

(c) *Implementation*

The finalisation of the plan drawn up by the agency and its production.

This function combines the following tasks:

- define the means in detail in light of the campaign and budgets;
- organise and administer their implementation;
- co-ordinate the liaison between advertiser and the agency.

(d) *Distribution and execution*

This function comprises three phases of activity:

- the in-depth and up to date knowledge of the advertising media;

- the purchase of time and space;
- the execution: orders and supervision as main contractor or for and on behalf of the advertiser.

Finally with respect to the public, by supervising that the messages are clear and define the product in circumstances such that it be informed as accurately as possible and may freely exercise its choice.

The above remarks show the range of skills which the advertiser must expect from its agency, to be carried out while respecting the consumer.

The age of 'simplistic advertising' is over. In a market characterised by rising demand, one could be content with approximations and improvisations of which certain were, however, brilliant. In the contemporary market, influenced by an offer in perpetual competition (national and international), the producer, obliged himself to reconsider permanently the quality of the image of its products, must be more and more attentive to the quality and efficiency of its advertising.

For their part, the agencies, concerned for the reputation of their profession and conscious of their liabilities, may no longer allow their function to be caricatured by pseudo-professionals unsuitable for the exercise of an activity which they unduly claim as their own.

In reality, by reason of the evolution of the techniques of investigation of the market and the setting up of more and more precise controls that advertising must develop, put in place and master, as well as by reason of the liabilities of all nature (and not only in the domains referred to) that it assumes, it has become a complex profession.

It is therefore indispensable, in the interest of all, that it be exercised by skilled persons who are recognised as such.

It is to this end that both the characteristics of the agency worthy of such name and the duties that it must assume vis à vis client advertisers, while respecting the consumer have been defined.

## CHARACTERISTICS OF THE ADVERTISING AGENCY

### 1 The qualification

(a) *Guarantee of qualification*

The advertising agency must offer essential guarantees in order to accomplish the four functions listed above.

Its qualification must depend on the individual skills of one or several persons whose abilities result both:

(a) from the possession of a recognised diploma conferring the necessary qualifications;

(b) from an acquired experience justified by the presentation of a comprehensive file.

The qualification thus defined will be the object of regular checks.

(b) *The service*

To fulfil its role as defined above, the advertising agency must be capable of assuming at least the four essential functions of the agency:

- commercial – marketing;
- creation and execution;
- media (strategy – media planning – purchase of advertising space)
- research.

This is the minimum necessary for the carrying out of the tasks which fall to an agency. These services may form an integral part of the agency. If its internal structure does not cover all these services, the agency must nevertheless be the main contractor and procure the carrying out under its liability and control of the tasks that it does not execute itself:

- must use qualified staff, who specialise in the various tasks defined above;
- must, moreover, be capable of acting as main contractor in dealing with companies specialised for the sales promotions or public relations campaigns. It is a known fact, that it is beneficial to interweave all the activities designed to interest consumers.

## 2 Conditions of exercise

(a) *Nature of the activity*

The activity defined above must be the exclusive activity of the advertising agency and it is indispensable for the qualification as an 'advertising agency'.

(b) *Independence*

In accordance with international rules and in particular those drawn up by the International Chamber of Commerce, the advertising agency must be independent both with regard to its clients and its suppliers:

- vis à vis its clients: its independence guarantees the objectivity of its advice. It may therefore only claim the qualification to the extent that it does not belong to an advertiser or a group of advertisers;
- vis à vis its suppliers: this objectivity, which characterises the service rendered to the client advertiser requires the advertising agency not to combine the functions described above with the activities of media sales for advertising or generally with the representation of suppliers.

## 3 Remuneration

Advertising agencies are remunerated either by commission or by fee, or a combination of the two.

## 4 Speculative campaigns

- The AACC is opposed to the principle of speculative campaigns; the choice of agency should be made on the basis of criteria including professional, sociological, psychological information and experience and availability, going beyond the mere production of a proposal and artwork.

- By definition, a speculative campaign is not a simple quotation for services but a service rendered necessarily at the request of the advertiser who must pay the cost thereof.

- The agency members of the AACC and their subsidiaries should, therefore, request remuneration of any speculative campaign at a reasonable price account given of the service provided.

- The advertiser cannot, in any event, use the ideas and realisations whether visual or written of the agency from whom it sought advice in the context of a speculative campaign and which has not been retained by it, by application in particular of the law of 11 March 1957 completed by the law of 3 July 1985, concerning literary and artistic property rights.

## DUTIES

The exercise of the profession of advertising agency results in the obligation to respect the rules set out in the preceding chapter but also the presentation of a request for qualification results automatically in the prior undertaking to respect a certain number of duties with regard to the profession as a whole, to advertisers and to consumers.

These duties concern in particular:

1 the responsibility for and the confidentiality of information entrusted to it by the advertiser;

2 intellectual and material independence;

3 the respect of fair practice with regard to the consumer, in particular, those defined in the Code of fair practice in advertising by the International Chamber of Commerce, in addition to the legal and regulatory rules concerning particular domains and advertising, to truthfulness and the decency of the messages;

4 the respect of the professional disciplines and duties imposed by the laws and regulations as well as those for the defence of the honour and dignity of the moral interests of the profession;

5 membership of the BVP and compliance with its decisions;

6 the demonstration of the value and the utility of advertising from an economic point of view both with respect to individual interests entrusted to it and in the general interest, which may not be disassociated one from the other;

7 it must take into account the share of responsibility that the business incurs in the advertising campaign as a whole as a result of its effect on the psychology and behaviour of individuals, especially when it is addressed to children and, in so doing, undertake to apply the 'advertising charter' which is applicable to it;

8 the respect of the fundamental liberty of the individual, the dignity of the human person and the aspirations of development of each person while respecting third parties, in the context of the motivations put forward by the business.

# USEFUL ADDRESSES

Bureau de Vérification de la Publicité (BVP)
5 rue Jean Mermoz
75008 Paris
Tel: + 01 43 59 89 45

International Chamber of Commerce
Cour Albert 1er
75008 Paris

Association des Agences Conseils en Communication (AACC)
40 boulevard Malesherbes
75008 Paris
Tel: + 01 47 42 13 42

Conseil Supérieur de l'Audiovisuel (CSA)
39, quai André Citroën
75015 Paris

Union des Annonceurs
53 avenue Victor Hugo
75116 Paris
Tel: + 01 45 00 79 10

Direction Générale de la Concurrence, de la Consommation
et de la Repression des Fraudes
59 boulevard Vincent Auriol
75013 Paris

Centre d'Etudes des Supports de Publicité (CESP)
32 avenue Georges Mandel
75116 Paris
Tel: + 01 45 53 22 10

## CHAPTER 7

# GERMANY

*Ralf Dresel*

## INTRODUCTION

In Germany, there is no single legal area called 'advertising law'. The rules of law which are applicable to advertising are essentially those of competition law, which in turn is extensively characterised by judicial development by means of the interpretation of general statutory clauses and flexible legal terms (and therefore also case law); furthermore, public law regulations are, at least in the area of public television stations, of increasing importance.

Due to the differences in the applicable legal rules, this area is very complex. It is, therefore, not possible to deal exhaustively with advertising law. The following passages can only offer an introduction.

## GERMAN ADVERTISING LAW

### Definition of advertising

The subject of advertising law covers the marketing of goods or services through the use of commercial advertising in all areas of the media. Due to the fact that the EC Directive on Misleading Advertising of 1984 is in force, the definition contained therein should be used.

Accordingly, advertising is every expression made in practice of trade, industry or of a profession with the goal of promoting the sale of goods or the provision of services, including immovable property, rights and obligations (Art 2(1) of the EC Directive on Misleading Advertising of 1984).

Alongside this, the law concerning marketing measures such as sales promotion by special events, prize competitions, gifts and discounts also counts as advertising law in Germany, as do professional regulations; for example, the specific practice guidelines of professionals such as lawyers and doctors.

# Freedom of advertising and its limits

Most importantly, freedom of advertising exists in Germany. This freedom is derived from the basic rights of the Constitution.

The applicable articles of the Constitution here are, in particular, Arts 2, 5, 12 and 14.

## Freedom of speech: Art 5 of the Constitution

Covering, as it does, freedom of expression and information, Art 5(1)(1) of the Constitution also extends to commercial advertising. Article 5(1)(2) protects the freedom of the press and extends to the advertisement sections of newspapers and magazines.

Both can be restricted by statute and must be considered in the light of the interpretation of other statutes. The object of this is to find a reasonable balance between freedom of expression and the interests put forward for its restriction. This is to be within the framework of the legislation and achieved by the balancing of legally protected rights by the judge.

## Professional and entrepreneurial freedom: Arts 2, 12 and 14 of the Constitution

Advertising law is a typical 'regulation for the practice of a profession' in the sense of Art 12 of the Constitution, which regulates professional freedom and is only applicable to German nationals; Art 2 of the Constitution is valid for foreigners in this case (general freedom to trade). This concerns the so called entrepreneurial freedom present in Arts 12 and 14 of the Constitution. Intervention with professional freedom (and therefore also with entrepreneurial freedom) must always be proportionate; along with this, the public interest in a regulation and the interest of the advertiser must also be precisely balanced.

According to the modern view, expressions made within the framework of commercial advertising (so called commercial speech) come under the influence of Art 10 of the European Convention on Human Rights (ECHR) which regulates the freedom of speech. However, restricting regulations in the area of the expression of political opinion are possible: see Art 10(2) of the ECHR.

# Advertising law and competition law

## Principles

In Germany, advertising law is widely understood to be part of competition law. The restraints to advertising set by the law exist for the interest of other market participants, consumers and the general public. One advertiser's restriction is another's protection of his market position. Also part of advertising law is the protection of advertisers from the imitation of their advertisement by others, and from advertising which interferes with the success of their own advertisement. The right to advertise is designed to guarantee fair competition in the fight to win market share.

## Characteristics

The Act Against Unfair Competition (*Gesetz gegen den unlauteren Wettbewerb* (UWG)) exists in Germany to guarantee this fair competition. In Arts 1–8, particular forms of advertising are regulated more closely. Through this, either the circumstances under which the businessman advertises (for example, clearance sale) or the form of advertising used (for example, pyramid advertising) are taken into account. What is important is that the possibility of sanction in both civil and criminal law is established. In addition to the general clause in Art 1 of the UWG, both supplementary and special statutes are to be applied in the decision as to whether a particular case is unconscionable. For example, the professional regulations of lawyers and doctors, or the medicine advertising law.

# Characteristics of advertisements in particular media

## Advertisements in newspapers and magazines

One of the main problems arising in the area of advertising in newspapers and magazines is 'editorial advertisements' (disguised advertising). In this situation, the danger is that the customer does not realise that the basis of the promotion is not a real and neutral evaluation of the product's qualities.

For this reason, there is a principle which dictates a clear separation between the advertising and editorial sections of a newspaper or magazine; this is mostly achieved through the use of the indication *Werbung* or *Anzeige* before the beginning of the advertisement text. It is important that even the average reader, or one who is skimming through, must be able to recognise that a passage is an advertisement.

By the end of the 1950s, the Central Committee of the Advertising Industry (*Zentralausschuß der Werbewirtschaft* (ZAW)) had already produced guidelines for the appearance of 'editorial-like' announcements. Groups from the media, advertising agencies and others have organised themselves under the umbrella grouping of the Central Committee of the Advertising Industry and have bound themselves to a code of practice, to which they adhere voluntarily.

Since legislative competence in relation to the press is in principle a matter for the individual States in Germany, and only in exceptional cases may regulations be made on a national level, the respective State press laws must also always be complied with. There are differences between the individual States. When an advertisement is produced, it is the laws of the place of production (for example, the place of printing) which are to be applied. When an advertisement is published, it is the laws of the place where the advertisement has its effect (for example, the place of distribution) which are to be applied.

In the case of an infringement, the publisher, responsible editor and any other collaborator who in some way wilfully or negligently contributed to the advertisement can be sued.

## Radio and TV advertising

The principles of advertising in newspapers and magazines are similarly valid here. The German Association of Broadcasting Organisations (*Arbeitsgemeinschaft der Rundfunkanstalten Deutschlands* (ARD)) adopted its own guidelines for advertising, corresponding to those of the Central Committee of the Advertising Industry, for the implementation of a division of programmes and advertisements and for sponsoring (the current version is that of 24 January 1992).

Furthermore, the so called 8 o'clock advertising watershed is, in principle, still in force for publicly regulated broadcasters. This prohibits advertisements after 8 pm on publicly regulated stations. However, various new forms of advertising (programme sponsoring) are increasingly breaking through this ruling. In the near future, a general abolition of the watershed is to be expected, due to the advertising practices of the private radio stations which have been licensed since the mid 1980s.

## Telephone, telex and fax advertising

In principle, it is not permitted for those running a business to advertise using private telephone lines. The special protection in the private sphere requires that – as for junk mail and handbill advertising – private individuals can have this kind of advertising stopped in order to avoid irritation. This legislation was also extended to the commercial area; it is not permitted to advertise in this manner to businessmen who have no obvious direct professional interest in receiving the call. The fact that the receivers of advertising may, in some way, have made their address and telephone number public does not mean the call is permitted. Basically, explicit agreement is required from an individual businessman regarding which calls of professional interest he will accept. An advertiser may not send a commercial recipient promotional material which is outside his stated field of activity.

This jurisprudence is now being applied to the fax machine. In particular, an advertiser is not permitted to block a business fax line with advertisements. In individual cases, however, it is possible that the transmission was agreed to implicitly or explicitly.

### Letterbox and handbill advertising

In principle, any businessman is allowed to draw attention to his service or product by means of handbills and letterbox leaflets. In reality, this method of advertising has increased to such an extent that the courts have had to define limits of permissibility.

In more recent law, reference is made to the personal right to self-determination stemming from Art 2 of the Constitution. Every businessman has the responsibility not to allow advertising handouts to penetrate the private sphere of the unwilling consumer. Printed papers or samples of merchandise mailed in bulk are also subject to this.

## Content requirements of advertisements

### Offences against common decency

*Comparative advertising*

In Germany, there is no general prohibition of comparative advertising. Although this has not always been the case in German jurisprudence, the Federal Court of Justice stressed it in an important judgment based on an EC Directive in 1998. Guided by the General Clause of Art 1 of the UWG, it must be decided in each specific case whether there exists a more legitimate comparison of services and products. A competition offence occurs when an advertisement contains an untrue belittling of competitors (either singly or as a group).

As is established in the law, the advantages of the advertiser's own product may be presented comprehensively in the advertisement only to satisfy the general public's need for information. For this, the advertiser's older products may also be used as a point of comparison. The advertising slogan must always remain truthful.

It is not permitted for the advertiser to take advantage of the good reputation of a competitor, nor to belittle the competitor's product in a critical manner. A sweeping devaluation is not permitted.

A comparison which centres on the different manufacturing processes or types of product used by advertiser and competitor is permitted if it remains neutral, abstract and also true.

*Advertisements inducing fear, emotion or a psychological need to purchase*

Fear advertising gives rise to an impression of threat in the targeted persons. This is, understandably, not permitted. Even when the advertising is orientated around facts, it is not permitted to stir up fears through the use of these facts.

The situation is similar for emotional advertising, which can trigger off both positive and, in the case of so called shock advertising, negative emotions. In case law, this problem occurs mostly about advertising which is connected to fundraising campaigns, which factually have nothing to do with the advertised product; here, the readiness of the target group to help is exploited to increase the sales of a product.

The illegitimate psychological inducement to purchase is defined as the exercising by the advertiser of a non-factual influence over the customer which is over and above the normal amount of influence put on potential purchasers. In doing this, the businessman trades anti-competitively, failing to conform with the market conditions regarding psychological sales strategy. Usually, the moral feeling arises of being obliged to purchase.

*Health advertising*

Health is one of the most important legally protected rights. In an economic sense, the medication and health care market is very interesting. In advertising law health, therefore, also plays a significant and special role.

As far as Art 1 of the UWG is concerned, the Pharmaceutical Products Advertising Act, which contains particular points of prohibition, also applies in this area. Most of the offences against the Pharmaceutical Products Advertising Act also give rise to offences against Art 1 of the UWG. Articles 3 and 11 of the Pharmaceutical Products Advertising Act are of particular importance, containing the regulations concerning misleading advertisements and advertisements targeted outside of specialist circles, that is, non-pharmacists and non-doctors, for which special requirements apply. Only product advertising measures as such fall within the competence of the Pharmaceutical Products Advertising Act and not, for example, image advertising from pharmaceutical companies.

*Misrepresentation of origin: imitation*

This misrepresentation can also be brought about through advertising.

Any person involved in business can make use of specific layouts of products which are not under special legal protection, be they of a technical or non-technical type.

In the technical area, special rights are essentially those deriving from the patent and the utility model and in the non-technical area, those from the registered design and the copyright.

The freedom to copy infringes on these rights if, in the marketplace, the imitated product leads to an avoidable misrepresentation regarding origin. The basic presupposition is the so called competitive individuality of the product. In the non-technical area, this refers to the special characteristic of the layout, for example, the design. In the technical area, it is when the product exceeds that which is the current state of the art.

It does not have to give rise to a perception of a special quality for the consumer. However, the advertiser must be guilty of having caused the misrepresentation, that is, it could have reasonably been avoided. The advertiser must, for example, make reference to the 'mother product'.

### Advertising through laymen

Often, laymen are used in advertising in order to promote products. This is done by using bonuses to encourage existing clients to canvass new clients. This is only permitted as long as the advertising is not otherwise illegal. The problem is especially evident with advertising bonuses which have a substantial value, or when the consumer does not know that the lay advertiser is receiving valuable bonuses. What is more, as soon as this method of advertising achieves a large circulation, it can become an irritation to the population and therefore be evaluated as being contrary to public policy.

### Illegal competitive advance

In advertising law, the topic of illegal competitive advance is of the utmost importance.

This topic especially concerns product identification. In the areas of pharmaceuticals, medicines and cosmetics, statutory provisions regulate what information about the product may and must be passed on to the ultimate consumer and therefore to the targeted advertising group and how this must be undertaken. Essentially, the regulations here are the Advertisement of Medicines Act (*Heilmittelwerbegesetz*), the Pharmaceuticals Regulation and the Cosmetics Regulation.

### Exploitation of reputation

It is not permitted for an advertiser to exploit the reputation of his competitor in order to market his product more successfully. In such cases, it is important to distinguish between hidden and open support of the positive reputation of the other. In case of open support, the advertiser makes reference to the product names of the competition in order to utilise the consumer's perception of the competing product's particular qualities.

Hidden support concerns 'scrounging' from the reputation of another. Without making any direct reference, the advertiser creates an advertising situation which implies a non-existent connection with the reputable product of another manufacturer. As this connection does not exist in reality, it is not permitted to advertise in this way.

Since 1 January 1995, the German Brand Law has been in force. This is a result of a harmonisation of the legal regulations of the EU Member States, as prescribed by EU law. The owner of a known brand or business logo can now defend himself against illicit exploitation of his reputation more strongly than under the law which existed up until now, namely, by means of a compensation or injunction claim or a claim for cancellation.

*Tie-in transactions, introductory offers*

Jurisprudence differentiates between open and concealed tie-in transactions. An open tie-in transaction occurs as soon as the relevant market can recognise the individual prices of the connected goods by reason of the pricing given on the product's packaging. The tie-in transaction is concealed when the trader only shows a joint price.

The criterion for assessing the legality of a tie-in transaction is whether the connected products are related or not. A non-factual influence on the consumer is more likely when unrelated products are tied in together than when related products are linked. (It is possible that such a transaction could also come under the Regulation on Bonuses. This will, however, not be considered here.)

*Value advertising*

Alongside advertising using pictures and words exists the possibility of gift advertising, for example, by giving away items, prize draws and prize competitions and/or product samples. Specifically, value advertising is regulated by the Regulation on Bonuses and the Discount Act.

Product testing is allowed, providing that a new product is being introduced onto the market. A normal commercial quantity may be distributed amongst consumers. It is essential that the testing purpose is obvious and that no obligation to purchase is implied.

Gifts of money to the ultimate consumer are, for example, also unconscionable, since this subjects the ultimate consumer to a strong stimulus to buy. The parameters of permitted attention-drawing advertising are exceeded. In this manner, the purchaser is forced into buying.

*Misleading advertisements according to Arts 3, 4 and 5 of the UWG*

Advertising information can be misleading if it is directed at the general public and a not inconsiderable section of the general public connects all images with the untrue information.

*Composition*

Composition is the main topic in this area. Information concerning composition is misleading:

(a) if the actual material of an article does not agree with the given material specification of the article;

(b) if the material specification is nominated by statute, the relevant market knows the statutory nomination and therefore assumes a specification conforming to the statute, but which does not apply to the advertised article;

(c) if the article is advertised with statements regarding its effectiveness which are actually incorrect;

(d) a branded product is feigned in order to exploit a predominant brand image with regard to branded goods in the market, without the prerequisites for a branded article existing.

Important statutory regulations here are the Specification of Raw Materials Act, Description of Foodstuffs Regulation, the Pharmaceutical Products Act and the Medicines Advertising Act.

If a trader advertises using a brand name, he must make it clear whether it is a dealer's or a producer's brand name. If the market assumes that it is a producer's brand name, despite the fact that it is actually a trader's brand name, the advertisement is misleading. Advertising with the producer's brand name may only occur if the goods actually originate from a specific production point and are of constant or continually improving quality.

For pharmaceutical products, the properties which the product is advertised as having must actually exist. If a product is presented as being healthier than the competitor's product, it must be healthier. Examples of this are diet and slimming products, amongst others.

In Germany, a product may not be advertised with a guarantee which does not have an expiry date, since the statutory regulations do not allow this.

Anybody who deals in imported motor cars must, for example, also point out the considerable ways in which the production and equipment characteristics of the imported car vary from those of the same car produced in Germany.

*Company or geographical specifications of origin*

The specifications of origin are problematic (for example, Lübeck Marzipan, Dresden Stollen, Dresden Poppy Slice, Nürnberger Bratwürste, Worcester Sauce, etc). The specifications of origin must also comply with the high regard of the advertisement's target group. If this is unclear in a dispute, the judge must carry out an opinion poll in order to investigate the accepted standards in the relevant market segment since, after a certain length of time, the specification of origin is often seen as specification of quality. Therefore, there is an exactly defined amount of prescribed ingredients contained in a Dresden Stollen.

If the advertiser uses foreign language terms or decorates his product in the colours of foreign flags, it is to be assumed, as a rule, that a not insignificant section of the audience will make a connection between the data and the origin of the product which will cause them to be misled if it is not the case.

If there is misleading information about the company origin, the following texts contain special statutory regulations: Art 12 of the Civil Code (general right to bear a name), Art 5 of the Trade Mark Act (business name) and Art 15 of the Trade Mark Act (exclusive right of the owner of a business name, injunction and compensation claim). In the appropriate cases in which these are not effective, Art 3 of the UWG is applicable.

## Selected special regulations

### Producer and wholesaler advertising: Art 6a of the UWG

So that there is no actual danger of the ultimate consumer being misled, the advertiser must, in principle, refrain from making reference to his capacity as producer or wholesaler. Exceptions to this are regulated in Art 6(1)(1)–(3) and 6(2) of the UWG.

The advertiser may only make reference to his capacity as wholesaler or producer if he either sells exclusively to the ultimate consumer when the ultimate consumer actually receives the commercial retailers' or commercial consumers' clearance price or when he makes reference to the fact that prices to the ultimate consumer are actually higher than to the commercial retailer or commercial consumer.

### Special events: Art 7 of the UWG

Special events in the retail trade are prohibited if they are not end of season sales, regulated by Art 7(3)(3) of the UWG, or jubilee sales regulated by Art 7(3)(2) of the UWG. The announcement of this kind of sales event is also anti-competitive.

A special event is not permitted if it is not just single, defined articles being advertised, but whole groups of articles or a variety of goods which are to be sold. In this case, the consumer believes that he has discovered a special chance which he must take immediately as it will not be offered to him again. He is therefore under excessive pressure.

Special events are allowed if a sufficient quantity of the advertised goods are available; exaggerated and therefore improper attraction to the customer must be avoided, however.

Generally, special events are permitted providing that they are end of season or jubilee sales (for example, July and January sales).

### Discount Act

Despite intense political debate, the Discount Act is still in force in Germany. This statute regulates the discounting of prices for certain persons and certain occasions.

The Discount Act differentiates between cash purchase discounts, special discounts, quantity discounts and loyalty discounts on branded goods.

A discount is created when a businessman offers the ultimate consumer two prices, namely, the normal or general price and the exceptional or special price. Whether or not two different prices are really been offered by the businessman is defined, as is the case throughout advertising law, by the opinion of the market. A discount exists if the ultimate consumer has the impression that the businessman is guaranteeing him an exceptional price.

## Cross-border advertising and international private law

In the judicial assessment of cross-border advertising, as is always the case in cross-border matters, at least two national legal systems are always to be considered. Which legal system is to be relied on must be decided through the rules governing the conflict of laws. Most States have their own rules on this.

In the area of competition law under which advertising in Germany mostly falls, there are no statutory regulations concerning the conflict of laws. In the meantime, however, it has been recognised in jurisprudence that, reasonably, it must connect to the place where the conflict of interests occurs. This means that for an advertisement which is based on English contract law, which appears in Germany in a newspaper printed in England, and which causes problems in German competition law, it is German law which is to be used for the judging of the case. According to the general rules of jurisdiction, and since the damage occurred in Germany, a German court would, as a rule, be geographically competent.

In this way, the law in Germany corresponds to the international regulations which have, in the meantime, manifested themselves and are usually connected to the advertisement's area of effectiveness, and find their validity in the legal system of the market in which the advertisement appears.

# INTERNATIONAL LAW/EUROPEAN LAW

Advertising law in Germany is extensively competition law and is supported by the General Clause of Art 1 of the UWG. With reference to this general clause, international regulations also find application, such as EC Directives, which can themselves have direct applicability, provided that they are sufficiently definite, contain individual claims, and that the implementation deadline has expired. (Nevertheless, in April 1998 the Federal Court of Justice applied an EC Directive indirectly, even though its implementation date is not until 1 July 2000.) Furthermore, within the framework of judicial interpretation of the law, European law as a whole must always be followed.

An actual example of this is the prohibition of advertisements for tobacco products decided by the Council of the European Union in June 1998. The order says that any kind of advertisement for tobacco products in any way will be illegal. Being an order, it will be applicable to the national law systems of the EU Member States directly, without any implementation. Germany voted against the prohibitive rule and took the matter to the European Court of Justice in September 1998.

Even if the Federal Republic of Germany has not adopted a specific advertising statute on the basis of international or European law, the regulations of the European Council and the European Community find application. (For example, the Directives concerning Misleading Advertising and Comparative Advertising.)

The rules of the ECHR are directly applicable in German law, since every citizen involved in a legal dispute can call on them and the judges are compelled to follow the rules in their application of the law.

# LAYOUT OF AN ADVERTISING CONTRACT

Due to the extensive private autonomy in German law, the layout of the advertising contract complies to the greatest possible extent with the requirements of the Contracting Parties. For this reason, the following specimen contract can only be offered as an example of one type of layout. However, as with every other contract, the parties should always observe the following points:

(a) the parties and the service are to be described or nominated in as detailed a manner as possible;

(b) the charge for the service, method of payment and possibly the bank account details are to be included;

(c) if the Contracting Parties are of differing nationalities, the law to which the contractual relationship is subject should be established (jurisdiction could also be agreed upon);

(d) without exception in a long term contract, the opportunity to give notice or set the contract aside and the conditions therefor should be complied with.

The specimen contract below deals with a fictitious contract layout for a newspaper advertisement, which is still the most common kind of advertisement. Since it makes little economic sense to advertise only once, the advert will appear 10 times. In this case, a choice of law is unnecessary, since the Contracting Parties are a German publisher and a company with its registered office in Germany, and the advert is to appear in Germany.

**CONTRACT**

Gundermann and Sons Building Limited

Managing Director Herr Manfred Müller

Burgstraße 4

76895 Millerstadt

and

Millerstädter News – Heiermann Publications Limited

Managing Director Frau Anna Elster

Druckstraße 67

76895 Millerstadt

conclude the following contract:

1   In the editions of the Millerstädter News dated 1 April 1996, 8 April 1996, 15 April 1996, 22 April 1996, 29 April 1996, 4 May 1996, 11 May 1996, 14 May 1996, 15 May 1996 and 17 May 1996, the half-page advertisement for Gundermann and Sons will appear on page five.

2   At the latest, a print copy of the advertisement is to be with the publishers two working days before it is to appear. At the signing of this contract Gundermann and Sons received information concerning the format of the advertisement.

3   The fee for the printing and publishing of the advertisement is payable upon publication of each respective advertisement and is to be transferred at the latest on the day of publication into account 12345 of the Millerstadt Savings Bank, sort code 56780090.

4   The amount of the fee is in accordance with Advertisement Price List 4 dated 14 December 1995. A copy of this has been given to Gundermann and Sons.

5   This contract can be terminated by either party without reason by giving a two week period of notice via registered post with notification of delivery.

[Signatures of the parties]

[Place and date of conclusion of contract]

# FUTURE DEVELOPMENTS

Due to the strictly regulated health advertising law and alongside the order concerning the prohibition of tobacco products advertising passed by the Council of the European Union, the German Government is working on regulations concerning alcoholic products.

There is no doubt that the rules made by the European institutions (European Union, European Council) are becoming increasingly important (as stressed above, p 458). As a result of the far-reaching integration of the European markets and the standardisation or harmonisation of the industrial protective regulations, the national governments will increasingly be taking a back seat.

However, it is unlikely that Germany will soon have its own advertising statute. The established system has proven its worth and through its generality also shows itself to be adaptable to newer marketing methods. Competition therefore has a standardised legal footing which definitely increases legal certainty and legal clarity for businessmen in Germany.

# USEFUL ADDRESSES

The Central Association of the German Advertising Industry (Central Committee of the Advertising Industry). (The Advertising Council (*Werberat*) is the Committee's institution responsible as self-control organ and complaints body.) It can be contacted at the following address:

Zentralverband der Deutschen Werbewirtschaft ZAW
Villichgasse 17
D-53177 Bonn
Deutschland
Tel: + 49 228 82092 0

The German Association of Broadcasting Organisations for Advertising Media and Marketing (ARD-Werbung Media Marketing) can be contacted on the following number: Tel: + 49 8131 58150

The address for the Central Office for the Combat of Unfair Competition is as follows:

Zentrale zur Bekämpfung unlauteren Wettbewerbs
Karlstraße 36
D-80333 München
Deutschland
Tel: + 49 89 592219

Also, all German and International Chambers of Commerce.

## CHAPTER 8

# GREECE

*Takis G Kommatas and Vassilis S Constandinides*

## INTRODUCTION

Advertising is treated as a special form of science and advertising studies were added to Greek universities in the early 1990s. Given the media's progress and evolution and their power to influence people, Greek law was obliged to treat the media as a special sector of social life, introducing rules, restrictions and conditions to their function.

More specifically, Greek law has recently adopted certain rules and restrictions referring mainly to the advertising message as a product of the advertising process, but the approach of the law may be characterised as a 'negative definition' of advertising. This means that the majority of legal provisions referring to advertising treat this last as a 'means' that might harm the public interest and not as a 'good' or a 'right' itself.

## DEFINITION OF ADVERTISING

### The 'positive' side of advertising – advertising as an intellectual right and its protection

The most general definition of advertising in Greek Law is the one included in para 1 of Art 9 of Law 2251/1994 (protection of the consumer) according to which:

> Advertising is any announcement made into the frame of trade, business, craft or professional activity in order to promote the supply of goods or services.

The above definition excludes from advertising announcements or messages made outside the framework of the above-mentioned activities (humanitarian, artistic, cultural, etc) probably because those activities may not be considered as 'harmful' to the public or the consumer.

The right to advertise and/or to be advertised is founded in Arts 5 (right to freedom of personality), 14 (freedom of press and opinion) and 16 (freedom of art) of the Greek Constitution. Based on the above, all persons (not only Greek citizens) have the right to develop freely their personality and to express their thoughts, ideas or messages 'under the conditions of the law'.

Freedom of advertising is considered as a basic element of financial freedom. This freedom refers mainly to commercial advertising, which aims to influence the recipients of the message to buy the advertised goods or to make use of the advertised services. Under the above definition, advertising includes the freedom of advertised persons to advertise their products or services and also the freedom for the performance of the profession of the advertiser.[1]

The advertising message has a further protection if it may be considered as a product of intellectual property, more specifically if said message fulfils the requirements of Law 2121/1993 on the protection of intellectual property. According to the provisions of Art 2 of Law 2121/1993, 'work' – the product of intellectual property protected by the Law – covers every original intellectual creation (work) of literature, art or science and especially written or oral texts, musical compositions (text/lyrics included or not), choreographic, audio-visual works, etc.

The one and only condition required by the Law, to define an audio-visual, written or musical work as an intellectual property work protected by the Law, is its originality. The theory (based on the former law) requires also the condition of the originality of the work in order to distinguish 'work of art' from patterns and sketches.[2]

Consequently, an advertising message, in no matter what form (for example, television spot, radio or picture), is protected by the provisions of the intellectual property law if it is an original work (with a certain 'creative depth').

The creator of the advertisement is also the original beneficiary of the 'property right', meaning that he has the power of financial exploitation of the work and also the power to protect his personal relationship with the work (moral right). This last 'moral right' over his intellectual property grants to the author (creator) the right to choose the time, place and form of the presentation of the work to the public, the right to ask for recognition of his creation, the right to forbid all amendments, transformations or offences against his personality, etc.

---

1   Dagtoglou, 'Advertising and the Constitution' (1993) Greek Justice 1612.
2   Patterns and sketches are also protected by the provisions of Law 2417/1996, which ratified the Hague Convention.

Given that the majority of advertising messages are the results of the work of several persons (for example, the television spot), Law 2121/1993 (Art 7, para 1) recognises all the contributors equally as beneficiaries of the intellectual property rights of the work. In the case of creation of an audio-visual work, Greek law recognises the film director as author and beneficiary. According to the law, if an advertising message is created by an employee, the original beneficiary of the right remains the employee, and the employer, if not agreed differently under the employment contract, gets only those powers of the 'financial' right.

Advertising as an intellectual property work is transferable as far as its financial side (the 'moral right' is, by definition, untransferable) among living persons. The financial right, or some of the powers included in it, may also be assigned (transferred) to other persons under the terms of contracts and licences of exploitation. Those contracts may be exclusive or not, and in case of doubt they are considered as non-exclusive. Said contracts should be made in written form, otherwise they are considered null and void. The object of these contracts may be the total or some of the powers included into the author's right, but not the future methods of exploitation of the right (if not known at the time of the conclusion of the contract) and should not include the total of the future work of the author.

These contracts should also have a definite duration, otherwise their duration is a maximum of five years. The contract should also mention the territory and the extension of the powers to be transferred or assigned and also the means of exploitation, otherwise the territory of the contract is the one of its conclusion, and the powers and means of exploitation transferred or assigned are those indispensable for the performance of the contract.

The original beneficiary (the author) continues to be the only beneficiary of the 'moral right', meaning that, even after the transfer or assignment of all the financial powers of exploitation, the author has the right to demand from his contracting party that he present the relevant work to the public, and to exercise all possible forms of redress in order to protect that right.

## The negative side of advertising

The title of this section indicates that we will examine advertising as a 'harmful' fact or a situation likely to 'harm' other legitimate rights or interests of the public: for example, property, health, the private life or economic behaviour of its recipient.

The Greek legislator, facing the fact of the evolution and increase of the power of the media (and consequently of advertising), to influence and 'manipulate' the thoughts, beliefs and the general behaviour of the recipient of their messages, has adopted, by several laws, a protective structure for the recipient of the advertising message.

The restrictions on advertising of certain products which are legally sold, are considered permissible for reasons of protection of a constitutionally protected merit (such as public health or youth), as long as said restrictions follow the principle of proportionality and do not violate financial freedom.

## General protection

The Greek legislation for the protection of the consumer consists of Law 2251/1994 (and also Law 146/1914) by which EC Directive 84/450 on 'misleading advertising' and other directives on consumer protection are adopted. Law 2251/1994 *abolished* the previous one, Law 1961/1991.

The provisions of Art 9 of Law 2251/1994 cover the matters of misleading advertising, illicit advertising, comparative and indirect advertising and have a more general character affecting all forms of advertising.

## Definitions

### Consumer and supplier

According to the terminology of Law 2251/1994, a consumer is defined as:

> A physical person or legal entity, to whom the products or services offered in the market are addressed, or the person making use of such products or services, provided that he is their end user. The recipient of an advertising message is also considered as a consumer.

The Law expressly declares the recipient of the advertising message as a consumer worthy of its protection. It is noteworthy that the Law also protects legal entities as consumers, though these last are not considered as consumers by the provisions of the EC Directives. Relevant provision was not included or adopted by the previous legislation (Law 1961/1991). This wide definition of 'consumer' is severely criticised by Greek legal authors, who proposed the strict interpretation of the provision and the application of the restrictions implemented by the principles of Art 281 of the Civil Code (referring to the *bona fide* principle and the 'abusive exercise' of a right).[3]

On the other hand, a supplier is defined as the 'physical person or legal entity supplying goods or performing services to consumers and acting for purposes related to his trade, business or profession. The advertised person is

---

3   Perakis, 'Consumer protection and illicit competition', in DEE, *Enterprises' and Corporations' Law Review*, 1995, pp 32, 34; Alexandridou, *Consumer Protection Law*, 1996, Sakkoulas, A (ed), p 39; Delouka-Inglessi, *Greek and European Community Consumer's Law*, 1998, Sakkoulas, A (ed), p 55 *et seq*.

also considered as a supplier.' (The definitions of the supplier in this Law, as well as that of the consumer, are not included in the text of Council Directive 84/450 on 'misleading advertising').

According to the provisions of this Law, all public and municipal services may also be considered as 'suppliers' (Art 1, para 3 of Law 2251/1994) in combination with the recently issued Law 2328/1995 (Art 17), according to which listeners and viewers are also considered consumers of the services provided by television and radio stations and are also protected by the protective structure of Law 2251/1994.

By the above-mentioned provisions, the legislator has introduced into Greek legislation and theory two new 'dimensions' of the definitions of the consumer and supplier respectively. By defining as consumer the recipient of the advertising message, and as supplier the advertised person (without, at the same time, relating these definitions to the nature or form of the message), the legislator managed to enlarge the framework of the application of the Law and to offer consumers substantial protection, for example, by including 'advertised person' with 'advertiser' is enlarging the 'volume' of people liable for the violation of the Law, and indirectly established a form of control of the advertiser on the part of the advertised to the advertiser as to what regards the compliance of the advertising message with the provisions of Law 2251/1994.

*Advertising*

The definition of advertising is given in para 1 of Art 9 of Law 2251/1994 as 'any announcement made in the framework of trade, business craft or professional activity in order to promote the supply of goods or services'. This definition is a copy of the definition of para 1 of Art 2 of Council Directive 84/450 on 'misleading advertising', except for the reference to 'immovable property, rights and obligations' which is not included in the Greek definition.

This definition has a very wide field of application, given that the means of broadcast and the form of the message are irrelevant, and its application depends only on the nature of the activity in respect of which the message was made. In general, this activity should have a financial motivation and character and includes all professional activities (for example, physicians, lawyers, engineers, architects) as well as commercial or business activities. It is understood that public service activities are also included.

We are of the opinion that, from the above definition and consequently from the application of this Law, political 'advertising' messages and those made by religious and other (cultural, etc) organisations and institutions should be excluded, given that their activities are not strictly financial in character and do not aim to promote products or services to consumers.

*Misleading advertising*

The Greek legislator has introduced a general prohibition clause on all kinds of misleading advertising, defined as 'any advertising, the context and form of which in any way deceives or is likely to deceive the persons to whom it is addressed or whom it reaches and which by reason of this deception is likely to affect their economic behaviour'.

The above-mentioned definition is considered as an innovation in Greek legislation, given that the law (and consequently the judge) is not now oriented to the discovery of any inaccurate announcement (required by the Law 146/1914 on illicit competition) or advertising exaggerations which may provoke in the consumer the 'impression of a favourite offer', but to the result or the eventual result of the advertising message. The conditions for the implementation of the protective provisions on 'misleading advertising' required by Law 2251/1994 are fulfiled if:

(a) an advertising message (no matter in what form, or through what media, etc);

(b) deceives, or is likely to deceive, the consumer (recipient of the message); and

(c) affects, or is likely to affect, the economic behaviour of the consumer.

The problem is to find out who is the consumer of the above definition. Which kind of consumer will be the subject of the implementation of the law, the average consumer or the actual recipient of the advertising message who was deceived by the message?

We are of the opinion that the *ratio legis* and the aim to offer the public (consumers in general) a protective structure of their interests (after taking into consideration the fact that the special forms of redress adopted by Law 2251/1994 have a more collective form and are granted, mainly, to the consumers' union) defines as the recipient of the advertising message of Art 9, para 2, the average, common or garden consumer and not only the consumer offended by the message (a certain person deceived, whose interests were harmed by the message). Otherwise, the eventual result ('likely to deceive') of the message required by the law, to implement its provisions would approximate a *lex imperfecta*, and would depend on the goodwill of a certain consumer.[4] This may not lead to the conclusion that a sole consumer is deprived by the protection of the Law, but a different ground for its claim is required (that is, the damage of its personal interests). Regarding the entitlement of the consumer, see below.

---

4   Some of the Greek writers are orientated – probably influenced by the German jurisprudence – to a quantitative criterion for the definition of the forms of the restricted (misleading) advertising – requiring a minimum percentage of consumers to be affected by the message: Kotsiris, *Competition Law*, 2nd edn, 1986, Sakkoulas, A (ed), pp 111–13; Delouka-Inglessi, *op cit*, fn 3, pp 47–148.

## Criteria for the definition of misleading advertising

Further to the above-mentioned criterion for the determination of whether advertising is misleading or not, para 3 of Art 9 of Law 2251/1994 also gives three categories of criteria to be considered for said determination, namely:

(a) the characteristics of goods or services, such as their availability, nature, execution, competition method and date of manufacture or provision, fitness for purpose, uses, quantity, specification, geographical or commercial origin or the results to be expected from their use, or the results and material features of checks carried out on goods or services;

(b) the price or the manner in which the price is calculated and the conditions under which the goods are supplied or the services are provided; and

(c) the nature, attributes and rights of the advertiser, such as his identity and assets, his qualification and ownership of industrial, commercial and intellectual property rights, or his awards and distinctions.

## Forms of misleading advertising

Law 2251/1994 also adopts four categories of advertisement that are 'misleading', namely when:

(a) appreciation of the advertisement is based on statements made by persons who appear as scientists, specialists or authorities on a matter without actually being so, or persons who have not given their written approval for the use of their statement for the advertising;

(b) appreciation of the advertisement is based on the idea that the technology or the scientific achievements of a certain country, different from the one of origin, prove the quality of the goods;

(c) the advertisement is presented as the result of journalist research, comment or scientific announcement without being expressly stated that it is advertising;[5] or

(d) the advertisement includes scientific terms or idioms, results of research, or parts of text of a scientific or technical character, in order to represent the advertisement as based on scientific work when it is not.

---

5    One Member First Instance Court of Athens, Decision No 26583/1996, DEE, *op cit*, fn 3, 1997 pp 84–85. In that case, the competent consumer union filed a request for the issue of cease and desist provisory measures against a tobacco industry, because this last made a press announcement of certain quasi-scientific results referring to 'harmful cigarette smoke in the air'. The Union considered the announcement as misleading advertising for the reason that it did not mention that it was an advertisement (given that it represented industry trade marks and made direct references to it) as well as illicit, because it alleged that the message was directly targeted at the subconscious of the consumer without him or her being able to proceed to a rational criticism of the message. The court seemed to adopt these grounds but did not proceed to the substantial examination of the request, for the reason that the campaign in question had already stopped, and therefore rejected the request.

## Misleading advertising and consumer protection

The special forms of redress adopted by Law 2251/1994 have a more collective character, meaning that consumers' unions, recognised by the provisions of Art 10 of Law 2251/1994, have the right to exercise them. The recent introduction of the Law has meant that Greek courts have not yet been able to interpret its provisions, in particular, the matter of entitling the individual consumer to file the actions of paras 8–15 of Art 10 of Law 2251/1994.

The following should be also noted in this matter.

The Law 2251/1994 aims to provide consumers, and consequently the whole market, with a protective structure for the interests of the public and for the freedom of competition. Greek law, in general, is not tolerant of forms of advertising or policies that affect the interests of the public (consumers) and are falsifying the competition. This last (protection of freedom of competition) may be characterised as the subsequent and auxiliary aim of the legislator of Law 2251/1994, given that the relevant special legislation (Law 146/1914) already exists. On the other hand, the individual consumer has a variety of forms of judicial protection offered to him by the general provisions of the Civil Code, etc.

The character of the provisions of Law 2251/1994 and the above-mentioned *ratio legis* of its provisions is leading us to the conclusion that the special forms of redress of Art 10 of the Law may be exercised exclusively by the consumer's unions. The entitlement of the individual consumer to bring actions under Law 2251/1994 before the competent court should be strictly excluded.

This is grounded *de lege lata* as follows.

Law 2251/1994, in its basic principles, aims to protect the *public* from the harmful result that the deceitful message can create or is likely to create to the financial detriment of the public. For the implementation of its provisions, the Law has assigned the right to litigation in the relevant cases to certain independent organisations, the consumers' unions (being the most representative entities). But we have to admit that those unions and organisations have a more or less bureaucratic structure and function, which is most likely to make them omit the idea of filing a lawsuit against the producer or supplier of a misleading or illicit advertisement. On the other hand, if any consumer, even without being harmed or affected by the relevant policy, was free to proceed to litigation against the supplier, this would lead to a judicial pandemonium that would provoke the financial and moral extortion of the supplier, who would be obliged to face lawsuits all over the country. It is clear that the aim of the Law is not to extinguish the violator, but to prevent the danger and protect the public. This target an be achieved only through the collective statutes of the consumers' unions, and not by the will of some individual consumers. It is another point if *de lege ferenda* the legislator should adopt a system for the prosecution of the violator indirectly by the individual consumers, in order to prevent the suspension of the implementation of the Law and to bypass the bureaucratic structure of the unions. For example, a *de lege ferenda* solution might be for the board of directors of the union to be obliged to proceed to the relevant prosecution of the violator when this is requested by a certain number of the union's members. (This condition may be adopted as a ius cogens provision of the union statutes.)

## Illicit advertising

The provisions of para 5 of Art 9 of Law 2251/1994 define as 'illicit' any advertising which 'offends the morality'. The above definition, compared to that of 'misleading advertising', is wider and does not set any criteria for the concrete definition of this kind of forbidden advertising.

Furthermore, para 6 of said Art adopts an indicative description of what illicit advertising is. The forms of advertising listed in para 6 of Art 9 of Law 2251/1994 are *de lege* proof of the illicit form of an announcement.

'Illicit' advertising is described as an advertising which:

a) aims to or is likely to provoke anger, fear or annoyance or to exploit those sentiments and the superstitions of the consumer, or lead them to criminal acts;

(b) is discriminating and offends social groups, races, religions, sexes, ages, their nationality, origin, beliefs and physical or spiritual differences;

(c) creates the image of an extremely tempting offer, especially to children, youngsters and to the most vulnerable groups of the population;

(d) directs the advertising message directly to the subconscious, without leaving its recipient the opportunity to judge it; or

(e) indirectly promotes goods different from those which are the apparent context of the advertising message, without this promotion being the intellectually central or indispensable part of the message.[6]

We are of the opinion that this last form of 'illicit advertising' should be included in the list of the criteria set by the Law for the definition of 'comparative' advertising (see below, p 470).

Finally, Law 2251/1994 (Art 9, para 7) provides that television and radio special regulations in the matter of the definition of illicit advertising for the protection of minors and other vulnerable groups of the population may define other forms of advertising as illicit.

---

6   Multi Member Court of First Instance of Athens Decision No 3717/1996 DEE, *op cit*, fn 3, 1997, p 82 *et seq.*

## Comparative advertising

The provisions of para 8 of Art 9 of Law 2251/1994 define 'comparative' advertising as that which indicates directly or indirectly the identity of a certain competitor or some products or services offered by that competitor, if that advertising compares objectively the main, similar, verifiable and objectively chosen features of the competitive goods or services.

Such advertising is mainly prohibited and should be allowed only if the advertising:

(a) is not misleading;

(b) does not provoke confusion in the market between the advertiser and his competitor(s) or their trade names or other distinctive features or the products or services of the advertiser and his competitor or competitors;

(c) does not belittle or slander a competitor or his trade marks or other distinctive features, products, services or his activities; and

(d) does not aim to exploit the reputation of the trade mark or of other distinctive features of the competitor.

## Other provisions of the Law regarding the content of advertisements

In Art 9, paras 10–13 of Law 2251/1994, certain provisions are adopted relating to the protection of the consumer's private life. More specifically, it is provided that direct advertising should not offend the privacy of the consumer, and that advertisers should not use information known to them from former transactions, or from other generally accessible sources, such as business catalogues, etc, regarding elements of the consumer's private life, unless the consumer so permits. The consumer has the right to ask the supplier to erase all such personal information and to cease all relevant advertising.

In para 9 of Art 9 of Law 2251/1994, it is provided that the reproduction or mention of the results of comparative tests of goods or services made by third parties in an advertising message is allowed only after the written consent of those responsible for the test has been given. In that case, the advertiser is responsible for this test as if it had been made under his supervision or by himself.

Law 2251/1994 has restricted the special forms of redress granted to the consumer by the former Law 1961/1991 (in Art 21, para 1) but has granted greater 'power' to the consumers' unions (see below, p 471). The consumer offended or harmed by illicit or misleading advertising has the power (if he can prove 'legitimate interest') to proceed to the courts with the 'general' forms of redress provided by the law.

Finally, in Art 14 of Law 2251/1994 (para 3) it is provided that the Ministry of Commerce has the right to impose a fine of between Drs 500,000 and Drs 20 m on violators of the provisions of this Law. In case of repetition of the violation, the ministry has the right to double the above fine and if the violation is repeated a second time, the Ministry of Commerce has the right to order violating business or its subsidiary to cease trading for a period up to one year.

## Law 146/1914 and consumer protection

After the discussion of the provisions of the above-mentioned new Law, it will be useful to examine the matter of the relation between Law 2251/1994 and Law 146/1914 on illicit competition. The practical interest for such a comparison is apparent when considering the matter of the entitlement of consumers and suppliers and the matter of the substantial conditions set by these Laws for the fulfilment of their legal results. In other words, when a policy is considered to be in violation of Law 2251/1994, should it also be considered as an act of illicit competition? Has the supplier the right to establish litigation against its competitor only through the provisions of Law 146/1914, or should it also be examined under Law 2251/1994?

Law 146/1914 was considered, for many years, as the only legal structure protecting the consumer's rights but only competitors have the right to seek relevant protection from the courts. Law 146/1914 deals mainly with the matters of 'healthy' and free competition in the market and, secondly, the protection of the consumer. The ratio of this Law was the protection of the consumer, but this was not the direct aim of the Law, given that this purpose was satisfied when behaviour considered as illicit competition (misleading advertising was also considered as an action of illicit competition) was suspended or stopped by the court following a relevant request filed exclusively by 'harmed' competitors.

The majority of legal writers and the Greek courts did not recognise the consumer's right to seek legal protection through the provisions of Law 146/1914 (with the exception of Professor Liakopoulos[7] and Professor Alexandridou).[8] It should be noted that Professor Alexandridou supported direct recognition, under Law 146/1914, of the consumer's right to seek damages as well as the right to demand the cessation of the tort.[9]

After the introduction of Law 2251/1994 (which abolished the previous similar Law No 1961/1991), Greek legal theory examined whether its application suspends or affects the provisions of Law 146/1914, or if their parallel application is admissible.

---

7   Liakopoulos, *The Financial Freedom as Object of Protection in the Competition Law*, 1981, Sakkoulas, PN (ed), p 328 *et seq*.
8   Alexandridou, *Illicit Competition and Consumer Protection*, 1993, Sakkoulas, PN (ed), p 223.
9   See also Multi Member Court of First Instance of Athens 97/1986 NoB, Legal Tribunal, 1987, p 937.

Before proceeding to the relevant discussion, we should note that para 2 of Art 14 of Law 2251/1994 provides that 'the provisions for illicit competition are not affected' and para 5 of the article provides that 'if the common law gives the consumer better protection than the special regulations of this Law, the common law is applicable'.

In view of the aforesaid, various theories were introduced regarding the parallel or combined application of the provisions of said Laws. One of these theories is that the remedies granted to the consumer through the provisions of Law 146/1914 should be in addition to those specifically provided by the rules of Law 2251/1994.[10] According to this theory, the consumer should be entitled to the best protection granted by both Laws even after their combination. The theory supports the opinion that a 'harmed' competitor should also be able to obtain protection of its interests through the provisions of Law 2251/1994. Nevertheless, the second part of this theory seems to be doubtful, because the ratio of Law 2251/1994 was not to grant competitors special, additional remedies to their protection from illicit competitive acts.[11] This might be the reason why the legislator decided to provide that the illicit competition rules are not affected by Law 2251/1994.

The question is what will happen if an advertising message is considered by Law 2251/1994 as misleading without, at the same time, being considered as such according to the provisions of Art 3 of Law 146/1914 (requiring impression of most favourite offer). Moreover, should the misleading advertising of Law 2251/1994, when considered as illegal action (and consequently as a violation of the Law), be also considered under the general principles of Art 1 of Law 146/1914 as illicit?[12] The legislator of Law 2251/1994 does not seem to respond to these questions.

It seems that the solution to the above-mentioned problem will be given by the courts. It is too early for the extraction of solid conclusions from the relevant jurisprudence. In two cases, the courts examined the entitlement of the litigants (competitors) and that was under different legal provisions (Law 1961/1991 and Law 2251/1994 respectively). The One Member Court of First Instance of Athens, in its Decision 5874/1994[13] interpreting the provision of Art 21 of Law 1961/1991, judged that the persons who have lawful interest and consequently are entitled to exercise the rights of the Law, were 'obviously and mainly' the supplier's competitors, and only then the consumers, when represented by their unions.

---

10  Perakis, in DEE, *op cit*, fn 3, p 117.
11  Introductory Report of the Law 2251/1994.
12  Alexandridou, Armenopoulos, 1996, p 295, fn 17.
13  [1994] Commercial Law Review 668.

On the other hand, the Multi Member Court of First Instance of Athens, in its Decision 2339/1997[14] in the case of an action brought by a union of merchants against a newspaper (based on the provisions of Law 146/1914), for the reason that this last offered products sold by the merchants at lower prices (compared to those of the relevant shops) has judged that 'competitors are entitled to request their protection under the provisions of Law 2251/1994, to the extent that they are not covered by those of 146/1914, for example, in case of comparative slanderous advertising, which is specifically forbidden by the provisions of para 8 of Art 9 of Law 2251/1994'.

Concluding, the court rejected the action as legally groundless on the basis that: (a) the claimants were not in 'competitive' relations; (b) the claimants are not entitled to bring the 'collective action' of Art 10 for the reason that they are not representing the consumers and that they do not allege damages as consumers; and finally (c) the claimants did not prove the prerequisites for the implementation of the provisions of para 8 of Art 9 of Law 2251/1994.

## The new legal remedies introduced by Law 2251/1994

Law 2251/1994, as we have mentioned before, in its first part (Art 2(9)) includes provisions of substantial law and in its second part, the structural and procedural provisions for the protection of the consumers' interests, through consumers' unions and the 'collective action' or 'class action'.

Article 10 of said Law provides the requirements of the law for the formation and functioning of the consumers' unions, that is: (a) the subscription of at least 100 members; and (b) the registration of the union at the competent prefecture (Nomarchia).

Every union of consumers abiding by the above-mentioned legal requirements is recognised as a legal entity competent to proceed to and seek the judicial protection of consumers' interests, through two different forms of entitlement. The first is the procedural exercise of the rights of its members/individual consumers, and the second is the protection of the non-individualised/general interests of the consumer/public, exercised by the union through the collective action. It is noteworthy that, when exercising this last remedy 'in the name' of the public, the union is entitled to request from the court the condemnation of the supplier to the payment of compensation, defined by the law as 'pecuniary compensation for the recovery from moral damages'.

In the following paragraphs we will examine those two remedies (a) from the point of view of the precedent (*res judicata*) of the relevant decision, and (b) of the pendency of the action affecting third parties.

---

14   DEE, *op cit*, fn 3, p 470.

**The exercise of the rights of the individual consumer by the union**

According to the provisions of para 8 of Art 10 of 2251/1994, every consumers' union is entitled to seek any form of lawful protection of the rights of its members as consumers, judicially or administratively, and specifically, is entitled to exercise an action, a petition for provisory measures, etc.

The matters of the *res judicata* produced by the decision issued in the case of such an action are treated in accordance with the general principles of the Civil Procedure Code (requiring identity of the litigants, the claim and the historical and legal ground of the trial), but it is also noted[15] that the enforceability of the judgment in such cases is expanded to the real beneficiary of the right (the consumer) when it is in his favour.

As to what regards the pendency of this action and its effect if the case is brought before the courts by the affected consumer, the legal writers[16] consider that the general principles of the Civil Procedure Code apply.

On the other hand, an action referring to the protection of a consumer (member of the union), does not affect any similar cases (even against the same supplier) when brought before the courts by other consumers (members of the litigant union) or different unions.

**Collective action/an *erga omnes* result**

According to the provisions of para 9 of Art 19 of Law 2251/1994, 'consumer unions with more than 500 active members and registered at the registries of the competent authority (prefecture) at least two years before the start of the litigation, are entitled to exercise all kind of actions for the protection of the general interests of the consumer public ('collective action')'.

The above requirements of the Law referring to the number of the members of the Union and their 'seniority', show the intention of the legislator to grant this power to the unions that are 'the most representative' entities and with a relative experience in the 'consumer movement'.[17]

The wording of the provision, and the fact that it is also provided that the unions have the power to prosecute and seek the 'cessation of the illegal behaviour of the supplier, even before an appearance', leads to the conclusion that the relevant procedural right granted is a sui generis 'action', because the court is not judging a substantial and specific right or claim or even a lawful relationship between the litigants, but the object of the litigation is the judicial confirmation of an anti-consumer policy and its prohibition, in order to avoid policies which damage consumers' interests.[18]

---

15  Nikas, Armenopoulos, 1996, p 1176.
16  Matthias, 'The legal nature and the results of the collective action' (1997) Hellenic Justice 1, p 1 *et seq*.
17  *Ibid*.
18  *Ibid*.

The Law also provides that the relevant judgment issued in the case of a collective action has an *erga omnes* result (para 12 of Art 10 of Law 2251/1994). This wording might lead to a misunderstanding as regards the force of the *res judicata* of the relevant judgment, because it may be alleged that this affects every similar case.

On that ground, legal theory has defined the following thoughts.

As regards the existence or not of a force of *res judicata* of the relevant decision, it is accepted[19] that the decision does not produce a *res judicata* because of the sui generis procedural nature of the action (the union is not the beneficiary of the claim, the object of the litigation is the judicial recognition of an illegal policy, etc) and of the procedural rules applied in the case, that is, those of the 'voluntary' procedure (Arts 739–866 of the Civil Procedure Code). The decisions issued by the courts do not have the result of res judicata, but simply 'exist' between the litigants, that is, the filing of a new application between the same litigants is not allowed (Art 778 of the Civil Procedure Code).

Therefore, in that case, it is not correct to make reference to an *erga omnes res judicata*,[20] but to a *quasi res judicata*, covering only the consumer unions and not their members. These last are free to establish and prosecute litigation against the infringer when personally harmed by the illegal policy.

### Pecuniary compensation for recovery from moral damage

In the framework of the exercise of collective action, the Law also provides (Art 10, para 9(b)) the right of the union to request 'pecuniary compensation for recovery from moral damage' by the supplier, the violator of the Law. The Law also implements certain criteria that help the court to estimate the level of compensation, such as the size of the enterprise of the violator, the force of the damaging policy and the 'need for general and specific prevention'.

Greek legal theory supported two different opinions as to the nature of this compensation.

The first, strongly influenced by the civil law doctrines, does not recognise any other type of compensation than the classical restitutional one.[21]

---

19  Matthias, *op cit*, fn 16.
20  The character of the judicial decision as a quasi-administrative measure when issued according to the procedural rules of the 'voluntary' procedure, is strongly alleged by the Greek legal literature. See *ibid*.
21  Karakostas and Paparseniou, in DEE, *op cit*, fn 3, p 475 *et seq*.

This is the main concept of the nature of compensation for recovery from moral damage under several provisions of the Civil Code (Arts 299, 59, 932) and adopted by the majority of writers and the jurisprudence.[22]

The scope of compensation sought in the framework of collective action is, according to this theory, the restitution of the 'pre-existing situation'; the restoration to the previous moral and social order and the payment of a certain amount in compensation leads to the re-establishment of the damaged moral and social balance.[23]

As to the criterion of 'general and special prevention' set by the Law, the above theory denies the preventative or exemplary nature of the compensation, alleging that the intention of this provision is not to blame personally the violator or to disavow its policy, but that the measure of payment of pecuniary compensation leads to the restitution of the moral damage to the victim (the public).

On the other hand, other writers[24] support the theory of the punitive or exemplary nature of the compensation.

It is true that the historical legislator aimed to introduce the example of 'punitive damages' as provided by Anglo-Saxon law.[25]

According to the above-mentioned theory, the criteria for quantification of the compensation set by the Law show the nature of the compensation as a punitive one. Therefore, it is accepted that the legislator did not set the moral belittlement of the union as a criterion for the quantification, but the 'force of the insult of the legal order' and 'the needs for general and specific prevention'. The punitive character of the compensation is also grounded by the fact that condemnation of the violator for the payment of compensation is taking place 'just once' (Art 10, para 13(a)), which is a form of the principle which rules all sanctions, that is, *ne bis in idem*. Finally, this nature of the compensation, it is alleged, is based on the wording of para 13(b) of Art 10 of Law 2251/94, providing that the amount paid as compensation will be used for the public good and especially for the protection of the consumer.

We are of the opinion that the second theory is correct, taking into consideration that the Law permits the exercise of collective action 'before the appearance of the violating policy' and consequently allows the union to

---

22 Stathopoulos, in Georgiadis-Stathopoulos, *Civil Code*, Art 299, No 3, Sakkoulas, A and Sakkoulas, P (eds), Karakatsanis NoB (Legal Tribunal) 24, p 667; Paterakis, *Pecuniary Compensation for Recovery from Moral Damages*, 1995, Dikery and Ikouomla (eds), p 81 *et seq*.

23 *Ibid*, p 479.

24 Matthias, *op cit*, fn 16; Spyrakos, 'Collective and Public Law Protection of the Consumer', NoB (Legal Tribunal), 1998, p 437 *et seq*; Kritikos, Hellenic Justice, 1997, p 699 *et seq*, Commentary under decision No 1114/1996 of the First Instance Court of Athens; Delikostopoulou, in DEE, *op cit*, fn 3, p 10 *et seq*.

25 *Ibid*, Kritikos; and Delikostopoulou.

request 'compensation' before any moral or social disturbance occurs and before the social balance is damaged. This shows the preventative aim of the legislator. Moreover, since the criteria set by the Law for the quantification of compensation are orientated to the violator and not the victim (as is accepted in cases of 'classical' compensation under Art 932 of the Civil Code), we consider that the relevant concept is adjusted to the principles of the Penal Code instead of the Civil Code.

The jurisprudence has not yet adopted one of these two doctrines. The Multi Member Court of First Instance of Athens, in two decisions, No 1114/96[26] and No 3717/96[27] has simply repeated the criteria of the Law without proceeding to any further specifications.

The same court, judging on the validity of the general clauses (Decision No 3229/1996)[28] has stated that 'the scope of the claim for compensation for recovery from moral damages may be either restitutional or punitive or preventative', without proceeding to any further comment, but simply repeating the legal criteria. It is only Decision No 2411/1997 of the same court which makes reference to the 'punitive' nature of the compensation. Finally, the same court, very recently (June 1998) issued Decision No 1208/1998, in which it is clearly declared that the above-mentioned pecuniary compensation for recovery from moral damages has 'only punitive character' (civil fine) and, therefore, no provision of the Civil Code with reference to moral damages is applicable. The court, after taking into consideration the size of the bank, its place in the market, the bank's assets, etc, the extent of the violation of the legal order and the need for general and specific prevention, condemned the bank to a fine of Drs 150 m payable to the claimant consumers' union.

In any case, we should note that, even if the nature of the compensation is considered punitive, the sanction should be defined in such a way as to prevent the repetition of the policy by the violator and the rest of their competitors without, at the same time, leading to the supplier's downfall.

## FREEDOM OF PERSONS/COMPANIES TO ESTABLISH THEMSELVES AS ADVERTISING AGENTS AND TO UNDERTAKE ADVERTISING BUSINESS

The advertising sector may be considered as a *terra libera* for all persons aiming to establish themselves as advertisers and to undertake the relevant business.

---

26  DEE, *op cit*, fn 3, p 519 *et seq.*
27  *Ibid*, p 82 *et seq.*
28  Armenopoulos, 1997, p 551 *et seq.*

No licence or permission is required by Greek law, and all persons, whether Greek or foreign, have the right to provide advertising services. The above freedom is considered a specific result of financial freedom and is covered by the constitutional protection of the latter (Administrative Supreme Court 25/1986, 727/1985, 630/1979, 436/1979 and 458/1979).

It is noteworthy that, under para 18 of Art 12 of Law 2328/1995, the owners of a television or radio station, when functioning under the legal form of a company limited by shares (private company) must have registered shares. This obligation is extended, by the provisions of para 3 of Art 2 of the Presidential Decree 261/1997 (referring to the clarity of advertising promotion in the public sector, harmonising the Greek legislation with the provisions of EC Directive 92/50/EEC dated 18 June 1992), to all advertising agencies when providing relevant services (including planning and organising of advertising strategy) to the public sector and functioning under the legal form of a private company.

The above-mentioned Presidential Decree also founded the public sector advertising persons registry (Art 3). This registry is kept by the Ministry of Press and Mass Media and includes 'companies of all legal forms providing advertising services defined in para 2(a), (b) and (c) of Art 2' of the Presidential Decree (with the exception of television and radio stations) having (a) a share capital or company capital or property of at least Drs 10 m and (b) adequate experience in the sector, which can be proved by the presentation of the 'relevant contractual and legal documents as well as the relevant audio-visual or printed samples'. Companies in the public sector must appoint advertising promotion companies which are so registered.

# SPECIAL FORMS OF ADVERTISING

In this section we will look at the different forms of advertising as presented and dealt with by Greek legislation. For our approach, we will examine these forms of advertising first, as defined by the media (for example, television commercials); secondly, as defined by the subject of the advertised persons (for example, advertising of medical services); and finally, by the contents of the advertised product itself (for example, tobacco).

# Special forms of advertising as defined by the means of advertising

## *Television and radio advertising*

### *Introduction*

For many years, the Greek legislator and the State interpreted very strictly the clause of para 2 of Art 15 of the Greek Constitution according to which 'radio and television shall be under the immediate control of the State and shall aim at the objective broadcast, on equal terms, of information and news reports as well as works of "literature and art"' forbidding the operation of any 'private' television and radio stations.

An example of this approach of the legislator to the matter of 'freedom' of television is that the public television stations run by ERT SA (Hellenic Radio Television) were operating for about 12 years without any kind of special legal provisions, only some ministerial decisions and, as recently as 1987, with Law 1730, Parliament tried to bring in the above-mentioned Constitutional Order.

The main provisions of the Law (Art 3, para 1), as amended and being in force, define that all radio and television programs of ERT SA should be inspired by the ideals of 'freedom, democracy, national independence, peace and friendship among the peoples' and the general principles to be followed by them are:

(a) objectivity, completeness and actuality of the information;

(b) polyphonism – the right of every political party, social group, etc, to express its ideas, make announcements, etc;

(c) good programme quality;

(d) maintenance of the quality of the Greek language;

(e) respect for the personality and private life of the individual; and

(f) maintenance, promotion and dissemination of Greek civilisation and tradition.

Law 1730/1987 adopts certain provisions regarding the matter of the television and radio advertising, according to which:

(a) the time granted for the broadcasting of advertising messages should not exceed 8% of the total daily broadcasting time;

(b) advertising messages are forbidden during television broadcasts.

ERT SA also had the right to prevent the broadcast (para 8, Art 3 of Law 1730/1987) of an advertising message if said advertising:

(a) goes against the aims and principles of ERT SA and, especially, the principles of respect for women, protection of reasonable interests and sensitivity of the young, as well as respect for the national cultural heritage;

(b) includes expressions of violence likely to affect the personality of the individual;

(c) is misleading. Misleading advertising is any advertising that, no matter how, even by its presentation, creates or is likely to create deceitful impressions, or affects the economic behaviour of the recipients (viewers or listeners), or harms a competitor;

d) is inelegant or anti-aesthetic.

Under the provisions of para 9 of Art 3 of Law 1730/1987, advertisements for the following are strictly forbidden:

(a) children's games and toys;

(b) tobacco products and cigarettes; and

(c) indirect advertising.

Finally, para 10 of Art 3 of Law 1730/1987 granted immunity to ERT SA, according to which the company was not liable for any compensation to be paid to advertisers or third parties for eventual damages arising from broadcast, cancellation or improper transmission of advertising.

The State television and radio monopoly, as provided by Law 1730/1987 (and severely criticised by legal theory and literature), was curbed two years later, when the government accepted the operation of private radio and television stations.

The Greek legislator, in view of this development, has amended the above Law by Laws 1866/1989, 1941/1991, 1943/1991, 2173/1993 and Presidential Decree 234/1993, and has issued Ministerial Decision No 609/11 of 18 July 1991, a sort of 'code of conduct' for television and radio commercials (and several decisions of the National Radio-television Council, Nos 20/1991, 609/1991 and Regulations 1/1991, 2/1991, 3/1991, 4/1991 and 5/1991 on the matter) and Presidential Decree 236/1992, which harmonises Greek legislation with the provisions of Directive 89/552/EEC (Law 298/1989).

Most recently, the Greek legislator has introduced Law 2328/1995, which deals with the matters of the foundation and operation of private television and local radio stations and adopts several special provisions on television and radio advertising. This law amends the provisions of Law 1730/1987 and also applies to ERT SA.

*The general principles of television and radio advertising*

In para 1(a) of Art 3 of Law 2328/1995, the legislator adopts the general clause or principle of operation of a television or radio station, which is the same as for ERT SA, as defined by Law 1730/1987. Respect for those principles is also the main condition of an operating licence for private stations.[29]

The second passage of the paragraph adopts the special principles to be followed on the broadcasting of all kinds of television and radio shows and advertising, which are respect for the personality, honour, substance, family and/or private life, professional, social, scientific, artistic, public or other activity of any person, the image of which or the name or characteristics of which are presented on screen or otherwise transmitted. Furthermore, according to the provisions of para 3(a) of Law 2328/1995, 'television advertising shall be readily recognisable as such and kept quite separate from other parts of the programme by optical and/or acoustic means'.

Paragraph 3 of the article also imposes principles according to which television advertising should not:

(a) prejudice respect for human dignity;

(b) include any discrimination on grounds of race, sex, religion or nationality;

(c) be offensive to religious or political beliefs;

(d) encourage behaviour prejudicial to health or safety; and

(e) encourage ways of behaviour prejudicial to the protection of the environment.

The provisions of Art 3, para 3(d) imposed the same strict criteria as in Art 16 of Directive 89/552/EEC, which should be followed for the protection of the moral and physical well being of young people. More specifically, television stations are obliged not to transmit advertising which violates the provisions of the article, such as advertising which:

(a) directly encourages minors to purchase products or services, by exploiting their inexperience or credulity;

(b) directly encourages minors to persuade their parents or third parties to purchase goods or services being advertised;

(c) exploits the special trust minors have for parents, teachers and other persons; and

(d) shows minors in dangerous situations without good reason.

*Restrictions on the advertising of alcoholic beverages and tobacco products*

Article 3, para 3(e) of Law 2328/1995 defines the rules with which television advertising for alcoholic beverages should comply. According to those criteria, advertising:

---

29  The same principles set by Art 3, paras 1–12, 14, 17 and 22 of the Law 2328/1995 are adopted by the recent Law 2644/1998 (Art 10) 'for the supply of radio and TV services by subscription and other relevant provisions'.

(a) must not be aimed specifically at minors or, in particular, depict minors consuming these beverages;

(b) must not link the consumption of alcohol with enhanced physical performance or driving;

(c) must not create the impression that the consumption of alcohol contributes towards social or sexual success;

(d) must not claim that alcohol has therapeutic qualities or that it is a stimulant or a sedative;

(e) must not encourage immoderate consumption of alcohol or present abstinence or moderation in a negative light; and

(f) must not place emphasis on high alcoholic content as being a positive quality of the beverage.

The last passage of para 3 of Art 3 of Law 2328/1995 adopts, as a general principle, the obligation of television stations to prohibit the broadcast of advertising messages violating the provisions of that paragraph (for example, on the protection of minors or regarding the advertising of tobacco products) or offending directly or indirectly a physical person or legal entity or political party or referring to those persons in a way giving them a legitimate interest to exercise their right to reply under Art 3, para 11 of Law 2328/1995.

The Greek legislator, harmonising the national legislation with the provisions of Directive 89/552/EEC, prohibits all forms of television advertising for cigarettes and tobacco products and of medicinal products or treatments available only on prescription, as well as the advertising of telecommunications services of a sexual character.

On the other hand, Greek law (para 7 of Art 3) adopts the 'freedom to be advertised', providing that television stations may not deny the broadcast of advertising messages referring to similar products or services under the same terms if those messages do not violate the provisions of this article or of other laws.

*Restrictions on the matter of time limits and the duration of advertising on television*

Paragraphs 5 and 6 of Art 3 of Law 2328/1995 set out the principles for the broadcasting of advertising messages with reference to time limits and duration.

The general principle imposed by these provisions is that all advertising messages should be inserted between television programmes.

The above-mentioned general clause has the following exceptions:

(a) the advertising message may be transmitted during the broadcast of a 'normal' programme, on condition that the integrity and value of the programme, taking into account natural breaks, the duration and nature of the programme and the rights of the rightholders, are not prejudiced;

(b) in programmes consisting of autonomous parts or in sports programmes and similarly structured events and performances including intervals, advertising messages may be only inserted between those independent parts or intervals;

(c) the broadcast of audio-visual works, such as feature films and films made for television (with the exception of series, television serials, light entertainment television shows and documentaries), whose duration exceeds 45 minutes, may be interrupted by advertising messages once only in each complete period of 45 minutes, in which case, the interruption should not exceed 9 minutes. Further interruption is allowed only if the overall duration is at least 20 minutes longer than two or more complete periods of 45 minutes;

(d) if programmes other than those mentioned under (b) are interrupted by the broadcast of advertising messages, a period of at least 20 minutes should elapse between successive interruptions made during the programmes;

(e) no advertising messages may be broadcast during the broadcast of religious services. Television news, current affairs programmes, talk shows of a political nature, documentaries, religious programmes and children's programmes with a duration of less than 30 minutes should not be interrupted by advertising messages. If their duration is greater than 30 minutes, the provisions of the above paragraphs shall apply.

In para 6(a) of Art 3, the time limits for the broadcasting of advertising messages, which should not exceed 15% of the total daily broadcasting time, are defined. However, this percentage may be increased to 20% of the total daily broadcasting time to include forms of advertising such as direct offers to the public for the sale, purchase or lease of products or services, provided that the amount of spot advertising does not exceed 15%.

According to the provisions of para 6(b) of Art 3, the permitted total broadcasting time of advertising messages within a given period of one hour should not exceed 20%. Interruptions to programmes for the broadcasting of advertising messages should not exceed four minutes, with the exception of the provisions of para 5(c) of Art 3 (above, under (c)).

According to the provisions of para 6(c) of Art 3, without prejudice to the provisions of para 6(a), all forms of advertising such as direct offers to the public for the sale, purchase or lease of products or for the provision of services shall not exceed one hour per day.

For the purposes of calculation of said maximum time, it is provided (para 5(f) of Art 3) that any reference or appearance of the trade mark of a product or service, or the trade name or title of an enterprise, or the announcement of any event of artistic or commercial character, on the screen during any television broadcast, is considered advertising and all the relevant conditions and restrictions on the matter of its content and duration apply equally.

Furthermore, all programme announcements or other activities of the television station (for example, trailers) interrupting a programme, count towards the total daily permitted advertising time and the number and pattern of the commercial breaks. The total daily permitted time for the broadcast of advertising messages may reach 20% for such announcements. The permitted time may be exceeded by a further 20% when such announcements or trailers are transmitted between regular programmes.

*Television sponsorship*

Sponsorship, as a special form of advertising and promotion in general, is also covered by the provisions of para 8 of Art 3 of Law 2328/1995. Under these provisions, sponsored television programmes shall meet the following requirements:

(a) the contents and scheduling of sponsored programmes may in no circumstances be influenced by the sponsor in such a way as to affect the responsibility and editorial independence of the broadcaster in respect of programmes;

(b) they must be clearly identified as such by the name and/or logo of the sponsor at the beginning and/or the end of the programme. The permanent or occasional appearance of the name and logo of the sponsor, and particularly of the trade mark of the products or services offered by the sponsor, on the screen during the broadcast is prohibited and in any case is treated as advertising to which all the relevant provisions apply;

(c) they must not encourage the purchase or rental of the products or services of the sponsor or a third party, in particular, by making special promotional references to those products or services.

Furthermore, in paras 9 and 10 of Art 3 of Law 2328/1995 it is also provided that television programmes may not be sponsored by natural persons or legal entities whose principal activity is the manufacture or sale of products, or the provision of services, the advertising of which is prohibited, and that news and current affairs programmes may not be sponsored.

*Special protection of minors*

In para 14(a) of Art 3 of Law 2328/1995, the regulation of the provisions of Art 22 of Directive 89/552/EEC on the special protection of minors is adopted.

According to those provisions, ERT SA and private television stations are obliged not to include or transmit programmes which might seriously impair the physical, mental or moral development of minors, in particular, those that involve pornography or gratuitous violence, or to transmit television news involving natural scenes of violence without this being necessary for public information about a certain event. The above-mentioned programmes should not contain any incitement to hatred on grounds of race, sex, religion or nationality.

In para 14(a)(c) of Art 3 of Law 2328/1995, the legislator makes a distinction between programmes harmful to minors' physical, mental or moral development, providing that so called 'soft' programmes (which do not seriously impair minors' development) should be transmitted after 9.30 pm, and other programmes after midnight. By those provisions, the law adopts the system of 'zones' of television broadcasting, which subsequently affects the broadcasting of television advertising, given that television advertisements regarded as 'hard' for the development of minors should be transmitted after midnight. A relevant provision, which restricts the time of broadcasting of advertisements referring to children's toys and games, is adopted by Law 2251/1994 (Art 14, para 8) according to which all such advertising should be broadcast after 10 pm and before 7 am.

## The right of reply

The Greek legislator, by harmonising the legislation with the provisions of Directive 89/552/EEC, has also introduced the statute of 'the right of reply' in Law 2328/1995 (Art 3, para 11). This legal right was also adopted by the former Law 1730/1987 (paras 12–14 of Art 3) which is amended by the provisions of the new Law.

According to those provisions (as amended), any natural person or legal entity whose personality, honour or reputation or whose private or family life or whose professional, social, scientific, artistic, political or similar activities are harmed by a television or radio programme, the spouse and relatives (up to third remove) of a deceased whose memory is insulted, as well as the legal representative of a legal entity whose reputation or business interests are harmed, have the right to request a remedy from the station transmitting the broadcast within an exclusive period of 10 days from the date of the broadcast or re-broadcast.

Among the persons to whom the law grants this right are political parties and their members and trade unions and their members when their beliefs or statements are falsified or presented incorrectly in a way creating a false impression to the viewer or listener.

The relevant application may be filed to the broadcasting station by any appropriate means, especially by fax, telex, telegram, registered letter or extra-judicial notice and should include:

(a) the identity of the insulted physical person or legal entity, as well as the identity of the spouse or the relative of the deceased and of the representative of the legal entity;

(b) the date and hour of the broadcast of the harmful programme;

(c) the reasons for which the programme was insulting; and

(d) the text of the reply or an application for the appearance of the applicant at the same or similar broadcast or for the registration of the relevant (and respective) reply.

The reply should not constitute a criminal act or provoke the civil liability of the station or insult morality. The reply is considered as respective or equal when its duration is at least the same as that of the harmful reference and is transmitted after the next equivalent programme (in the case of a series of similar programme) or after the respective (as far as the time of broadcast) television news or in general, to the same viewers. The right of reply is not a substitute for the civil or penal liability of the station, but if the reply is judged (by the court) as complete, it may be considered as actual penitence or as compensation in materiae.

The competent authority (at first instance) to decide on the application for reply is the station itself, informing the applicant of its decision within 48 hours. In case of disallowance of the application, the station is obliged to forward it to the National Council of Radio-television within 24 hours. The latter decides on the matter within three days and its decision is final and binding on the station.

## Radio advertising

All the above-mentioned conditions and restrictions imposed for television advertising apply similarly to advertising messages transmitted by local radio stations (Art 8 of Law 2328/1995).

## Administrative sanctions

Under the provisions of Art 4 of Law 2328/1995, in the case of violation of national legislation, of European Union legislation, or of international law ruling directly or indirectly on the function of private television, Law 2121/1993 (on the protection of intellectual property) and the rules of conduct as imposed by the provisions of Art 3 of Law 2328/1995, the Minister of Press and Mass Media, with the positive opinion of the National Radio/Television Council has the right to impose the following sanctions and penalties on television and radio stations:

---

30   These fines were doubled in cases of violation of the above mentioned provisions, in accordance with Art 12 of the Law 2644/1998 referring to the holders of a licence for the supply of radio and TV services by subscription (eg, cable TV).

(a) recommendations or warnings;

(b) fines from Drs 5 m up to Drs 500 m;[30]

(c) temporary cessation of the function of the station of up to three months; and

(d) revocation of the station's broadcasting permit.

These extremely severe fines are inflicted jointly and severally to the station, to the station's legal representative, all members of its board of directors and to all its shareholders holding more than 2.5% of the share capital.

The severe nature of the above-mentioned sanctions and penalties obliges the competent bodies, in our opinion, to interpret the relevant provisions very strictly in order to avoid unfair results and the ultimate destruction of the freedom of the Press.

Furthermore, accordance of the provisions of this article with the Constitution is very doubtful, given that the legislator once again excludes public television and radio from the implementation of these sanctions, effectively granting them immunity.

## Advertising in the press

Greek legislation over press matters may be characterised as conservative, considering that the relevant sector is governed mainly by the provisions of Law 1092/1938.

This Law, and several others of mainly administrative and criminal character, deal with matters of newspaper and magazine publication.

Law 1092/1938 does not include any special provisions on the presentation of an advertisement. Consequently, the advertisement should itself be treated as a 'publication' (article, photograph, etc) and the provisions of Arts 39–47 apply equally to advertisements.

According to these provisions, the following are prohibited:

(a) the publication of comments relating either to the litigant parties or to the judged crime and the publication of any document referring to the procedure during the process of a criminal trial (Art 39);

(b) the publication of articles, photographs, etc, encouraging or approving or otherwise describing the acts and life of criminals in a way which offends against public morals (Art 40);

(c) the publication of plans concerning army, navy or air force mobilisation and the publication of announcements, descriptions or photos relating to installations useful for the defence of the country or associated therewith;

(d) the publication of articles, photos, sketches, pictures which are obscene and offend against public morals. Works of art and of science are not considered as obscene publications.

Law 1092/1938 provides, in the case of violation of the above prohibitions, a variety of penalties (depending on the gravity and number of violations), from the imprisonment of the editor or the publisher, or the director and/or the journalist, to the seizure of the newspaper or the magazine (in case of violation of the obscene publication prohibition). The above crimes are always considered as 'caught in the act' and their prescription is determined to 18 months. Law 2243/1994 abolished the criminal (substantial and procedural) provisions of the above Law.

Moreover, according to the provisions of Law 1178/1981, as amended by Law 1941/1991, in the case of a civil dispute regarding a publication offending the honour of a particular person (or legal entity), the proprietor of the newspaper or magazine is liable for the indemnification of the harmed person, even if the harmful event is caused by the journalist.

If the relevant petition is included in the lawsuit, the Law recognises that the court has the right to oblige the magazine or newspaper to publish, in the same place, the court's decision in brief including:

(a) the decision number;

(b) the issuing court;

(c) the name of the plaintiff;

(d) the phrases, words or pictures found defamatory; and

(e) the relevant date of the harmful publication.

In case of delay in publication of this briefing, a fine is imposed equal to five times the price of the governmental publications for each and every day of delay.

Finally, the above Law as amended by Law 2243/1994 provides that the indemnity of a harmed person should be not lower than Drs 10 m for daily newspapers and magazines published in Athens and Thessaloniki and Drs 2 m for all other newspapers and magazines.

It is self-evident that the provisions of general laws concerning advertising apply also to press advertising.

## Advertising with posters

Advertising messages targeted at the public in the street or other open areas in the form of posters stuck to surfaces are dealt with by the provisions of Law 1491/1984.

Under this Law, all relevant conditions are defined by the local municipal authority (Art 1, para 1 of Law 1491/1984).

The local authority will define, one month before the end of each year, the special areas and places on which billposting of advertising messages is allowed.

Any kind of billposting is prohibited on:

(a) monuments, statues and historic buildings;

(b) surfaces of public sector technical works such as bridges, tunnels, pavements, etc;

(c) official public information signs, traffic signs, timetables and bus stations;

(d) archaeological sites, traditional villages as well as areas of outstanding natural beauty;

(e) public buildings and all places of worship;

(f) private buildings.

The hanging of banners over roads, squares and other public places and the placing of signs indicating the location or address of private enterprises or shops without the prior permission of the municipal authority is also prohibited.

Article 5 of Law 1491/1984 provides that any form of 'commercial' advertising (expressly excluding the 'advertising' messages of political parties – Arts 3 and 4 of Law 1491/1984) is allowed only after a relevant permit or licence is issued by the competent authority (mayor, etc) and after payment of the relevant advertising tax, permitting billposting in places defined by the municipality. Signs placed on the walls, windows or roofs of the business or office whose activities are being advertised are excluded from the above provisions. Moreover, Art 11 of the Code of Traffic provides that signs indicating the trading name, title or trade mark of a business operating in a particular street should be placed parallel with that street.

Subject to the restrictions provided in Art 2 of Law 1491/1984, commercial advertising may take place in streets, pavements, squares, public buildings and areas only with permanent, stable frames or temporary, movable frames made under the supervision and at the expense of the advertiser.

All posters should mention the trading name or name and the address of the business advertised or the advertiser or the name of the printer as well as the number of the relevant permit granted by the competent municipality.

By Art 6 of the Law 1491/1984, 'commercial' advertising is allowed:

(a) at ports, airports, railway stations and stadiums;

(b) inside railway carriages, trolley buses and buses;

(c) at bus stops and kiosks;

(d) in shops, cinemas, theatres and other relevant places;

(e) in restaurants, coffee shops, etc.

Law 1491/1984 also imposes penal sanctions and penalties on the violators of its provisions. More specifically:

(a) on violators of the provisions of para 1(a) of Art 2 of Law 1491/1984 (billposting on monuments, statues, etc), a penalty of up to one year's imprisonment and a fine of Drs 300,000 is imposed;

(b) on violators of the other provisions of para 1 of Art 2 of Law 1491/1984, a penalty of up to 6 months' imprisonment and a fine of up to Drs 100,000 is imposed;

(c) on violators of Arts 5 and 6 of the Law (advertising without permission), a penalty of up to 6 months' imprisonment and a fine of Drs 300,000 is imposed.

### Advertising on taxis

Under the provisions of Ministerial Decision No 8/1994, 'commercial' advertising may be placed on the exterior part of taxis, and specifically:

(a) stuck on the doors of the vehicle, unless those doors contain a written reference to the taxi's area and to the fact that it is a radio taxi;

(b) placed on the roof of the vehicle, behind the sign with the word 'taxi', in the form of a prismatic pyramid, on the parallel sides of which the advertisement may be placed. This pyramid should be illuminated or fluorescent and its dimensions may be:

- height – 30 cm maximum;
- top angle – 50°; and
- length – 85 cm maximum.

Only one sort of advertising may be stuck or placed on the taxi; it should not affect the appearance of the car or offend against morality and public order and should, in general, comply with the current laws and decrees on advertising. Any advertising of a political party or generally of a political nature is strictly prohibited.

The organisation and general management of this sort of advertising is granted to the most representative labour union of taxi owners of the capital of each prefecture, which is also responsible for the implementation of the above provisions.

## Advertising as defined by the subject of the advertised persons

In this section, we shall examine the special forms of advertising under the criterion of the advertised person.

## Advertising of physicians

Under the provisions of Law 2194/1994 (Art 6), as amended by Law 2256/1994, all kinds of 'medical' advertising are prohibited. Paragraph 1 of Art 6 provides that:

From the publication of this Law, medical advertising as well as advertising of private and dental hospitals, private clinics, dental centres, centres of medical diagnosis and laboratories is prohibited.

The Law specifically prohibits advertising, defined as any placement of advertising posters, panels or signs, announcements, publications or printed documents in order to promote the supply of medical services (para 2 of Art 6 of Law 2194/1984).

On violators of these provisions, the following administrative sanctions are imposed:

(a) a fine of between Drs 1 m and Drs 10 m for each violation and suspension of all relevant contracts existing between the violator and the State for a period of one month to one year;

(b) revocation of the medical practice licence for up to one year. In case of repeated violation, the sanction of permanent revocation of the medical practice licence is imposed.

## Advertising of pharmacies and chemists

Presidential Decree No 340/1993, 'Code of Conduct of Greek Chemists', adopts a prohibition of all forms of advertising of pharmacies and the services supplied by chemists. Under the provisions of para (a) of Art 25 of the Code, advertising of medicines or pharmaceutical products or the promotion of advertising messages contrary to the provisions of this Code (such as actions and means contrary to human dignity or the value of the chemist as a scientist in the service of public health – Art 22, etc) is strictly prohibited in any kind of mass communication or other media.

Advertising messages promoting certain parapharmaceutical activities of the pharmacies, such as beauty and diet products departments, are allowed on condition that the strict pharmaceutical services supplied by the pharmacy are not promoted.

## Advertising of hotels and travel agencies and businesses

Law 2160/1993 provides for several administrative sanctions on suppliers (hotel owners, travel agents, etc) who falsely advertise services. More specifically:

(a) according to the provisions of Art 4, para 5(b)(3) of Law 2160/1993, a travel agent, hotel owner or supplier of tourist services in general, who fails to provide its clientèle with the service, level of comfort and/or goods promised or advertised in writing, or whose goods or services are obviously of inferior rate or quality, is punished with a fine of Drs 200,000;

(b) in addition, a fine of up to Drs 5 m will be imposed on travel agents (and suppliers in general) who advertise tourist facilities different from those described in the relevant contracts (Art 4, para 9 of Law 2160/1993).

### Advertising of private institutes of professional education (colleges)

The Greek legislator has also adopted some special restrictions on the form and context of an advertising message which refers to private colleges, which are new to Greek legislation. Under the provisions of Art 10 of Ministerial Decision No 6987/1993, the advertising of:

(a) private colleges (IIEK) should contain a reference to the registered number of the college;

(b) all advertising material (for example, signs, posters, panels and television spots) must be approved by the competent organisation of the Education Ministry (OEEK) which, within 10 working days, should decide to approve or reject the advertisement;

(c) all advertising of colleges without the approval of said organisation is prohibited.

In cases of violation of the provisions of the above Ministerial Decision, the following sanctions are imposed:

(a) fine;

(b) temporary revocation of the licence to operate; and

(c) permanent revocation of the licence to operate.

### Advertising of banks and credit institutions

Certain restrictions on the advertising of the services supplied by banks and other credit institutions are adopted by Art 13 of Law 2076/1992 (Operation of Credit Institutions), mainly referring to the advertising of services supplied by credit institutions registered in other Member States of the EU and operating in Greece, which is allowed on condition that the advertising conforms with the relevant provisions (referring to advertising in general). The Bank of Greece, after consultation with the Union of Greek Banks, has the right to order the prohibition of misleading advertising.

Furthermore, by Ministerial Decision (Ministries of Justice – Commerce and National Economy) No F1-983/1991, the Greek legislator has harmonised Greek legislation with the provisions of Directive 87/102/EEC on the matter of consumer credit.

Under the provisions of Art 8 of the said Decision:

(a) the provisions referring to advertising apply respectively to all advertisements, written or electronic or other, in which the advertiser declares that he is offering credit or acting as an intermediary in order to achieve credit;

(b) if the advertisement includes references to arithmetical factors relating to the cost of the credit, the advertisement should include at least the following:

- the price of the product/or service if paid in cash and the price of the product and/or service if paid by credit;
- the amount of the advance payment;
- the amount, number and frequency of the installments;
- the compound interest; and
- the annual real compound interest (which is defined in Art 3 as the interest, which, on an annual basis, balances the values of the total of the obligation (loans, charges and payments), future and current, concluded between the credit institution and the consumer.

If the annual real compound interest cannot be defined otherwise, the advertisement should include a representative example.

### Advertising of legal services

The 'Code of Lawyers' (Decree 3026/1954, as amended by Law 1336/1983) forbids all kinds of advertising by lawyers and by third parties offering legal services.

Furthermore, under the provisions of para 2 of Art 40 of the above-mentioned Code of Lawyers:

Any civilian, not being a lawyer, or without the assistance of a lawyer, or with the assistance of a lawyer of his choice, undertaking or presenting or advertising himself as being able to manage cases and to proceed to actions of which lawyers are exclusively authorised, is punished with the sanction of imprisonment for at least six months and a fine of at least Drs 50,000.

## Tobacco advertising

The advertising of tobacco products, especially cigarettes, is strictly restricted. As already mentioned, such advertisements are strictly prohibited from being broadcast by television and radio stations.

Under the provisions of Law 1802/1988 (Art 12):

On all packaging of tobacco products that circulate and are consumed in Greece, as well as on all printed advertising of tobacco products, medical warnings concerning the harmful effects of smoking to health must appear in Greek, according to the Ministerial Decisions of the Ministry of Health.

The conditions and terms under which the advertising of tobacco products is allowed is defined by Ministerial Decision No A2c/1591/1989, which provides that advertisements for tobacco products are allowed in the press, magazines, printed matter, stickers, newspapers and posters, provided they include the relevant medical warning.

This medical warning consists of the phrase: 'Ministry of Health warning: SMOKING IS SERIOUSLY DAMAGING TO HEALTH.'

The same wording should be included and printed on all packaging (packets of cigarettes, cigars, etc) and permanent advertising installations (for example, kiosks, panels, etc). The frame in which the above-mentioned Ministry of Health warning should be printed must have a surface area equal to 10% of the whole surface area of the advertisement and the words 'SMOKING IS SERIOUSLY DAMAGING TO HEALTH' should cover at least 50% of the said frame and should be printed in black bold letters.

In the case of advertising in cinemas (which is allowed during the projection of a film inappropriate for minors), after the advertising message for the tobacco product the warning 'Ministry of Health warning: SMOKING IS SERIOUSLY DAMAGING TO HEALTH' should be shown for at least three seconds and should cover at least 30% of the screen.

Finally, all kind of advertising of tobacco products is prohibited inside hospitals, clinics, educational institutions of all degrees and all youth and sports centres (stadiums, gymnasiums, etc).

In case of violation of the provisions of the Law and of the relevant Ministerial Decision, the sanction of up to 6 months' imprisonment, or a fine of up to Drs 10 m (and in any case not less than 100% of the cost of the said advertising) or both, are imposed.

# CODE OF CONDUCT (THE CODE OF ADVERTISING PRACTICE)

The Greek Code of Advertising Practice was adopted by the Greek Union of Advertising Enterprises in 1977. This Code is based on the provisions of the relevant Code of Advertising Practice of the International Chamber of Commerce. The Code is based on the system of self-control of the advertisers and is also adopted by several legal entities involved in advertising as the Union of Hellenic Industries, the Consumers' Institutes, radio and television stations, Union of Newspaper Proprietors, the Association of Advertised Persons, etc.

## Scope of the Code

The Code applies to all advertising for any kind of goods and services. The Code sets the standards of ethical conduct to be followed by all persons concerned with advertising, whether as advertisers, advertised persons or media.

## Interpretation and application

(a) The Code is to be applied in the spirit as well as in the letter.

(b) The final criterion for the definition of an advertisement as ethical should be the eventual danger of the misleading of the consumer.

(c) The Code applies to the entire content of an advertisement, including all words and numbers (spoken or written) usual presentations, music and sound effects, in general, to the whole advertising message, in no matter what form (simple or complex).

(d) For the purpose of this Code, the term 'advertising' is to be taken in its broadest sense to embrace any form of advertising for goods, services, irrespective of the medium used and including advertising claims on packs, labels and point of sale material. The term 'product' includes services. The term 'consumer' refers to any person to whom advertising is addressed or who is likely to be reached by it, whether as a final consumer or as a trade customer or user.

## Basic principles

All advertising should be legal, decent, honest and truthful.

Every advertisement should be prepared with a due sense of social responsibility and should conform to the principles of fair competition, as generally accepted in business.

No advertising should be such as to impair public confidence in advertising.

*Rules*

**Decency**

Article 1

Advertising should not contain statements or visual presentations which offend prevailing standards of decency.

## Honesty

Article 2

Advertising should be so framed as not to abuse the trust of the consumer or exploit his lack of experience or knowledge.

Article 3

1 Advertising should not, without justifiable reason, play on fear.

2 Advertising should not play on superstition.

3 Advertising should not contain anything which might lead to or lend support to acts of violence.

4 Advertising should avoid endorsing national matters, sacred texts, the national and cultural heritage and discrimination based upon race, religion, etc.

## Truthful presentation

Article 4

1 Advertising should not contain any statement or visual presentation which directly or by implication, omission, ambiguity or exaggerated claim is likely to mislead the consumer, in particular with regard to:

(a) characteristics such as nature, composition, method and date of manufacture, fitness for purpose, range of use, quantity, commercial or geographical origin;

(b) the value of the product and the total price actually to be paid;

(c) other terms of payment such as hire, purchase, leasing, installment sales and credit sale;

(d) delivery, exchange, return, repair and maintenance;

(e) terms of guarantee;

(f) copyright and industrial property rights such as patents, trade marks, designs and models and trade names;

(g) official recognition or approval, awards of medals, prizes and diplomas.

2 Advertising should not misuse research results of quotations from technical and scientific publications. Scientific terms should not be misused; scientific jargon and irrelevancies should not be used to make claims appear to have a scientific basis they do not possess.

## Comparisons

Article 5

Advertising containing comparisons should be so designed that the comparison itself is not likely to mislead, and should comply with the principles of fair competition. Points of comparison should be based on facts which can be documented and should not be unfairly selected.

## Testimonials

Article 6

Advertising should not contain or refer to any testimonial or endorsement unless it is genuine and related to the experience of the person giving it. Testimonials or endorsements which are obsolete or otherwise no longer applicable should not be used.

## Denigration

Article 7

Advertising should not denigrate any firm, industrial or commercial activity or profession or any product, directly or by implication.

## Protection of privacy

Article 8

Advertising should not portray or refer to any persons, whether in a private or a public capacity, unless prior permission has been obtained; nor should advertising without prior permission depict or refer to any person's property in a way likely to convey the impression of a personal endorsement.

## Exploitation of goodwill

Article 9

1   Advertising should not make unjustifiable use of the name or initials of another firm, company or institution.

2   Advertising should not take undue advantage of the goodwill attached to the name of a person, the trade name and symbol of another firm or product, or of the goodwill acquired by an advertising campaign.

## Imitation

Article 10

1   Advertising should not imitate the general layout, text, slogan, visual presentation, music and sound effects etc, of other advertising in a way that is likely to mislead or confuse.

2   Where an international advertiser has established a distinctive advertising campaign in one or more countries, other advertisers should not unduly imitate this campaign in the other countries where he operates, thus preventing him from extending his campaign within a reasonable period of time to such countries.

## Identification of advertising

Article 11

Advertising should be clearly distinguishable as such, whatever its form and whatever the medium used; when advertising appears in a medium which contains news or editorial matter, it should be so presented that it will be readily recognised as advertising.

**Regard to safety**

Article 12

Advertising should not, without reason, justifiable on educational or social grounds, contain any visual presentation or any description of dangerous practices or of situations which show a disregard for safety. Special care should be taken in advertising directed towards or depicting children or young people.

**Children and young people**

Article 13

1   Advertising should not exploit the natural credulity of children or the lack of experience of young people.

2   Advertising addressed to or likely to influence children or young people should not contain any statement or visual presentation which might result in harming them morally, mentally or physically.

**Responsibility**

Article 14

1   Responsibility for the observance of the rules of conduct laid down in the Code rests with the advertiser, the advertising practitioner or agency and the publisher, media owner or contractor:

    (a)   the advertiser should take the overall responsibility for his advertising;

    (b)   the advertising practitioner or agency should exercise every care in the creation, preparation or promotion of advertising to be in conformity to the present Code. Furthermore, he should point out to the advertiser any deviation from the letter and/or the spirit of the Code and help him to observe the Code;

    (c)   the advertising media should exercise due care in the acceptance of advertisements and their presentation to the public.

Article 15

The responsibility for observance of the rules of the Code embraces the advertisement in its entire content and form, including testimonials and statements or visual presentations originating from other sources. The fact that the content or form originates wholly or in part from other sources is not an excuse for non-observance of the rules.

Article 16

Descriptions, claims or illustrations relating to verifiable facts should be capable of substantiation. Advertisers should have such substantiation available so that they can produce evidence without delay to the self-regulatory bodies responsible for the operation of the Code.

Article 17

Advertisers, advertising practitioners or agencies, media owners, publishers or contractors should not contribute to the public presentation of an advertisement found unacceptable by the competent regulatory body responsible for the operation of the Code.

Article 18

The competent regulatory body, at first instance, to judge whether an advertisement is in conformity with the provisions of the Code is the board of directors of the Greek Union of Advertising Enterprises. At second instance, the said board of directors will propose the formation of a wider committee with the participation of the media, advertisers and other organisations, as soon as they sign the Code.

This committee is formed and constituted of eight members with the participation of representatives of the media, the Ministry of Commerce, etc.

Article 19

The observance of the provisions of the Code and the decisions of the Judgment Committee is the responsibility and obligation of the members ratifying the Code.

The above-mentioned Code of Advertising Practice has also certain annexes and special guidelines referring to special forms of advertising.

## *Annex I*

Specifically, Annex I of the Code deals with the matter of advertising targeted at children (defined as children under 14 years of age), and covering communications referring to products that are directly aimed at children or products that are mainly and in normal circumstances used by children. Finally, Annex I also covers the matter of the participation of children in advertising messages and, especially, their behaviour. The Annex also covers all advertising and all kind of products and/or services as defined in the Code.

The Annex, in its basic principles, provides that advertising encouraging children to purchase products by phone or by post is prohibited and that all indirect advertising (advertorials/editorials) should be easily recognised as advertising.

On the subject of children's behaviour, para 3 of the Annex provides that the behaviour of children participating in advertising should conform with generally accepted good manners. Furthermore, it is provided that advertising should not misrepresent or doubt the responsibility and judgment of parents. Finally, any kind of advertising which shows children consuming alcoholic beverages, or in any way approving the consumption of alcoholic beverages, is prohibited.

In para 4 of this Annex, certain restrictions are adopted on the matter of promises included in advertising targeted at children and, more specifically, it is provided that:

(a) such advertising should not persuade a child that happiness, social recognition or success will be reached directly by the purchase of the product;

(b) advertising of a product should not promise children that its purchase will make them superior to other children;

(c) advertising or any communication should not include any exhortation to children to persuade other persons to buy the advertised products;

(d) in any case, emphasis should be given to the proper evaluation of the size and quality of the promoted product and, more specifically, to the nature and use of the product;

(e) in case of reference to the price, advertising should not include references to compared prices, for instance, by using the words 'just' or 'only', etc, or to suggest that the product may be easily acquired by everyone.

Finally, the Annex includes certain provisions on matters of security, according to which advertising should not contain any statement or visual presentation of children performing dangerous acts, consorting with strangers, or entering, or being in, places which are unsuitable for children.

In general, the provisions of para 5 of Annex 1 prohibit advertising containing actions whose effect could be to bring children into hazardous or unsafe situations, such as showing children using matches, medicines, gas or climbing on trees, ladders, or bridges, or driving vehicles, etc, without parental supervision.

## Annex II

In Annex II of the Code, certain restrictions are adopted on the advertising of tobacco products.

According to these provisions, advertising of tobacco products should be aimed only at adults and not to persons under the age of 18 and, in any case, should not encourage people to start smoking. Furthermore, such advertising should not be shown in or near places frequented by minors, such as schools, or in magazines aimed mainly at minors.

In addition, such advertising should not show or use (a) images of famous people, or (b) persons under the age of 25 years.

Finally, all advertising of tobacco and related products (lighters, matches, pipes, etc) should be moderate and, moreover, should include all the usual references and warnings on the damage to health that smoking may cause.

## Annex III

In Annex III of the Code of Conduct certain dispositions are adopted relating to advertising referring to ecology or the environment. The scope of the

Annex is to determine 'the framework of such advertising in all kinds of media of products or services, including promises related to the ecology or the environment'.

Under the provisions of Arts 1–2 of this Annex, advertising should be honest and decent, meaning that it should not be formulated in a way likely to exploit the interest of the consumer on environmental matters or his lack of experience or knowledge of ecology, and should not encourage acts contrary to generally accepted ecological or 'environmental' behaviour.

Article 3 of Annex III deals with truthful presentation of advertising, which should not contain statements or acts likely to mislead consumers with regard to the ecological prescriptions or advantages of the product, or activities of the advertiser for the benefit of the environment. Advertising of businesses should not refer to the ecological practice or values of the business if these do not represent their total activity.

Moreover, the second paragraph of Art 3 prohibits the use of phrases such as 'environmentally friendly' or 'ecologically safe', etc, by which a product or service is presented as having no effect, or positive consequences, on the environment, unless this is totally proved.

Regarding the use of scientific research, Art 4 of Annex III provides that the use of 'technical' presentations or scientific achievements relating to a positive effect on the environment should be included in advertising only when those factors are substantially and scientifically based. It is also provided that scientific or ecological terminology should be accepted only if it is presented in a certain way which is easily comprehended by consumers.

According to the provisions of Art 5, the use of testimonials in advertising should not be inaccurate when they present an ecological promise, especially when this is based on a change of composition of the product. The ratio of these provisions is founded on the rapid evolution of technology and environmental science, and it is also provided that special care should be paid to the genuineness of the promises at the time when the advertising campaign is taking place.

Furthermore, Art 6 of this Annex provides that the superiority of a product on ecological matters, when compared to another competitive product, should be shown only when this product has a substantial and important advantage which can easily be understood by the consumer, and its superiority can be substantiated by comparison.

A promise founded on the absence of a harmful ingredient, or of a disastrous effect on the product when compared to competitive products, is allowed only when the other products of the same class and category have this ingredient or are causing the above-mentioned effect.

Furthermore, according to the provisions of Art 7 of Annex III: 'An ecological value applying to one stage of the production or distribution of a product should not be implied to refer to all stages, eventually if non-ecological.' Paragraph (b) of this article also provides restrictions on advertising containing ecological messages and promises, which should specify to which stage or nature of the product they are referring. Finally, paragraph (c) of the article provides that, when advertising refers to a decrease in harmful ingredients or components, these should be specified.

On the use of ecological symbols, it is provided that this should not allude falsely to any official certification or authorisation, and also that such symbols should not be presented in a way likely to mislead (Art 8).

Finally, Art 9 provides that the use of a competitor's trade mark for comparison is prohibited.

## Annex IV

The final Annex (IV) of the Code refers to political advertising and is aimed at 'all political parties, groups and persons, involved in any way in the political life of the country'.

According to the definitions in para 5 of the introduction to the said Annex:

(a) 'politician' means physical persons, political parties and political groups;

(b) 'political message' means a message addressed in no matter what form or means, to one or more persons;

(c) 'misleading' is political language whose context, wording or form misleads or is likely to mislead its recipients, and affecting as a result their political or social behaviour and opinion or harming other politicians.

Para 2 of Annex IV (general principles) adopts the guidelines to be followed by the politician and the creator of the political message according to which:

(a) they should try to convince the citizen by addressing to his rational judgment with arguments, proof and opinions;

(b) they should respect both human personality and the right of every person to create and express his opinion freely;

(c) they should be sincere;

(d) they should contribute to the creation of the proper practical, intellectual, moral and psychological conditions for the conduct of a sincere debate;

(e) they should not apply or encourage methods that could be regarded as an attempt to corrupt the integrity and independence of the press and/or the electronic mass media;

(f) they should not use methods, means or techniques which provoke subconscious motivation in the recipients of the political message, thus depriving them of free judgment;

(g) they should protect and keep any secrets confided in them in the exercise of their duties.

In s 3 of this Annex the rules to be followed by political advertising are adopted:

(a) the political message should not be misleading or illicit;

(b) the political message should be moral, honest, national, legitimate, sincere and decent and be composed and expressed in the spirit of social responsibility and in a way that does not damage the trust of people in politicians and does not undermine their credibility.

According to those principles the political language should not:

(a) include false or disputable (unconfirmed) numbers, facts, statements and information;

(b) exploit the ignorance, lack of experience or credulity of the recipients;

(c) exploit the fears, hopes and general instincts and emotions and superstitions of the recipients;

(d) promise widely and generally the solution of all personal, collective and national problems, without mentioning a substantiated report of the methods and practice to be followed for their solution;

(e) present the results of market research generally and/or in fragments in such a way as to alter and/or deform the real results of the research;

(f) include elements which may lead, directly or indirectly, to dangerous social behaviour and/or acts of violence;

(g) speculate matters of national interest, holy texts, Greek cultural heritage, national defects, national or religious or international symbols;

(h) offend against the human dignity and personality of persons and/or social groups, discriminating on the basis of age, race, sex, religion, nationality, political or ideological beliefs and physical or intellectual features;

(i) include elements that, directly or indirectly, by allusion, omission, exaggeration and/or ambiguity, mislead its recipient;

(j) include comparative features, chosen in a certain way, in order to provoke doubt or confusion or to mislead;

(k) make false use of scientific terms, idioms and points irrelevant to the matter, in order to substantiate their positions on a scientific basis without being so.

Furthermore, the political message, when referring to other politicians should not:

(a) include insulting or disparaging expressions and/or allusions;

(b) refer disparagingly to their personal or family life when those references do not affect their political and public life;

(c) accuse them groundlessly and without proof of a political or other act or omission;

(d) imitate the message of other politicians in a way that may provoke confusion and/or mislead the recipient.

The responsibility for the observance of the rules of Annex IV rests with the same persons as the Code in general and with all parties, political groups and politicians.

# ADVERTISING CONTRACTS

Below is a draft of a contract for the provision of advertising services. This contract has been chosen for its general character (given that it refers to 'advertising services' without relating them to the advertising media) and for its combined legal character, which will be discussed below, p 508.

## LETTER OF AGREEMENT

### FOR THE PROVISION OF ADVERTISING SERVICES

_____

represented by _____

(hereinafter called the Agency)

and _____

(hereinafter called the Client) agreed today the _____ of

_____, the following:

1   ASSIGNMENT OF ADVERTISING SERVICES

The Client appoints the Agency and the Agency agrees to act as its advertising agent as of _____. This agreement covers the Client's following product/services (hereinafter called the Products):

1 _____

2 _____

3 _____

4 _____

5 _____

This agreement is in effect until terminated by 90 days' written notice by either party. The 90 days' notice period may be shortened subject to agreement between the two parties.

2   SERVICES PROVIDED BY THE AGENCY

The Agency shall:

1   study the market, the consumer and the various marketing variables, formulate strategies, as well as create and produce advertising copy and visual material for usage in media (for example, newspapers, magazines, radio, television, outdoor posters, cinema);

2   formulate media plans on the basis of the media budget agreed with the Client;

3   carry out approved media plans on behalf of the Client;

4   check all advertising insertions (including radio and television spots) by applying the methods and procedures that are generally used by advertising agencies;

5   follow up and assess the advertising activities and media expenditure of the clients' major competition;

6   formulate and execute in part or in whole, sales promotion activities, public relations, events, dealer meetings, etc;

7   create and produce logos, brand names, packaging and any other material which may be required for the proper product presentation;

8   create and produce print material and point-of-sale material;

9   undertake the supervision of print or other production of any advertising material;

10  co-operate in an advisory capacity in the formulation of the marketing plan of a product;

11  undertake the design and supervise the execution of marketing research.

3   REMUNERATION

1   The Agency will charge ....% commission on the gross cost of any advertising appearance of the Clients' products in any advertising medium (television, radio, newspapers, magazines, outdoor posters, cinema). The gross cost for the Client is considered the price of the advertising medium plus the stamp duty contribution and the special 30% television levy. The Agency shall return to the client the 20% discount it receives from the media as an agency.

2   For finished artwork, colour separations and films, radio tapes, cinema and television copies and any other material used in any advertising media, the Agency will charge the Client the internal production cost of such agreed material together with any payments to thirds parties, plus a commission of 17.65% on the external costs for the supervision of such work.

3   For the following jobs, as authorised by the Client, the Agency will charge all payments to third parties plus 17.65% commission, as well as the internal cost for the development and production of the material.

Indicative list of such jobs:

- design and/or artwork for print material;
- print production;
- design of logos and packaging;
- design and/or production of point-of-sale material;
- storyboards and artwork for television/Cinema commercials.

To ensure a clear understanding of the cost involved in performing the jobs listed above (2 and 3), the Agency issues once a year a price list based on the average cost of these jobs and on the price prevailing in the advertising market (see attached Appendix 2). The Client can accept the price list and charges will then be made based on it. The price list represents the internal Agency cost. As a result, payments to suppliers and the 17.65% commission on the latter will be added to each invoice. Should a specific job mentioned in the price list appear to be more complicated or, on the contrary, simpler than the average taken as a basis for the price list, the Client will receive an ad hoc cost estimate together with the necessary explanations.

For all other services, such as development of new product ideas, organising and/or co-operating in the organisation of sales meetings and conferences, exhibitions, public relations projects, sales promotion campaigns, marketing studies, etc, the Agency will charge a previously agreed fee.

4    If and when orders, pending jobs, plans or other cost generating jobs are cancelled or changed at the Client's request, the Agency will charge the actual expenses/costs/charges incurred up to the point of cancellation.

The Client commits himself to release the Agency promptly from all commitments vis à vis third parties related to cancelled or altered jobs.

5    Market research, advertising research, investigations and inquiries:

(a) the Agency subscribes to audience rating services and other types of media research, uses it for generating media plans and does not charge the Client for it;

(b) any other research that the Agency has recommended and the Client has approved or research that has been requested by the Client, will be charged at cost;

(c) competitive television commercials and press cuttings that the Agency purchases from outside suppliers will be charged at cost.

4    NON-BILLABLE SERVICES

1    Strategy proposals, creative recommendation for mass media campaigns, television scripts, layouts, media plans and sales promotion plans that are necessary for the setting up of a proper presentation, whether approved or not.

2    General administrative Agency costs.

3   Postage, telephone, fax, telex and local travel expenses that are incurred in the routine conduct of business. Expenses that the Agency undertake following the client's request for special jobs are charged at cost. Examples of such costs are long distance telephone calls, travelling out of the Athens area, transportation of material, etc.

4   Checking presence in all media used to ensure that advertising is run as agreed (time, position, reproduction quality).

5   Follow-up of competitive media advertising, including translation cost of competitive advertising copy.

6   Co-operation in an advisory capacity in the preparation of a product's marketing plan.

7   Advisory analysis of the Client(s) integrated communication's needs.

## 5   TERMS OF PAYMENT

The Client settles all invoices pertaining to approved costs within eight days from the date of issue.

## 6   COPYRIGHT

The whole material of the advertising campaign of the products, given that it includes the advertising ideas of the Agency and has been produced by it, after the transfer of the property rights of the creator employees, or of the external collaborators to it, is the copyright of the Agency. As a result, any kind of use, even of part of this material or of the advertising idea, by a third party without a previous agreement of the Agency, even after the termination of this contract, is not possible.

## 7   SECURITY

The Agency will not, while this agreement is in force, act as advertising agent of any other advertiser, for products which are competitive to the Client's products. It is the Agency's responsibility to discuss doubtful cases with the Client.

The Agency is bound to regard as a trade secret and maintain in the strictest confidence all information and material given to it by the Client, as well as work that the Agency will perform or propose to be performed for the Client.

The Agency will refrain from disclosing any such information to anyone, either inside or outside its organisation, except to those individuals who need it to implement the advertising plans effectively.

## 8   TERMINATION OF AGREEMENT

The Client will pay the Agency's remuneration as described in this document for all activities performed up to the day this agreement expires.

After the agreement's termination and independence of its cause, the Agency will turn over to the Client or his designate only such unused portion thereof, as concerns the Client's account.

All terms and conditions herein will be interpreted and have effect according to the laws of Greece.

FOR THE CLIENT                                    FOR THE AGENCY

Signature _____               _____

Name _____                    _____

Title _____                   _____

## The legal character of the contract

The description of the services to be provided by the 'Agent', the lack of any clause referring to the duration of the contract and the references to the remuneration of the Agent lead us to the conclusion that the above contract should be characterised as a 'leasing of work' contract as defined by the provisions of Arts 681–702 of the Greek Civil Code.

The definition of that kind of agreement derives from the provisions of Art 681 of the Civil Code, according to which 'leasing of work' is a bilateral, transient, contractual agreement according to which the contractor undertakes the obligation of the execution of the work and the other contracting party (the employer) undertakes the obligation of the payment of the agreed remuneration.

The object of this contract is the creation of a certain agreed result. The labour to be provided towards the execution of this result is not treated as an essential element of this contract. The obligation of the contractor is considered as fulfiled at the time of the 'delivery' of the work to the employer. If a time period is agreed for the delivery of the work to the employer, this fact does not define the duration of the contract but simply defines the time period when the employer has the right to demand the delivery/execution of the work or to exercise his rights of withdrawal and/or indemnity.

Greek theory and jurisprudence also characterise the provisions of Arts 681–701 of the Civil Code as provisions of jus dispositivum, meaning that the contracting parties have a wide contractual freedom to formulate their relations differently to the above-mentioned provisions.

The contract for the provision of advertising services that we are examining consists of several and different 'partial' jobs as described in clauses 2.1–2.9, but those parts may be considered as stages or parts of one and only 'work' that is the advertising promotion of the client.

Moreover, said contract includes also some elements of the agency contracts, given that in order to achieve the agreed result it is required that the contractor shall have the right to conclude contracts on behalf of the employer with third parties (media owners, printers, publishers, etc).

## Contractor's obligations

The main obligation of the contractor in a 'leasing of work' contract is the execution or creation of the work. This execution shall be as per the agreement, which derives from the general principles of the Civil Code (Arts 200, 281, 288). The contractor is obliged to follow any conditions, terms and plans included in the contract, but is not obliged to follow the instructions of the employer, unless the employer has expressly reserved the right to issue instructions in the contract.

In the contract that we have examined, it does not seem that the employer has reserved the right to issue instructions regarding the execution of the work agreed.

Furthermore, under the provisions of Arts 681–701 and the general principles of the Civil Code (Arts 686 and 320, 322) the contractor is obliged to begin the work on time, in order that it be complete and delivered to the employer on time. If no relevant time period for the commencement of work is agreed, the rule under Art 323 of the Civil Code applies, according to which execution of the contractual obligations should commence immediately.

The work to be created and delivered to the employer should also be free from all real and legal defects and include all the agreed qualities. In the contract that we have examined, no special quality of the work to be created is defined. In addition, and taking into account the fact that the description of the 'services' to be provided is not very clear, it is difficult to define whether those services are defective, unless they refer to the visual material of clause 2.1, or the logos and the printed material of clauses 2.7 and 2.8.

## Employer's obligations

(a) The main obligation of the employer deriving from the provisions of Art 681 of the Civil Code is the payment of the agreed remuneration. This remuneration, if not otherwise agreed, should be paid when the work is delivered to the employer (Art 694). In the contract we have examined, the contractor's remuneration may, by agreement, be paid either as the work progresses or against preparation and delivery of the components of the work (Art 694, para 2).

(b) According to the provisions of Arts 692, 693 and 698 of the Civil Code, the employer is obliged to accept and approve the work delivered. The unreserved acceptance and approval of the work by the employer consequently frees the contractor from all responsibility for potential defects of the work and. therefore. the contractor has the right to demand his remuneration. According to the provisions of Art 692(b), the contractor is not released from his responsibility if, at the time of the delivery of the work (and the acceptance on the part of the employer), those defects could not have been discovered by means of a simple examination or were intentionally concealed by the contractor.

The law does not require this approval to be expressed and equates the actual delivery and acceptance of the work to the approval.

Furthermore, in case of unreasonable denial by the employer to approve or accept the work, the contractor has the right to demand his remuneration and can claim interest on it. The main consequence of this denial (non-execution of the employer's obligation) is the default of the employer which has as a consequence the transfer of the danger (of the destruction, damage or loss of the work) to the employer and the right of the contractor to demand payment for the expenses and maintenance cost of the work.

## Abnormal evolution of the agreement – rights of the employer

Under the provisions of Art 686 of the Civil Code, in case of delay in commencement of the work on the part of the contractor, or when the contractor, at no fault of the employer, delays the execution of the work in a way which breaches the contract or makes the prompt execution of the work impossible, the employer has the right to withdraw from the contract before it expires.

Greek legal theory (with few exceptions) does not require, for the application of the above provisions, the existence of fault on the part of the contractor. As to the manner of the withdrawal, according to prevailing opinion, the employer should proceed to the withdrawal by means of a notice, addressed to the contractor, giving reasons. The right of withdrawal is not subject to a time limit or lapse, but its exercise can be deemed null and void as abusive and exceeding the limits of good faith (Art 281 of the Civil Code). In that case, the null and void withdrawal is treated as termination of the contract (Art 700 of the Civil Code).

Moreover, the results of a valid withdrawal are the ex tunc (from the beginning) amortisation of the contractual obligations of both parties, which oblige the return to the other contracting party of all the work supplied, meaning that the contractor should return to the employer the executed part of the work and the material provided by the employer and, on the other hand, the employer should pay the contractor, not the agreed remuneration, but the profit gained by him on to the partial execution of work (which has been delivered to the employer).

Furthermore, if in the contract the time of the commencement, or execution/delivery of the work, or of some of the work's stages are defined, the contractor becomes in default after the simple elapse of this time. Otherwise (if the time of delivery of the work is not expressly defined, or if the time of commencement of the work should be immediate according to the provisions of Art 323 of the Civil Code), a notice should be addressed to the contractor fixing a time limit for the execution or commencement of the work. The right of withdrawal, when based on the contractor's default, requires the existence of a contractor's negligence or intent.

In the case of contractor's default, the employer has the right to demand:

(a) the prompt and punctual execution of the work; and

(b) to be indemnified for all damages provoked by the delay; or

(c) to fix a time limit for the execution of the work declaring that, in case this time limit is passed, he will decline the inappropriate and delayed performance.

During this time, the employer has the right to demand full indemnity for the non-performance of the contract or to withdraw from it and demand reasonable indemnity. Such reasonable indemnity consists of the damage caused to the employer by the non-performance of the contract and, mainly, of the cost of the continuance of the work by another contractor or the employer personally.

Further to this right of withdrawal (reserved to the employer under the terms and conditions of Art 686 of the Civil Code) the law also recognises his right to 'correction' of the defects of the work, meaning that if, during the execution of the work, a certain defect or execution contrary to the agreement is foreseen and this defect is the fault of the contractor, the employer has the right to fix a time limit for the contractor to correct the defect and, in case of non-correction by the contractor, to proceed to correction at the contractor's expense (Art 687 of the Civil Code).

In Arts 688–90 of the Civil Code, the right of the employer to demand indemnity, or decrease of the contractor's remuneration, or even to reverse the contract is provided. Those rights are reserved to the employer when the delivered work presents substantial defects or lacks the agreed qualities and is therefore useless for the purpose of the contract. Those rights of the employer are considered to be in disjunctive inflow and the employer may choose among them. Furthermore, it should be noted that the exercise of the right of indemnity by the employer requires the existence of the fault of the contractor.

In any case, the employer is deprived of all the above rights if the defects in the work are due to his instructions or his fault and if the contractor has objected to those instructions (Art 691 of the Civil Code).

Finally, the Greek Civil Code recognises the employer's right of termination of the contract (Art 701 of the Civil Code). This last may be exercised during the execution of the work and until its completion. This termination should not be reasoned or founded on certain conditions and has as consequence the amortisation of the contract ex nunc and the obligation of the employer to pay the agreed remuneration. From this last are subtracted all the expenses and profits due to the conclusion of the contract gained or intentionally omitted to be gained by the contractor.

Prescription: the law recognises a short prescription of the rights of the employer and rather longer to the contractor, of six months and five years respectively.

# USEFUL ADDRESSES

ΕΔΕΕ
(Advertising Companies' Association of Greece)
7 Iperidou St, 105 58 Athens
Tel: + 30 1 3246 214 8
E-mail: edee@techlink.gr
http://www.techlink.gr:8080/edee

ΕΑΗΓΕ
(Creative Offices' Association of Greece)
9 El Venizelou St
154 51 N Psychiko
Tel: + 30 1 6756 716

ΕΙΗΕΑ
(Daily Newspapers of Athens Owners' Association)
14 Mourouzi St
106 74 Athens
Tel: + 30 1 3624 102 6

EIHEE
(Daily Newspapers of Provinces Owners' Association)
4, Vissarionos St
106 72 Athens
Tel: + 30 1 3624 651/3630 058

EIM
(Greek Institute of Marketing)
200 Ionias Ave and Iakovaton St
111 44 Athens
Tel: + 30 1 2112 000 9

Cinematography-Television Producers' Association
4 Angelikara St
117 42 Athens
Tel: + 30 1 9248 100

Greek Photoreporters' Association
22 Har Trikoupi St
106 79 Athens
Tel: + 30 1 3604 340

ΕΣΗΕΑ
(Athens Daily Newspapers Journalists' Association)
20 Akadimias St
106 71 Athens
Tel: + 30 1 3632 601 5

ΕΣΠΤ
(Magazines Editors' Association)
9 Valaoritou St
106 71 Athens
Tel: + 30 1 3636 039

ΕΦΕΔΗΦ
(Association of Photographers of Applied and Creative Photography)
63 Karea Ave
162 33 Kareas
Tel: + 30 1 7650 942

ΠΟΦ
(Panhellenic Federation of Photographers)
13 Ipokratous St
106 79 Athens
Tel: + 30 1 3610 345/3647 257

ΣΔΕ
(Advertised Persons' Association of Greece)
17 Mouson St
115 24 Athens
Tel: + 30 1 6483 917 8

ΣΕΔΕΑ
(Association of Gallup and Market Research Companies)
PO Box 17223
100 24 Athens
Tel: + 30 1 8951 355

## CHAPTER 9

# REPUBLIC OF IRELAND

*Walter Beatty and Robert Beatty*

## INTRODUCTION

This chapter looks at advertising law in Ireland. Advertising is a form of public announcement intended to promote the sale of goods or services or to bring about some other effect desired by the advertiser. It is a form of communication through such media as handbills, newspapers, magazines, billboards, radio and television broadcasts, and the cinema.[1] An authoritative definition is given in relation to broadcast advertising in the Code of Standards, Practice and Prohibitions in Advertising, Sponsorship and Other Forms of Commercial Promotion in Broadcasting Services (the Broadcasting Code) where an advertisement is defined as:

> ... any form of announcement which is inserted in a programme service in consideration of a payment or payments or other remuneration made to the broadcaster, including references to advertising matter in sponsored programmes, that is, programmes supplied for advertising, commercial or promotional purposes by or on behalf of an advertiser or programmes financed, in whole or in part, by advertisers for advertising, commercial or promotional purposes.[2]

Part I of this chapter deals with the different advertising media, the sources of law that affect advertising, misleading advertising, comparative advertising, the law of copyright and the law of trade marks in relation to advertising. Part II deals with the specific legislative and voluntary rules and guidelines that exist in relation to the advertising of particular goods or services and in relation to children and advertising.

---

1    *Encyclopaedia Britannica*, 15th edn, p 105.
2    However, this does not include the accreditation of a sponsor.

# ADVERTISING MEDIA, THE LAW
# AND REPRESENTATIVE BODIES

## MEDIA FORMS IN IRELAND

### Television

In Ireland, Radio Telefis Eireann (RTE) holds a large part of the Irish television audience and in April 1998 its two channels, RTE 1 and Network Two, held 57% of the Irish television audience during prime time television. TnaG is an Irish language national television station and an offshoot of RTE, but quite independent. It began broadcasting in October 1996 and accommodates English and Irish language advertising. In September 1998, an independent television broadcasting station, entitled TV3, commenced broadcasting. It operates under a licence granted to it by the Irish Radio and Television Commission (IRTC) which was established under the Radio and Television Act 1988 to oversee the granting of licences for independent radio and television operators.

Ireland is serviced to a large extent by cable transmission and satellite broadcasting, and therefore the Irish television audience has access to many of the operators transmitting from the UK and Europe, and in particular the British Broadcasting Corporation, Independent Television, Channel 4 and BSkyB.

RTE's Code of Standards for Broadcast Advertising (the RTE Code) represents the general principles which govern the acceptance and presentation of broadcast advertising by RTE. Although the RTE Code was published as far back as May 1985, it is comprehensive. Further, on 11 May 1995, the Codes of Standards, Practice and Prohibitions in Advertising, Sponsorship and Other Forms of Commercial Promotion in Broadcasting Services (the Broadcasting Code) was drawn up by the Minister for Arts, Culture and the Gaeltacht under s 4(1) of the Broadcasting Act 1990 (the 1990 Act). The Broadcasting Code is now the primary code of advertising standards for radio and television broadcasting in Ireland and comes under the purview of the Broadcasting Complaints Commission in relation to both RTE and those radio and television stations operating under licences granted by IRTC.

Section 2 of the Broadcasting Authority (Amendment) Act 1993 provides that the total daily and hourly times for television advertising fixed by RTE is subject to the approval of the Minister of Arts, Culture and the Gaeltacht. The average period permitted to be allocated to broadcasting advertisements in any one hour is six minutes. However, a maximum of seven and a half minutes per hour can be allocated to broadcast advertisements, provided that the total time allocated in any one day does not exceed 10% of the total transmission time. Council Directive 89/552/EEC (the 1989 Directive) has been partly implemented into Irish law by the European Communities (Television Broadcasting) Regulations 1991. The 1989 Directive has since been amended by European Council Directive 97/36/EC to include 'teleshopping' as a form of television advertising. Television advertising will be defined as any form of announcement broadcast whether in return for payment or for similar consideration or broadcast for self-promotional purposes by a public or private undertaking in connection with a trade, business, craft or profession in order to promote the supply of goods or services, including immovable property, rights and obligations, in return for payment.

## Radio

RTE has three national radio stations and once held a monopoly in relation to radio broadcasting in Ireland. However, as already mentioned, IRTC was established under the Radio and Television Act 1988 to oversee the granting of licences for radio and television, and has issued 23 licences to operate local commercial radio stations throughout Ireland and one national commercial radio station (which only commenced broadcasting in the spring of 1997), under the name 'Radio Ireland', which has since been changed to 'Today FM'.

The national radio market share figures for the first quarter of 1998 are:

| | |
|---|---|
| Independents | 28% |
| RTE Radio One | 33% |
| RTE Radio Two (2FM) | 31% |
| Today FM | 8%[3] |

## Newspapers

Notwithstanding the staggering advances of information technology, this medium is still extremely important.

The share of readership can be broken down as follows:

Daily newspaper readership:

| | |
|---|---|
| Irish Independent | 598,000 |
| Evening Herald | 379,000 |
| The Star | 373,000 |
| Irish Times | 286,000 |
| The Sun | 223,000 |

---

3   The Joint National Listenership Research Group interim report.

| The Examiner | 219,000 |
|---|---|
| Irish Mirror | 137,500 |
| Evening Echo | 67,000 |

Sunday newspaper readership:

| Sunday Independent | 1,126,000 |
|---|---|
| Sunday World | 977,000 |
| News of the World | 441,000 |
| Sunday Times | 300,000 |
| Sunday Tribune | 261,000 |
| Sunday People | 162,500 |
| Ireland on Sunday | 138,000 |
| Sunday Business Post | 131,000 |
| Sunday Mirror | 115,000[4] |

## Cinema

There has been a growth in cinema advertising due to an increase in the popularity of cinema amongst the public, due mainly to the introduction of the 'multiplex' cinema centre concept. Annual admissions have increased from 5 m in 1986 to 12.2 m in 1998.

The number of screens in Ireland has increased from 140 in 1986 to 243 in July 1998 and is expected to grow to over 300 by the year 2000.[5]

## Outdoor advertising

The Outdoor Media Association (OMA) was formed in 1984 to promote and protect the interests of its members, who are confined to outdoor media owners. The current membership comprises David Allen Outdoor Advertising, More Group Ireland and TDI-Metro Limited. The owners account for 97% of all poster advertising and 100% of all transport advertising in Ireland. In 1991, the OMA established a poster database recording the details of every poster panel, including the 'visibility factor' of each location. The data is used to predict the levels of visibility of poster or billboard sites in each location by the passing motorised and pedestrian traffic. The Joint National Poster Research database carries out quarterly surveys to assess the

---

4    The Joint National Readership Research Group.
5    Carlton Screen Advertising/Screen Digest/Taylor Nelson MRBI.

impact of selected poster campaigns, across 35 demographic and special interest groupings.

Poster sites are regulated by the Local Government (Planning and Development) Acts 1963–93.


# LAWS AND RULES PERTAINING TO ADVERTISING

## Introduction

The rights to and the limitations on one's freedom to advertise whatever material in whatever manner derive, in the main, from the Constitution, legislation, the common law and voluntary codes. There are a number of voluntary advertising codes, the most noteworthy of which is the Code of Advertising Standards for Ireland (the Code), published by the Advertising Standards Authority for Ireland (ASAI).[6] The other voluntary codes relate, in the main, to particular industries or professions. Examples are the Medical Council's Guide to Ethical Conduct (Advertising and the Media) and the Code of Conduct for the Bar of Ireland.

The European Association of Advertising Agencies (EAAA) has drawn up what is known as the 'Red Book', which incorporates all the voluntary codes and advertising legislation in Europe. The Institute of Advertising Practitioners in Ireland (IAPI), which is the Irish member of the EAAA, edits the Irish chapter of the Red Book.


## The Constitution

The 1937 Constitution established, among other things, a number of personal rights. While the Constitution does not refer to the advertising industry itself, it does refer to some of the media forms through which advertisements are communicated to members of the public, such as the radio, the press and the cinema.[7] The Constitution, in Article 40.6.1.i, also prohibits advertising through any media form if that would 'undermine public order or morality or the authority of the State'. Advertisers and advertising agencies benefit from a number of the constitutional rights conferred on individuals, such as the right to own private property,[8] the right to earn a livelihood,[9] and the right to

---

6   See Appendix 1.
7   Irish Constitution, Art 40.6.1.i.
8   *Ibid*, Art 43.
9   *Ibid*, Art 40.3.

express opinions freely.[10] These rights are subject to restrictions imposed by law for the common good.

## Legislation affecting the advertising industry

In Ireland there is no composite legislation dealing with advertising law or the advertising industry. The principles in relation to advertising have to be sourced from a wide range of primary and secondary legislation, such as the Sale of Goods and Supply of Services Act 1980, the Consumer Information Act 1978, the Defamation Act 1961, the Copyright Acts 1963–87, the Trade Marks Act 1996, the European Communities (Misleading Advertising) Regulations 1988 and specific legislation governing professions and products.

### *The law of contract and the sale of goods and supply of services*

The Sale of Goods and Supply of Services Act 1980 (the 1980 Act) regulates the obligations of the supplier of goods and services and safeguards the rights of consumers. The 1980 Act does not regulate advertising per se, but an advertisement can be construed as an inducement to encourage one person (the consumer) to enter into a contract with another person (in this case the advertiser) in that a consumer often purchases goods or services from an advertiser based on a representations contained in an advertisement.[11] An example would be where a consumer buys a product relying on the description given in relation to the produce by the trader/advertiser. If it turns out that the product does not approximate to its description and is therefore of no use to the consumer then the consumer may return the product and get a full refund.

Section 11 of the 1980 Act makes it an offence for an advertiser to restrict the rights conferred onto the consumer by the 1980 Act by any of the following means:

(a) displaying on any part of any premises a notice that includes any such restriction; or

(b) publishing or causing the publication of an advertisement which contains any such restriction; or

(c) supplying goods bearing, or goods in a container bearing, any such restrictions; or

(d) otherwise furnishing or causing the furnishment of a document including any such restriction.

---

10   Irish Constitution, Art 40.6.
11   See para 3.6.1.

Part V of the 1980 Act deals with misrepresentation and allows an injured party to sue for damages or rescind a contract in certain circumstances. Section 45 of the 1980 Act entitles a person who has entered into a contract based on a misrepresentation to sue for damages if as a result of the misrepresentation that person has suffered loss. It is irrelevant whether the misrepresentation was made fraudulently or not.

### Consumer information

The Consumer Information Act 1978 (the 1978 Act) established the Office of the Director of Consumer Affairs (the Director).

Section 9(6) of the 1978 Act provides that the Director must keep advertising practices under review and provide members of the public with information concerning the descriptions of goods and services. The Director may request advertisers to make such alterations to or deletions from advertisements or to provide such definitions as would increase the precision of or the amount of information contained in, or facilitate the understanding of, the expressions contained in the advertisement. The Director is obliged to publicise legislative provisions that protect consumers and encourage the establishment and adoption of voluntary codes of standards.

Section 11 of the 1978 Act provides that the Minister for Enterprise, Trade and Employment may impose a requirement that additional information be given to the public in relation to an advertisement, or at least an indication of the means by which this information may be obtained.

Section 13 of the 1978 Act, as amended by s 30 of the 1987 Act, provides that where an advertisement in relation to the supply or provision of any goods or services is published and does not include the name and address of the person who procured such publication or his agent, the publisher of the advertisement must, if the Director so requests, give the name and address of the advertiser or his agent to the Director within 12 months of the publication of the advertisement.

Section 32 of the Restrictive Practices (Amendment) Act (the 1987 Act) inserts into the 1980 Act additional functions for the Director, who shall keep under general review practices in relation to any of the obligations imposed on persons by the 1980 Act, including the power to have recourse to the High Court to enforce the provisions of the 1980 Act.

## Misleading advertising

Advertisers are obliged not to mislead the public. Misleading advertising is governed by the 1978 Act and the European Communities (Misleading Advertising) Regulations 1988 (the 1988 Regulations).

Section 8 of the 1978 Act prohibits an advertiser from publishing an advertisement if it is likely to mislead members of the public, thereby causing them material loss or damage.

The 1988 Regulations[12] go further than the 1978 Act in that they define misleading advertising as any advertising which in any way deceives or is likely to deceive the persons to whom it is addressed or whom it reaches and which, by reason of its deceptive nature, is likely to affect their spending patterns or which, for those reasons, injures, or is likely to injure, a competitor.

In determining whether an advertisement is misleading or not, the 1988 Regulations set out those constituent parts of the advertisement which should be examined. These include the nature of goods and services, such as their availability, composition, uses, origin, price, conditions of supply and information about the advertiser including its identity and the ownership of industrial, commercial or intellectual property rights in relation to the goods or services on offer.

The Director may request advertisers to discontinue or refrain from misleading advertising, and if that request is not complied with, then the Director may apply for injunctive relief where necessary. The Director is under no obligation to prove:

(a) actual loss or damage; or

(b) recklessness or negligence on the part of the advertiser.

The Broadcasting Code provides, in relation to false or misleading advertisements, that advertisements shall not be misleading or shall not prejudice the interest of consumers and that advertisements must not contain anything which is calculated to mislead members of the public either directly or indirectly in relation to the merits of the product or service advertised or its suitability for the purpose recommended.

## Comparative advertising

Comparative Advertising is amply defined in Council Directive 97/55/EC[13] (the 1997 Directive). The 1997 Directive defines comparative advertising as any advertising which explicitly or by implication identifies a competitor, or goods or services offered by a competitor.

An advertiser must be aware that in engaging in comparative advertising it is exposing itself to the possibility of (a) infringing the trade mark of a competitor; (b) infringing any copyright material of a competitor; (c) passing

---

12  These implement Council Directive 84/450/EEC.

13  This has not, as yet, been implemented into Irish law, but the definition of comparative advertising is a useful one. When it is made Irish law, it will amend the 1988 Regulations on misleading advertising to include comparative advertising.

off the goods or services of a competitor; (d) being involved in misleading advertising; and (e) committing an injurious falsehood.

Section 14(6) of the Trade Marks Act 1996 (the 1996 Act) expressly permits comparative advertising by providing that the use of a registered trade mark by any person for the purposes of identifying goods or services as those of the proprietor or licensee of the registered trade mark will not be an infringement if done in accordance with honest practices in industrial and commercial matters. However, comparative advertising will be deemed to have infringed the registered trade mark of another if the comparative advertising without due cause takes unfair advantage of, or is detrimental to, the distinctive character or reputation of the trade mark. In *Vodafone Group plc and Vodafone Ltd v Orange Personal Communications Services Ltd*,[14] Orange's advertisements contained the following slogan 'on average, Orange users save £20 every month in comparison to Vodafone's "equivalent tariffs"'. The court acknowledged that s 14(6) of the 1996 Act[15] permits comparative advertising provided that advertisers do not use their competitors' trade mark where such use, without due cause, would take unfair advantage of, or be detrimental to, the distinctive character or reputation of their competitors' trade mark. In this case, Vodafone failed in its claim for trade mark infringement as it failed to show that the comparative advertisement was not an 'honest practice', or that it took unfair advantage, or was detrimental to the distinctive character of its trade mark.

It is worth noting that s 24 of the Consumer Credit Act 1995 provides that where an advertisement purports to compare the level of repayments or cost under one or more forms of financial accommodation, the advertisement shall contain the relevant terms of each of the forms of financial accommodation referred to in the advertisement.

The 1997 Directive must be implemented by April 2000, and provides that comparative advertising will be permitted if:

(a) it is not misleading;

(b) it compares goods or services meeting the same needs or intended for the same purpose;

(c) it objectively compares one or more material, relevant, verifiable and representative features of those goods or services, which may include price;

(d) it does not create confusion in the market place between the advertiser and a competitor or between the advertiser's trade marks, trade names, other distinguishing marks, goods or services and those of a competitor;

---

14  [1996] 10 EIPR D-307.
15  In fact, the court was discussing s 10(6) of the Trade Marks Act 1994, being the equivalent English section to s 14(6) of the Trade Marks Act 1996.

(e) it does not discredit or denigrate the trade marks, trade names, other distinguishing marks, goods, services, activities, or circumstances of a competitor;

(f) for products with designation of origin, it relates in each case to products with the same designation;

(g) it does not take unfair advantage of the reputation of a trade mark, trade name or other distinguishing marks of a competitor or of the designation of origin of competing products;

(h) it does not present goods or services as imitations or replicas of goods or services bearing a protected trade mark or name.

Article 2 of the 1997 Directive establishes a commission to study the feasibility of a European complaints procedure in relation to comparative advertising.

The 1997 Directive amends Council Directive 84/450/EEC so as to include the policing by the Director of 'unpermitted comparative advertising' alongside that of misleading advertising.

The 1997 Directive grants Member States certain derogations from the Directive in relation to the advertising of professional services.

The General Rules of the Code of Advertising Standards for Ireland (the Code) briefly outlines the voluntary rules adhered to by the advertising industry in relation to comparative advertising.[16]

## The common law

### Contract

A legally binding contract comes into existence when there has been: (a) an unconditional offer (in this case by the advertiser of the goods or services); (b) an unconditional acceptance of the offer by the offeree; (c) an adequate consideration paid; and (d) an intention by the parties to create a legally binding contract.

In *Carlill v Carbolic Smoke Ball Co,*[17] the defendant advertiser was held liable to pay £100 to the plaintiff, who contracted flu symptoms after using its smoke ball medicine, which the advertiser claimed prevented flu symptoms. The defendant advertiser had claimed that its advertisement, to pay £100 to any person who contracted flu symptoms after using its medicine, was not intended to create legal relations. The Court of Appeal held that a contract did exist and that the consumer who relies on such an advertisement is protected by contract law.

---

16  See Appendix 1, para 2.47–2.51.
17  [1893] 1 QB 256.

## The law of tort

A tort is a civil wrong, not being a breach of contract or trust, and is mainly concerned with compensating an injured party for the acts of a wrongdoer. Generally, liability for the commission of a tort can only arise if the wrongdoer owes a duty of care to the injured party and by his action or inaction the wrongdoer has breached that duty resulting in the injured party suffering damage.

A detailed analysis of the law of tort goes beyond the scope of this chapter, but it will briefly deal with the torts of deceit, injurious falsehood, negligence, negligent misstatement, confidentiality, defamation[18] and passing off.[19]

### Deceit

The tort of deceit can and does affect advertisers and advertising agencies. The tort of deceit is committed when a person falsely represents a fact to another knowing that that other will act upon the representation and as a consequence of which he suffers loss or damage. An advertiser, for example, who knows that an advertisement is inaccurate and allows it to be used falsely to entice consumers to act to their detriment will be liable in the tort of deceit. In the case of *Pasley v Freeman*,[20] the defendant falsely represented to the plaintiff that a third party was creditworthy. As a consequence, the plaintiff suffered loss and was able to bring a claim in deceit.

### Injurious falsehood

The tort of injurious falsehood will arise if an advertiser maliciously makes an untrue statement about a competitor or a competitor's goods or services and as a consequence of which the competitor suffers either a direct financial loss or a loss of business. There are two conditions which have to be met for liability to be imposed. First, the statement must be untrue, and secondly, the statement must be made for an improper motive. In *Vodafone Group plc and Vodafone Ltd v Orange Personal Communications Services Ltd*,[21] it was held that for Vodafone to succeed in its claim for injurious falsehood it must show that: (a) the words complained of were false; (b) they were published maliciously; and (c) they were calculated to cause the plaintiff pecuniary damage. In deciding whether words contained in an advertisement are false or not, the court will construe those words as they would be understood by ordinary, reasonable, fair minded people.

---

18  See para 3.6.4.
19  See para 4.3.
20  [1789] 3 TR 51.
21  [1996] 10 EIPR D-307.

## Negligence

There are five main elements to the tort of negligence:

(a) the existence in law of a duty of care;

(b) careless behaviour by the defendant which results in a breach of that duty;

(c) that the injured party suffers damage;

(d) that there is a causal connection between the defendant's careless conduct and the damage suffered by the injured party;

(e) that the defendant's careless conduct would foreseeably result in damage to the injured party.

It is noteworthy that, in discussing negligence and the extent of the duty of care that is owed, Nolan LJ, in the case of *Alcock v Chief Constable of South Yorkshire*,[22] used the promotions industry to exemplify his point. He said that if a promotions organisation at a large, televised promotional event made arrangements for a party of children to go up in a balloon and the balloon tragically crashed, then it would be difficult, if not impossible, not only for the organiser of the promotion to deny that it was under a duty of care to the children but also to deny that it was under a duty to avoid causing mental injury to the parents of the children who were watching the event on television.

## Negligent misstatement

In *Hedley Byrne and Co v Heller and Partners Ltd*[23] it was established that a person who makes a negligent statement may owe a duty of care to a person who suffers financial loss as a consequence of relying on that statement. There must be a 'special relationship' and no contractual exclusion of the duty of care.

In this case, the plaintiff was an advertising agency who entered into a contract on behalf of a new client. It was to be personally liable if its client was in breach of the contract. Through its bankers, it obtained a favourable credit reference in relation to the new client from its bankers. It relied on this statement to its detriment as the client became insolvent. The House of Lords held that the defendants had been careless and would have been liable in negligent misstatement except for the fact that there was a contract in place which contained an exclusion of liability clause.

## The law of confidentiality

The law of copyright will not protect ideas or concepts *per se*. No matter how original or creative they are, the law of copyright will only protect the

22  [1992] 1 AC 310, pp 386–87.
23  [1964] AC 465.

expression of those ideas in some permanent form.[24] So when 'pitching', or making a presentation, to a potential client, advertising agencies must ensure that confidentiality is maintained by the potential clients and their employees and agents. It is essential, therefore, that a prospective client, and the employees and agents, enter into a confidentiality agreement with the advertising agency. While it will be difficult, in the event of there being a breach of confidentiality, to prove that the particular potential client was in breach, the very existence of a confidentiality agreement will give the agency some degree of comfort.

Even if an agency fails to include a confidentiality clause in an agreement, it may still succeed in a claim for breach of confidentiality if it can prove that:

(a) the information was seen to be of a confidential nature;

(b) there was an apparent obligation on the person receiving the information to hold such information in confidence. Megarry J suggested, in the case of *Coco v AN Clark (Engineers) Ltd*,[25] that if a reasonable man 'standing in the shoes of the recipient of the information would have realised that upon reasonable grounds the information was being given to him in confidence, then this should suffice to impose upon him the equitable obligation of confidence';[26] and

(c) there must have been an unauthorised use of the information to the detriment of the advertising agency communicating it.

## Defamation

Defamation is the wrongful publication of a false statement about a person, which tends to lower that person in the eyes of right-thinking members of society or tends to hold that person up to hatred, ridicule or contempt.

Defamatory material published in transient form, that is, orally, is slander, and defamatory material published in permanent form (including television and radio broadcasts) is libel.

Libel is actionable *per se*, whereas slander is actionable only on proof of actual damage except in certain circumstances, that is, slanders affecting a person's official, professional or business reputation.[27] The vast majority of media forms used by the advertising industry are what would be considered 'permanent form' media and so it is the law of libel that concerns advertisers and advertising agencies.

In the area of advertising, it is important not to publish defamatory statements about a person or persons that may give them a right of action.

---

24  Eg, video tape recording or written script.
25  [1969] Reports of Patents, Designs and Trade Mark Cases 41.
26  *Ibid*, p 48.
27  Defamation Act 1961, s 19.

Advertisers should be vigilant in avoiding the publication of defamatory statements about persons or personalities. Accordingly, they should obtain the written consent from personalities or models, as the case may be, to exploit their name in an advertising campaign.

# INTELLECTUAL PROPERTY AND ADVERTISING

## Introduction

Intellectual property rights are the most important rights in relation to the creation and publication of advertisements in all forms of media. The relevant forms of intellectual property are copyright, trade marks and the law of passing off. If an advertisement is an original work, it will be protected by the law of copyright. If the advertisement is infringing a third party's intellectual property rights, then this will normally be a breach of copyright, trade mark infringement or a passing off. The laws of copyright, trade marks and passing off and their relevance to the advertising industry will be examined in turn.

### Copyright in advertising

*Works in advertising which are capable of being the subject matter of copyright protection*

Copyright subsists in practically everything that can be termed an original work, whether it is published or not, and of which the author was a qualified person[28] at the time when the work was made, or if the making of the work extended over a period of time, was a qualified person for a substantial part of that period.

Copyright subsists in the following works:

(a) literary, dramatic and musical works;[29]

(b) artistic works;[30]

(c) recordings;[31]

(d) films;[32]

(e) broadcasts;[33]

---

28  Copyright Act 1963, s 7.
29  *Ibid*, s 8.
30  *Ibid*, s 9.
31  *Ibid*, s 17.
32  *Ibid*, s 18.
33  *Ibid*, s 19.

(f) computer programs;[34]

(g) typographical arrangements in published editions.[35]

## Copyright law in Ireland

The law of copyright in Ireland is governed primarily by the Copyright Act 1963 ('the 1963 Act') as amended by the Copyright (Amendment) Act 1987.

### Ideas or concepts for an advertising campaign

Ideas and opinions for an advertising campaign are not and cannot be the subject matter of copyright. For a work to be the subject matter of copyright, it must be concrete or permanent in its form. No copyright protection is afforded to ideas or opinions, no matter how original or creative they are.[36] In *Norowzian v Arks Ltd and Others*,[37] Arks advertising agency took ideas of a quirky dance rhythm and jump cutting in the film *Joy* and was held not to have infringed the plaintiff's film *Joy*. The two films were similar (due to the rhythm and editing techniques), whereas the subject was not.

### Literary works

**Definition**

A literary work includes any table or compilation[38] and would include advertisements in printed media.

**Level of creativity required in literary works – advertising slogans**

It has long been established that the term 'literary' in the context of copyright does not require any degree of creativity. Thus, in *Exxon Corporation v Exxon Insurance Consultants International Ltd*,[39] it was held that once there was information and instruction, then this was sufficient for the work to be a literary work. However, advertising slogans are not sufficiently substantial to be deemed to be a literary work.[40]

---

34  This principle is given statutory force in relation to computer programs by virtue of the European Communities (Legal Protection of Computer Programs) Regulations 1993, which states that 'ideas and principles which underlie any element of a computer program, including those which underlie its interfaces, are not protected by copyright'.

35  Copyright Act, s 20.

36  SI 26/1993.

37  (1998) unreported, 17 July, High Court, *per* Rattee J.

38  Copyright Act, s 2(1).

39  [1982] RPC 69.

40  *Sinanide v La Maison Kosmeo* (1928) 139 LT 365.

## Dramatic works

**Definition**

A 'dramatic work' includes 'a choreographic work or entertainment in dumb show if reduced to writing in the form in which the work or entertainment is to be presented, but does not include a cinematograph film, as distinct from a scenario or script for a cinematograph film'.[41]

Therefore, to come within the statutory definition of a dramatic work, the drama has to be reduced to writing.

The definition in the UK of a 'dramatic work' is different from the definition under the 1963 Act, but notwithstanding this, the UK case of *Norowzian v Arks Ltd and Others*[42] is informative. Rattee J held, *inter alia*, that a film of a choreographic work cannot be a dramatic work as it was not reduced to writing. In this case, the choreographic work by the plaintiff, entitled *Joy*, was recorded on film. The plaintiff claimed that he was entitled to the copyright in the choreographic work as a dramatic work. He also claimed that the choreographic work was being used by the defendant advertising agent in its advertisement for Guinness in the advertisement entitled 'Anticipation'. The court held that the choreographic work was not a dramatic work, as it had not been reduced to writing or otherwise recorded.[43]

## Musical works

**Definition**

A 'musical work' is not defined in the 1963 Act. The *Concise Oxford English Dictionary* defines music as 'the art of combining vocal or instrumental sounds (or both) to produce beauty of form, harmony and expression of emotion'.[44]

**Music must be in permanent form**

For a musical work to be the subject matter of copyright, it must be recorded in writing or otherwise made permanent in its form.[45] Many modern musicians record their songs directly onto tape or compact disc, which gives them the same protection as if the music had been written down. The recording, of course, creates a second or separate copyright in the second recording.[46]

---

41  Copyright Act 1963, s 2(1).

42  (1998) unreported, 17 July, High Court.

43  It is important to note that, under the UK Copyright, Designs and Patents Act 1988, the definition of the dramatic work is slightly broader than the definition of the 1963 Act, but the principle in this case still applies. The words 'otherwise recorded' do not appear in the 1963 Act.

44  11th edn, p 781.

45  See para 4.1.2.

46  Copyright Act 1963, s 17.

## Artistic works

### Definition

Section 9(1) of the Copyright Act 1963 defines 'artistic work' as a work of any of the following descriptions:

(a) paintings, sculptures, drawings, engravings and photographs, irrespective of their artistic quality;

(b) works of architecture, being either buildings or models for buildings; and

(c) works of artistic craftsmanship not falling within the description contained in para (a) or (b) above.[47]

A 'drawing' is defined by the 1963 Act as including 'any diagram, map, chart or plan'[48] and a 'photograph' is defined as 'any product of photography or of any process akin to photography other than a part of a cinematograph film'.[49]

## Sound recordings

### Definition

The 1963 Act defines 'sound recordings' as 'the aggregate of the sounds embodied in, and capable of being reproduced by means of, a record of any description, other than a soundtrack associated with a cinematographic film'.[50]

Clearly, this definition includes compact discs[51] and digital tapes.

## Films

### Definition

Section 18(10) of the 1963 Act defines cinematograph film as 'any sequence of visual images recorded on material of any description (whether translucent or not) so as to be capable, by use of that material:

(a) of being shown as a moving picture; or

(b) of being recorded on other material (whether translucent or not) by the use of which it can be shown.'

Clearly, this definition would extend to videos and compact discs. In *DPP v Irwin*,[52] Barron J stated that: 'a video cassette tape comes within the definition

---

47  Copyright Act 1963, s 9.
48  *Ibid*, s 2(1).
49  *Ibid*.
50  *ibid*, s 17(14).
51  *Polygram Records Inc v Raben Pty Ltd* [1996] 35 IPR 426.
52  (1984) unreported, 25 October, High Court, *per* Barron J; see also *Universal City Studios Inc v Mulligan* (1998) unreported, 25 March, High Court, *per* Laffoy J.

of a cinematograph film for the purposes of the Copyright Act 1963.'[53] It would also include a television advertisement.[54]

*Broadcasts*

Section 19(12) of the 1963 Act defines 'television broadcasts' as meaning 'visual images broadcast by way of television, together with any sound broadcast for reception along with those images'.

'Sound broadcasts' are, on the other hand, an addition to this, defined as 'broadcasts otherwise than as part of a television broadcast'.

*Typographical arrangements of published editions*

Copyright subsists in typographical arrangements of published editions of any one or more literary, dramatic or musical works where either the first publication of the edition took place in the State or the publisher of the edition was a qualified person at the date of first publication.[55] This relates to the layout, print size and so on. No copyright subsists in an edition which reproduces the typographical arrangement of a previous edition of the same work or works.[56]

*Works contrary to public policy*

Certain works cannot be the subject matter of copyright, even if they come within a work as defined by the 1963 Act. Copyright cannot subsist in a blasphemous[57] or an immoral advertisement.[58] Similarly, an advertisement that is libellous will not attract copyright protection.

*Copyright protection is afforded by operation of law*

Copyright in an advertisement attaches to the advertisement by operation of law. Unlike the law in relation to patents, industrial designs and trade marks, there is no need to have the work registered in the Patents Office for protection to be afforded.

---

53  (1984) unreported, 25 October, High Court, *per* Barron J, p 1.
54  *Norowzian v Arks Ltd and Others* (1998) unreported, 17 July, High Court, *per* Rattee J.
55  Copyright Act 1963, s 20(1).
56  *Ibid*, s 20(2).
57  *Lawrance v Smith* [1882] Jac 471.
58  *Glyn v Weston Feature Films Co* [1916] 1 Ch 262.

*Subsistence of copyright in an advertisement or part of an advertisement*

## Introduction

Whether copyright subsists in a work or other subject matter will depend, first, on whether the author,[59] maker,[60] or publisher[61] (as the case may be) was a qualified person[62] within the meaning of the 1963 Act as amended, secondly, in relation to published works, the place of publication, and thirdly, on whether the work or other subject matter was original.

## Originality

### Copyright Act 1963

The 1963 Act requires that an advertisement is original before copyright will subsist in it.

### Requirement for skill and labour

Notwithstanding that there is originality in ideas in an advertisement, if no skill and labour is used to express this, then clearly no copyright subsists in it. If an advertisement is copied *per se*, then it will not be original and no copyright will subsist in the copy.[63] There are no guidelines on the degree of skill or labour required,[64] but at the same time a sufficient degree of 'labour, skill and capital'[65] should be used by the agency in creating the advertisement. In *Interlego AG v Tyco Industries Inc*,[66] Lord Oliver pointed out that 'only certain kinds of skill, labour and judgment' will 'confer originality'.[67] Lord Oliver went on to say:

> There must in addition be some element of material alteration or embellishment which suffices to make the totality of the work an original work ... Of course, even a relatively small alteration or addition quantitatively may, if material, suffice to convert that which is substantially copied from an earlier work into an original work. Whether it does so or not is a question of degree, having regard to the quality rather than the quantity of the addition. But copying *per se*, however much skill or labour may be devoted to the process,

---

59  Copyright Act 1963, ss 8 and 9 refer to 'author' in relation to literary, dramatic, musical and artistic works.

60  *Ibid*, ss 17 and 18, refer to 'maker' in relation to sound recording and films respectively.

61  *Ibid*, s 20, refers to the 'publisher' in relation to published editions of works.

62  *Ibid*, s 7.

63  *Interlego AG v Tyco Industries Inc* [1989] 1 AC 217, p 265.

64  *Cambridge University Press v University Tutorial Press Ltd* [1928] 45 RPC 336.

65  *Macmillan and Co Ltd v Cooper* [1923] 93 LSPC 113, p 117.

66  [1989] 1 AC 217.

67  *Ibid*, p 262.

cannot make an original work. A well executed tracing is the result of much labour and skill but remains what it is, a tracing.

## Composite advertisements

Many advertisements can contain a variety of copyrights. Take, for example, a television advertisement relating to Russian caviar, using clips from the movie *From Russia with Love*, with a background voice reading excerpts from Alexander Solzhenitzyn's *Full Circle*, and background music composed by U2. Each work has its own copyright protection as well as being part of the overall copyright of the complete advertisement. It is extremely important that the advertiser obtains the written consent of the various owners of the different copyrights.[68]

## Ownership of copyright in an advertisement or part of an advertisement

### Initial ownership

Subject to certain exceptions, the first owner of copyright is the author of the work in relation to literary, dramatic, musical and artistic works and the maker in relation to film and sound recordings, the broadcaster in relation to broadcasts and the publisher in relation to published editions.

### Literary, dramatic, musical and artistic works

By virtue of s 10 of the 1963 Act, the author of an original literary, dramatic, musical or artistic work is the first owner of copyright.

### Definition of author

The 1963 Act does not, in general terms, define author. However, the term author is the person who actually writes the work, composes the music or paints the artwork for the advertisement. In *Gormley v EMI Records (Ireland) Ltd*,[69] Costello P held that 'the court should construe 'author' as meaning the originator of an original work'.[70]

The compiler of a composite advertisement will be the author of the advertisement, while there will be separate copyright in the individual contributions that make up the advertisement.[71]

An author of a photograph for an advertisement is defined under the 1963 Act as the person who, at the time when the photograph was taken, is the owner of the material on which it is taken.

---

68  See para 4.1.3.7.
69  [1998] 1 ILRM 124.
70  *Ibid.*
71  *Walter v Lane* [1900] AC 539, p 554.

**Works made in the course of employment of an advertising agency**

Under s 10 of the 1963 Act, where artwork is made in the course of the author's employment by an advertising agency under a contract of service or apprenticeship, the advertising agency shall be the author and so be entitled to any copyright that subsists in the artwork. This is subject to certain exceptions in relation to works of employees of newspapers, magazines and the like and commissioned works. The general rule will not apply if there is an agreement to the contrary (s 10(5) of the Copyright Act 1963) or an assignment of the future copyright in the work (s 10(6) and s 49 of the Copyright Act 1963). In-house photographers, designers, artists and draughtsmen will generally be full time employees, and the copyright in everything they create will belong to the advertising agency. However, there should be a written contract of employment specifying the scope of the employment, the job specification, and the hours of work to ensure that any work created comes within s 10 of the 1963 Act, so that any copyright subsisting in the work vests in the advertiser.

**Commissioned works**

As already mentioned, the owner of copyright in a work which will form part or the whole of an advertisement is the creator of the work. However, a person who commissions and pays or agrees to pay for certain artistic works is entitled to any copyright subsisting in the works.[72] Section 10(3) of the 1963 Act states that where an advertiser commissions the taking of a photograph or the painting or drawing of a portrait, or the making of an engraving, and pays or agrees to pay for it in money or money's worth, and the work is made in pursuance of that commission, the advertiser is entitled to any copyright subsisting in the work. The commission does not have to be in writing, though it is advisable that it is in writing.

The exception that the commissioner would be the first owner of the copyright in photographs, drawings or paintings of a portrait or engravings is itself subject to certain exceptions, namely:

(a) where the works are works of employees of newspaper proprietors and the like;

(b) where there are any agreements to the contrary; and

(c ) where there is an assignment of future copyright in the work.

---

72  Copyright Act 1963, s 10(3).

*Sound recordings*

Copyright vests in the maker of a sound recording,[73] who shall be entitled to any copyright subsisting in the recording[74]

*Films*

Copyright vests in the maker of a film or television advertisement,[75] who is the person by whom the arrangements necessary for the making of the film are undertaken.

*Broadcasts*

Copyright in broadcasts vests in the broadcaster,[76] which is the body by whom, at the time when, and from the place from which, the visual images or sounds in question, or both, as the case may be, are broadcast.[77]

*Published editions*

The general rule is that the publisher of an edition is entitled to any copyright subsisting in the edition.

*Multi-copyright advertisements*

Composite advertisements or compilation advertisements will contain a variety of copyrights as well as the overall copyright of the advertisement, unless all the constituent parts of the advertisement have been carried out by the advertiser or have been commissioned by him. Advertisers should identify the relevant copyrights and their respective owners in order to get copyright clearance from the owners before using the copyright material. This should be ascertained in relation to both printed media and television advertisements.

**Printed media**

It may be difficult for advertisers to identify third party owners of copyright material. For example, an advertisement in relation to football boots could contain an extract from a football magazine which endorses the football boots. The extract could be reproduced with torn edges to identify it as an exact copy of the original extract. The reproduced extract could contain a copy of the article in the extract which is perfectly legible, and photographs of the boots.

---

73  Copyright Act 1963, s 17(3).
74  *Ibid*, s 17(10).
75  *Ibid*, s 18.
76  *Ibid*, s 19.
77  *Ibid*, s 19(13).

Depending on the substantiality of the various parts of the extract, separate copyrights may subsist in the article, the published edition or in any accompanying photographs. It is essential that the advertiser gets the appropriate clearances from the third party owners.

In addition, the copyright in Irish banknotes vests in the Central Bank of Ireland.[78]

### Television and radio advertisements

Television and radio advertisements contain a number of copyrights for which clearance will have to be obtained from the third party owners. Third party consents will have to be obtained in relation to the following:

(a) Any music used in the advertisement

The advertiser will need the written consent of the owner of the copyright in the music (usually the music publisher) and the owner of the recording (usually the record company).

The use of music in advertisements, can be sourced in five ways.

(1) public domain music

Musical work which is in the public domain, such as Beethoven's Fifth Symphony, will not require any copyright consent. However, advertisers will require the consent of the music publisher or composer if the public domain musical work is in fact an original arrangement of the music. Advertisers should check with the Irish Music Rights Organisation (IMRO), the body representing composers and publishers in Ireland. Advertisers should also obtain the consent of the record company in relation to the copyright in the recording which is obtained in Ireland through the Mechanical Copyright Protection Society (MCPS).

(2) background music

Where an advertiser wants background music, it can get it from specialist studios and libraries which have recordings of various kinds of background music. Again, the appropriate consent is obtained through MCPS in relation to the copyright in the recording.

(3) commissioned advertising television jingles

Original music can be commissioned by an advertising agency for television or radio advertisements through bands or companies which produce television and radio soundtrack jingles. Alternatively, original music can be adapted for the purposes of an advertisement recording.

---

78 By virtue of the Copyright Act 1963, the Forgeries Act 1913 and the Central Bank Acts, 1942–98.

Generally 'jingle companies' insist on retaining the copyright in relation to music which they create and will generally only grant a limited licence to the advertising agency to use the music for the soundtrack of the radio or television advertisement.

Jingle music that is used in television or radio advertisements will generally be registered with IMRO, who will collect royalty payments whenever the original music is played on television or radio or in other public places such as shops, restaurants and bars.

(4) the use of existing popular recordings

Advertising agencies often use extracts from popular hits, and in this regard the agency should ensure that it gets clearance from both IMRO and MCPS. Levi Strauss has used various hits from the 1950s to promote 'Levi 501 jeans'.

(5) commissioned music

As an alternative to using music produced by 'jingle companies' an agency can commission a composer to compose original music, and in these circumstances the advertising agency can negotiate the terms of any assignment or licence in the music.

(b) Any footage of film

The advertiser will need the written consent of the owner of the copyright in the film.[79]

(c) Any printed material

The advertiser will need the written consent of the owner of the copyright in the printed material, such as newspaper clippings.[80]

(d) Irish banknotes

The advertiser will need clearance from the Central Bank to use Irish banknotes.[81]

(e) Dramatic works

If a dramatic work has been reduced to writing, then the advertiser should obtain consent of the owner of the dramatic work before using it.

*Obtaining clearance to use copyright material*

*Introduction*

Copyright in an advertisement is an intellectual property in the advertisement, which is freely transferable in whole or in part. Exploitation of copyright in advertisements can be extremely valuable. Take, for example, an

---

79  This applies to television advertising only.
80  This applies to television advertising only.
81  This applies to television advertising only.

advertisement in relation to a popular beer. There are a multiple of rights that may arise, such as the television rights, the translation rights, poster rights, etc. Irish copyright law facilitates the free transmission of copyright. Section 47(1) of the 1963 Act provides that the copyright is transmissible by assignment, testamentary position or by operation of law, as personal or movable property.

Advertisers will often want to become the owner of the copyright in the advertisement and so it is very important that their agencies have obtained clearance in respect of, or the beneficial right to transfer, the copyright in the advertisement to the advertiser, or at least have obtained the right to enable the advertiser to use the copyright.

Copyright can be transmitted in a number of ways.

## Assignments

### Assignments must be in writing

An assignment of copyright (whether total or partial) will only be effective if it is in writing and signed by or on behalf of the assignors, and advertisers must ensure that any assignee of the copyright in an advertisement is made in writing.

### No registration system for copyright transactions

Unlike other forms of intellectual property, there is no public registration system in relation to dealings in copyright and so the advertiser is taking a risk that there are no prior assignments which would take priority over it. If there are, then the advertiser's rights will be against the assignor.

### Partial assignments

The owner of copyright subsisting in a work can assign the copyright in part. Section 47(2) of the 1963 Act specially provides that an assignment of copyright to the advertiser or advertising agency may be limited in any one of the following ways or in any combination of two or more of those ways, that is to say:

(a) the class of act granted (for example, television advertisement as opposed to printed media);

(b) form of reproduction (for example, it may be reproduced for newspaper advertising but not billboard advertising);

(c) the geographical boundaries in which the copyright is to operate (for example, the Republic of Ireland only);

(d) the period during which the copyright in the advertisement is to operate (for example, the right to reproduce artwork for 20 years as opposed to 70 years after the death of the author).

## Formal requirements to effect an assignment

The 1963 Act does not provide any particular form that an assignment in the copyright of the advertisement or any part of it should take, other than stating that it must be in writing and signed by or on behalf of the assignor.

The assignment of the copyright in the advertisement (or any part of it) should contain words sufficient to effect an assignment of the copyright. Insufficient words may effect no transmission whatsoever, or only a licence or an equitable assignment of the copyright. However, because no formal words are required, it is often a matter of construction as to whether the particular document is an assignment or licence.[82]

## Assignor's obligations and rights

The assignor would usually have two obligations: first, to deliver the completed work to the advertiser or advertising agency and, secondly, to assign the copyright or so much of it as is agreed to the advertiser or advertising agency with good title. The assignor is obliged to comply with the terms of the assignment and is not permitted to exploit the rights that have been assigned.

## Assignee's obligations and rights

Once the assignment has been effected, the advertiser or advertising agency is liable to pay the assignor in whatever form is agreed in the contract. The advertiser or advertising agency only has the benefit of exactly what has been assigned and therefore, if there has been a partial assignment, the advertiser or advertising agency does not obtain the benefit to that which the assignor retained, assigned or licensed to another party. If the assignment specifies the advertiser or advertising agency's obligations in relation to the publishing, assigning or licensing of the copyright, then the advertiser or advertising agency must adhere to the terms of the contract.

The legal assignment or partial assignment of copyright vests the copyright (or such part of it that is assigned) in the advertiser or advertising agency, and so it is the advertiser or advertising agency who can permit any exploitation of the right assigned and who can take proceedings in its own name against any person who infringes it without joining any other party. The advertiser or advertising agency obtains a good title to the right assigned vis à vis a subsequent assignee irrespective of whether the subsequent assignee had notice of the first assignment. The advertiser or advertising agency's rights will be governed by the contract, and the advertiser or advertising agency should consider whether it can assign, licence or publish the right assigned to

---

82   *Re Jude's Musical Composition* [1907] 1 Ch 651.

it and the extent of the right assigned.[83] If the contract is silent, then the advertiser or advertising agency of the copyright can act as it pleases.

### Assignment of future copyright

Section 49 of the 1963 Act enables the prospective owner of copyright to assign the copyright in a work before the work or the copyright has come into existence. Where the prospective owner purports to assign the future copyright (wholly or partially) to an advertiser or advertising agency, then if, on the coming into existence of the copyright, the advertiser or advertising agency or a person claiming under it, would be entitled as against all other persons to require the copyright to be vested in him (wholly or partially as the case may be), the copyright shall, on its coming into existence, vest in the advertiser or advertising agency (as the case may be), or his successors in title accordingly, by virtue of s 49 of the 1963 Act, without the need for any further assurance.

The prospective owner of copyright may make partial assignments of a future copyright to different persons. For example, the prospective owner of the copyright subsisting in a cartoon advertisement could assign the future printed media rights to agency X and the future television rights to agency Y. When the copyright comes into existence, agency X will be entitled to the printed media rights and agency Y will be entitled to use the television rights.

### *Licences*

### Introduction

If the owner of copyright does not wish to transfer the copyright outright, then he can permit certain acts to be done in relation to the work in question which would normally be an infringement of the copyright subsisting in the work.

Copyright in a work is infringed by any person who, not being the owner of the copyright and without the licence of the owner, does, or authorises another person to do, certain acts which are restricted by the copyright.[84]

There is no particular format for a licence, though it is advisable that it should be in writing.

A licence granted in respect of any copyright by the person who, in relation to the matters to which the licence relates, is the owner of the copyright, shall be binding on every successor in title to his interest in the copyright, except a purchaser in good faith for valuable consideration and

---

83 For example, whether the copyright has been restricted in any way, such as by geographical limitation or duration, etc.
84 Copyright Act 1963, s 7(3).

without notice (actual or constructive) of the licence or a person deriving title from such a person.[85]

The future owner of any copyright may grant a licence of the prospective copyright in the same manner as the owner of any subsisting copyright, and the same rules apply.[86]

### Exclusive licences

Under the 1963 Act, the owner of copyright can grant an exclusive licence in relation to the copyright and the advertiser or advertising agency can institute proceedings for the infringement of the copyright.

Unlike a bare licence, an exclusive licence has to be in writing.

### Implied licences

Often, licences to use a copyright are implied by virtue of the circumstances surrounding a particular transaction. For example, if a car manufacturer commissions an advertising agency to carry out an advertising campaign on behalf of an advertiser without any agreement between them in relation to the ownership of the copyright subsisting in the various advertisements, the courts will often imply the right of the advertiser to use the copyright in the advertising campaign if the campaign has been paid for by the advertiser. The extent of the licence will depend on the particular circumstances.

### Extended copyright under SI 158/1995

Where the copyright subsisting in a work or related right has been extended or revived by virtue of the European Communities (Term of Protection of Copyright) Regulations 1995, then such extension or revival will only vest in the advertiser or advertising agency if the deed of assignment expressly provided for such extension or revival in the copyright.[87] Therefore, if photographer X licensed the copyright in his photographs to agency Y to enable agency Y to reproduce them for an advertising campaign and the copyright expired in 1993, then agency Y will need a further licence from photographer X to reproduce the photographs for the copyright so revived under the 1995 Regulations.

---

85  Copyright Act 1963, s 47(4).
86  *Ibid*, ss 49(3) and 47(4).
87  SI 158/1995, reg 13(2).

## Duration of copyright

*Introduction*

The periods of copyright under the 1963 Act have been amended by Council Directive 93/98/EEC of 29 October 1993, harmonising the law of protection of copyright and certain related rights which was brought into Irish law by the European Communities (Term of Protection of Copyright) Regulations 1995.[88]

The effect of the 1995 Regulations has been that many works which have been outside the term of copyright have been brought back into copyright, and so an advertiser or advertising agency should check whether a work is in the public domain or whether it has been brought back into copyright.

From an advertising point of view, the extension in the term of copyright may not be relevant, as many advertisements tend to date. However, often, the advertisers want a complete assignment of the copyright in the advertisement, including the residue of the term then unexpired.

*Literary, dramatic, musical and artistic works*

**General position**

Generally, the term of copyright subsisting in a literary, dramatic, musical or artistic work is the lifetime of the author and 70 years after the author's death, irrespective of the date when the work is published or otherwise lawfully made available to the public.[89]

**Works of joint ownership**

The term of copyright is calculated from the date of death of the last of the co-authors. Therefore, if X and Y were joint authors of an advert, and X died on 11 January 1968 and Y died on 1 January 1998, then the term of copyright would expire on 1 January 2069.

*Films*

The term of copyright subsisting in a television advertisement is the end of the period of 70 years after the death of the following persons, namely:

(a) the principal director;

(b) the author of the screenplay for the television advertisement;

(c ) the author of the dialogue; or

(d) the composer of music specifically created for use in the television advertisement.[90]

---

88   SI 158/1995.

89   *Ibid.*

90   *Ibid.*

The 1995 Regulations get away from the notion that 'publication' is the commencement date of the term of copyright. It is important to note that no copyright is conferred on the principal director, the author of the screenplay or dialogue or the composer of the music for the film, as the copyright vests in the maker.[91]

### Sound recordings

The term of protection subsisting in a sound recording is 50 years after the recording has been made.[92] The term of copyright in a sound recording runs from when the recording is made, and not from when it has been published.

### Broadcasts

The term of protection in relation to the rights of a broadcasting organisation in a broadcast is 50 years after the first transmission of the broadcast.[93]

### Calculation of the term of copyright

The term of copyright laid down by the 1995 Regulations expires on the first day of January of the year following the event which gives rise to them.[94] For example, if the composer of an advertising jingle were to die on 16 January 1999, the copyright in his works would expire on 1 January 2070.

### Revival of rights

One of the contentious effects of the extension of the term of copyright by the 1995 Regulations is that works in which copyright no longer subsisted because the term had expired have been brought back into copyright. Regulation 12 of the 1995 Regulations provides that the extended term of copyright (where it has been extended) applies to all literary, dramatic, musical and artistic works, sound recordings, films and broadcasts which are protected in at least one Member State of the European Union as of 1 July 1995.[95] For example, an advertiser may want to use a substantial excerpt of *Ulysses* by James Joyce to promote a Dublin beer. Under the 1963 Act, the term of copyright in the work *Ulysses* expired on 1 January 1992 (being 50 years from the end of the year on which James Joyce died (he died on 13 January 1941)). However, it was still protected in Germany, which provides for 70 years' protection after the death of the author. Under the 1995 Regulations, therefore, *Ulysses* has been brought back into copyright until 1 January 2012.

---

91  Copyright Act 1963, s 18(3).
92  SI 158/1995.
93  *Ibid.*
94  *Ibid.*
95  *Ibid*, reg 12.

*Protection of acquired rights and exploitation in good faith of revived public domain works*

Where exploitation or preparation of a substantial nature to exploit a public domain work occurred before the 1993 Directive was adopted on 29 October 1993, exploitation may continue unhindered and without any liability to the owner for the duration of the term of the copyright so revived.[96] Therefore, if advertising agency X had gone to substantial trouble to tape excerpts of *Ulysses* by James Joyce (the copyright of which had expired on 1 January 1992) on 1 January 1993 by making a radio advertisement using the excerpts, and had entered into contracts with the advertiser, producers, etc, then advertising agency X can continue the making of the radio advertisement for the duration of the term of copyright so revived without any fear of any action against him for copyright infringement by the copyright owner.

In addition, where exploitations or preparations of a substantial nature to exploit a public domain work took place between the date of adoption and the date of implementation of the 1993 Directive (namely, between 29 October 1993 and 1 July 1995) and the person so doing can show that they were not aware and had no reasonable grounds for suspecting that the copyright in the work would be revived by the 1993 Directive, the exploitation may continue unhindered without any liability to the copyright owner for the duration of the term of copyright so revived.[97]

This provision is trying to prevent persons from exploiting works who may well have had reasonable grounds for suspecting the copyright in a work would be revived. For example, a producer of a television advertisement who regularly talks to his legal advisers and negotiates contracts with advertising agencies and starts to make a television advertisement using excerpts from *Lady Chatterly's Lover* (the copyright of which expired on 1 January 1981) on 1 June 1994 and continues to make the film, he may be infringing the copyright subsisting in *Lady Chatterley's Lover*.

Bear in mind that the onus is on the television advertisement maker to show that he was not aware, and had no reasonable grounds for suspecting, that the copyright in *Lady Chatterley's Lover* had been revived.

## Infringement of copyright

*Introduction*

Infringement of copyright can be divided into primary and secondary infringement. Primary infringement is the unauthorised exercise of rights restricted by the Copyright Act 1963, while secondary infringement relates to

---

96  SI 158/1995, reg 14(1)(a).
97  *Ibid*, reg 14(1)(b).

infringement by sale or other dealings with articles where these articles are themselves an infringement of copyright.

## Primary infringement

Copyright is really a statutory right to prevent other people from doing certain acts. The 1963 Act refers to these acts as 'restricted acts'.

## Infringement of literary, dramatic and musical works

Copyright in a literary, dramatic or musical work of an advertisement is infringed if a person, who, not being the owner of the copyright and without the licence of the owner, does, or authorises another person to do, any of the following acts:[98]

(a) reproduce the work in any material form;

(b) publish the work;

(c) perform the work in public;

(d) broadcast the work;

(e) cause the work to be transmitted to subscribers to a diffusion service;

(f) make an adaptation of the work;

(g) do, in relation to an adaptation of the work, any of the acts listed in (a)–(e) above.[99]

### Reproducing the work in any material form

The 1963 Act does not actually define 'reproduction', but merely provides that it includes a reproduction in the form of a record or film. The reproduction of a work means the copying of the work.[100] Obviously, it will often be very difficult to prove that a work has been copied as only the defendant will know from where he sourced the material for the alleged infringement.

The courts have resisted putting in strict rules as to what amounts to copying or reproducing a work or other subject matter, and each case should be judged on its own facts, but there are a number of guidelines which are of assistance:

(a) There must be a causal connection

The plaintiff in an infringement action must show that the defendant has made use, either directly or indirectly, of his work.[101]

---

98 Copyright Act 1963, s 7(3).
99 *Ibid*, s 8(6).
100 *Ladbroke (Football) Ltd v William Hill (Football) Ltd* [1964] 1 WLR 273, p 276.
101 *House of Spring Gardens and Others v Point Blank Ltd* [1984] IR 611.

There must be a causal connection between the copyright work and the infringing work for an infringement to be established. In *House of Spring Gardens Ltd and Others v Point Blank Ltd and Others*,[102] Costello J stated that 'there must ... be a 'causal connection' between the copyright work and the infringing work, but indirect copying will amount to an infringement once the chain of connection between the two has been established'.[103] Costello J pointed to the useful test to establish if there has been a reproduction within the meaning of the 1963 Act as laid down by Willmer LJ in *Francis Day and Hunter Ltd v Bron*[104] and which he quoted from *Copinger on Copyright*.[105] Willmer LJ stated that:

- there must be a sufficient degree of objective similarity between the two works; and

- some causal connection between the plaintiff's and the defendant's work;

- it is quite irrelevant to inquire whether the defendant was or was not consciously aware of such causal connection;

- where there is a substantial degree of objective similarity, this of itself will afford prima facie evidence to show that there is a causal connection between the plaintiff and the defendant's work; at least, it is a circumstance from which the inference may be drawn;

- the fact that the defendant denies that he consciously copied affords some evidence to rebut the inference of causal connection arising from the objective similarly, but is in no way conclusive.[106]

In *House of Spring Gardens Ltd and Others v Point Blank Ltd and Others*,[107] Costello J held that there had been an infringement of the second plaintiff's copyright in the design of an armoured vest, as a causal connection had been established because of the similarity of the overall shape and configuration of the two garments, notwithstanding that there had been obvious differences of detail between the two vests.

(b) Subconscious copying

Where a person subconsciously copies an advertisement or words used in an advertisement, it will be necessary for the court to consider the following:

- the degree of familiarity that the defendant had with the plaintiff's work;

- the objective similarity of the defendant's work;

---

102 *House of Spring Gardens and Others v Point Blank Ltd* [1984] IR 611.
103 *Ibid*, p 670.
104 [1963] Ch 587.
105 12th edn, 1980, p 460.
106 *House of Spring Gardens and Others v Point Blank Ltd* [1984] IR 611, p 670.
107 *Ibid*.

- the inherent probability that such similarity as is found between the two works could be due to coincidence;

- the existence of other possible influences on the defendant;

- the quality of the defendant's own evidence on the presence of the plaintiff's work in his mind.[108] However, the defendant's evidence is to be no way conclusive in rebutting the *prima facie* case that the defendant has copied the plaintiff's work.[109]

(c) A substantial part of the work must be copied

Where a work used in an advertisement has been reproduced in its entirety without alteration, then there is no difficulty in proving infringement. Proof of infringement becomes more problematic where the work in the advertisement has not been reproduced in this fashion. Essentially, all that the 1963 Act requires is that a substantial part of the work be copied. Section 3(1) of the 1963 Act provides that any reference in the 1963 Act to the doing of an act in relation to a work or other subject matter shall be taken to include a reference to the doing of that act in relation to a substantial part of the work or other subject matter, and any reference to a reproduction, adaptation or copy of a work shall be taken to include a reference to a reproduction, adaptation or copy of a substantial part of the work. The courts have resisted putting in place rules as to what amounts to taking a 'substantial part' of a work or other subject matter; each case should be assessed on its own facts.

**Publishing the work**

The unauthorised publication of a literary, dramatic or musical work in an advertisement is an infringement of copyright. The 1963 Act does not define publication. However, in determining for the purposes of infringement whether:

(a) a work has been published; or

(b) publication of a work was a first publication thereof; or

(c) the work was published or otherwise dealt with in the lifetime of a person,

no account can be taken of any unauthorised publication or the doing of any unauthorised acts.[110] Publication is taken to be unauthorised if the copyright subsisted in a work and the act in question was done otherwise than by, or with the licence of, the owner of the copyright, or if the copyright did not subsist in the work, and the act in question was done otherwise than by, or with the licence of, the author or person lawfully claiming under him.

---

108 *Francis Day and Hunter Ltd v Bron* [1963] Ch 587.
109 *House of Spring Gardens and Others v Point Blank Ltd* [1984] IR 611.
110 Copyright Act 1963, s 3(3).

In *House of Spring Gardens Ltd and Others v Point Blank* Ltd *and Others*,[111] the defendant was held to have published the copyright of the plaintiff's design of armoured vests by issuing to the public the three component parts made up into its own armoured vest which was a reproduction of the second named plaintiff's copyright in the design of the armoured vests.

## Performing the work in public

The copyright subsisting in a literary, dramatic or a musical work is infringed if the work is performed in public without the copyright holder's authorisation. The 'performance of a work' is defined by the 1963 Act and includes delivery, in relation to lectures, addresses, speeches or sermons and, in general, includes any mode of visual or acoustic presentation, including any such presentation by the operation of wireless telegraph apparatus, or by the exhibition of a film, or by the use of a record, or any other means.[112]

## Broadcasting the work

## Causing the work to be transmitted through a diffusion service

## Making an adaptation of the work

It is an infringement of copyright to make an adaptation of a literary, dramatic or musical work. This would include an adaptation of a substantial part of the work, for example, in the following ways:

(a) conversion of a non-dramatic work into a dramatic work;

(b) conversion of a dramatic work into a non-dramatic work;

(c) where a work has been translated, an advertiser wishing to use the translated work should obtain a licence not only from the owner of the original work but also from the owner of the translation;

(d) a pictorial representation of a literary or dramatic work can be an adaptation of the work. For example, a cartoon strip used in an advertisement indicating the plot of a play may be an infringement even though there may be no words used. An adaptation in relation to a musical work is defined as meaning an arrangement or transcription of the work.[113]

---

111 [1984] IR 611.
112 Copyright Act 1963, s 2(1).
113 *Ibid*, s 8(7).

*Infringement of artistic works*

Copyright in an artistic work is infringed if an advertiser who, not being the owner of the copyright and without the licence of the owner, does or authorises another person to do any of the following acts:[114]

(a) reproduce the work in any material form;

(b) publish the work;

(c) include the work in a television broadcast;

(d) cause a television programme which includes the work to be transmitted to subscribers to a diffusion service.

*Sound recordings*

Copyright in a sound recording is infringed if an advertiser who, not being the owner of the copyright and without the licence of the owner, does or authorises another person to do any of the following acts:[115]

(a) make a record embodying the recording;

(b) cause the recording or any reproduction of it to be heard in public or to be broadcast or transmitted to subscribers to a diffusion service, without the payment of equitable remuneration to the owner of the copyright subsisting in the recording;

(c) cause the recording or any reproduction thereof to be heard in public, or to be broadcast, or to be submitted to subscribers to a diffusion service.[116]

*Copyright in films*

Copyright in films is infringed if an advertiser who, not being the owner of the copyright and without the licence of the owner, does or authorises another person to do any of the following acts:[117]

(a) make a copy of the film;

(b) cause the film, in so far as it consists of visual images, to be seen in public, or, in so far as it consists of sounds, to be heard in public;

(c) broadcast the film;

(d) cause the film to be transmitted to subscribers to a diffusion service.

In the case of *Norowzian v Arks Ltd and Others*,[118] it was held that there is no infringement of film copyright where the defendant advertising agent does not copy the plaintiff's film. In this case, the plaintiff produced a very short

---

114 Copyright Act 1963, s 7(3).

115 *Ibid*, s 7(3).

116 *Ibid*, s 17(4).

117 *Ibid*, s 7(3).

118 (1998) unreported, 17 July, High Court, *per* Rattee J.

film called *Joy*, with no dialogue, consisting of one man, casually dressed, performing a strange dance to music. It was held by the court that, because the defendant advertising agency's famous television advertisement for Guinness entitled 'Anticipation' did not copy any of the frames of the film *Joy*, that it was not in breach of copyright.

## Television and sound broadcasts

Copyright in a television and sound broadcast is infringed if an advertiser who, not being the owner of the copyright and without the licence of the owner, does or authorises another person to do any of the following acts:[119]

(a) in the case of a television broadcast in so far as it consists of visual images, make, otherwise than for private purposes, a film of it or a copy of such a film;

(b) in the case of a sound broadcast, or of a television broadcast in so far as it consists of sounds, make, otherwise than for private purposes, sound recording of it or a recording embodying such a recording;

(c) in the case of a television broadcast, cause it, in so far as it consists of visual images to be seen in public or in so far as it consists of sounds, to be heard in public, if it is seen or heard by a paying audience;

(d) in the case of either a television broadcast or a sound broadcast, re-broadcast it.[120]

## Published editions

Copyright in a published edition is infringed if an advertiser who, not being the owner of the copyright and without licence of the owner, does or authorises another person to make a photographic or similar process of a reproduction of the typographical arrangement of the edition.[121]

## General principles in relation to an action for primary infringement

There are a number of criteria which should be taken into account in relation to an action for primary infringement.

### Infringement by authorisation

Primary infringement will also take place if a person authorises infringement by others.[122]

---

119 Copyright Act 1963, s 7(3).
120 *Ibid*, s 19(5).
121 *Ibid*, s 20(5).
122 *Ibid*, s 7(3).

## Burden of proof

The burden of proof is on the plaintiff to show that there has been an infringement.

### Secondary infringement

Secondary infringement relates to commercial dealings in works which infringe copyright. It includes most kinds of commercial dealings, namely, selling, letting for hire, importing, exposing for sale or exhibiting infringing copies.[123] However, such infringement is limited to dealings where those persons know that the articles in question are an infringement of copyright.[124]

### Defences to a claim for breach of copyright in an advertisement

There are a number of defences which a defendant can plead in a claim for breach of copyright which are as follows:

### The advertisement is not a copy

The law of copyright does not confer a monopoly on the owner of copyright. It confers an exclusive right to prevent others from exploiting the works in question. Therefore, it is entirely conceivable that two people can create an identical work. If, for example, an advertiser had created an identical advertisement to its competitor and was able to provide evidence to this effect, then this would be a defence in any proceedings brought by the competition for breach of copyright.

### Third party consent obtained

It is a full defence if the advertiser can show that he has obtained third party consent to use the copyright material by way of licence or assignment.

### Protection of acquired rights and exploitation in good faith of public domain work

This enables advertisers and others, where they have exploited works in good faith or revived public domain works, to plead this as a defence by virtue of the European Communities (Term of Protection of Copyright) Regulations 1995.[125]

---

123 Copyright Act 1963, s 11(2).
124 *Ibid*, s 11(2).
125 SI 158/1995.

## Fair use defences

The fair use defences apply to literary, dramatic, musical and artistic work and are as follows:

Criticism or review (with an acknowledgment).

Reporting current events in a newspaper or other periodical (with an acknowledgment) or broadcasting them or including them in a film.

Educational use and private copying for research or private study ...

## Exceptions in relation to literary, dramatic and musical works

There are additional exceptions in relation to the reproduction of literary, dramatic or musical works for use in judicial proceedings or a report of such proceedings. A reading or recital in public or broadcast by one person of a reasonable extract from a published literature dramatic work (with an acknowledgment) will not be an infringement of copyright in that work. Advertisers should be aware that an acknowledgment means a sufficient acknowledgment, whereby the author should be identified together with the title of the work which is being used.

## Exceptions in relation to artistic works

Where a piece of architecture, sculpture or artistic craftsmanship is situated in a public place, there will be no infringement of the work by its inclusion in a television advertisement or broadcast, or if there is a painting, drawing or engraving, or photograph made. Accordingly, advertisers may not concern themselves with such works.

## Miscellaneous exceptions

Advertisers need not concern themselves with the incidental or background inclusion of a work in television advertisements.

## Exceptions in relation to sound recording in films and broadcasts

If the advertiser pays the equitable remuneration to the collection society in the use of the sound recording, it will not be treated as an infringement of the sound recording.

## *Remedies*

Advertisers should be aware that, if an advertiser breaches copyright, the owner of the work will be entitled to redress through the courts. The copyright owner will sue the advertiser and not the advertising agency. Therefore advertisers, if sued for breach of copyright, should join its advertising agency into the proceedings and seek an indemnity from the advertising agency. Frequently, advertisers seek an indemnity from the advertising agency in relation to any claim that may be brought against them by third party copyright owners.

### Injunction

The copyright owner may seek an injunction to prevent the advertiser from continuing with the use of the advertisement and the court order would require an immediate withdrawal from circulation of any advertisements whether in the form of printed material, videos, compact discs or any other medium and will also require that the advertiser immediately ceases publishing and distributing or broadcasting the advertisement.

### Damages

The courts can award the payment of damages to the copyright owner, which are normally calculated on the basis of the direct loss sustained by the copyright owner.

### Account of profits

Where the advertiser has received any profits, the court may order that those profits are paid over to the copyright owner.

### Punitive damages

The court may award additional damages in the form of penal damages, and in assessing the penal damages will have regard to the flagrancy of the infringement, any benefit that has accrued to the advertiser and whether any other forms of relief would be ineffective for the copyright owner.

### Costs

In addition, advertisers should be aware that if a copyright owner takes legal action against an advertiser and is successful, the advertiser will be liable to pay the legal costs of both parties.

## Trade marks in advertising

### Introduction

Trade marks have a direct bearing on advertising in that an advertiser, when advertising its product or name, will want any brand name protected, so that its competitors do not use the name for similar products once they become aware of it. In addition, an advertiser should be careful not to infringe the trade mark of any other person.

The legislation governing trade marks in Ireland is the Trade Marks Act 1996 (the 1996 Act). The 1996 Act defines a trade mark as 'any sign capable of being represented graphically which is capable of distinguishing goods or services of one undertaking from those of other undertakings'.[126] It can consist of words (including personal names, designs, letters, numerals) on the shape of goods and their packaging.

### Registration of trade marks

In order for an advertiser to have the benefit of a registered trade mark it has to register the mark successfully under the 1996 Act. Once it has done this, it will have the exclusive rights in the trade mark in respect of the goods or services which relate to the trade mark and can take infringement proceedings against any person who uses the trade mark in the State without the advertiser's consent.[127] It is advisable that advertisers register any trade marks where possible, as otherwise, they will be relying on the common law tort of passing off.[128]

### Trade mark infringement

Trade mark infringement takes place if one person uses in the course of trade:

(a) a sign which is identical with the trade mark in relation to goods or services which are identical to the proprietor's goods or services for which it is registered;

(b) a sign, where:

- the sign is identical with the proprietor's trade mark and is used in relation to goods or services similar to those for which the trade mark is registered; or

- the sign is similar to the trade mark and is used in relation to goods or services identical or similar to those for which the trade mark is registered,

and there is a likelihood of confusion on the part of the public, which includes the likelihood of association of the sign with the trade mark;

(c) a sign which is:

- identical with or similar to the proprietor's trade mark; and

- used in relation to goods and services which are not similar to those for which the proprietor's trade mark is registered, where the advertiser's

---

126 Trade Marks Act 1996, s 6.
127 *Ibid*, s 13.
128 See para 4.3.

trade mark has a reputation in Ireland and the use of the sign, being without due cause, takes unfair advantage of, or is detrimental to the distinctive character or the reputation of the proprietor's trade mark.

### Remedies

There are a number of remedies available to an advertiser who successfully brings infringement proceedings against the party using its trade mark, which are as follows.

### Injunction

The court can order that the defendant immediately ceases to use the trade mark of the advertiser.

### Delivery up

The court can order that the defendant delivers up all goods to which the advertiser's trade mark was applied.

### Disposal or destruction of goods

The court can order the disposal or destruction of goods, having considered whether or not other remedies are available which will adequately compensate and protect the interest of the advertiser.

### Search and seizure

The district court is given jurisdiction under s 35 of the 1996 Act to order the seizure of any infringing articles using the trade mark.

### Damages

The court can award the payment of damages to the proprietor of the trade mark which are normally calculated on the basis of the direct loss sustained by the proprietor of the trade mark.

### Account of profits

Where the advertiser has received any profits, the court may order that the profits are paid over to the proprietor of the trade mark.

### Consent to use of trade marks

Advertisers must proceed with caution before using trade marks belonging to another, including logos, in advertising campaigns or promotions. Take, for example, a department store that produces its own cheap brand of T-shirts. In order to give the T-shirts some popular credibility, it decides to undertake a television advertising campaign. In the campaign, the models wear the T-shirts with Levi jeans. The models are eating, drinking and dancing in Planet Hollywood with the camera focusing on the T-shirts, as well as the Levi Jeans and Planet Hollywood logos. This is not comparative advertising, as there is no competition in relation to the goods, but clearly, the advertiser is using the trade mark of Levi Strauss and Planet Hollywood to enhance its T-shirts. In this scenario, the advertiser will be infringing the trade marks of Levi Strauss and Planet Hollywood unless it has obtained the prior consent of those trade mark proprietors to use the trade marks.

Third party trade mark proprietors (such as Levi Strauss in this example) may not be willing to associate its goods with inferior goods.

## Passing off and advertising

### Introduction

Passing off has been defined as a misrepresentation made by a trader in the course of trade to prospective customers or ultimate consumers of goods for services supplied by him, which is calculated to injure the business or goodwill of another trader and which causes actual damage to the business of that trader.[129]

For example, if advertiser A decides to promote its new car called 'Beemer', which is an expensive and luxurious car with a prominent radiator grille and the logo of an oval green and black chequered coat of arms on top of the radiator grille, it is clear that advertiser A is trying to advertise its car with a brand name similar to that of BMW. BMW may or may not have a trade mark in the name of Beemer, but will almost certainly not have a trade mark in the oval logo, as it doesn't use it. However, the get up of 'Beemer' is confusingly similar to the BMW trade mark, so as to cause confusion among consumers familiar with the BMW car. In this scenario, BMW would have a good cause of action in passing off.

The remedies which a successful plaintiff is entitled to in an action in passing off are injunction, damages and an account of profits. The court may also award additional damages in a passing off action in the form of penal damages, and in assessing the penal damages will have regard to the flagrancy of the infringement, any benefit that has accrued to the advertiser and whether any other forms of relief would be ineffective relief.

In addition, advertisers should be aware that in a successful passing off action against an advertiser, the advertiser will be liable to pay the legal costs of both parties.

---

129 *Erven Warnink Besloten Vennootschap v J Townsend and Sons (Hull) Ltd* [1979] AC 731.

# ADVERTISING INDUSTRY ORGANISATIONS

## ASAI

As mentioned above, the main code for voluntary restrictions in relation to advertising in Ireland is the code published by ASAI. ASAI is a self-regulatory organisation which has three categories of membership, namely, advertising members, media members and agency members. The complaints committee of ASAI includes members nominated by the Director. The complaints committee may initiate corrective action and may issue appropriate directives. The self-regulatory system does not represent any curtailment of the freedom of commercial speech as enshrined in Art 10 of the European Convention on Human Rights, and it complements legislative control on advertising.

## IAPI

IAPI was founded in 1964, and represents the advertising agencies in Ireland. Its 38 members handle over 95% of advertising agency business. The wide range of services which IAPI offers include expenditure data (Ad-Stat) and other market and media research, together with the production of a range of publications. It provides an audio-visual equipment hire service and facilities for casting, teleconferencing and research. It organises an annual media conference and the International Advertising Festival of Ireland. It operates educational courses with the Dublin Institute of Technology. IAPI is actively involved in national and international issues, including the law, the maintenance of standards, the development of electronic services and business terms with the media and other third party suppliers. It takes a close interest in broadcasting, publishing, printing and production matters, and is an active member of the EAAA.

# RULES RELATING TO SPECIFIC PRODUCTS AND SERVICES

# ALCOHOL

## Television advertising

Television advertising of this product is governed by the Broadcasting Code, but emanates from Art 15 of Council Directive 89/552/EEC.

The RTE Code prohibits advertising of 'hard' liquor products, while advertising in relation to other alcoholic beverages is restricted in content and broadcast time. No alcoholic advertising is permitted during afternoon sports programmes. The same alcoholic advertisement may not be shown more than twice per night on any one RTE channel and must not contain any reference to a prize, competition or similar scheme. In multiple sequences of people drinking, great care must be taken to convey moderate, mature consumption.[130]

## Radio advertising

It is prohibited to advertise spirits on radio, and there is a restriction on other alcoholic beverages.[131]

## Cinema advertising

It is prohibited to advertise spirits in the cinema, and there is a restriction on other alcoholic beverages.

## Newspaper advertising

Advertising of alcoholic products is restricted voluntarily.

## Voluntary guidelines

The following restrictions are imposed on the content of alcohol advertising by the Code:

(a) advertising alcohol (that is, those drinks that exceed 1.2% alcohol by volume) should be socially responsible and should not exploit the young or the immature. It should neither encourage excessive drinking, nor present abstinence or moderation in a negative way;

(b) alcoholic advertising may refer to the social dimension or refreshing attributes of a drink but should not:

- emphasise alcohol as a stimulant, sedative or as having a tranquillising effect, or imply that it can improve physical performance;

- imply that drinking alcohol is necessary to social or business success or distinction or that those who do not drink are less likely to be acceptable or successful than those who do;

---

130 See also Appendix 2, para 12.
131 *Ibid.*

- suggest that alcohol can contribute towards sexual success or make the drinker more attractive to the opposite sex;

(c) alcohol advertising should not portray drinking as a challenge, nor should it be suggested that those who drink are brave or daring;

(d) alcohol advertising should not be directed at young people or in any way encourage them to start drinking. Accordingly:

- anyone depicted in an alcohol advertisement should appear to be over 25;

- advertisements in relation to alcohol should not feature real or fictitious characters who are likely to appeal particularly to people under 18 in a way that would encourage them to drink;

(e) the social consequences of alcohol should be recognised:

- alcohol advertising should not suggest that any product can mask the effects of alcohol in tests on drivers; advertisements for breath testing devices should include a prominent warning on the dangers of drinking and driving;

- immoderate drinking and regular solitary drinking should not be encouraged. Buying of large 'rounds' should not be depicted or implied;

- advertisements in relation to alcohol should not depict activities or locations where drinking alcohol would be unsafe or unwise. In particular, advertisements should not associate the consumption of alcohol with operating machinery, driving or any activity relating to water or heights, or any other occupation that requires concentration in order to be done safely;

- factual information can be given about the alcoholic strength of a particular drink but it should not be the principal theme of any advertisement. Drinks should not be promoted as being more intoxicating or presented as preferable because of their higher alcoholic content;

(f) advertisers should ensure that low alcoholic drinks (that is, those that contain 1.2% alcohol by volume or less) are not promoted in a way that encourages their inappropriate consumption.

## COSMETICS

### Voluntary guidelines

The following restrictions are imposed by the Code:

(a) claims about health and beauty products and treatments should be backed by substantiation, including the results of practical trials on human subjects of sufficient rigour, design and execution as to warrant general acceptance of the results;

(b) no reference should be made to tests, trials or endorsements by any college, hospital, clinic, laboratory or similar establishment unless there exists a bona fide establishment corresponding to the description used and it is under the effective supervision of a registered medical practitioner or other appropriate professional. Reference to such establishment should be made only with the permission of the appropriate authorities;

(c) an advertisement should not offer any product or treatment for serious or prolonged ailments or for conditions requiring the attention of a registered medical or other qualified practitioner;

(d) an advertisement for a health or beauty product or treatment should not:

- contain any offer to diagnose, advise, prescribe or treat by correspondence;
- encourage indiscriminate, unnecessary or excessive use of the product or treatment;
- suggest that the product or treatment is safe or effective merely because it is 'natural', nor should it refer to the omission of any ingredient in a way that suggests that the ingredient is unsafe or harmful;
- employ words, phrases or illustrations that claim or imply the cure of any ailment, disability, illness or disease, as distinct from the alleviation or relief of symptoms;
- contain any claim to provide rejuvenation, that is to prevent, retard or reverse the changes brought about by or associated with increasing age;
- use unfamiliar scientific terms for common conditions;

(e) consumers should be encouraged to take independent medical advice before committing themselves to significant treatments;

(f) an advertisement for a medicinal product should not contain an offer to refund money to dissatisfied customers;

(g) claims about the effect that a cosmetic has on or in the skin should distinguish between the composition of the product and any effects caused by the mode of application, such as massage.

# SLIMMING PRODUCTS

## Voluntary guidelines

The following are the rules in relation to the advertising of slimming products:

(a) a programme in which the intake of energy is lower than its output is the main self-treatment for achieving weight loss. Any claims made for the effectiveness of a slimming plan, method or product should be backed by rigorous practical trials on human subjects. Testimonials do not constitute substantiation, and the opinions expressed in them should be supported, where necessary, by independent evidence;

(b) claims that long term slimming, weight loss or inch loss can be achieved either generally or from specific areas of the body by any means other than dieting (for example, by expelling water, speeding up the metabolism, using mechanical devices, wearing garments or applying substances to the skin) should not be made unless they can be substantiated. Slimming claims in respect of an unproven weight loss method can not be justified merely by offering a diet or exercise scheme with it;

(c) advertisers should be able to show that their diet plans are nutritionally well balanced. These will be assessed in relation to the subjects who would be using them. Vitamins and minerals do not contribute to weight loss, but can be offered to slimmers as a safeguard against any shortfall when dieting;

(d) an advertisement should not suggest that persons of normal weight need slim. 'Crash diets' should not be advertised, because of the danger such diets can pose to the health of dieters not under medical supervision. An advertisement should not offer treatment for conditions that require medical treatment, such as obesity or anorexia;

(e) advertisements for diet aids, such as low calorie foods, food substitutes, appetite depressants and meal replacements should make it clear that they can be effective only as part of a calorie controlled diet. Prominence should be given to the role of the diet, and advertisements should not give the impression that particular methods cannot fail, or that dieters can eat as much as they like and still lose weight;

(f) advertisers should not make general claims that specific amounts of weight can be lost within a stated period. Claims that individuals have lost specific amounts of weight should be compatible with good medical and nutritional practice, should give details of the time period, and should not be based on unrepresentative experience;

(g) advertisements for intensive exercise programmes should encourage users to check with a doctor before starting.

# NON-PRESCRIPTION MEDICINAL PRODUCTS

## Legislation

Article 4 of the Medical Preparations (Advertising) Regulations 1993 (the 1993 Regulations) provides that a person shall not advertise a medical preparation in respect of which a product authorisation has not been granted. Article 5 of the 1993 Regulations prohibits the advertising of drugs requiring a prescription or controlled drugs. Article 8 of the 1993 Regulations provides that, in the case of advertisements to the general public, it must conform to the requirements laid down in Sched 2, which provide that those requirements are as follows: The advertisement must:

(a) be set out in such a way that it is clear that the message conveyed is an advertisement;

(b) contain:

- a clear identification by name that the product being advertised is a medical preparation, as well as by the common name if the preparation contains only one active ingredient;

- the information necessary for the correct use of the medical preparation;

- a warning to read carefully the instructions on the package leaflet, or on the outer packaging, as the case may be;

(c) not contain any material which:

- gives the impression that a medical consultation or surgical operation is unnecessary, in particular by offering a diagnosis or by suggesting treatment by mail;

- suggests that the effects of taking the medicine are guaranteed, are unaccompanied by side effects or are better than, or equivalent to, those of another treatment or medical preparation;

- suggests that the health of the subject can be enhanced by taking the medicine;

- suggests that the health of the subject could be affected by not taking the medicine. This prohibition shall not apply to vaccination campaigns;

- is directed exclusively or principally at children;

- refers to a recommendation by scientists, health professionals or persons who are neither of the foregoing but who, because of their celebrity, could encourage the consumption of medical preparations;

- suggests that the medical preparation is a foodstuff, cosmetic or other consumer product;

- suggests that the safety or efficacy of the medical preparation is due to the fact that it is natural;
- could, by a description or detailed representation of a case history, lead to erroneous self diagnosis;
- refers, in improper, alarming or misleading terms, to claims of recovery;
- uses improper, alarming or misleading terms, pictorial representations of changes in the human body caused by disease or injury, or of the action of a medical preparation on the human body or parts thereof;
- mentions that the drug has been granted a marketing authorisation.

In the case of a broadcast advertisement, for the purposes of 'reminding' the general public, one must give the name of the product and also advise people to read the leaflet. In printed media, both the number of the product authorisation and the name and address of the holder of that product authorisation are to be included in the advertisement.

# TOBACCO PRODUCTS

## Legislation

The Tobacco Products (Control of Advertising, Sponsorship and Sales Promotion) Act 1978, s 2, gives the relevant minister power to make regulations for the control and regulation of:

- advertising of tobacco products;
- sponsorship;
- any other activities which are intended or are likely to promote the sales of tobacco products.

The Tobacco Products (Control of Advertising, Sponsorship and Sales Promotion) Regulations 1991, in reg 8, provides that tobacco can only be advertised:

(a) in newspapers, magazines or other similar publications, other than comics or other publications directed at children;

(b) internally in premises which are points of retail sale of tobacco, provided that such advertising is not by means of visual electronic media or by sound;

(c) in duty free zones at airports and ferryports by means of permanent signs; and

(d) on packages of tobacco products.

Regulation 10 restricts what can be included in a tobacco advertisement, but it must include a recognised health warning. Regulation 12 states that advertisements of tobacco products shall not:

(a) claim or imply that smoking is free from risk to health or that it is less harmful to smoke one brand rather than another;

(b) describe filters, additives, tobacco substitutes, and so on, so as to suggest that they render the product less harmful to health; or

(c) to include or imply any testimonial for a particular brand.

Regulation 13 states that advertisements of tobacco products must not contain any representations of the tobacco product during or after combustion, or any representation of smoke or any other tobacco by-product.

Regulation 15 (as amended by the Tobacco Products (Control of Advertising, Sponsorship and Sales Promotion) (Amendment) Regulations 1996) provides that references to or representations of tobacco products or smoking utensils shall not be included in any advertisement or in any article or feature in any magazine, newspaper or other similar publication, where such reference or representation is intended or is likely to promote the sale of tobacco products.

Regulation 16 states that offers, vouchers, coupons, tokens and such like (including gifts of tobacco products) cannot be used to promote sales.

Regulation 18 states that a person shall not be allowed to induce a retailer to advertise tobacco products. Regulation 19 (as amended by the aforementioned 1996 Regulation) states that advertising expenditure must be approved by the relevant minister, and this is to mean total expenditure, but does not include expenditure on the design and production of packages.

Regulation 20 disallows the sponsorship of events where either the participants or the audience is predominantly under the age of 18. Regulation 21, as amended, states that a person engaged in the manufacture, importation, marketing, advertising, distribution or sale of tobacco products shall not incur expenditure on sponsorship unless such expenditure has been approved by the minister and shall not exceed an amount as determined, from time to time, by the minister and they shall not commence sponsorship of any event or activity in the State which was not sponsored in the State in the 12 months prior to 1 May 1986 without the prior approval of the minister, who may, at the same time, determine the expenditure which such person may expend on such sponsorship during a specified period.

## Recent European legislation

European Council Directive 98/43/EC, which was adopted on 6 July 1998, provides that all forms of advertising and sponsorship of tobacco products shall be banned in the European Union but that brand names already used in good faith both for tobacco products and for other goods and services may still be used under certain circumstances. The Directive prohibits any free distribution or promotion of tobacco products, but does not apply to communications or to the presentation of tobacco products offered for sale accompanied by a price index at tobacco sales outlets, or to advertising aimed at tobacconists, or to the sale of publications containing advertising for tobacco products which are published and printed in third countries, where those publications are not principally intended for the European Union. Article 5 of the Common Position allows Member States to implement stricter requirements as they deem necessary, and Art 6 allows Member States to defer the implementation of the total ban in Art 3 for:

(a) one year in respect of the press;

(b) two years in respect of sponsorship.

In exceptional cases, Member States may continue to authorise the existing sponsorship of events or activities organised at world level for a further period of three years ending not later than 1 October 2006, provided that:

(a) the sums devoted to such sponsorship decrease over the transitional period,

(b) voluntary restraint measures are introduced in order to reduce the visibility of advertising at the events or activities concerned.

# FINANCIAL SERVICES AND INVESTMENTS

## Voluntary guidelines

The following restrictions are imposed by the Code:

(a) advertisements for financial services and products should be prepared with care and with the conscious aim of ensuring that members of the public fully grasp the nature of any commitment into which they may enter as a result of responding to an advertisement. Advertisers should not take advantage of people's inexperience or gullibility;

(b) advertisements which invite a response by mail should contain the full address of the advertiser separate from any response coupon;

(c) advertisements should indicate the nature of the contract being offered and provide information on any limitations on eligibility, any charges, expenses or penalties attached and the terms on which withdrawal may be arranged. Alternatively, where an advertisement is short or is general in its content, free explanatory material giving full details of the offer should be made available before a binding contract is entered into;

(d) when an advertisement contains any forecast or projection, it should make clear the basis on which the forecast or projection is made, explaining, for example, whether:

- reinvestment of income is assumed;
- account has been taken of any applicable taxes;
- any penalties or deductions will arise on premature realisation or otherwise;

(e) advertisements should make it clear that the value of investments is variable and, unless guaranteed, can go down as well as up. If the value of the investment is guaranteed, details should be included in the advertisement;

(f) advertisements should specify that past performance or experience does not necessarily give a guide to the future. Any examples used should not be unrepresentative;

(g) attention is also drawn to any codes of standards or other requirements of trade associations/professional bodies (for example, the Irish Insurance Federation, the Irish Brokers Association, the Irish Association of Investment Managers) including:

- Code of Practice on Advertising and Sales Material of the Irish Insurance Federation;
- Code of Conduct for Insurance Intermediaries;
- Code of Advertising Practice of the Irish Association of Investment Managers.

## Legislation

Advertisements for financial products and services, including investment opportunities, deposits and credit facilities, are subject to a number of statutory requirements and primarily the Central Bank Acts 1942–98 and the Consumer Credit Act 1995.

# LOANS, CREDITS AND MORTGAGES

## Voluntary guidelines

The following restrictions are imposed by the Code:

(a) advertisements must comply with all relevant legal requirements;

(b) no advertisement is acceptable which directly or indirectly invites the remittance of money direct to the advertiser or any other person without further formality;

(c) advertisements must present the financial offer or service in terms which do not mislead the public, whether by exaggeration, omission or in any other way and:

- references to income tax and other tax benefits must be properly qualified to show what they mean in practice and to make it clear, where appropriate, that the full advantage may only be received by those paying income tax at a particular rate;

- reference to interest on savings and investments must be stated clearly and be factually correct at the time of the transmission of the advertisement. Calculations of interest must not be based on unstated factors (for example, minimum sum deposited, minimum deposit period, or minimum period of notice for withdrawal) which might affect the sum received by the individuals or be capable of misunderstanding in any other way. It should be clear whether the interest is gross or net of tax. Interest rates related to variables must be so described;

- there must not be any reference to specific rates or sums charged against borrowers unless the quoted rate or sum is fixed and applies universally to all borrowers; or is accompanied by a clear statement of the factors which might affect the position of individual borrowers; or is the highest currently charged; or is clearly and justifiably presented as an example only;

- no advertisement referring directly or indirectly to benefits to be derived from a purchase of units may state or imply that they are other than a medium to long term investment. There may be no projection of specific rates of growth or returns and no implication that past performance will inevitably be repeated. All references to past achievements or future possibilities must be qualified by a clear and unambiguous reference to the fact that the price of units and the income from them may go down as well as up;

- reference to rates and conditions in connection with insurance must not be inaccurate or misleading, and in specifying rates of premium or cover there must be no misleading omission of conditions. In life insurance advertising, references to specific sums assured or guaranteed bonuses must be accompanied by all relevant qualifying conditions, for example, age and sex of the assured at the outset of the policy, period of policy and amount and number of premiums payable. In reference to 'with profit' policies and bonuses, there must be no implication that past performance will inevitably be repeated. In advertisements for life insurance linked with unit trust investment, any reference to a specific maturity value, unless guaranteed, must be qualified by reference to the variables which might affect the quoted figure;

(d) actors may not purport to be chairmen, directors, officers or other employees of an advertiser. No one may appear to give independent professional advice on any investment offer. Celebrated entertainers, writers or sportsmen may not present, endorse or recommend any investment offer;

(e) full and detailed information will be required in connection with any financial offer or service to be advertised.

## Part II of the Consumer Credit Act 1995

Part II of the 1995 Act provides, by s 22, that an advertisement in which a person offers to provide or arrange the provision of credit shall, if mentioning a rate of interest, contain a clear and prominent statement of the annual percentage rate (APR), using a representative example if no other means is practicable, and no other rate of interest shall be included in the advertisement. The section also states that all charges must be specified in relation to the credit offered, and if security is a prerequisite to obtaining credit, that fact must also be specified in all advertisements.

Section 22 of the 1995 Act provides that where an advertisement refers to the availability of a financial accommodation in relation to the acquisition of goods or the provision of a service, it shall include a statement of the following:

(a) the nature of the financial accommodation;

(b) the cash price of the goods or services;

(c) where applicable, the total cost of credit or the hire purchase price;

(d) the number and amount of installments;

(e) the duration of the intervals between installment payments;

(f) the number of any installments which have to be paid before delivery of the goods; and

(g) details of any deposits payable.

Section 23 of the 1995 Act provides that an advertisement in which a person offers to arrange the letting of goods under a consumer hire agreement, or indicates the availability of such a letting, shall include a statement to the effect that the agreement is for letting, hiring or leasing only and the goods remain the property of the owner.

Section 24 of the 1995 Act provides that, where an advertisement purports to compare the level of repayments or cost under one or more forms of financial accommodation, the advertisement shall contain the relevant terms of each of the forms of financial accommodation referred to in the advertisement.

# EMPLOYMENT AND BUSINESS OPPORTUNITIES

## Voluntary guidelines

The following restrictions are imposed by the Code.

Advertisers and media should distinguish clearly between offers of employment, business opportunities and training courses:

(a) employment advertisements should correspond to genuine vacancies and should not require interested respondents to send money for further details. Terms and conditions should not be misrepresented and any earnings forecast should be realistic. If income is earned from a basic salary and commission, or commission only, this should be made clear;

(b) advertisements for business opportunities should not mislead participants as to the:

- nature of the work involved;
- amount of support available;
- extent of any financial investment required;
- potential earnings.

Where an advertisement does not contain the name and address of the advertiser, it is the responsibility of the media to be satisfied as to the advertiser's identity and honesty;

(c) advertisements for home work schemes in which respondents make articles, perform services or offer facilities at or from home should contain a clear description of the work and should make clear whether the home worker will be an employee of the company or will be self-employed. Any forecast of earnings should be based on the experience of current home workers. If it is a new scheme, no realistic forecast of earnings can be made and none should be given in the advertisement. Where an advertisement does not contain the name and address of the advertiser, it is the responsibility of media to be satisfied as to the advertiser's identity and honesty.

Details of charges imposed by the advertiser for machines, components or raw materials should be available to respondents before they are committed to any scheme.

If the advertiser intends to buy back the goods produced by the home worker, all relevant information should be supplied before any binding obligation or investment is made by the respondent. Home workers should know if there are any limitations that might affect their decision to accept the advertiser's offer before being committed to participate;

(d) advertisements for training and instruction courses should make no promise of employment unless a job is guaranteed.

The duration of the course and the level of attainment needed to embark on it should be made clear;

(e) advertisements for directories giving details of employment or business opportunities should indicate plainly the nature of what is being offered.

# CHARITY ADVERTISING

## Voluntary code

The Code imposes restrictions on promotions claiming that participation will benefit a charity or good cause. Such promotions should:

(a) name the charity or good cause that will benefit, and be able to demonstrate that those benefiting consent to the advertising or promotion;

(b) define the nature and objectives of the charity or cause unless that information is already widely available;

(c) specify the extent and nature of the advantage to be gained by the charity or cause;

(d) state if the promoters have imposed any limitations on the contribution they will make;

(e) not limit consumers' contribution. Any extra money collected should be given to the named charity or cause on the same basis as contributions below that level;

(f) not exaggerate the benefit to the charity which will be derived from any one individual's contribution;

(g) make available on request a current or final total of contributions made;

(h) take particular care with charity-linked promotions that may involve children and young people.

# CHILDREN AND ADVERTISING

## Legislation

The 1989 Directive[132] in relation to children and advertising was the basis for the wording of the section dealing with children in the Broadcasting Code.[133]

---

132 Council Directive 89/552/EEC on the co-ordination of certain provisions laid down by law, regulation or administrative action in Member States concerning the pursuit of television broadcasting activities, has been amended by Directive 97/36/EC to include 'teleshopping'.

133 See Appendix 2, para 11.

In the European Communities (Television Broadcasting) Regulations 1991,[134] reg 7 provides that a broadcaster is prohibited from broadcasting programmes that might seriously impair the physical, mental or moral development of minors, in particular those that involve pornography or gratuitous violence, and that other programmes which might impair the physical, mental or moral development of minors may only be shown where the broadcaster ensures, by selecting the time of the broadcast or by any technical means, that minors would not normally be expected to hear or see such broadcasts.

## Voluntary guidelines

Further restrictions in relation to children and advertising are imposed through the Code, the EAAA Red Book and the RTE Code:

(a) an advertisement should contain nothing that is likely to result in physical, mental or moral harm to children and:

- children should not be portrayed in a manner that offends against accepted standards of good taste and decency;
- they should not be encouraged to enter strange places or talk to strangers, for example, for the purpose of making collections or accumulating labels, wrappers, coupons and the like;
- they should not be shown in hazardous situations or behaving dangerously, inside the home or outside. Children should not be shown unattended in street scenes unless they are old enough to take responsibility for their own safety;
- they should not be portrayed engaging in anti-social behaviour; where they appear as pedestrians or cyclists they should be seen to observe the rules of the road;
- they should not be shown using, or in close proximity to, dangerous substances or equipment without direct adult supervision. Examples include matches, petrol, gas, medicines, certain household substances as well as certain electrical appliances and machinery, including agricultural machinery;
- an open fire in a domestic scene should always have a fireguard clearly visible when a child is included in the scene;

(b) an advertisement should not exploit the loyalty, vulnerability or lack of experience of children:

- they should not be made to feel inferior or unpopular for not buying the advertised product;

---

134 Implementing Art 22 of the 1989 Directive.

- they should not be made to feel that they are lacking in courage, duty or loyalty if they do not buy or do not encourage others to buy a particular product;
- they should not be encouraged to make a nuisance of themselves to parents or others with the aim of persuading them to buy the advertised product;

(c) an advertisement addressed to children should:

- not feature products that are unsuitable for children;
- make it easy for them to judge the actual size, characteristics and performance of any product advertised;
- not exaggerate what is attainable by an ordinary child using the product;

(d) if there is to be a reference to a competition for children in an advertisement, the value of the prizes and the chances of winning must not be exaggerated;

(e) to help in the portrayal of free gifts for children, television advertisements should, where necessary, make it easy to see the true size of the gift by showing it in relation to some common object against which its scale can be judged;

(f) the personalities or characters on children's programmes shall not be used to promote products, premiums, or services around their own programmes;

(g) nationally known persons, other than professional actors or presenters, shall not be used in advertising directed to children under 12 years of age, to endorse products or premiums either directly or indirectly;

(h) the cost of products should not be minimised by the use of such words as 'only' or 'just';

(i) when any parts that a child might reasonably suppose to be part of the purchase are available only at extra cost this must be made clear.

Advertisements for toys, games and other products of interest to children must not mislead and in particular:

- the true size and scale of the product must be made easy to judge. In any demonstration it must be made clear whether the toy is made to move mechanically or through manual operation;
- treatments which reflect the toy or game seen in action through the child's eyes, or in which real life counterparts of a toy are seen working, must be used with due restraint. There must be no confusion as to the noise produced by the toy;
- where advertisements show results from a drawing, construction, craft or modelling toy or kit, the results shown must be reasonably attainable by the average child and ease of assembly must not be exaggerated;

- advertisements for toys, games and similar products must include an indication of their price.

# GUARANTEES

## Legislation

The 1980 Act provides, by s 16, that the offer of a guarantee in relation to goods must be unambiguous and fair. Such guarantees do not exclude the rights of consumers at common law or their rights pursuant to statute. This applies to the use of guarantees in the advertisements of goods.

Subject to the above, there is no objection to the use of 'guarantees' in a colloquial sense; for example, where a film is 'guaranteed to cheer you up'.

## Voluntary guidelines

Voluntary guidelines provide that where an advertisement refers to a guarantee, the full terms of the guarantee should be available for consumers to inspect before they are committed to purchase. Any substantial limitations (for example, one year, parts only) should be clearly indicated in the advertisement.

# TESTIMONIALS AND ENDORSEMENTS

## Voluntary guidelines

The following restrictions are imposed by the Code:

(a) testimonials should be genuine, not more than three years old, and related to the experience of the person giving it;

(b) no testimonials or endorsements to be given by members of the medical professions;

(c) advertisers who use testimonials should be able to provide relevant supporting documentation to the ASAI. Testimonials by persons named or depicted in an advertisement may be used only with the prior permission of those persons;

(d) testimonials may be misleading if the formulation of the product or its market environment changes significantly. They should therefore relate to the product as currently offered;

(e) testimonials do not constitute substantiation and the opinions expressed in them should be supported, where necessary, with independent evidence of their accuracy. Claims based on a testimonial should conform with the Code;

(f) endorsements by fictitious or historical characters should not be presented as though they were genuine testimonials;

(g) references to tests, trials, professional endorsements, research facilities and professional journals should be used only with the permission of those concerned. Any establishment referred to should be under appropriate professional supervision.

## USEFUL ADDRESSES

Institute of Advertising Practitioners in Ireland
8 Upper Fitzwilliam Street
Dublin 2
Tel: + 353 1 6765991

Association of Advertisers in Ireland
Rock House, Main Street
Blackrock
Co Dublin
Tel: + 353 1 2780499

Independent Radio and Television Commission
Marine House
Clanwilliam Court
Dublin 2
Tel: + 353 1 6760966

Association of Independent Radio Stations
62, Lower Mount Street
Dublin 2
Tel: + 353 1 6629444

National Newspapers of Ireland
Clyde Lodge
Clyde Road
Dublin 4
Tel: + 353 1 6689099

Provincial Newspapers' Association of Ireland
33, Parkgate Street
Dublin 8
Tel: + 353 1 6793679

Outdoor Media Association
6 Sandyford Park
Burton Hall Road
Dublin 18
Tel: + 353 1 2958170

Radio Telefis Eireann
Donnybrook
Dublin 4
Tel: + 353 1 2083111

Advertising Standards Authority for Ireland
IPC House
Shelbourne Road
Dublin 4
Tel: + 353 1 6608766

Consumer Affairs Office of the Director
4 Harcourt Road
Dublin 4
Tel: + 353 1 4025500

# THE GENERAL RULES OF THE CODE OF ADVERTISING STANDARDS FOR IRELAND (4TH EDN)

**1   Scope and application**

1.1   The primary objective of the Code is the regulation of commercial advertisements in the consumer interest.

1.2   For the purposes of the Code:

(a)   an advertisement is defined as a paid-for communication addressed to the public or a section of it, the purpose being to influence the behaviour of those to whom it is addressed. It is characteristic of an advertisement that an advertiser pays a third party to communicate his message;

(b)   a product can encompass goods, services, facilities, opportunities, fund raising, prizes and gifts;

(c)   a consumer is anyone who is likely to see a particular advertisement or promotion;

(d)   a claim can be direct or implied, written, spoken or visual;

(e)   references to advertisers should be interpreted as including promoters unless the context indicates otherwise;

(f)   where for the sake of clarity and brevity the singular form of a word is used this should be construed as including legal persons and groups as appropriate;

(g)   every word importing the masculine gender should be construed as if it also imported the feminine gender unless the contrary intention appears. Every word importing the feminine gender should be construed as if it also imported the masculine gender unless the contrary intention appears.

1.3   The Code applies to:

(a)   advertisements in newspapers, magazines and other printed publications, including 'free sheets';

(b)   posters and aerial advertisements;

(c)   brochures, leaflets, circulars, mailings and facsimile transmissions;

(d)   commercials broadcast on television or radio or screened cinemas;

(e)   advertisements carried on audiotapes, videotapes, viewdata services and other electronic and computer systems;

(f)   sales promotion material;

(g)   advertisement features and promotions.

1.4 The Code does not apply to:

(a) statutory, public, Garda and other official notices;

(b) material published as a matter of record only;

(c) flyposting;

(d) packages, wrappers, labels and tickets unless they advertise another product or a sales promotion or are recognisable in an advertisement;

(e) point of sale displays;

(f) advertisements whose principal purpose is to express the advertiser's position on a political, religious, industrial relations, social or aesthetic matter or on an issue of public interest or concern;

(g) classified private advertisements;

(h) press releases and other public relations material;

(i) the content of books and editorial material in media;

(j) private correspondence;

(k) oral communications by telephone;

(l) works of art;

(m) specialised advertisements addressed to the medical and allied professions.

1.5 The Code is applied in accordance with the following criteria:

(a) an invitation from the ASAI to comment on a complaint does not mean that the Authority accepts the complainant's view. Each case is considered on its merits;

(b) the Code rules are indivisible; advertisers must conform, where appropriate, with all rules;

(c) conformity with the Code is assessed in the light of an advertisement's probable effect when taken as a whole and in context. Particular attention is paid to:

- the characteristics of the likely audience;

- the media by means of which the advertisement is communicated;

- the location and context of the advertisement;

- the nature of the advertised product and the nature, content and form of any associated material made available or action recommended to consumers;

(d) the Code does not deal with contractual relationships between advertisers and consumers. It does not presume to judge whether a product represents good value for money, nor does it seek to regulate terms of business;

(e) ASAI does not act as an arbitrator between conflicting ideologies;

(f)   no legal advice can be given or should be presumed in communications from the ASAI (Board, Complaints Committee or Secretariat);

(g)   the judgment of the ASAI on any matter of interpretation is final.

## 2   General rules

### Principles

2.1   All advertisements should be legal, decent, honest and truthful.

2.2   All advertisements should be prepared with a sense of responsibility to consumers and to society.

2.3   All advertisements should respect the principles of fair competition generally accepted in business.

2.4   The Code is applied in the spirit as well as in the letter.

2.5   An advertisement should not bring advertising into disrepute.

2.6   Primary responsibility for observing the Code rests with advertisers. Others involved in the preparation and publication of the advertisements, such as agencies and media, also accept an obligation to abide by the Code.

2.7   Any unreasonable delay in responding to ASAI's inquiries may be considered a breach of the Code.

2.8   ASAI will observe advertisers' requests to treat any material they supply in strict confidence unless the courts or an official agency acting within its statutory powers compel its disclosure.

### Substantiation

2.9   Before offering an advertisement for publication, advertisers should be able to provide documentary evidence to substantiate all claims, whether direct or implied, that are capable of objective assessment. Relevant evidence should be sent without delay if requested by the ASAI and should be adequate to support both detailed claims and the overall impression created by the advertisement.

2.10   If there is a significant division of informed opinion about any claim made in an advertisement it should not be portrayed as universally accepted.

2.11   Where claims contained in books, tapes, videos and the like cannot be independently substantiated, advertisements should not exaggerate the value or usefulness of what is claimed.

### Legality

2.12   Advertisers have primary responsibility for ensuring that their advertisements are legal. An advertisement should not contain anything that breaks the law or incites anyone to break it, nor omit anything that the law requires.

### Taste and decency

2.13 An advertisement should contain nothing that is likely to cause grave or widespread offence. Particular care should be taken to avoid causing offence on grounds of age, disability, gender, race, religion, sex or sexual orientation.

2.14 Advertisers should take account of public sensitivities in the preparation and publication of advertisements and avoid the exploitation of sexuality and the use of coarseness and undesirable innuendo. They should not use offensive or provocative copy or images merely to attract attention.

2.15 The fact that a product is offensive to some people is not in itself sufficient basis for objecting to an advertisement for that product. Advertisers should nevertheless avoid causing offence in such advertisements.

2.16 Compliance with the Code is assessed on the basis of the standards of taste, decency and propriety generally accepted in Ireland, taking account of the product involved, the media used, the location and context in which the advertisement is placed and the characteristics of the audience addressed.

### Sexism and stereotyping

2.17 Advertisements should respect the principle of the equality of men and women and the dignity of all persons.

2.18 Advertisements should recognise and reflect women's role in society and should avoid stereotyping, taking account of the following considerations:

(a) women as well as men pursue a wide range of contemporary occupations, hobbies, recreational activities and interests;

(b) both women and men take major purchasing decisions in the workplace and at home;

(c) men and women perform and share household management and domestic tasks.

2.19 Advertisements should, where appropriate, use generic terms that include both the masculine and feminine gender; for example, the term 'business executive' covers both men and women.

### Vulnerable persons

2.20 Advertisements which portray or refer to persons with disabilities or to persons who are vulnerable by reason of age or other condition or circumstance:

(a) should fully respect the dignity of such persons and not undermine their confidence or independence;

(b) should avoid stereotyping or other insensitive approaches which could promote negative images or prove hurtful or distressing to such persons or their families;

(c)    should not subject such persons to ridicule or offensive humour;

(d)    should not exploit disability, age or other condition for unrelated commercial purposes.

## Honesty

2.21  Advertisers should not exploit the credulity, inexperience or lack of knowledge of consumers.

2.22  The design and presentation of advertisements should allow them to be easily and clearly understood. Where footnotes are used, they should be of sufficient size and prominence and easily legible; where appropriate, they should be linked to the relevant part of the main copy.

## Truthfulness

2.23  An advertisement should not mislead by inaccuracy, ambiguity, exaggeration, omission or otherwise.

2.24  Obvious untruths or deliberate hyperbole that are unlikely to mislead, incidental minor inaccuracies and unorthodox spellings are not necessarily in conflict with the Code provided they do not affect the accuracy or perception of the advertisement in any material way.

2.25  Claims such as 'up to' and 'from' (for example, 'up to X miles per gallon' and 'prices from as low as Y') should not exaggerate the value or the range of benefits likely to be achieved in practice by consumers.

## Matters of opinion

2.26  Advertisers may state an opinion about the quality or desirability of a product provided it is clear that what they are expressing is their own opinion rather than a matter of fact and that there is no likelihood of consumers being misled about any matter that is capable of objective assessment. Assertions or comparisons that go beyond subjective opinions are subject to substantiation.

## Fear and distress

2.27  An advertisement should not cause fear or distress without good reason such as the encouragement of prudent behaviour or the discouragement of dangerous or ill-advised actions. In such cases the fear aroused should not be disproportionate to the risk.

## Safety

2.28  An advertisement should not encourage dangerous behaviour or show unsafe practices except in the context of promoting safety. Particular care should be taken with advertisements directed at or depicting children.

### Violence and anti-social behaviour

2.29 An advertisement should contain nothing that condones or is likely to provoke violence or anti-social behaviour.

### Protection of privacy

2.30 Subject to the exceptions referred to in 2.31 below, advertisers should have written permission in advance from anyone portrayed or referred to in an advertisement. Permission is also required before anyone's house or other possessions can be featured in a manner which identifies the owner to the public.

2.31 Exceptions include the use of crowd scenes or property depicted in general outdoor locations or where the purpose of the advertisement is to promote a product such as a book or film of which the person concerned is a subject.

2.32 Advertisements should not exploit the public reputation of persons in a manner that is humiliating or offensive. Advertisements should not claim or imply an endorsement where none exists. Advertisers are reminded that persons who do not wish to be associated with the advertised product may take legal action against them.

2.33 References to deceased persons should be handled with particular care to avoid causing offence or distress.

### Testimonials and endorsements

2.34 Advertisers who use testimonials should be able to provide relevant supporting documentation to ASAI. Testimonials by persons named or depicted in an advertisement may be used only with the prior permission of those persons.

2.35 Testimonials may be misleading if the formulation of the product or its market environment changes significantly. They should therefore relate to the product as currently offered.

2.36 Testimonials do not constitute substantiation and the opinions expressed in them should be supported, where necessary, with independent evidence of their accuracy. Claims based on a testimonial should conform with the Code.

2.37 Endorsements by fictitious or historical characters should not be presented as though they were genuine testimonials.

2.38 References to tests, trials, professional endorsements, research facilities and professional journals should be used only with the permission of those concerned. Any establishment referred to should be under appropriate professional supervision.

### Prices

2.39 If a price is stated in an advertisement, it should relate to the product depicted or specified in the advertisement. Care should be taken to ensure that prices and illustrated products match.

2.40 Except in advertisements addressed exclusively to the trade, prices quoted should include VAT. It should be immediately apparent whether any prices quoted exclude other taxes, duties or inescapable costs.

2.41 If the price of one product is dependent on the purchase of another, the extent of any commitment required of consumers should be made clear.

**Free offers**

2.42 An offer should be described as free only if consumers pay no more than:

(a) the current public rate of postage;

(b) the actual cost of freight or delivery;

(c) the cost, including incidental expenses, of any travel involved if consumers collect the offer.

In all cases, consumers' liability for such costs should be made clear and there should be no additional charges for packaging or handling.

2.43 Advertisers should not attempt to recover their costs by reducing the quality or composition, by imposing additional charges or inflating incidental expenses or by increasing the price of any other product that must be purchased as a precondition of obtaining a free item.

**Availability of products**

2.44 Except where supplies of a product are subject to an inherent limitation (for example, theatre seats), or where it is clear from the advertisement that there is a limit on availability, advertisers should be in a position to meet any reasonable demand created by their advertising. If a product proves to be available in insufficient quantity, advertisers should take immediate action to ensure that any further advertisements are amended or withdrawn.

2.45 Products should not be advertised as a way of gauging possible demand unless the advertisement makes this clear.

2.46 Advertisers should not use the technique of switch selling, where sales staff criticise the advertised product or suggest that it is not available and recommend the purchase of a more expensive alternative. Advertisers should not place obstacles in the way of purchasing the product or delivering it promptly.

**Comparisons**

2.47 Comparisons are permitted in the interests of public information and vigorous competition. They can be explicit or implied and can relate to advertisers' own products or those of their competitors.

2.48 Comparisons should be fair and should be so designed that there is no likelihood of a consumer being misled. The basis of selection should be clear and the elements of comparison should not be unfairly selected in a way that gives the advertisers an artificial advantage.

2.49 A claim that any product is superior to others should be made only where there is clear evidence to support the claim. Wording which implies superior or superlative status such as 'number one', 'leading', 'largest' and the like should be capable of substantiation with market share data or similar proof.

2.50 Advertisers should not unfairly attack or discredit other businesses or their products.

2.51 The only acceptable use of broken or defaced competitive products in advertisements is in the illustration of comparative tests, and the nature and results of these should be clear.

## Guarantees

2.52 Where an advertisement refers to a guarantee, the full terms of the guarantee should be available for consumers to inspect before they are committed to purchase. Any substantial limitations (for example one year; parts only) should be clearly indicated in the advertisement.

2.53 'Guarantee' when used in a colloquial sense should not cause confusion about consumers' statutory rights.

## Exploitation of goodwill

2.54 Advertisers should not exploit or make unfair use of the goodwill attached to the name, trade mark, brand, slogan or advertising campaign of any other person.

## Imitation

2.55 An advertisement should not so closely resemble another as to be likely to mislead or cause confusion.

## Recognisability

2.56 An advertisement should be designed and presented in such a way that it is immediately apparent that it is an advertisement.

2.57 A political advertisement should be recognisable as such and the identity and status of the advertiser should be clear.

2.58 An advertisement feature, announcement or promotion published in exchange for a payment or other reciprocal arrangement where the content is controlled by the advertiser should comply with the Code. It should also be clearly identified and distinguished from editorial matter.

**Other requirements**

2.59 Advertisements relating to credit must comply with the requirements of consumer credit legislation in regard to the showing of the Annual Percentage Rate (APR) and with any other relevant statutory requirement.

# THE CODES OF STANDARDS, PRACTICE AND PROHIBITIONS IN ADVERTISING, SPONSORSHIP AND OTHER FORMS OF COMMERCIAL PROMOTION IN BROADCASTING SERVICES

1.0 These Codes are intended to be applied in the spirit as well as in the letter

2.0 General standards

    2.1 Advertising shall not:

        (i) prejudice respect for human dignity;

        (ii) include any discrimination on grounds of race, sex or nationality;

        (iii) be offensive to religious or political beliefs; or

        (iv) encourage behaviour prejudicial to the protection of the environment.

3.0 False or misleading advertisements

    3.1 Advertisements shall not be misleading or shall not prejudice the interest of consumers.

    3.2 No advertisement shall contain any element of spoken or visual presentation which is calculated to mislead either directly or by implication, with regard to the merits of the product or service advertised or its suitability for the purpose recommended.

4.0 Programme separation

    4.1 Advertisers shall not exercise any editorial influence over the content of the programmes. No advertisement may include anything that states, suggests or implies, or could reasonably be taken to suggest or imply, that any part of any programme broadcast by a service has been supplied or suggested by an advertiser.

5.0 Identification of advertisements

    5.1 Advertisements shall be clearly distinguishable as such and recognisably separate from the other items of the programme service by optical and/or acoustic means. In principle, they shall be transmitted in blocks and isolated advertising spots shall remain the exception.

    5.2 Surreptitious advertising, meaning the representation in words or pictures of goods, services, the name, the trade mark or the activities of a producer of goods or a provider of services in programmes when such representation is intended by the broadcaster to serve advertising purposes and might mislead the public as to its nature, shall be prohibited. Such representation is considered to be intentional in particular if it is done in return for payment or for similar consideration.

5.3 Advertisements shall not feature, visually or orally, persons regularly presenting news and current affairs programmes, and the expression 'news flash' must not be used as an introduction to an advertisement, even if preceded by an advertiser's name.

5.4 Situations and performances reminiscent of broadcast programmes must not be used in such a way as to blur the distinction between programmes and advertisements. References to programmes are unacceptable in advertisements.

6.0 Insertion of advertisements

6.1 Advertisements shall be inserted between programmes. Provided the conditions contained in paras 6.2–6.5 are fulfiled, advertisements may also be inserted during programmes in such a way that the integrity and value of the programme taking into account natural breaks in and the duration and nature of the programme and the rights of the rights holders are not prejudiced.

6.2 In programmes consisting of autonomous parts, or in sports programmes and similarly structured events and performances comprising intervals, advertisements shall only be inserted between the parts or in the intervals.

6.3 The transmission of audio-visual works such as feature films and films made for television (excluding series, serials, light entertainment programmes and documentaries), provided their programmed duration is more than 45 minutes, may be interrupted once for each complete period of 45 minutes. A further interruption is allowed if their programmed duration is at least 20 minutes longer than two or more complete periods of 45 minutes.

6.4 Where programmes, other than those covered by para 6.2, are interrupted by advertisements, a period of at least 20 minutes should elapse between each successive advertising break within the programme.

6.5 Advertisements shall not be inserted in any broadcast of a religious service. News and current affairs programmes, documentaries, religious programmes, and children's programmes, when their programmed duration is less than 30 minutes, shall not be interrupted by advertisements. If their programmed duration is for 30 minutes or longer, the provisions of the previous paragraph shall apply.

7.0 Subliminal advertising

No television advertisement may include any technical device which, by using images of very brief duration or by any other means, exploits the possibility of conveying a message to, or otherwise influencing the minds of, members of an audience without their being aware or fully aware, of what has been done.

8.0 Health and safety

Advertisements should not encourage behaviour prejudicial to health or safety. Advertisements should not without justifiable reason depict or describe situations which show dangerous practices or a disregard for safety. Special care should be taken in advertisements directed towards or depicting children.

9.0 Time limits on certain forms of advertising

Forms of advertisements such as direct offers to the public for the sale, purchase or rental of products or for the provision of services shall not exceed one hour per day on any broadcasting service.

10.0 Cigarettes and tobacco

All forms of advertising for cigarettes, cigars and other tobacco products shall be prohibited. An advertiser who markets more than one product may not use advertising copy devoted to an acceptable product for purposes of publishing the brand name or other identification of an unacceptable product.

11.0 Advertising and children's programmes

11.1 Advertisers must exercise the utmost care and discrimination with regard to the content and presentation of advertisements transmitted during breaks within or near or adjacent to programmes designed for children.

11.2 Advertisements shall not exhort children to buy a product or service by exploiting their inexperience or credulity.

11.3 Advertising shall not exploit the special trust minors place in parents, teachers or other persons.

11.4 Advertisements shall not directly encourage minors to persuade their parents or others to purchase or make inquiries about the goods or services being advertised.

11.5 Advertisements shall not unreasonably show children in dangerous situations.

12.0 Alcoholic drink

The advertising of alcoholic drink may be accepted by broadcasters provided it complies fully with the following criteria:

(a) alcoholic drink advertising must not encourage young people or other non-drinkers to begin drinking. It must be cast towards brand selling and identification only;

(b) this Code recognises a voluntary code whereby spirit-based alcoholic drinks (that is, whiskey, gin, vodka, brandy, etc) are not advertised on radio and television. The Code is framed on the assumption that this situation will continue;

(c) this Code will apply to all other alcoholic drinks, that is, beers, wines, sherries, fortified wines, vermouths, liqueurs, etc;

(d)  where soft drinks are promoted as mixers, this Code will apply in full. When promoted as refreshments in their own right, soft drinks are not subject to this Code, but due care should be exercised if a bar or similar locations are used;

(e)  broadcasters will ensure that alcoholic drink advertisements are not transmitted in or around programmes primarily intended for young viewers or listeners; advertisers are required to take account of the age profile of the viewers and listeners so that advertisements are communicated, so far as it is possible, to adults;

(f)  advertising shall not encourage immoderate consumption of alcohol or present abstinence or moderation in a negative light;

(g)  advertisements shall not claim that alcohol has therapeutic qualities or that it is a stimulant, a sedative, tranquilliser or a means of resolving personal conflicts;

(h)  advertising shall not place emphasis on high alcoholic content as being a positive quality of the beverages;

(i)  advertisements for alcoholic drink may not be aimed specifically at minors or, in particular, depict minors consuming these beverages;

(j)  the advertising of alcoholic drinks should not create the impression that consumption of such beverages contributes towards sexual attraction and success, or social success;

(k)  advertisements shall not link the consumption of alcohol to enhanced physical performance or to driving.

13.0  Protection of privacy and exploitation of the individual

Individual living persons should not normally be portrayed or referred to in advertisements without their permission. However, reference to living persons may normally be made in advertisements for books, films, radio or television programmes, newspapers, magazines, etc, which feature the persons referred to in the advertisement, provided it is not offensive or defamatory.

14.0  Politics, religion and industrial relations

In this regard, the provisions of s 20(4) of the Broadcasting Authority Acts 1960–93, in the case of broadcasting services operated by the RTE Authority, and s 10(3) of the Radio and Television Act 1988, in the case of services established under that Act, and any amendments thereof, shall apply.

15.0  Advertising for medicinal products and medical treatments which are available only on prescription is prohibited.

## CHAPTER 10

# ITALY[1]

*Riccardo Rossotto and Vincenzo Guggino*[2]

## INTRODUCTION

The word 'advertising' in Italy essentially means television. Along with the strengthening of both the role and position of commercial television, which has little by little been broadcasting in parallel to the to RAI (the State broadcasting authority), over 55% of advertising investment is concentrated in this medium.

An extremely peculiar situation, then, as is the whole Italian scenario in the communications field. The business and political phenomenon, entrepreneur Silvio Berlusconi, has no doubt affected the history of Italian advertising over the last 15 years. Quite apart from any disputes, sometimes even violent ones, between the supporters of the *Berlusconi* case and his critics, one is bound to admit impartially that Berlusconi has succeeded in giving a decisive boost to the entire field. The figures speak for themselves: in Italy, the ratio between the overall advertising investment and the gross national product was 0.33% until 1982, when Canale 5 began. In 1998, the ratio was around 1.18%, and it is expected to rise to 1.21% in 1999.

Berlusconi's decision to enter politics in 1994 in a rather overbearing manner has actually engendered new and complex problems of an institutional and legal order (the much debated 'conflict of interests'). These problems have yet to be solved, even after the victory of the left wing coalition in April 1996.

After a three year slow down in the development of advertising investment, due mainly to the economic recession, in 1996, the advertising market started to grow again steadily. Growth in 1996 and 1997 reached the levels of the 1980s, and, although 78% of new investment has been made by companies which were already in the market 10 years previously, and by the same communication subjects (media intermediaries, agencies, etc), the way the advertising market is seen by the management of Italian companies has changed radically.

---

1   This chapter has been compiled thanks to the valued and active contribution of Massimo Tavella, Roberta Rizzolo and Luca Saglione, members of the Bar of Turin.

2   Dr Guggino's contribution on the self-regulatory system, p 607 *et seq*.

In fact, as stated in the UPA annual report (a yearly report on the advertising market), 'from a 'cultural' point of view, companies have the perception of advertising as an important factor for the development of business; on the other hand, immediate results in terms of sales compared with the investments have yet to be recorded'. This means that, unlike in the past, companies are now willing to invest in advertising strategies, even though the financial return in terms of sales is not immediately satisfactory.

In 1998, Italy was admitted to the group of Member States whose economies will be regulated by the Euro currency system: this has also created great expectations in the advertising market, since Italy has seemingly entered an economic environment characterised by stability and reliability.

# DOMESTIC LAW OVERVIEW

## Article 2598 of the Civil Code; advertising self-regulation; Law No 74/92

From the post-war period until the mid 1960s, it can be said that the only provision dealing with legal issues relating to the field of advertising in Italy was Art 2598 of the Civil Code, laying down regulations on matters of unfair competition.

For our purposes here, a careful examination is called for of that part of Art 2598 (the third section, in particular) which sets out the principle of professional fairness as the essential criterion in evaluating the lawfulness of a competitor's behaviour:

> ... acts of unfair competition are committed by anyone who ... avails him/herself either directly or indirectly of any means not complying with the principles of professional fairness and capable of damaging another person's business.

First, we must emphasise that all the provisions of Art 2598 pertained solely to actions carried out to the detriment of a competitor. Central to the provision is the competitor acting in the course of a business, not the consumer.

Case law has consolidated the principle according to which a competitor's advertising is unlawful with reference to Art 2598, n 3, namely whenever this is performed in a devious and malicious manner, and contrary to professional fairness so as to engender either disrepute or prejudice for the business competitor.

Besides this specific article of the Civil Code, and except for a few particular rules relevant to specific products – as we shall see – no other legal provision had applied to advertising up to the mid 1960s.

Since 1966 (the first Code of Advertising Self-regulation dates from 12 May 1966), the economic operators, following the setting up of the self-regulatory system, and in view of the almost complete lack of State regulation governing these matters, have aimed at 'ensuring that advertising, in the course of its particularly useful role in the economy, be carried out as a service to the public with special consideration given to its influence on the consumer'.

Up to 1992, when both the law on misleading advertising (Law No 74 of 25 January 1992) and the Vizzini Decree were enacted, relating to television advertising of tobacco and alcoholic products, as well as to the protection of minors (Decree No 425 of 30 November 1991), the two reference points on the matter have been the Self-regulation Authority on one hand, and the judiciary on the other.

## Relevant criminal provisions

To be precise, the protection of consumers' interests has always been subject to both criminal and administrative regulation, the former being aimed at repression, the latter at preventing specific kinds of advertising misuse by means of an authoritative system.

Relevant in this sense are Arts 528 (obscene publications and shows), 529 (obscene acts and objects: notions), 565 (attacks on family morality committed through the periodical press), 725 (business of writings, drawings or any other object contrary to public decency, obscene language) of the Criminal Code, all aimed at the protection of public morality.

Article 440 and those subsequent to it in the Criminal Code pertain to offences against public safety, and also include adulteration and counterfeiting of foodstuffs (Art 440), trade in and supply of spoiled, decayed or deteriorated medicines (Art 443), trade in noxious foodstuffs (Art 444). Their main goal is to protect public health and, indirectly, they set restrictions and sanctions for advertising in those fields.

The Criminal Code also includes other sets of provisions, either for the maintenance of public order (for example, misuse of popular credulity, Art 661) or to protect the regular course of competition between enterprises (selling of non-genuine substances as genuine, Art 516), (selling of industrial products with misleading signs, Art 517). Because the Italian system has lacked a criminal provision of general importance concerning misleading advertising, legal doctrine has always applied the above-mentioned Arts 516 and 517 of the Criminal Code to make up for this omission.

The inspiring principle of these provisions is that of 'truthfulness', with the consequent prohibition of any false representation capable of misleading the buyers.

## Other relevant special regulations

There are also laws which deal with the advertising of specific products. We mention here only the most important ones: Law No 2033 of 15 October 1921 on the suppression of fraud in the preparation and trade of agricultural products; Law No 567 of 30 May 1953 on the production and selling of nutritional extracts and similar products; Law No 578 of 30 May 1953 governing the production and trade of infants' foodstuffs as well as diet products; Law No 1354 of 16 August 1962 on the production and trade of beer; Law No 930 of 12 July 1963 on the protection of the original name of musts and wines; Law No 35 of 27 January 1968 on olive oil and vegetable seed oil, and last, Act 116 of 23 February 1968 on the production and trade of syrups and almond based drinks.

In Italy, then, the normative framework – not homogeneous at least until 1992 – is characterised by scattered articles of the Civil and Criminal Codes and special statutes enacted from time to time to solve problems connected to a specific product or service.

An overall framework has always been lacking, and still is: a single complete legislative text on the matter is strongly needed.

The recent enactment of Law No 74/92 on misleading advertising has at least aligned Italy with other Member States of the European Community.

# THE *BERLUSCONI* CASE: A 'PASSWORD' TO UNDERSTANDING TELEVISION COMMUNICATIONS IN ITALY

## The Italian situation in the mid 1970s

A step back into the mid 1970s, the outset of the Berlusconi phenomenon, is useful for a better understanding of the evolution of the normative discipline related to communications in general, and more specifically to advertising, in Italy. Only by re-examining that historical period can we attain a correct framework for understanding the present Italian situation.

In Italy, the entire television system was under public control up to the mid 1970s, as the State had been granted a complete monopoly in this area.

As the first private television stations began to broadcast, albeit in a strictly local environment, they actually started to weaken the public monopoly, which gave rise to the debate over the legitimacy of the State monopoly.

## The Constitutional Court's decisions

The Constitutional Court, being the appropriate authority for dealing with such a question, set out some basic principles for the regulation of radio and television for the first time, by issuing its landmark judgment 202 of 28 July 1976.

In short, the court declared that a public monopoly is unlawful when it forbids private broadcasting locally, and at the same time it stated that Parliament would have to deal with this matter by enacting provisions to regulate this activity (which in the meanwhile had become free and legitimate, or at least partially so).

The Constitutional Court, when again summoned to make a pronouncement on the legitimacy of the monopoly in 1981, not regarding the local level, but the national one, answered: 'There must be an Act regulating the field, as the risks for misuse and power concentration are very high and dangerous.'

Without a specific law in place, private sector radio and television could not operate on a national scale. Despite this fact, new technologies were already making the broadcasting of nationwide programmes possible, practically getting round the RAI's monopoly and the two above-mentioned Constitutional Court judgments as well.

As it happened, interconnection had enabled the three large private groups operating in this area (Fininvest, that is, Berlusconi with Canale 5; Rusconi with Italia 1; and Mondadori with Rete 4) to broadcast the same programme at the same time from the north to the south of Italy, therefore covering the whole of the Italian territory.

The risk the Constitutional Court had most feared had become reality: the Fininvest Group, after having first taken over Italia 1 from Rusconi, had stepped in to save Rete 4 as well within one year. This latter enterprise was threatening to sink the glorious cornerstone of the Italian publishing world: the publishing house of Mondadori.

So Fininvest now stood out alone within this scenario, which was characterised by the total lack of written code of practice. The 'struggle' by then had become exquisitely political: as often happens, a legislative substitute power was entrusted to the judiciary.

## The 'Berlusconi' decree

The courts then began their struggle against the new, unlawful, 'monopoly' of private sector nationwide television broadcasting. In October 1994, Fininvest was forbidden to broadcast through its three networks over the entire national territory by three separate and autonomous judgments.

At this point, the government could just wait and see. In exactly four days it issued a Law Decree, to be enforced immediately, allowing Berlusconi to broadcast nationwide, but only for the restricted period of time remaining until the enactment of the Act regulating this area, which had been so eagerly awaited. After a very troubled parliamentary debate, the Law Decree became an Act only four months later, in February 1985.

## Law No 223/90, referred to as the Mammì Act

In 1987, when the so called Berlusconi Act had already undergone several extensions, a bill by the MP Oscar Mammì was submitted to debate: the ensuing elaborations on the text resulted in a definite regulatory provision, according to which no private body can own more than three networks, while the advertising return is jointly shared between the public and private sectors.

The so called 'zero option' also came into existence: anyone who controls television networks cannot own newspaper businesses as well, and vice versa.

Once again, the Constitutional Court crucially hastened the evolution of the law.

The court, in its judgment 828 of 1988, did not declare the 'Berlusconi' Act to be unconstitutional, even if it did not believe it to be in keeping with the Constitution.

The court underlined its temporary peculiarity and invited legislators to replace it with a more general set of provisions, failing which, the court would declare the Act to be unconstitutional and would repeal it.

This seemed to be an opportune moment, and everyone accepted their responsibility and sought a way out of the impasse, despite the complexity of the subjects and the significance of the interests at stake.

The presiding judge of the Constitutional Court had to intervene again in public to urge the issuing of the Act, at the beginning of 1990, but then eventually the parliamentary task was carried out.

The Bill was passed by the Chamber of Deputies on 1 August 1990. Following some amendments, it then had to go to the Senate for consideration again, before being finally approved on 5 August 1990.

With the passing of the Act, the functions of the existing Authority for Publishing (established in 1981 by Law No 416) were extended, becoming the Authority for Publishing and Broadcasting.

Italy at last has a form of regulation of its television system. The 'Far West' attitude is over, or at least, it should be.

## A first evaluation

This review of the last 15 years of Italy's television history, however brief, has not been, in our opinion, superfluous, but strictly relevant to the advertising issues. In fact, the burgeoning of new commercial radio and television enterprises has caused the domestic advertising market virtually to explode, by doubling the investment volume and, most of all, by bringing commercials into millions and millions of Italian homes.

Italy is now on a par with the European average after starting from an advertising investment percentage which was definitely low by reference to the national product, when compared to other industrialised countries.

The Mammì Act, as we have seen, was unfortunately passed as a result of too many political and power compromises, which have affected both its validity and efficiency.

The initial concern was to safeguard the RAI's position and that of its three nationwide networks. Such peculiar development (no European government controls three networks directly) has affected the whole remaining legislation, thus leading to a phenomenon, which is both identical and contrary to itself (no private European entrepreneur controls three networks directly). Unfortunately, the starting point was determined by choices that were merely political and not technical, but whose effects have then turned out to be extremely dangerous.

On the basis that the RAI is entitled to own three networks, the Fininvest Group has been acknowledged to have the same right, being the RAI's direct competitor. Because of this perverse logic, Italy already has a total of six national television networks, which obviously affect the other entrepreneurs' opportunities for entering into competition. Pluralism of information, which theoretically was one of Mammì's legislative aims, has remained just theory.

## Berlusconi's entry into politics

Towards the end of 1993, Berlusconi decided to take up the political challenge of the early elections scheduled for March 1994. Within a few months, he managed to establish and organise a party called 'Forza Italia', which immediately achieved a large following, in a country undergoing a complete transformation and engaged in a struggle to emerge from the First Republic, dominated by the Christian Democrats and its partners.

The Centre-right coalition, allied as it was to Umberto Bossi's Lega (Northern League), won the elections and was awarded a large majority in the Chamber of Deputies, and a slight majority in the Senate. Berlusconi, even after being elected Prime Minister, continued to arouse controversy because of his contemporaneous capacity as the leader of the government and as the owner of the principal Italian commercial group operating in the communications and advertising field.

## The referendums of June 1995

Once his government was dismissed, in December 1994, in one of the many political 'reversals', so typical of Italy, Berlusconi managed to win important national electoral support in the referendum of 11 June 1995.

Two issues submitted to the electors specifically pertained to advertising and the repeal of two rules of the widely criticised Mammì Act.

The first referendum issue related to the repeal of Art 15, subpara 7, of Law 223/90 on advertisement raising by advertising intermediaries. A repeal of this rule would enable its promoters to limit, by a new specific regulation, the advertisement raising power by either private or public broadcasters to a maximum of two national networks and three local ones.

The second issue concerned the possible repeal of Art 8, subpara 3, second sentence, of Law 223/90 on the maximum number of commercial breaks during the broadcasting of films. Had the 'yes' vote won, its promoters would have restricted the permitted commercial breaks, by confining them to the usual breaks between the first and the second part of the performances, thus respecting the author's copyright, performance integrity, and the audience's rights.

However, the referendum ended instead in a victory for the 'no' vote. The result was the demonstration of the voters' will to keep the existing advertising and television system in place, as it guaranteed pluralism, in their opinion, and, most of all, the quality of television programmes.

## A 'third pole' comes into being

Meanwhile, a new entrepreneur, Vittorio Cecchi Gori, appeared on the RAI-Fininvest scene.

Cecchi Gori, following a great success in the cinema business and having bought the Florence based Fiorentina football team (Berlusconi, incidentally, owns 'Milan', a team from Milan), after having been elected to Parliament, took over two important commercial television channels: Videomusic, first, and Telemontecarlo at a later stage, thus challenging his two big competitors. This gave hope that a market, which had been too static thus far, and with prohibitive costs for anyone trying to enter it, was witnessing the birth of a third pole.

## The government of the Left

On 21 April 1996, the left of centre parties (the so called 'Ulivo coalition') won the general election for the first time in the history of the Italian Republic. The price of the victory was the alliance with the former Communist Party, renamed the PDS, and the far left party of Communist Refoundation, whose votes were necessary to obtain a relative majority in Parliament. This led to the birth of a 'dual majority', meaning that the votes of the centre-right coalition in opposition were necessary on some political issues. As a consequence, the government managed to resolve some thorny matters, such as the fulfilment of the required Maastricht parameters for monetary union and the introduction of the Euro currency from its outset, but could not solve definitively the problems related to the conflict of interests, given the importance of Berlusconi's party in opposition, for the fulfilment of the left of centre government programme.

## The Maccanico Act: the birth of the Authority for Communications

One of the thorny matters which the government has been able to resolve concerns the coming into force of a new law taking the place of the Mammì act, after years of debate. On 31 July 1997, Parliament approved Law No 249/97, dealing with the 'Institution of the Authority for Communications and dispositions on the telecommunication and radio and televisual systems'.

The newly created Authority consists of two commissions: one for 'infrastructures and communications', the second one for 'products and services'. The president of the Authority is nominated by the government, after a compulsory preliminary hearing of the competent parliamentary commission.

The commission for infrastructure and communications mainly deals with the planning of assignments of radio and television frequencies, while the commission for products and services has control and directive powers in some fields strictly related to telecommunications, among which is advertising.

Law 249/97 also contains some anti-trust regulations: Art 2 provides that no one can own more than 20% of the national television channels and get more than 30% of the income in the television and radio fields; the same limits apply for cable and satellite television. The Authority has the power to order a company exceeding these limits, and acquiring a dominant position in the market, to abandon the frequencies. If the 30% threshold is overridden due to the development of the company, these rules do not apply. Another exemption is contained in Art 2, subpara 19, for the RAI and Telecom, allowing them not to get sanctioned if they take part in the digital platform and in the channels of Telepiù, Italy's first pay-TV channel. This exemption is not valid for Mediaset or for the Cecchi Gori channels.

Four members from the commission for infrastructure and communications and four from that for products and services, together with the president of the newly created Authority for Communications, Mr Enzo Cheli, have taken over the functions of the former Authority for Publishing and Broadcasting, as from 21 July 1998. The new Authority, whose headquarters are in Naples, now deals with three fundamental issues: interconnection fees, the reorganisation of telephone tariffs and the assignment of frequencies.

The first two matters are connected to the issue of the liberalisation of telephone communications. Indeed, from 1 July 1998, Telecom Italia will have two new competitors: Albacom and Infostrada, at least as far as services provided to companies are concerned. These new companies will partially use Telecom's communication network and will pay a fee which, according to EU provisions, will have to be 'fair'. The fee list will be drafted after the tariff scheme has been updated, to balance the difference between urban calls (considered to be too cheap at present) and long distance calls (considered to be too expensive).

As far as the assignment of frequencies is concerned, the deadline of 31 October 1998 was set, but due to the number of subjects involved (1,500 radio and 700 television stations), this deadline was postponed. The Authority became operational on 10 June 1998, but it took a few months before it had all the necessary equipment and was assigned all of its functions.

At present, the only regulation enacted – on 1 December 1998 – is the one concerning the assignment by the Ministry of Telecommunication of Terrestrial Frequencies (both at national and local level) to private television broadcasters using the analogic system.

The technical requirements necessary for the assignment of the frequencies are the following:

(a) broadcasting from frequency ranges authorised by the applicable regulation on radio communications of the International Union of Telecommunications in compliance with the international treaties, the European Union and national law, as well as the national frequency assignment plans;

(b) layout of one or more broadcasting stations or of the complete broadcasting network (including the link systems connecting the production seats with the transmitters);

(c) exclusive use of equipment certified according to the applicable law and testing of the same equipment by bodies of the Ministry of Telecommunications at the assignee's expenses.

The applications for assignment must be submitted by citizens of the European Union or of the EES (European Economic Space – *Spazio Economico Europeo*). Unless the broadcaster is a non-profit making business company, the assignment of frequencies at national level can only be granted to limited companies with an entirely paid-in capital of L 12 bn or more (while a paid-in capital of L 300 m or more is required for assignment of frequencies at local level).

The applicants must constitute a reserve fund destined to future increases of capital which must be paid in within 30 days from the assignment. Particular conditions are required to foreign broadcasters subjected to the Italian law according to the European Union rules. Furthermore, there are limitations linked to geographical and population element in case of assignment of frequencies in more than one audience basins, as well as specific obligations concerning the type and extension of programs broadcasted. Specific requirements are needed for the authorisation of broadcasting of identical programs in different audience basins even when this type of broadcasting is not carried out through structural interconnection systems.

The applicants for frequencies at national level must specify whether they are going to be national commercial, telepromotion or pay-TV broadcasters, as well as the extent of broadcasting programming time attributed to the different programs, the extension of the audience basin targeted, the undertaking to comply with the broadcasting regulations on advertising and (except for pay-TV broadcasters) the undertaking to transmit daily at least 3 editions of self-produced TV news programs.

As far as the applicants for local frequencies are concerned, there are limitations to the change of type of assignment as well as to transfer of parts or total of the broadcaster's assets or equipment.

The assignment last 6 years. It can the renewed and transferred only in conjunction with the sale of the broadcasting television company.

## STATISTICAL REPORTS

Some statistical data relevant to the Italian advertising field may help to grasp further how atypical the Italian case is.

Figures 1, 2 and 3 below show the following indexes:

Figure 1: Advertising investment in the 1995–97 three year period, with an estimate for 1998 (in billions of lire) and percentage shares of each medium.

Figure 2: Percentage ratio between advertising investment and GNP.

Figure 3: Percentage ratio between advertising investment and home consumption.

**Figure 1 Advertising investment during 1995–97, with an estimate for 1998 (in billions of lire) and percentage shares of each medium**

|  | 1995 | 1996 | 1997 | 1998 |
|---|---|---|---|---|
| Newspapers | 1,497 | 1,601 | 1,776 | 1,874 |
| Share % | 6.95 | 6.97 | 7.215 | 7.173 |
| Magazines | 1,668 | 1,778 | 1,850 | 1,891 |
| Share % | 7.744 | 7.74 | 7.515 | 7.238 |
| Television | 5,290 | 5,682 | 6,215 | 6,638 |
| Share % | 24.559 | 24.732 | 25.247 | 25.41 |
| Radio | 413 | 455 | 505 | 543 |
| Share % | 1.917 | 1.98 | 2.051 | 2.079 |
| Cinema | 32 | 35 | 39 | 43 |
| Share % | 0.149 | 0.152 | 0.158 | 0.165 |
| External | 402 | 425 | 468 | 505 |
| Share % | 1.866 | 1.850 | 1.901 | 1.933 |
| Direct response | 2,920 | 3,113 | 3,306 | 3,531 |
| Share % | 13.556 | 13.55 | 13.430 | 13.516 |
| Promotions | 5,299 | 5,659 | 6,010 | 6,388 |
| Share % | 24.601 | 24.632 | 24.414 | 24.453 |
| Public relations | 2,157 | 2,286 | 2,435 | 2,593 |
| Share % | 10.014 | 9.95 | 9.892 | 9.926 |
| Sponsorship | 1,862 | 1,940 | 2,013 | 2,118 |
| Share % | 8.644 | 8.444 | 8.177 | 8.107 |
| **Grand total** | **21,540** | **22,974** | **24,617** | **26,124** |
| **Share %** | **100** | **100** | **100** | **100** |

**Figure 1 Percentage ratio of investment compared to Gross National Product and total home consumption**

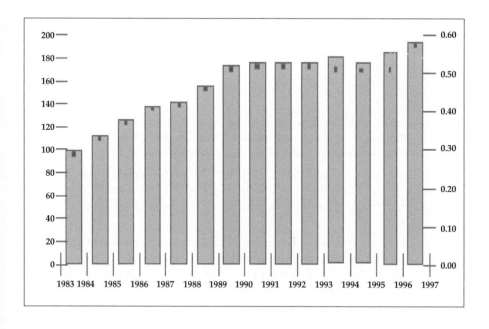

**Figure 2 Percentage ratio between advertising investment and home consumption**

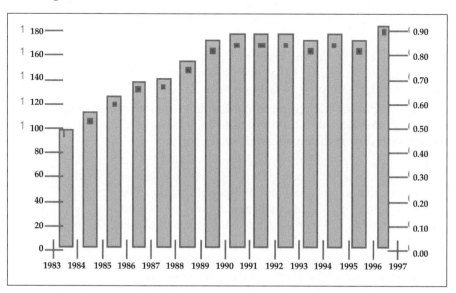

# ITALY'S SYSTEM OF ADVERTISING LAW

## The Mammì Act (Law No 223/90: Art 8)

We now examine the main aspects of Law 223 of 6 August 1990 named after its promoter, the MP Mammì, especially considering the articles relating to advertising.

The core of Law 223/90 as far as advertising is concerned is Art 8, which states that:

> Radio and television advertising must not offend a person's dignity, must not recall any racial, sexual or nationalist discrimination, and must not offend any religious or other ideals, be they political, philosophical, etc.

The legislator has thus set himself the prior goal of defining the general limits pertaining to the content of the advertising message, by instituting a barrier which is much wider than that of misleading advertising, in order to protect the consumer.

As already stated, in EC Directive 89/552, the forerunner of the Mammì Act, the prohibition of offensive advertising as mentioned above is firmly emphasised, as stated, following the Authority's provision for advertising self-regulation, in a well known decision in 1980, 'not all that is permitted while expressing one's thoughts, is likewise permitted during advertising'.

The function of advertising is commercial, not political, so its messages must not directly 'involve' the citizens' inner convictions concerning politics, religion and ethics.

Article 8 sets out that advertising must not induce the consumer to behave in ways that might be dangerous to his or her health and safety, or to the environment.

Even on this point, the layout of Directive 89/552 has been followed, prohibiting those messages that may lead to behaviour capable of damaging one's health and safety, or the environment.

Finally, the first paragraph of Art 8 emphasise that advertising must not cause any moral or physical damage to minors and forbids the insertion of commercials during the broadcasting of cartoons.

After listing the general prohibitions pertaining to the message content, Art 8 then deals with the advertising regulations concerning specific products (medicines, alcohol, tobacco) and for special categories of recipients (minors). Although referring to subsequent regulations (issued on 30 November 1991 under Decree No 425, named after the Postmaster General, Vizzini), the Act sets out some basic principles, in compliance with EC Directive 89/552:

(a) absolute prohibition of advertising of those medicines obtainable only against a prescription from a medical practitioner;

(b) absolute prohibition of advertising tobacco related products, whether it be direct or indirect (Art 1 of the Vizzini Decree);

(c) legitimacy of advertising wines and spirits, provided it is carried out according to specific criteria, as precisely laid down in Art 2 of the Vizzini Decree;

(d) legitimacy of advertising targeted at minors, or having minors playing the main character roles, provided it is carried out according to the criteria set out in Art 3 of the Vizzini Decree.

The third area of intervention by Mammì Act concerns the delicate issue of how to recognise advertisements: 'Television advertising must be clearly recognisable as such, and must be clearly separated from the rest of the programmes by visual and/or acoustic means.'

This issue, which has in the past led to heated debates and numerous decisions by the Authority (Art 7 of the Code deals with these problems), has been solved by drastic means, especially with regard to 'editorial advertising'.

Those messages which may induce the consumer to believe that the communication is reflecting the 'impartial' opinion of a third party or, worse still, of an independent journalist and not merely a business goal, must be recognisable and not misleading.

Lastly, Art 8 governs the crowding of television advertisements during the transmission of any given television programme ('advertisement crowding'). Since the rules set out therein are numerous, we shall mention only the essential ones:

(a) during transmissions with either a high artistic value or an educational or religious character, as well as during cartoons, no advertising breaks are allowed;

(b) during theatre, cinema, operatic programmes and musical performances, advertising is only allowed during the intervals, unless the performance is scheduled to last over 45 minutes.

In short, a 45 minute performance may be interrupted only once during the interval between one act and the next; a performance lasting more than 45 minutes may be interrupted twice, where one interruption is the interval; a performance lasting 110 minutes may be interrupted four times, including the interval. The legislator has also assigned the Authority the difficult task of selecting and singling out the highly artistic performances to which the above-mentioned restrictions apply.

Paragraphs 6 and 7 of Art 8 deal with regulations on advertisement crowding and its effect on broadcasting as a whole.

The Mammì Act has set out a discipline which is more structured and, at any rate, different for public and private advertising broadcasters, whereas the EC Directive only set out a maximum advertising limit of 15% in relation to the daily broadcasting time, with a 20% maximum per transmission hour. (Article 8, para 6 states: 'Broadcast advertising messages by the public broadcaster cannot exceed 4% of the weekly programming schedule and 12% per hour; any possible excess, however, no longer than 2% per hour, will be recovered during either the previous or the subsequent hour.' Paragraph 7 states: 'Television advertising messages by private licensees for broadcast at the national level cannot exceed 15% of daily broadcasting time and 18% per hour; any possible excess, however, no longer than 2% during the hour, will be recovered during either the previous or subsequent hour. An identical limit has been established for private sector broadcasters who, according to Art 21, are authorised to broadcast at the same time over a minimum of 12 user areas, with reference to the simultaneous programming time.')

As far as private sector television broadcasters over the national territory are concerned, the maximum daily time allotted to advertising is increased to 20%, if teleshopping (an offer directly made to the public) is included.

## The Maccanico Act (Law No 249/97, Arts 1 and 2)

Subsequently, on 31 July 1997, with the enactment of Law No 249 (dubbed the Maccanico Act, from the name of its promoting MP), the Authority for Communications was established.

Within such an Authority, a commission for services and products was created, to supervise compliance with statutory provisions of services and products supplied by the telecommunications providers/licensees.

Apart from controlling the general quality level of the services provided, this commission, subject to respect for the jurisdictions of other authorities, supervises the conditions of distribution of services and products, including any form of advertising broadcast (Art 1.6(b), n 3).

The commission also implements the statutory provisions relating to any form of advertising, including teleshopping, as well as regulating the relations between the provider/licensee or the service and product supplier with the public (Art 1.6(b), n 5).

Another domain of intervention of the commission concerns the compliance, in the radio/television communication systems, with the provisions regarding communications targeted at children, the protection of ethnic minorities and the provisions regarding equal access to political advertising and propaganda (nn 6, 7 and 9).

Finally, Art 2 of Law No 249 regulates the prohibition of abuse of dominant positions in the area of radio and television communications. Specific provisions in this section of the Act regulate the income limits which can be earned through advertising and sponsorship activities by media companies and their intermediaries.

# The self-regulatory system

Any analysis pertaining to the legal aspects of the commercial advertising phenomenon as it has been developed in Italy cannot but concentrate on the matter of self-regulation.

Self-regulation, of course, is the phenomenon by which a plurality of subjects shares the need to make their own behaviour conform to some rules of fairness, and determines to obey some common rules of behaviour, as well as some instrumental rules aimed at the observance of the former by specific coercive methods.

However, if all self-regulating experiences are based on the taking up of a field responsibility established on professional deontology rules (the historical one which medical doctors conform to is a good example), the results being achieved by the Italian self-regulating experience in the field of advertising assign some intrinsic meaning to it, both unique and unrepeatable, because of the particular implications in the advertising control its setting up has disclosed.

## An historical outline

The first self-regulatory code in advertising was formally issued by organisations operating in this field on 12 May 1966.

The first 10 years of self-regulation had been rather difficult, because of factors such as criticism from some advertising sectors, scepticism on the part of both consumer organisations and public opinion (these being also affected by the wave of objections particularly directed against advertising), and the disbelief of the legal world that a social group could seriously decide to limit its own freedom within a much narrower framework than the one established by law.

This is why, during the first decade (1966–75), progress was rather moderate, with a yearly average of 15 resolutive interventions (compared with over 300 today). Furthermore, there were also some disturbing signs, such as the resignation from associations by some individual enterprises which had experienced the strictness of self-regulating decisions.

Some concurring factors helped to start what was to become the system's revival. Amidst these factors was the decision, not provided for by the Code, to appoint a high-ranking judge to the chairmanship of the adjudicating body – the 'Jury', also referred to in this chapter as the Advertising Self-regulation Authority. An extremely positive inspiration it was too, which was to become a consistent feature: the present Advertising Self-regulation Authority's chairman is the retiring president of the Constitutional Court, Professor Antonio Baldassare.

Another consolidating element was the firm upholding of the commitments by those bodies which had first established the Interfederal Board for Advertising and, between 1971 and 1976, the Advertising Italian General League, followed by the present Istituto dell'Autodisciplina Pubblicitaria (Institute of Advertising Self-regulation – IAP).

A revision of the Code, after the first five years, was another positive contribution, as it required the obligation to declare the names of the parties involved in judgments, thus signalling a clear confirmation of a public responsibility being taken. Four years later, in 1975, a second revision was carried out. This was characterised by greater emphasis on consumer protection, together with an incisive series of new essential regulations (advertising transparency; respect of moral, civil and religious beliefs; obligation to warn of possible dangers inherent in products; restrictions on advertising of wines and spirits, cosmetics and organised travel). Two years later (1977) it was also agreed that all the members of the Self-regulation Authority should be appointed from among the experts, all of whom should come from outside the advertising world. This was a turning point, transforming the system into a unique system worldwide, but most of all it was to give a decisive boost to the elimination of any doubt about its seriousness.

The evolutionary process, which was to constitute one of the peculiarities of self-regulation, began at that stage. Very soon, revisions of the Code started occurring almost yearly: for example, the Code is currently (1997), in its 26th edition. This means that rule updating is occurring quickly and steadily, which is vital for keeping up with the fast moving developments in advertising, within an increasingly expanding and free market.

At the same time, the formal aspects of Code's regulations were being improved, and unanimously praised for their clarity and intelligibility – a long way off from certain older legislative provisions, and thus easily understandable by anyone.

The Code increasingly widened its scope to the point where today's text is more than double the length of the original one.

All other changes affecting the rules of proceedings (which will be detailed further on) were aimed at extending the role of the self-regulating examining body, the Review Board, as well as to allow for increasingly more direct and productive contributions on the part of the Secretariat in the achievement of its institutional purposes.

Thanks to changes of this kind, there has been increasingly rapid action on the part of self-regulatory bodies, another essential characteristic enabling them to stop the effects of either unfair or misleading advertising at its inception.

It has thus become possible to solve several cases within a week, the more difficult ones within two weeks, and those considerably more complicated ones, which are transferred to the Self-regulation Authority, are solved within four weeks on average. Here, in talking about figures that are here assessed in weeks, it is important to keep in mind that one has to talk about years when referring to proceedings in courts of law, and months for the new authorities.

## The institutional framework

Evaluating the juridical nature of self-regulation is a matter for scholars: it involves an analysis from arbitration to arbitrage to the contractual theory of obligations.

Its basic principle is voluntary participation and, therefore, a willingness to abide by the rules. The Code of Self-regulation is mostly joined freely: its rules are observed and the judgment of the appointed bodies (Review Board and Jury) respected on the basis of a free and willing adherence through those associations joining the Institution.

The self-regulatory system's autonomy cannot run counter to the general purposes and principles of State regulations, while not necessarily involving an absolute coincidence with the rules of the latter. It may turn out to be stricter because of its voluntary spirit, and it might be more open to future developments in advertising communications.

The IAP is a free association, as well as forming the structure on which the system is based. Its aim is to see that advertising becomes more and more 'honest, truthful, and fair' (as in Art 1 of the Self-regulation Code), and this is pursued by applying the Code of Advertising Self-regulation.

The IAP is, therefore, composed of the most important and qualified associations (and bodies) of the advertising world, which represent about 90–95% of the total investment.

The Board of Directors is the IAP's driving force: it appoints the legislative body, in co-operation with the Commission of Study, while providing at the same time for the system's control and management, through the Secretariat.

Overall, more than 100 qualified people are, on the basis of their particular function, and partially by rotation, directly engaged in the management of advertising self-regulation.

We must not forget, either, the members of the Commission of Study, in addition to the members of the Board and its President; the IAP's Secretariat, with the General Secretary and the other members; the auditors and their President; the 14 experts, for the most part being distinguished university professors, who form the basis of the adjudicating body, the Jury; the 15 experts who compose the Advertising Review Board and some other consultants.

## *Aim and application of the Self-regulatory Code*

The aims of the Code of Advertising Self-regulation (see Appendix 2) are clearly set out in the general and preliminary rules. It aims at 'ensuring that advertising, in the course of its particularly useful role in the economy, be carried out as a service to the public with special consideration given to its influence on the consumer':

> The Code of Advertising Self-regulation defines those activities which, though in compliance with current State legislation, conflict with the above-mentioned aims; the rules of the Code, being an expression of the behaviour to which advertising practice must conform, constitute the legal basis of advertising self-regulation.

The Code's application framework is indicated in the same preliminary rules as well:

> The Code of Advertising Self-regulation is binding for advertisers, agencies, consultants, all advertising media, and for anyone who has accepted the Code directly or through membership in an association, or by underwriting an advertising contract ... Signatory associations commit themselves to observe the rules of the Code and to have them accepted by their members, to make the decision of the Jury adequately known, and to adopt appropriate measures regarding those members who do not comply with the decisions of the Jury.

> In order better to ensure full compliance with the decisions of the Jury, the sponsoring organisations undertake that their members insert in their contracts a special clause of acceptance of the Code and of the decisions of the Jury, including orders to publish such decisions.

The Code is accepted and has been signed by all the associations and bodies composing the IAP and, therefore, by the main associations of advertisers, advertising agencies and advertising media (press, radio, television, cinema, bill posting, etc).

Furthermore, because of the acceptance clause, even the advertising of an advertiser, an agency or a media who does not belong to any association adhering to the system is subject to the Code and will have to comply with the decisions of its bodies. Such a clause is considered as a contract in favour of a third party, and it is acknowledged to be valid by the courts of law.

The Code's regulations are also accepted as 'business customs' by several chambers of commerce (Milan, Turin, Vicenza, Bari, etc) and, therefore, are to be considered among the sources of law. In short, while originating as a voluntary discipline, Italian advertising and the vast majority of Italian advertisers are subject to the Code.

## *Proceedings of the Advertising Self-regulation Authority*

The Jury, with its decisions, is the most qualified reference point for the application of the Code's rules and principles to real cases. Its members are of a high professional and cultural calibre, with specific authority in those disciplines which are most suitable to their office. In order better to guarantee independent decisions, none of the members are directly or personally involved in advertising activities.

The chairman, who, from the very beginning of self-regulation, as we have said, has been a high-ranking judge, every four months establishes the roles, that is, he determines the composition of each individual commission of the Jury (five members and two substitutes selected by rotation from the 14 available members), by taking into consideration the cases to be submitted to the Body for its decision and the necessary distribution of experts in law, psychology, sociology and communications.

Requests for decisions are set forth by the Review Board (ordinarily or by appealing for a summary order of discontinuance) or directly by private parties – by consumers' associations or competitors for advertising deemed to be unfair.

These latter petitions, while prevailing at one time, currently represent only 15–20% of the total number of resolutive actions, thus highlighting the clear prevalence of actions protecting consumers.

Upon receipt of a petition by either the committee or a party involved, the chairman appoints a referee for the individual case and assigns the parties a time limit for exchanging memorials and preparing their respective defences, which ranges from eight to 12 days.

In respect of the basic principles for appeal, an extensive verbal explanation of the reasons of both the petitioner and the respondent is allowed for during the hearing, with the possibility of a short reply. Lawyers, experts and witnesses are admitted and heard, as well as a representative of the Review Board with the specific task of supporting the interests of the citizen-consumer and of advertising in general.

The discussion will centre on those aspects of the argument which could not be dealt with in the preliminary notes of either the plaintiff or the defence. Should any breach, not provided for earlier, emerge during the proceedings, the Authority will acknowledge, notify and judge them, and will call for any necessary investigation.

At this point, the Authority meets in council with the Board for the decision, which will then be edited by the reporter.

Generally, within an afternoon, the Authority (which meets up to three times a month) deals with and defines on average two arguments: an average of two hours is necessary to debate and take a decision.

In the case of a 'guilty verdict', suspension of the advertisement in question will be ordered (in the more serious cases, the decision will be published), with immediate communication to the parties involved and to all those who, while not being part of the decision, have nevertheless accepted compliance with the self-regulatory system. The judgment is subsequently lodged in court and then published.

## Some peculiarities of self-regulation

### Who is qualified to act?

The legitimacy to act is one of the qualifying aspects of the Code, which does not limit the undertaking of the initiative.

Indeed, Art 36 states:

> Anyone who believes he has suffered prejudice from advertising activities contrary to the Code may request the intervention of the Self-regulation Authority against those who, having accepted the Code in one of the forms set out in the preliminary and general rules, have undertaken the activities alleged to have caused damage to the petitioner.

Natural legal persons and companies, bodies and associations in general may, therefore, take the initiative for action. In fact, the basic task of the self-regulatory system is to meet the collective interests of its members for self-regulatory rules. In short, the interests of the latter are so important that power for action has been granted to non-members as well.

### The burden of proof

Article 6 already determines the principle, according to which: 'Whoever makes use of advertising must be able to substantiate, at the request of the Jury or of the Advertising Review Board, the truthfulness of the data, descriptions, statements, illustrations and testimonials used.' Concerning this point, we refer back to Art 32, which states:

> At any time, the Jury and the Review Board can ask the advertiser to supply documentation in support of the truthfulness of the data, descriptions, statements, illustrations and testimonials used. The Jury and the Board may avail themselves of experts for the evaluation of the documentation produced.

This being the case, it follows, no matter how implicitly, that because of the speed of self-regulatory actions, it is in the advertising operators' interest to provide for and always have at hand those probative elements supporting their advertising statements.

### Sanctions

If the restraining order is the basic sanction, there are additional important ones, consisting of the publication of abstracts of the decisions, both when the Jury considers the cases to be serious and deserving of special public emphasis, and when the breaches are repeated (in the latter case the publication is binding).

These sanctions have to be assessed from at least three points of view:

(a) the moral value of the 'guilty verdict', to which possible consequences may be added at a membership level;

(b) the economic damage deriving from the failure to use an advertising campaign, whose preparation (as far as co-operation, research and materials are concerned) often implies extremely high costs, and is normally in proportion to the importance of the campaign;

(c) the serious damage caused to the users' commercial activity (as an example, one can think of frequent cases of 'seasonal' products) and to the company's image.

### Protection of advertising ideas

Protecting advertising ideas from possible imitation and the consequent need to prove they are antecedent – in case of disputes – have always been strong requirements for those who are professionally engaged in creating and developing an advertising project. One cannot exclude the risk of planning a campaign with elements (words, sentences, images, symbols, etc) whose originality and priority in time may be objected to in the future, with unavoidable consequences for both the relationship with the client and towards the competing agency.

It is then in the advertising operator's legitimate interest to establish the firm evidence of the date of creation.

This evidence, due to the lack of specific directions, cannot but become a publication of the message, preceding the launch of the campaign – within a reasonable time limit – a message that has to show its clear advertising nature and be provided with as much originality as to represent the premise for guaranteed protection within the self-regulatory system, by Art 13 of the Code of Advertising Self-regulation.

The Board of Directors, at the end of 1989, singled out and put into legal form a suitable tool to prevent controversy pertaining to priorities in an advertising creation (of course, if these ideas are original and new), by establishing and regulating a registry (within the IAP's Secretariat) of 'isolated press advertisements, used to anticipate and protect a campaign' – pre-emption – and carried out in a newspaper (in order to give a certain date) being indicated by the same IAP. The protection efficiency is fixed at 12 months to duly balance conflicting needs of guaranteeing protection of ideas, while avoiding possible and unjustified intellectual monopolies with no time limits.

This instrument, codified by Art 44 of the Self-regulatory Code, has been proved to meet fully the requirements of the parties involved, which have made extensive use of it over the last few years (over 1,000 registrations).

## Social advertising

At the beginning of 1995, the IAP's Board of Directors approved the insertion of a new Title VI in the Code of Advertising Self-regulation, devoted to 'social advertising' (messages aimed at soliciting voluntary contributions of money, goods or services for purposes beneficial to society).

Article 46, 'Appeals to the Public', is a part of it. At the same time, the Board modified the 'preliminary and general rules' of the Code by extending the standard definition of advertising to include 'social advertising'. This limit had undergone debate within the IAP, considering several requests, both internal and external.

It is common experience to be faced with advertising campaigns, appealing to the public's generosity to collect funds to be granted for social purposes, for humanitarian, health or whatever other aims, without being in a position to verify the genuineness of these initiatives. It is also common to be confronted with advertisements resorting to especially shocking appeals, sometimes even capable of arousing an unjustified disturbance within the public, both of adults and, especially, minors.

The increase in campaigns which might be defined as 'social' – with hundreds of milliards in lire being invested per annum – has contributed to hasten the debate within the IAP, a debate which has been going on for some time now, on the basis that unfair social advertising would discredit advertising in general in the public eye, as much as any other unfair commercial advertising would.

The IAP then elected to insert a separate title in the original Code. This was considered to be the correct way of enhancing the concept of the 'exceptional' rule of the article on social advertising with respect to the Code's main text, which still only deals with commercial advertising. On the other hand, a further possibility was left open for a later development, which, in theory, intended to address and regulate other profiles of non-profit aspects of advertising.

The character of an 'exception' to the new Title VI has also been emphasised under the preliminary and general rules. As far as the substance of the regulation is concerned, emphasis and predominance were given to social advertising aimed at fund raising.

**Table 2  30 years of activity of advertising self-regulation**

| Years by Decades | 30 YEARS' ACTIVITY | | | | | | | | | |
| | REVIEW BOARD'S ACTIVITY | | | | | | JURY'S DECISIONS | | TOTAL CASES HANDLED | |
| | Cases Examined by CAP | Advance Opinions | Cases Investigated and Filed | Cases Solved by Quick Procedure | Desist Orders | Petitions to Jury | On Party's Claim | Total No of Decisions | Decade | Yearly Average in Decade |
|---|---|---|---|---|---|---|---|---|---|---|
| First decade | 104 | — | * | 3 | — | 101 | 45 | 146 | 149 | 15 |
| Second decade | 625 | 53 | * | 247 | 36 | 289 | 148 | 437 | 773 | 77 |
| Third decade | 3,439 | 877 | * | 1,121 | 1,128 | 313 | 369 | 682 | 3,808 | 380 |
| TOTAL | 4,168 | 930 | * | 1,371 | 1,164 | 703 | 562 | 1.265 | 4,730 | 472 |

*\* Data available only since 1995*

**THE LAST TWO YEARS**

| Years by Decades | Cases Examined by CAP | Advance Opinions | Cases Investigated and Filed | Cases Solved by Quick Procedure | Desist Orders | Petitions to Jury | On Party's Claim | Total No of Decisions | Decade | Yearly Average in Decade |
|---|---|---|---|---|---|---|---|---|---|---|
| 1996 | 907 | 210 | 319 | 96 | 246 | 36 | 36 | 72 | 943 | |
| 1997 | 806 | 132 | 282 | 80 | 283 | 29 | 43 | 72 | 849 | |
| TOTAL | 1,713 | 342 | 601 | 176 | 529 | 65 | 79 | 144 | 1,792 | |

- By the active role of the Secretariat, the Review Board is able to solve a number of cases quickly (within a few days) and informally thanks to the ready availability of the interested parties.
- Jury's decisions in three cases out of four involve a 'sentence' and the immediate discontinuation of the advertisement, which takes place regularly.
- The increase in the number of cases handled by the self-regulatory system follows an increased number of campaigns and media, as well as the increasingly incisive character of the rules and interventions by the self-regulatory bodies.

**Table 3 Self-regulation Board's orders and Advertising Self-regulation Authority's decisions according to the type of product or service being advertised (1995 percentage data)**

| Product or service | % |
|---|---|
| Telephone services | 22.5 |
| Aesthetic and physical treatments | 17.0 |
| Electrical appliances/computers | 9.0 |
| Cosmetics | 7.0 |
| Personal belongings | 6.1 |
| Clothing/fabrics | 6.1 |
| Courses/schools | 6.1 |
| Foods/beverages | 5.6 |
| Commerce | 3.3 |
| Agriculture | 2.8 |
| Financial products | 2.3 |
| Miscellaneous | 12.2 |
| **Total** | **100.0** |

## Misleading Advertising Act (Law No 74/92)

Since 1992, Italy has had its own Act concerning misleading advertising. After a long series of Bills which were debated and never approved, the Italian Parliament eventually implemented EC Directive 84/450 on 25 January 1992. This is the first step taken by the Italian legislature towards systematic and unitary regulations for advertising.

On an adjudicating level, in addition to the judiciary, the Advertising Self-regulation Authority and the Authority for Broadcasting, a new specific authority with preliminary and restraining powers, have been established.

The legislature has designated the Authority for Competition and the Market (created by the so called Anti-trust Act 287/90) as the administrative body with specific competence, thus complying with the requirement of one single, independent judge competent on a national level, as required by EC Directive 84/450.

This choice has met with a favourable opinion as it may, quite apart from the relationship with other authorities, give rise to the development of a constant and specific jurisprudence on the issue, which should assist the operators in this area.

We turn now to examine in detail the basic principles contained in Legislative Decree No 74/92.

Article 1 of the Act sets out the general principle, according to which advertising must be evident, truthful and correct, while singling out the scope of the regulation to protect from misleading advertising those who are engaged in commercial, industrial, handicraft, professional and/or consumers and general recipients of the advertising message.

Articles 2 and 3 aim to identify minimum objective criteria to detect the deceitfulness of an advertising message.

Specifically, Art 2 singles out those who are bound to observe the rules as well as liable to undergo sanctions: the message buyer, its author, and the owner of the media through which the message is being broadcast (the latter being so only if he does not allow the identification of the former two subjects).

Article 4 deals with 'editorial' or 'non-evident' advertising. It explains the principle already mentioned in Art 1 of the Act, according to which advertising must be evident.

Articles 5 and 6 (information on dangerous products and regulations of advertising targeted at minors) essentially imitate those rules already set out in the Code of Advertising Self-regulation.

Article 7 is the most important article in the whole Legislative Decree and it is also the one governing both administrative and jurisdictional protection in the matter of misleading advertising.

As we have seen, the competent authority is the Authority for Competition and the Market; the provision identifies the subjects who may request administrative protection against those messages deemed to be misleading. The innovation consists in the fact that even the individual consumer can file a claim directly to the Authority.

This is where concerns among the operators, as to a possible exploitation of this rule for purposes quite separate from the spirit of the Legislative Decree, have originated.

In the case of special urgency, the Authority may suspend, ex parte and with immediate effect, the advertising message which is the subject of complaint.

The Authority has, moreover, wide investigative powers, as it can order the operator to prove the truthfulness of the message which is the subject of the complaint, the lack of which would indicate a presumption of inexactitude of the facts being advertised.

The other authority, the one in charge of broadcasting, is entrusted with a compulsory consultative function for those cases of misleading advertising being published by the press or broadcast on radio or television.

The Legislative Decree has deferred the preliminary discipline to the issuing of subsequent regulation, which must nevertheless safeguard the debate, the complete production of evidence, as well as its recording.

Lastly, Art 8, in compliance with EC Directive 84/450, has acknowledged the full validity of self-regulatory voluntary and autonomous bodies by granting the parties the right to file claims for consideration by such institutions, as well as the right to abstain from applying to the Authority for Competition and the Market until after the Self-regulation Authority, to which an application has been made, has made a final judgment.

The parties concerned may also request the suspension of proceedings pending before the Authority for Competition and the Market while awaiting the judgment of the Self-regulation Authority, provided that the latter decides within 30 days.

This rule has led to different interpretations as to the possible result of two diverse judgments on the same case, one from the Advertising Self-regulation Authority, the other from the Authority for Competition and the Market, with the obvious concerns for the operators.

Different concurring proceedings and the lack of a discipline regulating the interactions between such proceedings may actually cause some discrepancies in the judgments, not only as to the application of the different regulations, but as to different preliminary verifications or to contrasting personal evaluations as well.

Seven years after the enactment of the Legislative Decree No 74/92, it is now possible to draw the first conclusions as to its application.

After getting over the running-in stage, the authority (which was initially chaired in 1992 by the late Prof Saja, former President of the Constitutional Court, and which has been chaired since 1 January 1998 by Giuseppe Tesauro) has taken on more staff over the last few years, while establishing a specific department called the 'Misleading Advertising Department', devoted to issues pertaining to the control and suppression of misleading advertising.

As regulations for the preliminary procedure have, as yet, remained on paper only, instead of being issued by the industry ministry within 90 days of enactment (as should have happened according to the Act (Art 7, subpara 8)), the Authority has so far dealt with it autonomously, by referring to the regulations set out in Law No 241/90 as to the discipline of administrative proceedings. During December 1992, the Authority deliberated a first procedural scheme to be applied, within the delays of the formative course of regulations, to pending cases, and which essentially takes into consideration the principles contained in Art 7, subpara 8 of the Legislative Decree No 74/92 (guarantee of debate, full cognisance of acts, recordings). As already mentioned, the Authority has fixed the maximum duration of the proceedings to 90 days (180 in the case of a temporary interruption of the same proceedings) while trying to find a balance between the necessary speed in issuing a judgment concerning advertising and the timing and typical procedures of the administrative machine.

When reviewing the host of judgments issued and published periodically in the Authority's Official Bulletin, and considering the reports that the same Authority has to edit and address to the head of the Cabinet each year, according to the Act, one gets a rather voluminous and stimulating general picture.

From the early 166 judgments in 1993, there were 213 in 1994, 220 in 1995 and 582 in 1997; 59 complaints led to a verdict in 1993, 105 in 1994, about 145 in 1995: during the last two years the ratio of verdicts to the total of complaints has settled at around 60%. The escalation in activity (in 1995, complaints notified to the Authority numbered over 680) is quite obvious and – in our opinion – is based on three specific reasons:

(a) an increasingly higher awareness and level of information on the part of consumers, and of the wider public concerning the Authority's role and functions regarding misleading advertising;

(b) increased co-operation between the subjects involved (consumers' associations, etc) and the Authority;

(c) the cost free nature of proceedings.

## Pay-TV

Italian legislation regulated the pay-TV field through a new Law Decree of November 1995, which had immediate effect. This law was established to break the actual monopoly of the two commercial television channels: Telepiù 1 and Telepiù 2. This law applies to all broadcasters already operating in Italy as well as to all foreign networks which can transmit over Italian territory.

All businesses operating in this field were required to have begun satellite broadcasting by 31 December 1996 and to have stopped terrestrial transmission by 31 August 1997.

## An overview of procedural aspects

Having examined the different sources of advertising regulations in Italy, we now sum up the procedures of the competent authorities, as well as the various sanctions.

### Courts of law – breach of Art 2598 of the Civil Code

A competitor being either directly injured or threatened by someone's tort is entitled to action within the civil discipline for competition. It is unquestionable that unfair competition can take place only where there is a competitive relationship between active and passive subjects, and both parties must be acting in the course of business.

Contrary to trade mark and patent regulations, those on unfair competition do not provide for the typical preventive remedies, so it is necessary to apply to the measures as set out in Art 700 of the Code of Civil Procedure.

The competent court is located where the plaintiff fears the injury is about to occur.

Therefore, in the case of an advertisement being broadcast on television or published, the judge where the broadcaster is established or where the publication is being issued will have jurisdiction on the matter.

The party willing to use the precautionary measure relating to Art 700 of the Code of Civil Procedure will have to prove the existence of the injured right as well as the irreparability of the injury, should it not be possible to achieve an immediate judicial measure.

In the case of misleading or denigrating or unfair advertising, the most frequent measure adopted is the inhibitory one, that is, ordering the other party to abstain from the behaviour in dispute (the advertising campaign) until the settlement of the relevant judgment.

The issue of an inhibitory measure gains an importance as a further measure to either eliminate or attenuate the impending and irretrievable detriment, amidst the supplementary remedies. Among the various remedies available within the precautionary measures set out in Art 700 of the Code of Civil Procedure, the 'inhibitory measure' (that is, restrictive injunction) is probably the most relevant and effective one in order to eliminate or reduce the amount of pending damages (that is, damages with are *very likely to occur* according to the actual circumstances of the case).

When declaring the measure, the judge must fix a mandatory period within which the petitioner must begin compliance with the specific judgment. The purpose of this judgment is to ascertain whether the issuing of the urgent measure is legitimate.

Sanctions provided for unfair competitive actions presume either deceit or blame on the part of the acting subject and consist of compensation for damages as well publication of the verdict.

### *Self-regulation – breach of the Code of Advertising Self-regulation*

We have already examined in detail both the bodies and procedures involved in self-regulation.

In short, anyone who is deemed to have suffered damage from an advertising activity not in accordance with the Self-regulatory Code is entitled to apply to the Advertising Self-regulation Authority for redress.

The judgment is not subject to appeal and immediately enforces the order on the parties involved to refrain from allowing the specific advertising to be circulated.

In the case of non-compliance with a decision, the Advertising Self-regulation Authority orders the decision to be published according to Art 42 of the Code of Advertising Self-regulation.

The Advertising Self-regulation Authority may likewise order the publication of the decision whenever reasons of special gravity exist.

## The Authority for Publishing and Broadcasting – breaches of Law No 223/90 and Decree No 425 of 30/11/91 (television advertising of tobacco related products, wines and spirits, and advertising directed at minors)

Article 6 of the Mammì Act established the Authority for Publishing and Broadcasting as the competent authority for controlling and issuing administrative sanctions, as set out in Art 31 of the same Act. Article 31 also established the procedures for the preliminary stage of the different cases of possible sanction, by assessing the administrative sanction in an amount ranging from L 10 m to L 100 m, or, for more serious cases, the suspension of the licence or the permit for a period ranging from one to 10 days.

On 22 April 1998, however, the Authority ceased to exist and part of its functions were taken over by the newly constituted Authority for Communications.

The Authority acts autonomously.

Anyone is entitled to notify the Authority of instances of possible non-compliance with the Act.

Breaches of the Vizzini Decree are also part of the provisions as articulated in the above-mentioned Art 31 of Mammì Act.

It is possible to appeal to the Administrative Court of the Lazio Region (the administrative region in which Rome is located) against the Advertising Self-regulation Authority's judgments, within 60 days from the service of the measure.

## The Authority for Competition and the Market – breaches of Law No 74/92 on Misleading Advertising

The Authority for Competition and the Market is competent for breaches of regulations pertaining to misleading advertising, and was established by Law No 287 of 10 October 1990, known as the Anti-trust Act.

The Authority is not qualified to act autonomously, but at the request of competing business operators, consumers and their associations, the industry ministry, or any other body of public administration, provided that the latter has some interest at stake.

The Authority adheres to a certain procedure as detailed in Art 7 of the Act to develop the preliminary stage, while still safeguarding the principle of debate.

If it considers that the advertising being complained of is in conflict with the regulation, it can order its discontinuance as well as provide for the publication of the judgment in the press.

The advertising operator who fails to comply with the measures taken by the Authority will be punished with a maximum three month prison sentence and a maximum fine of L 5 m.

Should any party refuse to supply the required information, the Authority may inflict an administrative sanction ranging from 2 m to 5 m lire.

It is possible to appeal to the Administrative Court of the Lazio Region against the Authority's judgment, within 60 days from the service of the measure.

## Specific areas

### Alcoholic products

By issuing Decree No 425 of 30 November 1991, generally referred to as the Vizzini Decree after the signatory minister, the Italian legislature has provided Italy with specific regulations for television advertising of wines and spirits.

Before then, the Advertising Code of Self-regulation (Art 22) was the only provision regulating such matters, and referred to all kinds of media, not only television.

The Vizzini Decree sets out the principle related to television advertising of wines and spirits in Art 2.

Such advertising is lawful, and therefore permitted, but it must not:

(a) target minors expressly nor, specifically, show any minor having such alcoholic drinks;

(b) relate the drinking of alcohol to physical performance of special importance or to driving vehicles;

(c) give the impression that drinking alcohol helps achieve social or sexual success;

(d) lead anyone to believe that wines and spirits have either stimulating or relaxing therapeutic properties or that they might help solve situations of psychological conflict;

(e) encourage excessive and uncontrolled use of wines and spirits or show abstinence or sobriety in a bad light;

(f) use the indication of high alcoholic content as a positive quality of the drink.

Sanctions for those who do not comply with the above-mentioned Decree are those set out in Art 31 of Law No 223 of 6 August 1990 (the Mammì Act):

1   The Authority provides for the necessary verifications, and notifies the charges to the parties involved, in the case where the provisions in Arts 8, 9, 20, 21 and 26 have not been complied with, while giving a period no longer than 15 days for any justifications.

2   Once this term has elapsed, or where the justifications are inadequate, the Authority warns the parties involved to cease the unlawful behaviour within a period no longer than 15 days, as may be assigned to this end.

3   When the unlawful behaviour persists beyond the period set out in the second subparagraph or, in the case of incomplete, tardy compliance with the obligation of correction, or of the lack of it, as set out in subparas 2, 3 and 4 of Art 10, or in those cases of non-compliance with prohibitions set out in subparas 8 and 15 of Art 15, the Authority deliberates upon the infliction of an administrative sanction for the payment of an amount ranging from 10 m to 100 m lire and, in the more serious cases, the suspension of the validity of either the licence or the permit for a period ranging from 1–10 days. Sanctions are enforced if the correction is carried out because of the proceedings as stated in subpara 4 of Art 10, unless the Authority determines otherwise when justified reasons occur.

4   As regards the administrative sanctions consequent to the breach of regulations set out in subpara 1, the regulations contained in item 1, s I and II of Act 689 of 24 November 1981 still apply, as there are no provisions otherwise.

5   In the case where the same breach is repeated within 365 days, the Authority provides for the suspension of the validity of the licence and the permit for a period ranging from 11–30 days and, in the most serious cases, it may propose the repeal of the licence or permit.

As mentioned, there is a specific article dealing with this area of marketing in the Self-regulatory Code as well. Article 22 of the Code singles out in detail the regulating criteria for advertising wines and spirits, by stating: 'The advertising of alcoholic beverages must not be in contrast with the need to provide models of consumption which project moderation, correctness and responsibility.'

The sanction for those who break the rule is defined as prohibition from further broadcasting of the infringing message.

In especially severe cases, publication of the judgment may be imposed.

Recently, the proposal of a Bill, requiring the warning 'Alcohol can be seriously harmful to health' to be printed on the labels of alcoholic drinks bottles, has given rise to strong debate.

## Tobacco related products

In Italy, the absolute prohibition of advertising of tobacco related products remains in force.

Since 1962, by Law No 165, there has been a prohibition of this type of advertising. Later, administrative sanctions were raised from a minimum of 5 m lire to a maximum of L 50 m by Law No 52 of 22 February 1983.

Until the enforcement of the Vizzini Decree, the administrative jurisprudence had considered indirect advertising of tobacco related products to be legitimate, that is, advertising relating to diverse products that nevertheless use the trade marks of famous tobacco related products.

The Vizzini Decree, which only takes television advertising into consideration, has also prohibited this kind of advertising, by establishing the following principle in Art 1:

> Television advertising of cigarettes and of any other tobacco related product is forbidden, even if carried out indirectly by using names, trade marks, symbols or any other element typical of tobacco related products or of enterprises whose main business is the production or selling of said products, when by ways, modes, and the media being utilised, that is, on the basis of any other unequivocal element, this use is appropriate to attain the purpose of advertising the same products.

> To establish which is the main business referred to in subpara 1 above, it is necessary to refer to the turnover of the individual businesses, so that the main one is the one which prevails over each of the other business activities within the national territory.

Sanctions against infringers are the same as set out in Art 31 of the Mammì Act. The competent authority is the Authority for Publishing and Broadcasting.

As to sponsorship, the absolute prohibition is confirmed, even for those sponsorships indirectly using cigarette trade marks for products other than the tobacco related ones.

After an initial liberal approach adopted by the Italian courts (during which, only messages likely to generate or increase the individual's desire or personal inclination to smoke were forbidden), a recent judgment of the Supreme Court under combined divisions (No 10508 of 6 October 1995) has solved the issue drastically by once again including any evocative form, be it direct or indirect or hidden, of tobacco related products with an advertising effect, including sponsorships, in the prohibition of advertising, as set out in the above-mentioned Law No 165/62.

The stricter 1995 approach had been preceded and introduced by two previous decisions of the Supreme Court (No 7209 of 11 July 1990 and No 10906 of 16 October 1990), in which it was held that the ban stated in Law No 165/62 covered any form of advertising of tobacco related products, either direct or indirect, including those advertising messages which do not openly reveal their purpose to increase the use of tobacco related products.

With the 1995 decision, the Supreme Court outlawed any advertising behaviour, regardless of the intensity of the message, the ways in which the message is conveyed, or the final goal to which the message is directed. The facts examined by the court in this decision concerned the sale of children's pencil cases decorated with pictures of packets of a well known cigarette: the court held that, notwithstanding the different nature of the product sold (the pencil case), which excluded any possibility of confusion with the product portrayed in the decoration, the use of the cigarette packets constituted an evocative message, even though there was no commercial co-operation between the manufacturers of the two products in question.

The only limit to the ban is represented by the immanent advertising function residing in the offer for sale to the public (which is allowed) of tobacco related products identified by their trade marks. The Supreme Court seems to have distinguished between the normal, immanent distinctive function of the trade marks and the abuse of the further 'exceeding' advertising function; how this theoretical distinction can be translated into practical terms, the court did not say.

In addition, it is necessary to point out the problems of co-ordination and compatibility of the content of this decision which have arisen in relation to the provisions of the internal legal system.

First of all, reference was made to the problems of compatibility with the *constitutional provisions* aimed at protecting the freedom of personal expression of individual opinions (Art 21) and, most of all, of economic private initiative (Art 41). The conflict was resolved in the light of the limits which Art 41 of the Italian Constitution lays down for the protection of private initiative, that is, the contrast with principles of social usefulness and with prevailing different constitutional values. The prevailing nature of the fundamental right of protection of individual and public health justified the conclusion of the Supreme Court's decision.

Secondly, there is a problem of co-ordination with the Italian provisions on trade mark protection law. In point of fact, the decision in question examined the case of a trade mark originally used to identify a tobacco related product, which was subsequently used as the distinctive sign of a totally different type of product.

According to Art 11 of the Italian Trade Mark Protection Act, the use of a trade mark which has previously been used by another manufacturer is permitted to the extent that this will not create confusion between the two different products bearing such a mark. This is in accordance with the initially liberal approach of the Supreme Court, as well as with the recent decisions of the Advertising Self-regulation Authority; the latter held (in a decision of 9 June 1992) that the ban referring to a product will concern exclusively the product itself and not its trade mark, which could legally be used to identify other products as a legitimate way to profit from 'the symbolic value capitalised by the trade mark'.

But the Supreme Court decided that the lack of confusion between two products identified by the same mark could not prevent the ban from being applicable, if one of the goods bearing the mark is a tobacco related product. This stricter approach was justified by the fact that the interest protected by trade mark protection law is radically different from that protected by the limitations contained in advertising law. The two respective sets of legal provisions have to be co-ordinated, in the sense that the use of a trade mark initially adopted to define a tobacco related product shall be considered forbidden by law, independently from any lack of confusion, if and when such use will maintain an evocative effect and the function of advertising the tobacco related product.

This position clearly undermined the fundamental basis of the protection of a trade mark having a prominent market reputation, being in conflict with the concept of a trade mark which, for its highly distinctive qualities, has to be considered as having a different value from the product to which it has initially been related.

But with such a decision, the Supreme Court expressly declared the prominence given to public values to the detriment of private interests, limiting to a very restricted area the legitimate use of a mark connected to a tobacco related product: this shall be allowed only when the trade mark has acquired complete independence from the tobacco related product and is, therefore, devoid of any evocative power of it.

According to the Supreme Court, this situation is likely to occur in two different situations:

(a) a trade mark originally identifying a tobacco related product and subsequently acquiring an independent notoriety as a distinctive mark of a different good;

(b) a trade mark originally identifying a certain product and subsequently used in relation to a tobacco related product.

In the first case, the mark has acquired the capacity to define directly a product which is totally different from the original one, and so has lost the original evocative power; the second case, since the mark is apt to advertise a non-tobacco related product, does not come within the ban of the statutory provisions.

Finally, until very recently the 1995 Supreme Court decision involved problems of compatibility with EC provisions.

Until the beginning of this year, in the absence of a definitive, uniform set of EC provisions regarding the ban on tobacco related product advertising, as well as the ban on indirect promotion through merchandising activities, the 1995 Italian decision could have ended up being considered a 'measure equivalent to a restrictive trade practice' among Member States under the terms of Arts 30–36 of the Treaty on European Union.

Indeed, the result of such a decision would have been to forbid the Italian importation of merchandising goods legitimately manufactured and distributed in the other Member States.

Besides that, case law of the European Court of Justice expressly included Member States' internal courts' decisions among the range of 'restrictive trade measures'.

It could be said that the case in question could be justified by the protection of public health covered by Art 36 of the Treaty. However, this could be in contrast to the usual restrictive interpretation that the European Court gives to the concept of public health interests.

This particular problem will soon cease to be of practical relevance: on 12 February 1998, after eight years of debate, a Green Paper proposing the prohibition of direct advertising of tobacco related products within the next three years was approved by the majority of Member States.

The aim of harmonising Member States' provisions has already led the European Commission to present a Green Paper for a Directive regarding labelling of tobacco related products (622/89), inspired by strict criteria of health interest protection.

The same results deriving from the 1995 Italian Supreme Court decision will soon be achieved with the next legislative step: by the year 2006 indirect advertising of tobacco related products, including sponsorship of sports and cultural events, will be banned by the EC legislation.

The EC ban will include 'any direct or indirect form of reproduction of tobacco related products, including the use of names, symbols, trade marks and any other distinctive signs'. It would also expressly forbid the use of trade marks of tobacco related products for different types of goods, unless the turnover of the non-tobacco related products is at least twice that of the tobacco related products. Finally, advertising would only be allowed within the sales premises, unless it is visible from the outside.

Also, by the year 2006, licences of non-tobacco related products bearing the same trade marks as cigarette companies will be drastically reduced.

The reason why the ban on indirect advertising is being postponed to 2006 by the EC legislation is explained by the fact that this type of advertising activity, and especially sponsorship, have always been the main source of financial income supporting world motor racing. Some of the Member States were quite reluctant to cut off such a vital source of investment, so it was decided to delay the elimination process for as long as possible.

Sponsorship of world motor racing seems effectively to be the last area of privilege granted to the big multinational cigarette manufacturers.

Since the 1995 decision, although the Italian Authority for Competition and the Market has recently excluded its jurisdiction on violation of provisions regarding advertising of tobacco related products, the no smoking policy has exerted its influence in basically every area of law considered by the Italian courts of justice. The protection of non-smoking individuals has in fact been subject to the attention of both the Constitutional Court (decision of 20 December 1996, No 399, on employers' duties towards non-smoking workers) and the regional administrative courts, which held the public administration responsible for the damage caused by an employee's exposure, in the course of his employment, to other workers' tobacco smoke (decision of 20 March 1997 of the *Tribunale Amministrative Regionale* (TAR), Lazio).

## Financial and real estate operations

Any kind of advertising relating to financial operations is subject to the supervision of a national committee for companies and the stock exchange, the *Commissione Nazionale per la Società e la Borsa* (CONSOB) (CONSOB Regulations 1739 of 10 July 1985).

Law No 771 of 23 March 1983 (Art 12), governing the investment of common funds, provides that any kind of advertising aimed at potential savers and carried out through any kind of media is subject to the CONSOB's supervision.

Law No 142 of 19 February 1992, which has implemented Directive 90/88, contains some regulations on consumer credit, while the Law of 17 February 1992 has regulated the rules on banking services' transparency.

As regards regulations for product advertisements, financial services or transactions, CONSOB regulations 6243 of 3 June 1992 and 6378 of 28 July 1992 on the matter of public offers for the purchase and exchange of shares are worth emphasising.

Article 27 of the Code of Advertising Self-regulation governs both financial and real estate operations. Such advertising must not encourage any investment, undertaking and deposit without proper guarantees being offered. It must also provide for clear and exhaustive information on the nature and exact conditions of the operations being offered.

## Pharmaceuticals

All advertising of medicines and medical treatments only available against prescription, either on traditional billboards or through sponsorship, is forbidden (Art 8, subpara 5 and 14.1 Law 223/90, the Mammí Act).

In all other cases, advertising of the products and activities listed in the title must have been previously authorised by the health ministry (as regards nursing homes, the competent local office of the national health authority has to give its approval).

Ministry authorisation relates to the type of advertising message as well as to its content, by imposing special forms of communication on the advertising message, if necessary, such as 'please read instructions extremely carefully'. This statement has to appear on television for a minimum of eight seconds (Art 2 of Ministerial Decree of 5 June 1981).

The advertising communication, thus authorised, must quote both the number and the date of the authorising Ministerial Decree.

In the case of a breach, criminal sanctions (a fine and, for the most serious cases, arrest) for both the client and the media are provided for, besides the possible attachment of the product being advertised.

Law Decrees Nos 540 and 541 of 30 December 1992, enacted in compliance with Directives 92/27 and 92/28 respectively, mark a significant turning point by regulating in a more specific and updated way the labels and instruction sheets of medicines for human use (Law Decree No 540/92) as well as the relevant advertising (Law Decree No 541/92).

Mineral waters which have been registered as proprietary medicines claiming special therapeutic effects may be advertised according to the procedures and in compliance with the obligations previously indicated and pertaining to proprietary medicines.

Finally, Law Decree No 105 of 25 January 1992 has implemented Directive 80/777 in Italy on the matter of the marketing of natural mineral waters.

A provision (Art 201 of the Single Act on Medical Laws of the Royal Decree No 1265 dated 27 July 1934) generically applying to natural or artificial mineral waters, although non-registered as proprietary medicines, is, however, generally provided for and states that the advertising of these products must have been previously authorised by a Decree from the health ministry.

The Decree that authorises the advertising of mineral waters normally requires that the number of the Decree is quoted for the duration, if any, thereby indicated and it is always advisable to ask the client for it.

In the case of a breach, the same sanctions as provided for proprietary medicines will be applied to both the client and the media.

Article 25 of the Self-regulatory Code deals with medicines and curative treatments by setting out very strict principles on the matter, essentially based on the concept that: 'Advertising of medicinal products and curative treatments must take into consideration the sensitiveness of the matter and be made with the utmost sense of responsibility.'

## Food and agricultural products

As already mentioned, regulations on advertising are scattered in a series of different Acts. This is particularly true as far as food products are concerned. The following statutes are pointed out as a mere example.

The Royal Law Decree No 2033 of 15 October 1925 stipulates a fine ranging from 250,000 lire to L 2.5 m lire for anyone who puts agricultural products up for sale by using inappropriate names not corresponding to either the characteristics or the nature of the products themselves or which might howsoever mislead the consumer, by any advertising media.

Law No 283 of 30 April 1962 stipulates a fine ranging from L 600,000 to 15 m lire for anyone who spreads, by any advertising media, advertising messages for food products or drinks by using inappropriate names, trade marks or quality certificates, which might somehow cheat the consumer's good faith, or which might howsoever mislead as to the nature, the essence, the qualities, or the nutritional properties of the said products, or which might even claim special therapeutic effects.

As to the numerous special Acts related to individual food product categories, please refer to the material above, p 594.

Lastly, a series of Acts implementing important EC Directives in this area are worth noting: Republic Presidential Decree No 902 of 23 August 1982, enforcing Directive 79/581 on the price indications for foodstuffs to protect consumers; Law Decree No 76 of 25 January 1992, enforcing Directive 88/315, also regarding foodstuff prices; Law Decree No 109 of 27 January 1992, enforcing Directives 88/395 and 89/396 on the labelling, displaying, and advertising of foodstuffs; Law Decree No 111 of 27 January 1992, enforcing Directive 89/398 on diet products; Law Decree No 77 of 16 February 1993, enforcing Directive 90/496 on labelling regarding the nutritional values of food.

Finally, Art 2 of the Self-regulatory Code and Law No 74/92, pertaining to misleading advertising, perform an especially important role in the food field and specifically to the general and strict prohibition of misleading the consumer by assigning untruthful characteristics to the product.

## Advertising targeted at minors

The first subparagraph of Art 8 of Law No 223/90 (which has since been applied thanks to the Vizzini Decree) sets out the following:

(a) radio/television advertising must not be morally or physically detrimental to minors;

(b) its inclusion within cartoon programmes is forbidden.

Article 3 of the Vizzini Decree specifies the criteria regulating television advertising to minors:

1   In order to prevent any moral or physical detriment to minors, television advertising shall not:

   (a) directly encourage minors to purchase a product or a service by abusing their inexperience or credulity;

(b) directly encourage minors to ask their parents or other people to purchase said products or services;

(c) abuse minors' specific trust in their parents, teachers or anyone else;

(d) show minors involved in dangerous situations when this is not necessary to convey the message of the advertisement.

Article 11 of the Self-regulatory Code had long since singled out a series of principles on the matter by emphasising the idea that 'Particular care must be taken in advertising messages addressed to children and adolescents or which could be received by them'.

Finally, Art 28 *bis* of the Self-regulatory Code considers those advertising messages whose subject is children's toys. Article 28 *bis* declares that:

Advertising for games and toys for children must not mislead:

* in the nature, performance and dimensions of the advertised product;
* on the degree of ability needed in order to use the product;
* on the amount of the expenditure, especially when the purchase of complementary products is needed to make the product work.

In any case, this advertising must not minimise product price or imply that its purchase is normally compatible with any family budget.

## Cosmetics

Royal Decree No 478 of 3 March 1927 considered beauty products and other toiletries in the same way as medicines, by assigning them particular therapeutic effects.

Consequently, the specific regulations have always been entirely based on the principle that, if beauty products claimed therapeutic properties during advertising, they would automatically be included in the same regulations as medicines, thus requiring the ministerial authorisation.

A recent Act (Law No 713 of 11 October 1986), passed in order to comply with EC Directive 76/768 on the matter, stated that the advertising of beauty products cannot assign these products any characteristic other than those peculiar to modern beauty products.

Finally, on 10 September 1991, Law Decree No 300 was enacted to enforce the above-mentioned Directive 76/768.

The Self-regulatory Code has long since been regulating the issue. Article 23 states that advertising of beauty products must not lead the consumer to believe that such products have any other characteristics apart from that of application onto the skin or other parts of the human body, with the sole purpose of cleaning, deodorising, perfuming, or superficially improving a person's looks, that is, of protection in order to maintain the body in a good shape.

This advertising – still according to Art 23 of the Self-regulatory Code – must not lead the consumer to mistake beauty products for medicines, as if the former had medico-surgical effects or qualities and therapeutic benefits.

# SPONSORSHIP OF PROGRAMMES

## The Italian form of sponsorship and limits to advertising clutter

For a long time now, sponsorship and television promotions have been the focus of strong controversy, which has pitted Italian advertising operators in opposition to one another for economic and ideological reasons.

The controversy has arisen from the fact that both investors and television networks have been using atypical forms of sponsorship for many years, which do not conform to any specific statement of Directive 89/552, and which have been defined as 'telepromotions' or even 'Italian-style telesponsorships'.

In fact, the European Directive, while regulating the issue of advertising crowding limitation, does provide for sponsored television programmes, which do not undergo any crowding limit: 'they must not encourage the purchase or rental of the products or services of the sponsor or a third party, in particular by making special promotional references to those products or services' (Art 17(1)(c)).

Law No 223 of 6 August 1990 (the Mammì Act), which was meant to assimilate and introduce Directive 89/552 in Italy, has actually left out the above-mentioned rule, thus causing severe problems of interpretation.

Within this contradictory framework between the Italian and the European framework, the leading private sector Italian television channels, owned by the Fininvest Group, devised a new advertising tool called 'telepromotion', wherein performance and entertainment co-exist with other spaces allotted to advertise certain products: so what we have is not separate and autonomous commercials, but ones that are organically part of the television programmes.

With the use of telepromotions which, according to the Mammì Act, could have been included in the category of sponsorship (then considered to be advertising messages covering a minimum 2% of a programme's duration, to be included within the daily limit for advertising crowding: Art 8, subpara 15 of the Mammì Act), television companies were able to broadcast an extremely high quantity of advertising for some years; in fact, once the percentage time limits established for the traditional scheduled advertising had been reached, they 'flooded' television programmes by means of telepromotions.

This situation has, however, been modified by the passing of Law No 408 of 17 December 1992, which made some significant amendments to the Mammì Act to make the Italian regulations conform to the European ones.

A new paragraph (Art 8, subpara 13, para B *bis*) has been added to the Mammì Act, which states that 'sponsored programmes ought not to encourage the purchase or rental of any product or service of either the sponsor or a third party, especially by specific promotional references to the said products or services'. Moreover, all limits on television sponsorships were abolished. To complete the legislative overhaul, a new Art 8, subpara 9 *bis* was inserted, which states that 'the maximum daily transmission time allotted to advertising by private concessionaires for television broadcasting within the national territory has been increased to 20%, if they include advertising methods such as offers directly proposed to the public for the sale or rental of products or the supply of services, without prejudice to the daily crowding and timing limits as established for traditional advertisements (15% daily timing, 18% per hour).

These changes have put an end to the Italian anomaly, by excluding telepromotions from the sponsorship riverbed, and including them in the more traditional forms of advertising.

Therefore, sponsorships and telepromotions may both be carried out in Italy today: the only difference is that the former do not have to meet any advertising crowding limit, while for the latter, the common time limits established for advertisements, as set out in Art 8, subpara 8 of the Mammì Act, are in force.

## Sponsorship: rules and regulations

Following the amendments to the Mammì Act brought about by Law No 483 of 7 April 1993, it was necessary to set some additional rules, which would specify the definition, performance, and limits of television sponsorship.

The Ministerial Decree No 581 of 9 December 1993 was then enacted under the title of 'regulations regarding sponsorships, television programmes, and offers to the audience', which, in some ways, repeats the previous, obsolete Ministerial Decree of 4 April 1991, while in others, it completes and specifies the Directive concerning television sponsorship.

Article 4 states that sponsorship may be carried out as follows:

(a) by inviting to watch, and thanking for having watched a particular programme, where the sponsor's name or trade mark [Art 4, subpara 1] is simply mentioned;

(b) by announcements or invitations, each one lasting at least eight seconds, to watch programmes being scheduled for broadcasting, which are followed by the mention of the sponsor's name or trade mark only. Each programme is allowed to contain a maximum of three announcements [Art 4, subpara 2];

(c) should the sponsored transmission last at least 40 minutes, the appearance of the sponsor's name or trade mark during the sponsored transmission is allowed once, and for no longer than five seconds [Art 4, subpara 3];

(d) should the sponsorship be aimed at financing a game or a contest programme, the sponsor's products and services may be awarded as prizes to private winners, even while specifying that the prize has been supplied by the sponsor. It may be displayed to the audience in a precise and reasonable way at the prize award only. This rule also provides that, if the admission to the game or contest, that is, the prize award, is subject to proof of purchase of either the sponsor's or third parties' products, the message is no longer considered to be sponsorship [Art 4, subpara 4].

It is clearly forbidden to insert in the programme 'any kind of advertising slogan and presentation of products and services' (Art 4, subpara 1). The logical consequence to this is Art 4, subpara 5, according to which, if the programme contains either advertising slogans or explicit invitations to purchase the sponsor's goods, the case again falls within the category of telepromotions, which in turn are subject to advertising crowding regulations.

## Programmes which may be sponsored

Ministerial Decree No 581 of 9 December 1993 likewise provides some rules concerning programmes which may be sponsored, and fixing limits to the sponsor's influence within the programme itself.

As regards the kinds of programmes which can be sponsored, Art 7 states that 'news and radio news ... and at any rate radio/television news of a political, economic, and financial character cannot be sponsored'. Moreover, 'sponsorship of consumer advice programmes is not allowed'.

In any case, the sponsor cannot influence the content and the programming of the programme being sponsored so as to be prejudicial to the editorial responsibility and autonomy of the broadcaster in relation to the transmissions (Art 3, subpara 1(a)); moreover, sponsored programmes must be clearly recognisable as such, and must show the sponsor's name and/or trade mark at the beginning and/or at the end of the programme.

## Products which may be sponsored

Italian regulations also provide for some restrictions concerning products which may be sponsored during a radio/television transmission.

In fact, Art 8 of Ministerial Decree No 581 of 9 December 1993, by recalling what had already been stated in Art 8, subpara 14 of the Mammì Act, provides that 'programmes cannot be sponsored by natural legal persons or by artificial legal persons whose main activity consists of the manufacture or sale of cigarettes or any other tobacco related products, the manufacture or sale of spirits, or the manufacture or sale of medicines, that is, the administration of medical treatments which are only available against a prescription'.

These prohibitions, however, are easily understood considering that, within the Italian regulations, even the traditional advertising of products and services indicated in Art 8 of Ministerial Decree No 581 is forbidden (cigarettes and tobacco related products), or is subject to administrative authorisation (medicines and nursing homes), or is subject to very strict rules (spirits).

The rule, however, has even sought to provide a stratagem which would effectively deal with tobacco multinationals which have tried to get round the absolute prohibition on the advertising of their own products: while using their famous trade marks to distinguish the most diverse products (clothing, watches, sporting goods, etc), they were also making an extremely high advertising investment in these other products. The unquestionable result was strong indirect advertising of cigarettes and tobacco related products.

Ministerial Decree No 581 has tried to obviate these setbacks not by forbidding the advertisement of certain products, but by forbidding those businesses, whose main activity consists of manufacturing or marketing the products quoted in the rule, from carrying out their sponsorships.

With the very purpose of restricting the framework of this prohibition, Art 8 subpara 2 of Ministerial Decree No 581 has also provided that 'in order to determine which is the main activity according to subpara 1, one must refer to the turnover of the individual activities, the main one being that which prevails when compared to the other business activities within the national territory'.

This rule, while it has come to grips with an important and real problem, has not fully accomplished the task, as it has not regulated the problems connected with merchandising at all, especially those referring to the possibility that subjects who are third parties to the one who manufactures or markets cigarettes or tobacco related products, and who may have acquired the right to use the said trade marks in certain market areas, may use the same trade marks to sponsor television transmissions as well.

This possibility, which is not regulated by the provisions on television matters, would be, at any rate, forbidden by another legal provision, Law No 52 of 10 April 1983, which forbids any kind of advertising dealing with tobacco related products. This law has been very widely interpreted by the Supreme Court (No 10508, 6 December 1995), to the extent of forbidding any form of merchandising on famous cigarette trade marks. On this point, please refer to what has already been stated above, p 620.

# COMPARATIVE ADVERTISING

## State regulation

Italy does not have a specific national regulation concerning comparative advertising, as is the case in many other European countries. However, this legislative lacuna has not prevented advertising professionals from utilising this significant tool, but they have done so while using the necessary prudence and respecting the obvious limits in a situation not characterised by any specific regulation.

The applicable general regulation which one needs to remember when referring to comparative advertising is Art 2598, item 2 of the Civil Code, which provides that '... Acts of unfair competition are carried out by anyone ... who spreads news and opinions concerning a competitor's products and activity so as to throw discredit on them ...'.

On first reading of this regulation, a rather liberal orientation of the Italian legislator might seem to emerge, as it appears not to forbid the spreading of any piece of news pertaining to competitors, but only that aimed at discrediting them.

But what kind of news might throw discredit on competitors? The answer to the question is not as easy as it may seem; if anything, by noting that even a true piece of news, be it proven and/or to be proven, is potentially capable of discrediting somebody else's enterprise.

Law has already intervened several times on these interesting principles; specifically on the following points:

(a) comparative advertising methods which turn into a tendentious or incorrect disclosure of news about the competitor, regardless of the truthfulness of the news being spread, are unlawful (Court of Appeal, Milan, 8 February 1983, in *Foro Padano* 1985, I, 63; Court of Milan, 24 March 1978, in *Giurisprudenza annotata diritto industriale*, No 1043);

(b) comparative advertising methods which, though not being characterised by tendentiousness or incorrectness, make use of false news, are likewise considered to be unlawful (Court of Milan, 16 September 1982, in *Giurisprudenza annotata diritto industriale*, No 1620; Court of Milan, 12 July 1976, in *Giurisprudenza annotata diritto industriale*, No 850). For example, comparisons made by using relative superlatives or expressions such as 'the only, 'unique', 'real', – when not corresponding to the actual characteristics of the products being advertised, and when completed by comparative references aimed at belittling and discrediting the competitor's products – have been condemned;

(c) on the contrary, comparative advertising containing a low opinion of the competing products has been considered to be lawful, if this tool is the only way to respond to somebody else's attack: these are so called cases of self-defence;

(d) emphasising the technical equivalence of advertised products with the competitor's ones by referring to objective data has been likewise considered as lawful (Supreme Court, 3 August 1987, No 6682; Supreme Court, 12 October 1987, No 7530);

(e) again, emphasising the cheaper price of the advertised product compared to the competitor's one has been considered to be lawful, provided that the two products being compared have similar characteristics (Court of Milan, 30 March 1978, *Giurisprudenza annotata diritto industriale*, No 1044).

Although these two latter cases seem to leave many possibilities open to business enterprises to make use of comparative advertising on paper, they do present some serious difficulties as to tests, as they actually impose the onus on the business enterprises themselves of proving that the products being compared have the same characteristics or the same performance.

If considering both the difficulty and risks that such proof could reserve and the sanctions provided for by the regulations in case of breach of Art 2598 of the Civil Code (prohibition of spreading censured advertising, payment of damages suffered by the competitor, publication of the judgment), one can well understand why comparative advertising in Italy has been used only under specific circumstances and with peculiar methods so far.

There is another comparative method that deserves to be mentioned separately: the so called *Warentests* (that is, by using the results of comparisons between homogeneous products) and carried out by either subjects or bodies, which are specialised, independent and autonomous from the producers of the goods and services being analysed and compared.

If the comparison is performed in an objective, impartial and accurate manner, then the law allows for the use of such tests, provided that the ways in which the test results are inserted in the advertisement are not of a kind to disparage the other competitors.

European Directive 97/55/EC has set out the 'standards' by which comparative advertising can be allowed. The Directive requires legislators of all EC countries to enact, by March 2000, national rules to enforce the conditions outlined in the Directive. As a consequence, in Italy, a new law covering comparative advertising is being worked on, so the situation could change within the next few months.

## Advertising self-regulation

Notwithstanding the persistent indifference shown by the Italian legislators to the phenomenon of comparative advertising, the Italian self-regulatory system for advertising has regulated the issue, in Art 15 of the Code of

Advertising Self-regulation, according to which 'indirect comparison is allowed to illustrate technical and economic aspects of objectively relevant and verifiable advantages and characteristics of advertised goods and services'.

The first remark has to do with the subject of this rule, which excludes any possibility of direct comparison, that is, advertisements containing unequivocal references (illustrations, brands or any other distinctive sign) to the competitor's products, while only governing the possible methods of indirect comparison performance.

The Jury, that is, the Advertising Self-regulation Authority, has also stated that easy identification of the competitor's product will not be sufficient to consider something as a direct comparison – which is forbidden in any case. For example, in a duopoly market situation, advertising one of the products containing a vague reference to the 'other' one, without displaying any distinctive mark, does not represent a case of direct comparison, even if it is perfectly suitable to single out the competitor.

Indirect comparison methods are therefore lawful, provided they are based on strictly truthful data, they are limited to significant and important aspects to the consumer, and are justified by the need to describe or situate the advertised product in the market.

A further limit is represented by Art 14 of the Code of Advertising Self-regulation, according to which 'the denigration of others' activities, companies or products, even if not specifically mentioned, is prohibited'.

In fact, a 'plus' that may be present in the advertised product, does not legitimate the use of either verbal or visual excess by the manufacturers of the above-mentioned products, which might discredit the competitor's products.

The Advertising Self-regulation Authority, then, while enforcing this principle, has steadily condemned advertising which has made comparisons by methods which are aggressive: for example, the commercial for a detergent, where the actor's hand, with great energy, was sweeping away from a table a different cleaning product (Decision 32/79), or the comparison between two brands of batteries, carried out by presenting two puppets, one being driven by the advertised batteries, and lifting up the other one, driven by rival batteries, before putting it into a waste paper basket (Decision 58/88).

Only in two circumstances will the self-regulatory system tolerate the comparison of methods which put competing products in a bad light: the need to position a new product in an already settled market, or the need to react to an especially aggressive advertising communication by competitors.

Comparisons using superlatives ('the biggest', 'the only', etc) have been generally censured, when product characteristics do not justify such a statement of superiority, but they have been allowed where they have turned out to be clear and recognisable advertising exaggerations (the following claims are an example: 'The most precise watch in the world. Absolutely.' (Decision 10/77); or 'The (door) handle is only ... Valli and Colombo'. (Decision 84/85)).

As to the use of *Warentests*, the Advertising Self-regulation Authority has deemed this procedure to be legitimate, provided the tests are reliable. To be reliable, *Warentests* must be carried out on a sample of consumers being sufficiently representative, and must also relate to the main characteristics of products being compared.

The leading comparative advertising methods deserve special note. The text of Art 15 of the Code of Advertising Self-regulation, by requiring that comparison be performed on the basis of real information (price, performance, etc), excludes the possibility that comparison may be carried out on the basis of mere suggestion.

On the basis of the few cases being mentioned, it should be obvious that the Jury, after acknowledging the extreme conciseness of Art 15 of the Self-regulatory Code, has elaborated several principles, which, if known in depth, would enable advertising operators to make use of the comparative advertising tool.

## RULES RESTRICTING ADVERTISING AGENTS/COMPANIES FROM ENTERING INTO OR HOLDING LICENCES

Any entrepreneur, whether Italian or a foreign national, who wishes to start an activity as an advertising operator in Italy, may do so without the need to obtain public authorisation. He or she can establish a company, and start his/her own activity after having received the approval by the competent court.

For several years – and some cases occurred even recently – the interior ministry, through the local police headquarters, has requested advertising agencies to obtain a 'Public Safety Licence', an administrative document, which, upon payment of a concessionary tax, allows the licensee to carry out this type of enterprise. The request was engendered by the interpretation of a very old rule within the Single Act on police regulations (Art 115 of Royal Decree No 773 of 18 June 1931) which, while referring to business agencies, imposed the concession of such a public authorisation.

Although a specific rule on the matter is still lacking at present, in reality, the analysis of an advertising agency's activity has made positive clarification with the competent authorities possible, which is quite different from the one carried out by the business agencies referred to in the above-mentioned Art 15: there should not be any more problems in the future!

However, one cannot be completely sure of that, as yet!

# ADVERTISING CONTRACTS

The Italian Civil Code was issued in 1942, when advertising in Italy was limited to a few press releases and a few street billpostings. So it comes as no surprise that legislators did not regulate so called advertising contracts governing relationships among advertisers, agencies and media. As the market developed, operators in this field of activity adopted the Anglo-Saxon original contractual schemes, while looking for a reasonably successful harmonisation with the general principles of Italian regulations.

Even if it has been recommended, evidence in writing is not that essential to validate an agreement. It is, however, useful for proving both the terms and the modes of the agreements reached by the parties. Up to a few years ago, most of contracts among advertisers, agencies, and media were verbal, and only administrative procedures had to be formulated in writing. Today, the market situation has to be divided into two areas: nearly all advertiser/agency contracts are in writing; while those with media or their concessionaires are still concluded over the telephone! Or even by a simple handshake.

An analysis of these two contractual types follows.

## Advertiser/agency contracts

The agreement, in legal terms, may be traced back to the tender (Art 1655 of the Civil Code), which is a contract by which the client (the advertiser) entrusts the contractor (the agency) with the task of carrying out a job (the advertising campaign) with his/her own business organisation and against payment of a consideration (the agency's fee).

The client entrusts the contractor with the power to deal with third parties (media and general suppliers), to purchase products (advertising time and space) or services (photographs, actors, etc) within this task.

This power may be accomplished by representation, Art 1704 of the Civil Code (the agency deals with third parties *in the name and on behalf of the advertiser*, while the legal effects of the contract fall on the client directly); or without representation, Art 1705 of the Civil Code (the agency deals with third parties *in the name and on behalf of the advertiser*, while the legal effects fall on the agency itself). The majority of cases adopt the first scheme.

Advertising and agency associations (UPA on the one hand, AssAP, Otep and Aipas on the other) have provided for standard contract schemes, which obviously reflect the different subjects to be protected. The two typical contractual models differ from each other essentially in three basic aspects:

(a) campaign property;

(b) agency responsibility;

(c) third party rights.

Associations are now trying to standardise the basic text for standard contracts. As long as this standardisation is lacking, the parties will have to negotiate all the terms of the contract each time.

## Advertiser-agency/media contract

This specific field is characterised by the absolute lack of written agreements. 'Advertising orders', stating the general purchasing conditions for space, and usually not signed, do exist. The interests at stake and the commercial remedies (replacement, delay, free space, etc) prevent contention in most cases.

The key elements of the agreements are:

(a) the date by which the advertisement must be issued;

(b) quality of diffusion;

(c) payment of fee.

# FUTURE DEVELOPMENTS

Solving the 'conflict of interests' posed by Berlusconi's media ownership, the enactment of specific regulations by the Regulatory Authority of Telecommunications, the prompt assimilation of EC Directives, as well as the regulation of new media such as the internet will be the essential steps to develop this field over the next few years in Italy. In fact, once the lack of political settlement has been overcome, and once the 'conflict of interests' issue existing for those who own important national media and hold a State office at the same time has been clarified and legally regulated, Italy will be in a position to define a general regulatory framework aligned with the European context. The programmes closest to completion are:

(a) *The enactment of implementing regulations by the Authority for Telecommunications*: according to Law No 249/1997, which established the Authority for Telecommunications, further to the regulation on the assignment of terrestrial frequencies to private television broadcasters (enacted on 1 December 1998) the Authority itself will emanate regulations and directives to set out the other technical standards generally referred to by law: for example, the implementing regulations of the law concerning advertising.

(b) *EC Directives*: Italy, despite some delay, has recently aligned itself with the other Member States on a legislative level. The prompt and precise assimilation of the next EC Directives will be important in the future, especially in the matters of:

- comparative advertising,
- new interactive media,
- pay-TV and satellite systems.

(c) *Relationships between self-regulation and the watchdog authorities*: so far we have seen that there are several competent legal advertising bodies in Italy. Of contentious cases today, 90% go through the Advertising Self-regulation Authority (the Jury) or the Authority for Competition and the Market, which is competent according to Law No 74/92. A better co-ordination between the two bodies could avoid any duplication of judgments, and especially the consequent legal uncertainties.

While perfectly respecting the different role positions, a substantial division of tasks between the two bodies, which would consider the different time requirements (the administrative procedure being longer than the self-regulatory one) would be hoped foras well as the different efficiency of decisions (the self-regulatory one being more limited, the State one being wider).

After the enactment of the European Directive 97/55/EC, in the subsequent debates for the approval of a national law on comparative advertising, it has been decided that the comparative advertising issue will be dealt with by the Authority.

(d) *A single text on advertising issues*: today, in Italy, rules on these matters are scattered, sometimes being referred to in legislative texts where the advertising issue is only a marginal one. An overall review of this issue, by the elaboration of a single text containing the entire regulatory framework in force is to be hoped for (as already done for the fiscal and health fields). Such a text could considerably assist those operating in this field, by taking away the excuse from the 'typical clever ones' who do not apply the regulations on the pretext that they are either unknown or difficult to retrieve.

A last consideration on the Italian market: with the exception of the Armando Testa Agency, by far the leader in terms of 'billing' and turnover, all the 'Top 10' Italian agencies are actually agencies which are connected to or owned by large international networks. This situation is also occurring in many other countries, with the result that in Italy, too, the advertising agency world is essentially placed in foreign hands. However, this has not prevented small creative entities from coming into existence and developing, which, while facing a difficult comparative situation, are carving out for themselves an increasingly noteworthy niche in the market. This situation helps to foster modern professionalism, capable of withstanding competition, and ready for the international challenge, with clear benefits in terms of a 'healthy' development of the market.

# USEFUL ADDRESSES

Autorità Garante della Concorrenza e del Mercato
(Regulatory Authority for Market Competition)
via Liguria 26
Rome

Autorità Garante per la Radiodiffusione e l'Editoria
(Regulatory Authority for Radio and Publishing)
via Santa Maria in Via 12
Rome

Camera di Commercio Internazionale
(International Chamber of Commerce)
via XX Settembre 5
Rome

Ministero della Sanità
(Ministry of Health)
Direzione Generale del Servizio Farmaceutico
(Central Office, Pharmaceuticals)
viale Civiltà Romana 4
Rome

*Organisations which form part of the Istituto Autodisciplina Pubblicitaria*
*(Institute of Advertising Self-regulation)*

Associazione Aziende Pubblicitarie Italiane (AAPI)
(Association of Italian Advertising Agencies)
via Larga 7
Milan

Associazione Albo Officiale delle Organizzazioni Pubblicitarie (ALBO)
(Official Registry of Advertising Organisations)
via Larga 15
Milan

Associazione Consulenti Pubblicitari Italiani (ACPI)
(Italian Association of Advertising Consultants)
viale Col di Lana 12
Milan

Associazione Italiana Agenzie di Promozione (ASP)
(Italian Association of Promotional Agencies)
via Larga 15
Milan

Associazione Italiana Agenzie di Pubblicità a Servizio Completo (ASSAP)
(Italian Association of Advertising Agencies Offering a Comprehensive Service)
via Larga 23
Milan

Federazione Italiana Editori Giornali (FIEG)
(Italian Federation of Newspaper Publishers)
via Piemonte 64
Rome

Federazione Radio Televisioni (FRT)
(Radio and Television Federation)
viale Regina Margherita 26
Rome

Federpubblicità – Federazione Sindacale Operatori della Pubblicità
(Trade Union Federation of Publishing Agents)
via Farini 5
Rome

Pubblicità Progresso
(Progress in Publishing)
via Larga 13
Milan

Radiotelevisione Italiana (RAI)
(Italian State Television Authority)
viale Mazzini 14
Rome

Unione Stampa Periodica Italiana (USPI)
(League of the Italian Periodical Press)
via Battista Bardanzellu 95
Rome

Utenti Pubblicità Associati (UPA)
(Association for Users of Advertising Services)
via Larga 13
Milan

# THE CODE OF ADVERTISING SELF-REGULATION

**26th edition effective 1 October 1997**
**First edition dated 12 May 1966**

### Preliminary and general rules

(a) *Purpose of the Code*

The Code of Advertising Self-Regulation has the objective of ensuring that advertising, in the course of its particularly useful role in the economy, be carried out as a service to the public with special consideration given to its influence on the consumer.

The Code of Advertising Self-Regulation defines those activities which, though in compliance with current State legislation, conflict with the above mentioned aims; the rules of the Code, being an expression of the behaviour to which advertising practice must conform, constitute the legal basis of advertising self-regulation.

(b) *Complying Parties*

he Code of Advertising Self-Regulation is binding for advertisers, agencies, consultants, all advertising media, and for anyone who has accepted the Code directly or through membership in an association, or by underwriting an advertising contract as described in point (d).

(c) *Obligations of Signatory Associations*

Signatory associations commit themselves to observe the rules of the Code and to have them accepted by their members, to make the decision of the Jury adequately known, and to adopt appropriate measures regarding those members who do not comply with or use to break the decisions of the Jury.

(d) *Clause of Acceptance*

In order to better ensure full compliance with the decisions of the Jury the sponsoring organizations undertake that their members insert in their contracts a special clause of acceptance of the Code and of the decisions of the Jury, including orders to publish such decisions.

(e) *Definitions*

In relation to the Code the term 'advertising' comprises any communication, institutional as well, having the objective of promoting sale of products or services regardless of the media used, as well as communications ruled in Title VI.

The term 'product' refers to anything that is the subject of the advertising communication and therefore also includes services, methods, treatment, and the like.

The term 'message' refers to any type of presentation of a product to the public and it is therefore also extended to the packaging presentation, and the like.

The term 'consumer' comprises any person the advertising message is addressed to or any person likely to receive it.

The Code of Self-Regulation does not consider the distribution of advertising material for teaching purposes as advertising, when the material is requested by private or public schools and when it is used under the control of teachers.

## Title I

### Rules of behaviour

### Art 1 Fairness in Advertising

Advertising must be honest, truthful and correct. It must avoid anything likely to discredit it.

### Art 2 Misleading Advertising

Advertising must avoid any statement or representation likely to mislead consumers, even by means of omissions, ambiguity or exaggeration that are not obviously hyperbolical, particularly regarding the characteristics and effects of the product, its price, any free offer, its conditions of sale, its distribution, the identity of persons shown, prizes or awards.

### Art 3 Terminology, Quotations, Technical and Scientific Tests, Statistical Data

Terms, quotations and references to scientific and technical tests must be used in an appropriate manner. Technical and scientific tests and statistical data with limited validity must not be presented in such a way as to make them appear generally valid.

### Art 4 Testimonials

Testimonials must be authentic, responsible and verifiable.

### Art 5 Guarantees

Mandatory guarantees cannot be advertised in such a way as to lead to believe that their contents are wider or different. Should wider or different guarantees to the mandatory ones be advertised, such advertising must specify contents and conditions of the proposed guarantee, or alternatively a concise, yet meaningful information thereof together with a contextual reference to the written sources of information available at the sale point or together with the product.

### Art 6 Substantiation of the Truth of the Message

Whoever makes use of advertising must be able to substantiate, at the request of the Jury or of the Advertising Review Board, the truthfulness of the data, descriptions, statements, illustrations and testimonials used.

### Art 7 Identification of Advertising

Advertising must always be recognisable as such. In those media in which information and other contents are presented to the public together with advertising, the advertising must be made distinguishable as such by appropriate means.

### Art 8 Superstition, Credulity, Fear

Advertising must avoid in every form the exploitation of superstition and credulousness and, except in justifiable cases, of fear.

### Art 9 Violence, Vulgarity, Indecency

Advertising must not contain statements or representations of physical or moral violence or such which can be considered indecent, vulgar or repugnant according to the good state and sensibility of consumers.

### Art 10 Moral, Civil, and Religious Beliefs and Human Dignity

Advertising must not offend the moral, civil and religious beliefs of citizens.

Advertising must respect human dignity in all its forms and expressions.

### Art 11 Children and Adolescents

Particular care must be taken in advertising messages addressed to children and adolescents or which could be received by them.

These messages must not contain anything which might damage them psychologically, morally or physically and, further, should not take advantage of their natural credulity, inexperience or sense of loyalty. In particular, this advertising must not induce children and adolescents to:

– violate rules of generally established social behaviour;
– act dangerously or expose themselves to dangerous situations;
– believe that lack of ownership of the advertised product means either inferiority or parents' failure to fulfil their duties;
– solicit other people to purchase the advertised product.

The use of children and adolescents in advertising messages must avoid the exploitation of adults' natural sentiments regarding the young.

### Art 12 Health, Safety and Environment

The advertising of products likely to present dangers, particularly to health, safety and environment, must indicate them clearly, mainly when such dangers cannot be easily recognised.

In any case advertising should not contain descriptions or representations likely to cause consumers to neglect normal safety procedures nor to relax their sense of watchfulness and responsibility towards their health and safety, and that of others.

### Art 13 Imitation, Confusion and Exploitation

Any advertising that copies or imitates slavishly must be avoided even if relating to non-competitive products, particularly if likely to create confusion with other advertising.

In addition, any exploitation of the name, trademark or notoriety of others must be avoided, if intended to generate an undue advantage.

### Art 14 Denigration

The denigration of others' activities, companies or products, even if not specifically mentioned, is prohibited.

### Art 15 Comparison

Indirect comparison is allowed to illustrate the technical and economic aspects of objectively relevant and verifiable advantages and characteristics of advertised goods and services.

### Art 16 Variability

A message which is acceptable for a certain medium or a certain product is not necessarily acceptable for others, in consideration of the different characteristics of the various advertising media and the various products.

In the cases indicated in Articles 17, 18, 21, 27, 28 and 46, messages not containing all the information required therein are permitted when messages are limited to general statements.

Compliance of advertising with the rules of the Code does not exclude the possibility of individual media to reject, on the basis of their own contractual autonomy, any advertising which may not comply with their own more stringent criteria for the acceptance of advertising.

### Title II

### Special rules

### (A) Sales Systems

### Art 17 Sales on Credit

Advertising relating to sales on credit must indicate clearly the amount of the initial down payment and the following installments, the interest rates and other charges, and the total cost of the product. In particular, it should specify conditions of ownership and property, as well as leasing or rent with redemption rights.

### Art 18 Distance selling

Advertising relating to distance selling sales must clearly describe the products offered for sale, prices, payment and delivery conditions as well as cancellation or return clauses when applicable.

It must also clearly indicate the full name and address of the advertiser.

### Art 19 Unsolicited Supply of Goods

Advertising is forbidden which aims at obliging the recipient of unsolicited goods to pay should he not refuse the products supplied or should he fail to return them to the supplier.

### Art 20 Special Sales

Advertising relating to special sales, and in particular to promotional sales, must clearly specify in what is the favourable purchasing opportunity, as well as the expiration of the offer. This last indication is not required on the packaging.

### Art 21 Promotional Activities

Promotional advertising, either contests or premium operations, must let the public be aware clearly and easily of the conditions of participation, expiry dates and prizes, as well as – as far as contests are concerned – number and value of the prizes, award conditions, and media where the results are announced.

### (B) Product categories

### Art 22  Alcoholic Beverages

The advertising of alcoholic beverages must not be in contrast with the need of providing models of consumption which project moderation, correctness and responsibility.

Advertising must particularly avoid:

- encouraging an immoderate and uncontrolled, and hence detrimental, consumption of alcoholic beverages;
- representing situations of unhealthy attachment to the product, and generally of addiction to alcohol;
- addressing or representing minors, even if indirectly;
- associating the consumption of alcoholic beverages with driving of vehicles;
- making the public believe that consumption of alcoholic beverages promotes clearness of mind and physical efficiency, or that the non-use of the product leads to physical, psychological or social inferiority;
- inducing the public to disregard the different ways of using the product that must be considered depending on the specific characteristics of individual products and on the personal conditions of the consumer;
- indicating the alcoholic content of a beverage as the principal topic of the advertising.

### Art 23  Cosmetics and Personal Hygiene Products

Advertising relating to cosmetics and personal hygiene products must not lead the consumer to believe that such products have characteristics, properties and functions other than that of being applied to skin, mouth or teeth for the exclusive or primary purpose of cleaning them, deodorizing them, perfuming them, correcting their appearance or protecting them, in order to keep them in good condition.

Such advertising, therefore, may present these products as having additional characteristics which prevent particular pathological conditions, provided that they actually contain ad hoc specific ingredients or formulations; under no circumstances, however, should this kind of advertising lead consumers to consider cosmetic or personal hygiene products as substitutes for medicines, medical aids or therapeutic treatments.

### Art 23 *bis* Food supplementers and Dietetic Products

Advertising of food supplementers and dietetic products must not claim properties which do not correspond to the real specific characteristics of the products, or not really possessed by them. Furthermore, such advertising must be produced in such a manner as not to lead consumers into nutritional error and must avoid reference to recommendations or statements of medical nature.

These rules also apply to infant formula and baby food, to products which wholly or partially substitute mother's milk, to products used in the weaning period and to children's dietetic supplements.

### Art 24 Physical and Aesthetic Treatments

Advertising relating to physical and aesthetic treatment must not lead consumers to believe that such treatment has a therapeutic and restorative function, or is able to achieve radical results, and must avoid reference to recommendations or statements of medical nature.

### Art 25 Medicinal Products and Curative Treatments

Advertising of medicinal products and curative treatments must take into consideration the sensitiveness of the matter and be made with the utmost sense of responsibility as well as in compliance with the technical summary of product characteristics.

Such advertising must draw consumer attention to the need of appropriate cautions in using the product, encouraging in a explicit and clear way the reading of the package warnings and advising against incorrect use of the product itself.

Specifically, advertising of over-the-counter products to consumers must include the denomination of the medicinal product as well as the common name of the active ingredient; this latter information being not compulsory if the medicinal product contains more than one active ingredient or the advertising is intended solely as a generic reminder of the product denomination.

Advertising of over-the-counter medicinal products and curative treatments must avoid:

- suggesting that the efficacy of the medicine is unaccompanied by side effects or that its safety or efficacy are due to the fact that it is a natural substance;

- claiming that the efficacy of the medicine or the treatment is equal to or better than others;
- suggesting that a medical consultation or surgical operation is unnecessary or inducing to erroneous self diagnosis;
- being addressed exclusively or principally to children or inducing minors to a use of the product without appropriate supervision;
- making use of a recommendation by scientists, health professionals or persons well-known to the public, or of the fact that the medicinal product has been granted a marketing authorisation or referring in improper or misleading terms to claims of recovery;
- comparing the medicinal product with a foodstuff, cosmetic or other consumer product;
- suggesting that the medicinale or the curative treatment can improve normal good health or the effects of avoiding a product or a treatment can be prejudicial, unless this refers to vaccination campaigns;
- using in improper, misleading or appaling ways representations of changes in the human body caused by disease or injury, or of the action of a medicinal product.

### Art 26 Instruction Courses and Study or Teaching Methods

Advertising relating to instruction courses and study or teaching methods must not contain any promise of work nor exaggerate employment or salary opportunities for those persons who follow such courses or adopt the proposed methods, neither must it offer degrees or qualifications which are not recognised or are not obtainable by such means.

### Art 27 Financial and real estate transactions

Advertising aimed at soliciting or promoting financial transactions and in particular transactions for savings and investments on movable or real estate property must supply clear and exhaustive information in order not to mislead on the promoter, the nature of the proposal, the quantity and characteristics of the goods or services being offered, the terms of the transaction, the relevant risks, so that those who receive the message, though they are inexperienced in this field, can make conscious choices about the use of their own resources.

In particular, such advertising:

(a) must avoid, when referring to yearly interest rates, making use of terms like 'income' and 'return' meant as a sum of unearned income and increase in property values;

(b) must refrain from inducing to take commitments and make advance payments without appropriate guarantees;

(c) must not present past performance as valid for the future; must not claim returns obtained by computing over periods that are not sufficiently representative with reference to the particular nature of the investment and to the fluctuations in results.

Advertising for real estate transactions must be set out in such a way to avoid deceptiveness by mistaking movable investments for real estate investments or by favouring the economics of a real estate without informing adequately that the nature of the investment is actually on movables.

The provisions of this article apply also to advertising of bank and insurance services; for these latter services if there is a need to highlight that it is an investment.

### Art 28 Package Tour

Advertising of any form relating to package tours must give complete and accurate information, particularly with reference to the services included in the minimum price for participation. The message must emphasise a suggestion to carefully consider the conditions of participation, payment and cancellation reported in the informative material or in the registration form.

### Art 28 *bis* Games, Toys and Educational Products for Children

Advertising for games, toys and educational products for children must not mislead:

– in the nature, performance and dimensions of the advertised product;
– on the degree of ability needed in order to use the product;
– on the amount of the expenditure, especially when the purchase of complementary products is needed to make the product work.

In any case, this advertising must not minimise product price or imply that its purchase is normally compatible with any family budget.

### Title III

### Bodies and areas of responsibility

### Art 29 Composition of the Jury

The Jury is composed of a number of members from nine to fifteen, designated by the Istituto dell'Autodisciplina Pubblicitaria, and chosen from among experts in law, consumer problems, and advertising communications.

The members of the Jury remain in office for a two-year term and can be reconfirmed.

The Istituto dell'Autodisciplina Pubblicitaria appoints from among the Jury members the President and two Vice-Presidents who stand in for the President in his absence.

The members of the Jury cannot be chosen from among experts who practice their professional activities in advertising self-regulation matters.

### Art 30 Composition of the Advertising Review Board

The Advertising Review Board is made up of from ten to fifteen members appointed by the Istituto dell'Autodisciplina Pubblicitaria and selected among experts in consumer problems, advertising technique, communication media and legal matters.

The members of the Board remain in office for a two-year term and can be reconfirmed.

The members cannot be chosen from among experts who practice their professional activities in advertising self-regulation matters. The IAP appoints from among the Board members the President and the Vice-Presidents.

The Board can act divided into working sections of at least three members, each section chaired by the President or a Vice-President.

### Art 31 Principles of Judgment

The members of the Jury and of the Advertising Review Board carry out their duties according to their own free convictions and not in the representation of interest of classes of subscribers to the Code.

In the execution of their task the members of the Jury and of the Board are expected to observe the utmost discretion.

### Art 32 Function of the Jury and of the Advertising Review Board

The Jury examines the advertising submitted to it and judges it according to the Code of Advertising Self-Regulation.

In disputes where the interests of consumers are not involved, the Jury, at the mutually agreed request of the parties, can constitute itself as a court of arbitration and decide the dispute with an award. The President of the Jury decides the procedure to be adopted on a case-by-case basis.

The Advertising Review Board:

– submits to the Jury autonomously also on the grounds of indications received, cases of advertising which it considers not to comply with the rules of the Code protecting the interests of consumers or of advertising in general;

– expresses consulting opinions at the request of the President of the Jury;

– may request for prevention modifications to advertising which appears to be in conflict with the rules of the Code;

– can issue a desist order, according to Article 39;

– can provide an advance opinion, at the request of an interested party, on whether the final but not yet publicised advertising submitted to it conforms to the rules of the Code protecting the interests of consumers. The opinion is expressed based on the validity and completeness of the data and information supplied by the requesting party. Under these conditions, approval binds the Board to not intervene against the approved advertising. The Parties in the interest of whom an advance opinion has been given must refrain from any exploitation of said opinion for advertising purposes.

At any time, the Jury and the Review Board can ask the advertiser to supply documentation in support of the truthfulness of the data, descriptions, statements, illustrations and testimonials used.

The Jury and the Board may avail themselves of experts for the evaluation of the documentation produced.

Apart from what is set out in the present Code, the Jury and the Board carry out their function without formalities.

### Art 33 Secretariat

The Secretariat of the Istituto dell'Autodisciplina Pubblicitaria also performs the secretarial work for the Jury and the Advertising Review Board.

The Secretariat certifies the existence of a case pending at the Jury and, on request of those who may have an interest, issues a written statement of it.

### Art 34 Location and Meetings

The Jury, the Advertising Review Board and the Secretarial Office are located in the offices of the Istituto dell'Autodisciplina Pubblicitaria.

The Jury and the Review Board with its sections meet whenever it is required. The meetings are called by their respective Presidents with at least a three days advance notice. Such notice may be reduced in case of extreme urgency. The meetings of the Jury and of the Review Board are not held in open court.

The Jury is validly constituted with the presence of at least three members; the Review Board, in plenary session, with at least five members.

In the absence of the President and the Vice-Presidents, the meeting is chaired by the senior member in age. The Jury and the Review Board, the latter when a plenary session takes place, make decisions based on the majority vote of the members present. In the case of a tied vote, the President of the meeting casts the deciding vote.

Decisions in the Sections of the Board must be taken unanimously; if unanimity is not possible, decisions are delegated to a plenary session of the Board. The Sections of the Board are validly constituted with the presence of a least three members.

During the course of their meetings the Jury and the Board are assisted by an official from the Secretariat who is sworn to secrecy and who leaves the meeting during the resolutions of the Jury.

### Art 35 Administration

Administrative rules concerning petitions are decided by the Istituto dell'Autodisciplina Pubblicitaria.

### Title IV

### Procedural rules and sanctions

### Art 36 Petitions to the Jury and to the Review Board

Anyone who believes he has suffered prejudice from advertising activities contrary to the Code may request the intervention of the Jury against those who, having accepted the Code in one of the forms set out in the preliminary and general rules, have undertaken the activities alleged to have caused damage to the petitioner.

The interested party must submit a written request containing a description of the advertising which is being submitted to the Jury, the reasons for such request and the supporting documentation.

Petitions for Jury's action including those for arbitration must be addressed to the President of the Jury; those for advance opinion must be addressed to the President of the Review Board.

### Art 37 Procedure Before the Jury

Upon receipt of a petition, the President appoints a referee from among the members of the Jury, arranges for copies of the petition to be sent to the parties concerned, assigns them a time limit, not less than eight nor more than twelve clear working days, for the filing of possible comments and documents, and convenes them before the Jury within the shortest possible time for the verbal discussion of the dispute, which focuses primarily on those aspects which could not be treated in writing.

A specially delegated member of the Review Board participates in the discussion.

In procedures originated by interested parties the President of the Jury may request a written opinion from the Review Board, in which case a time limit is set for its response.

At the end of the discussion, the Jury:

(a) will issue its decision, if it considers the case sufficiently debated.

(b) If it should consider it necessary to acquire additional evidence, will refer the available material to the referee who will arrange immediately and without formality to obtain further evidence and documentation. This being done, he will submit the material to the Jury for the resumption of the case.

(c) If during the proceedings new facts emerge likely to constitute violation of the Code not considered in the petition, will acknowledge, notify and judge suo officio said facts unless further investigation is ordered.

At any time during the proceedings the Jury may ask, without formality, for the opinion of the Review Board on any matter.

The interested parties may be assisted or represented by their lawyers or consultants in front of the Jury.

### Art 38  Decision of the Jury

At the end of the discussion the Jury renders its decision. A summary of the findings is immediately communicated to the interested parties.

When the decision establishes that the advertising is contrary to the rules of the Code, the Jury orders that the interested parties refrain from using it.

In the summary of the decision, information on the censured aspects of the advertising can be provided, if necessary.

Within ten days of its decision, the Jury deposits its verdict with the Secretariat which than sends copies to the parties and to the other interested organizations.

The Jury's decisions are unappealable.

### Art 39 Desist Order

Should any advertising submitted for examination appear to clearly violate one or more articles of the Code of Advertising Self-Regulation, the President of the Review Board can order it to be discontinued by the advertiser.

The order, accompanied by a summary of the reasons that justify such decision, is communicated to the parties concerned by the Secretariat, together with the notice that each party may appeal the decision stating reasons for opposition before the Review Board within a maximum term of ten days.

Failure to file opposition or to respect the prescribed term for appeal or to state reasons for opposition is ascertained by the President of the Review Board. In such cases the order becomes final. The Secretariat certifies the enforceability of the decision which is then communicated to the parties concerned for compliance.

Should there be any grounded opposition within the prescribed term the order will be revoked. The President of the Review Board, having considered facts and reasons alleged by the parties, may decide, after having heard the Board, that the order is revoked and the case is filed. The parties are informed of the President's decision.

On the contrary should the Review Board hold that the reasons for opposition are not convincing, the file is handed over to the President of the Jury with the rationale of the Board's decision. Should even the President of the Jury hold that the reasons for opposition are not convincing, the file is sent back to the President of the Review Board who acts according to the preceding third paragraph. On the contrary the President of the Jury who holds it appropriate that the Jury takes a decision upon provides that the proceeding should continue according to the ordinary procedure; in such a case the order is revoked.

### Art 40 Publication of the Decisions

Extracts of all decisions are published by the Secretariat in the bulletin of the Istituto dell'Autodisciplina Pubblicitaria with the names of the parties concerned.

The Jury may order that abstracts of decisions be disclosed to the public by the Istituto, also with the name of the interested parties under the terms and in media that are deemed appropriate.

The extract is prepared by the referee and signed by the President. The parties concerned cannot use the decision for advertising purposes.

### Art 41 Binding Effect of the Decision of the Jury

The advertising media which directly or through their Associations have accepted the Code of Advertising Self-Regulation, even if they were not involved with the proceedings before the Jury, are obliged to observe its decisions.

### Art 42  Non-Observance of Decisions

Should compliance with the decisions of the Jury or of the Advertising Review Board be refused, the Jury orders to the Istituto dell'Autodisciplina Pubblicitaria that public notice of such uncompliance be given through communication media specified by the Jury itself.

### Title V

### Protection of advertising ideas

### Art 43  Advertising Projects

Advertisers who in consideration of a future assignment of their advertising budget ask an advertising agency or a professional consultant to present, in the framework of a bidding or a series of selecting contacts, one or more creative projects, shall refrain from using or imitating creative and inventive aspects of the project(s) rejected or not selected for a three-year term as from the filing date of such material with the Secretarial Office of the Istituto dell'Autodisciplina Pubblicitaria, such material being filed in a sealed envelope by the advertising agency or professional consultant concerned.

### Art 44 Protective aids

For the protection of advertising ideas, isolated aids used in anticipation of and for protection of a campaign must be filed and published in compliance with the rules of the Istituto dell'Autodisciplina Pubblicitaria. The filings are published in the IAP bulletin. The protection is valid for a twelve-month period, on print ads. and a eighteen-month period for audio visual ads starting from the date of publication.

### Art 45 Advertising carried out abroad

Advertisers wishing to protect from possible imitation in Italy advertising they have carried out abroad, can file copies of such advertising with the Secretarial Office of the Istituto dell'Autodisciplina Pubblicitaria.

The filing confers a priority right valid for a period of five years from the date of filing.

### Title VI

### Social advertising

### Art 46  Appeals to the Public

Messages aimed at soliciting, directly or indirectly, a voluntary contribution of money, goods or services of any kind, in the framework of initiatives designed to generate awareness in the public about the achievement of objects, specific too, of general and social interest are subject to the rules of this Code. To allow a clear understanding and easy identification, such messages must include name and address of the promoter as well as the social objective that should be achieved. If social advertising is linked with initiatives of commercial promotion, the amount or the percentage intended for the social cause must be specified.

Promoters of such messages can freely express their opinions but must specify, in a clear way, that these are opinions of promoters and are not verified facts.

In any case such message cannot:

(a) exploit inappropriately the human misery by hurting the dignity of the human being; resort to shocking calls that can generate unwarranted claim, feeling of fear, or serious anxiety;

(b) make those who don't agree to the appeal feel guilty or liable;

(c) make direct comparison with other social campaigns;

(d) present in an exaggerate way the degree and the nature of the social problem for which the appeal was made;

(e) overestimate the specific or potential value of the contribution from the public to the initiative;

(f) solicit money offers from minors.

The above rules must be observed, to the applicable extent, also for messages of social advertising different from those specified herein.

## CHAPTER 11

# LUXEMBOURG

*Alex Schmitt*

## INTRODUCTION

### Forms of advertising

In Luxembourg, the different forms of advertising fall into three main categories:

(a) television broadcasting (Arts 26 and 28 of the Law of 27 July 1991);

(b) radio (RGD 13 February 1992 and Art 7 of the Law of 27 July 1991);

(c) billposting and hoardings (RGD 4 June 1984 and Law of 18 July 1983).

#### *Television*

Television advertising is defined as any type of broadcast message paid for by a public or a private undertaking in order to promote the supply of goods and services, including immovable property, rights and obligations. The regulations prohibit clandestine and comparative advertising, although there is currently a debate on whether comparative advertising is acceptable or not. In France, for instance, it is a burning issue, as some people think that this type of advertising promotes competition between traders. Nevertheless, comparative advertising is still prohibited in both Luxembourg and France.

The duration and the frequency of advertising spots are controlled. For instance, the broadcasting of works such as films made for television can be interrupted once in every 45 minute period, on condition that the programme is longer than 45 minutes in duration. However, another interruption is permitted if the programme's scheduled duration is at least 20 minutes longer than two or more complete 45 minute periods.

Any television news, documentaries, religious broadcasts or broadcasts for children, whose duration is less than 30 minutes, may not be interrupted by advertising.

The content of advertising shall not be prejudicial to the respect of human rights, or make any discrimination in consideration of race, sex, nationality, political or religious convictions.

Any advertising of tobacco or tobacco products is prohibited.

Television advertising for medicines and medical treatments, which are only available under medical prescription, is forbidden.

Any advertising for alcoholic drinks is subject to strict conditions; for instance, it cannot be targeted at minors or associate the consumption of alcohol with the improvement of physical or sexual performance. This type of advertising must neither suggest that alcoholic drinks have a medicinal effect, nor must it encourage immoderate consumption of alcohol.

Where minors and children are the targets of the advertising spots, the advertisers must not take unfair advantage of their inexperience and credulity.

With regard to sponsored programmes, sponsors must respect certain requirements, for example, the elements of sponsored programmes must be clearly identified by the name or logo of the sponsor at the beginning and/or the end of the elements of the programme. A sponsor is not permitted, under any circumstances, to interfere with the independence and responsibilities of the operator with regard to the content and programming of any element of a sponsored programme. Luxembourg law prohibits the sponsoring of broadcasts such as television news and political debates.

The time allocated for advertising may not exceed 15% of the daily broadcasting time, but, under certain conditions, it can reach 20%. The time allocated for advertising spots inside any one hour period shall not exceed 20%, and offers made directly to the public in order to sell or buy products or supply services cannot exceed one hour per day.

### Radio

Luxembourg provisions are not particularly exhaustive.

Local radio programmes may contain advertising messages under certain conditions provided in Art 1 of the relevant grand-ducal regulation; for instance, the time allocated for advertising may not be more than 10% per trader, firm or group of firms.

The same article provides that advertising messages are limited to an average of six minutes per hour broadcast in one day, as well as to a maximum of eight minutes in any specific hour of the day.

The marketing of advertising messages in local radio programmes can only be made by the authorised operator itself. It may not be handled by a State agency, a private advertising firm or any other professional.

Advertising income can neither exceed the programme's costs, including depreciation of the transmitter and other technical equipment, nor the amount of LFr 500,000 per annum.

## Billposting and hoardings

In this section, 'advertisement' means any optical device set up for the purposes of advertising, whatever the object of the advertisement or the location of the device. The principle of the law is that an advertisement can only be placed on the main facades of a building occupied by the business, or having a direct relation to the object of the advertisement.

The law provides some conditions concerning format, whether the advertisement is placed flat or projects from the building:

(a) if flat, a firm's sign or advertisement can neither exceed 1.5 m2 nor protrude beyond the edges of the facade;

(b) if a flat sign is made with letters with cut outlines (that is, each letter protruding independently), the surface limit is increased to 2.5 m2, on condition that the letters do not each exceed 30 cm in height and are indirectly illuminated;

(c) if the advertisement projects from the building, it must be less than 1.2 m from the facade and shall neither protrude beyond the upper edge nor have edges exceeding 0.5 m;

(d) without prejudice to these provisions, the whole advertising surface, whether flat or projecting, cannot exceed, frame included, 1.5 m2 per facade.

Each firm can have a sign on each main facade. Only one advertisement for each object is permitted.

For an advertisement on an immobile object other than a house, authorisation from the Secretary of State for Culture is required.

# Specific restrictions on tobacco advertising

Like many other countries, Luxembourg has adopted a specific regulation concerning tobacco advertising and any other products derived from tobacco: the Law of 24 March 1989. This Law implements the European rules in this matter and is reproduced below, pp 668–70.

The principle contained in this Law is that any advertising of tobacco and its products is forbidden, as is smoking, in some areas.

Tobacco products are regarded as those intended for smoking, chewing or snuff, as long as they are made of tobacco.

Article 3 of this Law is very exhaustive and provides, for instance, that it is forbidden to advertise tobacco on radio or television, on handbills, on stickers, signs, etc. However, the simple indication on a hoarding of the name of the product, so long as it is not surrounded with text or graphics, is permitted in stadia, in public or private sports grounds and in swimming pools.

However, it is permitted to promote tobacco and its products inside a tobacconist's, and also in pubs or clubs. This Law does not regard as advertising the simple indication, on a commercial vehicle delivering tobacco, of the name of the product, its composition, and the name and address of the manufacturer or the distributor.

The above-mentioned Law tolerates tobacco advertising in newspapers or on hoardings under three conditions:

(a) the advertising message cannot be targeted at minors;

(b) health considerations cannot be suggested;

(c) advertising cannot contain any representation of famous personalities known to the public.

It is forbidden to advertise tobacco in magazines for minors, and producers, manufacturers and traders of tobacco or its products cannot sponsor meetings designed for children and minors. As a consequence, in order to protect minors, educational information relating to tobacco will be taught at school.

A special health warning must be written on each unit of tobacco or its products.

The Grand-Duc is entitled to determine the rules relating to this warning, which must, at least, indicate the grade of toxic substances released by combustion, and the maximum grade of tar and other toxic substances contained in cigarettes.

In any case, this warning must be visible and legible and should not be hidden, masked or interrupted by another message or picture.

## Example of a code of practice: advertising by law firms

The example of the advertising rules in the legal profession will be of interest. This code is very strict and is particularly respected. Two main regulations apply: the Circular of 15 June 1987 and Art 36 of the Law of 10 August 1991.

## Independent bodies concerned with media advertising

The Law of 27 July 1991 describes these bodies. To join, please contact the Fonds National de l'Audiovisuel 5 or the Secretary of State for the Culture (see Appendix 1, 'Useful Addresses').

# RESTRICTIONS ON ADVERTISING

## Rules restricting advertising on television

The relevant regulation is the Law of 27 July 1991 on electronic media. Article 26 of this Law defines television advertising:

### Article 26(4)

Television advertising is any type of broadcast message paid for by a public or private undertaking and made as part of a commercial, industrial, or craft activity in order to promote the supply of goods, including property, services, rights and obligations.

### Article 26(5)

Clandestine advertising is the verbal or visual representation of goods, services or the name, trade mark or activities of a supplier of goods or a provider of a service in parts of a programme, if it is made intentionally for advertising purposes and may mislead the public as to its real nature. A representation is considered intentional if, for instance, it is made in exchange for payment or any similar consideration.

Article 28 of this Law enumerates all the restrictive rules applicable on television advertising:

### Article 28

(1) Television advertising shall be easily identifiable as such and shall be distinguished from the rest of the programme by optical or acoustic means.

(2) Isolated advertising spots shall be exceptional.

(3) Advertising shall not use subliminal techniques.

(4) Clandestine advertising is forbidden.

(5) Advertisements shall be inserted between elements of the programme. Except as provided in paras (6) and (9) hereafter, advertisements may also be inserted during programmes in such a way that the integrity and value of the programme taking into account natural breaks in and the duration and nature of the programme and the rights of the rights holders are not prejudiced.

(6) In programmes consisting of autonomous parts, or in sports programmes and similarly structured events and performances comprising intervals, advertisements shall only be inserted between the parts or in the intervals.

(7) The broadcasting of works such as full-length films and films made for television (with the exception of series, serials, or documentaries), provided their programmed duration is more than 45 minutes, may be interrupted once for each complete period of 45 minutes. A further interruption is allowed if their programmed duration is at least 20 minutes longer than two or more complete periods of 45 minutes.

(8) When the elements of programmes other than the ones described at para (6) are interrupted by advertising, at least 20 minutes should elapse between each successive interruption inside the elements of the programme.

(9) Advertising may not be inserted into religious broadcasts. Television news, news magazines, documentaries, religious broadcasts and broadcasts for children, whose scheduled duration is less than 30 minutes, may not be interrupted by advertising.

When their scheduled duration is at least 30 minutes, the provisions of the previous paragraph apply.

(10) Television advertising shall not:

(a) be prejudicial to the respect of human dignity;

(b) make any discrimination in consideration of race, sex or nationality;

(c) make an attempt on religious or political convictions;

(d) encourage behaviour prejudicial to security and health;

(e) encourage behaviour prejudicial to the protection of the environment.

(11) Any form of television advertising for cigarettes and other tobacco products is forbidden.

(12) Television advertising for medicines and medical treatments which, in the Grand-Duchy, are only available under medical prescription, is forbidden.

(13) Television advertising for alcoholic drinks shall meet the following criteria:

(a) it shall not be targeted at minors or, in particular, show minors drinking alcohol;

(b) it shall not associate the consumption of alcohol with the improvement of physical performance or with car driving;

(c) it shall not imply that the consumption of alcohol improves social success or sexual performance;

(d) it shall not suggest that alcoholic drinks have medical, stimulating or sedative effects;

(e) it shall not encourage the immoderate consumption of alcoholic drink or portray abstinence in a bad light;

(f) it shall not stress the strength of alcoholic drinks as a positive quality.

(14) Television advertising shall not be prejudicial to minors and thus it shall meet the following criteria for their protection:

(a) it shall not directly incite minors to buy a product or service by taking unfair advantage of their inexperience or their credulity;

(b) it shall not directly incite minors to persuade their parents or third parties to buy the products or services concerned;

(c) it shall not take advantage of the confidence that the minors have in their parents, teachers or other persons;

(d) it shall not, without reason, present minors in a situation of danger.

(15) The elements of sponsored programmes shall meet the following requirements:

    (a) a sponsor is not permitted, under any circumstances, to interfere with the independence and responsibilities of the operator with regard to the content and programming of any element of a sponsored programme;

    (b) they shall be clearly identified by the name and/or the logo of the sponsor at the beginning and/or at the end of the elements of the programme;

    (c) they shall not incite the purchase or rent of the sponsor's products or services, or the products and services of a third party, particularly by making special offers for those products or services.

(16) The elements of a programme cannot be sponsored by individuals or legal entities who have as principal activity the manufacture or sale of products or the supply of services for which advertising is forbidden pursuant to paras (11) and (12).

(17) Television news and political broadcasts cannot be sponsored.

(18) The time allocated for advertising shall not exceed 15% of the daily broadcasting time. However, this percentage can reach 20% if it includes offers made directly to the public in order to sell, buy or rent products, or to supply services, on condition that the volume of the advertising spots does not go beyond 15%.

(19) The time allocated for advertising spots inside any one hour period shall not exceed 20%.

(20) Without prejudice to the provisions of para (18), offers made directly to the public in order to sell, buy or rent products, or to supply services, shall not exceed one hour per day.

## Rules restricting advertising on radio

Article 7 of the Law of 27 July 1991 describes the content of radio advertising:

### Article 7(1)

Luxembourg radio programmes can contain advertising messages as long as this law, its implementations and specifications do not provide any prohibition or limitation.

The Grand-ducal Regulation of 13 February 1992 makes the following provisions concerning advertising in programmes broadcast by local radio stations:

### Article 1

Programmes of the local radio stations described in Art 17 of the Law of 27 July 1991 relating to electronic media are authorised to contain advertising messages to the following extent:

(a) the advertising income can neither exceed the programme's costs, including the depreciation of the transmitter and other technical equipment, nor the amount of Lfr 500,000 per annum;

(b) the time allocated for advertising cannot be more than 10% per trader, firm or group of firms;

(c) advertising messages are limited to an average of six minutes per hour broadcast in one day, as well as to a maximum of eight minutes in any specific hour of the day.

### Article 2

The marketing of advertising messages in local radio programmes can only be made by the authorised operator itself. It may not be handled by a State agency, a private advertising firm or any other professional.

### Article 3

If the local radio operator has declared, at the time of its application for a broadcasting licence, that it will not broadccast advertisements, it may not do so thereafter unless it obtains a new authorisation to this effect.

### Article 4

The amount stipulated at Art 1(a) can be adapted by grand-ducal regulation.

## Rules restricting advertising on hoardings

The Law of 18 July 1983 relating to the conservation and the protection of national sites and monuments provides the following:

### Article 37

According to the current law, 'advertisement' means any optical device set up in order to advertise, whatever the object of the advertisement or the location of the device, except for advertisements producing their effect exclusively towards the inside of a building.

The Grand-ducal Regulation of 4 June 1984 relating to Art 37 above provides for the following:

### Article 1

Advertising, whether illuminated or not, can only be installed on the main facades of the building occupied by the establishment, or having a direct relation with the object of the advertising.

### Article 2

If flat, a firm's sign or advertisement can neither exceed 1.5 m2 nor protrude beyond the edges of the facade.

## Article 3

If a flat sign is made with letters with cut outlines, the surface limit is increased to 2.5 m$^2$, on condition that the letters do not each exceed 30 cm in height and are indirectly illuminated.

## Article 4

If the advertisement projects from the building, it shall be less than 1.2 m$^2$ from the facade and shall neither protrude beyond the upper edge nor have edges exceeding 0.5 m$^2$.

## Article 5

When the advertisement, whether flat or projecting, has a frame of an artistic or historical nature, the surface of the frame is not included in these limits.

## Article 6

Without prejudice to the exceptions provided in Arts 3 and 5, the whole of the advertising surface, whether flat or projecting, cannot exceed, frame included, 1.5 m$^2$ per facade.

## Article 7

A sign, whether flat or projecting, can appear for each firm on each main facade.

## Article 8

Advertisements, whether flat or projecting, can only be installed on the main facade.

Only one advertisement is permitted for each object.

## Article 9

By special request to the Municipality, the Secretary of State for Culture can allow derogations to the above provisions under certain conditions [see paras (1)–(5) of this article for the conditions].

## Article 10

Any advertisement on an immobile object other than a house shall be authorised by the Secretary of State for Culture. This authorisation is granted on the recommendation of the Commission for National Sites and Monuments.

## Article 11

Any advertisement on a mobile object which is in reality used as an immobile object is prohibited.

## Article 12

In the areas designated at Art 13 below, and in the sites therein, any advertising pursuant to Art 37 of the Law of 18 July 1983 is subordinated to the authorisation of the Secretary of State for Culture.

This provision is also applicable to the advertisements referred to in Arts 1 and 2 of this regulation.

### Article 13

The provision of Art 12 applies to:

(1) areas listed below and in the sites therein:

Beaufort, Berdorf, Bourglinster ...;

(2) sectors protected by the city of Luxembourg as designated in the 'projet général d'aménagement' of 17 April 1967.

# SPECIFIC RESTRICTIONS FOR TOBACCO ADVERTISING

The Law of 24 March 1989 relating to the advertising of tobacco and its products, and the prohibition of smoking in some places, provides the following rules:

### Article 1

This law aims, in the interest of public health:

(a) to forbid or to restrict advertising of tobacco and its products; and

(b) to forbid smoking in some areas.

### Article 2

Tobacco products are regarded as those intended for smoking, chewing or snuff, as long as they are made, even in part, of tobacco.

### Article 3

No advertising of tobacco and its products can be done:

(1) using signs or advertisements in entertainment rooms or other public places;

(2) in radio or television broadcasts or recordings;

(3) on handbills, stickers or signs, whether illuminated or not. However, these provisions do not apply to advertising inside a tobacconist's or in pubs as mentioned in the Law of 12 August 1927 relating to clubs. These provisions also do not apply to signs indicating pubs, nor to those indicating the premises where products referred to in Art 1 are manufactured or stored. This article does not regard as advertising the simple indication, on a commercial vehicle delivering tobacco and its products, of the name of the product, its composition, the name and address of the manufacturer or the distributor, the graphic or photographic representation of the product, or its packing and mark;

(4) on aeroplanes or ships;

(5) by distributing samples of tobacco and its products;

(6) by using the trade mark or the name of the tobacco or its products, or by using any other representation which could refer to it on common articles other than the ones directly connected with the use of tobacco. This provision is not applicable to articles which were already on the market before the implementation of this law, under names, marks or signs similar to the ones of the tobacco and its products;

(7) in newspapers and magazines intended for minors;

(8) in stadia, public and private sports grounds and in swimming pools. However, this provision does not apply to the simple indication of the name of the product on a hoarding, so long as it is not surrounded with text or graphics.

### Article 4

Advertising of tobacco and its products in newspapers or on hoardings is subject to the following restrictions and conditions:

(1) the advertising message cannot be targeted at minors;

(2) health considerations cannot be suggested;

(3) advertising cannot contain any representation of famous personalities known to the public.

### Article 5

The Grand-Duc is entitled to determine, by means of grand-ducal regulation, rules relating to the health warning which must be written on each unit of tobacco or its products, indicating the grade of toxic substances released by combustion, and the maximum grade of tar and other toxic substances contained in cigarettes. This same regulation will provide the text of the health warning that every advertisement for tobacco and its products must contain. This warning must be visible and legible and should not be hidden, masked, or interrupted by another message or picture.

### Article 6

Advertising of tobacco and its products is forbidden during athletics meetings. However, this provision does not apply to a simple indication on a hoarding or a commercial vehicle, so long as it is not surrounded by text or graphics.

### Article 7

It is forbidden for producers, manufacturers and traders of tobacco or its products to sponsor meetings designed for children and minors; the promoters of such meetings must not accept such sponsorship.

### Article 8

Preventative and educational information must be taught at school.

### Article 9

[This article only deals with places where it is forbidden to smoke.]

**Article 10**

Infringements against the provisions of Chapter 1 of this Law, including those of the grand-ducal regulation referred to in Art 5, are punishable by a fine of Lfr 2,501 to 200,000. Infringements against the provisions of Chapter 2 of this Law are punishable by a fine of Lfr 250 to 2,500. In case of repetition of an offence within the two years following a definitive judgment, the fines referred to in this article can be doubled.

**Article 11**

In case of infringement against Arts 3, 4 and 6 and the grand-ducal regulation referred to in Art 5 of this Law, the following will be prosecuted as principal offenders:

(1) producers, manufacturers and traders of tobacco or tobacco products who produce illegal advertising or propaganda;

(2) advertising agents who have produced illegal advertising;

(3) the director of a theatre or other public place, in which a forbidden advertisement has been shown or broadcast;

(4) anyone who has agreed to affix an advertisement, hoarding or irregular sign on a building which he owns.

**Article 12**

The provisions of Arts 3, 5 and 6 become effective only after a period of two years since the publication of this Law in the Memorial.

**Article 13**

Any propaganda or advertising made in compliance with a contract signed before the implementation of this Law is still valid until the term stipulated in the contract, unless this term exceeds two years after the publication of this law in the Memorial.

**Article 14**

The grand-ducal regulation taken in execution of Art 5 of this Law comes into effect after a period of two years since its publication in the Memorial.

# EXAMPLE OF A CODE OF PRACTICE: ADVERTISING BY LAW FIRMS

According to Art 36(2) of the Law of 10 August 1991 relating to the profession of lawyer, any prospecting or canvassing by lawyers is forbidden.

A professional circular of the Luxembourg Bar, dated 15 June 1987, explains the code of conduct concerning advertising by lawyers:

The main principles of this code are as follows:

(a) any individual advertising is forbidden;

(b) any declaration describing the lawyer, his activities, his clients, his special lines of business and success is regarded as advertising;

(c) newly installed lawyers may publish, in one or more newspapers in Luxembourg, one notice indicating their name, professional address and phone number, and the name of the association to which they belong;

(d) lawyers may publish their new address in case of transfer of their chambers.

No authorisation from the Luxembourg Bar is needed for these types of publication.

## INDEPENDENT BODIES CONCERNED WITH MEDIA ADVERTISING

The Law of 27 July 1991 lists the different bodies and institutions who control media advertising.

Article 29(1) provides that in the government administration, attached to the Secretary of State for Culture, there is a special service called 'Service des médias et de l'audiovisuel'.

Article 30 stipulates that an independent commission for radio broadcasting is created, called 'Commission indépendante de la radiodiffusion'. According to Art 30(2), this Commission must check that legal provisions are followed.

Article 33 provides for the creation of a consultative commission for the media, called 'Commission consultative des médias'. This Commission represents the businesses, associations, and trade unions of the media sector in the government, especially in the field of the newspapers, television, radio, videotext, satellites and cable broadcasting.

## USEFUL ADDRESSES

Fonds National de l'Audiovisuel 5
route de Zoufftgen
L-3598 Dudelange
Tel: + 352 24 24 27/24 24 1

Ministère de la Culture
20 Montée de la Pétrusse
L-2912 Luxembourg

Ministère d'Etat
Service des Médias et de l'Audiovisuel
5 rue Large
L-1917 Luxembourg

Mediaport Luxembourg
5 rue Large
L-1917 Luxembourg
Tel: + 352 478 2176

Ministère d'Etat
Service Information et Presse
43 bd Roosevelt
L-2450 Luxembourg

## CHAPTER 12

# THE NETHERLANDS

*J Harmeling-de Maa*

## INTRODUCTION

There is a whole set of rules restricting advertising in The Netherlands. It is not always easy for advertisers to find their way through this jungle of rules, bodies and institutions to activity which is permissible. Below is an overview of Dutch advertising law, focusing on substantive standards which, incidentally, can be found in various sources of law applicable to advertising law. A distinction is made between general and more specific rules for advertising. The general rules apply, in principle, to all forms of advertising, regardless of the products or services offered. The scope of such general standards is that advertising may not be deceptive, derogatory or needlessly parasitic. Advertising may not, furthermore, be contrary to the standards of public decency and good taste. The specific rules in principle only apply to advertising for a certain product or service, or apply only to advertising through certain channels of communication or distribution. Examples of such specific standards are the special codes of practice of the Advertising Standards Authority (Reclame Code Commissie), such as the code for tobacco products. In addition to a discussion of the substantive rules of law, there is a survey of the various bodies and institutions, each of which maintains its own procedures, regulations and sanctions in enforcing the above standards.

## RULES RESTRICTING ADVERTISING AGENTS/COMPANIES FROM ENTERING INTO OR HOLDING LICENCES (FOREIGN AND DOMESTIC COMPANIES)

No establishment permit is required to set up an advertising agency in The Netherlands. After its incorporation (which should be recorded in a notarial instrument), however, the business should register with the Commercial Register. Various details should be registered, such as particulars of the agency's executive officers, powers of representation, and branch offices, if any.

Foreign companies which have their headquarters within the territory of the European Community are, by virtue of Art 52 of the EC Treaty, entitled to locate elsewhere in the Community in accordance with the provisions set for the subjects of the country of establishment. They may also set up a subsidiary, branch office or agency in another Member State of the Community.

Businesses which have their headquarters outside the Community may, by virtue of Art 58 of the EC Treaty, start a business in accordance with the law of one of the Member States. From that business, they may then incorporate subsidiaries and branch offices elsewhere in the Community.

## ADVERTISING LIMITS ON THE FREQUENCY OF COMMERCIALS AND ADVERTISING INTERRUPTIONS

The European advertising regime is based on the EC Directive on the co-ordination of certain provisions laid down by law, regulation or administrative action in Member States concerning the pursuit of television broadcasting activities (Television Without Frontiers Directive 89/552/EC, OJ L 298, 3.10.89, pp 23–30). In the EC Member States and, consequently, in The Netherlands, television advertising must comply with this Directive, which envisages, among other things, protection of the consumer against the growing commercial expressions in television programmes and promotion of the (transfrontier) trade in goods and services through over the air commercials.

At present there is a dual broadcasting system in The Netherlands, where public broadcasting organisations and privately owned commercial broadcasting organisations exist side by side. Other possibilities are public regional and local broadcasters. Both the public non-commercial and the private commercial broadcasting organisations are bound by rules of media law (the Media Act, Media Decree and directives issued by the Media Commission) with regard to commercials and other forms of advertising. Commercials are understood to mean:

Messages which unmistakably aim at inducing the general public to buy a certain product or to use a certain service or to win their favour towards a certain company, a branch of industry or a certain institution to promote the sale of products or services (Article 1 of the Media Act).

### Public national non-commercial broadcasting

In The Netherlands, the national public broadcasters are not permitted to transmit commercials (Art 52 of the Media Act), nor may their broadcasts contain forms of advertising which, although not envisaging a sales promoting effect, still convey such effect. Only if the form of advertising cannot be avoided, or is explicitly permitted, is such advertising allowed. Whether or not a form of advertising is avoidable is determined by the Media Commission (*Commissariaat voor de Media*) (see below, p 690), which evaluates the form of advertising against the law (Art 26 *et seq* of the Media Decree) and the aspects of policy issued by it.

The ratio of the advertising ban imposed on national public broadcasting organisations is that they have a service function for the viewers and listeners who are interested in a varied programme output. This viewpoint leaves no room for profit making, nor for servitude to profit making by third parties, nor for advertising.

Within the national public broadcasting system, the Radio and Television Advertising Association (Stichting Ether Reclame (STER)) has been given exclusive power to produce a programme consisting of advertising spots aimed at the Dutch consumer (Art 39 of the Media Act). Part of the revenue is earmarked for public national broadcasting.

Each year, the STER may use a yet to be established percentage of the total airtime. At present, the STER is entitled to about 6.5% of the total television airtime per year of the national broadcasting corporations. The STER is governed by strict standards: their airtime may not exceed 15% per day per channel, with a maximum of 12 minutes per clock hour.

In addition, the STER is bound by a strict interruption regime (Art 41a of the Media Act). Only programmes which consist of a (comprehensive) report of sports events, stage shows or similar shows or events may be interrupted, on condition that such breaks are scheduled in the natural intervals in the show or event and the body responsible for the programme in question does not object to the break.

## Public regional and local broadcasters

Since 1991, a separate advertising regime has applied to regional and local stations, which, before 1991, were also bound by the general advertising ban. Currently, these stations may exploit commercial airtime with the permission of the Media Commission. To do so, the stations must be a member of the Advertising Standards Organisation (Stichting Reclame Code) (see below, p 688 *et seq*). Otherwise, the same content related regulations apply as to the STER.

## Dutch commercial stations

Effective from mid-1992, national commercial stations have been allowed in The Netherlands.

The rules on advertising have been laid down in the Media Decree (Arts 52b–52f, 52j of the Media Decree) and are, to a great extent, based on the

Television Without Frontiers Directive: advertising messages should be recognisable as such, and commercials may make up 15% maximum of the daily airtime, with a maximum of 12 minutes per hour of programming.

The Media Act imposes a more stringent interruption regime on Dutch commercial stations than required by the EC Directive. Unlike the Directive's stipulations, religious programmes may not be interrupted, and news and children's programmes only on certain conditions. Commercial breaks should last at least two minutes and within one programme, a period of at least 20 minutes should elapse between each successive advertising break.

## CONTENTS BASED RESTRICTIONS (GOOD TASTE, TRUTH) AND PROHIBITIONS

### General standards

#### Misleading advertising

*Introduction*

Unlike most other EC Member States, Dutch legislation has incorporated special provisions about deceptive advertising in the Civil Code (CC). Sections 6:194–96 of the CC contain these provisions. They form a *lex specialis* of the general provision on tort (s 6:162). The reason is that the legislator believes the consumer should be protected against misleading statements.

By s 6:194 of the CC, statements about goods or services made professionally which are deceptive in one or more respects are tortious. Sections 6:194–96 do not cover religious, political or idealistic statements. In this area, deception should be evaluated against the general standard set out in s 6:162 of the CC.

Section 6:194 of the CC contains a non-exhaustive list of examples of misleading advertising. Statements can be misleading with regard to:

(a) the nature, composition, quantity, quality, properties or possibilities for use;

(b) the origin, manner or time of manufacture;

(c) the size of the stock;

(d) the price, or the way of calculating the price;

(e) the reason for the making of the offer;

(f) the awards granted, testimonials or other appraisals or statements made by third parties, or the scientific or professional terms used, technical inventions or statistical data;

(g) the conditions on which goods are supplied or services rendered or on which payment is to be made;

(h) the scope, content or duration of the warranty;

(i) the identity, qualities, skills or authority of the person by whom, under whose direction or supervision or with whose co-operation the goods have been or are manufactured or offered or the services are rendered;

(j) comparison with other goods or services.

In appraising whether advertising is misleading, a court of law will first examine whether the advertiser has observed the truth. In doing so, the court must consider the intelligence and conceptive faculty of the average audience which is aware of, but not influenced by, the fact that some exaggeration is inherent in advertising. In some cases, the target audience should be of concern. Advertising directed at children, for instance, should be appraised differently from that directed at a professional.

Any interested party may file a claim under s 6:194 of the CC, including consumer organisations and other interest groups.

By s 6:195 of the CC, anyone responsible for the content of the misleading statement should prove its accuracy and completeness, unless this would be unreasonable. The onus of proof, therefore, lies with the advertiser, the advertising agency or the medium which determined the content and presentation of the advertisement.

The court may prohibit misleading advertising on forfeiture of a penalty, award damages, and, by virtue of s 6:196 of the CC, order retraction. The prohibitory order and retraction do not require that the deceptive statement is attributable to the party making it.

The Advertising Standards Authority may, by virtue of Art 16 of the Dutch Advertising Code (*Nederlandse Reclame Code* (NRC)), evaluate such statements against the following criteria: breach of the law or truth, deception and imitation. The misleading statement must have been made in public, regardless of the manner of dissemination.

### Passing off or parasitic advertising

Dutch law defines passing off as: 'The profiting from the achievements of one or several specific competitors by using the achievements or reputation of those competitors to one's own advantage.' The literature and case law are based on the assumption that the profiting of the reputation and goodwill of a competitor in itself is not unlawful, not even if it prejudices the latter. The Supreme Court decided so in 1961 in the *Leesportefeuille* judgment. The Supreme Court held that tort only applies if additional conditions are met, such as risk of confusion, serious dilution, deception or derogatory effect.

Needless or excessive passing off is not permitted, however. Excessive passing off exists where insufficient proportionality is observed by the passer off between the advantage gained by him on the one hand and the damage inflicted on the other party on the other hand.

The same applies, *mutatis mutandis*, to passing off with regard to celebrities or institutions, provided that an additional condition could be the fact that, if the person portrayed had granted prior permission, a financial compensation could have been stipulated. Moreover, the use of portraits of celebrities without their permission can be rebutted by invoking the right of portrayal (Art 21 of the Copyright Act).

## Derogatory advertising

In *De Haan's Ochtendvoer* (22 November 1934), the Supreme Court ruled that derogatory and denigrating advertising is, in principle, tortious. Derogatory and denigrating advertising is defined as negative statements about the person of the competitor or needlessly hurtful statements about the competitor's product. Even if the advertisement is truthful, such behaviour still constitutes tort.

## Standards of public decency, etc

The NRC (see below, p 688) stipulates that advertising should be in accordance with the law, the truth, good taste and public decency (Art 2 of the NRC), that advertising may not conflict with general interests or public order, or be immoral (Art 3). Moreover, advertising may not be needlessly hurtful, nor may it pose a threat to mental and/or physical health (Art 4). By its form and content, advertising should be such that it does not damage public confidence in advertising. In examining advertising for public decency and good taste, the Advertising Standards Authority applies as a general criterion that anything considered by many to be in conflict with the standards of public decency and good taste should be regarded as such. The Authority's case law, furthermore, shows that application of the standards to sensitive products or services, such as fur coats, war toys and religious topics, does not, in itself, result in such advertisements being banned. However, such advertisements should be treated with extra care. With the application of the standards of public decency and good taste, erotic or sexual advertisements are held to be impermissible if the advertisement should be qualified unreasonable or chauvinist. The Advertising Standards Authority generally considers the use of names of private individuals, or the (ab)use of the suffering of others, to be improper and in bad taste.

# Specific standards

## Special codes

In addition to the general regulations of the Dutch Advertising Code mentioned above, 24–28, special codes apply to certain products, such as tobacco, alcohol, drugs and health products.

### Tobacco products

The Tobacco Product Code (Code voor Tabaksprodukten) applies to advertisements for tobacco products. It contains several specific provisions relating to health, minors, sports sponsorship and non-users of tobacco products. For instance, an advertisement may in no way whatsoever propagate a link between the consumption of tobacco products and human health. It should also include the message: 'Smoking may seriously damage your health.' Moreover, the advertisements may not be aimed at influencing minors, nor may they relate to or establish a link with sports.

In addition to the Code, there is the Tobacco Act, which also regulates advertising for tobacco products. Article 4 contains an absolute ban on commercials for tobacco products on radio and television.

### Alcoholic beverages

The Code on Alcoholic Beverages (Code voor Alcoholhoudende Dranken) contains specific standards for alcoholic beverages, as does a special supplementary Code to the Dutch Advertising Code. This Code is based on the assumption that advertising may not aim to increase alcohol consumption as such. Only advertisements for alcohol of a specific brand or trade name, or for wine from a specific locality or region, are permitted. Collective advertising for a certain type of drink is not allowed. In no way may advertisements link alcohol consumption and human health, nor may advertisements target minors or feature youth idols. Alcohol advertisements may not show 'dangerous' situations. For instance, a connection between alcohol consumption and active traffic participation is prohibited, as is the connection between alcohol and sports. Two out of five television commercials should be provided with an educational slogan such as 'Enjoy, but in moderation'. The Code also contains regulations on other sales promoting activities.

### The environment

The Environmental Advertising Code (Milieu Reclame Code (MRC)) covers the regulation of information about the environmental aspects of products and services. Article 1 stipulates that the Code applies to environmental claims or statements about the environment, that is, advertisements in which the advertiser implicitly or explicitly refers to environmental aspects connected with the production, distribution, consumption or waste disposal of goods and services.

In the event of such environmental claims, the provisions of the MRC apply which impose on the advertiser the obligation to prove so called 'absolute' claims, such as 'good for the environment', 'clean' and 'green'. The Code, furthermore, contains a ban on testimonials by non-experts and requires advertisers to indicate clearly the origin of the environmental symbols used.

It is not permitted to encourage environmentally unfriendly behaviour. The MRC allows environmental claims which meet the specific regulations imposed by the authorities.

*Medicinal products*

Medicinal products are also subject to special advertising regulations. Medicinal products which are available on prescription only may not, in principle, be advertised. This ban does not apply to advertising aimed at the professional target audience. Advertising for prescription-free medicinal products is bound by the regulations of the Code for Public Promotion of Medicines (*Code voor de Publieksreclame voor Geneesmiddelen*). However, the Television Directive was also modified with regard to advertising for medicinal products (pharmaceuticals), which were slightly broadened. If production and sales of pharmaceuticals amount to less than 50% of total production and turnover of a pharmaceutical company, such a company will be allowed to sponsor television programmes. It should be noted that such sponsorship may only promote the company's reputation, bearing in mind that advertising for pharmaceutical products themselves remains forbidden. Provided certain conditions are met, pharmaceuticals may also be sold through teleshopping.

The Public Promotion of Medicines Inspection Board (*Keuringsraad Openlijke Aanprijzing Geneesmiddelen* (KOAG)) supervises the enforcement of the Code (see below, p 681). The Code stipulates, among other things, that the form and content of advertisements should be such as to make clear that they are advertisements. It should be worded in understandable language and comply with the standards of public decency and good taste. No suggestions may be made that the effect of the medicinal product is guaranteed. No references may be made to endorsements by scientists, professionals or celebrities who, by their reputation, could stimulate the use of medicinal products. The advertisements may not be aimed at children.

*Health products*

The Health Products Promotion Code (*Code voor Aanprijzing van Gezondheidsprodukten*) contains specific standards for health products. These are products in a pharmaceutical form (tablets, capsules, etc), or with a pharmaceutical appearance (presentation), or products to which a health related function is attributed. They are not intended to be used as a medicinal product. Because they do have affinity with medicines, this Code is attuned to the Code for the Public Promotion of Medicines, referred to above, p 680.

Health promotions may relate only to the furtherance or maintenance of good health. The Promotion of Health Products Inspection Board (*Keuringsraad Gezondheidsprodukten* (KAG)) is entrusted with the preventive supervision of enforcement of the Code.

Like advertisements for medicinal products, the form and content of advertisements for health products should be such as to identify them clearly as advertisements. No suggestions may be made that the effect of the health product is guaranteed. No references may be made to endorsements by scientists or celebrities and the advertisements may not be aimed at children.

Besides the codes referred to above, there are the following special codes:

(a) Code on Letterbox Advertisements, House Sampling and Direct Response Advertising;

(b) Code on Distribution of Unmailed Print Advertising;

(c) Advertising Code on Casino Games;

(d) Code on Passenger Cars;

(e) Code on Sweepstakes;

(f) Confectionery Code.

*Novel food products*

The Regulation regarding the acceptance of novel foods came into force in 1997 (EC/258/97). Article 8 of this Regulation contains rules on labelling. The consumer must be informed with regard to all characteristics which qualify the novel foods as dissimilar to existing foodstuffs.

The Board of Appeal of the Advertising Code Commission has interpreted this Art 8 provision in line with the provisions on misleading advertising as contained in the Code. As a result, it is not permitted to suggest that the quality of the novel food is the same in comparison with the traditional product (Board of Appeal, 11 September 1997, file 944/97.0136).

*The Restriction of Free Gift Schemes Act* (Wet Beperking Cadeaustelsel *(WBC)*)

The giving of articles, 'premiums at a reduced price', and other gift schemes were greatly restricted by the Restriction of Free Gift Schemes Act, by which the legislator envisaged protection of the consumer against price disguises. The predominant reason for abolishing the WBC (which occurred on 7 May 1997) was that this legal mechanism appeared to be an impediment to free competition rather than a means of protection against unfair competition. The intended protection against unclear pricing was considered to be no longer necessary, considering that the consumer, by 1998, had developed into an independent and well qualified individual as regards industry and retailers, one who was prepared to speak up for himself (Parliamentary Documents 1996–97, No 25).

It should be noted that, with regard to individual product groups, like tobacco, alcohol, books and insurances, special rules apply with regard to gifts. These rules are often of a self-regulatory nature and were not abolished together with the WBC.

### Betting and Gaming Act (Wet op de Kansspelen)

It is not permitted to give the opportunity to compete for prizes or premiums if the winners are chosen randomly and the entrants in general have no significant influence on the outcome. The opportunity is given if the game of chance incites persons to participate, and thus to compete, with the object of qualifying for prizes. Games of chance are allowed in closed private circles. Only if the revenue from the game of chance is earmarked for some public interest goal can the Minister of Justice grant a licence. No licence can be obtained for commercial promotional games of chance.

The Betting and Gaming Act does not permit lotteries, since here, a drawing of lots decides who wins a prize. The entrants have no influence whatsoever on the winning of the prize.

Contests are allowed if two conditions are met:

(a) the contestants should have a significant influence on the designation of the winners. This means that there should be a so called 'judgable achievement';

(b) the maximum value of the prize may not exceed NLG 5,000, whereas the total of prizes is not restricted to a maximum.

It is essential to a contest that third parties, judging by criteria set beforehand, decide who is the funniest, the best, etc. By making an effort, the contestants can influence the outcome.

In a sweepstake, prizes are awarded in advance to several numbers in a series, after which the numbers are sent to the entrants on an unsolicited basis. The entrants are invited to report whether their number carries a prize. Case law has decided that such a scheme also comes under the Betting and Gaming Act. The Supreme Court held that, even if the entrants can take action after designation (by returning the entry form), this is a 'random decision on which the entrants in general have no significant influence'.

Incidentally, advertising accompanied by sweepstakes is also subject to the Sweepstakes Code. This Code defines 'sweepstake' as a scheme in which the available prizes are awarded depending on the draw of a number allotted in advance, or on the return or other way of verification of that number by its recipient. One of the conditions is that the sweepstake should be clear and should not raise false expectations.

## RULES RESTRICTING RETRANSMISSIONS OF COMMERCIALS IN THE NETHERLANDS WHICH VIOLATE ADVERTISING CODES

As a result of the stricter regime for Dutch commercial broadcasters (see above, 15), they are restricted in their advertising options as compared to foreign stations which reach the same audiences and which are subject to a less stringent regime. The Television Directive, after all, determines that the country of reception shall not restrict the retransmission of commercials from other EU Member States where they comply with the media laws. This free traffic of commercials is effectuated by the so called 'transmitting State principle' (Art 2 of the Directive), which implies that the reception and cable transmission of television programmes broadcast from an EU Member State may not be interfered with in another Member State. Only the media laws of the transmitting country are relevant. Broadcasting organisations are subject only to the domestic laws of a Member State from which the broadcasts are transmitted, and only that Member State may supervise the television programme. Meanwhile, upon modification of the Television Directive, the respective criteria applicable to determine whether a broadcasting organisation is subject to the rules and authorities of a particular country are specified in more detail. The most important point of reference is, of course, still the Member State where the broadcasting organisation has its official seat. The argument that the Television Directive sets rules only for broadcasting organisations and not for advertisers is incorrect. This is illustrated by the decision of the EFTA Court in the *Mattel/Lego* case (16 June 1995). The advertiser's possibility of expression is in principle, therefore, also determined by the domestic regime of the transmitting country. This is not altered by the fact that, as a result, advertisers prefer transmission from a country with a less stringent regime to a Member State with a stricter regime, where the commercial in question is not permissible. The EFTA Court observed that the Directive's principal objective is to ensure freedom of services with regard to the provision of television programmes. In this context, the court even regarded the evasion of domestic laws as a logical and inevitable consequence of the transmitting State principle and the envisaged freedom of television services.

The Television Directive does not provide for a regulation which allows for the filing of content-specific complaints against transfrontier commercials.

Advertising is transfrontier if a person or organisation in one country complains about a commercial transmitted in that country while it originates from another country. The regulation of such complaints is left to the national authorities. In The Netherlands, the Advertising Standards Organisation evaluates the complaint against the Dutch Advertising Code (see below, p 688 *et seq*). The Advertising Standards Organisation is a member of the European Advertising Standards Alliance (EASA) in Brussels. Meanwhile, 18 self-regulatory organisations from 15 European countries are members of this alliance. One of EASA's objectives is to ensure that complaints about advertisements in all media are dealt with quickly and effectively, even if advertisers or media in other countries are concerned. To attain this objective, the EASA has drawn up a procedure on transfrontier advertising.

In The Netherlands, complaints should be filed in writing to the Advertising Standards Organisation. The chairman of the Advertising Standards Authority then decides whether the complaint concerns transfrontier advertising, after which the complaint is forwarded to the EASA member of the country of origin, which is then responsible for further consideration of the complaint. The Advertising Standards Organisation acts as an intermediary between the complainant and the EASA member of the country of origin.

In principle, the Advertising Standards Authority has no remedies against a commercial transmitted in The Netherlands by a foreign broadcasting organisation. Foreign broadcasting organisations are not a member of the Advertising Standards Organisation and for that reason do not consider themselves to be bound by the Dutch Advertising Code. It is typical of the Dutch Advertising Code, however, that complaints are directed against the advertiser and not the foreign broadcasting organisation. Advertisers based in The Netherlands can therefore not evade complaints by having their commercials transmitted by foreign broadcasting organisations.

# ADVERTISING THROUGH PROGRAMME SPONSORSHIP

## The Television Without Frontiers Directive

The Dutch laws on sponsorship are based on the EC Television Without Frontiers Directive (see above, p 676). By virtue of Art 17 of the Directive, broadcasting organisations may have their programmes sponsored on certain conditions. The Directive requires that the sponsor is mentioned at the beginning or at the end of a programme. Article 17 also ensures the editorial independence of the broadcaster. News and political information programmes may not be sponsored. Sponsorship by the alcohol, tobacco and pharmaceutical industries is not permitted either. As to the last mentioned category, this restriction only applies to medicinal products and medical actions which are available on prescription only. The Directive also contains an explicit prohibitionary provision regarding surreptitious advertising (Art 10, para 4).

The Television Directive requires the Member States to introduce the minimum framework established by the Directive into their national television laws. In doing so, the Member States have the right to incorporate rules which are more stringent than required by the Directive. Meanwhile the Television Directive has been implemented in the Media Act, both in terms of sponsorship of the public and the commercial stations.

The Media Act and the Media Decree lay down the conditions of sponsorship and what programme components may be sponsored. The Dutch Media Act defines sponsorship as 'the grant of financial or other contributions by government institutions or privately owned companies for the production or purchase of a programme component to promote or enable transmission of the same'.

One condition of sponsorship is that the sponsors must be mentioned at the beginning or the end of a sponsored programme component. This is an exception to the ban on avoidable forms of advertisement. It is also relevant that the content of the sponsored programme component may not be influenced by the sponsor.

Unlike the Directive, the Dutch law further stipulates that the sponsorship regulation applies to both radio and television. For this reason, domestic commercial and public radio stations should also comply with the sponsorship regulation in the Media Act and the Media Decree.

By virtue of the sponsorship regulations, a distinction should be made between national public broadcasting organisations, domestic commercial stations and foreign commercial stations. Different sponsorship rules apply to these different stations, which exist side by side.

## Public broadcasting organisations

With regard to sponsorship for public broadcasting, (new) Arts 52a–52c, 56a, 64b and 64c of the Media Act should be considered. In its Policy on Sponsorship, the Media Commission also explains several terms used in these new provisions for public broadcasting organisations (WM/3839/TV).

The sponsorship rules for public broadcasting determine that programmes may be sponsored, with the exception of news and current affairs programmes, political information, children's and consumers' programmes. Moreover, the following requirements must be met:

(a) the sponsor should be mentioned at the beginning or the end of the sponsored programme; this mention may not exceed five seconds and should take the form of a name, word mark or logo. The mention may consist only of stills, may not fill the entire screen (a text should be added) and may not become a commercial message;

(b) sponsorship by manufacturers of tobacco and medicinal products is not allowed;

(c) in a sponsored programme, products or services of the sponsor may be shown in the context of the programme, in such a way as not to affect the programme formula or the integrity of the programme and without exaggerated, excessive or specific promotional references to the products or services;

(d) the sponsor contribution should be paid to the broadcasting organisation directly; the sponsorship should, furthermore, be regulated in a written agreement;

(e) the broadcasting organisation should have editorial independence towards the sponsors.

Within one week after conclusion of the sponsorship contract, and, at any rate, before transmission, the public broadcasting organisation should send a copy of the contract to the day to day management of The Netherlands Broadcasting Corporation (*Nederlandse Omroep Stichting* (NOS)). The NOS may prohibit transmission if it deems the contract to be contrary to the joint interest of the public broadcasting organisations. Every year, the public broadcasting organisations should, furthermore, submit a written report to the Media Commission, stating the revenue from sponsorship, the quality of the sponsors and the sponsored programme parts.

Not only must sponsorship comply with Arts 52a–52c and 56a of the Media Act, but also with Arts 55 and 56 of the Media Act. These articles do not relate to the contents of the programme, but to the functioning of the broadcasting organisation as such.

## Domestic commercial broadcasting organisations

The sponsorship regulations for domestic commercial broadcasting organisations are set out in Arts 52h–52j of the Media Decree. The regime on sponsorship by domestic commercial broadcasting organisations largely corresponds with the regime on sponsorship by public broadcasting organisations. The broadcasting organisation must, however, have set up editorial regulations setting out guarantees for the editorial independence of the programme makers with regard to the sponsors.

Commercial broadcasting seems to offer somewhat better opportunities for broadcasting trade marks and logos. The 'sponsor bans' relate only to programmes that involve news, current affairs or political information. Furthermore, commercial broadcasting organisations need not submit their sponsorship contracts to the NOS and need not report (in writing) every year to the Media Commission.

## Foreign commercial broadcasting organisations

With regard to foreign commercial broadcasting organisations, only the Directive and the media laws of the country of origin must be observed. The implementation of the Directive may lead to the situation where advertisements that are not permitted in a specific country are broadcast by a foreign broadcasting organisation that falls under a favourable or more favourable national advertising regime and whose broadcasts are directed or also directed at the Member State where a stricter regime applies. This so called 'channel hopping' is considered permissible for advertisers.

## Teleshopping

So called 'teleshopping' is a new phenomenon in the field of advertising and sponsorship. A product or service is offered directly to consumers in television broadcasts, specifying where the consumer can order the product or service, by telephone or by post.

Article 52g of the Media Decree regulates teleshopping for Dutch commercial broadcasting organisations: they may broadcast no more than two hours of teleshopping per 24 hour period.

No specific regulations apply with regard to the content of such broadcasts. They must, however, meet the standards of the Advertising Code. The Act does not regulate the times at which teleshopping may be broadcast. The Media Decree classifies teleshopping as a form of advertising. Under the above-mentioned 'servitude ban', the public broadcasting organisations are therefore not permitted to broadcast teleshopping.

Modification of the Television Directive results in the advertising regime becoming fully applicable to teleshopping. Teleshopping may be not be aimed at minors and it may not last for more than a total of three hours per day.

## REGULATORY BODIES

In addition to the Civil Court, which has jurisdiction in the field of advertising forms and notices, The Netherlands has various self-regulatory bodies, which are concerned with the assessment of their admissibility.

The main self-regulatory bodies in the field of advertising are:

(a) the Advertising Standards Authority (*Reclame Code Commissie* (RCC));

(b) the Public Promotion of Medicines Inspection Board (*Keuringsrad Openlijke Aanprijzing Geneesmiddelen* (KOAG));

(c) the Promotion of Health Products Inspection Board (*Keuringsraad Aanprijzing Gezondheidsprodukten* (KAG));

(d) the Media Commission (*Commissariaat voor de Media* (CvdM)).

## The Civil Court

The Dutch judiciary consists of the county court, district court, Court of Appeal and Supreme Court. In principle, proceedings on advertisements are conducted at the level of the district court. Practice has shown, however, that many cases in the field of advertising benefit from a faster course of proceedings. For urgent cases, Dutch law offers the possibility of summary proceedings before the President of the district court. In summary proceedings, injunctive relief may be claimed. The judgment in summary proceedings is provisional, and may be appealed. Also, proceedings on the merits of the case may be initiated.

## The Advertising Standards Authority

The Advertising Standards Organisation (*Stichting Reclame Code*) was set up to ensure that advertising in The Netherlands is soundly organised. Some 12 organisations participate in this foundation, including media organisations (NDP, NOTU), advertisers (BVA), advertising agencies (VEA) and a consumer organisation (*Consumentenbond*). The Advertising Standards Organisation has formulated a number of rules for the realisation of its objectives. These rules must be observed when advertising and have been laid down in the Dutch Advertising Code (*Nederlandse Reclame Code* (NRC)), which consists of a general section and so called 'special codes of practice' that apply to specific branches (such as the Confectionery Code, Tobacco Code and Environmental Advertising Code). Furthermore, a number of codes are presented in the form of general recommendations (for instance, on children's fireworks, the use of the term 'recommended retail price', and magnetic health bracelets).

The Advertising Standards Authority assesses whether advertisers and other people responsible for advertisements have observed the Advertising Code.

In principle, the Advertising Code applies to all advertisements, regardless of the medium used, unless it is expressly provided otherwise. Within the meaning of the Advertising Code, an 'advertisement' is:

Any public recommendation of goods, services and ideas. Advertising also includes the promotion of services.

Anyone who believes that a certain advertisement conflicts with the Advertising Code may file a complaint (in writing) with the Advertising Standards Authority. Furthermore, the Advertising Standards Authority may also assess an advertisement ex officio. After hearing the advertiser, the Advertising Standards Authority assesses whether the advertisement is in conflict with the Code. If the Authority considers a complaint unfounded, the complainant may file an appeal with the Advertising Standards Authority, which will then decide on the appeal.

If the Advertising Standards Authority considers the complaint justified, the following sanctions may be imposed on all forms of advertising, with the exception of those which relate to the propagation of ideas:

(a) unofficial recommendation

The recommendation is announced only to the parties involved, and is not publicised;

(b) public recommendation

The decision is published, stating the parties' names. The criteria as to whether a recommendation is publicised include the seriousness of the infringement of the Code, intent, public interest, and the interests of other parties in the relevant branch of industry. The Advertising Standards Authority may also make the recommendation subject to conditions, such as the term within which the recommendation must be followed and, with regard to television and radio advertisements, the time of broadcasting;

(c) general recommendation

The object of such a recommendation is to draw attention to generally undesirable advertising practices and to try and avoid them.

(d) penalty

In principle, the Advertising Standards Authority is not entitled to impose penalties. Only in a limited number of cases may the Advertising Standards Authority impose a fine on an advertiser by virtue of an agreement that it has concluded with a trade organisation. At present, the Advertising Standards Authority is entitled, under such agreements, to impose a penalty if the Tobacco Code, the Alcoholic Beverages Code, the Sweepstakes Code and the Casino Code are violated.

A decision of the Advertising Standards Authority may be appealed within 14 days with the Appeals Tribunal. In urgent cases, the appeal term is seven days. The Appeals Tribunal will then rule, after hearing the parties either orally or in writing.

## KOAG/KAG

On 1 January 1995, the Public Advertising of Medicines Code and the Health Products Promotion Code came into force. The former sets out the relevant provisions of the Medicines Advertising Decree. This decree is the implementation of the EC Directives on the advertising of medicinal products for human consumption. The Health Products Promotion Code is the implementation of Arts 19 and 20 of the Commodities Act. These articles stipulate that it may not be claimed or suggested that certain commodities have properties that prevent, treat or cure diseases.

The Public Promotion of Medicines Inspection Service (KOAG) has been entrusted, since 1926, with the preventive supervision of public advertisements for medicinal products. Since 1 January 1995, it has been in charge of the preventive supervision of the observance of the Public Advertising of Medicines Code. This Code lists the conditions which an advertisement for medicinal products must meet (see above, 36 et seq).

If the KOAG considers an advertisement permissible, it is given an authorisation certificate with a validity of 12 months. If the KOAG, after hearing the advertiser, does not consider the advertisement in keeping with the Code, such a certificate will not be granted. A decision of the KOAG may be appealed with the Medicines Advertising Code Organisation (Stichting Code Geneesmiddelenreclame) or with the Appeals Tribunal of the Advertising Standards Authority. If the Code is violated, the KOAG may request the Advertising Standards Authority to impose a sanction on the violator.

Since 1 January 1995, the KAG, formerly called the KAMA, exercises preventive supervision of the enforcement of the Health Products Promotion Code. Within the meaning of the Code, 'health products' are:

... products that have a pharmaceutical form or a pharmaceutical appearance or that claim to have a primary function related to health.

The scope of the Health Products Code does not include food and beverages and medicinal products within the meaning of the Medicines Act. The KAG assesses the advertisement in the same manner as the KOAG.

## Media Commission

Television and radio advertising is regulated in the Media Act and the Media Decree based on that Act. The Media Commission is an independent organisation, whose powers are regulated in the Media Act.

One of the Commission's main tasks is to supervise the enforcement of the Media Act and the enforcement of the regulations. The Media Commission also has a service function. It advises programme makers on camouflaged advertising and sponsorship, for instance. In performing its task, the Commission is authorised to impose sanctions when the Media Act or the decrees based on that Act are violated. These sanctions may consist of penalties, reduction or withdrawal of broadcasting time, or withdrawal of the permit. A notice of objection to the sanction may be filed, after which the sanction may also be appealed before the Civil Court.

## Other self-regulatory bodies

In addition to the above self-regulatory bodies, the following organisations are also concerned with advertising:

(a) the ROTA (press);

(b) the Direct Marketing, Distance Selling and Sales Promotion Association (DMSA) (direct marketing);

(c) disciplinary bodies of organisations in the professions that supervise the publicity activities of their members (lawyers, doctors, architects).

On 1 January 1990, the publicity regulation of the Dutch Bar Association came into force, which allowed lawyers to advertise. Until then, in principle, every form of publicity was prohibited.

# COMPARATIVE ADVERTISING

## Individual comparative advertising: the current situation

The Dutch legislator has provided, in s 6:194(j) of the Dutch Civil Code, with regard to comparative advertising, that it may not be misleading. The question whether comparative advertising is permitted must, therefore, as a rule, be answered on the basis of the criteria for liability on the grounds of tort (s 6:162 of the Dutch Civil Code).

It has been provided in case law that comparative advertising is permitted, provided that it does not involve any derogatory statements or passing off (see above, p 677 *et seq*). If a manufacturer compares his own product with a competitor's, stricter standards apply than when he is merely advertising his own product.

Comparative advertising is also permitted as long as only essential, relevant and (objectively) verifiable properties of competitive products or services are compared. Comparative advertising may not contain any misleading statements (see above, p 676 *et seq*). Misleading is, for instance, any failure of the advertiser to mention (disadvantageous) properties or other characteristics of the manufacturer's own product, such as its price, origin or composition. In one case the court ruled, for instance, that the comparison of a specific product with a competitive product was misleading and hence unlawful when it turned out that the manufacturer's own product (in an entirely new form) had been compared with a competitor's product that was already being used.

Making derogatory statements about a competitor's product, as part of a comparative advertisement aimed at dissuading consumers from buying the product concerned, is also unlawful if the statements are untrue or misleading or if the statements (which may be true in themselves) are needlessly offensive or derogatory (see above, p 678).

Since 1 January 1992, the Advertising Code contains a provision on comparative advertising. Under Art 14 of the Code, comparative advertising is permitted, provided that it meets the following requirements:

(a) the comparison must relate to similar products;

(b) the comparison must relate to all relevant properties of the product;

(c) the comparison may not be misleading or needlessly derogatory.

## Comparative advertising and use of trade marks

It is tempting, in comparative advertising, to refer to the competitor's product by its trade name. The question is whether this is permitted.

On 1 January 1996, the Benelux Trade Mark Act was amended.

### Old Benelux Trade Mark Act

Under the old Benelux Trade Mark Act, the use of another party's trade mark in comparative advertising almost always constituted an infringement of that trade mark.

Under the provisions of the (old) Benelux Trade Mark Act, the rightful owner could invoke its trade mark to oppose any form of use of his trade mark in so far as it took place in commerce and under such circumstances that the trade mark owner might be 'prejudiced'.

Reference to another party's protected trade mark in comparative advertising must be regarded as use of the trade mark 'in the course of trade', since the use takes place in the pursuance of a profession or business. If an independent and impartial body (such as a consumers' organisation) publishes the results of a comparative test of products or services, the trade mark is not used in the course of trade. Such a comparative test serves to provide consumers with objective and impartial information, not to promote the sale of certain products or services. The trade mark holder will, therefore, not be able to oppose this as use of his trade mark.

Damage is deemed possible, for instance, in the event of loss of sales or loss of profit, or if the trade mark's capacity to generate sales is affected. Only if the user of another party's trade mark can provide a valid reason for such use will the trade mark owner be unable to oppose such use.

It has been provided in case law that a valid reason is an urgent, insurmountable necessity to use another party's trade mark. In the case of comparative advertising, the existence of such an urgent reason will not easily be assumed; after all, there are many other ways of advertising one's own product or service.

### Current Benelux Trade Mark Act

Under the amended Act, the trade mark owner can oppose, among other things, any use that is made of his trade mark in commerce without a valid reason, other than to distinguish commodities or services, if such use may lead to unjustified advantage from or damage to the trade mark's distinctive power or reputation. 'Use' of the trade mark includes 'the use of the trade mark in documents for business purposes and in advertising. In practice, this amended provision has not yet been invoked in court.

## Future EC developments

On 2 July 1991, the European Commission filed a proposal with the Council of the European Communities for a Directive on Comparative Advertising and – in that context – for an amendment of the Directive on Misleading Advertising (Council Directive of 10 September 1984 on Misleading Advertising and Comparative Advertising).

The proposal aims at allowing comparative advertising in the Member States, provided that a number of provisions have been met. Article 3 (bis) of the Directive provides that:

Comparative advertising is permitted if it compares only essential, relevant, always verifiable and soundly selected representative characteristics of competitive goods or services, and it:

(a) is not misleading;

(b) does not lead to confusion in the market between the advertiser and the competitor or between the trade marks, trade names, other distinctive characteristics, goods or services of an advertiser and those of a competitor;

(c) does not make any disparaging or contemptuous statements about the trade marks, trade names, goods, services or activities of a competitor and does not discredit the same, or primarily profit by the reputation of a competitor's trade mark or trade name;

(d) does not relate to the competitor's person or personal situation.

To guarantee that specific regulations in the area of advertising (such as advertisements for medicinal products and tobacco) are not thwarted by the above rules on comparative advertising, the Directive includes a provision that such specific regulations may not be infringed pursuant to the Directive.

The European Directive with regard to comparative advertising was finally published in 1997 (Directive 97/55/EC, OJ L 290, 6.10.97, p 18).

## CONTRACT BETWEEN ADVERTISER AND ADVERTISING AGENCY

The legal relationship between the advertiser and the advertising agency may be characterised as a commission contract. The provisions on commissions are laid down in s 7:400 *et seq* of the Dutch Civil Code, in which 'order' means:

> ... an agreement by which one party (the commissionee) undertakes towards the other party (the commissioner) to perform activities outside employment that consist in more than realising a work of a material nature, taking custody of goods, publishing works or transporting or arranging the transport of persons or goods [s 7:400].

Although, in principle, no two advertisers or advertising agencies are alike, and despite all the specific requirements involved, a standard commission contract drawn up by the BVA and the VEA is often used in practice in The Netherlands.

The basic text of the standard contract includes various options that may serve as a guideline in drawing up the agreement between the advertiser and the advertising agency.

The standard contract presents a number of guidelines in this respect and contains rules with regard to:

(a) the nature of the advertising agency's activities;

(b) the subject of the agreement (the activities required of the agency, such as strategy and concept development, realisation, sales promotion, direct marketing, PR);

(c) the term of the agreement;

(d) the advertising agency's fee, commission and hourly rate in addition to fixed fee and margin systems;

(e) regulation of intellectual property rights

The standard contract includes two options:

- the copyright vests in or is transferred to the advertiser;
- the copyright vests in the agency.

A commission contract does not affect the main principle of the Copyright Act, that is, that the copyright vests in the maker of a work. In the case of a commission, the copyright also vests in the maker of the work. The advertising agency and the advertiser must therefore reach agreement on either a transfer of the copyright or the granting of a right of use. In other words, the advertising agency has the exclusive right to its own creative work;

(f) guarantee and liability

The liability of the advertising agency towards the advertiser on the grounds of an unlawful act towards third parties is usually excluded by contract;

(g) secrecy;

(h) exclusivity of the co-operation;

(i) applicable law and jurisdiction clause.

## FREEDOM OF ADVERTISING

Article 7 of the Constitution provides that, in principle, no one requires any prior permission to express and publicise ideas or feelings, save for everyone's liability under the law. Under Art 7(4) of the Constitution, however, this constitutional freedom does not apply to commercial advertisements. The question is whether Art 7(4) of the Constitution does not conflict with Art 10 of the European Convention for the Protection of Human Rights and Fundamental Freedoms, since the European Court of Human Rights has ruled in the case of Market Internal (20 November 1989) that commercial advertising falls entirely or largely within the concept of freedom of expression. Article 10 of the Convention provides that everyone is entitled to freedom of expression, a right which also includes the freedom to pass on information or ideas. This provision has direct force of law. The Supreme Court, the highest judicial body in The Netherlands, has already accepted the position of the European Court of Human Rights. The advertising sector, however, pleads in favour of substantive concordance between Art 10 of the European Convention for the Protection of Human Rights and Fundamental Freedoms and Art 19 of the BUPO (International Convention on Civil and Political Rights), because practice has shown that these provisions are not sufficiently observed.

The right to express a commercial opinion, and hence to broadcast advertisements, does not relate to the content of the advertisement. In this respect, the law provides that such contents may not be insulting or discriminatory and may not conflict with public decency or good taste. Any limitation of the freedom that serves a legitimate purpose is legally valid, by virtue of Art 7 of the Constitution, Art 10(2) of the European Convention for the Protection of Human Rights and Fundamental Freedoms, and Art 19(2) of the BUPO.

In Dutch advertising practice, freedom of expression is relevant with regard to, for example, limitations on advertising in the professions (lawyers, dentists), on advertising medicinal products, tobacco and alcohol, on door to door selling of books and magazines, on the distribution of letterbox advertisements, limitations resulting from the use of trade mark rights and limitations on the grounds that advertising must comply with the standards of good taste and public decency.

## USEFUL ADDRESSES

Commissariaat voor de Media
Emmastraat 51-53
1213 AK Hilversum
Postbus 1426
1200 BK Hilversum
Tel: + 31 35 6721721

Consumentenbond
Enthovanplein 1
Postbus 1000
2500 BA Den Haag
Tel: + 31 70 4454545

Genootschap voor Reclame
Hogehilweg 8
1101 CC Amsterdam ZO
Postbus 12876
1100 AW Amsterdam ZO
Tel: + 31 20 697301

Keuringsraad Openlijke Aanprijzing Geneesmiddelen (KOAG)
Keuringsraad Aanprijzing Medische Aspecten (KAMA)
Falckstraat 49-I
1017 VV Amsterdam
Tel: + 31 20 6225917

Nederlandse Vereniging van Erkende Reclame-Adviesbureaus (VEA)
AJ Ernststraat 169
1083 GT Amsterdam
Tel: + 31 20 6425642

Reclame Code Commissie
Paasheuvelweg 15
1105 BE Amsterdam SO
Tel: + 31 20 6960019

Stichting Etherreclame STER
Laapersveld 70
1213 VD Hilversum
Postbus 344
1200 AH Hilversum
Tel: + 31 35 6725500

## CHAPTER 13

# PORTUGAL[1]

*José Miguel Alarcão Júdice and Camila Pinto De Lima*

## INTRODUCTION

### Structure and organisation of media advertising in Portugal and general information regarding all forms of advertising

The characteristics of the Portuguese advertising market are similar to those existing in other EC countries. The market is strongly disputed by the media advertising agencies and media buyers' agencies (whose activity consists of selling advertising space and time) whose main purpose is influencing the consumers.

The main mass media and other means used for advertising are television, press, outdoor advertisements and radio.

Television is the leading medium used by advertisers to broadcast their advertising messages, currently holding 58% of the advertising investment share. This situation is obviously due to the easy access television has to every segment of the population, to its national coverage and to the price reduction policies practised by the television stations, caused by the fierce competition between them. In Portugal, there are four broadcasting stations, RTP 1, RTP 2 (both public companies), SIC and TVI (both private companies).

Presently, the private broadcasting station SIC is the undisputed audience share leader, followed by RTP 1 and TVI. RTP 2, which broadcasts cultural programmes, only broadcasts institutional advertising, and at the moment stands in last place in the publicity and audience share ranking.

As regards advertising investment, the press is in second place in the mass media ranking, holding a market share of 26%. In this type of advertising medium, daily newspapers are the most popular with advertisers. In fact, 40% of press advertising spend is directed towards daily newspapers, followed by weekly newspapers, with an investment share of 19%.

The remaining advertising investment in the press is shared by women's magazines (8%), sports newspapers (5%), society magazines (5%), sports and

---

1    The authors thank Professor José Luis Cruz Vilaça, also a partner of AM Pereira, Sáragga Leal, Oliveira Martins, Júdice e Associados, for his co-operation in preparing this work, particularly as regards the proposed Ad-ban Directive.

car magazines (4%), business and economics magazines (4%), television magazines (3%), fashion and decorating magazines (2%) and others.

Outdoor advertising stands in third place in the advertisers' preference rank, holding a market share of 8%. In Portugal, there are about 70 companies whose main activity consists of developing this kind of advertising. They already offer quite a wide range of advertising means, including illuminated advertisements, advertisement boards, electronic boards, murals, columns, advertising stands, street furniture, advertising on vehicles, etc.

Finally, radio, as an advertising medium, is positioned in last place in the advertisers' preference ranking, holding a market share of 8%.

In Portugal, there are about 150 advertising agencies, of which the top 10 companies hold 45% of the market. In general, the advertising agencies, incorporated as commercial companies, conceive, plan and control the advertising in the mass media.

The activities of the advertising agencies include a preliminary campaign stage, consisting of market studies, defining targets, communication strategies and global advertising campaign budgeting. In the second stage, the advertising agency carries out 'conception and production', that is, the drafting and production of the contents and form of the models (sketches and finished artwork of the structure) for each advertising message or commercial to be included in the campaign.

The advertising agencies may eventually intervene in the 'planning of means' and 'space and time contracting and control' stages, selecting the nature of the media to be used and their location, the frequency of insertion and the negotiation and establishment of contracts for assignment of space and time with the mass media titleholders.

Another participant in this process is the media buyers' agency. These are companies which, on behalf of the advertiser or the advertising agency, enter into contracts with the media and eventually take part in the planning and control of campaigns. In Portugal, since the main media buyers' agencies concentrate on the most important advertising agencies, they hold a strong negotiating position regarding the media. For example, 95% of the turnover of the advertising broadcast by RTP 1 (public television) belongs to only six media buyers' agencies.

Besides these organisations, there are others which may also take part in advertising activities, carrying out a specific task, such as the 'concessionaire' of the rights belonging to the titleholder of the advertising means, or the 'sponsor' (a role which, in sponsorship contracts, is similar to that of the classic advertiser).

The recent opening up of television stations to private initiatives, which doubled the number of stations, and the increase in the number of written publications, has caused fierce competition on rates and has been responsible for an increase in advertising space, accompanied by a gradual increase in advertising investment in Portugal.

The number of commercials per square metre has grown surprisingly; however, because of the reduction in rates, advertising investment has not followed the same pace, with values below the European average. In fact, the growth of the media (television and press) has caused price competition which is clear from the constant application of special rates, discounts, rappels, etc. Another symptom that has been occurring is the advertisers' preference for 'below the line advertising' (sales promotions, merchandising, etc).

Nowadays, there has been an increasing tendency to invest in promotions, television contests, leaflets and other initiatives promoted at sales outlets. This type of promotional policy already holds a wide share of the budgets allocated by companies for promotion of their products, and is on an upward trend.

The new technologies and media, such as the internet, will play an essential role in the future of this business, changing the way advertising is carried out. On the other hand, procedures such as audiometrics and research will more and more assume a fundamental role to maximise the efficiency of an advertising campaign.

Following this summary of the advertising business in Portugal we will now continue with an analysis of the rules of law applied to advertising and advertising activity.

# ADVERTISING LAW

## Advertising Code

Advertising activity is generally governed in Portugal by the so called Advertising Code, approved by Decree-law No 330/90 of 23 October and modified by Decree-law No 74/93 of 10 March, Decree-law No 6/95 of 17 January, Decree-law No 61/97 of 25 March and Decree-law No 275/98 of 9 September.

The first statute to cover advertising activity and advertising in Portugal was Decree-law No 421/80 of 30 September. That statute was reviewed and reformulated through Decree-law No 303/83 of 28 June. The present Advertising Code revoked Decree-law No 303/83, except for the provisions of Art 25 and sub-ss (c) and (d) of No 1 of Art 30, which relate to motor vehicle advertising and the relevant penalties for violation.

The latest amendment to the Advertising Code, contained in Decree-law No 275/98, was meant to reinforce the guarantees of health protection and consumer safety by introducing a prohibition on advertising so called 'miraculous' products. The concept of deceitful advertising was clarified.

This amendment also implements the harmonisation of the Advertising Code with the latest EC legislation, in particular, Directives 97/36/EC of 30 June and 97/55/EC of 6 October, both from the European Parliament and Council, published in the Official Journal of the European Communities, 30 June and 23 October 1997, respectively.

The Advertising Code establishes the General Regime on Advertising, laying down the principles of advertising, establishing restrictions regarding the content and object of advertising, which makes it the basis of advertising law in Portugal.

The rules of civil law and commercial law are subsidiarily applicable to advertising. Also to be considered as a source of advertising law are the rules of the Constitution, community law and conventional international law, as well as the rules contained in detached legislation, regulations, contracts, and ethics.

By way of example, the Legal Regime on Broadcasting Activity and the Press Law contain rules for advertising broadcasts, which approximately reproduce the principles contained in the Code. However, the fundamental rules are contained in the Advertising Code.

Since it contains the fundamental discipline on advertising, the Advertising Code is applicable to any form of advertising, irrespective of the medium used. Directly influenced by Art 2 of No 1 of Directive 84/450/EEC, the concept of advertising is defined by the Portuguese legislator as 'any form of communication, by public or private entities, in the scope of a commercial or industrial activity, craftsmanship or independent profession, aimed directly or indirectly at:

(a) promoting any goods or services with a view to their sale or transfer;

(b) promoting ideas, principles, initiatives or institutions.

As far as political propaganda is concerned, far from being considered as advertising, it has always been excluded from such in the Portuguese legal system.

On the other hand, advertising activity is defined by the Portuguese legislator as 'the set of operations relating to the broadcast of an advertising message to its recipients, as well as the legal and technical relations thereby arising between advertisers, professionals, advertising agencies and businesses exploiting the advertising media or exercising the referred operations'. This includes such operations as the conception, creation, production, planning and distribution of advertising.

The Portuguese Advertising Code also supplies the legal concept of subjects intervening in advertising activity. Thus, it defines *advertiser* as an 'individual or legal entity in whose interest the advertising is performed'. *Professional or advertising agency* is defined as an 'individual engaged in advertising or a commercial company existing for the sole purpose of carrying on the advertising business'. *Advertising medium* is the means used for transmitting the advertising message. *Recipient* is the individual or legal entity at whom the advertising message is aimed or who is in any way reached by it.

## The principles of advertising

The Advertising Code requires those involved in advertising activity to observe various general principles, which must always guide the content as well as the object of advertising. The fundamental principles of advertising law in Portugal are: lawfulness, identifiability, veracity and respect for consumers' rights.

The *principle of lawfulness* prohibits any type of advertising which, for its form, object or purpose, would offend fundamental values, principles and institutions constitutionally sanctioned.

This principle is meant to prevent a disparaging use of institutions, national or religious symbols, or historical figures. The prohibitions that result from the application of this principle will cover any messages likely to stimulate or appeal to violence or to any illegal or criminal activity, including any messages offending against the dignity of the human person or containing any discrimination in relation to race, language, territory of origin, religion or sex.

The legislator further prohibits the use of somebody's image or words without his/her authorisation, the use of obscene language, the encouragement of behaviour damaging to the environment, and any advertising of ideas with a unionist, political or religious content.

Still on the scope of the application of this principle, the Portuguese legislation only allows the use of foreign languages in advertising, even where used together with Portuguese, when it is aimed exclusively or mainly at foreigners. However, the use of words or expressions in foreign languages is now exceptionally accepted when required to obtain the effect the message was deigned to achieve. This restriction is a fundamental requirement for the exercise of the right to information, which is one of the most important rights of consumers.

The second principle laid down in the Advertising Code is the *principle of identifiability*. Advertising must be unequivocally identified as such, whatever the media used for its broadcasting. Advertising broadcast by radio or television must be clearly separated from the remaining programmes, through the introduction of a separator at the beginning and end of the advertising space.

Such separators consist of acoustic signals on radio and optical or acoustic signals on television, with the word 'advertisement' appearing in a way perceptible to television viewers in the separator preceding the advertising space. Failure to observe these provisions subjects the transgressors to a fine.

The chapter on principles includes the *prohibition of subliminal* or *dissimulated advertising*. Portuguese law forbids the use of subliminal images or other dissimulating means which exploit the possibility of broadcasting advertising without the recipients being aware of the advertising nature of the message.

In television or photographic broadcasts of any events or situations, whether real or simulated, it is forbidden to focus directly and exclusively on advertising appearing on the site. The law considers as subliminal any advertising which, through the use of some technique, might arouse in the recipient any sensory perceptions of which he remains unaware.

Another fundamental principle according to Portuguese legislation is that of *veracity*. Advertising must respect the truth, not distort the facts. Assertions concerning the origin, nature, composition, ownership and purchase conditions of the advertised goods or services must be exact and at all times verifiable with the appropriate companies. This principle, the consumers' right to information, and comparative advertising discipline, are fundamental elements in a market where free competition prevails.

By transposition of Directive 84/450/EEC to internal law, *the prohibition of deceitful advertising* becomes another principle of advertising activity. All advertising is forbidden which, in any way, including its presentation, and by its deceitful character, might mislead its recipients or be detrimental to a competitor.

It is also considered deceitful advertising to promote any message which in any way misleads or is likely to mislead its recipient by creating the idea that some prize, gift or promotion will be granted without any economic consideration or order required.

In order to determine whether a message is deceitful, it is necessary to take into account all its elements and, specifically, all indications relating to:

(a) the characteristics of the goods or services, such as their availability, nature, execution, composition, mode and date of manufacture or delivery, their appropriateness, uses, quantities, specifications, geographic or commercial origin, results that can be expected from their use, or even essential results and characteristics of the tests and controls carried out on the goods or services;

(b) the price, the mode of its determination or payment, as well as the conditions of supply or provision of service;

(c) the nature, characteristics and rights of the advertiser, such as his identity, qualifications and industrial, commercial or intellectual property rights, or the awards or distinctions received;

(d) the rights and duties of the user, as well as the terms for provision of warranties.

In these cases, the appropriate entity for conducting the respective proceedings may require the advertiser to submit proof of the material accuracy of the data in fact contained in the advertising. The data are presumed to be inaccurate if the required proof fails to be submitted or is insufficient.

These provisions are based on Art 6 of Directive 84/450/EEC. However, influenced by Community law, Portuguese law created the possibility of cautionary measures being decreed to stop, suspend or forbid advertising in cases of deceitful advertising or advertising prejudicial to the health and safety of consumers. This instrument may also be applied to advertising with a political or religious content.

These cautionary measures are a innovation to the Advertising Code, by transposition of Directive 84/450/EEC. However, the application of these measures seldom occurs, notwithstanding the many cases of advertising qualifying as deceitful that the press and television broadcast everyday.

The *principle of respect for consumers' rights* is another fundamental principle of advertising activity. Law No 24/96 of 31 July, which establishes the legal rules applicable to the defence of consumers' rights, contains many essential rules bearing on the contents and value of advertising messages.

The right to information for consumption takes the principles of veracity and identifiability as aforementioned and, in addition, gives advertising messages a contractual binding value or force. In fact, the concrete, objective information contained in advertising messages on particular goods or services are considered as integrated into the contents of the contracts that are established after the broadcast of such advertising, and any clauses stipulating otherwise will be considered null and void.

Finally, the last general principle adopted by the legislator is *respect for the health and safety of consumers*, which specifies the principle mentioned previously. Any advertising is forbidden which would encourage behaviour harmful to consumers' health and safety, for example, by giving insufficient information regarding the danger involved or the possibility of accidents occurring with the use of the product.

Advertising should not contain any visual presentation or description of situations where safety is not respected, except if justified on educational grounds. These situations require special care in the case of advertising aimed mostly at children, adolescents, the aged or handicapped.

As practical regulations based on this principle, we have, for example, the rules on toy safety and advertising, contained in Decree-law No 140/90 of 30 April.

## Freedom of advertising

Freedom of advertising or freedom of advertising expression does not have any specific legal sanctioning in Portugal, but consists of a corollary of the constitutional principle of freedom of expression. Thus, everybody has the right to divulge his thoughts freely by words, through images or any other means, as well as the right to inform, to inquire and to be informed, without impediment or discrimination.

The exercise of these rights and, specifically, the freedom of advertising expression, may not be prevented or limited by any type of any form of censorship. However, as we shall see below, the freedom of advertising expression is strongly conditioned by the legal provisions contained in the Advertising Code.

According to the prevailing principle, anything that is not forbidden is allowed. Therefore, freedom of advertising, or freedom of content of the advertising message, is an undeniable right, subject to the limitations deriving from third parties' rights, such as consumers' rights, and to the limitations deriving from the law.

To begin with, any advertising message must respect and be conditioned by the rights of consumers. On the other hand, this freedom is limited by the legislator imposing the protection of fundamental values, such as fair competition, truth, health and safety.

The next chapters deal with limitations to the object and content of advertising, rules that set bounds to the freedom of advertising.

## Restrictions on the content of advertising messages: comparative advertising

Portuguese law sets out the general principles that must rule any form of advertising and, in addition, it specifically regulates, in certain cases, the content of advertising messages, thereby limiting the freedom of advertising.

The content of advertising aimed at minors, testimonial advertising and comparative advertising are subject to legal restrictions imposed by Portuguese legislation.

(a) Advertising specifically aimed at minors is specifically regulated by the Advertising Code and, in certain cases, by detached legislation, as happens with toy advertising. The legislator's main concern was to safeguard the so called psychological vulnerability of minors, whose inexperience makes them particularly susceptible to influence. Thus, any advertising is forbidden which would incite minors directly, by exploiting their inexperience or credulity, into acquiring particular goods or services or persuading their parents or third persons to buy such goods or services.

Advertising is illegal if it contains elements likely to endanger the physical or moral integrity of minors, or their health or security, in particular, through pornographic scenes or by inciting to violence. Nor is any advertising permissible which exploits the special confidence minors have in their parents, guardians or teachers.

Minors may only play leading roles in advertising messages where there is a direct link between them and the product or service advertised.

(b) The contents of testimonial advertising are also limited by Portuguese legislation.

Testimonial advertising must include personalised statements, genuine and verifiable, relating to the experience of the person testifying himself or of someone he represents. Depersonalised statements are allowed as long as they are not ascribed to a specially qualified witness, for example, through the use of uniforms, military clothing or apparel characteristic of a given profession.

(c) Finally, still on the subject of legal restrictions on the content of advertising, Portuguese law limits the use of 'comparative' advertising.

In Portugal, it is considered 'comparative' advertising to advertise any message explicitly or implicitly identifying a competitor or the goods or services offered by a competitor.

It is forbidden to advertise by using comparisons without relying on essential, similar and objectively demonstrable characteristics of the goods or services, or by comparing them with other goods or services that are unknown or not similar.

As far as comparison is concerned, comparative advertising is now allowed, providing it fulfils the following conditions:

(1) it must not be deceitful;

(2) the goods or services compared must fulfil the same needs or have the same objectives;

(3) it must compare objectively one or more characteristics which are essential, relevant, verifiable and representative of those goods or service, among which the price can be included;

(4) it must not cause confusion in the market between the advertiser and a competitor, or between trademarks, trade names, other distinctive signs, goods or services of the advertiser and the competitor;

(5) it must not discredit or disparage a competitor's trademarks, trade names, other distinctive signs, goods, services, activities or status;

(6) in all case of products with origin denomination, it must refer only to products with the same denomination;

(7) it must not take undue advantage from the renown of a competitor's trademark, trade name or other distinctive sign or from the origin denomination or other competitor products;

(8) it must not present a product or service as being an imitation or reproduction of a product or service with protected trademark or trade name.

The burden of proof about the truth in comparative advertising falls to the advertiser.

## Restrictions on the object of advertising

*Tobacco and alcoholic drinks and medicines*

Portuguese law imposes restrictions on the freedom of advertising through limitations to the object of advertising.

Advertising of alcoholic drinks is subject to the following legal restrictions: irrespective of the medium used, advertising of alcoholic drinks is only allowed when:

(a) it is not specifically aimed at minors and, in particular, does not show them consuming such drinks;

(b) it does not encourage excessive consumption;

(c) it does not denigrate non-drinkers;

(d) it does not suggest that success, social prominence or special aptitudes result from consumption;

(e) it does not suggest the existence, in alcoholic drinks, of therapeutic properties or stimulating or sedative effects;

(f) it does not associate the consumption of those drinks with physical exercise or vehicle driving;

(g) it does not emphasise the alcoholic content of the drinks as a positive quality.

Finally, advertising of alcoholic drinks on television or radio is forbidden from 7 am to 9.30 pm.

These legal restrictions to liquor advertising have been much protested against by Portuguese advertisers, who refute the existence of a direct causal link between advertising and consumption. In their turn, advertising agencies consider those limitations to be unjustified offences against the freedom of advertising.

Another object of advertising that is strongly limited by Portuguese legislation is tobacco.

At present, all forms of tobacco advertising through media under the Portuguese jurisdiction are forbidden, except in motor racing championships, where tobacco advertising is specially authorised.

Portuguese legislation on tobacco advertising goes far beyond the provisions of the proposed directive on advertising of tobacco products, as it forbids any form of tobacco advertising. This limitation also meets with protests from advertisers and advertising agencies who argue that, according to existing evidence, these restrictions do not reduce tobacco consumption.

Also forbidden is advertising of medical treatments and prescription medicines, except for the publicity contained in technical publications for doctors and other health professionals.

The Medicine Statute, which lays down the rules on medicine labelling and advertising, approved by Decree-law No 72/91 of 8 February, adopted to internal law the following directives of the EC Council:

(a) Directive 65/65/EEC of 26 January 1965;

(b) Directive 75/319/EEC of 20 May 1975;

(c) Directive 83/570/EEC of 26 October 1983;

(d) Directive 87/21/EEC of 22 December 1986;

(e) Directive 87/22/EEC of 22 December 1986;

(f) Directive 89/105/EEC of 21 December 1988;

(g) Directive 89/341/EEC of 3 May;

(h) Directive 89/342/EEC of 3 May;

(i) Directive 89/343/EEC of 3 May;

(j) Directive 89/381/EEC of 14 June.

Enormous importance is given in this statute to such matters as labelling and attached literature. With the latter, the main concern is to ensure that consumers be provided with correct information, especially in case of medicines sold over the counter.

Whether aimed at the general public or intended for health professionals, the advertising of medicines is subject to specific regulations, namely on such aspects as medicine labelling requirements and contents, packaging and attached literature. In addition, the legal regime introduced into Portuguese law specific norms on medicine advertising, which complement the legal provisions contained in the Advertising Code.

To begin with, any form of communication alluding to medicine, with the objective of promoting its acquisition or consumption, is considered as advertising of medicine.

It is stipulated that advertising will be prohibited where no authorisation has been granted for a medicine to be introduced in the market. On the other hand, the advertising may not diverge from the information contained in the summary describing the characteristics of the medicine, as authorised.

Advertising must encourage a rational use of the medicines, doing so in an objective way and without exaggerating its properties. Advertising must be conceived so that the advertising message will appear clearly, indicating that it relates to a medicine.

Like the rule contained in the Advertising Code, the Medicines Statute sets out that prescription medicines may only be advertised in technical publications or audio-visual information media exclusively intended for doctors and other health professionals.

Advertising of medicines to the public must contain the following minimum information:

(a) the name of the medicine;

(b) therapeutic indications and special precautions;

(c) indispensable information on how to use the medicine properly;

(d) a recommendation that the attached literature should be read carefully and, in case of doubt, the patient should see a doctor if the symptoms persist.

When the advertising is solely intended to call attention to the name of a medicine by alluding to advertising messages broadcast in the previous 30 days in compliance with the indications mentioned above, the repetition of such information is dispensed with.

The public advertising of medicines may not contain any element which would:

(a) lead to the conclusion that seeing a doctor or undergoing surgery would be superfluous, especially by suggesting a diagnosis or recommending treatment by correspondence;

(b) suggest that the effect of the medicine is guaranteed;

(c) suggest that the patient's health may be affected if he does not use the medicine;

(d) aim exclusively or mostly at minors;

(e) refer to a recommendation emanating from scientists or health professionals;

(f) confuse the medicine with food or cosmetics;

(g) suggest that the safety or efficacy of the medicine is due to the fact that it is considered a natural product.

In such advertising, therapeutic indications are prohibited which could lead to self-medication, for example, in such diseases as tuberculosis, sexually transmittable diseases, grave infectious diseases, cancer, chronic insomnia, diabetes and other metabolism disorders. All forms of comparative advertising are prohibited.

Any public advertising of medicines that contain narcotics or psychotropic substances is forbidden, as is any gratuitous distribution of medicines to the public with promotional purposes.

Advertising aimed at health professionals, or at technicians qualified to prescribe or supply medicines, must include:

(a) a summary of the characteristics of the medicine;

(b) indication of obligatory medical prescription, where applicable;

(c) price for the different forms in which the medicine is available;

(d) subsidised price regime.

When dealing with medicines that qualify for a subsidy, in addition to this information, the advertising must specify, in escudos, the State aid amount as well as the amount to be paid by the buyer.

Advertising documents transmitted as promotional materials, and intended for technicians qualified to prescribe or supply medicines, must include at least the above information.

The information contained in such documents must be exact, up to date, verifiable and sufficiently complete to enable the recipient to form a correct idea of the therapeutic value of the medicine.

On the other hand, free promotional samples of medicines may not be given to persons qualified to write prescriptions unless the following conditions are met:

(a) delivery must take place within a period of two years from the date of introduction into the market;

(b) it must occur at the recipient's request;

(c) the samples must be identical to the smallest form in which the medicine is available for sale;

(d) the samples must contain the phrases 'free sample', 'not for sale', or the like;

(e) the samples must be accompanied of a copy of the summary of characteristics of the medicine.

No samples of medicines may be given out which contain narcotics or psychotropic substances.

Advertisers, advertising agencies and any other entities doing business in advertising, as well as the titleholders of the advertising media used, or their concessionaires, are jointly and severally responsible, in general terms, for damage caused to third parties on account of broadcasting illicit advertising messages. Advertisers will be released from such liability if they prove that they had no previous knowledge of the message transmitted. This rule establishes the civil liability for damages caused to third parties, in the same terms as its counterpart does in the Advertising Code; the provisions of this Code will always be subsidiarily applicable.

Finally, violation of these rules on advertising is a transgression liable to an accessory penalty of up to two years' suspension of medicine advertising.

The competent body for application of the penalties listed in this statute is the Director Geral de Assuntos Farmaceuticos.

Advertising in schools is also subject to legal restrictions. Advertising of alcoholic drinks or tobacco or any type of pornographic materials are forbidden in schools as well as in publications, programmes or activities aimed mainly at minors.

Because of their social consequences, games of chance may not be advertised as the essential object of a message, except for lotteries promoted by *Santa Casa da Misericórdia de Lisboa* (Institution of Social Solidarity).

Advertising messages relating to courses or any other training activities or intellectual, cultural or professional improvement must indicate the nature of the courses or activities, according to the designation officially accepted by the competent services, as well as their duration.

Advertising for promoting the sale of motor vehicles is also subject to legal limitations. Portuguese law prohibits any motor vehicle advertising containing situations or suggesting uses of the vehicle in ways involving risk to the personal safety of the driver or third parties, or likely to cause environmental disturbance. Such advertising must also comply with rigorous consumer information requirements.

Advertising is forbidden which presents situations transgressing traffic rules, namely excessive speed, dangerous driving, non-use of safety accessories and disregard for traffic signs or for pedestrians.

The advertising of miraculous products or services is also clearly forbidden. Advertising of 'miraculous' products or services is considered to be that:

> ... which, exploiting the recipients' ignorance, fear, belief or superstition, presents any goods, products, objects, apparatus, materials, substances, methods or services as having specific, automatic or guaranteed effects on the health, well being, luck or happiness of consumers or other people, in particular, for allowing prevention, diagnosis, healing or treatment of disease or pain, providing professional, economic or social advantages, or changing one's physical features or appearance, without objective scientific proof of the advertised or suggested properties, characteristics or effects.

Portuguese legislation is very particular about advertising of securities operations. The text of the Securities Market Code stipulates that any information, whether obligatory or optional, given to the public by any means by the issuing body, organisations responsible for public subscription or transaction offers, financial brokers, or entities managing secondary markets, must conform with rigorous principles of lawfulness, veracity, objectivity, timing and clarity.

The said entities may not, for example, by divulging insufficient, inaccurate or false information, by giving indicators, forecasts or value judgments that are lacking in rigour or foundation, by using a dubious or confusing manner of expression, by presenting the information in a certain manner or in a certain context, by being outdated or ill timed, by failing to provide the necessary clarification for correct understanding and assessment, or by any other circumstances where knowledge, clarification or consideration could reasonably be demanded from such entities, mislead the public about the reality of facts, situations, activities, results, business, prospects, values, rates of yield or appreciation for the capital invested, or any other matters that may be the object of such information.

These rules are applicable to any advertising made by the said entities:

(a) with a view to the placing or transaction of securities of whatever nature;

(b) which may directly or indirectly affect the quotation of such securities on the Stock Exchange or their selling price in other secondary markets where they may be negotiated;

(c) which may be likely to influence the behaviour of investors in respect of the entity being advertised and with regard to the subscription or negotiation of the securities issued or traded, the exercise of any inherent rights, or the hiring of brokerage services such entity is authorised to provide. This type of advertising must always be identified as such, whatever the media used for its broadcasting.

## Domiciliary advertising (direct mail) and sponsorship

Portuguese advertising legislation regards domiciliary advertising and sponsorship as special forms of advertising. Under the Portuguese Advertising Code, domiciliary advertising consists of 'advertising delivered to the recipient's domicile, by correspondence or by any other means'.

With regard to the particular character of this form of advertising, and in order to protect the interests and rights of consumers, Portuguese law provides that all domiciliary advertising must contain, in a clear and precise form:

(a) the name, address and other data sufficient to identify the advertiser;

(b) indication of the place where the recipient may obtain the information he may require;

(c) a rigorous and faithful description of the goods or services advertised and its characteristics;

(d) the price of the goods or services and the representative form of payment, as well as acquisition conditions, guarantee and after sale assistance.

The law also determines that this special form of advertising may only concern articles with samples available for the recipient's examination. However, the recipient is not obliged to acquire, keep or return any goods or samples sent or delivered to him without his request.

Sponsorship is described in the Advertising Code as:

... the participation of individuals or legal entities not engaged in the television business or in the production of audio-visual works, in the financing of any audio-visual works, programmes, reports, editions, features or sections, broadcast by whatever means, for promoting their name, trademark or image, as well as their activities, goods and services.

There are nowadays several television contests in Portugal sponsored by companies involved in mass consumption, representing electrical appliance and motor car manufacturers and banks. Generally, these companies also sponsor musical shows, football teams and television shows of public interest.

However, sponsorship is also subject to legal limitations similar to the ones imposed on traditional advertising; for instance, individuals or legal entities whose main activity is the manufacture or sale of tobacco and medicines may not sponsor television programmes.

Newscasts and television programmes for political information may not be sponsored.

The law also determines that sponsored programmes must be clearly identified as such by means of indication, at the beginning or end of the programme, of the name or logo of the sponsor.

Under no circumstances may the content and programming of a sponsored broadcast be influenced by the sponsor to affect the editorial responsibility and independence of the broadcaster. Sponsored programmes must not incite viewers to buy or hire the goods or services of the sponsor or those of a third party, for example, through specific promotional references to such goods or services.

These rules reflect the contents of the European Convention on Transfrontier Television and Council Directive 89/552/EEC.

## Advertising on television: time reserved for advertising

As regards the regulation of advertising activity in the mass media, the Portuguese Advertising Code only contains special rules regarding advertising on television, for which it establishes some restrictions and limitations.

First, and with respect to the identifiability principle, advertising broadcast on television must be clearly distinguished from the programmes themselves, by means of a separator at the beginning and end of the advertising spot.

The Advertising Code generally forbids the broadcast on television of any events or situations, real or simulated, in the form of subliminal or dissimulated advertising and television broadcasts of any events may not focus on advertising present on the site.

Advertising of alcoholic drinks on television is forbidden from 7 am to 9.30 pm.

Advertising on television must be inserted between programmes, and their interruption is limited. In fact, advertising may only be inserted during programmes provided it does not offend against their integrity and takes into account their natural breaks, as well as their duration and nature, and without damaging any credit titles.

The transmission of religious services may under no circumstances be interrupted by any advertising.

Newscasts, political information programmes, reports of current events, news reviews, documentaries, religious broadcasting and programmes for children, scheduled to last less than 30 minutes, may not be interrupted for advertising.

In programmes composed of autonomous parts, sports broadcasting, demonstrations or entertainment with a similar structure, which have intervals, advertising may only be inserted between those autonomous parts or during the intervals.

There must be a period of at least 20 minutes between two successive interruptions of the same programme, for the broadcast of advertising.

The transmission of audio-visual works scheduled to last more than 45 minutes, such as full length pictures and films conceived for television, except serials, soap operas, entertainment and documentaries, may only be interrupted once in each complete period of 45 minutes. Another interruption will only be admitted if the scheduled duration of the broadcast should exceed, by at least 20 minutes, two or more full periods of 45 minutes. Isolated advertising messages may only be inserted in exceptional circumstances.

The law considers as 'scheduled duration' of a programme the effective time the programme lasts, not counting the periods taken up by advertising and other interruptions.

Before Decree-law No 61/97 of 25 March was published, the restrictions relating to advertising insertions in programmes composed of autonomous parts, sports broadcasting, demonstrations or entertainment with a similar structure, as well as the restrictions relating to advertising insertions in audio-visual works scheduled to last for more than 45 minutes, were not applicable to broadcasting exclusively destined for the national territory or to those that could not be picked up, directly or indirectly, in other EC countries.

These restrictions, introduced by the above-mentioned Decree-law, transposed to the Portuguese legal system some of the rules provided by Art 11 of the EEC Directive on Transfrontier Television. Since that Directive foresaw the possibility of Member States establishing different rules relating to advertising insertions in broadcasting exclusively destined for the national territory and which could not be picked up in other EC countries, Portugal decided not to impose these limitations merely to local broadcasting.

After the publication of Decree-law No 61/97, the legal provision that determined the non-application of restrictions to merely local broadcasting was revoked. In consequence, the restrictions regarding interruptions for advertising insertions in programmes, sports broadcasting, entertainment and audio-visual works came fully into force in the Portuguese legal system.

Law No 31-A/98 of 14 July, which establishes the Television Activity Regime, now regulates the time reserved for advertising determining that the time allocated for advertising on nationwide channels with non-reserved access may not exceed 15% of the daily broadcast time. However, if that period of time includes other forms of advertising or teleshopping messages, such percentage may be increased to 20%.

On nationwide channels with reserved access, the time allowed for advertising or teleshopping messages must not exceed 10% of the daily broadcasting time. The same rule applies to theme channels for teleshopping or self-promotion, where the time allocated for advertising must not exceed 10% of the daily broadcasting time.

Broadcasting time allocated for advertising and teleshopping in each period comprised between two hour units may not exceed 10 or 20%, depending on whether they are reserved access channels or not. However, information messages broadcast by television operators concerning their own programmes and teleshopping spots are not subject to these limits.

In Portugal, nationwide channels with non-reserved access may broadcast up to eight teleshopping spots per day, provided the total duration does not exceed three hours. Each teleshopping spot must have an uninterrupted duration of at least 15 minutes.

Advertising broadcast by satellite television is not subject to the limitations provided by the rules and principles established in the Advertising Code. Broadcasting incorporated from other EC countries should respect the legislation applicable in the original State.

The above applies in Portugal in accordance with the European Convention on Transfrontier Television and Council Directive 89/552/EEC of 3 October 1989.

## Radio: time reserved for advertising

Advertising broadcast on radio is also regulated first by the Advertising Code, which, as we have previously seen, contains the general regulations applicable to all forms of advertising, regardless of the medium.

The legal regime that governs radio broadcasting activity includes the advertising ruling principles.

The 'Radio Law', approved by Law No 2/97 of 18 January, respects the general advertising principles, described above, as well as the provisions regarding advertising identifiability, sponsorship, deceitful advertising and products harmful to health.

Finally, regarding the question of the time allowed for advertising, the legislation establishes that broadcasting of advertising by national, regional and local radio stations may not exceed 20% of the daily broadcasting time. In general, radio stations broadcast 12 minutes of advertising per hour.

## The press

Advertising published by the press is generally governed by the Advertising Code provisions. The Press Law dedicates only one article to advertising, which, in very brief form, establishes some specific rules.

First, the Law considers it necessary to protect the freedom of press even as far as advertising is concerned. Therefore, it is not possible to impose the insertion in any publication, of any advertising, written works or images, if they are considered contrary to the publication guidance.

On the other hand, no journalistic company may subject the insertion of any advertising written works or images, to the obligation of their non-insertion in any other publications extraneous to that company.

Also as a result of the application of the principle of identifiability, the legislation determines that all written and graphic advertising not immediately identifiable as such should be identified with the word 'advertisement', in upper case, at the top of the advertisement, and should also contain, whenever it is not evident, the name of the advertiser.

The Law understands as written and graphic advertising all text or images included in a periodical publication whose insertion has been paid for, even without respect to the advertising rate of the relevant publication.

Last but not least, it is obligatory to publish communications, notices or advertisements ordered by the courts, in the legal terms of the judicial procedure.

Besides the need for observance of these rules, there are no other limitations regarding advertising in the press, and it may therefore include an infinite number of advertising insertions.

## Video

In Portugal, advertisers do not traditionally use video as an advertising medium.

In general, advertising on video is submitted to the same legal regime as any cinematographic or audio-visual work, since Portuguese law (Decree-law No 39/88 of 6 February) does not make a distinction.

Such activities as video editing, reproduction, distribution and selling, hiring or exchanging, are subject to the control of the Direcção-Geral dos Espectáculos e do Direito de Autor (Entertainment and Copyright General Department).

The distribution, for instance the hiring, selling and public screening of videos, depends on their qualification by the Comissão de Classificação de Espectáculos (Entertainment Qualification Commission).

The contents of the video for distribution or exhibition must be previously qualified by request of the titleholders of the rights to exploit it. The application for qualification must be accompanied by all the elements relating to the work, in particular, the documents that prove the applicant's quality as titleholder of the right to exploit it, and the authorisation of the sponsor or advertiser.

Any video that has not been qualified is considered to be unlawfully produced and its distribution or exhibition is punishable by law.

## VIOLATION OF THE ADVERTISING CODE

In the preceding sections we have described the essential content of the Portuguese Advertising Law in force. The violation of imperative advertising provisions is a tort liable, in general, to a penalty of Esc 200,000 to Esc 1 m, for instance, for unlawful advertising aimed at minors, on alcoholic drinks, tobacco and medicines. The amount of the penalty varies depending on whether the transgressor is an individual or a legal entity, being greater for the latter.

Negligence is always liable to penalty, except in cases where the advertiser had no previous knowledge of the advertising message transmitted.

When the rule providing for the introduction of a separator in the radio or television broadcast is violated, negligence is not liable to penalty if the advertising medium titleholder or any other entity have done no more than promote materially the broadcast of the advertising message. This also applies to subliminal or dissimulated advertising, violation of the rules relating to alcoholic drinks and sponsorship situations.

Besides penalties, accessory penalties may also be applicable, such as confiscation of objects used in carrying out the violations, temporary withdrawal, up to a maximum of two years, of the right to carry on an advertising business, withdrawal of the right to grants or benefits accorded by public entities or services, temporary shutdown of the facilities or establishments where the advertising activity is carried on, and cancelling of licences or charters.

However, it is not common to apply these accessory penalties, but only to condemn the violator to the payment of relatively reasonable penalties, taking into account the values in abstract applicable to the infractions.

The advertiser, the professional, the advertising agency or any other entity exercising the advertising activity, the advertising medium titleholder or the respective concessionaire, as well as any other party involved in the broadcasting of the advertising message will be liable to penalty, as co-perpetrators, for any of the transgressions listed in the Advertising Code.

Without prejudice to the competence of the police and administrative authorities, it is especially incumbent on the Instituto do Consumidor to oversee the observance of the provisions contained in this statute, and therefore all records of transgressions or denunciations must be delivered to this body.

The tort investigation proceedings also fall under the competence of the Instituto do Consumidor.

Finally, the competent body for the application of the penalty is a Commission composed of a judicial magistrate, by the president of Insituto do Consumidor, the president of Instituto da Comunição Social.

In case of application of an accessory penalty jointly with a penalty, the final decision shall be issued by the member of the government with responsibility for consumer protection.

As previously mentioned, Portuguese legislation has foreseen the possibility of ordering cautionary measures, in case of deceitful advertising, illicit comparative advertising or any advertising that, for its object, form or purpose, may involve or be likely to involve risks to the health, safety, rights or legally protected interests of those such advertising is aimed at, of minors or of the public. These cautionary measures consist of stopping, suspending or prohibiting such advertising, irrespective of guilt or evidence of loss. However, these cautionary measures must be applied, whenever possible, after hearing the advertiser, who has a period of three days for that purpose.

The entity competent for ordering the cautionary measure may demand the submission of evidence concerning the material exactness of the data of fact contained in the advertising, and also may accord a period of time for suppression of the illicit elements contained in the advertising.

The act whereby a cautionary measure is applied for suspension of advertising must expressly fix its duration, which may not exceed 60 days.

When required by the gravity of the case or when it may minimise the effects of illicit advertising, the supervisory authority may order that the advertiser or the advertising medium concessionaire titleholder, as the case may be, broadcast corrective advertising at his own expense, determining the terms of the respective diffusion. This legal regime is laso applicable to the advertising of ideas with political or religious contents.

The advertisers, professionals, advertising agencies and any other entities carrying out an advertising activity as well as the titleholders of the advertising media used or their concessionaires, are civil and severally responsible, in general terms, for the damages caused to third persons as a result of the broadcast of illicit advertising messages.

In this case, the advertisers may be exempted from liability provided that they prove that they had no previous knowledge of the broadcast advertising message.

# ADVERTISING AGENCIES

The Advertising Code defines 'advertising agency' as a 'commercial company existing for the sole purpose of carrying on advertising business'.

Besides the determination of the corporate object of advertising agencies, Portuguese Law does not establish any other legal requirement or restrictions to the incorporation or performance of their activity. In fact, there is no licensing procedure or any special authorisation to allow the carrying out of this activity in Portugal. Therefore, any person may set up an advertising agency, provided that it is incorporated as a commercial company with the above-mentioned object.

The incorporation of commercial companies is governed by the provisions of the Portuguese Companies Code. According to this Code, commercial companies may be incorporated as limited companies, joint stock companies, secret partnerships, or statutory partnership associations.

To create a legal regime that, without prejudice to the exercise of the companies' activity, would ensure the protection of consumers' rights and dignify the companies involved, the 'Certified Advertising Agencies' legal statute was established by Decree-law No 34/94 of 8 February. This legal statute aimed to establish a quality guarantee system based on ISO/9000 (1, 2 or 3) of the International Standards Organisation. The certification may be freely requested by the advertising agencies from the Portuguese Quality Institute, where they will register.

The importance of the certification of advertising agencies relies on the fact that State advertising should be carried out by certified agencies. Notwithstanding this, there is not a single certified advertising agency in Portugal. Therefore the award of State advertising requires a previous order of the competent body justifying the motives that made it impossible to award the advertising campaign to a certified advertising agency.

Despite its lack of practical relevance, State advertising campaigns should be awarded to advertising agencies regularly certified and which fulfil the following requirements:

(a) be responsible for rendering all the services relating to each campaign;

(b) have been in operation for more than 12 months before the beginning of the awarding process;

(c) hold a minimum capital stock of Esc 4 m;

(d) present the necessary profile items stating the soundness and professional competence required for execution of the contractual tasks, for instance, in the field of State advertising.

Besides the need to fulfil all these requirements, the provision of collateral or a bank guarantee may also be demanded, based on a percentage of the aggregate amount of the campaign.

Consequently, no legislation exists in Portugal to rule and govern advertising agencies, in spite of many unsuccessful attempts to create a legal status.

## SELF-REGULATION

Because of this lack of legislation, the advertising agencies have organised themselves into associations to defend their interests, dignify their activity and protect consumers' rights.

The Portuguese Advertising and Communication Companies Association (AAPAP) is a private institution which advertising agencies, media titleholders or concessionaires and even advertisers may freely join. This Association has adopted an internal ethical code, the 'Fair Advertising Code', which binds its members.

This ethical code establishes ethical rules and principles that should be observed in the exercise of the advertising activity, such as decency, loyalty, veracity, prohibition of comparative advertising and respect for the image and reputation of third parties.

In Portugal there are two other outstanding associations in the advertising sector, the Portuguese Advertisers Association and the Portuguese Outdoor Advertising Companies.

These associations have jointly created the Civil Institute for Self-regulation in Advertising (ICAP) in order to establish an ethical code on advertising communication, similar to the existing Fair Advertising Code, in respect of the relationship between the various parties involved in the advertising process, such as advertising agencies, mass media, advertisers, consumers and others.

ICAP has created consultancy and technical structures and aims to study advertising legislation and regulations and issue legal opinions and recommendations, investigation and comment on particular cases of relevant interest. The Institute assumes a preventive role regarding the content of advertising messages, and may examine campaigns that are submitted to it and deliver its legal opinion.

It may also assume the role of arbitrator or conciliator, for instance, in competition cases, taking as reference the International Chamber of Commerce Code of Practice and others that may be meaningful.

Besides these functions, ICAP represents its members, pursuing the maintenance of advertising ethics.

## ADVERTISING CONTRACTS

The different groups involved in advertising activity – advertisers, agencies and media – are free to establish the rules that will govern their relations, by entering into a contract. Contractual freedom is a prevailing principle of Portuguese law, as provided under Art 405 of the Civil Code, according to which the parties are free to stipulate the contents of their obligations, within legal limits.

However, because there is no legal regime for advertising contracts, this convention will be an unnamed or non-typical contract, falling under the general rules of Portuguese contract law and those provided by the services contract and building contract regimes.

The fundamental contractual relationship established under an agreement between an advertiser and an agency is as follows:

The advertiser entrusts the agency with the creation, programming and execution of an advertising campaign, for a certain consideration which normally consists of a commission calculated on the value of such campaign.

In any contract, the parties must, from the outset, establish their objectives and specify the tasks that will not be entrusted to the agency, such as, for example, market surveys, promotions, public relations, fairs and exhibitions, and technical publications.

The parties may include an exclusiveness clause, whereby the agency undertakes not to do advertising for products or services which are in direct competition with the products or services covered by the contract.

The duration of the contract must be expressly stipulated.

The parties are free to establish a fixed or uncertain term, depending on the duration of a given campaign. If the contract is for a fixed term, it may be renewable automatically for equal or different periods.

In such cases, it is usually provided that either party may terminate the contract by notifying the other party, usually in writing, with a stipulated prior notice, of its wish to terminate the contract or not to let it be renewed automatically.

As far as the parties' obligations are concerned, all the tasks, duties or services to be provided must be specified in detail.

The specification of the services that may fall to the agency may include:

(a) market surveys, conception and development of a complete advertising plan;

(b) procurement of the most appropriate media;

(c) creation of all the texts and graphics for all the advertising messages required under the plan of action;

(d) execution of all the technical work subsequent to creation and such as may be necessary for broadcasting;

(e) acquisition of space and time (press, television, outdoor, cinema, printed matter, etc), seeking to obtain, on behalf of the advertiser, the best price/quality/term ratio;

(f) controlling the good performance of all orders booked for the advertiser's account, and presenting the respective vouchers to the advertiser;

(g) controlling and gathering the invoicing elements;

(h) study and assessment of the impact the advertising message will have;

(i) study and design of packages;

(j) study and implementation of sales conferences;

(k) study and production of stands, etc.

The parties may specify the obligations of the agency to as detailed an extent as they wish.

It is advisable to distinguish clearly what services will be paid by agreed commission and what actions or tasks will be paid for separately.

The agency's fees must be clearly agreed upon between the parties and stated in the contract.

The services provided by a *complete service* agency are normally paid by commission on the amount of advertising spend entrusted to them.

According to current practice, the fees consist of a commission varying from 15%–20% on the nominal value, net of taxes, of invoices issued by the media, or 17.65% on the net value of billings, net of discounts granted by the media titleholders.

However, other forms of remuneration may be agreed, such as a lump sum, payable annually or monthly. Certain services may be subject to special billing.

In some cases, the parties may stipulate that the advertiser will be obliged to bear certain expenses which, though not provided for in the budget, turn out to be absolutely indispensable.

The methods of billing and payment must be expressly stipulated.

As far as billings are concerned, the parties may agree on certain requirements, such as:

(a) all the accounting documents (invoices, debit or credit notes) for the services provided by the agency or by third parties must be detailed;

(b) for the advertiser's information, the agency must make available all the necessary accounting elements and vouchers;

(c) all commissions and discounts granted by the media or by suppliers on the orders or reservations booked by the agency must be granted to the advertiser, and such credits must be expressly stated on the invoices relating to the services concerned;

(d) the amount of taxes or rates on the invoices issued by the media or by the agency's suppliers must be debited to the advertiser;

(e) settlement terms of invoices are usually 30 days or more;

(f) invoices for distribution must be issued at the end of each month;

(g) invoices for production and other special services must be issued after completion of the work;

(h) in cases where the media or suppliers invoice in advance, the agency should be able to invoice such services in advance.

The question of reproduction rights or copyright on the work created must be clearly established in any advertising contract.

The Advertising Code prohibits the use for any purpose, other than where agreed, of any idea, information or advertising material supplied for contractual purposes relating to advertising conception, creation, production, planning and distribution.

Advertising creation is still protected by the legal provisions on copyright, and it is assumed by law that proprietary rights on advertising creations belong exclusively to the respective intellectual author.

As regards graphics, messages or other creations approved and paid for by the advertiser, it is normally stipulated that the agency may not use the object of their copyright except for the exclusive benefit of the advertiser. In addition, the assignment or transfer on behalf of the advertiser of the proprietary copyrights or reproduction rights must be provided by agreement – sometimes a separate agreement. If nothing is agreed with regard to this important question, the law will be applied and the rights will belong to the advertising agency.

The parties may also agree on ways to control the advertising budget. All the elements of the actions planned for in the budget must be previously approved by the advertiser, such as texts and models, execution schedules, preparation and execution cost estimates.

Sometimes, the parties establish clauses to regulate advertising liability, for example, by having the advertiser assume all responsibility for the advertising booked and approved by him, particularly with regard to a correct description of his products or services as well as to compliance with the rules of fair competition.

Finally, the parties may agree on the jurisdiction that will be competent to settle any disputes. They may opt to resort to arbitration or to judicial courts. If the choice is for judicial courts, the parties may determine that the competent court will be that with territorial jurisdiction or that of either the defendant's or the plaintiff's domicile.

# THE PROPOSED AD-BAN DIRECTIVE

The proposed Council Directive for the harmonisation of legislative, regulatory and administrative provisions of Member States on advertising, hereinafter referred to as the Ad-ban Directive, was preceded by a proposed Council Directive presented by the Commission in 1989. The main objectives of that first proposal presented by the Commission were:

(a) a prohibition on advertising tobacco products in publications aimed at minors under 18 years (Art 1);

(b) the establishment of rules and regulations regarding the form and content of advertising in the general press and on placards (Arts 2 and 3);

(c) to guarantee free circulation in the internal market of products that comply with the requirements of the Directive (Art 5(1)).

That proposal, based on Art 100a of the EEC Treaty, was aimed at:

> ... eliminating obstacles to the free circulation of certain supports for tobacco product advertising and the distortion of competition which may possibly result from differences between national regulations.

The project of the Commission was substantially modified in 1991 and 1992, and started to include a general prohibition regarding:

(a) all forms of tobacco advertising, whether direct or indirect (Art 2(1));

(b) the use of marks generally associated with tobacco products on products other than tobacco products (Art 2(2) and (3));

(c) the gratuitous distribution of tobacco products (Art 2(4)).

According to the latter proposal, Member States were reserved the right to determine that such prohibition would not be applicable to advertising within tobacco sales outlets, provided it could not been seen from the outside.

On the other hand, Member States were given the possibility of implementing such measures concerning tobacco product advertising as were deemed necessary to ensure health protection.

The proposed Directive, which was the object of recent discussion, is primarily aimed at:

(a) extending the prohibition to sponsorship;

(b) forbidding the use of tobacco names and trade marks, emblems and other distinctive signs on new products or services not related with tobacco;

(c) requiring that the appearance of the product name in advertising of products other than tobacco should be clearly distinct from the aspect of the name used for tobacco products.

Article 2 of the proposed Directive provides that: 'Without prejudice to the provisions of Directive 89/552/EEC, all forms of advertising and sponsorship as defined in Art 1 shall be banned in the Community.'

The concepts of advertising and sponsorship are defined in Art 1, as follows:

Advertising: any form of commercial communication with the aim, or direct or indirect effect, of promoting a tobacco product, including advertising which, while not specifically mentioning tobacco products, tries to circumvent any advertising ban by using brand names, trade marks, emblems or other distinctive features of tobacco products.

Sponsorship: any public or private contribution to an activity or event with the aim, or direct or indirect effect, of promoting a tobacco product.

The proposed Directive also aims to prohibit the gratuitous distribution of tobacco with the purpose or effect of promoting tobacco products.

The provisions and limitations contained in the Directive would not be applicable to: communications exclusively addressed to professionals in the tobacco trade; presentation of tobacco products offered for sale and the indication of their prices at tobacco sales outlets; advertising intended for purchasers at the tobacco points of sale and to the sale of publications containing advertising for tobacco products which are published and printed in third countries, where those publications are not principally intended for the Community market.

Member States would also be able to establish, in accordance with the Treaty, more rigorous measures with regard to tobacco advertising or sponsorship in order to ensure the health protection of individuals.

Regarding prohibition of sponsorship, the Directive provides that, in exceptional cases and for duly justified reasons, and for a period of three years, Member States may continue to authorise the existing sponsorship of events or activities organised at world level, provided certain conditions are complied with.

The proposed Directive caused a great controversy centred on its legal basis.

The text of the Directive is based on Arts 57(2), 66 and 100a of the EEC Treaty. Indeed, Art 100a could only be used as a legal basis for harmonisation Acts adopted by the Community with the main (not just accessory) objective of facilitating the establishment and operation of the internal market, promoting a free circulation of goods and services between Member States and ensuring that the competition conditions are not distorted.

According to Professor José Luis da Cruz Vilaça, former Advocate General at the Court of Justice of the European Communities and former President of the Court of First Instance of the European Communities, that would not be the case of a directive or proposed directive which imposed, without limitations as to scope, a general prohibition on tobacco product advertising, regardless of the type of support used and even if it were patent that such support (for example, static advertising, local press) or the type of trade involved (for example, gratuitous distribution of tobacco products) do not affect the free circulation of the products in the internal market.

In fact, the main objective of the proposed Directive seemed to be the protection of public health, rather than the removal of obstacles to trade in certain goods or services. Therefore, the proposed Directive could not be justified on the basis of achievement of the internal market.

According to the case law of the EC judicature, national rules on advertising are, in principle, considered as 'selling arrangements', since their objective is not to regulate the trade in goods and, therefore, they are not a measure of equivalent effect prohibited by Art 30 of the Treaty.

Thus, the rules of general character on advertising, such as the prohibition of tobacco advertising, as they would not affect the 'intrinsic characteristics' of the products which were the object of inter-community trade (be they advertised products or those consisting of the material support of advertising), do not represent obstacles to inter-community trade likely to be the object of harmonisation measures on the basis of said Art 100a.

On the other hand, considering that advertising is also a service, the general prohibition contained in the proposed Directive would be an effective denial of a free circulation of the services and goods concerned.

Notwithstanding the unfavourable opinion of the European Parliament's Juridical Commission regarding the legal basis of the proposed Directive on tobacco product advertising, the European Parliament passed its approval.

Now Member States must implement the appropriate legislative measures for compliance with the rules contained in the Directive, within a period of three years. In this regard, as far as Portugal is concerned, Art 18 of the Portuguese Advertising Code already prohibited all forms of tobacco advertising, through media under the jurisdiction of the Portuguese State. However, the very rule admits the exceptions listed in special legislation, like tobacco sponsorship and advertising in sports contests and car racing integrated in the World and European Championships.

Therefore, unless an appeal for annulment is lodged by the Member States who voted against the European Parliament's decision, Portuguese law must implement the rules recently approved in order to ban definitely, within a period of three years, and with only the exceptions listed in the Directive, all forms of tobacco product advertising, including sponsorship.

## THE FUTURE OF ADVERTISING LAW

The future of Portuguese advertising law will depend absolutely on the evolution of community rules on the matter. The trend will necessarily be for Portuguese legislation to adopt any Directives that have not yet been transposed, as well as any Directives that may be produced.

On the other hand, a trend can clearly be seen towards an increasing flow of regulations on the advertising of specific products, which will mean an increased issue of detached legislation designed to complement in concrete the principles contained in the fundamental statute, that is, the Advertising Code.

Against the wishes and despite the protests of the agents involved in advertising activities, it appears that freedom of advertising expression will tend to be restricted and limited by the defence of values globally assumed by the State, by consumers' rights and by fair competition.

# USEFUL ADDRESSES

Alta Autoridade para a Comunicação Social
(Superior Authority for the Media)
Av D Carlos I 128 6º
1200 Lisboa

Associação Portuguesa de Anunciantes
(Portuguese Advertisers Association)
Av da República 62 6º Frente
1050 Lisboa

Associação de Desenvolvimento das Comunicações
(Association for the Development of Communications)
Rua Tomás Ribeiro 41 8º
1050 Lisboa

Associação Portuguesa de Empresas de Publicidade e Comunicação
(Portuguese Association of Advertising and Communication Companies)
Rua Rodrigo da Fonseca 204 4º Dtº
1070 Lisboa

Instituto Civil de Auto-Disciplina da Publicidade
(Civil Institute for Self-regulation in Advertising))
Rua da Palmeira 15
1200 Lisboa

Instituto da Comunicação Social
(Media Institute)
Praça dos Restauradores
Palácio Foz
1100 Lisboa

# THE PORTUGUESE ADVERTISING CODE

Decree-law No 330/90 of 23 October

## CHAPTER I

### General Provisions

**Article 1 (Scope of the statute)**

This statute applies to any form of advertising, regardless of the medium used for its diffusion.

**Article 2 (Applicable law)**

Advertising is governed by the provisions of this statute and, subsidiarily, by the rules of civil law or commercial law.

**Article 3 (Concept of advertising)**

1   For the purposes of this statute, it is considered that advertising consists of any form of communication made by entities of a public or private nature, in the scope of a commercial or industrial activity, craftsmanship or independent profession, aimed directly or indirectly at:

(a)  promoting any goods or services with a view to their sale or transfer;

(b)  promoting ideas, principles, initiatives or institutions.

2   Also considered as advertising is any form of communication not covered in the preceding number, by the public administration, aimed directly or indirectly at promoting the supply of goods or services.

3   For the purposes of this statute, political propaganda is not considered as advertising.

**Article 4 (Concept of advertising activity)**

1   It is considered as advertising activity the set of operations relating to the broadcast of an advertising message to its recipients, as well as the legal and technical relationships thereby arising between advertisers, professionals, advertising agencies and business exploiting the advertising media or exercising the referred operations.

2   The operations mentioned in the preceding number include those of advertising conception, creation, production, planning and distribution.

**Article 5 (Advertiser, professional advertising agency, advertising medium and recipient)**

For the purposes of this statute, the following definitions apply:

(a)  advertiser: individual or legal entity in whose interest the advertising is carried out;

(b) professional or advertising agency: individual engaged in advertising or commercial company existing for the sole purpose of carrying on the advertising business;

(c) advertising medium: medium used for transmitting the advertising message;

(d) recipient: individual or legal entity at whom the advertising message is aimed or who is in any way reached by it.

## CHAPTER II

## General Regime of Advertising

## SECTION I

## General Principles

### Article 6 (Advertising principles)

Advertising is ruled by the principles of lawfulness, identifiability, veracity and respect for consumer's rights.

### Article 7 (Principle of lawfulness)

1 Advertising is forbidden which, by its form, object or purpose, would offend fundamental values, principles and institutions which are constitutionally established.

2 It is forbidden, in particular, any advertising involving:

(a) depreciative use of national or religious institutions or symbols, or historical figures;

(b) stimulus or appeal to violence, or to any illegal or criminal activity;

(c) attempt against the dignity of the human person;

(d) any discrimination in relation to race, language, territory of origin, religion or sex;

(e) the use of somebody's image or words without his/her authorisation;

(f) the use of obscene language;

(g) encouragement of behaviour damaging to the environment ;

(h) ideas of unionism, political or religious content.

3 The use of foreign languages in the advertising message, even if together with Portuguese language, is only allowed when the message is exclusively or mainly aimed at foreigners, without prejudice to the provisions contained in the next number.

### Article 8 (Principle of identifiability)

1 Advertising must be unequivocally identified as such, whatever the medium used.

2 Advertising broadcast by radio or television must be clearly separated from the remaining programmes, by means of the introduction of a separator at the beginning and end of the advertising space.

3    The separator referred to in the preceding number consists, on radio, of acoustic signals and, on television, of optical or acoustic signals, and in the case of television the word 'advertising' must appear, in some way perceptible to viewers, in the separator preceding the advertising space.

### Article 9 (Subliminal or dissimulated advertising)

1    It is forbidden to use subliminal messages or other dissimulated means exploiting the possibility of broadcasting advertising without the recipients understanding the advertising nature of the message.

2    In television or photographic transmission of any events or situations, real or simulated, it is forbidden to focus directly and exclusively on the advertising present on the site.

3    For the purposes of this statute, any advertising which, through the use of some technique, might arouse in the recipient sensory perceptions of which he remains unaware, is considered as subliminal advertising.

### Article 10 (Principle of veracity)

1    Advertising must respect the truth, not distort the facts.

2    Assertions concerning the origin, nature, composition, ownership and conditions for the acquisition of the advertised goods or services must be exact and at all times verifiable with the appropriate entities.

### Article 11 (Deceitful advertising)

1    All advertising is forbidden which, in any way, including its presentation, and by its deceitful character, misleads or is likely to mislead its recipients , irrespective of causing them any economic loss, or which could be detrimental to a competitor.

2    In order to determine whether a message is deceitful, it is necessary to take into account all its elements and, specifically, all the information respecting to:

   (a) the characteristics of the goods or services, such as their availability, nature, execution, composition, mode and date of their manufacture or provision, their appropriateness, uses, quantities, specifications, geographic or commercial origin, results that can be expected from their use, or even essential results and characteristics of the tests and controls effected on the goods or services;

   (b) the price, the mode of its determination or payment, as well as the conditions of supply or service provision;

   (c) the nature, characteristics and rights of the advertiser, such as his identity, qualifications and industrial, commercial or intellectual property rights, or the awards or distinctions received;

   (d) the rights and duties of the user, as well as the terms for provision of warranties.

3    It is also considered deceitful advertising, for the purposes of no 1, any message which in any way, including its presentation, misleads or is likely to mislead its recipient by creating the idea that some prize, gift or

promotion will be granted without any economic consideration, drawing of lots, or order being required.

4    In the cases foreseen in the previous numbers, the appropriate entity for conducting the respective contravention proceedings may require the advertiser to submit proof of the material accuracy of the data in fact contained in the advertising.

5    The data referred to in the preceding numbers will be presumed to be inaccurate if the required proof fails to be submitted or is insufficient.

### Article 12 (Principle of respect for consumers' rights)

Advertising must not offend against the rights of consumers.

### Article 13 (Consumers' health and safety)

1    Advertising is forbidden which would encourage behaviour harmful to consumers' health and safety, particularly by giving insufficient information regarding the danger involved or where there is a particular likelihood of accidents occurring as a result of normal utilisation of the product.

2    Advertising should not contain any visual presentation or description of situations where safety is not respected, except if justified on educational grounds.

3    The provisions contained in the previous numbers must be observed with particular care in the case of advertising specially aimed at children, adolescents, the aged or handicapped.

### SECTION II

### Restrictions on advertising content

### Article 14 (Minors)

1    Advertising specially aimed at minors must always take into account their psychological vulnerability, and must therefore refrain from:

(a) directly inciting minors, exploiting their inexperience and credulity, to acquire a given goods or service;

(b) directly inciting minors to persuade their parents or third parties to buy the goods or services in question;

(c) containing elements likely to endanger their physical or moral integrity, or their health or security, in particular through pornography scenes or by inciting to violence;

(d) exploiting the special confidence minors have in their parents, guardians or teachers.

2    Minors may only play leading roles in advertising messages where there is a direct relation between the message and the product or service advertised.

### Article 15 (Testimonial advertising)

Testimonial advertising must include a personalised statement, genuine and verifiable, relating to the experience of the person giving it himself or of someone he represents. Depersonalised statements are allowed as long as they are not ascribed to a specially qualified witness, such as through the use of uniforms, military clothing or apparel characteristic of a given profession.

### Article 16 (Comparative advertising)

1   Advertising is comparative when it explicitly or implicitly identifies a competitor or goods or services offered by a competitor.

2   Irrespective of the medium used for diffusion, comparative advertising is only allowed, as far as comparison is concerned, provided it respects the following conditions:

(a)  it must not be deceitful, according to the terms of Art 11;

(b)  the goods or services compared must fill the same needs or have the same objectives;

(c)  it must compare objectively one or more characteristics which are essential, relevant verifiable and representative of those goods or services, among which the price can be included;

(d)  it must not cause confusion in the market between the advertiser and a competitor or between trademarks, trade names, other distinctive signs, goods or services of the advertiser or of a competitor;

(e)  it must not discredit or disparage a competitor's trademarks, trade names, other distinctive signs, goods, services, activities or status;

(f)  it in all cases of products with origin denomination, it must refer to products with the same denomination;

(g)  it must not take undue advantage from the renown of a competitor's trademark, trade name, other distinctive sign, or from the origin denomination of other competitor products;

(h)  it must not present a product or service as being an imitation or reproduction of a product or service with a protected trademark or trade name.

3   Whenever the comparison refers to a special offer, it must contain a clear and unequivocal indication of its time limit or, if that is the case, that such special offer depends on the availability of the products or services.

4   When the special offer referred to in the preceding number has not started yet, it must also indicate the starting date of the period during which the special price or other specific condition will be applicable.

5   The burden of proof about the truth in comparative advertising falls to the advertiser.

## SECTION III

### Restrictions on the object of advertising

### Article 17 (Alcoholic drinks)

1   Advertising of alcoholic drinks, irrespective of the medium used, is only allowed when:

   (a) it is not specifically aimed at minors and, in particular, does not present them consuming such drinks;

   (b) it does not encourage excessive consumption;

   (c) it does not denigrate non-drinkers;

   (d) it does not suggest that success, social prominence or special aptitudes are an effect of consumption;

   (e) it does not suggest the existence, in alcoholic drinks, of therapeutic properties or stimulating or sedative effects;

   (f) it does not associate the consumption of those drinks with physical exercise or vehicle driving;

   (g) it does not emphasise the alcoholic content of the drinks as a positive quality.

2   Advertising of alcoholic drinks on television or radio is forbidden from 7 am to 9.30 pm.

### Article 18 (Tobacco)

Without prejudice to the provisions contained in special legislation, all forms of tobacco advertising through media under the jurisdiction of the Portuguese State are forbidden.

### Article 19 (Treatments and medicines)

Advertising is forbidden for medical treatments and medicines that require prescription, except for the publicity contained in technical publications for doctors and other health professionals.

### Article 20 (Advertising in schools)

Advertising of alcoholic drinks or tobacco or any type of pornographic materials is forbidden in schools as well as in any publications, programmes or activities specially aimed at minors.

### Article 21 (Games of chance)

1   Games of chance may not be the object of advertising if an essential object of the message.

2   The games promoted by Santa Casa da Misericórdia de Lisboa are excepted from the provisions contained in the preceding number.

### Article 22 (Courses)

The advertising message relating to courses or any other training activities or intellectual, cultural or professional improvement must indicate:

(a) the nature of those courses or actions, according to the designation officially accepted by the competent services, as well as their duration;

(b) the expression 'without official recognition', whenever recognition has not been granted by the appropriate official bodies.

### Article 22A (Automobiles)

1   Advertising of automobiles is forbidden:

(a) if it contains situations or suggestions for the use of the vehicle which could put at risk the personal safety of the user or third parties;

(b) if it contains situations or suggestions for the use of the vehicle in ways likely to cause environmental disturbance;

(c) if it presents situations transgressing traffic rules, namely excessive speed, dangerous driving, non-use of safety accessories and disregard for traffic signs or for pedestrians.

2   For the purposes of this Code, automobiles are any mechanically propelled vehicles designed to go by their own means on public ways.

### Article 22B (Miraculous products and services)

1   Without prejudice to the provisions contained in special legislation, the advertising of miraculous products or services is forbidden.

2   For purposes of this statute, it is considered as advertising of miraculous products or services that which, exploiting the recipients' ignorance, fear, belief or superstition, presents any goods, products, objects, apparatus, materials, substances, methods or services as having specific, automatic or guaranteed effects on the health, well being, luck or happiness of consumers or other people, in particular, for allowing prevention, diagnosis, healing or treatment of disease or pain, providing professional, economic or social advantages, or changing one's physical features or appearance, without objective scientific proof of the advertised or suggested properties, characteristics or effects.

3   The burden of scientific proof, as referred to in the preceding number, falls to the advertiser.

4   The entities competent for the investigation proceedings on contravention and for applying the cautionary measures and the penalties foreseen in this statute may require the advertiser to present proof of the scientific evidence referred to in no 2, as well as of the material exactness of the data of fact and of the advertised or suggested benefits.

5   The scientific evidence referred to in no 2, as well as the data of fact and the benefits referred to in the preceding number, are presumed to be non-existent or inexact if the required proof is insufficient or fails to be presented forthwith.

## SECTION IV

### Special forms of advertising

#### Article 23 (Domiciliary advertising)

1   Without prejudice to the provisions of special legislation, advertising delivered to the recipient's domicile, by correspondence or by any other means, must contain, in a clear and precise form:

   (a) the name, address and other data necessary to identify the advertiser;

   (b) indication of the place where the addressee may obtain the information he may require;

   (c) a rigorous and faithful description of the goods or services advertised, and their characteristics;

   (d) the price of the goods or services and the respective form of payment, as well as the conditions for acquisition, guarantee and assistance after sale.

2   For the purposes of subsections (a) and (b) of the preceding number, a mere indication of a PO box number or any other mention which would not allow the immediate location of the advertiser is not permitted.

3   The advertising referred to in no 1 may only concern articles with samples available for the recipient's examination.

4   The recipient of any advertising covered by the preceding numbers is not obliged to acquire, keep or return any goods or samples sent or delivered to him without his request.

#### Article 24 (Sponsorship)

1   For the purposes of this statute, sponsorship means the participation of individuals or legal entities not engaged in the television business or in the production of audio-visual works, in the financing of any audio-visual works, programmes, reports, editions, features or sections, hereafter abbreviated to programmes, diffused by whatever means, for promoting their name, trademark or image, as well as their activities, goods and services.

2   Television programmes may not be sponsored by individuals or companies whose main activity is the manufacture or sale of cigarettes or other tobacco byproducts.

3   Newscasts and television programmes for political information may not be sponsored.

4   Sponsored programmes must be clearly identified as such, through indication at the beginning and/or end of the programme, of the name or logo of the sponsor, but such indication may be made cumulatively at other moments, in accordance with the regime provided in Art 25 on inserting advertising on television.

5   Under no circumstances may the content and programming of a sponsored broadcast be influenced by the sponsor so as to affect the editorial responsibility and independence of the broadcaster.

6   Sponsored programmes must not incite people to buy or hire the goods or services of the sponsor or of a third party, specially through specific promotional references to such goods or services.

## CHAPTER III

### Advertising on television and teleshopping

#### Article 25 (Inserting advertising on television)

1   Advertising on television must be indicated between programmes.

2   Advertising may only be inserted during programmes provided it does not offend against their integrity and takes into account their natural interruptions, as well as their duration and nature, and without harming any credit titles.

3   Advertising may not be inserted during the broadcast of religious services.

4   Newscasts, political information programmes, reports of current events, news reviews, documentaries, religious broadcasting and programmes for children, scheduled to last less than 30 minutes, may not be interrupted for advertising.

5   In programmes composed of autonomous parts, sports broadcasting, demonstrations or entertainment with a similar structure, which have intervals, advertising may only be inserted between those autonomous parts or during the intervals.

6   Without prejudice to the provisions contained in the preceding number, between two successive interruptions of the same programme, for broadcast advertising, there must be a period of at least 20 minutes.

7   The transmission of audio-visual works scheduled to last for more than 45 minutes, namely, full length pictures and films conceived for television, except serials, soap operas, entertainment and documentaries, may only be interrupted once in each complete period of 45 minutes. Another interruption will only be admitted if the scheduled duration of the broadcast should exceed, by at least 20 minutes, two or more full periods of 45 minutes.

8   Isolated advertising messages may only be inserted in exceptional circumstances.

9   For the purposes of this article, it is understood as 'scheduled duration of a programme' the effective time a programme lasts, discounting the periods taken up by advertising and other interruptions.

#### Article 25A (Teleshopping)

1   For the purposes of this statute, it is considered as 'teleshopping' the broadcast of direct offers to the public through television channels, with a view to the supply of products or provision of services, including real estate, rights and obligations, for a consideration.

2   Without prejudice to the stipulations contained in the next numbers, the provisions of this Code on advertising are applicable to teleshopping, with the necessary adaptations.

3  The teleshopping of medicines subject to a trading authorisation and the teleshopping of medical treatments are forbidden.

4  Teleshopping must not incite minors to buy or hire any goods or services.

### Article 26 (Time reserved for advertising)

Revoked.

## CHAPTER IV

### Advertising activity

### SECTION I

### State advertising

### Article 27 (State advertising)

1  State advertising must be done by certified advertising professionals or agencies, without prejudice to the provisions contained in the next number.

2  When it is not possible to observe the preceding stipulation, the award of the advertising campaign at stake must be preceded through an order by grounded decision from the appropriate member of government.

3  A percentage of the advertising referred to in the preceding numbers, provided the relevant objectives or technical conditions are not against it, may be placed with local radios and regional papers, according to the terms and quantities to be defined by a regulation ('portaria') of the member of government responsible for the media area.

### SECTION II

### Relations between participants in advertising activity

### Article 28 (Respect for contractual purposes)

It is forbidden to use for any purposes other than those agreed, any idea, information or advertising material supplied for contractual purposes relating to any of the operations referred to in Art 4(2).

### Article 29 (Advertising creation)

1  The legal provisions on copyright are applicable to advertising creation, without prejudice to the provisions contained in the next numbers.

2  Except as otherwise agreed, property rights on an advertising creation are presumed to be assigned exclusively to its intellectual author.

3  It is illegal to use advertising creations without the authorisation of the holders of the respective rights.

### Article 30 (Civil liability)

1  Advertisers, professionals, advertising agencies and any other entities carrying on business in advertising, as well as the entities holding title to

the advertising media used, or their respective concessionaires, are jointly and severally responsible, in general terms, for the losses caused to third parties as a result of the broadcast of illicit advertising messages.

2   Advertisers will be released from the liability mentioned in the preceding number if they prove that they had no previous knowledge of the advertising message transmitted.

**Article 31**

[Revoked.]

**Article 32**

[Revoked.]

**Article 33**

[Revoked.]

## CHAPTER VI

### Surveillance and penalties

**Article 34 (Penalties)**

1   Violation of the provisions contained in this statute is a tort liable to the following penalties:

(a) Esc 350,000 to 750,000 or Esc 700,000 to 9 m, according to whether the transgressor is an individual or a legal entity, for violation of the provisions contained in Arts 7, 8, 9, 10, 11, 12, 13, 14, 16, 20, 22B, 23, 24, 25 and 25A.

(b) Esc 200,000 to 700,000 or Esc 500,000 to 5 m, according to whether the transgressor is an individual or a legal entity, for violation of the provisions contained in Arts 17, 18 and 19.

(c) Esc 75,000 to 500,000 or Esc 300,000 to 1,600,000, according to whether the transgressor is an individual or a legal entity, for violation of the provisions contained in Arts 15, 21, 22 and 22A.

2   Negligence is always liable to penalty, according to the general terms.

**Article 35 (Accessory penalties)**

1   Without prejudice to the provisions contained in the preceding number, the following accessory penalties may also be applied:

(a) confiscation of objects used in practising the transgressions;

(b) temporary withdrawal, up to a maximum of two years, of the right to carry on the advertising business;

(c) withdrawal of the right to grants or benefits accorded by public entities or services;

(d) temporary shutdown of the facilities or establishments where the advertising activity is carried on, and cancelling of licences or charters.

2   The penalties detailed in sub-sections (b), (c) and (d) of the preceding number may only be applied in case of fraud in the practice of the corresponding transgressions.

3   The accessory penalties listed in sub-sections (c) and (d) of no 1 have a maximum duration of two years.

4   In serious or socially relevant cases, the entity competent to decide on the application of the fine or accessory penalties may determine that the contravention penalty be publicised at the infractor's expense.

### Article 36 (Responsibility for the transgression)

The advertiser, the professional, the advertising agency or any other entity carrying out the advertising activity, the advertising medium titleholder or the respective concessionaire, as well as any other participant in the broadcasting of the advertising message, will be liable to penalty, as co-perpetrators, of any of the transgressions detailed in this statute.

### Article 37 (Surveillance)

Without prejudice to the competence of police and administrative authorities, it is especially incumbent on the Instituto do Consumidor to supervise the observance of the provisions contained in this statute, and therefore all records of transgressions or denunciations must be delivered to this body.

### Article 38 (Investigation proceedings)

It is incumbent on the Instituto do Consumidor to carry out the investigations on the contraventions foreseen in this statute.

### Article 39 (Application of sanctions)

1   The application of the penalties listed in this statute belongs to a commission composed of the following members:

(a)  The president of the commission referred to in no 2 of Art 52 of Decree-Law no 28/84 of 20 January, who shall preside;

(b)  The president of Instituto do Consumidor;

(c)  The president of Instituto da Comunicação Social.

2   Decree-Law no 214/84 of 3 July will be applicable, with the necessary adaptations, to the commission mentioned in the preceding number, assisted by Instituto do Consumidor.

3   Whenever the commission considers that, in addition to the fine, some of the accessory sanctions foreseen in this statute should be applied, it shall send the respective file, together with a grounded proposal, to the member of government in charge of consumer protection, who is entitled to decide on the proposed accessory sanctions.

4   The proceeds obtained from the penalties are allocated:

(a)  20% to the entity that applies the fine;

(b)  20% to the Instituto do Consumidor;

(c)  60% to the State.

### Article 40 (Special rules on competencies)

1 The supervision concerning compliance with the provisions of Art 19, as well as the respective contravention investigation proceedings and the application of the respective penalties and accessory sanctions fall to Direcção-Geral dos Cuidados de Saúde Primários, Direcção-Geral dos Assuntos Farmacêuticos and the respective competent services in the Autonomous Regions of Azores and Madeira.

2 The proceeds from the penalties applied under the provisions of the preceding number are allocated 40% to the entity that carries ou the investigation and 60% to the State.

### Article 41 (Cautionary measures)

1 In case of deceitful advertising, illicit comparative advertising or any advertising which, for its object, form or purpose, may involve or be liable to involve risks to the health, safety, rights or legally protected interests of those such advertising is aimed at, of minors or of the public, the entity competent for supervising advertising infractions may order cautionary measures for stopping, suspending or prohibiting such advertising, irrespective of evidence of loss.

2 Before the cautionary measures referred to in the preceding number are adopted, the advertiser or the respective media concessionnaire, titleholder, as the case may be, should be heard, for which purpose they have a period of three business days .

3 The entity competent for ordering the cautionary measure may demand the submission of evidence concerning the material accuracy of the data of fact contained in the advertising, according to the terms of Art 11(3) and (4).

4 The entity competent for ordering the cautionary measure may accord a period of time for suppression of the illicit elements contained in the advertising.

5 The act whereby a cautionary measure is applied for suspension of advertising must expressly fix the duration, which may not exceed 60 days.

6 The act applying the cautionary measures referred to in no 1 may determine the respective publicising, at the expense of the advertiser or of the advertising medium concessionnaire titleholder, as the case may be, fixing the terms of the respective diffusion.

7 When required by the gravity of the case, or when it may minimise the effects of illicit advertising, the entity referred to in no 1 may order that the advertiser or the advertising medium concessionaire titleholder, as the case may be, broadcast corrective advertising at his own expense, determining the terms of the respective diffusion.

8 The act ordering application of the measures listed in No 1 is liable to appeal, according to the terms of general law.

9 The regime stipulated in this article is also applicable to the advertising of ideas with political or religious content.

## CHAPTER 14

# SPAIN

*José Manuel Rey and Enrique J Batalla*

## INTRODUCTION

'Advertising', according to a definition by the Spanish Language Royal Academy, is the 'set of means used to divulge or extend news concerning things or events'. Advertising is as old as the human race itself, as, since man began trading with his fellows, he felt the need to make his products known in the widest possible way in order to encourage sales as much as possible. During the early days the system was bartering, later on claims were made by shouting, usually among competitors in markets, finally to give way, with access to more advanced technology, to murals and printing, thus beginning a diffusion at a much higher level.

In principle, advertising was restricted only to informing the public in a more or less artistic manner, using certain decorative elements and images in colour, although the ultimate purpose was mainly to capture the public's attention. In this sense, and as provided by the Statute of Advertising 1964, 'advertising activity was any dissemination destined to direct the public's attention or the attention of the media towards a specific person, product or service, with the purpose of promoting an acquisition or a contract either immediately or at a later date'.

Notwithstanding this, the advertising campaigns of today consist of the execution of a co-ordinated plan of announcements destined to produce or encourage the sale of an object, with the participation of a multitude of professionals, from economists and psychologists to all kinds of artist related to the creation business; and all that because the basic idea is to obtain the maximum possible result by joining efforts and using the technologies that have developed during the production and creation process.

The legal notion of advertising, found under the General Advertising Act, is described as 'any form of communication made by a public or private individual or legal entity, engaging in a commercial, industrial, craft or professional activity, in order to promote directly or indirectly the contracting of real or personal services, rights and obligations'.

Once the notion of advertising has been established, and in order to explain the legislation that operates in Spain, it is important to refer first to Art 20 of the Spanish Constitution, which provides the following:

1   The following rights are recognised and protected:

   (a) the right to express and freely disseminate thoughts, ideas and opinions through words, in writing or by any other means of reproduction;

   (b) literary, artistic, scientific and technical production and creation;

   (c) the freedom of expression and education;

   (d) the right to communicate and freely receive truthful information by any means of diffusion. The law also regulates the right to include a clause concerning ethics and professional secrecy within the exercise of these privileges.

2   The exercise of the above rights may not be restricted by any kind of private censorship.

3   The law regulates the organisation and parliamentary control of the media that operates in the State or any public entity guaranteeing the access of significant social and political groups and always respecting the pluralism of society and the several languages used in Spain.

4   These freedoms have their limit in the respect to the rights recognised by this title, in the provisions of the law, developing such rights and specially in the right to the honour, intimacy and own image and the protection of youth and childhood.

5   The seizure of publications, recordings and other means of information may only be made by virtue of court orders.

This article, defined in a wide and comprehensive manner, is the legal frame that develops the State as well as the autonomous regulations concerning advertising in all its aspects, being, because of its constitutional rank, the highest legal provision within a whole set of norms that regulate any advertising activity.

In order to organise our approach in this chapter, which simply aims to explain as clearly as possible the legislation applicable to the whole Spanish State in matters concerning advertising, and despite the fact that later on we will review the regulations approved by the European Community, which have to be implemented to the national regulations of each one of the Member States within the terms established by each of the norms, we will make the following classifications:

(a) first, legislation applicable in the Spanish territory in general (General Advertising Act, Unfair Competition Law, etc);

(b) secondly, following the provisions of Art 1 of the General Advertising Act that states that 'advertising shall be ruled by the provisions of this Law and by special rules that regulate specific advertising activities', we will refer to the legislation applicable specifically to each one of the activities or means where the advertising activity must comply with additional requirements besides those established by the laws applicable in general, which is the case of television advertising, advertising on highways, advertising of medicines and advertising by lawyers;

(c) thirdly, and considering the territorial division of Spain into autonomous communities and the powers of the State over all of them, with the exception of Ceuta and Melilla, we will refer to the rules applicable in each one of these communities;

(d) fourthly, we will review the most recent and relevant Community Directives concerning advertising activity;

(e) finally, we will refer to the latest developments in advertising regulations.

# GENERALLY APPLICABLE STATE LEGISLATION

## Law 34/88 of 11 November: General Advertising Act

This Law defines advertising under its article as 'any form of communication made by an individual or legal entity, public or private, engaging in a commercial, industrial, craft or professional activity in order to promote, directly or indirectly, the contracting of real or personal services, rights and obligations'.

According to this Law, advertising shall be illegal when 'it attacks self-respect and infringes the values and rights recognised in the Constitution, in particular as regards childhood, youth and woman'. It is misleading when 'it misleads or can mislead the recipients in any way, including by its presentation, and may affect their economic conduct or be capable of injuring a competitor'. Advertising is also misleading when 'it silences certain fundamental aspects of the goods, activities or services when such omission can mislead the recipients'.

Advertising is unfair when 'its contents, form of presentation or dissemination, directly or indirectly bring discredit on, disparage or show contempt of a person, company or their products, services or activities ... when it contravenes the standards of correction and good commercial usage'.

Comparative advertising is illegal when it 'fails to rely on essential, related and objectively demonstrable characteristics of the products or services, or when goods or services are set aside with others that are unlike or unknown or have a limited presence in the market'.

For the purposes of the Law, 'advertising shall be subliminal where, by means of techniques producing stimuli with intensities bordering the thresholds of the senses or the like, it may act on the receiving public without being consciously received'.

Any advertising infringing the regulations of specific products, goods, activities or services is also illegal.

Title III of the Law regulates several types of advertising contracts, making a distinction among:

(a) advertising contract: an advertising contract is an agreement whereby an advertiser commissions an advertising agency, for a consideration, to perform an advertising function and create, prepare and programme the same;

(b) advertising dissemination agreements: advertising dissemination agreements are agreements whereby, for a consideration fixed at preset rates, a medium agrees for the benefit of an advertiser or an agency to allow the use for advertising purposes of available units of space or time to perform the required technical activity to achieve the advertising result;

(c) advertising creation agreement: advertising creation agreements are agreements whereby, in exchange for a consideration, an individual or a legal entity agrees for the benefit of an advertiser or agency to devise and prepare a proposed advertising campaign, a part thereof or any other advertising element;

(d) sponsorship agreements: sponsorship agreements are agreements whereby the person sponsored, in exchange for financial aid to carry out a sports, charitable, cultural, scientific or other activity, agrees to assist the sponsor in its activity.

Lastly, under Title IV, the Law regulates the cessation and rectification processes as well as the proceedings used for such purposes. As opposed to the provisions of the Advertising Statute, according to this title, the ordinary courts shall be competent to deal with matters arising from advertising activities.

Directive 84/450/EEC on Misleading Advertising provides an additional procedure to stop unlawful advertising.

The cessation process is handled in accordance with the provisions of the Civil Procedural Law for lower scale proceedings with a number of modifications, arising, mostly, from Organic Law 2/1984 that regulates the right to rectification.

## Law 26/84 of 19 July: For the Defence of Consumers and Users

In order to comply with Art 51 of the Spanish Constitution, which supports the defence of consumers and users, protecting, through competent proceedings, their security, health and legitimate interests, the Law aims to endow the consumers and users with sufficient legal protection and defence.

For the purposes of this Law, consumers and users are 'the persons or legal entities that acquire, use or enjoy as end users, goods, products, services, activities or functions, regardless of their nature, and regardless of who produces, facilitates, supplies or forwards them'.

This consideration also includes 'those who without being final addressees, acquire, store, use or consume goods or services with the purpose of integrating them in a process of fabrication, transformation, commercialisation or rendering to third parties', and excludes 'those who without being final addressees, acquire, store, use or consume goods or services with the intention of integrating them to a process of production, transformation, commercialisation or rendering to third parties'.

The basic rights of consumers and users are the following:

(a) protection of health and security;

(b) protection of economic interests;

(c) right to get information;

(d) right to get education and information in matters concerning consumption;

(e) right of representation and participation;

(f) right to obtain legal administrative and technical protection in cases of inferiority, subordination or defencelessness.

All these rights must be respected when carrying out any advertising activity.

## Law 3/91 of 10 January: Unfair Competition

Several circumstances have made this initiative necessary:

(a) the opening of new markets, the freedom of our business life from corporate and protectionist links and the increased sensitivity of our entrepreneurs to new commercial strategies have opened new perspectives to our economy;

(b) the need to validate our system of competition at an international level;

(c) the need to adjust the rules of competition to values that have taken root in our economic constitution. Our economic system must rest on the principle of free enterprise and consequently, at an institutional level, on the principle of free competition. This means that the ordinary legislator is bound to lay the necessary foundations to prevent such principle from being breached by unfair practices, which may, in due course, upset the competitive operation of the market. This constitutional requirement is complemented and reinforced by that which derives from the principle of consumer protection.

As a general rule, the law provides that any conduct that is objectively against the requirements of good faith shall be deemed unfair, and in particular:

(a) misleading acts: any conduct that is objectively against the requirements of good faith shall be deemed unfair;

(b) deceptive acts: the use or dissemination of improper or false labels, the omission of true labels and any other practice whatsoever that may, in the circumstances in which it takes place, mislead the persons at which it is aimed or whom it reaches as to the nature, mode of manufacture or distribution, specifications, fitness for use, quality and quantity of products and, in general, as to the truly offered advantages, is deemed unfair (Art 7);

(c) gifts, bonuses and the like: the delivery of gifts for advertising purposes and like commercial practices shall be deemed unfair whenever, in the circumstances in which they take place, the consumer feels under the obligation to acquire the main goods and/or service (Art 8);

(d) disparaging acts: the making or dissemination of statements regarding the activity, rendering goods and/or services, establishment or commercial relations of another to bring discredit on such third party in the market, unless they are accurate, true and appropriate, is deemed unfair (Art 9);

(e) comparative acts: when the comparison refers to particulars that are neither similar, relevant nor verifiable it is deemed unfair;

(f) imitation acts: the imitation of third party rendering services shall, however, be deemed unfair whenever it is appropriate to lead a proportion of consumers into associating the rendering goods and/or services with, or it entails an undue appropriation of, the goodwill or effort of another;

(g) appropriating the goodwill of another.

Following the references to the advertising regulations currently in force which regulate the matter in general, we will refer to those that regulate advertising in specific areas.

## STATE LEGISLATION REFERRING TO SPECIFIC AREAS OF APPLICATION

### Law 25/94 of 12 July: Television Broadcasting

This Law, which incorporates into Spanish legislation Directive 89/552/EEC, on the co-ordination of legal dispositions of Member States concerning television broadcasting, regulates, among other matters, advertising and sponsorship on television.

For the purposes of this Law, television broadcasting is 'any form of television message broadcast in exchange for a fee, put on the air following the instructions of a public or private person or a legal entity, and concerning a commercial, industrial, craft activity or a liberal profession aiming to promote the contracting of goods, services, rights and obligations'.

This Law, besides the provisions of the General Advertising Law, provides the assumptions under which television broadcasting shall deserve the classification of unlawful advertising:

(a) advertising encouraging behaviour that may be hazardous to the health or the security of people or to the protection of the environment;

(b) advertising offending against respect, human dignity or religious and political beliefs;

(c) advertising that discriminates by reasons of birth, race, sex, nationality, opinion, or any other personal or social circumstance;

(d) advertising encouraging any violation or anti-social behaviour, appealing to fear or superstition, or which may encourage abuse, recklessness, negligence or aggressive behaviour;

(e) advertising instigating cruelty or maltreatment of persons or animals, or destruction of cultural or natural goods.

The use of certain products, such as cigarettes and other tobacco related products, are prohibited in direct as well as in indirect advertising.

The advertising of alcoholic beverages is likewise subject to very strict controls in terms of the persons to whom it may not be addressed (under age), the messages that should be avoided (success, improvement of personal relationships or beneficial properties) and the goals that should not be sought (encouraging excessive consumption or offering a positive image of alcohol).

Key aspects of the Law are the rules concerning the identification of advertising, its differentiation from the rest of the programme, the areas of programmes where it should be inserted and the terms and volume of interruption of the programme where advertising may be inserted.

The maximum percentage of broadcast time dedicated to advertising of the total programming is also regulated by this Law as follows:

(a) the duration should not exceed 15% of the time dedicated to broadcasting each day;

(b) advertising broadcasts should not exceed 12 minutes per hour.

Also, the Law dedicates a chapter to child protection in television broadcasting, in order to prevent the exploitation of children's lack of experience, their trust in parents or guardians or their credulity over the characteristics of the products advertised. In order to preserve their correct physical, mental and moral development, it also establishes the need to issue warnings on the content of programmes that may corrupt the young.

## Law 14/95 of 22 December: Electoral Advertising on Local Television Stations

This Law prohibits the contracting of electoral advertising on terrestrial local television stations, regardless of the manner in which they operate.

However, the free insertion of propaganda on these stations is allowed when operated directly by the city council for the benefit of political parties, federations, coalitions and groups that participate in municipal elections in those areas where such political parties present their candidates. This excludes the possibility of inserting these free spaces in campaigns other than municipal elections, where it would be too complicated to apply the standards of proportionality in the distribution of space, as they may be broadcast by an important number of local television stations.

## Law 25/88 of 29 July: Highways

This Law prohibits advertising outside urban areas on State highways in any places visible from the public part of the highway.

## Law 22/88 of 28 July: Coastal Routes

This Law prohibits advertising with posters, billboards, or acoustic or audio-visual means in those areas of rights of way located within 100 metres inland from the seashore.

## Law 1/82 of 24 February: Regulation of Special Cinemas, the Spanish Film Archive and the Rates for Dubbing Licences

This Law regulates the advertising of films for adults. This may only use information on the technical and artistic records of each film, excluding any symbolic representation reference to the storyline. The advertising in this case may only be shown inside the cinema premises and on billboards or in the advertising sections of the papers and other news media. Under no circumstances may the title of the film explain its pornographic nature or make any statement supporting violence in the film.

## Law 16/85 of 25 July: Spanish Heritage

This Law prohibits the placing of commercial advertising in historical places and over facades and roofs of monuments that have been declared of cultural interest.

Likewise, the placing of commercial advertising in archeological areas is forbidden.

## Law 14/86 of 25 April: General Health

This Law orders all public administrations, in accordance with the scope of their respective jurisdictions, to exercise 'control over advertising and commercial propaganda so both adjust to the truthfulness standards, thus avoiding any practice that may prove to be detrimental to people's health' (Art 27).

It also contemplates the inspection and control of the promotion and advertising of health centres (Art 20.1), and prior authorisation of advertising of medicines and health products (Art 102) recommending the State Health Administration 'to assess the security, effectiveness and efficiency of technologies that affect health and health care' (Art 110).

## Royal Decree 1416/94 of 29 July: Regulation of Advertising of Medicines for Human Use

Advertising of medicines is defined as 'any form of informative offer, prospecting or encouragement designed to promote the prescription, distribution, sale or consumption of medicines'.

The general advertising principles are the following:
(a) the prohibition of any advertising without its corresponding marketing authorisation;
(b) all advertising elements of medicines shall meet the specifications indicated under the corresponding sheet of instructions;
(c) the advertising shall always recommend reasonable utilisation, presenting the medicine in an objective manner without exaggerating its properties;
(d) the advertising shall not be misleading.

The Law makes a distinction between advertising aimed at the public and advertising aimed at persons entitled to prescribe or dispense medicines.

Advertising aimed at the public:
(a) should enhance the advertising nature of the message, clearly specifying that the product being advertised is a medication;
(b) should be clearly identified and must include the recommendations made by the health authorities.

It must include as a minimum:
(a) the denomination of the medicine;

(b) the basic information to promote reasonable utilisation;

(c) an express and visible invitation to read the instructions carefully;

(d) the reference 'in case of doubt please consult the pharmacist'.

A number of prohibitions are imposed under Arts 6–9 of this Royal Decree. For instance, it prohibits any advertising aimed at children, or any reference indicating that its use may increase sporting ability, etc.

## Control of advertising aimed at the public

(a) Any advertising aimed at the public must have prior authorisation by the competent health authority, which shall be valid for a maximum term of three years.

(b) Preliminary injunction: whenever the advertising of medicines is misleading, contrary to the Law, or involves a risk to the health or safety of people, the competent authority shall be able to:

- request the advertiser to cease or rectify the advertising;

- initiate and promote *ex officio* the relevant actions to do so;

- immediately suspend the advertising activity when implying an imminent risk to the health.

Advertising aimed at persons entitled to prescribe or dispense medicines must provide the technical and scientific specifications required so that the recipient may decide by himself the therapeutical value of the medicine, and as a minimum it should include:

(a) the basic information about the product (name, quantitative and qualitative composition, full clinical data, incompatibilities, instructions for use, and name and address of the holder of the authorisation);

(b) the prescription and administration recommendations;

(c) the different presentations of the product and the pharmaceutical formula.

This advertising should include the price of sale to the public, the conditions of the National Health System services, and, when possible, an estimate of the cost of the treatment.

## Control of advertising aimed at persons entitled to prescribe or dispense medicines

(a) Prior authorisation: by a grounded resolution, the Ministry of Health and Consumption may exceptionally demand the acquisition of a prior authorisation to advertise specific medicines.

(b) Precautionary measures: the competent health authority may suspend the advertising when:

- involving medicines submitted to previous authorisation;
- when the content of the advertising message is contrary to the provisions ruling the advertising of medicines; and
- in those cases when the assumptions determined by the Medicines Law are given.

This provision also regulates the technical information on the medicine, documentary advertising, free samples as well as the type of sanctions in case of non-compliance.

## Royal Decree 1907/96 of 6 August: Advertising and Commercial Promotion of Products, Activities or Services with Alleged Health Properties

This Law prohibits the advertising of secret medicines, of preparation formulae and of products that are going through the phase of clinical investigation. It also prohibits any kind of advertising of products, materials, substances, energies or methods with alleged health properties in the cases listed under Art 4 of the Law (for example, when designed for the prevention, treatment or cure of transmissible diseases, cancer and other tumoral diseases).

Likewise, advertising by health professionals aimed at the public when using their name, profession, specialty, or position to support alleged benefits of a medicine is expressly prohibited by the law.

The advertising of and information on health establishments and beauty centres, slimming facilities, and treatments for physical or aesthetic development must always meet the requirements of the authorisation expressly given to them to operate.

As a general rule, health advertising should always be transparent, accurate and truthful, avoiding any situation that could be dangerous to the health or security of people or frustrate their legitimate expectations regarding accurate and precise information. If this is not the case, the health authorities may immediately formulate a suitable warning through the media used to advertise.

## Royal Decree 1268/97 of 25 July: General Regulations for Labelling, Presentation and Advertising of Packaged Food

This regulation is applicable to the labelling of food products packaged to be sold directly to the consumer, as well as to food supplied by restaurants, hospitals and similar establishments.

It applies to the advertising and presentational aspects of food products and specifically affects their appearance, packaging, packaging material, manner of display and surroundings of the places where they are made available to the consumer (Art 1).

This regulation defines concepts such as labels, labelling, advertising, etc, providing the following general rules regarding food products:

(a) there should not be any doubt about the product's nature, quality, quantity, origin, or other essential aspects;

(b) there must not be references which attribute to the product any therapeutical, preventive or curative action;

(c) labelling, etc, shall not mislead or deceive through inscriptions, signs or graphics that may give rise to:

- attribution to the product effects or properties it does not have;
- suggestion that the product has some particular characteristics when all similar products do have the same characteristics;
- suggestions that may lead to confusion with another product;

(d) any printing or engraving on the inner side of the container in direct contact with the product is forbidden.

The regulation under Title IV refers to the mandatory information the label must contain; Title V covers the lettering and presentation of this information and, finally, Title VI covers optional labelling, which is developed through two attachments.

## Royal Decree 930/95 of 20 July: Modification of the General Regulations for Labelling, Presentation and Advertising of Packaged Food

This Royal Decree modifies the attachments to the General Regulation for labelling, presentation and advertising of packaged food. It also modifies Art 6, which refers to the product's denomination of sale, which will be ruled by the applicable legal provisions and in the absence of any reference, the denomination shall be the name usually given to the product in Spain or a description of the product or of its utilisation sufficiently precise as to allow the buyer to know its actual nature and to avoid confusion with similar products.

# Royal Decree 1908/95 of 23 January 1996: Modification of the General Regulations for Labelling, Presentation and Advertising of Packaged Food

This Royal Decree modifies Art 11 of the above-mentioned Regulation with respect to the instructions for conservation, which as therein provided for, must be indicated on the label. The modification adds a new paragraph and refers to food products packaged to last a long period of time by using gases authorised by Royal Decree 1111/1991 concerning food additives, which must include a special reference to that respect.

# Royal Decree 1599/97 of 31 October: Cosmetic Products

The Ministry of Health and Consumption has approved Royal Decree dated 17 October 1997 over cosmetic products that implements a number of new rules included in the previous regulations over cosmetic products, in existence since 1988, and also implementing the new European Directives.

The new Decree, under Chapter V, refers to the labelling and advertising of said products, and indicates that the receptacles and packaging must indicate the denomination of the product, the name, or corporate denomination, and address of the manufacturer, the nominal content at the time of packing, the use-by date, any special precautions as to the product's use, the serial number of fabrication, its function and, among other information, the list of ingredients.

The label shall also include the following reference: 'Notwithstanding the provisions of the rules concerning advertising, the text, denominations, marks, images and other signs shown on the label, the prospectus and advertising of cosmetic products shall not attribute to these products characteristics, properties or actions exceeding the cosmetic functions indicated therein', by which is meant curative properties, or false or misleading statements.

On the other hand, the denominations of said products shall not give rise to confusion with medicines, pharmaceutical specialities or food products. The packaging and presentation shall not lead to confusion with food or other consumer products, in order to avoid any health related risk.

Finally, the Decree provides that the Public Administrations, within the scope of their respective competencies, shall control advertising so that it meets the standards of veracity as far as health is concerned, restricting any element that could turn out to be harmful or detrimental.

# REGULATIONS CONCERNING ADVERTISING BY LAWYERS

The current Statute of Lawyers, in force since 1982, contemplates a total prohibition as far as advertising is concerned; however, the deep social changes, especially those arising from technological advances and cultural evolution, have made it necessary to review these rules and to create a new legal framework to regulate professional advertising.

Thus, the General Council of Spanish Lawyers unanimously approved an Advertising Regulation that was enacted on 1 January 1998, according to which, for the first time, law firms are allowed to advertise their services. Notwithstanding this, advertising has not been totally liberalised and some prohibitions have been maintained to avoid any attempt against professional dignity and also to defend consumers and users.

The basic principles on which this regulation is based are: 'objective, truthful and worthy information, in its contents as well as in the support used, which in any case must always respect the deontological standards of the profession.'

The advertising may include information about the personal identity of the lawyer, the year of association or the opening of the firm, location of the office, telephone, fax, working hours, denomination and logo of the firm, areas of professional expertise, degrees of the lawyers, educational background, etc.

Any reference as to the clients or professional matters handled is forbidden, as well as references to public or private positions, persuasive wording, references to ideologies, self-praise or comparison with other firms, providing erroneous information and promoting of results.

The information may be published in magazines, bulletins, guides, on the internet or electronic mail and it shall be restricted to one publication a week or one announcement per publication.

Finally, participation in conferences and round tables is authorised, along with the publication of writs, circulars and articles over legal issues, and the distribution of informative postcards or letters with objective information, which must be subject to the prior authorisation of the Bar Association.

# LEGISLATION APPLICABLE IN THE AUTONOMOUS COMMUNITIES

Currently, all autonomous communities hold exclusive competence in matters concerning advertising, regardless of the regulations dictated by the State for specific areas, with the exception of Ceuta and Melilla. A brief summary of the regulations currently in force in each one of these autonomous communities is as follows.

### Andalusia

Law 1/1996 of 10 January: Internal Trading in Andalusia. This Law regulates advertising with the different methods of sale.

Law 5/1995 of 6 November: Institutional Advertising Regulations.

### Aragon

Law 8/1997 of 30 October: Statute of Consumers and Users of the Autonomous Community of Aragon.

Law 6/1993 of 5 April: Highways Advertising in the Autonomous Community of Aragon.

### Balearic Islands

Law 5/1997 of 8 July: Advertising Dynamics in the Balearic Islands.

### Cantabria

Law 5/1997 of 6 October: Prevention, Assistance and Social Incorporation in Matters concerning Drug Addiction. This regulates tobacco and alcoholic beverage advertising.

### Castilla la Mancha

Law 2/1995 of 2 March: Sale of Alcoholic Beverages to Under Age People.

Law 6/1994 of 22 December: Advertising in the Official Gazette of Property, Rents and Activities of Public Administrators of Castilla La Mancha.

Law 2/1997 of 30 May: Fairs and Exhibition Activities in Castilla La Mancha.

### Catalonia

Law 31/1991 of 13 December: Pharmaceutical Ordinance of Catalonia. This regulates advertising of medicines.

Law 3/1993 of 5 March: Consumers' Statute.

Law 23/91 of 29 November: Foreign Commerce.

Law 10/91 of 10 May: Modification of Law 20/85: Assistance in Matters of Substances that may Generate Dependence. This restricts the offer and promotion of substances that may generate dependence, such as alcoholic beverages or tobacco products in under age people.

Law 8/95 of 27 July: Attention and Promotion of Childhood and Adolescence and Modification of Law 37/91 of 30 December. Protection measures for unprotected children and adoptions. This regulates the advertising aimed at and performed by children and adolescents, starting from the freedom standards enshrined by Article 20.1 of the Spanish Constitution.

## Extremadura

Law 4/1997 of 10 April: Protection Measures and Control of Sale and Advertising of Alcoholic Beverages to Under Age People.

Law 6/1996 of 26 September: Institutional Advertising.

## Galicia

Law 2/1996 of 8 May: Drugs. This regulates advertising of alcoholic beverages and tobacco.

Law 10/1988 of 20 July: Internal Trading in Galicia. This Law regulates the advertising of the several means of sale.

Law 9/1997 of 21 August: Ordinance and Protection of Tourism in Galicia.

Law 9/1988 of 19 June: Statistics in Galicia. This regulates the advertising of statistical results.

## Madrid

Law 12/1995 of 21 April: Statistics in the Autonomous Community of Madrid.

Law 6/1995 of 29 March: Guarantees and Rights of Childhood in the Autonomous Community of Madrid.

Law 8/1995 of 28 March: Tourism Regulations in the Autonomous Community of Madrid.

## Murcia

Law 3/97 of 30 May: Pharmaceutical Regulations.

## Valencia

Law 8/1986 of 29 December: Trading and Shopping Centre Regulations.

Law 5/1997 of 25 June: Social Services in the Community of Valencia.

Law 3/1997 of 16 June: Drug Addiction and Other Related Disorders.

Law 5/1990 of 7 June: Statistics in the Community of Valencia.

# COMMUNITY DIRECTIVES

## Directive 92/28/EEC: Advertising of Medicines for Human Use

The companies and pharmaceutical laboratories that fabricate medicines for human use must make their products known to health professionals as well as to consumers. To do so, they carry out a constant advertising task in order to inform about and sell their products.

Notwithstanding this, it is important to keep in mind that the advertising of medicines may affect people's health and because of that, the administration considers that such advertising should basically be of an informative nature.

This is the main reason why the above Directive was approved, and its main purpose is to eliminate the discrepancies existing between national legislations with respect to the advertising of pharmaceutical products. It has been incorporated to the Spanish Juridical Ordinance, through Royal Decree 1416/1994.

## Directive 97/4/EC of the European Parliament and of the Council amending Council Directive 79/112/EEC on the Approximation of the Laws of the Member States Relating to the Labelling, Presentation and Advertising of Foodstuffs for Sale to the Ultimate Consumer

The following modifications to Directive 79/112/EEC are provided by this Directive:

(a) the use of names that have become popular by their use in the State of production is also allowed for products to be sold in other Member States;

(b) in order to provide the consumer with more information and ensure fair trade, the regulations pertaining to labelling have been improved giving wider information about the nature and characteristics of the products;

(c) the provisions applicable to sales names remain subject to a principle according to which the consumer should never be misled about the characteristics of any food product;

(d) the Directive also includes the obligation, which had been imposed by case law, of providing details on the labels concerning, specifically, the nature of the product, which allows the consumer to make his choice in full knowledge of what he is buying, and thus creating fewest obstacles to the free trade.

# SPECIAL APPROACH ON COMPARATIVE ADVERTISING FROM THE MEMBER STATES' VIEWPOINT

In order to analyse the new Directive on Misleading and Comparative Advertising, we will now refer to what is understood by these concepts and continue with a review of comparative law.

Comparative advertising has been defined as 'advertising in which the advertiser compares his offer with the offer of one or several of his competitors, identified or unequivocally identifiable, with the direct or indirect result of enhancing the advantages of his own products or services in relation with others'.

## Advertising regulations in France

Until 1992, Comparative Advertising in France was prohibited, by Art 1382 of the French Civil Code in the absence of any special legislation in matters of unfair competition, because comparative advertising was considered as an assumption of indirect denigration of the shop, products or services of a competitor. Comparative advertising was considered as such when the affected competitor was sufficiently identifiable by the public receiving the message and regardless of whether or not the information was sufficiently truthful.

The following exceptions to the prohibition were established:

(a) *the right to criticism*, provided the criticism is objective and moderate, and not implying or making references to specific competitors or competitors who may be easily identified;

(b) *the right to legitimate defence.* Any comparative advertising conceived as a reply to a previous act of unfair competition is lawful;

(c) *the defence of legitimate interests*, that is, the defence of interests that are important from the legal viewpoint, which in practice found few occasions for application.

In 1992, the *Loi renforçant la protection des consommateurs* authorised comparative advertising in the assumptions provided for under Art 10: advertising comparing goods and services with those of others was authorised when faithful, truthful and not likely to mislead the consumer. The advertising must always refer to the essential and most significant and verifiable characteristics of the goods or services that are made available to the market.

The comparison of prices must always refer to identical products sold under the same conditions, indicating the period during which such prices will be maintained. It should never seek support from individual or collective associations and its main purpose should never be taking advantage of the renown of a specific trade mark. No advertising should show products or services covered with marks that have been previously registered.

In products enjoying the benefits of a denomination of origin, comparisons are not authorised, unless the comparison is made with products that enjoy the same denomination.

The advertiser defined in the present article must be able to prove at any time the accuracy of his statements, indications or presentations.

## Advertising regulations in Belgium

Comparative advertising is strictly prohibited in Belgium as a result of a tradition transmitted to the jurisprudence and finally to the law.

In the absence of specific legislation in matters of unfair competition, Belgian case law established the prohibition of comparative advertising based on the provisions of the Civil Code. This tendency remained during the enforcement of the *Arrêté Royal* of 1934, despite the fact the text did not include any regulation that prohibited comparative advertising. This doctrine finally was incorporated into the legislative framework by means of the Trade Practices Act 1971, which included a provision prohibiting comparative advertising, which appears again in the new Trade Practices Act 1991.

This prohibition is supported by:

(a) the protection of commercial credibility: the protection of the honour and the reputation of the competitor affected.

(b) the fact that 'the competitor is entitled to be ignored even if the truth about him is being told'.

The *Arrêté Royal* of 1934, by Art 2(b), provided that 'anybody in the business of trading who spreads false information about persons, companies, merchandise or personnel of a competitor shall be committing an act against the standards of fairness'.

The courts ignored the fact that the regulation failed to make any reference to comparative advertising, which meant that the total prohibition for comparative advertising was maintained using the same arguments. Notwithstanding this, the case law established a number of exemptions:

(a) *legitimate defence*: provided there was previous aggravation by a third party, who should be the person at whom the comparative advertising was aimed; that the attack was legitimate; that the comparison was correct, proportionate, truthful, objective and adequate for the purposes sought; that the defence was not exercised in an abusive manner. Such strict conditions have, in practice, had little impact;

(b) *right to criticism*: criticism of products and services is admitted, provided the statements in the message are unquestionable; that the message refers to the facts and never to the person of the competitor; that the advertising message is not aimed at one or more specific competitors and that the criticism is proportionate, objective and non-aggressive;

(c) *comparison at the request of the clients*: comparisons among products or services are considered legitimate when replying to a demand formulated previously by an interested client and provided they are truthful, objective and avoid unnecessary denigration of the competitor.

Today, with the *Loi sur les pratiques du commerce et sur l'information et la protection du consommateur* 1991, the above prohibition continues in force with the same exemptions previously detailed.

## Advertising regulations in Italy

Article 2598.2 of the Codice Civile provides that 'any dissemination of news or statements about the products or the activity of a competitor likely to cause discredit shall be considered unfair competition'.

The Italian case law still clinging to the prohibition of comparative advertising only allows it in an indirect manner, that is, when it refers to a specific competitor only and justifying it as follows: 'Magnification of the quality and the merits of the product, although exaggerated, does not give rise by itself to an assumption of unfair competition unless accompanied by explicit or implicit comparative references or hints about the activity or products of the competitor.'

Presently, Italy is one of the European States that prohibit comparative advertising. As regards this prohibition, only five exceptions are known:

(a) the right to criticism;

(b) legitimate defence;

(c) verbal comparisons at the request of clients;

(d) comparisons required by the market structure;

(e) comparisons of prices.

The maintenance of comparative advertising in Italy is due, to a very important extent, to the weakness of consumers' defence in this country.

## Advertising regulations in Switzerland

In Switzerland, comparative advertising is allowed, and has been since the last century, when a judgment of the Federal Court dated 23 November 1895 stated:

If the statements are truthful, there will not be any unlawful act when the advertiser only states that his products have specific characteristics that are not present in the competitors' products, or that his own products are free of those defects that are inherent in the products of the competitors.

The Act against Unfair Competition (*Gesetz gegen den unlauteren Wettbewerb* (UWG)) 1943 did not represent any change in the regulations on comparative advertising, as it did not include any rule concerning this kind of competition, although it regulated acts of defamation under Art 1.2, which provided: 'Acts of defamation shall be considered as unfair competition as they contradict the standards of good faith of others, their merchandise, their services or their commercial relationships by means of false or unnecessarily offensive statements.'

The UWG 1986, in order to provide legal protection and clearly determine the boundaries of comparative advertising, included in a specific regulation a doctrine that, until then, had been maintained by the courts.

Article 3(e) provides that 'unfair advertising shall be that which compares in an inaccurate, misleading, offensive and parasitic manner its person, merchandise, activities, services, and prices with those of other competitors'. This represents the legal 'glorification' of comparative advertising in Switzerland.

From the above, it may be inferred that the only assumptions of unlawful comparative advertising are:

(a) inaccurate comparative advertising: advertising based on information that does not correspond with reality or on information that objectively may not be compared;

(b) misleading advertising: advertising which, even if based on actual information, is likely to mislead the public, or which advertises products or services that may not be compared;

(c) unnecessarily offensive comparative advertising: advertising which is not objectively expressed or justified or which primarily tends to damage the competitor, or which includes pejorative statements of a disproportionate nature;

(d) parasitic comparative advertising: It is only prohibited when is not necessary.

## Advertising regulations in Germany

The German law of the beginning of the century considered that comparative advertising was a basic legal practice, unless affected by special circumstances that could make it unfair.

The enactment of the UWG of 1909 did not present any change in this doctrine. In *Persönliche und sachliche Reklame in der Grossendustire*, 1916, Josef

Kohler prompted the unlawfulness of comparisons in advertising; the advertiser should never declare that the products of the competition are more expensive or of lower quality, as any assessment should be made by the public and not by the advertiser, who, in view of his bias, may not act as a judge or as a party.

This author was a decisive influence on the development of German law. A judgment of the Constitutional Court of 11 March 1927 included the above-mentioned doctrine in a case pertaining to comparative advertising.

In 1931, the prohibition of comparative advertising finds a definitive expression in the judgment of the Constitutional Court dated 6 October 1931.

The following are the exceptions to this prohibition established by the judgment of the Constitutional Court of 17 April 1944:

(a) *legitimate defence*: comparative advertising is lawful when representing an act of defence in connection with a previous unlawful attack from a competitor, and must comply with the following requirements:

- there must be a previous illegitimate attack committed by the competitor at whom the comparative advertising is aimed, that is, the advertiser doing the comparative advertising must be the victim of the attack. Such an attack does not necessarily need to be a comparison, although it needs to be contemporary or current;

- the comparative advertising must be necessary for the advertiser to be able to defend himself from the attack suffered; the announcer must prove he could not defend himself from the attack by other means of defence, or that at least the self-defence was the most effective means to avoid the damage arising from the attack;

- the comparison must be genuine and objective, and besides, it should be restrained to whatever is strictly necessary for the defence against the illegitimate attack. The investigation in this respect must be done on a case by case basis;

- as a last requirement, it is necessary that the public realises without any doubt that the comparison is an act of defence against a prior attack from a competitor;

(b) *comparison at the request of the client*: for this advertising to be lawful, the following requirements must be met:

- there must be an express request by the client, demanding to be informed of the advantages and disadvantages of the competitor's services. The demand made by the client must be express and specific, a general interest in the offers made by the competitor not being sufficient. The initiative must always come from the client;

- the advertiser must restrict himself to provide only the information that was specifically requested by the client;

- the comparison must be truthful and objective and must avoid any unnecessary slander against the affected competitor;

(c) *comparison required to explain a technical or economic procedure*: the following are the requirements for this advertising to be lawful:

- there must be a technical progress on an objective basis;
- the comparison with the competitor's products must be required for the explanation of the technical or economic procedure. The comparison is considered necessary when the advertiser cannot exploit the progress achieved through other means and without making any reference to the competitors;
- it must be truthful and objective, avoiding any unnecessary denigration of the competitor.

Currently, as a general rule, comparative advertising continues to be prohibited and, exceptionally, it is considered lawful when there is 'sufficient motive' to justify it and provided the form and content are always kept within the boundaries of whatever proves to be necessary. These motives are:

(a) comparison in legitimate defence;

(b) comparison at client's request;

(c) comparison necessary to explain technical and economic progress;

(d) comparison necessary to provide information to competitors.

Following 30 years of debate, the German approach continues to demand a change allowing Germany to withdraw from the very much reduced group of countries that forbid comparative advertising.

## Advertising regulations in Spain

We will begin the review of this matter with the Statute of Advertising 1964.

It is important to point out that Art 6 provides that 'within the exercise of any advertising activity, the standards of legality, veracity, authenticity and free competition must always be observed', the free competition aspect being the factor that determines if the comparative advertising is or is not lawful.

Article 10 provided the grounds used by the Central Advertising Jury to determine the prohibition of comparative advertising under the following terms: 'any advertising activity designed to create confusion among goods or services or tending to discredit competitors or their products shall be considered unfair, as will, in general terms, any advertising contrary to the norms of good manners and correct trading standards'. However, during the times the prohibition was running, the Central Advertising Jury only applied the general clauses on two occasions identifying good manners and correct trading standards with the deontological standards arising from professional ethics.

The decision of the Central Advertising Jury of 4 November 1976 implied a fundamental change in the doctrine applied by this institution, as it left behind the prohibitions, proclaiming that comparative advertising was legal with the following words:

> ... the use of phrases of comparison may not always be considered punishable, provided of course they are truthful, because: (a) comparative advertising is not forbidden by the law; (b) should this be the case, there would be a clear attempt against the rights of consumers; (c) in some cases it would go against the truth; (d) its prohibition would restrict the freedom of creation.

The essential principle of legality of comparative advertising was later on picked up by the General Advertising Act under Art 6, which provided: 'Comparative advertising shall be unfair when it fails to rely on essential, related and objectively demonstrable characteristics of the products or services, or when the goods or services are set aside with others that are unlike or unknown or have a limited presence in the market'.

This was also recognised later on by the Unfair Competition Act, which considered that 'the public comparison of the activity, renderings or establishment of one's own or of another with those of a third party when the comparison refers to particulars that are neither similar, nor relevant or verifiable, is deemed unfair'.

Also, any comparison contradicting the rules concerning misleading and denigrating practices shall be considered unfair.

Advertising is misleading 'when it misleads or can mislead its recipients in any way, including by its presentation, and may affect their economic conduct or injure or be capable of injuring a competitor. Advertising is also misleading where it silences certain fundamental aspects of the goods, activities or services when such omission can mislead the recipients'.

An act of denigration shall be 'the production or diffusion of statements on the activity, rendering, establishment or the business relationships of a third party that may damage its standing within the market'.

### Requirements concerning the objects of comparison

(a) The General Advertising Act only refers to products and services, however, the Unfair Competition Act makes an extension to include products, services, activities, establishments or other third party services.

(b) The objects of comparison must be similar or comparable.

(c) The advertiser must avoid choosing as objects of comparison products or services that are unknown or have a limited presence in the market.

(d) The objects of comparison shall be similar and consequently comparable when belonging to the same generic category and are commonly used to satisfy identical needs.

(e) The comparison with unknown products or products with limited presence in the market may not be considered as a misleading comparison.

### Requirements concerning the areas of comparison

(a) The advertiser may choose a single area of comparison, but at the same time it should exhaust all precautions necessary in order to prevent the comparison from generating an incorrect image overall.

(b) The advertiser must refer to all the primary characteristics which are unconditionally associated with the comparison area(s) chosen and that are unknown to the consumer.

(c) The comparison areas must be similar or related.

(d) The comparison shall refer to relevant characteristics of the objects compared. A relevant characteristic will be any circumstance that in some manner may affect the buyer's decision.

### Requirements concerning the contents of the comparison

(a) Veracity of the comparison; for any comparison to be lawful it needs to be truthful, which also implies a certain degree of current importance of the information under comparison.

(b) To the greatest possible extent, the comparison must be restricted to comparable information and facts.

(c) The comparison must avoid any misleading characteristics.

(d) It shall lack any derogatory characteristics.

## Directive 97/55/EC of 6 October 1997, amending Directive 84/450/EEC on Misleading Advertising to include Comparative Advertising

The above Directive defines comparative advertising as 'any advertising involving directly or indirectly a competitor or its goods or its services'.

Regarding the regulations concerning this matter, the Directive starts from the principle of lawfulness of comparative advertising, which, however, is a principle of limited legality as it provides for some requirements that must be complied with by the comparison.

### Requirements concerning the objects

The Community Directive does not impose a representative selection of the objects of comparison, leaving these up to the advertiser, given that the comparison may be made between only two products or services, although these products or services must satisfy the same needs or have the same purpose.

### Requirements concerning the areas of comparison

According to Art 3(1)(c), comparative advertising is allowed when comparing, in an impartial manner, one or more essential, verifiable and representative characteristics of the goods and services involved.

### Requirements concerning the content of the comparison

(a) The comparison shall not be misleading.

(b) The comparison shall not jeopardise or denigrate trade marks, commercial names or any other distinguishing marks or circumstances of a competitor.

(c) The comparison shall not create confusion in the market between an advertiser and a competitor or among trade marks, commercial names or other distinguishing signs or goods or services of the advertiser and those of a competitor.

(d) The advertiser shall not take unfair advantage of the reputation of a trade mark, commercial name or other distinguishing mark.

(e) The presentation of goods and services as imitations or replicas of other goods or services bearing a protected trade mark or name shall not be allowed.

Besides, there are two additional requirements that are only applicable in specific circumstances:

(a) Comparative advertising of a specific product that has a denomination of origin must refer to products that enjoy the same denomination of origin.

(b) Comparative advertising referring to products under a special or limited offer shall clearly and unequivocally indicate the date when the offer ends, and, where appropriate, the fact that the special offer is subject to the availability of the goods and services involved, and where the offer has not yet begun, the date as from when the special price or other conditions shall be applied.

# IMPACT OF THE COMMUNITY DIRECTIVE ON COMPARATIVE ADVERTISING ON SPANISH LAW

There are substantial coincidences between the regulations on comparative advertising in the Community Directive and the regulations contemplated by the General Advertising Act and the Unfair Competition Law. The differences, however, are restricted to only two aspects:

(a) neither the General Advertising Act nor the Unfair Competition Law consider the following specific requirements for particular comparisons that are included within the Community text:

- comparisons in favour of products enjoying a denomination of origin;
- comparative advertising concerning products under special offer;

(b) the General Advertising Law includes a requirement not considered by the Community Directive and considers as unfair advertising the comparison of products or services with other unknown products or services or those with limited presence in the market. It is important to recall that the legality requirements provided by the Community Directive are maximum requirements, which means that after the period of adaptation, the States will not be able to establish or maintain requirements different to those provided for by the Community regulations.

In summary, the incorporation of the Community Directive to the internal regulations will only demand slight modifications of detail and will not require a global review of regulations pertaining to comparative advertising.

The final harmonisation must become effective within a term of 30 months, which means the Member States will have that period of time to adjust their regulations to the Community Directive.

## ASSOCIATION FOR ADVERTISING SELF-REGULATION

In 1937, the International Chamber of Commerce started to co-ordinate a common base for the creation and development of self-regulation systems. Today, 33 countries have an independent self-regulatory organisation, among them Spain, where it is called the *Asociación de Autocontrol de la Publicidad* (Association for Advertising Self-Regulation (AAP)).

The European Advertising Standards Alliance (EASA) was incorporated during 1991 and its purpose is to group together all the self-regulatory associations of the different European countries and represent the interests of its members, among which is the AAP. The basic job of the AAP, among other activities, is to settle cross-border complaints.

It is important to point out that the EC Directive of 12 February 1972 on consumer protection recommended the Member States to create organisations to take care of self-regulation in advertising, and to co-operate with public organisations and consumer associations in that respect.

Directive 97/36/EC on misleading and comparative advertising provides that the 'voluntary controls conducted by autonomous organisations to eliminate misleading advertising may prevent the seeking of an administrative or legal action and because of this, it should always be encouraged'. On the other hand, the General Advertising Act provides the regulations of a procedural nature that must rule the sanctions and repression of unlawful advertising, regardless of the voluntary control conducted by self-regulatory organisations.

On 13 June 1995, the AAP was incorporated with the purpose of defending and supervising good practice in the Spanish market, in reply to the need of resolving eventual conflicts and providing an ethical framework to develop responsible and truthful communication.

The specific tasks of the AAP are:

(a) to settle controversies and resolve claims arising from a specific advertising activity that may affect fair competition or the consumer;

(b) to draft codes of advertising conduct for general and territorial application;

(c) to draft opinions or other kind of reports over advertising matters requested by partners or third parties;

(d) to co-operate with public administrations, national and international organisations to check that advertising regulations conform to the law;

(e) to contribute to the development and improvement of Spanish law in matters concerning advertising.

All the above leads to an arrangement of advertising activities in Spain in such a manner that it makes State and social control unnecessary as advertising companies themselves, through their self-regulatory instruments, may offer the public sufficient guarantees as far as strictness and ethical standards are concerned.

Likewise, self-regulatory instruments allow the settlement of conflicts out of court in an efficient, fair and quick manner that otherwise would imply long and costly litigation before the courts.

The AAP, of the several legal organisations contemplated by European self-regulating procedures, has chosen an independent jury (tribunal of arbitration) which:

(a) prepares and approves the codes of ethics concerning advertising;

(b) settles out of court any claims concerning advertising lodged against associated members or third parties;

(c) prepares and delivers reports or opinions;

(d) acts as arbitrator if required.

This jury acts in accordance with its rules and the AAP's bylaws and guarantees the right to be defended, the equal rights between the parties and the respect to the principle of contradiction.

The jury operates through plenary sessions and in sections; the plenary session approves the codes and decides on the appeals concerning the resolutions pronounced by the sections, which, in turn, take care of resolving the ordinary matters supervised by an Executive Committee.

The jury may act at the request of the Executive Committee or in reply to a claim filed by anyone with a legitimate interest in proceedings against a specific advertisement.

The AAP, as far as possible, intervenes in the first place in order to avoid submitting the dispute to the ordinary courts. The procedure is regulated by arbitration law.

In accordance with the bylaws, the resolutions are binding among the associates and represent a serious moral obligation for those not associated.

The resolutions pronounced by the AAP are published in the journal *Revista de la Asociación de Autocontrol de la Publicidad* (Advertising Self-regulation Review).

# LATEST DEVELOPMENTS

## Tobacco

The Health Ministries of the European Union reached, on 4 December 1997, an agreement to prohibit tobacco advertising. A common approach was adopted, which contemplates the approval of a Directive that will prohibit any kind of advertising of tobacco as from 1 October 2006. This Directive will also allow the Member States to maintain or introduce more strict requirements in order to guarantee the protection of people's health.

The Member States will have a term of three years to implement this Directive, and as from the end of 2001, the tobacco manufacturers will have an additional year to advertise in the written press and two years to sponsor worldwide events.

However, the Directive will not apply to communications aimed exclusively at professionals who participate in the tobacco trade, or the sale of printed material with tobacco advertising published or printed in third countries, provided the material is not primarily aimed at the Community market and is sold only at tobacco shops.

Regarding indirect advertising of tobacco, a Member State may allow a name already used in good faith for tobacco products and other products or services, commercialised either by a same company or by different companies before the publication of the Directive, to be used to advertise other products or services also. However, this name may only be used if its appearance differs from the tobacco product and provided it does not bear any other sign already used for the tobacco product.

No product or service may carry the name, mark, symbol or any other sign of a tobacco product, unless said product or service were already marketed with that name or mark at the time of enforcement of the Directive. In such case, the name, symbol or other sign of the product or service shall clearly differ from those used for the tobacco product.

Besides, free distribution is forbidden when the aim or direct or indirect result is the promotion of tobacco products.

## Alcoholic beverages

Sources from the Community Executive have stated that the European Commission 'has no intention whatsoever' to propose a prohibition on advertising alcoholic beverages in the European Community similar to the tobacco prohibition.

A spokesman from the Health Commission stated that 'the Commission has not considered the possibility of proposing a prohibition on advertising alcoholic beverages or the sponsorship of sports events in the European Union'.

The European Health Commissioner considers it is not possible to compare tobacco and alcohol, as it is a known fact that tobacco is harmful for those smoking and for those nearby, whereas 'it is also known that alcohol in moderate quantities may be beneficial'.

## Television Without Frontiers

On 16 February 1998, the Cabinet of Ministers approved the Law amending Law 25/1994 which incorporated into Spanish law by Directive 89/552/EEC concerning the co-ordination of legal provisions of the Member States with respect to television broadcasting activities. This new Law will also incorporate into Spanish law the new Directive 97/36/EC of the European Parliament and Council which modified the 1989 Directive.

This draft Law presents three basic aspects:

(a) it assumes the new Community Directive;

(b) it regulates television activity with more precision; and

(c) it contemplates the guarantee of the rights of users in relation to specific forms of abusive advertising or advertising that may be detrimental to the recipients' legitimate interests.

The text regulates the scheduling of programmes and supervises teleshopping, adverts that encourage violence, or those that discriminate by reasons of sex. In this respect, the Law says that:

> ... any television advertisement and teleshopping activity which encourage behaviour that may be harmful to health, people's security, or the protection of the environment; attempt against the human dignity or religious or political beliefs or are discriminatory for reasons of birth, race, sex, religion, nationality,

opinion or any other personal or social circumstance, shall be deemed unlawful.

Subliminal procedures shall not be allowed in advertising, nor in teleshopping, and the spots shall not encourage violence or antisocial behaviour or appeal to fear or superstition or encourage abuse, recklessness, negligence or aggressive conduct.

The draft Law gives teleshopping special treatment, as a phenomenon totally different from advertising, and prohibits the use of subliminal procedures and those which encourage under age people to buy or rent goods or services. Self-promotion adverts of television stations are considered as advertising.

Another important issue refers to the sponsorship of television programmes by companies that manufacture, distribute or sell medicines, health products or medical treatments, which is allowed provided that only the name of the sponsor is mentioned, omitting any reference to the products or services offered.

## USEFUL ADDRESSES

Agencia de Protección de Datos
Paseo de la Castellana 41
28046 Madrid
Tel: + 34 91 308 48 82/91 308 49 08/91 308 49 77

Anuncios (advertising publication)
Principe de Vergara 15
28001 Madrid
Tel: + 34 91 435 78 47

Asociacón de Autocontrol de la Publicidad (AAP)
Paseo de Recoletos 18 Esc Izqda 6 Dcha
28001 Madrid
Tel: + 34 91 576 66 01

Asociacón Española de Anunciantes
Paseo de la Castellana 121
28046 Madrid
Tel: + 34 91 556 03 51/91 555 46 48

Asociación Usuarios de la Comunicación
C/Carranza 13
28004 Madrid
Tel: + 34 91 448 73 41/91 448 73 83

C/Principe de Vergara 25
28001 Madrid
Tel: + 34 91 556 03 51/91 556 46 48

Secretaría General de Comunicación del Ministerio de Fomento
C/Alcalá 50 (Palacio)
28014 Madrid
Tel: + 34 91 521 65 00/91 531 39 21

## CHAPTER 15

# SWEDEN

*Lennart Lindström and Mårten Stenström*

## INTRODUCTION

The structure and development of Swedish media advertising since 1990 has, not surprisingly, been affected by the commencement of television advertising in Sweden in 1991. Before 1 July of that year, television or radio advertising was not allowed in Sweden.

The total advertising and media spend in Sweden amounted approximately to SKr 35 bn (approx \$4.5 bn) in 1997. Of this amount, approx SKr 8.4 bn is attributable to the daily press, SKr 2.9 billion to television advertising and SKr 0.42 bn to radio advertising.

Forecasts suggest that the financial turnover of the advertising market will increase in 1998.

## The main alternative forms of advertising in Sweden

### *Daily press*

The commencement of television advertising has not materially affected the yearly advertising income, approx SKr 8 bn, of the Swedish daily press. Some of the biggest daily newspapers in Sweden are Dagens Nyheter, Svenska Dagbladet and Göteborgsposten (morning papers); Expressen and Aftonbladet (evening papers). Surveys have indicated that approx 80% of the Swedish population read a daily paper every day.

### *Trade press*

The quality of advertising in the trade press in Sweden is regarded higher by the consumers than other advertising. Surveys also indicate that the impact of the advertising is very high. The advertising income for the trade press in 1997 was approx SKr 1.25 bn. The published titles are represented by an interest organisation named 'Fackpressen'.

## Weekly press

Some of the largest publishers are Bonniers, Allers, Egmont, Medströms and Albinsson & Sjöberg, who together distribute some 100 titles. The annual advertising income is approx SKr 500 m. The impact of advertising in the weekly press is regarded as relatively low.

## Outdoor public advertising

Seven companies sell advertising space in this sector (hoardings, buses and elsewhere in public places). The two largest are Wennergren-Williams and ARE-bolagen. The annual advertising income in this sector is approx SKr 500 m. The impact of this advertising is regarded as high.

## Direct advertising

Three large advertisers dominate the field: Posten (the Sweden Post), Citymail and Svensk Direktreklam. The total annual spend in this field varies between SKr 2 and 2.5 bn, and is thus about the same as that for television advertising in Sweden.

## Television

More than 95% of Swedes have a television set in their home. Most of those people have access to TV 4, which is currently the only terrestrial television channel with nationwide coverage which is allowed to broadcast advertising (see below, 2.4.2). Other major channels where advertising is allowed are TV 3, Kanal 5, MTV, Eurosport and TV 6. The total annual income has risen substantially since the beginning of television advertising in Sweden. In 1995, the income was SKr 2.2 bn for TV 4, TV 3 and Kanal 5. TV advertising in Sweden is said to have a fairly high impact.

## Radio

Advertising is not allowed on the four existing Swedish channels of terrestrial radio with nationwide coverage. The most important source of radio advertising is the commercial local radio channels, which mostly broadcast music to the younger public. Four companies dominate the market: Radio Rix, Megapol, Energy (NRJ) and Radio City. The total turnover for radio advertising in Sweden in 1995 was approx SKr 230 m. The impact of radio advertising in Sweden is regarded as fairly good.

## The advertisers

Producers of day to day products, such as foodstuffs and clothes, clearly dominate the list of big spenders of advertising money. The big foodstuffs distributor, ICA-handlarnas AB, spent slightly less than SKr 600 m on advertising in 1997.

The 20 largest advertising buyers in Sweden spent in total approx SKr 4.3 bn on advertising in 1997.

## The advertising agencies

The Swedish advertising agencies employ approx 6,800 people and have an annual turnover of approx SKr 10–12 bn. Some of the major firms are Rönnberg McCann, Love Brindfors, Observa, Grey and Hall and Cederquist/Y & R. The Advertisers' Association of Sweden (Sveriges Reklamförbund) is the advertising agencies' trade association, and is a member of the European Association of Advertising Agencies (EAAA). As well as protection of the agencies' interests, the objectives of the association are, amongst others, to debate the ethics of advertising and to spread knowledge thereof. The association arranges an annual competition called the 'Golden Egg', to choose the year's best advertisement. Swedish advertising has also gained success internationally; for example, at the American CLIO competition and at the advertising week in Cannes.

# SWEDISH ADVERTISING LAW

## Background

The Swedish legislation pertaining to the media has a relatively short history, and could, in general, be said to have developed during the last 50 years. The structure of today's regulation was mainly shaped in the 1970s, when two central Acts were passed: the Improper Marketing Act (1970:412) and the former Marketing Act (1975:1418). The main purpose of the legislation was consumer protection.

A characteristic of Swedish marketing legislation is that the State has the primary responsibility for ascertaining that a sound ethical standard is exercised in advertising and other kinds of marketing. However, there was formerly an order according to which the market itself, through different organs, was expected to exercise such standards. During the 1960s, the most important organ was the Swedish Council on Business Practice (*Näringslivets opinionsnämnd*).

Certain international conventions, for example, the rules of the Paris Convention on the Protection against Unfair Competition and other international treaties regarding protection of labelling connected with geographical origin, have been of great importance for the development of Swedish marketing legislation. Recently, the rules pertaining to marketing and competition have been harmonised with the directives and regulations of the European Union.

Until 1996, the former Marketing Act of 1975 was the central Act in the field. The Act has now been replaced by a new Marketing Act, which came into force on 1 January 1996, and which is outlined below, pp 782–87. However, it is important to observe that the precedents of the last 20 years relate to the former Marketing Act and that the new Marketing Act is, to a great extent, a codification of court practice in the marketing area.

Like the former Marketing Act of 1975, the new Marketing Act covers all offers of products and services, although it is complemented by different Acts with more detailed provisions of marketing methods for certain products and services.

The former Marketing Act of 1975 was thus gradually complemented by Acts with more detailed legislation; partly by Acts which seriously restricted the marketing and advertising of alcohol and tobacco, partly by way of adding rules on marketing and advertising to existing Acts regarding the sale of finance and insurance to consumers.

## The structure of Swedish marketing legislation

### The new Marketing Act (1995:450)

The new Marketing Act (1995:450) has been in effect since 1 January 1996 and is outlined below, pp 782–87. The main aim of the Act is the interest of consumers and traders in connection with the marketing of products and services, and to prevent improper marketing to consumers and traders. The Act is applicable to all sectors of the media which could be used in marketing. There are also additional regulations regarding advertising on radio and television (outlined below, p 782.

The Act only concerns commercial marketing; broadcasting of news, politics and religion, etc, are thus not covered by the Act.

The Act contains, among other provisions, a general clause which enables actions against improper marketing. The general clause can also be applied to order a trader to provide certain information in connection with the marketing. The general clause has been complemented by provisions containing direct prohibitions against certain specified marketing methods, as well as provisions which require the trader to take certain courses of action.

There is also a provision which enables the prohibition of sale of products which are clearly unfit for their purpose.

## Special rules for certain kinds of products

There are complementary regulations to the Marketing Act which partially limit the freedom of traders to act in the market. These regulations relate to the manufacturing, marketing and sale of certain kinds of products.

### Tobacco and alcohol

By the Tobacco Advertising Act (*Tobakslagen* 1993:581) and the Liquor Advertising Act (*Lag med vissa bestämmelser om marknadsföring av alkoholdrycker* 1978:763) certain rules have been introduced which completely ban advertising in newspapers, on the radio or on television of tobacco, hard liquor, wine or strong beer. The latter Act is also complemented by certain regulations in the Beverages Production Act (*Lag om tillverkning av drycker m m* 1977:292) regarding marketing. A marketing action that violates any of these Acts shall also be regarded as violating the general clause of the Marketing Act and could hence be subject to the remedies available under the Marketing Act (below).

Matters concerning the marketing of alcoholic beverages and tobacco are dealt with by the National Board for Consumer Policies (*Konsumentverket*).

In the Tobacco Advertising Act, there are also regulations regarding labelling with warnings and a declaration of contents. The manufacturer and the importer are jointly responsible for such labelling. The National Board for Health and Welfare (*Socialstyrelsen*) is the supervising authority regarding matters of labelling.

As will be clear below (see p 790) a manufacturer of tobacco or alcoholic beverages is not allowed to be a sponsor of television programmes.

### Pharmaceutical products

Under the Pharmaceutical Products Act (*Läkemedelslagen* 1992:859), pharmaceutical products must not be sold until they have been examined and approved by the Medical Products Agency (*Läkemedelsverket*). Sections 4 and 21 contain certain regulations regarding the marketing and labelling of pharmaceutical products. The application of the Act is supervised by the Medical Products Agency.

### Foodstuffs

The Foodstuffs Act (*Livsmedelslagen* 1971:511), contains, for example, regulations of labelling of foodstuffs and also rules prescribing that certain designations of foodstuffs shall be exclusive to certain products. As an example of the latter, it may be noted that the Swedish word for milk should only be used if the products meet with certain restrictions regarding additives, etc. The National Food Administration is the main controlling authority in the country, but there are also regional and local boards which exercise control over foodstuffs.

### Chemical products

The Chemical Products Act (*Lagen om kemiska produkter* 1985:426) requires, amongst other things, the labelling of such products, but there are no specific regulations regarding advertising of chemical products in the Act (although such products are also covered by the Marketing Act). However, the Act requires the supervising authorities – mainly the National Chemicals Inspectorate (*Kemikalieinspektionen*) – to report to the Consumer Ombudsman if the authority finds that an action for prohibition of marketing of a chemical product is called for, for reasons of protection of health or the environment.

### Loans to consumers

The marketing of loans which traders grant consumers for individual purposes are dealt with in the Act on Loans to Consumers (*Konsumentkreditlagen* 1992:830).

Apart from mandatory rules regarding provision that apply to such loans, the Act contains rules on their marketing. In general, the Act calls for restricted and reasonable marketing. The Act provides that the marketing of such loans must not mislead the consumer as to their financial consequences or tempt him to make rash decisions to take out a loan – for example, by advertising it as totally problem free. The information that must be given shall be clear and correct, and shall declare the effective rate of interest, etc.

A trader who supplies insurance to consumers is also obliged to provide information. This is clear from the Consumer Insurance Act (*Konsumentförsäkringslagen* 1980:38).

The two Acts discussed above prescribe that the remedies provided by the Marketing Act shall apply if traders do not comply with the above provisions.

## Other marketing legislation

The Product Safety Act (*Produktsäkerhetslagen* 1988:1604) extends to products and services supplied by a trader to consumers for private use or consumption.

The aim of the Act is to counteract personal injuries or damage to property. In this regard, a trader could:

(a) be ordered to provide safety information in connection with the marketing of a product, if it is of particular importance in preventing personal injury or damage to property;

(b) be prohibited from marketing products or services which present a risk of personal injury or damage to property;

(c) be ordered to provide suitable risk information in connection with the marketing, if supplying goods or services which present a risk of personal injury or damage to property;

(d) be ordered to withdraw goods or services to a reasonable extent to prevent personal injury or damage to property;

(e) be prohibited from exporting goods presenting a risk of serious bodily harm.

The Act has been amended twice to comply with the relevant European directives.

The Swedish National Board for Consumer Policies (*Konsumentverket*) and the Swedish Consumer Ombudsman (*Konsumentombudsmannen* (KO)) are responsible for monitoring compliance with the Act. However, in the case of the products which are subject to special regulation (chemicals, foodstuffs, pharmaceutical products, etc), there are special authorities which carry out this monitoring. To ensure compliance with the Products Safety Act, the Consumer Ombudsman may either directly, or through the Market Court, serve a compliance order on the trader. Such orders are regularly issued under penalty of a fine.

*The Act on Use of Names and Pictures in Advertising*

This Act (*Lagen om namn- och bild i reklam* 1978:800) has introduced a prohibition on the use of names of private persons or their pictures in advertising without their prior consent. This is also the case regarding celebrities, such as film stars, actors or actresses and athletes.

## Provisions in private law relevant to marketing

Swedish Acts in the sphere of product law contain provisions stipulating when a product or service shall be regarded as in default. One of the criteria is thus the product's or service's conformity with information supplied in the marketing or advertising thereof. This is the case in s 18 of the Sale of Goods Act (*Köplagen* 1990:931), s 19 of the Consumer Sale of Goods Act (*Konsumentköplagen* 1990:932) and s 10 of the Consumer Services Act (*Konsumenttjänstlagen* 1985:716). The two latter Acts also state that a product or service is to be regarded as in default if sold in violation of a prohibition under the Marketing Act.

*Norms for business ethics and self-regulatory provision of the market*

The legal provisions outlined above are complemented by codes of practice which have developed in different sectors of business (see below). These codes of practice are usually not legally binding. The application of the general clause in the Marketing Act (s 4) prohibiting improper marketing is, however, often dependent on such codes of practice to judge whether a marketing action is improper or not.

*Rules relating to advertising on radio and television*

As will become clear below, and as already mentioned, the new Marketing Act applies to all kinds of media advertising, including radio and television advertising. Certain restrictions relating to advertising on radio and television are, however, laid down in a new Act, the Radio and Television Act (1996:844). These rules conform to the relevant EU directive and concern the shape of such advertising and its placement in programmes.

These rules will be covered in detail below, p 785.

## The new Marketing Act (1995:450)

As stated above, the new Marketing Act is applicable irrespective of what media are used for the advertisement and irrespective of the kind of products advertised. The aim of the Act is clear from its first section, namely, to promote the interests of consumers and traders in relation to the marketing of products and to counteract improper marketing to consumers or traders.

The Act rests mainly on a general clause, which requires conformity with good marketing ethics and provision of information. The general clause is complemented by sections with specific prohibitions against certain kinds of marketing measures and sections calling for certain measures to be observed in marketing.

Possible sanctions under the Act are administrative fines (*marknadsstörningsavgift*), damages to a party who has suffered from the improper marketing, prohibitions, and orders which normally shall be sanctioned under penalty of a fine.

*The general clause*

The general clause is to be found in s 4 of the Act, and reads as follows:

Marketing must be compatible with good marketing practice and in other respects be fair towards consumers and traders.

When marketing, traders must provide such information as is of particular importance from the consumer perspective.

In order to judge what is good marketing practice, one must look to what constitutes good business practice within the economy or industry, to recommendations issued by authorities in the field of marketing (such as norms issued by the Swedish National Board for Consumer Policies), which the authorities have developed in co-operation with different self-regulatory bodies within the economy or industry (see below), and to the practice and precedents developed over the years by the Market Court (Marknadsdomstolen) in its application of, above all, the former Marketing Act. Internationally applied norms can also be of importance.

The specific requirement, in para 2 of s 4, for the provision of relevant information in marketing, has no similarity to the marketing law of other countries (as far as the author is aware). In separate Swedish Acts relating to marketing, there are also detailed provisions for the provision of information in marketing. In the practical application, there could appear to be certain conflicts between, on one hand, the wish of a trader to make commercial announcements with a simple and powerful message and, on the other hand, the demands for the provision of information which could be expensive and heavy and which could also have an impact on the competitive situation. It is clear from the practice of the Market Court that a comparison should be made in such a situation between different needs and interests. In a case from 1981 (MD 1981:4) the Market Court required a trader to inform consumers that certain stoves were also supplied by the group under other trade marks.

Under s 15 of the Marketing Act, a trader who fails to provide information of importance may be ordered, under penalty of a fine, to provide such information.

### Certain demands under the Act

In ss 5–13 of the Act, specific rules have been enacted which, in reality, could already be applied using the general clause in s 4. Those specific provisions do, however, regard common violations and are based on the practice of the Market Court in its application of the general clause of the former Marketing Act.

The trader, or anyone acting on his behalf, can be ordered to pay an administrative fine (below, p 783) if he maliciously or negligently violates any of the following specific regulations. However, violation of the general clause is not sanctioned by such a fine.

Section 5 states that all advertising and other marketing must be made and presented in such a way that it does not create the risk of being understood to be non-commercial. It must also be clear which trader is behind the marketing.

Section 6, which concerns misleading advertising, emanates mainly from the European Misleading Advertising Directive (Council Directive 84/450) and Sweden's Treaty obligations to adopt the Madrid Convention 1981.

Under the section, a trader must not use expressions, etc, which are misleading as regards the trader's own or another trader's business. This concerns in particular expressions, etc, concerning prices, payment terms, quality, nature, amount, origin, manufacturing method, or effect on health or the environment.

In addition, the section deals with comparative advertising which, in a misleading manner, describes another trader's activities, goods or services or the advertising party's own activities, goods or services in relation to those of the other trader. Thus, the European Comparative Advertising Directive is implemented by this section and by the general clause in s 4 of the Act.

In s 7, a rule is introduced which prohibits the trader's use of packaging which, through its size or shape in general, is misleading with respect to the amount, size or character of the product.

To implement Art 10 *bis* of the Paris Convention on the Protection of Industrial Property, a rule has been introduced in s 8 of the Marketing Act which states that a trader in his marketing must not use imitations that are misleading by being easily confused with other traders' well known and distinctive products. An exception is made for products whose shape and distinction serves a mainly functional purpose.

The use of the expression 'bankruptcy', alone or combined with sales advertising, is banned by s 9 for sales other than those conducted by a bankruptcy estate or on its behalf.

Under ss 10 and 11, a trader may, in his marketing, use the expressions 'closing down sale', 'clearance sale', 'closing' or similar expressions (s 10), or 'bargain sale' or similar expressions (s 11) only under certain conditions detailed in the respective sections.

Section 12 prohibits a trader from misleading about obligation to pay by delivering products to someone who has not expressly ordered them.

Under s 13, there are certain provisions regulating the use of combination offers, for example, offers to obtain additional products free of charge or at a special price. In connection with such offers, the trader must provide clear information about:

(a) the conditions of the offer;

(b) the nature and value of the offer;

(c) the time limits and other limits of the offer.

## Sanctions under the Marketing Act

### Prohibitions and orders

Under s 14 of the Act, a trader whose marketing actions violate the above-mentioned general clause of s 4 of the Act may be prohibited from proceeding with such marketing or taking any similar action. Such prohibitions may also be directed towards an employee of the trader or anyone who acts on behalf of the trader (for example, an advertising agency) and anyone else who has contributed to the marketing.

If anyone does not comply with the liability under the general clause to provide information, he may, under s 15, be ordered to provide such information. Such an order can also be served on people other than the trader. The order can, for example, contain an obligation to provide the information either in advertisements, in other marketing measures which the trader uses in the marketing, or by labelling (on the product, or in some other way where the product is sold).

Someone who supplies products clearly unfit for their designated purpose can be prohibited from making such sales under s 17 of the Act.

The kinds of orders and prohibitions which follow will normally be imposed under penalty of a fine. The fine should be high enough that the person towards whom the order or prohibition is directed will refrain from violation thereof. There is no upper limit for such fines.

Orders and prohibitions can also, under s 20 of the Act, be given immediate effect if there are weighty reasons therefor. Such interim decisions are valid until replaced by a final decision in the district court or in the Market Court. A court will only issue an interim decision where the applicant shows that there are reasonable grounds for his action and reasonable grounds to believe that the defendant will diminish the importance of a future decision by certain actions or certain omissions. Hence, it is the applicant who carries the burden of proof for these prerequisites.

### Market Disruption Charge

A trader who violates the provisions of ss 5–13 with specific types of impermissible marketing measures can be obliged to pay an administrative charge to the State, the Market Disruption Charge. Under s 24, the Market Disruption Charge shall not fall below SKr 5,000, and shall not exceed SKr 5 m. However, the charge must not exceed 10% of the trader's turnover for the preceding fiscal year. Only intentional or negligent violations are sanctioned by the Market Disruption Charge. Someone who acts on the trader's behalf, for example, an advertising agency, can also be obliged to pay the Market Disruption Charge.

In ss 26–27 of the Act, a provision of limitation has been introduced regarding the Market Disruption Charge. The time of limitation is five years.

In order to secure a claim for Market Disruption Charge, a court may issue a decision of attachment.

## Damages

Under s 29 of the Act, a trader who intentionally or negligently violates one of the prohibitions or injunctions mentioned above, or who violates the specific provision of ss 5–13, shall be obliged to compensate the damage suffered by a consumer or another trader. A trader who has had costs accrued due to another trader's unlawful marketing may thus obtain compensation therefor.

Under s 30, a claim for damages becomes statute-barred unless an action for damages is commenced within five years from the date when the loss was suffered.

## Miscellaneous

If a trader ignores a prohibition issued against him or violates the provisions of ss 5–13, a court may, to a reasonable extent, decide that misleading information on a product or its packaging should be destroyed or altered. If the misleading effect cannot be prevented in any other way, the court may decide that the goods shall be destroyed (s 31). In addition, under s 32, a court may impose a suitable interim action in order to guarantee a possible future decision of destruction.

As a rule of thumb, the party losing a case under the Marketing Act will be obliged to compensate the winning party for his costs. A provision to this effect has been introduced in s 55, which mainly refers to the general rules of costs of procedure in Chapter 18 of the Swedish Code of Procedure.

### Supervising and deciding authorities under the Marketing Act

The general supervising and controlling body is the National Board for Consumer Policies (*Konsumentverket*). The authority obtains reports from the public and also controls marketing measures on its own initiative. Questions of possible violations can often be solved by negotiations with the traders.

The authority co-operates with the Consumer Ombudsman (*Konsumentombudsmannen* (KO)), who, in some cases, has been given authority to issue prohibitions or orders to provide information and who also has authority to commence actions before the relevant courts.

Regarding all remedies other than prohibitions and injunctions issued directly by the Consumer Ombudsman, the Stockholm City Court is the relevant court where the Consumer Ombudsman may commence actions. Along with the Consumer Ombudsman, traders and associations of consumers or traders have the authority to commence actions. As regards claims for the Marketing Disruption Charge, however, such authority is limited.

A judgment or decision issued by the Stockholm City Court may be appealed to the Market Court. Orders to pay fines for non-conformity with orders or prohibitions of authorities are, however, appealed to the Svea Court of Appeal in Stockholm.

### Codes of practice and regulatory bodies

At present, there are about 20 different programmes of measures which have been introduced by the market with a view to attaining good ethical standards in marketing. Some of the programmes cover all types of business, but most of them cover one type only.

Examples of codes of practice covering all types of business are the rules of advertising of the ICC. These rules are supervised in Sweden by a council founded by different bodies in the market and the Swedish National Committee of the ICC. Regarding questions of discrimination between the sexes in advertising, a council has been established by the Swedish Advertisers' Association (*Annonsörföreningen*) and the Advertisers Association of Sweden (*Sveriges Reklamförbund*). Furthermore, the Swedish Newspaper Publishers' Association (*Svenska Tidningsutgivareföreningen*), the Swedish Weekly Press Association (VECTU) and the Swedish Trade Press Organisation (*Fackpressen*) have together issued rules dealing with identification of advertising material.

## Specific rules relating to advertising on television and radio

### Introduction

Advertising on television or radio was not allowed in Sweden until 1 July 1991, when changes in the legislation were introduced together with the creation of a new commercial television channel (TV 4).

In 1992, a new constitutional Act was created: the Freedom of Speech Act, which regulates the freedom of speech on television and radio, etc. The Act contains, for example, a prohibition against censorship, freedom of establishment and protection for sources. Apart from the Freedom of Speech Act, the following Acts have been some of the more important ones in the field:

(a) the Radio Act (1966:755);

(b) the Local Radio Act (1993:120);

(c) the Cable Act (1991:2027);

(d) the Satellite Act (1992:1356).

In the summer of 1996, a new Act was introduced in Sweden, the Radio and Television Act (*Radio-och TV-lagen* 1996:844), which, as from 1 December 1996, has replaced these Acts, each of which regulated one different form of broadcasting. During a transitional period this will not, however, be the case for local radio, which will continue to be regulated separately, by the Local Radio Act. Only minor amendments are introduced in the substantive content of the relevant provisions. Thus, the reform now described was more a question of form and order than a question of change in policy.

The relevant provisions raise demands of impartiality and objectivity, and regulate questions of sponsorship of programmes and frequency of commercials. They also ban broadcasting in terrestrial television and radio programmes on behalf of others where the aim is to gain support for political or religious views.

As will become clear, the general statutes in the field of Swedish marketing law (primarily, the Marketing Act, see above) also apply to advertising on television and radio. Broadcasting of commercials is thus not protected by the Freedom of Speech Act, which otherwise applies to broadcasting. Under Swedish law, broadcast information is regarded as advertising if it has a commercial purpose and commercial content.

A checklist for television advertising has been issued by the Consumer Ombudsman, the Swedish Advertisers' Association and the Advertisers' Association of Sweden. This list, which is based on legal regulations as well as court practice and market norms, deals with the substantive content of the advertising, not the formal restrictions on placing of advertising in television programmes, etc.

It is of great interest to note that the provisions concerning advertising, etc, found in the Radio and Television Act, which are examined more closely below, p 787, are directed principally at the broadcasting companies. In no event can the trader who books the advertising be reached by the sanctions under the Broadcasting Acts. The trader's responsibility is covered by the Marketing Act and the other provisions mentioned above (see p 782). Those rules thus apply without restriction to advertising in all media, including television, radio, newspapers and hoardings.

As regards advertising and sponsorship in broadcasting, the provisions that apply to different broadcasting media vary to some extent. The law makes a distinction between:

(a) terrestrial radio and television with nationwide coverage;

(b) local radio;

(c) radio and television broadcast by cable;

(d) radio and television broadcast by satellite.

## The shaping of commercials in different broadcast media not covered by the general rules of the Marketing Act, etc

### Terrestrial radio and television with nationwide coverage

In Sweden, the large public service group comprising *Sveriges Radio* (SR) and *Sveriges Television* (SVT), which broadcasts on four radio channels (*Sveriges Radio*) and two television channels (*Sveriges Television*), provides the majority of terrestrial broadcasting with nationwide coverage. No advertising may appear on these channels, which are financed through licence fees. Since 1991, a new channel, TV 4, has been broadcasting terrestrial television nationwide. This channel is financed by advertising.

All terrestrial nationwide broadcasting is covered by the Radio and Television Act. The reason for the fact that advertising is allowed on TV 4 but not on *Sveriges Television* is that the two broadcasting companies have different agreements with the State. Thus, it is not the Radio and Television Act that restricts broadcasting of commercials, but the agreement between the State and the broadcasting companies. However, the Radio and Television Act has important restrictions for a broadcasting company allowed to broadcast advertising under agreement with the State.

In Ch 6, s 1 of the Radio and Television Act, there is a requirement that broadcasting is carried out in line with the fundamental ideas of democracy, the principles of equal value of every human being and the freedom and dignity of the individual.

Regarding the shaping of advertising, the following applies:

(a) persons who have prominent positions in news programmes may not appear in advertisements. This also applies to persons or characters with prominent positions in children's programmes;

(b) advertising must not be targeted at children below the age of 12 (note also the restrictions regarding the placing of advertisements in children's programmes; see below, p 791);

(c) advertising must not aim to support political or religious views.

### Local radio

Broadcasting of local radio in Sweden is only handled by private companies, which finance the broadcasting by advertising and sponsorship.

The Local Radio Act contains a provision which calls for impartiality and objectivity of broadcasting other than advertising.

There are only a few broadcasting regulations applicable to the shaping of advertising in local radio. In particular, persons with prominent positions in news programmes must not appear in advertising.

*Cable television*

Regarding advertising on television broadcast by cable, there are different rules for broadcasting by the owner of the cable network and broadcasting over the network by local cable television companies.

As for local cable television companies, no advertising is allowed at all (but regarding sponsorship, see below).

As for broadcasting by the owner of the cable network or someone broadcasting in agreement with the owner, however, advertising is allowed. The advertising must not be targeted at children under the age of 12 (note also the restrictions concerning the placing of advertisements in children's programmes; see below, p 791).

As regards the shaping of the advertising on satellite channels, the following applies:

(a) persons with prominent positions in news programmes must not appear in advertising. The same applies for persons or characters who have prominent positions in children's programmes;

(b) advertising must not be directed at children under the age of 12 (note also the restrictions concerning the placing of advertisements in children's programmes; see below, p 791).

## *Sponsorship of programmes in different broadcasting media*

*Terrestrial radio and television with nationwide coverage*

In the agreements entered into between the State and Sveriges Television and TV 4 respectively, it is stipulated that the broadcasting companies are allowed to finance some kinds of programmes by sponsorship. For TV 4, this is the case for all kinds of programmes except for news programmes or children's programmes.

The following restrictions apply for programme sponsorship:

(a) the name of the sponsor shall be stated before or after the programme;

(b) for broadcasting by Sveriges Television, the sponsor's logo must not be shown if it is also used as a logo for the sponsor's products or services;

(c) the logo or the company name may only be shown still;

(d) on TV 4, but not on Sveriges Television, the sponsor's message can, under certain circumstances, be accompanied by music;

(e) a programme may not be sponsored by a company whose main activity is the production or marketing of alcohol or tobacco.

## Local radio

As for sponsorship on local radio, the same rules apply as for cable and satellite television; see below.

## Cable and satellite television

For local broadcasting companies and for broadcasts by the owner of the cable network, the sponsorship of television programmes is allowed. For cable and satellite television, the Radio and Television Act provides that it shall be announced in a suitable manner at the beginning and at the end of the programme if the programme has been financed by anyone other than the company responsible for the broadcast. To decide what is a 'suitable manner', it should be possible to follow the rules which apply to national terrestrial broadcasting.

In addition, news programmes must not be sponsored. Companies supplying tobacco, alcohol or medical products may not act as sponsors.

## Placing of commercials or advertisements in different broadcast media

### Terrestrial radio and television with nationwide coverage

As stated above, only TV 4 is entitled to broadcast commercials. There is no terrestrial radio channel with nationwide coverage entitled to broadcast commercials.

Under the Radio and Television Act, the following provisions apply (Ch 7):

(a) advertising time must not exceed eight minutes per broadcast hour (with some exceptions, 10 minutes during prime time television). Blocks of commercials must not fall below one minute;

(b) a maximum of 10% of the broadcasting time per 24 hours may consist of advertising;

(c) advertising may be shown only between programmes, or between two complete parts of a programme, provided that neither part falls below 20 minutes;

(d) advertising may also interrupt programmes, but only if it is placed in longer interruptions in sports programmes, shows or events;

(e) advertising may not appear in children's programmes;

(f) a signature tune must commence and terminate commercial time, so that it is clear that advertising is starting or finishing.

*Local radio*

Under the Local Radio Act, advertising may not exceed eight minutes per broadcast hour (with some exceptions, 10 minutes).

*Cable television*

As is clear above, advertising is not allowed by a local cable broadcasting company. For broadcasts by the owner of the cable network, the same provisions apply as for terrestrial television channels with nationwide coverage, see above.

*Satellite television*

For the broadcasting of satellite television from Sweden, the same provisions apply as for terrestrial television channels with nationwide coverage, see above.

For TV 3, which is a satellite channel with broad coverage in Sweden, the Satellite Act does not apply, since the broadcasts are transmitted from Great Britain. Thus, the company can, for example, make interruptions for advertising in the middle of the programmes. However, TV 3 is bound by the European Broadcasting Directive, see below, p 791.

## Broadcasting of sales programmes (teleshopping)

Before the new Radio and Television Act came into force (1 December 1996), there were no specific rules relating to sales programmes or teleshopping – that is, television programmes in which the audience can order goods or services – in the legislation relating to advertising on television and radio. In the new Radio and Television Act it is stated (Ch 7, s 5, para 3) that channels purely designed for teleshopping shall be allowed in the future.

## Sanctions and supervising authorities

As with all kinds of advertising, the Marketing Act applies to advertising on radio and television. The provisions of the Act are primarily directed at the trader or the advertiser, but can also be directed at a broadcasting company. A government survey completed in 1994 (SOU 1994:105) did not find reasons to change the way these provisions are directed.

Compliance with the regulations pertaining to advertising on radio and television, described in this chapter, is controlled by the Swedish Broadcasting Commission (*Granskningsnämnden för Radio och TV*), which covers terrestrial broadcasting as well as broadcasting via cable or satellite. The most important sanction available under the relevant Acts are orders given by the broadcasting authority to comply with the relevant provisions. These orders may be given under penalty of a fine.

A separate authority, the Swedish Radio and Television Authority (*Radio-och TV-Verket*) exercises the control of granting of permits which are required to carry out broadcasting in Sweden.

# INTERNATIONAL RULES

## Introduction

EU legislation in the field of marketing has three fundamental aims:

(a) to abolish obstacles to trade;

(b) to support a well functioning consumer protection regime; and

(c) to co-operate in order to obtain efficient and fair competition.

Sweden entered the EU on 1 January 1995.

The two directives central to EU marketing legislation are:

(a) the Misleading Advertising Directive (84/450/EEC);

(b) the European Broadcasting Directive (89/552/EEC).

## The Misleading Advertising Directive

The Misleading Advertising Directive is the most comprehensive instrument covering advertising in the EU. Its aim is to protect consumers as well as traders from misleading advertising. The definition of what is to be regarded as advertising is wide. Under Art 3 of the Directive, all issues of advertising shall be taken into consideration to judge if it is misleading. Certain typical examples of misleading information are given in the Directive.

The fundamental obligation of the Member States of the EU under the Directive is to take sufficient and effective measures to control misleading advertising. There is, however, considerable freedom of choice for Member States as to how those measures are formed.

The new Marketing Act (above, p 780), which went into force on 1 January 1996, fully implements the Misleading Advertising Directive.

## The European Broadcasting Directive

The fundamental aim of the Directive is to promote free movement within the EU of broadcasting to the public, which is normally regarded, from a legal point of view, as a kind of service. The provisions cover, for example, the distribution and production of television programmes.

An important part of the Directive is Chapter 4, which provides detailed rules on advertising in television programmes and sponsorship thereof. These rules regard both the placing of advertising in broadcasts (Arts 10–11) and the shaping of advertising from an ethical/moral point of view (Art 12). Article 13 contains general restrictions on the advertising of certain kinds of products, for example, tobacco, alcohol and medical products.

The Directive was first implemented in Swedish law primarily by the Satellite Act (1992:1356) and certain amendments to the Radio Act (1996:755). These rules are now to be found in

the new Radio and Television Act, which came into force on 1 December 1996. Advertising on television or radio of tobacco and alcohol is banned in Sweden under the Tobacco Advertising Act (1993:581) and the Alcohol Advertising Act (1978:763). In addition, the new Marketing Act, with its demands of compatibility with good marketing practice (see above, p 783), also applies to broadcasts via satellite transmitted from Sweden and directed towards other EU countries.

## Other international rules

Besides the European Broadcasting Directive, the Council of Europe has adopted a convention – the European Convention on Trans-frontier Television – which also contains rules for advertising on television and radio. This came into force on 1 May 1993 and is intended to be applied to the Member States of the Council of Europe. However, as regards the Member States of the EU, the European Broadcasting Directive shall primarily be applied. The provisions are generally the same, but the two do contain important differences, especially regarding remedies. Because of those differences, Sweden has decided to wait to ratify the Convention of the Council of Europe. However, Swedish ratification is likely once the expected harmonisation of the remedies under the Convention with those of the European Broadcasting Directive has taken place.

Section 6 of the Marketing Act deals, among other things, with comparative advertising which describes, in a misleading way, another trader's activities, goods or services or the advertising party's own activities, goods or services in relation to those of the other trader. Thus, the European Comparative Advertising Directive is implemented by this section and by the general clause in s 4 of the Act.

In 1992, the Council of the EU issued a detailed directive dealing with advertising of medical products (the Advertising Medical Products Directive (92/28/EEC)). The Directive prohibits advertising directed at the public of medical products which are available only on a doctor's prescription. The Directive also raises quite strict provisions regarding the form of advertising for other medical products and regarding the information which must be provided therewith.

The new Radio and Television Act, which came into force on 1 December 1996, contains in s 10 a prohibition of advertising of those medical products and treatments detailed in the Directive.

As regards the proposed EU directive on the advertising of tobacco products, it should be noted that Sweden has, for a long time, had restrictions on the advertising of tobacco. The national rules are currently to be found in the Swedish Tobacco Advertising Act (1993:581) and in the various provisions relating to different kinds of broadcasting, that is, the new Radio and Television Act and the Local Radio Act (1993:120). Thus, implementation of a European directive on advertising of tobacco products will not be a problem in Sweden.

# ADVERTISING CONTRACTS

Below is a brief description of the general conditions applicable to advertising on one of Sweden's major advertising-financed television channels and the general conditions applicable to advertising in newspapers, as suggested by the three interest organisations for newspaper publishers and often incorporated in newspaper advertising agreements.

## General conditions applicable to television advertising

The conditions are drawn up under the following headings:

(a) introductory provision;

(b) the client's delivery of the commercial to the broadcaster, etc;

(c) the shaping of the commercial;

(d) copyright, etc;

(e) cancellation of booked advertising time;

(f) prices and terms of payment;

(g) changes in the programme schedule, etc;

(h) the right of the television company to cancel the broadcast of a commercial;

(i) the responsibility of the television company if the broadcasting of a commercial is cancelled or incomplete;

(j) the client's responsibility;

(k) sponsorship;

(l) applicable law, etc.

In addition, schedules to the above-mentioned headings technical requirements for the advertising material.

Chapter 2 of the conditions regulates, among other things, when a recorded broadcasting spot should be delivered to the broadcasting company. The main rule is five working days before the scheduled broadcast. The broadcasting company reserves the right to charge an additional fee if delivery takes place later than this. The chapter also states that the broadcasting company should examine the delivered material in order to judge whether or not the advertising is compatible with the general conditions concerning the content or the technical quality of the material. There is an exemption clause regarding damage to delivered tape.

Chapter 3 stipulates that the advertisement should be compatible with relevant legislation and other rules, such as the Radio and Television Act, the Marketing Act, the agreement between the television company and the government and the rules of advertising of the ICC. Relevant provisions are enclosed with the general conditions. Chapter 3 also states that a commercial must not be shorter than 10 seconds and must not exceed 60 seconds. However, commercials exceeding 60 seconds can be broadcast by specific agreement.

Chapter 4, Regulating Questions of Copyright, etc, stipulates, *inter alia*, that the advertiser is responsible for ensuring that the contents of the advertisement do not infringe copyright, and hence, that necessary agreements have been entered into with copyright holders and actors, etc. The television company also reserves the right to make copies of commercials for internal use and copies required for the National Archive of Recorded Sound and Moving Images (*Arkivet för Ljud och Bild*). The television company also reserves the right to sell copies of the commercials to third parties for private use.

Chapter 5 stipulates that cancellation of booked advertising time shall be made in writing, and also regulates matters of advertising fees in the case of cancellation.

In Chapter 8, the television company has reserved the right to cancel the broadcast of a commercial which does not conform with the content or technical quality requirements in the general conditions. Provided that the television company has reasonable grounds for a decision of cancellation, the advertiser must still pay for the advertising even if the decision means that the advertising time cannot be used. The chapter also gives the television company a wider, unconditional, right of cancellation than that mentioned above. Such a cancellation does not, however, give the television company the right to charge the advertiser for the cancelled broadcasting time.

Chapter 9 regulates the responsibility of the television company for defective or incomplete broadcasting of commercials. The broadcasting company may compensate the advertiser by way of re-broadcasting at an equally good time within seven days from the expiry of the intended advertising period. Unless the television company compensates the advertiser by such rebroadcasting, the advertiser may withhold payment for defective broadcasting time either partially or fully. The advertiser is entitled to compensation only if he notifies the television company of his complaints in writing within five working days from the day of the defective broadcasting.

Except for the liability described above, an exemption clause in Chapter 9 declares the television company free from any liability for direct or consequential loss which the advertiser or a third party may suffer due to any lack of advertising in the broadcast, whatever the reason may be.

Chapter 10 of the general conditions stipulates that the advertiser shall reimburse the television company for any loss due to non-conformity of the advertising with applicable provisions or for any infringement which the advertising may cause to the rights of a third party. This is also the case for material which the television company has checked in advance without objections.

A reference in Chapter 11 of the conditions stipulates that the conditions concerning advertising are applicable also to sponsorship.

Chapter 12 of the general conditions stipulates that Swedish law applies to the agreement, and that disputes in relation to the agreement shall be settled in Sweden by arbitration. The television company is, however, entitled to seek compensation for agreed fees for advertising in regular Swedish courts.

## General conditions for newspaper advertising

These general conditions, 'norms for advertising and recommendations regarding the identification of advertising' (*normer för annonsering samt rekommendationer angående reklamidentifiering*), regulate relations between a newspaper and an advertiser or another purchaser of advertising in agreements of purchase, sale and intermediation of advertising unless other conditions have been agreed upon.

Sections 5 to 7 lay down the responsibilities of the advertiser/purchaser, and stipulate, for example, that the advertiser has the responsibility to the newspaper to ensure that the advertisement does not violate the relevant provisions or norms. The advertiser is also liable to the newspaper for any possible infringement of the copyright of a third party that the advertising may cause. Section 7 also stipulates that if a booked advertisement cannot be inserted in the newspaper by default of the advertiser/purchaser, liability therefor is limited to the cost of insertion.

Sections 8 to 11 stipulate what is to be included in the cost of the insertion of the advertisement in the paper. Among other things, it is stated that typesetting or composition is included in the cost of the insertion of the advertisement in a daily paper, whereas for magazines, such work is not included. Section 11 also stipulates that any advertising tax shall be included in the rate for the advertisement.

Sections 12 to 24 deal with technical issues concerning the advertisement.

Section 25 stipulates that title to advertisement originals produced by the paper shall rest with the paper. This is also the case for material produced within the framework of an offer, such as sketches and drawings.

Section 26 stipulates that payment for advertising shall be made in cash, in advance.

Sections 29 to 34 deal with defaults in the advertising. The first two of these sections stipulate that the paper is free from liability if the defaulting advertising is due to material provided by the advertiser/purchaser.

Section 32 limits the liability for the paper to the agreed insertion cost of the advertisement.

Section 33 requires the advertiser to give notice of complaint for any default in the advertisement within three days of publication, unless the advertiser has not seen the advertisement until later.

Section 34 stipulates that any complaint concerning errors in an invoice should be made immediately, and no later than 14 days after receipt thereof.

Section 35 limits the right of the advertiser to cancel a booked advertisement.

An exemption clause is included in s 37, giving the paper freedom from liability if the advertisement is not published on the exact date agreed between the parties.

If the advertisement cannot be published as agreed and the reason therefor is that the advertising material has been delivered to the paper after the last day agreed upon, s 38 still entitles the paper to charge the advertiser the sum agreed.

Section 39 unconditionally entitles the paper the right to refuse an advertisement booking.

The remaining provisions of the general conditions list identification requirements of the advertiser in the advertisement in question. The general rule is clear from s 41:0, stipulating that the advertisement shall contain give the reader clear information on the identity of the advertiser and making it easy for the reader to reach the advertiser.

## FUTURE DEVELOPMENTS

As described above, a new Marketing Act applicable to all media in Sweden came into force on 1 January 1996. This Act, which, among other things, implements the Misleading Advertising Directive of the EU, has been covered in detail above, pp 780–85. Thus, as regards the substantive content of advertising, no reforms are to be expected in the near future. In addition, a new Radio and Television Act, which contains specific provisions for advertising and sponsorship on radio and television, came into force in Sweden on 1 December 1996. This Act has also been outlined above, p 786. Advertising and other matters relating to Swedish commercial local radio channels, usually broadcasting music for the younger public, are still regulated separately by the Local Radio Act. Once the political decisions concerning the future of Swedish local radio have been taken, these issues will probably also be incorporated into the Radio and Television Act.

As reforms have recently been introduced into Swedish legislation, and as Sweden has reached a fairly high degree of implementation of the relevant EU directives in this field, the conclusion must be that no substantial amendments should be expected in the near future.

# USEFUL ADDRESSES

*Governmental and related bodies*

Granskningsnämnden för Radio och TV
(Swedish Broadcasting Commission)
Box 244
136 23 Haninge
Tel: + 46 8 606 79 70

Kemikalieinspektionen
(National Chemicals Inspectorate)
Box 1384
171 27 Solna
Tel: + 46 8 730 57 00

Konsumentombudsmannen
(Consumer Ombudsman)
118 87 Stockholm
Tel: + 46 8 429 05 00

Konsumentverket
(National Board for Consumer Policies)
118 87 Stockholm
Tel: + 46 8 429 05 00

Läkemedelsverket
(Medical Products Agency)
Box 26
751 03 Uppsala
Tel: + 46 18 17 46 00

Marknadsetiska rådet
(Council on Market Ethics)
Box 14025
104 40 Stockholm
Tel: + 46 8 662 00 98

Marknadsdomstolen
(Market Court).
Box 2217
103 15 Stockholm
Tel: + 46 8 24 41 55

Radio- och TV-Verket
(Swedish Radio and TV Authority)
Box 123
136 22 Haninge
Tel: + 46 8 606 90 80

Socialstyrelsen
(National Board of Health and Welfare)
106 30 Stockholm
Tel: + 46 8 783 30 00

Statens Livsmedelsverk
(National Food Administration)
Box 622
751 26 Uppsala
Tel: + 46 18 17 55 00

Stockholms tingsrätt (Stockholm City Court)
Box 8307
104 20 Stockholm
Tel: + 46 8 657 50 00

Svea hovrätt
(Svea Court of Appeal)
Box 2290
103 17 Stockholm
Tel: + 46 8 700 34 00

*Independent bodies*

Annonsörföreningen
(Swedish Advertisers' Association)
Box 1327
111 83 Stockholm
Tel: + 46 8 23 51 00

Etiska Rådet mot Könsdiskriminerande Reklam
(Trade Ethical Council Against Sexism in Advertising)
Box 3202
103 63 Stockholm
Tel: + 46 8 20 75 95

IRM
(Swedish Institute for Advertising and Media Statistics)
Vasagatan 5 A
411 24 Göteburg
Tel: + 46 31 711 56 62

Sveriges Reklamförbund
(Advertisers' Association of Sweden)
Box 1420
111 84 Stockholm
Tel: + 46 8 679 08 00

Svenska Tidningsutgivareföreningen
(Swedish Newspaper Publishers' Association)
Box 22500
104 22 Stockholm
Tel: + 46 8 692 46 00

## CHAPTER 16

# UNITED KINGDOM

*Lord Campbell of Alloway and Zahd Yaqub*

The major part of the advertising industry is based in England, so the law of Scotland and Northern Ireland will not be looked at in this respect. The legal controls affecting the form or content of advertisements covers a wide spectrum of statutory and common law. Many of the regulations are derived from legislation and, in addition to the legal controls, a comprehensive system of self-regulation has evolved over the years, promoted by means of codes of practice. Some of the codes have been drawn up to comply with the statutory obligations, namely the ITC Codes and the Radio Authority Codes. Others, while purely voluntary, are supported by the advertising industry and relevant trade associations, that is, the British Code of Advertising Practice.

## SELF-REGULATION IN THE ADVERTISING INDUSTRY

The self-regulatory system is not an alternative to legal control, but co-exists as a complementary system. The first self-regulatory code was introduced in 1955, when independent television began to broadcast commercials. It was followed, in 1961, by the first edition of the British Code of Advertising Practice (BCAP), which took, as its model, the International Code of Advertising Practice, first published in 1937. The BCAP applies to all non-broadcast advertising, whilst broadcast advertising is governed by different codes, drawn up by the Independent Television Commission (ITC) and the Radio Authority in accordance with their statutory duties. There are several other voluntary codes concerned with advertising, most of which contain a requirement that all advertising should be in accordance with the law, the BCAP and the Broadcasting Codes. Some of these have been adopted by trade associations in consultation with the Director General of the Office of Fair Trading, who has a duty to encourage trade associations and similar bodies to prepare and disseminate codes of practice giving guidance with regard to safeguarding and promoting interests of consumers, that is, s 124(3) of the Fair Trading Act 1973 and the Competition Act 1998. The codes of practice drawn up in consultation with the Director General of the Office of Fair Trading cover:

(a) consumer credit: a separate code of practice for the consumer credit industry has been negotiated with the Director General of the Office of Fair Trading by the Consumer Credit Trade Association, the Consumer Credit Association UK, the National Consumer Trade Federation and the London Personal Finance Association;

(b) direct selling;

(c) domestic, electrical appliance services, etc.

In some cases, a breach of the code of practice can result in disciplinary action being taken against a member. Particular problems can arise in certain industries and the code concerned may contain requirements additional to those in the BCAP or broadcasting codes. The Proprietary Association of Great Britain (PAGB) has drawn up its own Code of Standards of Advertising Practice, and the Code of Practice for the Motor Industry contains specific provisions concerning advertising by manufacturers and dealers in relation to the supply of new and used cars.

# NON-BROADCAST ADVERTISING

## The British Codes of Advertising Practice (BCAP)

The BCAP are published by the Committee of Advertising Practice, now in an eighth edition (and presently being revised). This body of codes contains the general rules to be applied, as well as more detailed guidelines to be followed in relation to specific categories of advertisements. There are separate sections dealing with health claims; hair and scalp products; vitamins and minerals; slimming and cosmetics; mail order and direct response advertising; financial services; employment and business opportunities; sales promotions; children; alcohol; and tobacco (see Appendix 1).

### The Committee of Advertising Practice (CAP)

The membership of the CAP is composed of representatives from various professional and trade associations with substantial advertising contracts (see Appendix 2). The CAP's principal task is to secure compliance with the British Codes of Advertising Practice and the British Code of Sales Promotion Practice through co-ordination of the actions of its member associations – in this process, the role of the media associations is particularly important, as their members provide the main chance through which an advertisement can be brought to public attention. Not only do these associations check the acceptability under the BCAP of all advertisements submitted to them for publication, but they are able to exercise their discretion about which advertisements to accept and which to refuse so as to reflect any views expressed by the CAP or the Advertising Standards Authority about the interpretation of the codes. The CAP's other responsibilities include the continuous review and, as necessary, amendments of the BCAP, administration of the mandatory pre-clearance scheme for cigarette advertising, and advice which is given without charge on a confidential basis on how BCAP should be interpreted. Much of the detailed work of the CAP is remitted to two review panels, one of which deals with general media issues and the other with sales promotion and direct marketing.

## The Advertising Standards Authority (ASA)[1]

The ASA is a non-profit making limited company, governed by a council, whose members are appointed by the chairman and who sit as individuals. The task of the ASA is to deal with complaints from both the public and the industry about the contents of advertisements, to maintain and promote proper standards of advertising and to provide an external check on the self-regulatory system to ensure that it operates within the public interest. While the opinion of the ASA on any matter concerning the interpretation of the BCAP is final, decisions of the ASA are susceptible to judicial review (see *R v Advertising Standards Authority Limited ex p Insurance Services plc* [1989] 133 SJ 1545 and *R v Committee of Advertising Practice ex p Bradford Exchange* [1991] COD 43), as are those of the Committee of Advertising Practice.

## Complaints

The Advertising Standards Authority investigates complaints from any source against advertisements and promotions in non-broadcast media which are alleged to have broken the BCAP. Complaints from members of the public are dealt with without revealing the complainant's identity, whereas complaints from those with a commercial interest in the outcome are investigated on a named basis. The advertisers which are the subject of a complaint are told the outcome of the ASA Council's ruling and, where appropriate, are asked to withdraw or amend the advertisements or promotions. The adjudications reached by the Council at its monthly meetings, as well as editorial guidance on current topics, are published in the ASA's monthly report. This is distributed free of charge to the media, libraries, government departments, politicians, businesses, consumer bodies and the public.

The ASA gives equal emphasis to conducting a substantial research and monitoring programme by reviewing issues, advertisements and promotions that fall within its scope. Particular media and product categories are also selected for scrutiny. In this way, the ASA can identify trends and prevent further problems. Publicising the ASA's policies and actions is essential to sustain wide acceptance of the system's integrity. A comprehensive programme of seminars and speeches, advertising, leaflets, briefing notes on a wide range of topics video-targeted at consumers and educational establishments, and written articles for professional journals, newspapers and magazines all augment the ASA's extensive media coverage.

---

1   For up to date information on this, see the ASA website: http://www.asa.org.uk.

In 1997, 8,291 advertisements attracting a total of 10,678 complaints were the subject of ASA scrutiny. Following investigation, 512 advertisements had breached the codes and were withdrawn or amended (728 in 1996). Complaints in 1997 fell to 10,678 from 12,055 in 1996. The number of advertisements complained about also fell fractionally, down 1% from 8,408 to 8,291.

## Legal proceedings

Ultimately, the ASA can refer misleading advertisements to the Office of Fair Trading (OFT). The OFT can obtain an injunction to prevent advertisers using the same or similar claims in future advertisements.

## Cross-border complaints[2]

The European Advertising Standards Alliance (EASA) was founded in 1991 and was set up as a system whereby complaints about non-broadcast (and broadcast) advertisements can be dealt with on a cross-border basis. It is envisaged that a complaint about an advertisement originating in one country, but appearing in another, will be referred to the second country's self-regulatory body, and if the complaint is upheld, the necessary action will be taken by that body. The ASA has close links with the EASA, and the appointment, in 1996, of Christopher Ogden, the ASA's Deputy Director General, as chairman of the Alliance, has meant that the authority is more involved in Europe than ever before. By 1996, the EASA's membership comprised Austria, Belgium, France, Germany, Greece, Ireland, Italy, The Netherlands, Portugal, Spain, Sweden, Switzerland and the UK; Turkey joined in 1996, followed by Finland, so the European Union is now fully represented. The EASA now has 25 members from 22 countries, giving European advertising self-regulation its widest representation to date.

The system of cross-border complaints operated by the EASA has successfully resolved over 150 complaints made by customers or consumers – 47 cases were examined and resolved by EASA members in 1996, 13 of which were dealt with by the ASA. This mechanism offers consumers in member countries a pan-European opportunity to complain about misleading or offensive advertisements appearing in one country, but published in another.

## Funding

The costs of operating a self-regulatory system in the UK are met from a levy imposed on all display advertising, which is collected by the Advertising Standards Board of Finance Limited (ASBOF).

---

2    For up to date information on this, see the EASA website: http://www.easa-alliance.org.

## The British Sales Promotion Code

This code of good practice, currently in its sixth edition (and presently being revised), conforms to the principles of the International Code of Sales Promotion Practice published by the International Chamber of Commerce and is implemented by the CAP under the general supervision of the ASA. It is aimed at regulating, primarily, the interests of the consumer, the nature and the administration of those marketing techniques which are used, usually on a temporary basis, to make goods and services more attractive to the consumer or provide some additional benefit, whether in cash or in kind. The code covers such forms of promotion as premium offers of all kinds; reduced price and free offers; the distribution of vouchers, coupons and samples; personality promotions; and charity linked promotions. It also applies to sales and trade incentive promotions and to some aspects of sponsorship (see Appendix 1). All advertising material used to draw attention to the promotion should also conform to the British Code of Advertising Practice.

The principles governing the code stress legality, decency, fair competition and honesty. Primary responsibility for observance of the code is placed on promoters, but intermediaries and agents are also included.

# BROADCAST ADVERTISING

The duties of broadcasting authorities are enshrined in the Broadcasting Acts of 1990 and 1996. The Broadcasting Act 1990 refers to two broadcasting authorities, the Independent Television Commission (ITC) under s 1 and the Radio Authority under s 83, which replaced the Independent Broadcasting Authority (IBA). The function of the authority is to regulate television programmes (s 2) and radio services (s 84) provided by persons other than the BBC. Both authorities are required to do all they can to ensure that licensed services comply with the following rules concerning advertising; a licensed service must not include:

(a) any advertisement that is inserted by, or on behalf of, any body whose objects are wholly or mainly of a political nature;

(b) any advertisement which is directed towards any political end; or

(c) any advertisement which bears any relation to any industrial dispute, other than an advertisement of a public nature inserted by, or on behalf of, a government department (s 8(2)(a), television; s 92(2)(a), radio);

(d) in the acceptance of advertisements for inclusion in the licensed service, there must be no unreasonable discrimination either against or in favour of any particular advertiser (s 8(2)(b), television; s 92(2)(b), radio);

(e) a licensed service must not, without the previous approval of the Commission or other authority, include a programme which is sponsored by any person whose business consists, wholly or mainly, in the manufacture or supply of a product, or in the provision of a service, which the licence holder is prohibited from advertising (s 8(2)(c), television; s 92(2)(c), radio).

The Broadcasting Act 1990 imposes the following duties on both authorities:

(a) after the appropriate consultations, to draw up and from time to time review a code governing standards and practice in advertising and in the sponsorship of programmes. The ITC has drawn up a separate Code of Programme Sponsorship;

(b) to prescribe in the Code some methods of advertising or sponsorship to be prohibited, or to be prohibited in particular circumstances (s 9(1)(a), television; s 93(1)(a), radio);

(c) to do all they can to secure that the provisions of the Code are observed and the provisions of licensed services (s 9(1)(b), television; s 93(1)(b), radio).

The ITC and Radio Authority are required to consult the Secretary of State with regard to class and description of advertisements which must not be included in licensed services and the methods of advertising or sponsorship which must not be employed in, or in connection with, the provision of such services; and to carry out any direction which the Secretary of State may give in respect of such matters (s 9(4), television; s 93(4), radio).

The Act expressly reserves the right of both authorities to impose requirements as to advertisements and methods of advertising and sponsorship which go beyond the requirements of the code (s 9(5), television; s 93(5), radio). The methods of control open to the ITC and the Radio Authority include powers to give directions as to the exclusion not only of classes and descriptions of advertisements and methods of advertising and sponsorship, but of individual advertisements in particular circumstances (s 9(6), television; s 93(6), radio). The ITC is also empowered to give directions in relation to the times when advertisements are to be allowed and their distribution within programming (ss 9(7) and 97(8)). Further, the ITC rules on advertising breaks give effect to the requirements laid down in the EEC Directive on Television Broadcasting (89/552/EEC) under the 1989 Council of Europe Convention on Transfrontier Television. The relevant sections of the Broadcasting Act 1990 concerning advertising are reproduced in Appendix 3.

## Copy clearance

### Broadcasting Advertising Clearance Centre (BACC)[3]

From 1 January 1993 the ITC no longer played a role in approving commercials prior to transmission. In order to fulfil the conditions of their licences, as well as providing a service to advertisers and advertising agencies, the broadcasters set up the Broadcasting Advertising Clearance Centre (BACC), a specialist body responsible for the pre-transmission examination and clearance of television advertisements. The BACC also provides a similar service for radio advertising on behalf of the Association of Independent Radio Companies (AIRC). The BACC's services are free of charge to the advertiser or agency.

The BACC has two principal functions: examination and discussion of pre-production scripts and the pre-transmission clearance of finished television advertisements. With the exception of the minority of local advertisements, which may be cleared by the broadcaster concerned, all finished advertisements must be viewed and given clearance by the BACC prior to transmission. Although the submission of pre-production scripts is not compulsory, the great majority of advertising agencies avail themselves of this service; consequently, it is unusual for the finished commercial to be rejected when it is viewed by the BACC and only a small proportion requires amendment before being cleared for transmission.

The BACC is funded by broadcasters, its role being to examine advertisements before they are accepted for broadcasting, to decide whether they comply with the relevant code and to handle the resulting day to day negotiations with advertising agencies and advertisers. The BACC consults the ITC and the Radio Authority regularly on matters affecting the interpretation of the codes of practice.

Agencies are asked to send to the BACC the script of a proposed advertisement, so that it can be examined to see if it complies with the relevant code. If a script does not comply, the BACC will discuss amendments with the agency. When agreement is reached, a revised script is submitted by the agency and which the BACC then formally approves. There are advantages for advertisers, agencies and the consuming public in such a system of pre-clearance, but also for the broadcasters affiliated to the BACC, as it forms an important part of the procedures which they need to have in place in order to comply with their licence conditions.

## Advertisement and films

All advertisements for cinema exhibition must be approved by a panel of the Cinema Advertising Association. Commercials of 30 seconds or longer must also be submitted to the British Board of Film Classification.

---

3   For up to date information on this, see the Broadcasting Advertising Clearance Centre website: http://www.bacc.org.uk.

# The ITC: regulation of television advertising and sponsorship[4]

The ITC's regulatory powers derive from the Broadcasting Acts 1990 and 1996 and relate to the television companies which it licenses and their compliance with the ITC's codes on advertising and sponsorship (see below). It has the power to direct licensees to discontinue an advertisement or sponsorship which does not comply with the respective code. It may also impose scheduling restrictions. The ITC also has regulatory responsibilities concerning the sales of television advertising, such as to ensure 'fair and effective competition' and 'no unreasonable discrimination').

## The ITC's Code of Advertising Standards and Practice

This code, modelled closely on the former IBA and Cable Authority codes which it replaces, has many points in common with the British Code of Advertising Practice. In drawing up the code, the ITC had regard to the code of practice issued by the Broadcasting Standards Council and the need to give effect in the UK to the requirements relating to television advertising in Council Directive 89/552 and the Council of Europe's Convention on Transfrontier Television. The ITC Code applies to all television services regulated by the ITC. The term 'licensee' in the ITC Code should be taken as referring to all television broadcasting companies regulated by the ITC, whether as contractors or licensees. The ITC's Code of Advertising Standards and Practice can be read on its website: http://www.itc.org.uk.

## The ITC's Code of Programme Sponsorship

The ITC's Code of Programme Sponsorship gives effect in the UK to a number of requirements relating to television sponsorship in the EEC Directive (89/552) on television broadcasting and the 1989 Council of Europe Convention on Transfrontier Television. The Broadcasting Act 1990 reserves the right of the ITC to impose requirements as to the methods of sponsorship which go beyond the rules set out in the code (s 9(5)), and if the rules are breached or the licensee fails to comply with any directions by the Commission, the ITC may impose financial penalties or shorten (s 41), or in certain circumstances revoke (s 42), the company's licence.

A programme is deemed to be sponsored if any part of its costs of production of transmission is met by an organisation or person other than a broadcaster or television producer with a view to promoting its own or another's name, trade mark, image, activities, product or the direct or indirect commercial interests. Any television programme may be sponsored unless it falls into one of the expected categories which are set out in the ITC Television

---

4   For up to date information on this, see the ITC website: http://www.easa-itc.org.uk.

Sponsorship Code, which includes programmes and news flashes comprising local, national and international news items, business and financial reports containing interpretation and comment, and programmes containing explanation and analysis of current affairs.

No sponsorship will be permitted where there is any influence on either the content or the scheduling of a programme. Any sponsorship must be clearly identified at the beginning or at the end of the programme, or both, and the credit must explain the sponsor's connection with the programme, without suggesting that the programme has been made by the sponsor. Reference to the sponsor's product or service may be included in the credit, provided such product or service is not shown and no slogan description is included. No promotional reference to the sponsor, or to his product or services, is permitted within the programme he has sponsored. The code prohibits sponsorship by anybody whose objects are either wholly or mainly of a political nature, or by the manufacturers of tobacco products and pharmaceutical products available on prescription only. The previous approval of the ITC must be obtained before a programme can be sponsored by any other person whose business consists, wholly or mainly, in the manufacture and supply of a product, or in the provision of a service, which is not acceptable for television advertising under the ITC Code of Advertising Standards and Practice.

Programme coverage of events which have been sponsored, or at which advertising or branding is present, may itself be sponsored. Visual or oral references to any advertising, signage or branding at an event must be limited to what can clearly be justified by the editorial needs of the programme itself. There are specific rules covering the sponsorship of events by tobacco companies, in particular in relation to the branding or signage of the sponsor.

The present edition of the Code of Programme Sponsorship dates from 1997, and has, *inter alia*: widened the opportunity for sponsorship of consumer advice programmes; provided greater scope for the use of straplines in credits; and established that advertiser-supplied programmes would be treated in the same way as conventionally sponsored programmes. It also permits 'masthead programming' (that is, using the editorial and production resources of a magazine title) on all ITC licensed services other than Channels 3, 4 and 5. The ITC's Code of Programme Sponsorship can be read on its website: http://www.itc.org.uk.

## The Advertising Advisory Committee

The Advertising Advisory Committee (AAC) works in close collaboration with the ITC. The AAC meets quarterly and includes representatives from consumer groups, advertising interests, as well as individual experts. The AAC keeps the Code of Advertising Standards and Practice under review and makes recommendations to the ITC in this regard and also on the ITC's handling of advertising complaints. It is also consulted by the ITC on matters concerning sponsorship.

## The Radio Authority's Code of Advertising Standards and Practice and Programme Sponsorship[5]

The Radio Authority's code applies to all advertisements and sponsorship and radio services licensed by the Radio Authority, and licensees are responsible for ensuring any advertising and sponsorship they broadcast complies with the code. The first two sections of the code deal with presentation and standards, and the third section of the code deals with sponsorship. The code also contains seven appendices, dealing with the categories of advertisements which require particular care. The rules governing presentation and standards are very similar to those contained in the ITC's code.

The rules dealing with radio sponsorship are less stringent than those related to television sponsorship. All programmes may be sponsored, with the exception of news bulletins. A link between a sponsor's commercial activities and the subject matter of the programme is acceptable in all sponsored programmes, while ultimate editorial control of a sponsored programme must remain with the licensee. Sponsors may contribute to the editorial content of all sponsored programmes, except news features, news magazines, current affairs, business or financial news or comment and programmes addressing matters of political/industrial controversy or relating to current public policy.

## SELF-REGULATORY BODIES AND THEIR CODES OF PRACTICE

## The Code of Standards of Advertising Practice: the Proprietary Association of Great Britain (PAGB)

The PAGB's Code of Standards of Advertising Practice is concerned with the advertising of non-prescription medicines. Member companies of the PAGB are required to submit all material relevant to the labelling, packaging, advertising and promotion of their products to the PAGB for clearance under its aforesaid code of practice. It is a requirement of the code that all copy is resubmitted two years after approval is given. The code's provisions are supplementary to the requirements of the Medicines Act 1968 and the subordinate legislation, and it is unnecessary for members to comply with the BCAP. The PAGB's code does not apply to advertisements directed to help

---

5    For up to date information on this, see the Radio Authority's website: http://www. radioauthority.org.uk.

professionals or to persons or organisations connected with the wholesale or retail distribution of medicines. The PAGB is represented on the CAP.

## Mail order[6]

The code of practice of the Association of Mail Order Publishers was drawn up by the British Direct Marketing Association, in consultation with the Director General of Fair Trading. For the purposes of the code, advertisements include all forms of selling communication, written, visual, electronic or oral, between a member, its customers and the general public. The code contains detailed rules governing the obligations of members in relation to their advertising and promotions, and it is a requirement of the code that members comply with the British Advertising Code and Sales Promotion Code (Appendix 2).

The Mail Order Traders Association has also drawn up a code of practice. Furthermore, the British Advertising Code (Appendix 2) makes provision for mail order advertising. It requires that, except in limited circumstances, advertisers should fulfil orders within 28 days, and the name and address of the advertiser should be stated in the body copy of an advertisement, as well as in any coupon.

In terms of legal requirements, mail order advertising must contain the name and address of the seller; the name given must be the name under which the company is registered; a pseudonym may be used as long as the registered name is also given (Mail Order Transactions (Information) Order SI 1976/1812). When an advertisement contains a coupon by which goods can be ordered, the place of registration of the company, its registered number and the address of the registered office must be given. The fact that the company is a limited company should also be mentioned, where the company has been exempted from the requirements to use the word 'Limited' (Companies Act 1985, s 351). It is a requirement that any advertisement placed in the course of a business must make that fact clear. Normally, there will be no confusion about the word 'trade', should the advertisement otherwise appear to emanate from a private individual (the British Advertisement Disclosure Order SI 1977/1918). There are also various regulations dealing with particular aspects of mail order advertising, ranging from the Nightwear Safety Regulations SI 1985/2043 to the Trade Descriptions (Place of Production) Marking Order SI 1988/1771).

---

6   For up to date information on this, see the Mail Order Protection Scheme website: http://www.mops.org.uk.

## Mail order protection schemes

The National Newspaper Mail Order Protection Scheme (MOPS), a scheme operated by the Periodical Publishers Association (*and* the Scottish Daily Newspaper Society and the Scottish Newspaper Publishers Association) was introduced in 1975 as a means of safeguarding readers' money by compensating them in the event of a failure to deliver goods which they had ordered as a result of the advertiser going into liquidation or bankruptcy, or ceasing to trade. The scheme also covers readers who have returned goods and not received a refund from a failed member. It is necessary for all mail order advertising agencies to submit a formal application to join the scheme. The level of membership fees for advertisers is determined by advertising expenditure. It does not automatically follow that all advertising will then be accepted, since this decision ultimately rests with the publisher of the newspaper concerned. Where payment is made by Access or Visa credit cards, the MOPS protection covers only up to £100. In regard to any claim above this, the individual should contact his credit card company.

Certain categories of advertisement are exempt from the scheme:

(a) those for the sale of perishable foodstuffs;

(b) those asking readers to send for brochures/catalogues/details of products which are supplied free, or for a charge of less than £5 (if the combined charge for brochures is more than £5, MOPS approval is required; subsequent sales made from such brochures or inserted with goods ordered in response to mail order advertising are not covered by the scheme);

(c) those inviting readers to retail premises;

(d) those offering a service, such as club membership, magazine subscriptions, theatre tickets, film processing, etc (but, in the case of film processing, if an advertiser offers a replacement film to be purchased in addition to the charge for processing, the reader is protected for the cost of the replacement film, but not for the processing);

(e) those inviting readers to purchase goods up to the value of 25p;

(f) those offering goods on a self-liquidating basis or other premium basis (that is, where readers have to send, in addition to cash, some proof of the purchase, such as a label, stamps, etc, from products obtained through retail outlets;

(g) those offering goods on approval or on a 'cash on delivery' basis, or where the reader is required to send only a small sum to cover carriage or postage cost only;

(h) those offering to sell second hand products.

# PROVISIONS REGARDING BANK, BUILDING SOCIETY, INSURANCE, FINANCIAL, PENSIONS AND CREDIT ADVERTISING

## Advertising of interest bearing accounts

The Code of Conduct for the Advertising of Interest Bearing Accounts was drawn up by the Building Societies Association, the British Bankers Association and the Finance House Association; it is supported by the Bank of England and the Building Societies Commission. This will be overseen by the Financial Servcies Authority once the legislation comes into force. The code applies to the advertising of all interest bearing accounts maintained within the UK. For the purpose of the code, the term advertisement includes press and broadcast advertisements, direct marketing, window displays, posters, brochures, leaflets and automated teller machine displays. The principal objective of the code is to ensure that building societies, banks and other financial institutions use a common terminology to describe the various types of interest rates on offer in their advertisements. The code contains detailed provisions regarding the advertising of interest rates and the information to be included where such rates are quoted. The code also sets out the information to be included to indicate the type of deposit being advertised. Advertisements inviting deposits by immediate coupon response must include the full terms and conditions or state that they are available on request and must state the address where the advertiser can be contacted.

## Building societies

The Building Societies Commission has considerable powers in respect of an authorised building society to give directions on advertising, including prohibiting advertisements of a specified description or all descriptions, or those requiring a modification under the Building Societies Act 1986, s 50. Power to give directions directly arises where the Commission considers it expedient to do so in the interest of a prospective investor in the relevant society (s 50(1) of the Act). Treasury consent is no longer required for the exercise of these powers.

## Banking

The Bank of England is given powers under the Banking Act 1987 to issue directions where it considers any deposit advertisement issued or produced to be issued by or on behalf of an authorised institution is misleading (Banking Act 1987, s 33). Such directions can include provisions and modifications under s 33(2) of the Act as amended.

Under the Act, any person who makes a statement, promise or forecast which he knows to be misleading, false or deceptive, or dishonestly conceals any material facts or recklessly makes a statement, promise or forecast which is misleading, false or deceptive, is guilty of an offence if he does so for the purpose of inducing, or is reckless as to whether it may induce, another person to make or refrain from making a deposit, or to enter or refrain from entering into an agreement for the purpose of making such a deposit (s 35(1) of the said Act).

It is a defence under the Act for a person charged to prove that he took all reasonable precautions and exercised all due diligence to avoid the commission of such an offence by himself or any other person under his control. This provision is provided under s 96(4) of the Act.

Regulations made under the Act specify matters which must and must not be included in advertisements inviting the making of deposits and, in particular, require the inclusion of details about the person taking the deposit, and contain the figures in connection with reference to the deposit taker's assets and liabilities, deposit protection arrangements, interest on deposits and the currency in which deposits are made (Banking Act 1987 – Advertisement Regulations SI 1988/645). The defence of due diligence (s 96(4) of the Banking Act 1987) applies to allay defences against any regulations.

## Insurance

*Insurance advertisements* are defined as any advertisement 'inviting persons to enter into or to offer to enter into contracts of insurance'. An advertisement which contains information calculated to lead directly or indirectly to persons entering into or offering to enter such contracts shall be treated as an advertisement inviting them to do so (Insurance Companies Act 1982, s 72(5)). Insurance advertisements are governed by the Insurance Companies Regulations SI 1981/1654, apart from those which are issued by persons authorised under the Financial Services Act 1986 and which relate to an insurance contract, and which amount to advertisements within the meaning of the Act (Financial Services Act 1986, Sched 10, para 5(1)). (This will be amended by the new Financial Services Act.)

## Financial advertising[7]

The Financial Services Act 1986 has established a new and comprehensive framework of controls over investment advertising. An investment advertisement is defined as:

---

7 For up to date information on this, see the Financial Services Authority's website: http://www.fsa.gov.uk.

... any advertisement inviting persons to enter or offer to enter into an investment agreement or to exercise any rights conferred by an investment to acquire, dispose of, underwrite or convert an investment, or containing information calculated to lead directly or indirectly to persons doing so [s 57(2)].

Under the Act, investment business must be authorised by the Securities and Investment Board (SIB). At the time of writing, the self-regulatory bodies (the Security and Futures Authority, the Investment Management Regulatory Organisation and the Personal Investment Authority), the Bank of England team, the insurance section of the Department of Trade and Industry (DTI) and the SIB are being squeezed into a single super-regulator: the Financial Services Authority.

The Financial Services Authority (FSA) is now up and running, but for legal reasons has to delegate the actual regulation back to the antecedent bodies. Those bodies have the legal authority, whereas the FSA must await a new Financial Services Act from Parliament to formalise its powers. The Bill is presently completing its passage through the House of Commons and is not expected to become law before the year 2000. When the new law is in force, the FSA will assume the powers of the SIB over advertising of financial services and new regulations will be enacted.

Once authorised, the investment business must comply with the rules laid down by the relevant authorising body, which includes rules dealing with advertising (ss 7–14).

The authorised investment business should appoint a person within the company, nominally known as a Compliance Officer, with the responsibility for approving all advertisements. The Act makes it an offence for anyone other than the authorised person to issue, or cause to be issued, an investment advertisement unless the contents have been approved by an authorised person (s 57(1)). This means that advertising agencies which buy a totality of space or air time on behalf of an investment business will need to satisfy themselves that the content of the advertisement has been approved by an authorised person. The media will not be guilty of an offence if they can prove that they believed on reasonable grounds that the person on whose order the advertisement was issued was an authorised person, or that the advertisement was permitted by, or under, s 58 of the Act, which sets out exceptions from the restrictions on advertising. Others are exempted because they constitute exempt persons (Financial Services Act 1986, s 57(4)), or because they are covered by the Financial Services Act 1986 (Investment Advertisement Exemptions) Order SI 1988/316 or the Financial Services Act 1986 (Investment Advertisement Exemptions) Order SI 1992/274. All of the above will change on the coming into force of the new Act.

## Pensions

The Personal Pension Scheme (Advertisement) Regulations SI 1990/1140 apply to the content of advertisements for personal pension schemes where contributions are invested in interest bearing accounts. The Regulations specify the matters which must be included in such advertisements, and the basis on which projections of future benefit are to be made. These are likely to be amended in the foreseeable future.

## Consumer credit

The provisions of the Consumer Credit Act 1974 (CCrA 1974) concerned with advertising (ss 43–54) apply to any advertisement (s 189(1), for the purposes of a business carried on by the advertiser, indicating that he is willing to provide credit, or enter into an agreement for the bailment of goods by him (s 43). Credit is defined in the Act as 'any form of financial accommodation' (s 9(1)); this includes free credit. Advertisements for consumer hire and consumer credit must not contain information which, in a material sense, is false or misleading (s 46). It is unlawful to advertise that credit is available under a restricted use credit agreement relating to goods or services to be supplied to the advertiser if he is not, at the time of publication, holding himself out as prepared to sell for cash (s 45).

The Act gives powers to the Secretary of State to make regulations as to the form and content of advertisements to which Part IV applies under s 44. The regulations currently in force are the Consumer Credit (Advertisement) Regulations 1989 SI 1989/1125, which contain general rules as to the form and content of advertisements, and schedules setting out more detailed requirements regarding the information to be included which would depend on whether the advertising falls into a category of simple, intermediate or full credit advertisement. Certain consumer credit agreements are exempt from the requirements of the Regulations (Consumer Credit (Exempt Agreements) Order SI 1989/869, as amended by SI 1991/1393), and certain advertisements are excluded from the application of the Act under the Consumer Credit (Exempt Advertisements) Order SI 1985/621. The form and content of credit or hire quotations are governed by separate regulations – the Consumer Credit (Quotations) Regulations 1989 SI 1989/1126.

Advertisements to which the Consumer Credit (Advertisement) Regulations 1989 SI 1989/1125 and the Consumer Credit (Quotations) Regulations 1989 SI 1989/1126 do not apply are those which indicate any of the following:

(a) that the credit must always exceed £15,000 and is either unsecured or is not secured on land;

(b) that the credit is payable in four installments or less within a period of 12 months, and is for a debtor-creditor-supplier agreement (but the Regulations do apply to agreements financing the purchase of land);

(c) that the credit arises because the trader lets customers charge their purchases to an account and requires them to settle up in full at the end of each fixed period, for example, at the end of the month (but the Regulations do apply to agreements financing the purchase of land, hire purchase or conditional sale agreements secured by a pledge);

(d) that the credit is connected with foreign trade;

(e) for hire advertisements, wherein the hire will cost more than £15,000 or will not last for more than three months;

(f) that the credit or hire facility is advertised for business purposes only (but the Regulations do apply if the credit is available to both businesses and individuals);

(g) that the credit or hire is available only to limited companies (or corporate bodies);

(h) advertisements for agreements to finance insurance contracts where there are no more than 12 payments, or the APR does not exceed the greater of 13% or the clearing bank's base rate plus 1%.

It is provided that an advertiser commits an offence if his advertisement, being one to which the Act applies, indicates that he is willing to provide credit under a restricted use credit agreement relating to goods or services to be supplied by any person when, at the time the advertisement is published, that person is not holding himself out as prepared to sell the goods or services, as the case may be, for cash (CCrA 1974, s 45).

Even if an advertisement complies with all the provisions of any regulations as to form and content, the advertiser nevertheless commits an offence in respect of it if it conveys information which is, in a material respect, false or misleading (CCrA 1974, s 46(2)).

Where an advertiser commits an offence under the Act, a like offence is also committed:

(a) by the publisher of the advertisement (CCrA 1974, s 47(1)(a));

(b) by any person who, in the course of business carried on by him, devised the advertisement (CCrA 1974, s 47(1)(b)); and

(c) in the case where the advertiser did not procure the publication of the advertisement, by the person who did procure it (CCrA 1974, s 47(1)(c)).

The publisher will have a defence if he can prove that the advertisement was published in the course of a business carried on by him, and he received the advertisement in the course of that business, and did not know, and had no reason to suspect, that the publication would be an offence (CCrA, s 47(2)).

Further general defences are provided by the Act in relation to charges under the Act and the Regulations. It is a defence for the person charged to prove that his act or omission was due to a mistake or to reliance on information supplied to him, or to an act or omission by another person, in which an accident or some other cause beyond his control, that he took all reasonable precautions and exercised all due diligence to avoid such act or omission by himself or any person under his control (CCrA 1974, s 168(1)). When the defence involves the allegation that the actual omission was due to an act or omission by another person or to reliance on information supplied by another person, the person charged is not, without leave of the court, entitled to rely on the defence unless, within a period ending seven clear years before the hearing, he has served a notice in writing on the prosecutor giving such information identifying or assisting in the identification or what other person as was then in his possession (CCrA 1974, s 168(2)).

Further, where a body corporate commits an offence under the Act with the consent or connivance of, or because of the neglect by, any individual, that individual commits an offence if he is a director, manager, secretary or similar officer or is purported to act as such an officer, or if the body corporate is managed by its members of whom he is one (CCrA 1974, s 169).

# TRADE DESCRIPTIONS

Under the Trade Descriptions Act 1968, it is an offence in the course of any trade or business to apply a false trade description to goods, or to supply, or to offer to supply, goods to which a false trade description is applied (s 1). A *trade description* can be conveyed by the use of words, pictures, numbers or by implication, and a *false trade description* is one which is false to a material degree, or is misleading (s 3(1)).

Where a trade description is used in an advertisement in relation to any parts of goods, the trade description is to be taken as referring to all goods of the class, whether or not in existence at the time the advertisement is published for the purpose of determining whether an offence under the Act has been committed (s 5). Section 39(1) provides that an advertisement includes a catalogue, a circular and a price list.

It is an offence under the Act to make a false statement as to:

(a) the provision in the course of any trade or business of any services, accommodation or facilities;

(b) the nature of any services, accommodation or facilities provided in the course of business;

(c) the time of which, manner in which, or persons by whom any services, accommodation or facilities are so provided;

(d) the examination, approval or evaluation by any person of any service, accommodation or facilities so provided; or

(e) the amenities of any accommodation so provided under s 14(1) of the Act.

*False* means false to a material degree as set out in s 14(4) of the Act; the offence is committed where a person knowingly makes a false statement, or makes it recklessly, regardless of whether it is true or false as provided by s 14(1)(a) and (b).

It is unlawful under the Act to give any form of false indication that any goods, services or methods are of a kind supplied to or approved by Her Majesty or any member of the royal family; and it is an offence to use, without authority, any device or emblem signifying the Queen's Award to Industry or anything which so resembles it as to be likely to deceive (s 12). Furthermore, it is an offence to give any kind of false indication of any goods or services supplied by a person of a kind supplied to any person (s 13).

It is a defence for a person charged with that offence under the Act to show:

(a) that the commission of the offence was due to a mistake or to reliance on information supplied to him or to the act or default of another person, an accident or some other cause beyond his control;

(b) that he took all reasonable precautions and exercised all due diligence to avoid the commission of such an offence by himself or any other person under his control.

It is provided in s 24(1)(a) and (b) that, where the person charged alleges that the commission of the offence was due to the act or default of another person or to reliance on information supplied by another person, a notice in writing should be served on the prosecution at least seven days before the hearing (s 24(2)).

A person charged with an offence which has been committed by the publication of an advertisement will have a defence if he can prove that it is his business to publish or arrange for the publication of advertisements, and that he received the advertisement for publication in the ordinary course of business, without having any reason to suspect that publication would amount to an offence (s 25). Specific provision is made for offences committed by a body corporate where the offence was committed with the consent or the connivance of, or was attributable to, any neglect on any part of any director, manager, secretary or similar officer (including anyone who purported to act in such a capacity). Such a person, as well as a body corporate, is liable as provided in s 20(1).

There are special provisions relating to the marking of certain goods and the information to be contained in advertisements for such goods (ss 8 and 9). The relevant orders made under the Act are the Trade Descriptions (Place of

Production) Marking Order SI 1988/1771, and the Trade Descriptions (Seal Skin Goods) Information Order SI 1980/1150.

# PRICE

## The overall context

The Consumer Protection Act 1987 makes it an offence for traders to give consumers an indication which is misleading as to the price at which any goods, services, accommodation or facilities are available, whether general or from particular persons (s 20(1)). According to the new Directive 98/6/EC, shopkeepers will have to indicate the selling price as well as the unit price of a product. An offence is also committed if a price indication becomes misleading after it was given, is not correct and some customers may be reasonably expected to rely on it (s 20(2)). *Price* means the total amount to be paid by the consumer in respect of the supply of goods or provision of services, facilities or accommodation or any method which will be, or has been, used to calculate the amount (s 20(6)). Consumer means anyone who might wish to be supplied with the goods or provided with the services for private use (s 20(6)).

A price indication will be misleading if the information conveyed by the indications suggest:

(a) that the price is less than it in fact is;

(b) that the applicability of the price does not depend on facts or circumstances on which it is applicable, but it does in fact depend;

(c) that the price covers matters in respect of which an additional charge is in fact made;

(d) that there will be future price increases or reductions where in fact there is no real expectation of that happening;

(e) that facts or circumstances referred to for the purpose of comparison are not in fact what they are (s 21(1)).

The Code of Practice for Traders and Price Indications, issued by the Department of Trade and Industry, offers practical guidance on what would amount to an offence under the Consumer Protection Act 1987, and is designed to promote desirable practices in the giving of price indications. The provisions of the code give detailed guidance on the making of price comparisons in a wide variety of situations, including comparisons with previous prices, with other traders' prices and with the price of goods in different conditions or quantity. The state of the code is evidential. Compliance with its provisions is not an absolute defence, but will tend to show that the trader has not committed an offence. Failure to comply will tend to show that the price indication is misleading and will negative any defence (s 25(2)).

It is a defence for any person charged with an offence of giving a misleading price indication to show that he took all reasonable steps and exercised all due diligence to avoid committing the offence (s 39(1)). If the defence involves an allegation that the commission of the offence was due to an act or default of another or to reliance on information given by another, the persons charged will not, without leave of the court, be entitled to rely on the defence unless he has given the prescribed notice at least seven days before the hearing (s 39(2)–(5)).

Where a misleading price indication is published in a book, newspaper, magazine, film, radio or television broadcast, or in a programme included in a cable programme service, it is a defence for the person charged to show that indication was not contained in an advertisement (s 24(2)).

Where a misleading price indication is published in an advertisement, it is a defence for the person charged to show that he is a person who carries on a business of publishing, or arranging for the publication of advertisements, that he received the advertisement for the publication during the course of that business and that at the time of publication he did not know and had no reason or grounds for suspecting the publication would involve the commission of an offence (s 24(3)).

## Price marking

The Price Marking Order SI 1991/1382 requires the selling price, and in some cases the unit price, of retail goods (other than in the motor field) to be indicated in writing (Arts 3 and 4).

The order applies to advertisements which indicate the selling price or unit price of goods which are or may be for sale by retail (Art 21(b)). The order does not apply to advertisements which only give a recommended retail price or general indication of the price or range of prices at which it is expected that the goods may be sold by retail (Art 2(2)).

All mail order advertisements inviting customers to purchase goods must give an indication of price (Art 83(b)).

A catalogue, circular or price system amounts to an advertisement for the purposes of the order (Art (2)).

Where ancillary goods or services have to be paid for in order to obtain particular goods, the price of the goods must be indicated to show whether it is inclusive or exclusive of the ancillary goods or services (Art 10(1)). Where the price is indicated as being exclusive of ancillary goods or services, the price of the ancillary goods or services shall be indicated as prominently as the indication of the price of the goods (Art 10(3)).

Specific provisions apply to prices indicated in catalogues and price lists (Art 10(5)).

If a price is given for a motor vehicle being sold by a retailer and number plates are excluded from the price, there should be a statement to this effect (Art 10(4)).

In most cases the price indicator should be inclusive of VAT.

There are separate provisions where the sale of goods is mainly to persons carrying on business (Art 9).

# CONTROL OF MISLEADING ADVERTISEMENTS[8]

The Control of Misleading Advertisements Regulations SI 1988/915, as amended, were made under the European Communities Act 1972, s 2(2). They give effect to the EEC Council Directive on Misleading Advertising 84/450, as amended by Directive 97/55/EC. The Regulations impose a duty on the Director General of the Office of Fair Trading to consider any complaint made that an advertisement is misleading, unless the complaint is one that is fictitious or frivolous (see Control of Misleading Advertisements Regulations SI 1988/915, reg 4(1) and (2), as amended by the Broadcasting Act 1990, s 203(1), Sched 20, para 51(2)).

The duty only arises once the established means of dealing with the complaint have been invoked and have not dealt with the complaint adequately (reg 4(3)). It was made clear in consultation papers that this power is only intended to be used where the self-regulatory systems, principally the ASA, have failed to provide adequate redress or are unable to act quickly enough in a particular case. In exercising the powers conferred by the Regulations, the Director General must have regard to all the interests involved and, in particular, the public interest and the desirability of encouraging the control of advertisements by self-regulatory bodies (reg 4(4)).

The Director General has no power to investigate any complaint that can be dealt with by either the Independent Television Commission, the Radio Authority or the Welsh Authority (reg 42, as amended).

The Director General's powers come into play when a complaint about an advertisement is made to him. Complaints likely to be considered by the Director General will be those where:

(a) a complaint procedure to an existing body has not been used, but the complaint appears to raise such serious issues that it justifies seeking an immediate injunction in the High court in England and Wales, or the equivalent courts in Scotland or Northern Ireland;

---

8    For up to date information on this, see the OFT's website: http://www.oft.gov.uk.

(b) there is no existing body for dealing with the complaint;

(c) there is an existing body, but although it has been approached, and has had a reasonable opportunity to deal with the complaint, it has not done so adequately. (In the case where the Director General considers that the complaint has already been adequately dealt with by an existing body, he will not use his powers merely because the complainant is not satisfied with the outcome, or the way the case has been handled.)

It is for the Director General to decide how to deal with cases. In some instances, he may advise a complainant to seek redress in the courts.

Financial Services are excluded from the Regulations because of the separate regime established under the Financial Services Act 1986, as provided in reg 3. If, after considering a complaint, the Director General is of the view that an advertisement is misleading, he can apply for an injunction (interdict in Scotland) against any person concerned with the publication of the advertisement. Usually, this will be an application for an interlocutory injunction, until the case can be fully argued in court. An injunction will only be granted if the court is satisfied that the advertisement is misleading, and after considering all the interests involved (in particular the public interest), but an interlocutory injunction may be granted where there is *prima facie* evidence of misleading advertising, having regard to all the interests involved (reg 6). An injunction may relate not only to a particular advertisement, but to any advertisement in similar terms likely to convey a similar impression (reg 6(2)).

# ADVERTISING OF FOOD

The main statutory provisions governing food advertising are the Food Safety Act 1990 and the Food Labelling Regulations SI 1984/1305, which comply with EC Directive 97/4/EC, amending EC Directive 79/112/EEC. The framework is likely to change with the creation of the proposed Food Standards Agency.

Food is defined to include drink, articles and substances of no nutritional value which are used for human consumption, chewing gum and other products of a like nature and use, and articles and substances used as ingredients in the preparation of food under s 1 of the Act.

Where certain names, descriptions and qualifications are required to be used under the provisions of the Act, such names, descriptions and qualifications are deemed not to be a description as provided for under the Trade Descriptions Act 1968, s 25, as substituted by the Food Safety Act 1990, s 59(1), Sched 3, para 6.

Under the 1990 Act, advertisements include any notice, circular, label, wrapper, invoice or other document, and any public announcement made orally or by means of producing or transmitting light or sound (s 53). The Regulations provide that 'advertisement' is to have the same meaning as in the Act, except that it does not include any form of labelling (reg 2(1)).

Under the Act, it is an offence to publish or be a party to the publication of an advertisement which falsely describes any food or is likely to mislead as to the nature or substance or quality of any food (s 15). An advertisement may be false through omission, even though it may literally be true. The test of whether or not an advertisement is likely to mislead is whether or not an ordinary person would be misled by it. It is an offence under the Regulations to claim either that a food has tonic properties (Food Labelling Regulations 1984, reg 36, Sched 6) or that food which is intended for babies is equivalent or superior to the milk of a healthy mother (Sched 6, Part I of the Regulations).

The Regulations also contain detailed provisions for restricting the claims that can be made in relation to certain types of food (Sched 6, Part II) and make the use of certain words or descriptions in the labelling or advertising of food conditional upon compliance with conditions set out in the Regulations (reg 38, Sched 7, which sets out the conditions to give the right to the use of, *inter alia*, the following words: butter, cream, dietary milk, starch, reduced vitamins, alcohol-free, non-alcoholic, shandy, sweet, liquor, tonic, wine, vintage – the complete list is provided in Sched 7).

# ADVERTISING OF MEDICINES

The advertising of medical products for which a product licence is required is governed by the Medicines Act 1968, and regulations were made under it, namely:

(a) the Medicines (Advertising of Medicinal Products) Regulations 1975 SI 1975/298;

(b) the Medicines (Advertising of Medicinal Products) (No 2) Regulations 1975 SI 1975/1326, as amended by SI 1979/1760, SI 1994/1932;

(c) the Medicines (Labelling and Advertising to the Public) Regulations 1978 SI 1978/41, as amended by SI 1994/1932;

(d) the Medicines (Advertising) Regulations 1994 SI 1994/1932, as amended by the Medicines for Human Use (Marketing Authorisations, etc) Regulations 1994 SI 1994/3144;

(e) Marketing Authorisations for Veterinary Medicinal Products Regulations 1994 SI 1994/3142.

In addition, various self-regulatory codes contain supplementary rules relating to health claims, medicines and treatments, as provided in the ITC Code of Advertising Standards and Practice, in respect of health claims, medicines and treatments, and in the British Advertising Code (Specific

Rules), the Code of Practice for the Proprietary Association of Great Britain and the Code of Practice of the Association of the British Pharmaceutical Industry.

Where certain names, descriptions and qualifications are required to be used under the provisions of the Medicines Act 1968, such names, descriptions, and qualifications are deemed not to be trade descriptions under the Trade Descriptions Act 1968, s 2(5), substituted by the Food Safety Act 1990, s 59(1), Sched 3, para 6. Part VI of the Medicines Act 1968 contains detailed provisions concerned with the advertising of medical products (see Appendix 4 for ss 93–97 of the Medicines Act 1968).

*Advertisement* is defined as including any form of advertising, whether in a publication, or by the display of any notice, or by means of any catalogue, price list, letter (whether circular or addressed to a particular person) or other document, or by the words inscribed in any article, or by the exhibition of a photograph, or by cinematography, film, or by way of sound recording, sound broadcasting or television, or by inclusion in a cable programme service (s 92(1), as amended by the Cable and Broadcasting Act 1984, s 57(1), Sched 5, para 23(1)).

Under the Act, it is an offence for a commercially interested party (s 92(4)), or anyone acting at the request of, or with the consent of, a commercially interested party to issue, or cause another person to issue, a false or misleading advertisement relating to medical products of any description (s 93(1)), or an advertisement which consists of or includes recommendations which go beyond those specified in the licence (s 93(2)). *False or misleading advertisement* is one which falsely describes the description of the medical products to which it relates, or is likely to mislead as to the nature or quality of medical products of that description or as to their use or effects (s 93(7)).

It is a defence if the person charged is able to show that he did not know, or could not, with reasonable diligence, have discovered that the advertisement was false or misleading or that the recommendation made in the advertisement was unauthorised (s 93(5)). Furthermore, where a person can prove that it is his business to issue or arrange for the issue of advertisements, it is a defence if he can show that either:

(a) he received the advertisement for issue in the ordinary course of business and issued, or arranged for it to be issued, either unaltered or without any alteration except in respect of lettering or layout; or

(b) not being a commercially interested party, he received from a commercially interested party the information on which the advertisement was based and in the ordinary course of business prepared the advertisement in accordance with that information, but issued at the request of the party; and

(c) that if, in either case, he did not know and had no reason to suspect that the issue of the advertisement would amount to an offence under this section (s 93(6)), where a product licence is in force in respect of a medical product, it is an offence to issue or cause to be issued an advertisement without the consent of the licence holder (s 94).

The Medicines (Labelling and Advertising to the Public) Regulations 1978 prohibit advertising of medical products and other substances or articles likely to lead to the use of the product, substance or article for the treatment of certain specified diseases or for the purpose of procuring the miscarriage of a woman, as provided in reg 4. Whilst there is no statutory requirement for advertisements for medical products to be cleared prior to issue, the prohibitions, restrictions or requirements imposed by the Regulations will not apply to any advertisement where the holder of the product licence has submitted a copy of the advertisement to the licensing authority, that is, the Medicines Control Agency; and, if the authority has not notified the holder within 48 days, the advertisement should not be issued without the approval of the Medicines Control Agency, as provided in reg 8(1).

## ADVERTISING ON OUTDOOR SITES

Most outdoor advertising falls within the control of the Town and Country Planning (Control of Advertisement) Regulations SI 1992/666 as amended. Subject to a number of exceptions, anyone wishing to display an advertisement on an outdoor site must obtain the consent of either local planning authority or the Secretary of State.

Consent may either be expressed or deemed, depending on whether it is granted on application by operation under the Regulations (reg 5). Local planning authorities may only exercise their powers under the Regulations in the interests of amenity and public safety (reg 4). Where consent is refused or made subject to conditions, the local planning authority must give written reasons (reg 14). The applicant can appeal and take seek leave to have the authority's decision judicially reviewed.

## AERIAL ADVERTISING

The use of an aircraft while in the air for the emission or display of any advertisement or any other communication which is audible or visible from the ground is prohibited, except in certain prescribed circumstances, under the Civil Aviation Act 1982, s 82(1).

An aircraft, other than a kite, may identify on its body (by a mark or inscription that is other than an illuminated sign) a number of features including its owner, its manufacturer and its type of engine (the Civil Aviation

(Aerial Advertisement) Regulations SI 1983/1881, reg 4(2)). A free balloon may carry similar information on its body, or on a basket, car or a bit of equipment attached to it, as provided in reg 4(6).

The specified exceptions to the general prohibition allow the display of any mark or inscription on a banner, towed behind an aeroplane as provided in reg 4, s 3, on the body of an airship or an illuminated sign attached to an airship, as provided in reg 4(4), and on the body of a balloon which is not more than 1 m in any linear dimension, reg 4(5). Advertising is also permitted on captive balloons under the Civil Aviation (Aero Advertising Captive Balloons) Regulations SI 1984/474.

## INDECENCY AND OBSCENITY

The public display of indecent matter and the publication of obscene materials gives rise to a criminal liability under a variety of statutes, such as the Indecent Displays Control Act 1982, s 1(1), and the Obscene Publications Act 1959, s 2, as amended. In addition to the statutory controls, both the ITC Code and Radio Authority Code contain provisions dealing with taste and offence, and the Broadcasting Standards Council has statutory authority to monitor the portrayal of sex, violence and matters of taste and decency generally in broadcasting, as provided in s 151 of the Broadcasting Act 1990 and the Broadcasting Act 1996.

## CHILD PORNOGRAPHY AND ILLEGAL MATERIAL ON THE INTERNET

A self-regulatory body, the Internet Watch Foundation (IWF), has been set up to receive and process complaints about child pornography and other illegal material communicated on the internet or in usenet news groups, and to establish a classification system for legal material (drugs, sex, violence, etc) communicated over the net.

In those cases investigated by the IWF which appear to involve criminal activity, the IWF reports its findings to the police through the National Criminal Intelligence Service, which then forwards the matter to the relevant law enforcement agency in the UK or abroad.

The IWF provides a hotline service to enable the public to report potentially illegal material. In the first year of its operation, during 1996–97, 781 reports were received, concerning over 4,300 items of complaint.

In terms of the reports on which the IWF took action, 85% concerned child pornography, with less than 7% each on matters such as financial scams, other pornography, racism, etc.

The origin of these reports was mainly usenet news articles (45%) and websites (39%). Only 6% originated in the UK, 63% from the USA, 19% from Japan and 11% from Europe.

## MARINE BROADCASTING

Beaming of advertisements to the UK, as far as broadcasts from outside territorial limits are concerned, is generally prohibited under the Marine and Broadcasting Offences Act 1967, ss 1(1), 2(1) and 5. To advertise by means of such a broadcast is an offence, as is to invite another to advertise by means of such an advertisement (s 5(3)(e)). Advertising by means of such a broadcast is deemed to have taken place wherever the broadcast is received and wherever it is made (s 5(5)). It is also illegal to publish any details of an offending broadcast or to publish an advertisement calculated, directly or indirectly, to promote the interest of the business whose activities consist of or include the operation of a station from which the broadcast is, or is to be, made (s 5(3)(f)).

## RACIAL DISCRIMINATION

It is unlawful to publish, or cause to be published, any advertisement which indicates, or an intention which could reasonably be understood to indicate, an intention to discriminate on racial grounds (Race Relations Act 1976, s 29). There are some exceptions, as provided in s 29(2) and (3) of the Act, for example, where belonging to a particular racial group is a genuine occupational qualification for the job being advertised (s 5). Positive discrimination is also permitted (ss 35–38), as are advertisements for clubs where membership is to enjoyed by persons of a particular racial group defined otherwise than by reference to colour (s 26).

Enforcement is the responsibility of the Commission for Racial Equality (s 63(1)), which may seek an injunction in order to prevent further unlawful discrimination (s 63(4)). While the publisher of an offending advertisement will not be subject to any liability if he can show both that he relied on a statement to the effect that publication would not be unlawful and that his reliance was reasonable (s 29(4)), criminal proceedings can be brought against a person making such a statement knowingly or recklessly (s 29(5), as substituted by the Criminal Justice Act 1982, ss 38 and 46).

## SEX DISCRIMINATION

It is unlawful to publish or cause to be published an advertisement which indicates or might reasonably be understood as indicating an intention unlawfully to discriminate in the field of employment or education or in the provision of goods, facilities, services or premises under the Sex Discrimination Act 1975, s 38(1). The use of a job description with a sexual connotation such as waiter, sales girl, postman or stewardess will be taken as indicating an intention to discriminate, unless an indication to the contrary is shown (s 38(3)).

Enforcement of these provisions is the responsibility of the Equal Opportunities Commission (s 72), and its powers are in parallel to those of the Commission for Racial Equality. An individual may make a claim for unlawful discrimination in relation to the arrangements made for the purpose of determining who should be offered employment (s 61(a)), and it has been held that an advertisement may be part of such arrangements (see *Prindle and Tayside Health Board* [1976] IRLR 364). It is unlawful for a publisher to refuse to publish an advertisement for a resident domestic employee on the ground that there will be no female employer living in the household.

The publisher and advertiser rely on a similar defence to that of s 29(4) of the Race Relations Act 1976, in regard to racially discriminatory advertisements (Sex Discrimination Act 1975, s 38(4)).

The Disability Discrimination Act 1995 deals with advertising that is discriminatory towards disabled people.

## SURROGATE MOTHERHOOD

The publication and distribution of advertisements relating to arrangements for surrogate motherhood is unlawful under the Surrogacy Arrangements Act 1985, s 3. Such advertisements are defined as those which contain an indication, however expressed, that any person is, or may be, willing to enter into a surrogacy arrangement or to negotiate or facilitate the making of surrogacy arrangements, or for any persons looking for a woman willing to become a surrogate mother, or for persons wanting a woman to carry a child as a surrogate mother (s 3(1)). Whenever such an advertisement is published, whether in a newspaper or periodical in the UK, the offence committed by the proprietor, editor or publisher is one of strict liability (ss 6 and 3(2)). These offences are overseen by the Human Fertilisation and Emryology Authority.

## UNITED KINGDOM DISCOUNTS/TRADING STAMPS

Discounts, including coupons, are allowed. There is no specific legislation relating to discounting in the UK. The basic requirement is that any price indication should not be misleading (Consumer Protection Act 1987, Part III, and the Code of Practice for Traders on Price Indications 1989). There are also restrictions under competition legislation to deal with abuses of a dominant position. Consumer protection and fair trading practices are covered in the following: the Trade Descriptions Act 1968; the Fair Trading Act 1973; the Restrictive Trade Practices Act 1976; the Resale Prices Act 1976; the Competition Act 1980; the Supply of Goods and Services Act 1982; the Control of Misleading Advertising Regulations 1988; the Consumer Protection Act 1987; the Price Marking Order 1991; the Sale of Goods Act 1979 as amended by the Sale and Supply of Goods Act 1994; and the Competition Act 1998.

The Trading Stamps Act of 1964 requires trading stamps to bear a cash value which consumers can redeem when they have collected stamps worth 25p.

There are also codes of practice covering commercial communication activities such as the British Code of Advertising and Sales Promotion 1995 and the Direct Marketing Code of Practice 1998.

# TOBACCO ADVERTISING

There is a general prohibition on tobacco advertising on television (the ITC Code of Advertising Standards and Practice) and it is prohibited on radio. The CAP operates a mandatory pre-clearance procedure for the advertising of cigarettes and hand rolling tobacco, which is subject to the Cigarette Code (Appendix 1).

In May 1998, the European Parliament agreed to ban tobacco advertising, the industry spending £320 m a year on this kind of advertising in Europe. Further, it was agreed to exempt sponsorship by tobacco companies for a period of eight years (see above, Chapter 1).

In December 1998, the government published a White Paper on Tobacco 'Smoking Kills'. The White Paper set out the timetable to bring forward secondary legislation in the 1998–99 Parliamentary session to put the EC Directive into law in the UK. The intention is to end tobacco advertising on billboards and in the printed media at the earliest practicable opportunity. Member States are required to end most forms of tobacco advertising including billboards by 30 July 2006 to end all tobacco sponsorship. This last date is the date by which the Directive must be implemented in its entirety.

Allowance will be made for sports to find alternative sponsors and a group of sponsorship experts, chaired by the Minister for Sports will provide support and guidance when needed. Although, in allowing global sports, such as Formula One racing, a longer period of adjustment until 2006, evidence of diminished reliance on tobacco sponsorship must be demonstrated by 2003 at the latest.

Meanwhile, the sports' organising body, the *Fédération Internationale de l'Automobile* (FIA) are studying evidence,provided by Britain and others, of a direct link between tobacco advertising/sponsorship and smoking. If satisfied by the evidence, the FIA has announced publicly that it would ban tobacco advertising and sponsorship at Formula One events from 2002.

The EC Directive will also make it illegal to advertise tobacco products indirectly using other products, so called 'brand-stretching'. However, the use of a common product name may be allowed if presentational features are clearly distinct from those used with tobacco products. Member States may allow brand names in existence at 30 July 1998 to continue to be used.

The White Paper states that direct and indirect marketing aimed at providing incentives to smokers to keep on smoking will be phased out. Communications between those in the tobacco trade are to be exempt, as will be advertising in publications produced outside the EU and aimed mainly at a non EU market. However, the government intends to limit strictly shop advertising to protect children from exposure to pro-tobacco messages in shops will sell a range of goods and services. Under an agreement with the Associated Independent Tobacco Specialists, specialist tobacconist shops will be exempted from the ban, provided they fulfil criteria defining specialist traders, and refrain from advertising cigarettes in their shop windows. In addition to publishing the White Paper, the government published a current draft of the Regulatory Impact Assessment (RIA) which includes an employment impact assessment. This will be updated.

In September 1998, four major tobacco companies, British American Tobacco, Imperial Tobacco Ltd, Gallaher Ltd and Rothmans (UK) Ltd, announced their intention to challenge the legal basis of the EU Advertising Directive and leave to take this challenge to the ECJ was granted in December 1998 by Mr Justice Turner. The German government, whose six month presidency began on 1 January 1999, is also mounting a legal challenge to the directive. We await a judgment from the court.

## Sources

Independent Television Commission, *Annual Report*, 1998, London: ITC

Radio Authority, *Annual Report*, 1998, London: Radio Authority

Advertising Standards Authority, *Annual Report*, 1998, London: ASA

*Encyclopaedia of Forms and Precedents: Volume 1*, London: Butterworths

# THE BRITISH CODES OF
# ADVERTISING AND SALES PROMOTION

The Committee of Advertising Practice (CAP), devises, reviews and amends the codes.

A full set of the codes is available free from the Advertising Standards Authority website: http://www.asa.org.uk.

The codes are reproduced here by kind permission.

*Note*: at the time of going to press, the February 1995 edition of the codes was the current edition. A new edition of the codes is due to be published in 1999. Readers are advised to consult the ASA's website (cited above) or contact the ASA directly for information about availability of the new edition of the codes.

### Introduction

1.1 The Codes apply to:

    (a)    advertisements in newspapers, magazines, brochures, leaflets, circulars. mailings, catalogues and other printed publications, facsimile transmissions, posters and aerial announcements

    (b)    cinema and video commercials

    (c)    advertisements in non-broadcast electronic media such as computer games

    (d) viewdata services

    (e) mailing lists for business-to-business

    (f) sales promotions

    (g) advertisement promotions

    (h) advertisements and promotions covered by the Cigarette Code.

1.2 The Codes do not apply to:

    (a)    broadcast commercials, which are the responsibility of the Independent Television Commission or the Radio Authority

    (b)    the contents of premium-rate telephone calls, which are the responsibility of the Independent Committee for the Supervision of Standards of Telephone Information Services

    (c)    advertisements in foreign media

    (d)    Health-related claims in advertisements and promotions addressed only to the medical and allied professions

    (e)    classified private advertisements

    (f)    statutory, public, police and other official notices

(g) works of art exhibited in public or private

(h) private correspondence

(i) oral communications, including telephone calls

(j) press releases and other public relations material

(k) the content of books and editorial communications

(l) regular competitions such as crosswords

(m) flyposting

(n) packages, wrappers, labels and tickets unless they advertise a sales promotion or are visible in an advertisement

(o) point-of-sale displays except those covered by the Sales Promotion Code and the Cigarette Code.

1.3 The following definitions apply to the Codes:

(a) a product encompasses goods, services, ideas, causes or opportunities, prizes and gifts

(b) a consumer is anyone who is likely to see a given advertisement or promotion

(c) the United Kingdom rules cover the Isle of Man and the Channel Islands (except for the purposes of the Cigarette Code)

(d) a claim can be implied or direct, written, spoken or visual

(e) the Codes are divided into numbered clauses.

1.4 The following criteria apply to the Codes:

(a) the judgement of the ASA Council on interpretation of the Codes is final

(b) conformity is assessed according to the advertisement's probable impact when taken as a whole and in context. This will depend on the audience, the medium, the nature of the product and any additional material distributed at the same time to consumers

(c) the Codes are indivisible; advertisers must conform with all appropriate rules

(d) the Codes do not have the force of law and their interpretation will reflect their flexibility. The general law operates alongside the Codes; the Courts may also make rulings against matters covered by the Codes

[...]

(f) no spoken or written communications with the ASA or CAP should be understood as containing legal advice

(g) the Codes are primarily concerned with advertisements and promotions and not with terms of business, products themselves or other contractual matters

(h) the rules make due allowance for public sensitivities but will not be used by the ASA to diminish freedom of speech

(i)  the ASA may decide that it is not qualified to judge advertisements and promotions in languages other than English

(j)  the ASA does not act as an arbitrator between conflicting ideologies.

## Advertising Code

### Principles

2.1  All advertisements should be legal, decent, honest and truthful.

2.2  All advertisements should be prepared with a sense of responsibility to consumers and to society.

2.3  All advertisements should respect the principles of fair competition generally accepted in business.

2.4  No advertisement should bring advertising into disrepute.

2.5  Advertisements must conform with the Codes. Primary responsibility for observing the Codes falls on advertisers. Others involved in preparing and publishing advertisements such as agencies, publishers and other service suppliers also accept an obligation to abide by the Codes.

2.6  Any unreasonable delay in responding to the ASA's enquiries may be considered a breach of the Codes.

2.7  The ASA will on request treat in confidence any private or secret material supplied unless the courts or officials acting within their statutory powers compel its disclosure.

2.8  The Codes are applied in the spirit as well as in the letter.

### Substantiation

3.1  Before submitting an advertisement for publication, advertisers must hold documentary evidence to prove all claims, whether direct or implied, that are capable of objective substantiation. Relevant evidence should be sent without delay if requested by the ASA. The adequacy of the evidence will be judged on whether it supports both the detailed claims and the overall impression created by the advertisement.

3.2  If there is a significant division of informed opinion about any claims made in an advertisement they should not be portrayed as universally agreed.

3.3  If the contents of non-fiction books, tapes, videos and the like have not been independently substantiated, advertisements should not exaggerate the value or practical usefulness of their contents.

3.4  Obvious untruths or exaggerations that are unlikely to mislead and incidental minor errors and unorthodox spellings are all allowed provided they do not affect the accuracy or perception of the advertisement in any material way.

## Legality

4.1 Advertisers have primary responsibility for ensuring that their advertisements are legal. Advertisements should contain nothing that breaks the law or incites anyone to break it, and should omit nothing that the law requires.

## Decency

5.1 Advertisements should contain nothing that is likely to cause serious or widespread offence. Particular care should be taken to avoid causing offence on the grounds of race, religion, sex, sexual orientation or disability. Compliance with the Codes will be judged on the context, medium, audience, product and prevailing standards of decency.

5.2 Advertisements may be distasteful without necessarily conflicting with 5.1 above. Advertisers are urged to consider public sensitivities before using potentially offensive material.

5.3 The fact that a particular product is offensive to some people is not sufficient grounds for objecting to an advertisement for it.

## Honesty

6.1 Advertisers should not exploit the credulity, lack of knowledge or inexperience of consumers.

## Truthfulness

7.1 No advertisement should mislead by inaccuracy, ambiguity, exaggeration, omission or otherwise.

## Matters of opinion

8.1 Advertisers may give a view about any matter, including the qualities or desirability of their products, provided it is clear that they are expressing their own opinion rather than stating a fact. Assertions or comparisons that go beyond subjective opinions are subject to 3.1 above.

## Fear and Distress

9.1 No advertisement should cause fear or distress without good reasons. Advertisers should not use shocking claims or images merely to attract attention.

9.2 Advertisers may use an appeal to fear to encourage prudent behaviour or to discourage dangerous or ill-advised actions; the fear likely to be aroused should be disproportionate to the risk.

## Safety

10.1 Advertisements should not show or encourage unsafe practices except in the context of promoting safety. Particular care should be taken with advertisements addressed to or depicting children and young people.

10.2 Consumers should not be discouraged to drink and drive. Advertisements, including those for breath-testing devices, should not suggest that the effects of drinking alcohol can be masked and should include a prominent warning on the dangers of drink and driving.

## Violence and anti-social behaviour

11.1 Advertisements should contain nothing that condones or is likely to provoke violence or anti-social behaviour.

## Political advertising

12.1 Any advertisement whose principal function is to influence opinion in favour of or against any political party or electoral candidate contesting a UK, European parliamentary or local-government election, or any matter before the electorate for a referendum, is exempt from clauses 3.1, 7.1, 14.3, 19.2 and 20.1. All other rules in the Codes apply.

12.2 The identity and status of such advertisers should be clear. If their address or other contact details are not generally available they should be included in the advertisement.

12.3 There is a formal distinction between government policy and that of political parties. Advertisements by central or local government, or those concerning government policy as distinct from party policy, are subject to all the Code's rules.

## Protection of privacy

13.1 Advertisers are urged to obtain written permission in advance if they portray or refer to individuals or their identifiable possessions in any advertisement. Exceptions include most crowd scenes, portraying anyone who is the subject of the book or film being advertised and depicting property in general outdoor locations.

13.2 Advertisers who have not obtained prior permission from entertainers, politicians, sportsmen and others whose work gives them a high public profile should ensure that they are not portrayed in an offensive or adverse way. Advertisements should not claim or imply an endorsement where none exists.

13.3 Prior permission may not be needed when the advertisement contains nothing that is inconsistent with the position or views of the person featured. Advertisers should be aware that individuals who do not wish to be associated with the advertised product may have a legal claim.

13.4  References to anyone who is deceased should be handled with particular care to avoid causing offence or distress.

13.5  References to members of the Royal Family and the use of the Royal Arms and Emblems are not normally permitted; advertisers should consult the Lord Chamberlain's Office, References to Royal Warrants should be checked with the Royal Warrant Holders' Association.

**Testimonials and endorsements**

14.1  Advertisers should hold signed and dated proof, including a contact address, for any testimonial they use. Testimonials should be used only with the written permission of those giving them.

14.2  Testimonials should relate to the product being advertised.

14.3  Testimonials alone do not constitute substantiation and the opinions expressed in them must be supported, where necessary, with independent evidence of their accuracy. Any claims based on a testimonial must conform to the Codes.

14.4  Fictitious endorsements should not be presented as though they were genuine testimonials.

14.5  References to tests, trials, professional endorsements, research facilities and professional journals should be used only with the permission of those concerned. They should originate from within the European Union unless otherwise stated in the advertisement. Any establishment referred to should be under the direct supervision of an appropriately qualified professional.

**Prices**

15.1  Any stated price should be clear and should relate to the product advertised. Advertisers should ensure that prices match the products illustrated.

15.2  Unless addressed exclusively to the trade, prices quoted should include any VAT payable. It should be apparent immediately whether any prices quoted exclude other taxes, duties or compulsory charges and these should, wherever possible, be given in the advertisement.

15.3  If the price of one product is dependent on the purchase of another, the extent of any commitment by consumers should be made clear.

15.4  Price claims such as 'up to' and 'from' should not exaggerate the availability of benefits likely to be obtained by consumers.

**Free offers**

16.1  There is no objection to making a free offer conditional on the purchase of other items. Consumers' liability for any costs should be made clear in all material featuring the offer. An offer should only be described as free if consumers pay no more than:

(a)    the current public rates of postage

(b)    the actual cost of freight or delivery

(c)    the cost, including incidental expenses, of any travel involved if consumers collect the offer.

Advertisers should make no additional charges for packing and handling.

16.2    Advertisers must not attempt to recover their costs by reducing the quality or composition or by inflating the price of any product that must be purchased as a pre-condition of obtaining another product free.

**Availability of products**

17.1    Advertisers must make it clear if stocks are limited. Products must not be advertised unless advertisers can demonstrate that they have reasonable grounds for believing that they can satisfy demand. If a product becomes unavailable, advertisers will be required to show evidence of stock monitoring, communications with outlets and the swift withdrawal of advertisements whenever possible.

17.2    Products which cannot be supplied should not normally be advertised as a way of assessing potential demand.

17.3    Advertisers must not use the technique of switch selling, where their sales staff criticise the advertised product or suggest that it is not available and recommend the purchase of a more expensive alternative. They should not place obstacles in the way of purchasing the product or delivering it promptly.

**Guarantees**

18.1    The full terms of any guarantee should be available for consumers to inspect before they are committed to purchase. Any substantial limitations should be spelled out in the advertisement.

18.2    Advertisers should inform consumers about the nature and extent of any additional rights provided by the guarantee, over and above those given to them by law, and should make clear how to obtain redress.

18.3    'Guarantee' when used simply as a figure of speech should not cause confusion about consumers' legal rights.

**Comparisons**

19.1    Comparisons can be explicit or implied and can relate to advertisers' own products or to those of their competitors; they are permitted in the interests of vigorous competition and public information.

19.2 Comparisons should be clear and fair. the elements of any comparison should not be selected in a way that gives the advertisers an artificial advantage.

## Denigration

20.1 Advertisers should not unfairly attack or discredit other businesses or their products.

20.2 The only acceptable use of another business's broken or defaced products in advertisements is in the illustration of comparative tests, and the source, nature and results of these should be clear.

## Exploitation of goodwill

21.1 Advertisers should not make unfair use of the goodwill attached to the trade mark, name, brand, or the advertising campaign of any other business.

## Imitation

22.1 No advertisement should so closely resemble any other that it misleads or causes confusion.

## Identifying advertisers and recognising advertisements

23.1 Advertisers, publishers and owners of other media should ensure that advertisements are designed and presented in such a way that they can be easily distinguished from editorial.

23.2 Features, announcements or promotions that are disseminated in exchange for a payment or other reciprocal arrangement should comply with the Codes if their content is controlled by the advertisers. They should also be clearly identified and distinguished from editorial (see clause 41).

23.3 Mail order and direct response advertisements and those for one-day sales, homework schemes, business opportunities and the like should contain the name and address of the advertisers. Advertisements with political content should clearly identify their source. Unless required by law, other advertisers are not obliged to identify themselves.

## Sales Promotion Code

### Introduction

26.1 The Sales Promotion Code should be read, where appropriate, in conjunction with the rules in the Advertising and Cigarette Codes. [...]

26.2 The Sales Promotion Code is designed primarily to protect the public but it also applies to trade promotions and incentive schemes and to promotional elements of sponsorships.

26.3 The Sales Promotion Code regulates the nature and administration of promotional marketing techniques. These techniques generally involve providing a range of direct or indirect additional benefits, usually on a temporary basis, designed to make goods or services more attractive to purchasers.

**Principles**

27.1 All sales promotions should be legal, decent, honest and truthful.

27.2 All sales promotions should be prepared with a sense of responsibility to consumers and to society; they should be conducted equitably, promptly and efficiently and should be seen to deal fairly and honourably with consumers. Promoters should avoid causing unnecessary disappointment.

27.3 All sales promotions should respect the principles of fair competition generally accepted in business.

27.4 No promoter or intermediary should bring sales promotion into disrepute.

27.5 Sales promotions must conform with the Codes. Primary responsibility for observing the Codes falls on promoters. Intermediaries and agents also accept an obligation to abide by the Codes.

27.6 Any unreasonable delay in responding to the ASA's enquiries may be considered a breach of the Codes.

27.7 The ASA will on request treat in confidence any private or secret material supplied unless the courts or officials acting within their statutory powers compel disclosure.

27.8 The Codes are applied in the spirit as well as in the letter.

**Public interest**

28.1 Sales promotions should not be designed or conducted in a way that conflicts with the public interest. They should contain nothing that condones or is likely to provoke violent or anti-social behaviour, nuisance, personal injury or damage to property.

**Substantiation**

29.1 Promoters must be able to demonstrate that they have complied with the Codes by submitting documentary evidence without delay when asked by the ASA. The adequacy of evidence will be judged on whether it supports the detailed claims, on the way in which the sales promotion is administered and on the overall impression created by the promotion.

## Legality

30.1 Promoters have primary responsibility for ensuring that what they do is legal. Sales promotions should contain nothing that breaks the law or incites anyone to break it, and should omit nothing that the law requires.

## Honesty

31.1 Promoters should not abuse customers' trust or exploit their lack of knowledge or experience.

## Truthfulness

32.1 No sales promotion should mislead by inaccuracy, ambiguity, omission or otherwise.

## Protection of consumers and promoters

33.1 Promotions involving adventurous activities should be made as safe as possible by the promoters. Every effort should be made to avoid harming consumers when distributing product samples. Special care should be taken when sales promotions are addressed to children or when products intended for adults may fall into the hands of children. Literature accompanying promotional items should give any necessary safety warnings.

33.2 Promotions should be designed and conducted in a way that respects the right of consumers to a reasonable degree of privacy and freedom from annoyance.

33.3 Consumers should be told before entry if participants may be required to become involved in any of the promoters' publicity or advertising, whether it is connected with the sales promotion or not. Prizewinners should not be compromised by the publication of excessively detailed information.

33.4 Promoters and others responsible for administering sales promotions should ensure that the way they compiles and use lists containing personal information about consumers conforms to the Specific Rules on List and Database Practice.

## Suitability

34.1 Promoters should make every effort to ensure that unsuitable or inappropriate material does not reach consumers. Neither the sales promotions themselves nor the promotional items should cause offence. Promotions should not be socially undesirable to the audience addressed by encouraging either excessive consumption or inappropriate use.

34.2 Alcoholic drinks and tobacco products should not feature in sales promotions addressed to people who are under 18 and tobacco promotions should be addressed only to existing smokers (see Cigarette Code and Specific Rules on alcoholic drinks).

## Availability

35.1 Promoters should be able to demonstrate that they have made a reasonable estimate of likely response and that they are capable of meeting that response. This applies in all cases except prize promotions, where the number of prizes available to be awarded should be made clear to participants.

35.2 Phrases such as 'subject to availability' do not relieve promoters of the obligation to take all reasonable steps to avoid disappointing participants.

35.3 If promoters are unable to supply demand for a promotional offer because of any unexpectedly high response or some other unanticipated factor outside their control, products of a similar or greater quality and value or a cash payment should normally be substituted.

## Children

36.1 For the purposes of this Code, a child or young person is someone under the age of 16. Where appropriate, sales promotions should conform with the Specific Rules on Children.

## Participation

37.1 Sales promotions should specify:

   (a)   how to participate, including any conditions and costs

   (b)   the promoters' full name and business address in a form that can be retained by consumers

   (c)   a prominent closing date if applicable; where the final date for purchase of the promoted product differs from the closing date for the submission of claims or entries, this should be made clear to participants.

   (d)   any proof-of-purchase requirements; this information should be emphasised for example by using bold type, separating it from other text or using a different colour.

   (e)   where it is not obvious, if there is likely to be a limitation on the availability of promotional packs in relation to any stated closing date of the offer

   (f)   where applicable, geographical or personal restrictions, including whether permission is needed from an adult

   (g)   any other factor likely to influence consumers' decisions or understanding about the promotion

(h)   that any deadline for responding to an undated mailing will be calculated from the date the mailing was received by consumers.

## Administration

38.1   Sales promotions should be conducted under proper supervision and adequate resources should be made available to administer them. Promoters and intermediaries should not give consumers any justifiable grounds for complaint.

38.2   Promoters should allow ample time for each phase of the promotion: notifying the trade, distributing the goods, issuing rules where appropriate, collecting wrappers and the like, judging and announcing the result.

38.3   Promoters should fulfil applications within 30 days unless:

(a)   participants have been told in advance that it is impractical to do so

(b)   participants are informed promptly of unforeseen delays and are offered another delivery date or an opportunity to recover any money paid for the offer.

38.4   When damaged or faulty goods are received by consumers, promoters should ensure that they are either replaced without delay or that a refund is sent immediately. The full cost of replacing damaged or faulty goods should fall on promoters. If an applicant does not receive goods, promoters should normally replace them free of charge.

## Free offers and promotions where consumers pay

39.1   In the case of free offers and offers where payment is required, consumers should be informed if any other conditions apply.

39.2   There is no objection to making a free offer conditional on the purchase of other items. Consumers' liability for any costs should be made clear in all materials featuring the offer. An offer should only be described as free if consumers pay no more than:

(a)   the current public rates of postage

(b)   the actual cost of freight and delivery

(c)   the cost, including incidental expenses, of any travel involved if consumers collect the offer.

Promoters should make no additional charges for packing and handling.

39.3   Promoters must not attempt to recover their costs by reducing the quality or composition or by inflating the price of any product that must be purchased as a precondition of obtaining a free item.

39.4 Promoters should provide a cash refund, postal order or personal cheque promptly to consumers participating in 'try me free' offers with a money-back guarantee.

## Promotions with prizes

40.1 Promotions with prizes including competitions, free draws and instant-win offers are subject to legal restrictions. Promoters should take legal advice before embarking on such schemes.

40.2 Before making a purchase, participants should be informed of:

(a)   the closing date for receipt of entries

(b)   any geographical or personal restrictions such as location or age

(c)   any requirements for proof of purchase

(d)   the need to obtain permission to enter from an adult or employer

(e)   the nature of any prizes.

40.3 Before entry, participants should be informed:

(a)   of any restrictions on the number of entries or prizes

(b)   if a cash alternative can be substituted for any prize

(c)   how and when winners will be notifies of results

(d)   how and when winners and results will be announced

(e)   of the criteria for judging entries

(f)   where appropriate, who owns the copyright of the entries

(g)   whether and how entries will be returned by promoters

(h)   of any intention to use winners in post-event publicity.

40.4 Complex rules should be avoided and promoters should not need to supplement conditions of entry with additional rules. If further rules cannot be avoided, participants should be informed how to obtain them; the rules should contain nothing that would have influenced consumers against making a purchase or participating. Participants should always be able to retain entry instructions and rules.

40.5 The closing date for entry to a prize promotion should not be changed unless circumstances outside the reasonable control of the promoters make it unavoidable.

40.6 A poor response or an inferior quality of entries is not an acceptable basis for extending the duration of a promotion or withholding prizes unless the promoters have announced their intention to do so at the outset.

40.7 Promoters must either publish or make available on request details of the name and county of major prizewinners and their winning entries. They should make clear in promotional material how this will be done.

40.8 Unless otherwise stated in advance, prizewinners should receive their prizes no more than six weeks after the promotion has ended.

40.9 If the selection of winning entries is open to subjective interpretation, an independent judge, or a panel including one member who is independent of the competition's promoters and intermediaries, should be appointed. Those appointed to act as judges should be competent to judge the subject matter of the competition. The identity of judges should be made available on request.

40.10 Promoters should ensure that tokens, tickets or numbers for instant-win and similar promotions are allocated on a fair and random basis. An independent observer should supervise prize draws to ensure that participants have an equal opportunity of winning.

40.11 Participants in instant-win promotions should get their winnings at once or should know immediately what they have won and how to claim it without delay, unreasonable costs or administrative barriers.

40.12 When prize promotions are widely advertised, promoters should ensure that entry forms and any goods needed to establish proof of purchase are widely available.

40.13 The distinction between a prize and a gift should always be clear to consumers. Gifts offered to all or most participants in a promotion should not be described as prizes. If promoters offer a gift to all entrants in addition to giving a prize to those who win, particular care is needed to avoid confusing the two.

40.14 Promoters should avoid exaggerating the likelihood of consumers winning a prize.

**Advertisement promotions**

41.1 Advertisement promotions should be designed and presented in such a way that they can be easily distinguished from editorial.

41.2 Features, announcements or promotions that are disseminated in exchange for a payment or other reciprocal arrangement comply with the Codes if their content is controlled by the promoters.

41.3 Publishers announcing reader promotions on the front page or cover should ensure that consumers know whether they will be expected to buy subsequent editions of the publication. Major qualifications that may influence consumers significantly in their decision to purchase the publication should appear on the front page or cover.

**Charity-linked promotions**

42.1 Promotions claiming that participation will benefit registered charities or good causes should:

(a)   name each charity or good cause that will benefit, and be able to demonstrate to the ASA that those benefiting consent to the advertising promotion

(b)   when it is not a registered charity, define its nature and objectives

(c)   specify exactly what will be gained by the named charity or cause and state the basis on which the contribution will be calculated

(d)   state if the promoters have imposed any limitations on the contribution they will make out of their own pocket

(e)   not limit consumers' contributions; any extra money collected should be given to the named charity or cause on the same basis as contributions below that level

(f)   not exaggerate the benefit to the charity or cause derived from individual purchases of the promoted product

(g)   if asked, make available to consumers a current or final total of contributions made

(h)   take particular care when appealing to children (see 47.4(e)).

**Trade incentives**

43.1   Incentive schemes should be designed and implemented to take account of the interests of everyone involved and should not compromise the obligation of employees to give honest advice to consumers.

43.2   Promoters should secure the prior agreement of employers or of the manager responsible if they intend to ask for assistance from, or offer incentives to, any other company's employees. Promoters should observe any procedures established by companies for their employees, including any rules for participating in promotions. In the case of a trade-incentive scheme that has been generally advertised rather than individually targeted, employees should be asked to obtain their employer's permission before participating.

43.3   It should be made clear to those benefiting from an incentive scheme that they may be liable for tax.

**Alcoholic drinks**

46.1   For the purposes of the Codes, alcoholic drinks are those that exceed 1.2 per cent alcohol by volume.

46.2   The drinks industry and the advertising business accept a responsibility for ensuring that advertisements contain nothing that is likely to lead people to adopt styles of drinking that are unwise. The consumption of alcohol may be portrayed as sociable and thirst-quenching. Advertisements may be humorous, but must still conform with the intention of the rules.

46.3 Advertisements should be socially responsible and should not encourage excessive drinking. Advertisements should not suggest that regular solitary drinking is advisable. Care should be taken not to exploit the young, the immature or those who are mentally or socially vulnerable.

46.4 Advertisements should not be directed at people under 18 through the selection of media, style of presentation, content or context in which they appear. No medium should be used to advertise alcoholic drinks if more than 25 per cent of its audience is under 18 years of age.

46.5 People shown drinking should not be, nor should they look, under 25. Younger models may be shown in advertisements, for example in the context of family celebrations, but it should be obvious that they are not drinking.

46.6 Advertisements should not feature real or fictitious characters who are likely to appeal particularly to people under 18 in a way that would encourage them to drink.

46.7 Advertisements should not suggest that any alcoholic drink can enhance mental, physical or sexual capabilities, popularity, attractiveness, masculinity, femininity or sporting achievements.

46.8 Advertisements may give factual information about the alcoholic strength of a drink or its relatively high alcohol content but this should not be the dominant theme of any advertisement. Alcoholic drinks should not be presented as preferable because of their high alcohol content or intoxicating effect.

46.9 Advertisements should not portray drinking alcohol as the main reason for the success of any personal relationship or social event. A brand preference may be promoted as a mark of the drinker's good taste and discernment.

46.10 Drinking alcohol should not be portrayed as a challenge, nor should it be suggested that people who drink are brave, tough or daring for doing so.

46.11 Particular care should be taken to ensure that advertisements for sales promotions requiring multiple purchases do not actively encourage excessive consumption.

46.12 Advertisements should not depict activities or locations where drinking alcohol would be unsafe or unwise. In particular, advertisements should not associate the consumption of alcohol with operating machinery, driving, any activity relating to water or heights, or any other occupation that requires concentration in order to be done safely.

46.13 Low-alcohol drinks are those that contain 1.2 per cent alcohol by volume or less. Advertisers should ensure that low-alcohol drinks are not promoted in a way that encourages their inappropriate consumption and should not depict activities that require complete sobriety.

**Children**

47.1 The way in which children perceive and react to advertisements is influenced by their age, experience and the context in which the message is delivered. The ASA will take these factors into account when assessing advertisements.

47.2 Advertisements and promotions addressed to or featuring children should contain nothing that is likely to result in their physical, mental or moral harm:

(a) they should not be encouraged to enter strange places or talk to strangers. Care is needed when they are asked to make collections, enter schemes or gather labels, wrappers, coupons and the like.

(b) they should not be shown in hazardous situations or behaving dangerously in the home or outside except to promote safety. Children should not be shown unattended in street scenes unless they are old enough to take responsibility for their own safety. Pedestrians and cyclists should be seen to observe the Highway Code.

(c) they should not be shown using or in close proximity to dangerous substances or equipment without direct adult supervision. Examples include matches, petrol, certain electrical appliances and machinery, including agricultural equipment.

(d) they should not be encouraged to copy any practice that might be unsafe for a child.

47.3 Advertisements and promotions addressed to or featuring children should not exploit their credulity, loyalty, vulnerability or lack of experience:

(a) they should not be made to feel inferior or unpopular for not buying the advertised product

(b) they should not be made to feel that they are lacking in courage, duty or loyalty if they do not buy or do not encourage others to buy a particular product

(c) it should be made easy for them to judge the size, characteristics and performance of any product advertised and to distinguish between real-life situations and fantasy

(d) parental permission should be obtained before they are committed to purchasing complex and costly goods and services.

47.4 Advertisements and promotions addressed to children:

(a) should not actively encourage them to make a nuisance of themselves to parents or others

(b) should not make a direct appeal to purchase unless the product is one that would be likely to interest children and that they could reasonably afford. Mail-order advertisers should take care when using youth media not to promote products that are unsuitable for children

(c) should not exaggerate what is attainable by an ordinary child using the product being advertised or promoted

(d) should not actively encourage them to eat or drink at or near bedtime, to eat frequently throughout the day or to replace main meals with confectionery or snack foods

(e) should not exploit their susceptibility to charitable appeals and should explain the extent to which their participation will help in any charity-linked promotions.

47.5 Promotions addressed to children:

(a) should not encourage excessive purchases in order to participate

(b) should make clear that parental permission is required in order to participate

(c) should clearly explain the number and type of any additional proofs of purchase needed to participate

(d) should contain a prominent closing date

(e) should not exaggerate the value of prizes or the chances of winning them.

**Motoring**

48.1 Advertisements for motor vehicles, fuel or accessories should avoid portraying or referring to practices that encourage anti-social behaviour.

48.2 Advertisers should not make speed or acceleration claims the predominant message of their advertisements. However, it is legitimate to give general information about a vehicle's performance such as acceleration statistics, braking power, roadholding and top and mid-range speeds.

48.3 Advertisers should not portray speed in a way that might encourage motorists to drive irresponsibly or to break the law.

48.4 Vehicles should not be depicted in dangerous or unwise situations in a way that would encourage irresponsible driving. Their capabilities may be demonstrated on a track or circuit provided it is clearly not in use as a public highway.

48.5 Care should be taken in cinema advertisements and those in electronic media where the moving image may give the impression of exceptional speed. In all cases where vehicles are shown in normal driving circumstances on the public road they should not exceed UK speed limits.

48.6 When making environmental claims for their products, advertisers should conform with the Specific Rules on Environmental Claims.

48.7 Prices quoted should correspond to the vehicles illustrated. For example, it is not acceptable to feature only a top-of-the-range model alongside the starting price for that range.

48.8 Safety claims should not exaggerate the benefit to consumers. Advertisers should not make absolute claims about safety unless they hold evidence to support them.

**Environmental claims**

49.1 The basis of any claim should be explained clearly and should be qualified where necessary. Unqualified claims can mislead if they omit significant information.

49.2 Claims such as 'environmentally friendly' or 'wholly biodegradable' should not be used without qualification unless advertisers can provide convincing evidence that their product will cause no environmental damage. Qualified claims and comparisons such as 'greener' or 'friendlier' may be acceptable if advertisers can substantiate that their product provides an overall improvement in environmental terms whether against their competitors' or their own previous products.

49.3 Where there is a significant division of scientific opinion or where evidence is inconclusive, this should be reflected in any statements made in the advertisement. Advertisers should not suggest that their claims command universal acceptance if it is not the case.

49.4 If a product has never had a demonstrably adverse effect on the environment, advertisers should not imply that the formulation has changed to make it safe. It is legitimate, however, to make claims about a product whose composition has changed or has always been designed in a way that omits chemicals known to cause damage to the environment.

49.5 The use of extravagant language should be avoided, as should bogus and confusing scientific terms. If it is necessary to use a scientific expression, its meaning should be clear.

**Health and beauty products and therapies**

**General**

50.1 Medical and scientific claims made about beauty and health-related products should be backed by trials, where appropriate conducted on people. Substantiation will be assessed by the ASA on the basis of established scientific knowledge.

50.2 Advertisers should not discourage people from having essential treatment; medical advice is needed for serious or prolonged ailments and advertisers should not offer medicines or therapies for them.

50.3 Advice, diagnosis or treatment of any serious medical condition should be conducted face-to-face. Advertisers inviting consumers to diagnose their own minor ailments should not make claims that might lead to a mistaken diagnosis.

50.4 Consumers should not be encouraged to use products to excess and advertisers should not suggest that their products or therapies are guaranteed to work, absolutely safe or without side-effects for everyone.

50.5 Advertisements should not suggest that any product is safe or effective merely because it is 'natural' or that it is generally safer because it omits an ingredient in common use.

50.6 Advertisers offering individual treatments, particularly those that are physically invasive, may be asked by the media and the ASA to provide full details together with information about those who will supervise and administer them. Where appropriate, practitioners should have relevant and recognised qualifications. Consumers should be encouraged to take independent medical advice before committing themselves to significant treatments.

50.7 References to the relief of symptoms or the superficial signs of ageing are acceptable if they can be substantiated. Unqualified claims such as 'cure' and 'rejuvenation' are not generally acceptable.

50.8 Claims made for the treatment of minor addictions and bad habits should make clear the vital role of willpower.

50.9 Advertisers should not use unfamiliar scientific words for common conditions.

**Medicines**

50.10 The Medicines Act 1968 and its regulations, as well as regulations implementing European Community Directive 92/28/EEC, govern the advertising and promotion of medicines and the conditions of ill health that they can be offered to treat. Guidance on the legislation is available from the Medicines Control Agency (MCA).

50.11 Medicines must be licensed by the MCA before they are advertised and any claims made for products must conform with the licence. Unlicensed advertisers should not make medicinal claims. Advertisements should refer to the MCA, the licence or the EC only if required to do so by the MCA.

50.12 Prescription-only medicines may not be advertised to the public. Health-related claims in advertisements and promotions addressed only to the medical and allied professions are exempt from the Codes.

50.13 Advertisements should include the name of the product, an indication of what it is for, text such as 'Always read the label' and the common name of the active ingredient if there is only one. There should be no suggestion that any medicine is either a food or a cosmetic.

50.14 Advertisers must not use fear or anxiety to promote medicines or recovery from illness and should not suggest that using or avoiding a product can affect normal good health.

50.15 Illustrations of the effect or action of any product on the human body should be accurate.

50.16 Advertisements for medicines should not be addressed to children.

50.17 Advertisers should not use health professionals or celebrities to endorse medicines.

50.18 Advertisements for any medicine should not claim that its effects are as good as or better than those of another identifiable product.

50.19 Homeopathic medicinal products must be registered in the UK. Any product information given in the advertisement should be confined to what appears on the label. Advertisements should include a warning to consult a doctor if symptoms persist and should not make any medicinal or therapeutic claims or refer to any ailment.

### Vitamins, minerals and food supplements

50.20 Advertisers should hold scientific evidence for any claim that their vitamin or mineral product or food supplement is beneficial to health.

50.21 A well-balanced diet should provide the vitamins and minerals needed each day by a normal, healthy individual. Advertisers may offer supplements as a safeguard, but should not suggest that there is a widespread vitamin or mineral deficiency or that it is necessary or therapeutic to augment a well-balanced diet. Advertisements should not imply that supplements will guard against deficiency, elevate mood or enhance performance. Supplements should not be promoted as a substitute for a healthy diet.

50.22 Certain groups of people may benefit from vitamin and mineral supplementation. These include people who eat nutritionally inadequate meals, the elderly, children and adolescents, convalescents, athletes in training, those who are physically very active, women of child-bearing age, lactating and pregnant women and dieters. In assessing claims, the ASA will bear in mind recommendations made by the Department of Health.

50.23 Serious vitamin and mineral depletion caused by illness should be diagnosed and treated by a doctor. Self-medication should not be promoted on the basis that it will influence the speed or extent of recovery.

## Cosmetics

50.24 Claims made about the action that a cosmetic has on or in the skin should distinguish between the composition of the product and any effects brought about by the way in which it is applied, such as massage. Scientific evidence should also make this distinction.

50.25 Some cosmetics have an effect on the kind of skin changes that are caused by environmental factors. Advertisements for them can therefore refer to temporarily preventing, delaying or masking premature ageing.

## Hair and scalp

50.26 Advertisers should be able to provide scientific evidence, where appropriate in the form of trials on people, for any claim that their product or therapy can prevent baldness or slow it down, arrest or reverse hair loss, stimulate or improve hair growth, nourish hair roots, strengthen the hair or improve its health as distinct from its appearance.

## Slimming

51.1 A slimming regime in which intake of energy is lower than its output is the main self-treatment for achieving weight loss. Any claims made for the effectiveness or action of a slimming method or product should be backed where appropriate by rigorous practical trials on people; testimonials that are not supported by trials do not constitute substantiation.

51.2 Advertisements for any slimming regime or establishment should be neither directed at, nor contain anything that will appeal particularly to, people who are under 18.

51.3 Obesity is a condition in which the subject's weight is more than 20 per cent above the ideal range for their height or whose Body Mass Index is more than 30. Obesity requires medical attention and treatments for it should not be advertised to the public unless they are to be used under qualified supervision.

51.4 Advertisements should not suggest that it is desirable to be underweight.

51.5 Before claims are made that weight or inch loss can be achieved by expelling water, speeding up metabolism, using mechanical devices, wearing garments or applying substances to the skin they must be substantiated with scientific evidence of the method's effect on people.

Combining a diet with an unproven weight-loss method does not justify making slimming claims for the method.

51.6 Advertisers should be able to show that their diet plans are nutritionally well-balanced. This will be assessed in relation to the kind of subjects who would be using them.

51.7 Vitamins and minerals do not contribute to weight loss, but may be offered to slimmers as a safeguard against any shortfall when dieting.

51.8 Crash diets are those that fall below 400 calories a day. They should not be advertised to dieters unless they are to be used under direct medical supervision.

51.9 Diet aids such as low-calorie foods, food substances, appetite depressants and meal replacements should make clear how they work. They should state that they cannot aid slimming except as part of a diet in which total calorie intake is controlled. Prominence must be given to the role of the diet, and advertisements should not give the impression that dieters cannot fail or can eat as much as they like and still lose weight.

51.10 Advertisements should not contain general claims that precise amounts of weight can be lost within a stated period or that weight can be lost from specific parts of the body. Claims that individuals have lost exact amounts of weight should be compatible with good medical practice, should give details of the time period involved and should not be based on unrepresentative experiences.

51.11 Both physical and passive exercise improve muscle tone slowly and this can have an effect on body shape. An improvement in posture may also benefit the figure. Advertisers should be able to substantiate any claims that such methods used alone or in conjunction with a diet plan can lead to weight or inch loss. Advertisements for intensive exercise programmes should encourage users to check with a doctor before starting.

51.12 Short-term loss of girth may be achieved by wearing a tight-fitting garment. This should not be portrayed as permanent, nor should it be confused with weight loss.

**Distance selling**

52.1 Distance selling involves offering goods or services to consumers without the buyer and seller at any time meeting face-to-face. Advertisers, promoters and all others involved in handling responses must observe the Codes.

52.2 Advertisements should state the full name and address of the advertiser outside the coupon or other response mechanism so that it can be retained by consumers. A separate address for orders may also be given; this need not be a full address but could, for example, be a Freepost address or PO Box number.

52.3 Unless obvious from the context, advertisements should include:

    (a) the main characteristics of the product or service

    (b) the amount and number of any transport charges

    (c) any VAT payable, unless the advertisement is addressed exclusively to the trade

    (d) a statement that goods can be returned, if applicable

    (e) any limitation on the offer and any conditions that affect its validity

    (f) the estimated delivery time; consumers should be advised if orders cannot be fulfiled within 30 days. Those who have paid in advance should be offered a refund but if they prefer to wait they should be given a firm despatch date or fortnightly progress reports.

52.4 Advertisers should take no longer than 30 days to fulfil orders except:

    (a) where security is provided for purchasers' money through an independent scheme

    (b) for goods such as plants and made-to-measure products where the estimated time of delivery should be made clear

    (c) where the advertisers make clear that they do not intend to begin production unless a sufficient response is received

    (d) where a series of goods is sent at regular intervals after the first 30 days.

52.5 Before goods or services are supplied and accepted advertisers should, where appropriate, provide consumers with written information on:

    (a) payment arrangements, including credit and installment terms

    (b) how to exercise their right to withdraw

    (c) the cancellation of open-ended contracts

    (d) other terms and conditions, including guarantees

    (e) the most appropriate address to contact them.

52.6 Advertisers must refund money promptly when:

    (a) consumers have not received their goods or services; alternatively advertisers may, if asked, provide a replacement

    (b) goods are returned because they are damaged when received, are faulty or are not as described, in which case the advertisers must bear the cost of transit in both directions

    (c) unwanted goods are returned undamaged within seven working days of being received by the purchaser; consumers should assume they can try out goods unless the advertisement states otherwise. It should be made clear if consumers have to pay the return postage

(d) an unconditional money-back guarantee is given and the goods are returned within a reasonable period

(e) goods that have been returned are not received back, provided consumers can produce proof of posting.

52.7 Advertisers do not have to provide a full refund on:

(a) perishable, personalised or made-to-measure goods so long as all contractual obligations to consumers are met

(b) high-value products, or those to be delivered abroad, where an administration fee may be charged; this should be made clear to consumers before they are committed

(c) goods that can be copied unless they fall under 52.6(a), (b) or (c).

52.8 If advertisers intend to call on respondents personally this should be made clear in the advertisement or in a follow-up mailing. To allow consumers an adequate opportunity to refuse a personal visit, advertisers should provide a reply-paid postcard or Freephone telephone-contact instructions.

52.9 Advertisers should take particular care when packaging products that may fall into the hands of children.

**List and database practice**

53.1 List owners, brokers and users should:

(a) ensure that their lists are run against the most recent quarterly Mailing Preference Service (MPS) Suppression File and are accurate and up-to-date

(b) be able to identify anyone who has objected in the last five years, or who has not had an opportunity to object, to their inclusion on any list that is to be disclosed to others

(c) avoid duplication

(d) act promptly to correct personal information

(e) ensure that anyone who has been notified as dead is not mailed again and, where appropriate, should refer the notifier to the MPS

(f) comply with the provisions of the Data Protection Act 1984.

53.2 List users should:

(a) ensure, where possible, that those approached are not inappropriate for the offer

(b) not use lists or selections from lists that are more than six months old unless they have been updated

(c)    inform the list owner of any requested corrections within 60 days

(d)    if asked, give the sources of names on their list promptly to anyone listed or to the ASA.

53.3  List owners should:

(a)    satisfy themselves, and obtain an assurance from users, that any literature used in an offer complies with the Codes

(b)    make corrections or suppressions themselves, or ensure that list users do, if a mailing is delayed by more than six months

(c)    require list users to inform them of requests for correction within 60 days

(d)    be able to demonstrate their compliance with this Code regarding list rental.

53.4  Where it is not obvious from the context, consumers should be informed by anyone asking for personal information:

(a)    why it is being collected

(b)    who is collecting it

(c)    the reason for collecting extensive information and, if it is intended to disclose it to others, their names

(d)    whether it is intended to make the information available to others, including associated companies; before information is disclosed to any other company for the first time, consumers should be given the opportunity to object.

53.5  If, after collection, it is decided to use information for a purpose that is significantly different from the one originally intended, consumers must be advised and given 30 days to object.

53.6  The extent and detail of personal information held for any purpose should be adequate, relevant and should not be excessive for that purpose.

53.7  Personal information must always be held securely and should be safeguarded against unauthorised use, disclosure, alteration or destruction.

53.8  Individuals are entitled to have their names removed from any mailing list. However, if they want to reduce all their mailings significantly, they should be referred to the MPS.

53.9  Individuals who have asked for information about them to be suppressed should not be contacted again for a minimum of five years from the date of their request unless they ask to be reinstated.

53.10 Businesses are permitted to use any published information that is generally available, provided the individual concerned is not listed on the MPS Suppression File.

## Employment and business opportunities

54.1 Advertisers should distinguish clearly between offers of employment and business opportunities. Before publication, media normally require full details of the advertisers and any terms and conditions imposed on respondents.

54.2 Employment advertisements must correspond to genuine vacancies and potential employees must not be asked to send money for further details. Living and working conditions should not be misrepresented. Quoted earnings should be precise; if a forecast has to be made this should not be unrepresentative. If income is earned from a basic salary and commission, commission only, or in some other way, this should be made clear.

54.3 An employment agency must make clear in advertisements that it is an employment agency.

54.4 Homework schemes require participants to make articles, perform services or offer facilities at or from home. Consumers should be given:

(a) the full name and address of the advertisers

(b) a clear description of the work; the support available to homeworkers should not be exaggerated

(c) an indication of whether participants are self-employed or employed by a business

(d) the likely level of earnings, but only if this can be supported with evidence of the experience of current homeworkers

(e) no forecast of earnings if the scheme is new

(f) details of any required investment or binding obligation

(g) details of any charges for raw materials, machines, components, administration and the like

(h) information on whether the advertisers will buy back any goods made

(i) any limitations or conditions that might influence consumers prior to their decision to participate.

54.5 Advertisements for business opportunities should contain:

(a) the name and contact details of the advertisers

(b) where possible, a clear description of the work involved and the extent of investors' commitments, including any financial investment; the support available should not be exaggerated

(c) no unrepresentative or exaggerated earnings figures.

54.6 Vocational training and other instruction courses should make no promises of employment unless it is guaranteed. The duration of the course and the level of attainment needed to embark on it should be made clear.

54.7 The sale of directories giving details of employment or business opportunities should indicate plainly the nature of what is being offered.

**Financial services and products**

55.1 The rules that follow provide only general guidance. Advertisers, their agencies and the media must also comply with the numerous statutes that govern financial services and products including issuing advertisements, investment opportunities, credit facilities and the provision of financial information.

55.2 Offers of financial services and products should be set out in a way that allows them to be understood easily by the audience being addressed. Advertisers should ensure that they do not take advantage of people's inexperience or gullibility.

55.3 Advertisers asking for a commitment at a distance should make sure that their full address is given outside any response coupon or other mechanism.

55.4 Advertisements should indicate the nature of the contract being offered, any limitations, expenses, penalties and charges and the terms of withdrawal. Alternatively, where an advertisement is short or general in its content, free explanatory material giving full details of the offer should be readily available before a binding contract is entered into.

55.5 The basis used to calculate any rates of interest, forecasts or projections should be apparent immediately.

55.6 Advertisements should make clear that the value of investments is variable and, unless guaranteed, can go down as well as up. If the value of the investment is guaranteed, details should be included in the advertisement.

55.7 Advertisements should specify that past performance or experience does not necessarily give a guide for the future. Any examples used should not be unrepresentative.

**Cigarette Code**

**Introduction**

66.1 The Cigarette Code is exceptional in that it is the outcome of discussions between the UK Department of Health (DH), the manufacturers and importers of cigarettes (represented by the Tobacco Manufacturers Association and the Imported Tobacco Products Advisory Council respectively) and the Advertising Standards Authority (ASA). It runs in parallel with, and its rules are applied in addition to, those imposed elsewhere in the British Codes of Advertising and Sales Promotion.

66.2   The ASA is the final arbiter of the meaning of the Cigarette Code's rules. The ASA deals with complaints about advertisement content and also supervises the advisory and the mandatory pre-clearance procedure for cigarette advertisements operated by the Committee of Advertising Practice (CAP).

66.3   The Cigarette Code governs the content of advertisements. It is one part of a wider voluntary agreement between the DH and the tobacco industry. This agreement also covers advertising expenditure, media selection, health warnings and promotions. There is a separate agreement on sports sponsorship between the Department of National Heritage, on behalf of HM Government, and the tobacco industry. This includes a provision encouraging advertisers of sponsored sporting events to follow the Cigarette Code. Complaints relating to breaches of these two agreements should be addressed to the Committee for Monitoring Agreements on Tobacco Advertising and Sponsorship (COMATAS).

66.4   The rules are not intended to hamper fair competition. Advertisers of cigarettes and hand-rolling tobacco are free to attract attention to their products, provided both the spirit and the letter of the Codes are observed.

**Scope**

66.5   The Cigarette Code applies to advertisements for:
  (a)   cigarettes and their components such as tobacco and tobacco substitutes
  (b)   hand-rolling tobacco
  (c)   cigarette papers, filters and wrappings
  (d)   any product if the advertisement concerned features a cigarette or pack design of a recognisable brand available in the UK
  (e)   teasers
  (f)   special offers, competitions and other sales promotions
  (g)   products displaying the colours, livery, insignia or name of a cigarette brand in a way that promotes smoking rather than these other branded products.

66.6   The Cigarette Code does not apply to advertisements for:
  (a)   cigars, cheroots, cigarillos, pipe tobacco or snuff
  (b)   herbal cigarettes and tobaccos
  (c)   cigarette holders, matches, lighters and the like except when covered by 66.5 above
  (d)   schemes, events or activities sponsored or supported financially by manufacturers of products listed in 66.5 above, even where such advertisements are for sports sponsorship and are required

by the voluntary agreement on sports sponsorship to carry a health warning

(e)   advertisements and promotions addressed to the trade in media not targeted at the public.

**General principles and procedures**

66.7  The rules which follow in clauses 66.13–66.26 should be observed in the spirit as well as in the letter.

66.8  Claims encompass statements and visual presentations and can be direct or indirect. Claims which the ASA or CAP regard as eroding or diminishing the effectiveness of the rules will be judged contrary to the spirit of the Code; humour is acceptable provided it is used with care and is not likely to have a particular appeal to the young.

66.9  Advertisements for cigarettes or hand-rolling tobacco should have a signed, dated and numbered certificate of clearance from CAP before being displayed or published.

66.10 Certificates will be valid for advertisements in current campaigns after which time the copy must be re-certified. Clearance can be universal or may be media-specific in that certain advertisements might only be acceptable for publication in a limited circulation medium. Certificates will be endorsed accordingly.

66.11 Point of sale material featuring themes or elements already cleared in general media advertisements should normally need no additional clearance from CAP. However, the acceptability of extracted themes or elements will depend on the context and spirit in which they are used. These must not differ from the original advertisements. Whenever new treatments or developments of existing themes are introduced they should be checked with CAP to ascertain whether a certificate is needed.

66.12 CAP clearance does not automatically protect advertisements against complaints to the ASA Council which acts as the final arbiter of the meaning of the Code's rules.

**Rules**

66.13 No advertisement should incite people to start smoking.

66.14 Advertisements should not encourage smokers to increase their consumption or smoke to excess. Smokers should not be encouraged to buy or stock large quantities of cigarettes.

66.15 Advertisements for coupon brands should not feature products unless these can be obtained through the redemption of coupons collected over a reasonable period of average consumption.

66.16 Advertisements should never suggest that smoking is safe, healthy, natural, necessary for relaxation and concentration, popular or appropriate in all circumstances. Cigarettes should not be shown in the mouth and advertisements should not associate smoking with healthy eating or drinking.

66.17 No more than half of those shown in groups should be smoking; smoking should not be shown in public places where it is usually not permitted.

66.18 People can be shown smoking while engaged in work or leisure activities, provided that the advertisement does not illustrate inappropriate smoking situations.

66.19 Smoking should not be associated with social, sexual, romantic or business success and advertisements should not be sexually titillating, though the choice of a particular brand may be linked to taste and discernment. In particular, advertisements should not link smoking with people who are evidently wealthy, fashionable, sophisticated or successful or who possess other attributes or qualities that may reasonably be expected to command admiration or encourage emulation.

66.20 Advertisements should not contain actual or implied testimonials or endorsements from well-known people, famous fictitious characters or people doing jobs or occupying positions which are generally regarded as admirable.

66.21 No heroic figure, personality cult, pastime or fashion trend should be featured in advertisements in a way that would appeal to those who are adventurous or rebellious, particularly the young.

66.22 No advertisement should play on the susceptibilities of those who are physically or emotionally vulnerable, particularly the young or immature. Advertisements should therefore avoid employing any approach which is more likely to attract the attention or sympathy of those under the age of 18.

66.23 Anyone shown smoking should always be, and clearly be seen to be, over 25.

66.24 No advertisement should exaggerate the pleasure of smoking or claim that it is daring or glamourous to smoke or that smoking enhances people's masculinity, femininity, appearance or independence.

66.25 Advertisements that employ outdoor locations or those that depict people or animals should avoid any suggestion of a healthy or wholesome style of life. Any locations, people and objects depicted should not have undue aspirational, historical or cultural associations.

66.26 Advertisements should not associate smoking with sport or with active or outdoor games. Advertisements for sports sponsorship are governed by a separate voluntary agreement with the Department of National Heritage, on behalf of HM Government, and the tobacco industry.

# USEFUL ADDRESSES

Advertising Association
Abford House
15 Wilton Road
London SW1V 1NJ
Tel: + 44 (0) 171 828 2771

Advertising Standards Authority (and Committee of Advertising Practice)
Brook House
Torrington Place
London WC1E 7HN
Tel: + 44 (0) 171 580 5555
Website: http://www.asa.org.uk

Advertising Standards Board of Finance Ltd
Bloomsbury House
74–77 Great Russell Street
London WC1B 3DA
Tel: + 44 (0) 171 580 7071

Broadcast Advertising Clearance Centre
200 Gray's Inn Road
London WC1X 8HF
Tel: + 44 (0) 171 843 8265

Broadcasting Standards Commission
7 The Sanctuary
London SW1P 3JS
Tel: + 44 (0) 171 233 0544

Chartered Institute of Purchasing and Supply
Easton House
Easton-on-the-Hill
Stamford
Lincolnshire PE9 3NZ
Tel: + 44 (0) 1780 56777

Cinema Advertising Association
127 Wardour Street
London W1V 4AD
Tel: + 44 (0) 171 439 9531

Data Protection Registrar
Wycliffe House
Water Lane
Wilmslow
Cheshire SK9 5AF
Tel: + 44 (0) 1625 535777 (enquiries); + 44 (0) 1625 535711 (administration)

Direct Marketing Association (UK)
Haymarket House
1 Oxendon Street
London SW1Y 4EE
Tel: + 44 (0) 171 321 2525

European Advertising Standards Alliance, *see* p 81

European Commission (London Office)
Jean Monnet House
8 Storey's Gate
London SW1P 3AT
Tel: + 44 (0) 171 973 1992

Incorporated Society of British Advertisers (ISBA)
44 Hertford Street
London W1Y 8AE
Tel: + 44 (0) 171 499 7502

Independent Committee for the Supervision of Standards of Telephone
Information Services
3rd Floor, Kingsbourne House
229–231 High Holborn
London WC1V 7DA
Tel: + 44 (0) 171 430 2228

Independent Television Association
200 Gray's Inn Road
London WC1X 8HF
Tel: + 44 (0) 171 843 8000

Independent Television Commission
33 Foley Street
London W1P 7LB
Tel: + 44 (0) 171 255 3000

Institute of Practitioners in Advertising (IPA)
44 Belgrave Square
London SW1X 8QS
Tel: + 44 (0) 171 235 7020

International Advertising Association
166 Finchley Road
London NW3 6BP
Tel: + 44 (0) 171 431 7701
Website: http://www.iaaukchp.co.uk

International Chamber of Commerce (ICC UK)
E14–15 Belgrave Square
London SW1X 8PS
Tel: + 44 (0) 171 823 2811
Website: http://www.iccwbo.org

Internet Watch Foundation
East View
5 Coles Lane
Oakington
Cambridgeshire CB4 5BA
Tel: + 44 (0) 1223 237700
Website: http://www.internetwatch.org.uk

Institute of Sales Promotion
Arena House
66–68 Pentonville Road
London N1 9HS
Tel: + 44 (0) 171 837 5340

Institute of Trading Standards Administration
Units 4 and 5, Hadleigh Business Centre
351 London Road
Hadleigh
Essex SS7 2BT
Tel: + 44 (0) 1702 559922

Local Authorities Coordinating Body on Food and Trading Standards
(LACOTS)
PO Box 6
Robert Street
Croydon CR9 1LG
Tel: + 44 (0) 181 688 1996

Mail Order Protection Scheme
16 Tooks Court,
London EC4A 1LB
Tel: + 44 (0) 171 405 6806

Mailing Preference Service
5 Reef House
Plantation Wharf
London SW11 3UF
Tel: + 44 (0) 171 738 1625

Newspaper Publishers Association Ltd
34 Southwark Bridge Road
London SE1 9EU
Tel: + 44 (0) 171 928 6928

Outdoor Advertising Association of Great Britain
27 Sale Place
London W2 1YR
Tel: + 44 (0) 171 973 0315
Website: http://www.oaa.org.uk

Proprietary Association of Great Britain
3rd Floor Vernon House
23 Sicilian Avenue
London WC1A 2QH
Tel: + 44 (0) 171 242 8331

Radio Authority
Holbrook House
14 Great Queen Street
London WC2B 5DG
Tel: + 44 (0) 171 430 2724

Radio Authority Clearance Centre (RACC)
46 Westbourne Grove
London W2 5SH
Tel: + 44 (0) 171 727 2646

World Federation of Advertisers, *see* p 79

# BROADCASTING ACT 1990

**Reproduced with the permission of the Controller of Her Majesty's Stationery Office**

8  **General provisions as to advertisements**

1  The Commission shall do all that they can to secure that the rules specified in subsection (2) are complied with in relation to licensed services.

2  Those rules are as follows–

(a)  a licensed service must not include–

(i)  any advertisement which is inserted by on behalf of any body whose objects are wholly or mainly of a political nature,

(ii)  any advertisement which is directed towards any political end, or

(iii)  any advertisement which has any relation to any industrial dispute (other than an advertisement of a public service nature inserted by, or on behalf of, a government department);

(b)  in the acceptance of advertisements for inclusion in a licensed service there must be no unreasonable discrimination whether against or in favour of any particular advertiser; and

(c)  a licensed service must not, without the previous approval of the Commission, include a programme which is sponsored by any person whose business consists, wholly or mainly, in the manufacture or supply of a product, or in the provision of a service, which the licence holder is prohibited from advertising by virtue of any provision of section 9.

3  Nothing in subsection (2) shall be construed as prohibiting the inclusion in a licensed service of any party political broadcast which complies with the rules (so far as applicable) made by the Commission for the purposes of section 36.

4  After consultation with the Commission the Secretary of State may make regulations amending, repealing, or adding to the rules specified in subsection (2); but no such regulations shall be made unless a draft of the regulations has been laid before and approved by a resolution of each House of Parliament.

5  The Commission shall not act as an advertising agent.

**9    Control of advertisements**

1    It shall be the duty of the Commission–

  (a)    after the appropriate consultation, to draw up, and from time to time review, a code–

      (i)    governing standards and practice in advertising and in the sponsoring of programmes, and

      (ii)    prescribing the advertisements and methods of advertising or sponsorship to be prohibited, or to be prohibited in particular circumstances; and

  (b)    to do all that they can to secure that the provisions of the code are observed in the provision of licensed services;

and the Commission may make different provision in the code for different kinds of licensed services.

2    In subsection (1) 'the appropriate consultation' means consultation with–

  (a)    the Radio Authority;

  (b)    every person who is the holder of a licence under this Part;

  (c)    such bodies or persons appearing to the Commission to represent each of the following, namely–

      (i)    viewers,

      (ii)    advertisers, and

      (iii)    professional organisations qualified to give advice in relation to the advertising of particular products,

  as the Commission think fit; and

  (d)    such other bodies or persons who are concerned with standards of conduct in advertising as the Commission think fit.

3    The Commission shall publish the code drawn up under this section, and every revision of it, in such manner as they consider appropriate.

4    The Commission shall–

  (a)    from time to time consult the Secretary of State as to the classes and descriptions of advertisements which must not be included in licensed services and the methods of advertising or sponsorship which must not be employed in, or in connection with, the provision of such services; and

  (b)    carry out any directions which he may give to them in respect of such matters.

5    The Commission may, in the discharge of a general responsibility with respect to advertisements and methods of advertising and sponsorship, impose requirements as to advertisements or methods of advertising or sponsorship which go beyond the requirements of the code.

6   The methods of control exercisable by the Commission for the purpose of securing that the provisions of the code are complied with, and for the purpose of securing compliance with requirements imposed under subsection (5) which go beyond the requirements of the code, shall include a power to give directions to the holder of a licence–

(a)   with respect to the classes and descriptions of advertisements and methods of advertising or sponsorship to be excluded, or to be excluded in particular circumstances, or

(b)   with respect to the exclusion of a particular advertisement, or its exclusion in particular circumstances.

7   The Commission may give directions to persons holding any class of licences with respect to the times when advertisements are to be allowed.

8   Directions under this section may be, to any degree, either general or specific and qualified or unqualified; and directions under subsection (7) may, in particular, relate to–

(a)   the maximum amount of time to be given to advertisements in any hour or other period,

(b)   the minimum interval which must elapse between any two periods given over to advertisements and the number of such periods to be allowed in any programme or in any hour or day,

(c)   the exclusion of advertisements from a specified part of a licensed service,

and may make different provision for different parts of the day, different days of the week, different types of programmes or for other differing circumstances.

9   The Commission shall–

(a)   in drawing up or revising the code, or

(b)   in giving any directions under subsection (7),

take account of such of the international obligations of the United Kingdom as the Secretary of State may notify to them for the purposes of this subsection.

**92   General provisions as to advertisements**

1   The Authority shall do all that they can to secure that the rules specified in subsection (2) are complied with in relation to licensed services.

2   Those rules are as follows–

(a)   a licensed service must not include–

(i)   any advertisement which is inserted by or on behalf of any body whose objects are wholly or mainly of a political nature,

      (ii)   any advertisement which is directed towards any political end, or

      (iii)  any advertisement which has any relation to any industrial dispute (other than an advertisement of a public service nature inserted by, or on behalf of, a government department);

  (b)   in the acceptance of advertisements for inclusion in a licensed service there must be no unreasonable discrimination either against or in favour of any particular advertiser; and

  (c)   a licensed service must not, without the previous approval of the Authority, include a programme which is sponsored by any person whose business consists, wholly or mainly, in the manufacture or supply of a product, or in the provision of a service, which the licence holder is prohibited from advertising by virtue of any provision of section 93.

3    Nothing in subsection (2) shall be construed as prohibiting the inclusion in a licensed service of any party political broadcast which complies with the rules (so far applicable) made by the Authority for the purposes of section 107.

4    After consultation with the Authority the Secretary of State may make regulations amending, repealing, or adding to the rules specified in subsection (2); but no such regulations shall be made unless a draft of the regulations has been laid before and approved by a resolution of each House of Parliament.

5    The Authority shall not act as an advertising agent.

### 93  Control of advertisements

1    It shall be the duty of the Authority–

  (a)   after the appropriate consultation, to draw up, and from time to time review, a code–

      (i)   governing standards and practice in advertising and in the sponsoring of programmes, and

      (ii)  prescribing the advertisements and methods of advertising or sponsorship to be prohibited, or to be prohibited in particular circumstances; and

  (b)   to do all that they can to secure that the provisions of the code are observed in the provision of licensed services;

and the Authority may make different provision in the code for different kinds of licensed services.

2    In subsection (1) 'the appropriate consultation' means consultation with–

  (a)   the Independent Television Commission;

  (b)   such bodies or persons appearing to the Authority to represent each of the following, namely–

    (i)    listeners,

    (ii)   advertisers, and

    (iii)  professional organisations qualified to give advice in relation to the advertising of particular products,

as the Authority think fit, and

(c)    such other bodies or persons who are concerned with standards of conduct in advertising as the Authority think fit,

and (to the extent that the Authority consider such consultation to be reasonably practicable) consultation with every person who is the holder of a licence under this Part.

3    The Authority shall publish the code drawn up under this section, and every revision of it, in such manner as they consider appropriate.

4    The Authority shall–

(a)    from time to time consult the Secretary of State as to the classes and descriptions of advertisements which must not be included in licensed services and the methods of advertising or sponsorship which must not be employed in, or in connection with, the provision of such services; and

(b)    carry out any directions which he may give to them in respect of such matters.

5    The Authority may, in the discharge of a general responsibility with respect to advertisements and methods of advertising and sponsorship, impose requirements as to advertisements or methods of sponsorship which go beyond the requirements imposed by the code.

6    The methods of control exercisable by the Authority for the purpose of securing that the provisions of the code are complied with, and for the purpose of securing compliance with requirements imposed under subsection (5) which go beyond the requirements of the code, shall include a power to give directions to the holder of a licence–

(a)    with respect to the classes and descriptions of advertisements and methods of advertising or sponsorship to be excluded in particular circumstances; or

(b)    with respect to the exclusion of a particular advertisement, or its exclusion in particular circumstances.

7    Directions under this section may be, to any degree, either general or specific and qualified or unqualified.

8    The Authority shall, in drawing up or revising the code, take account of such of the international obligations of the United Kingdom as the Secretary of State may notify to them for the purposes of this subsection.

# MEDICINES ACT 1968, SS 93–97

**Reproduced with the permission of the Controller of Her Majesty's Stationery Office**

### 93 False or misleading advertisements and representations

1 Subject to the following provisions of this section, any person who, being a commercially interested party, or at the request or with the consent of a commercially interested party, issues, or causes another person to issue, a false or misleading advertisement relating to medicinal products of any description shall be guilty of an offence.

2 Where a licence under Part II of this Act is in force which is applicable to medicinal products of a particular description, and, in accordance with the provisions of the licence, the purposes for which medicinal products of that description may be recommended to be used are limited to those specified in the licence, then, subject to the following provisions of this section, any person who, being a commercially interested party, or at the request or with the consent of a commercially interested party, issues, or causes another person to issue, an advertisement relating to medicinal products of that description which consists of or includes unauthorised recommendations shall be guilty of an offence.

3 Subject to the following provisions of this section, any person who, in the course of a relevant business carried on by him, or while acting on behalf of a person carrying on such a business, makes a false or misleading representation relating to a medicinal product in connection with the sale, or offer for sale, of that product shall be guilty of an offence; any person who, in the course of such a business or while acting on behalf of a person carrying on such a business , makes a false or misleading representation relating to medicinal products of a particular description–

(a) to a practitioner for the purpose of inducing him to prescribe or supply medicinal products of that description, or

(b) to a patient or client of a practitioner for the purpose of inducing him to request the practitioner to prescribe medicinal products of that description, or

(c) to a person for the purpose of inducing him to purchase medicinal products of that description from a person selling them by retail,

shall be guilty of an offence.

4    Where in the circumstances specified in subsection (2) of this section any person, in the course of a relevant business carried on by him, or while acting on behalf of a person carrying on such a business–

(a)    in connection with the sale, or offer for sale, of a medicinal product of the description in question, makes a representation relating to the product which consists of or includes unauthorised recommendations, or

(b)    for any such purpose as is specified in paragraphs (a) to (c) of subsection (3) of this section makes a representation relating to medicinal products of that description which consists of or includes unauthorised recommendations,

that person, subject to the following provisions of this section, shall be guilty of an offence.

5    Where a person is charged with an offence under this section, it shall be a defence for him to prove–

(a)    where the offence charged is under subsection (1) or subsection (3) of this section, that he did not know, and could not with reasonable diligence have discovered, that the advertisement or representation was false or misleading;

(b)    where the offence charged is under subsection (2) or subsection (4) of this section, that he did not know, and could not with reasonable diligence have discovered, that the recommendations made by the advertisement or representation were unauthorised recommendations.

6    Without prejudice to the last preceding subsection, where a person is charged with an offence under this section in respect of the issue of an advertisement, it shall be a defence for him to prove that he is a person whose business it is to issue or arrange for the issue of advertisements, and that either–

(a)    he received the advertisement for issue in the ordinary course of business and issued it, or arranged for it to be issued, either unaltered or without any alteration except in respect of lettering or lay-out, or

(b)    not being a commercially interested party, he received from a commercially interested party the information on which the advertisement was based and in the ordinary course of business prepared the advertisement in accordance with that information for issue at the request of that party,

and (in either case) that he did not know and had no reason to suspect that the issue of the advertisement would amount to an offence under this section.

7    For the purposes of this section an advertisement (whether it contains an accurate statement for the composition of medicinal products of the description in question or not) shall be taken to be false or misleading if (but only if)–

(a)   it falsely describes the description of medicinal products to which it relates, or

(b)   it is likely to mislead as to the nature or quality of medicinal products of that description or as to their uses or effects,

and any reference in this section to a false or misleading representation shall be construed in a corresponding way.

8     The preceding provisions of this section shall have effect subject to section 121 of this Act.

9     Any person guilty of an offence under this section shall be liable–

(a)   on summary conviction, to a fine not exceeding [the prescribed sum];

(b)   on conviction on indictment, to a fine or to imprisonment for a term not exceeding two years or to both.

10    In this section 'unauthorised recommendations', in relation to the circumstances specified in subsection (2) of this section, means recommendations whereby medicinal products of a description to which the licence in question is applicable are recommended to be used for purposes other than those specified in the licence.

**94   Advertisements requiring consent of holder of product licence**

1     Where a product licence under this Act is in force which is applicable to medicinal products of a particular description, then, except with the consent of the holder of the licence–

(a)   no commercially interested party (other than the holder of the licence) shall issue, or cause another person to issue, any advertisement relating to medicinal products of that description; and

(b)   no person who is not a commercially interested party shall, at the request or with the consent of a commercially interested party, issue, or cause another person to issue, any such advertisement.

2     Subject to section 121 of this Act, any person who contravenes the preceding subsection shall be guilty of an offence and liable on summary conviction to a fine not exceeding [level 3 on the standard scale].

**95   Powers to regulate advertisements and representations**

1     The appropriate Ministers may by regulations prohibit any one or more of the following, that is to say–

(a)   the issue of advertisements relating to medicinal products of a description, or falling within a class, specified by the regulations;

(b)   the issue of advertisements likely to lead to the use of any medicinal product, or any other substance or article, for the purpose of treating or preventing a disease specified in the regulations or for the purpose of diagnosis of a disease so specified or of ascertaining the existence, degree or extent of a physiological condition so specified or of permanently or temporarily preventing or otherwise interfering with the normal operation of a physiological function so specified, or for the purpose of artificially inducing a condition of body or mind so specified;

(c) the issue of advertisements likely to lead to the use of medicinal products of a particular description or falling within a particular class specified in the regulations, or the use of any other substance or article of a description or class so specified, for any such purpose as is mentioned in paragraph (b) of this subsection;

(d) the issue of advertisements relating to medicinal products and containing a word or phrase specified in the regulations, as being a word or phrase which, in the opinion of the appropriate Ministers, is likely to mislead the public as to the nature or effects of the products or as to any condition of body or mind in connection with which the products might be used.

2    Where any regulations are made in accordance with paragraph (b), paragraph (c) or paragraph (d) of the preceding subsection, the regulations may prohibit the making of any representation likely to lead to the use of a medicinal product or other substance or article to which the regulations apply for a purpose specified in the regulations in accordance with paragraph (d) of that subsection, if the representation–

(a) is made in connection with the sale or supply, or offer for sale or supply, of a medicinal product or other substance or article to which the regulations apply, or

(b) is made to a person for the purpose of inducing him to purchase such a medicinal product, substance or article from a person selling by retail medicinal products or other substances or articles to which the regulations apply, or

(c) in the case of medicinal products of a description to which the regulations apply, is made to a practitioner for the purpose of inducing him to prescribe or supply medicinal products of that description or is made to a patient or client of a practitioner for the purpose of inducing him to request the practitioner to prescribe medicinal products of that description.

3    Without prejudice to the preceding provisions of this section, the appropriate Ministers may by regulations impose such requirements as, for any of the purposes specified in the next following subsection, they consider necessary or expedient with respect to any one or more of the following matters, that is to say–

(a)  the particulars which advertisements relating to medicinal products must contain;

(b)  he form of any such advertisements; and

(c)  in the case of advertisements by way of cinematograph films or television, the duration for which, and the manner in which, any part of such an advertisement which contains particulars of a description specified in the regulations must be exhibited;

and any such regulations may prohibit the use, in relation to medicinal products of a description specified in the regulations, of advertisements of any particular kind so specified.

4    The purposes referred to in subsection (3) of this section are–

(a)  securing that adequate information is given with respect to medicinal products;

(b)  preventing the giving of misleading information with respect to medicinal products;

(c)  promoting safety in relation to such products.

5    Without prejudice to the application of section 129(5) of this Act, any prohibition imposed by regulations under this section may be a total prohibition or may be imposed subject to such exceptions as may be specified in the regulations.

6    Any regulations made under this section may provide that any person who contravenes the regulations shall be guilty of an offence and–

(a)  shall be liable on summary conviction to a fine not exceeding [the prescribed sum] or such lesser sum as may be specified in the regulations; and

(b)  if the regulations so provide, shall be liable on conviction on indictment to a fine or to imprisonment for a term not exceeding two years or to both.

7    Section 92(3) of this Act shall not have effect for the purposes of paragraphs (b) to (d) of subsection (1) of this section.

## 96    Advertisements and representations directed to practitioners

1    On and after the relevant date, no advertisement relating to medicinal products of a particular description, other than a data sheet, shall be sent or delivered to a practitioner–

(a)  by a commercially interested party, or

(b)  by any person at the request or with the consent of a commercially interested party,

unless the conditions specified in subsection (3) of this section are fulfiled.

2    On and after the relevant date, no representation likely to promote the use of medicinal products of a particular description referred

to in the representation shall be made to a practitioner by a person carrying on a relevant business, or by a person acting on behalf of a person carrying on such a business, unless the conditions specified in subsection (3) of this section are fulfiled.

3    Those conditions are–

(a)    that a data sheet relating to medicinal products of the description in question is sent or delivered to the practitioner with the advertisement, or is delivered to him at the time when the representation is made, or that such a data sheet has been sent or delivered to him not more than fifteen months before the date on which the advertisement is sent or delivered or the representation is made; and

(b)    that the advertisement or representation is not inconsistent with the particulars contained in the data sheet.

4    For the purposes of this section the relevant date–

(a)    in relation to medicinal products of any description to which neither subsection (2) nor subsection (3) of section 16 of this Act is applicable, is the first appointed day; and

(b)    in relation to medicinal products of any description to which either of those subsections is applicable, is the date of expiry of the period of six months from the date (or, if more than one, the latest date) on which, by virtue of one or more orders under section 17 of this Act, those subsections cease (or, if only one of them is applicable, that subsection ceases) to have effect in relation to them.

5    Subject to section 121 of this Act, any person who contravenes subsection (1) or subsection (2) of this section shall be guilty of an offence, and, if he contravenes that subsection by not complying with the conditions specified in paragraph (b) of subsection (3) of this section, shall be liable–

(a)    on summary conviction, to a fine not exceeding [the prescribed sum], or

(b)    on conviction on indictment, to a fine or to imprisonment for a term not exceeding two years or to both,

and, in any other case, shall be liable on summary conviction to a fine not exceeding [level 3 on the standard scale].

6    In this and the next following section 'data sheet' means a document relating to medicinal products of a particular description, which is prepared by or on behalf of the holder of a product licence which is applicable to medicinal products of that description and which–

(a)    complies with such requirements as to dimensions and form, as to the particulars to be contained in it, and as to the manner (whether in respect of type, size, colour or disposition or lettering or otherwise) in which any such particulars are to be so contained, as may be prescribed for the purposes of this subsection, and

(b) does not contain any information relating to medicinal products of that description except the particulars so prescribed.

[7 Nothing in this section applies in relation to a relevant medicinal product, as defined by paragraph (1) of regulation 2 of the Medicines (Advertising) Regulations 1994, in respect of which there is required to exist a summary of product characteristics as defined by that paragraph.]

## 97 Power for licensing authority to require copies of advertisements

1 The licensing authority may serve on any person a notice requiring him, within such time as may be specified in the notice, to furnish to the licensing authority such number of copies (not exceeding twelve) as may be so specified of any advertisement (including any data sheet) relating to medicinal products or to medicinal products of a description or falling within the period of twelve months ending with the date of service of the notice, and which he has so issued, or caused to be issued–

(a) being a commercially interested party, or

(b) at the request or with the consent of a commercially interested party.

(2) Any person who without reasonable excuse fails to comply with any requirement imposed on him by a notice under this section shall be guilty of an offence, and shall be liable on summary conviction to a fine not exceeding [level 3 on the standard scale].

# INDEX